D0043197

"C"

ALSO BY ANTHONY CAVE BROWN

Bodyguard of Lies (1977)

On a Field of Red (with Charles B. MacDonald, 1980)

Dropshot: The Third World War (1981)

The Last Hero: Wild Bill Donovan (1982)

"C"

THE SECRET LIFE OF

Sir Stewart Graham Menzies

SPYMASTER TO WINSTON CHURCHILL

Anthony Cave Brown

COLLIER BOOKS

MACMILLAN PUBLISHING COMPANY

NEW YORK

CONCORDIA UNIVERSITY LIBRARY
PORTLAND, OR 97211

Copyright © 1987 by Anthony Cave Brown

All rights reserved. No part of this book may be reproduced or
transmitted in any form or by any means, electronic or mechanical,
including photocopying, recording, or by any information storage and
retrieval system, without permission in writing from the Publisher.

Macmillan Publishing Company
866 Third Avenue, New York, NY 10022
Collier Macmillan Canada, Inc.

Library of Congress Cataloging-in-Publication Data
Brown, Anthony Cave.
The secret life of Sir Stewart Graham Menzies: spymaster to
Winston Churchill/Anthony Cave Brown.
p.   cm.
Bibliography: p.
Includes index.
ISBN 0-02-049131-X
1. Menzies, Stewart Graham, Sir, 1890–1968.
2. World War, 1939–1945—Secret service—Great Britain.
3. Intelligence officers—Great Britain—Biography.
4. Churchill, Winston, Sir, 1874–1965.
I. Title.
D810.S8M464   1989
940.54'86'41—dc19   88-38527   CIP

Macmillan books are available at special discounts for bulk purchases
for sales promotions, premiums, fund-raising, or educational use.
For details, contact:

Special Sales Director
Macmillan Publishing Company
866 Third Avenue
New York, NY 10022

First Collier Books Edition 1989

10 9 8 7 6 5 4 3 2 1

Designed by Jack Meserole

PRINTED IN THE UNITED STATES OF AMERICA

CONCORDIA UNIVERSITY LIBRARY
PORTLAND, OR 97211

FOR D.C.B. AND D.V.B.,

WITH LOVE AND GRATITUDE

For "C":

My admiration for the work of your organization cannot be made public. It nevertheless arises from knowledge and constant use of all that has been done. The services rendered, the incredible difficulties surmounted, and the victories gained in the course of the war cannot be overestimated. Everyone who has taken part, working at such a ceaseless strain, deserves the most cordial expression of my approval. Will you, within the secret circle, convey to all possible my compliments and gratitude to a large band of devoted and patriotic workers.

—W.S.C.
May 9, 1945

CONTENTS

PROLOGUE   In Search of "C"

1

CHAPTER **One**   The Golden Lads 1890–1915

CHAPTER **Two**   On Secret Service 1915–1933

CHAPTER Ten   Into the Cold War 1945–1952

EPILOGUE   Wilderness of Mirrors

AUTHOR'S NOTE

APPENDIXES

SOURCES, NOTES, AND BIBLIOGRAPHY

INDEX

"C"

"G"

PROLOGUE

In Search of "C"

I arrived in Luckington at about 2:20 P.M. in a taxi from Chippenham railway station. The village proved to be a silent group of gray-stone cottages and houses gathered about a church with a belfrey, a lich-gate put up as a memorial to the villagers who had lost their lives in the Boer War, and a graveyard. There were high lichened walls, clouds of black crows, stark oaks and elms, old yews, and a deserted air—the soul of England, they used to say.

A little early for my appointment with "C," I marked time with a visit to the church and the graveyard. The graves in front of the church were so old that it was impossible to read the inscriptions on the tombstones, but Luckington was obviously a prosperous parish, for most of those buried there had been "esquires." There was a number of early-Victorian cherubim and seraphim; and there was one knight there, his stone effigy dressed in stone helmet, breastplate, surplice, his hands crossed on his chest and clasping his stone sword. All the stonework was, I noticed, chipped by time.

Inside the church were two or three flags hanging from flagstaffs and plaques set into the walls to mark the passage through life of local worthies such as colonels and squires. There was also a plaque from some Italians of the Young Fascist Brigade, men who had been taken prisoner in Cyreneica in 1941 and had been brought to Luckington to work in the fields. They had put up the plaque as a mark of their gratitude for the kindly treatment they had received from the parishioners.

Then the taximan drove me to Bridges Court, where I was to meet "C."

It was January 29, 1964, the eve of "C's" seventy-fourth birthday. The letter "C" was the ideogram of the chief of the British Secret Intelligence Service, a government post that did not exist, either in the statute book or in common law. By tradition and usage the service, too, was as secret as its chief was anonymous. Of course it was well

1

known among sensible men that there was a department of state called
the secret service, that it functioned to obtain the secrets of state of
foreign powers, and that it functioned, too, as a bureau through which
certain acts of foreign policy could be carried out without the British
government being seen to be involved. It was an institution whose
chiefs, I had been told in London, believed absolutely in a single
cardinal rule: To be effective, a secret service must be secret.

The secrecy of the service and the anonymity of its members was
then—as now—protected by an act of Parliament that made public
discussion of the service and its activities a serious crime. Even its
historical origins were supposed to be secret, although "C" told his
American counterpart during World War II that the service was established by Henry VII, the first of the Tudor kings, between 1485
and 1509. I looked it up and found that, according to Francis Bacon,
the English philosopher, essayist, and statesman, its purpose was to
defend Henry's realm and reign, which were under attack from York-
ist "*Moles* perpetually working and casting to undermine him." Owing
much to his spies, who may have reported to the Star Chamber,
Henry made the post of spymaster of England a royal gift, which,
technically, it remained into "C's" time.

The man I was going to see was Sir Stewart Graham Menzies,
Knight Commander of the Bath, Knight Commander of St. Michael
and St. George, Distinguished Service Order, Military Cross, Eton,
the Life Guards, GHQ in World War I, the War Office, "attached
to the Foreign Office," the Beaufort Hunt (an institution that was as
much a political cabal as it was an organization for the chase), White's
Club in St. James's, the central citadel of the Tory landowning aristocracy. My informant in London told me that "C" had the reputation
for being "discretion incarnate," and not without reason, for "C" must
have had, I was assured, over fifteen hundred meetings with Churchill
during the 2,064 days of World War II.

Furthermore, "C" had spent his entire working life in the secret
service of the state. In his twenties he had begun his career as chief
of counterespionage and security at British general headquarters in
France and, by the end of World War I, he had been responsible for
the direction of all counterespionage operations throughout the group
of five British armies in the field. Before he was thirty he had become
chief of the War Office secret service. When he was only just into
his thirties he joined the Secret Intelligence Service of the Foreign
Office as the representative of the War Office. There, he was known
as a "terrific anti-Bolshevik," and he was in turn chief of the military

section, then of the German section, and then deputy chief, acting chief, and finally chief—"C"—between November 1939 and May 1952.

Menzies had been in the secret world, therefore, throughout the twenties, the thirties, World War II, and the early years of the Cold War with Russia. He had reported to no less than four sovereigns— George V, Edward VIII, George VI, Elizabeth II—and the thirteen governments of David Lloyd-George, A. Bonar Law, Stanley Baldwin, J. Ramsay MacDonald, Neville Chamberlain, Winston Churchill, Clement Attlee, and Winston Churchill's second ministry.

I looked forward to my meeting with "C" with keen anticipation, for he must have known more about the inner secrets of the princes and the proletariat than any man alive. I had been surprised greatly when "C" agreed to see me on the strength of one telephone call. People such as "C" did not usually see people such as myself, reporters of nondescript origins. Why, therefore, did he agree to see me? Why did he greet me on the telephone as if I were known to him from the past? He was, after all, a man who by repute *never, ever* spoke to a newspaperman, except to muzzle him. I thought at first that "C" must be familiar with my name from his reading of the *Daily Mail*, for which I had worked for a decade as a reporter and then foreign correspondent. But then sadly I realized the truth: he had believed, as had others of his standing in life, that I was a member of the Cave-Browne-Cave family. That family had distinguished itself greatly before and during World War I for having played a major part in the establishment of the Royal Air Force and in the general development of early aviation in England.

In personality, I was told, he closely resembled a character in a John Buchan novel, Sir Richard Hannay. Indeed, Buchan and Menzies did have much in common. Both had close connections in Perthshire. Buchan was born at Perth, a generation ahead of "C." The Menzies family were whiskey barons in those parts for generations and had made a great fortune and had a great estate there. Both had close ties to the Church of Scotland. When Buchan was a boy of thirteen his father was called to the John Knox Free Church, while "C's" parents, and particularly his grandparents, were eminences in the general assembly of the Church of Scotland, of which Buchan became lord high commissioner in 1933.

Both were sons of Scots meritocrats. Both were Edwardians schooled in the virtues of endurance, hard work, and perseverance, qualities that became the hallmark of many of Buchan's novels as they became the hallmark of "C's" work in secret office. Both believed completely in the other canons of the times: God, king, empire, courage, industry, success. Buchan created a world of secret societies, talismans and tokens, fairylike heroines. "C" inhabited such a world from 1915 until 1952. Like Hannay, "C" was a creature of the London clubs, Highland moors, hunting great stags amidst the crags, country houses, and high politics and low tactics in old, grand London. One could easily imagine "C" stating, as did Hannay: "This murder of Karolides will play the deuce in the chancellories of Europe."

Like Hannay, Menzies was an excellent shot, an excellent horseman, and an excellent stalker, carrying a .240 Mannlicher. Unlike Hannay, however, "C" disliked travel to foreign countries and kept as close to St. James's as was possible throughout his life. Certainly Menzies and Buchan worked closely together on the grand staff of Field Marshal Lord Haig during World War I and came to know each other well.

Despite the similarities and associations, however, it seems improbable that Hannay was the incarnation of Stewart Menzies, although Stewart Menzies may well have been the incarnation of Hannay, except in one important respect. Unlike Hannay, "C" was reputed to have been "a bit of a lad with the ladies," although I was never able to discover how he could possibly have found the time for all the adventures he was supposed to have had. Nor in truth was he quite so successful with the ladies as he was said to be. Indeed, upon reflection, it seems to me that he was unlucky in his choice of mates. He had three, I learned: the first cuckolded him; the second was desperately ill when they married; and the third turned against him in the most resounding fashion when he most needed her support.

A few seconds after my car drew up outside the gates to Bridges Court, a blur emerged from the side door of the house. Stewart Menzies hurtled down the drive and greeted me warmly. I was quite taken aback with the speed with which he moved and the warmth of his smile. Far from being the Whitehall mandarin, a person who measured each word and movement with gravity, "C" was almost boyish. He proved to be very brisk for a man of almost seventy-four. He was about five feet ten, slim, a little shrunken with years and, it seemed, a slightly concave chest. His face was pale and slender, with pale blue eyes, what were called *fin de race* features, and his skin was good and his handshake firm and fresh. He wore three-piece tweeds, rather heavy brown *Veldtschoen*, the Life Guards' tie, and a fine gold chain at his waistcoat. Later I was assured this suit had come from the Fifty-Shilling Tailors, a house that then specialized in suits for working-class youths seeking to rise in life. That news impressed me, for it had looked to me as if it must have been "built" by Pope and Bradley. Menzies certainly wore his clothes well.

"C" said he hoped that I had had a pleasant journey and apologized for not being able to give me lunch, but his wife was away and the housekeeper had the day off. I noticed a groom in the yard, bandaging the fetlocks of a beautiful brown horse. This man was a Pole who had been in the SS; Stewart Menzies had found him somewhere in Germany after the war and brought him to England "because he had a way with horses." The whole place seemed to revolve not around motorcars but around horses, another sign of a gentleman.

"Well!" Menzies exclaimed. "Here you are, then. Come along." He led me down a passage in which there were old mackintoshes and coats, some Wellington boots, gardening shoes, and harness and horse furniture hanging from wooden pegs, some walking sticks, dogs' leads, a calendar, and, I think, a railway timetable pinned to the wall over a telephone. We settled into old armchairs. The room was furnished in the manner of country gentlemen, which was what Menzies appeared to be, and everything about the man and room was pure Hannay—comfortable, well appointed, well used, but not luxurious.

We sat side by side, with a small table between us. "C" then showed that he had made a blunder, one that in the context of events proved of high importance. He said to me that he had known my father in World War I and that they had been fast friends. That was when I realized why he had seen me at all. I looked anxiously through the window to ensure that the driver was being obedient to his instructions, which had been to wait for me, as I feared that I would not be with Sir Stewart very long. "C" had thought I was a member of the Cave-Browne-Cave family. I explained very carefully that in my case Cave was a Christian name, not a surname, that my father had been an air-frame mechanic in the Royal Flying Corps in World War I, and that Wing Commander Cave-Browne-Cave had known my father in a servant-and-master relationship. Wing Commander Cave-Browne-Cave had had much to do with airships, a subject that greatly interested my father, so that when I was born he recalled his youthful association with the wing commander, and as a tribute to a man whom my father thought was a great aviator, he had had me christened Anthony Cave Brown.

To my surprise, and my delight, "C" loved the story, patting the fat little mongrel in his lap at the conclusion of each sentence in my story. "Well!" he declared. "When you rang up I thought you must be Meyrick Cave-Browne-Cave's grandson. *That* was why I had you down so quickly." He possessed a very quick smile. It came on. It went off. "Dammit!" he exclaimed. "Now what was all this about Canaris?" We were, I realized, over the hurdle and into the straight.

It was still daylight as I began to explain why I had sought the meeting. I was writing a book about the intelligence operations for D-Day in Normandy. Part of that book concerned the activities of Admiral Wilhelm Franz Canaris, one of "C's" German adversaries during the war and then almost a collaborator in the ideological struggle against Hitler and national socialism. "Ah!" exclaimed "C" at the mention of Canaris's name. "Damned brave." Pause. "And damned unlucky." "C" was quite right: Hitler had Canaris hung in the last days of the war, his crime, it was alleged, that he had committed high treason—high treason aided and abetted by "C," the man sitting next to me.

Now in the course of my career up until that time I had interviewed many famous men. Most of them had been boring, but the talk I had with "C" was pure delight, a truly memorable talk and a very rare one. "C's" recollections took much time, perhaps an hour, and he had a most interesting voice, a neutral but educated accent with much authority in it. It was a voice made the more engaging by his occasional use of Edwardianisms. No great flow of words issued from his lips. Each sentence was most beautifully framed, and he was most quotable. My pencil flew across the pages as I took down the statements in pidgin Pittman. And I remember recalling having the sudden thought that he actually welcomed my presence, that he had not had such a discussion in a long time, that he was a lonely man. Indeed, it seemed to me there was a sadness about him and about the room itself. The house was empty, and there was nothing for "C" to do except talk to a stranger on the eve of his birthday.

"C" was a frank man and answered most if not all my questions, which I at least thought must involve the highest matters of state, quite freely. There was, however, a second side to him. He showed a flash of steel when, tactlessly but courteously, I asked him why it was that the secret service had the reputation of having done little or nothing in the war. In that instant he became official and cross. "That's quite enough," he declared. "Now you've had a good innings." It seemed that I would have to go. But he went on unexpectedly. "I think we were rather badly beaten in the beginning," he confessed. "But the service did some good work." Pause. "The espionage branch got the secrets of the missiles in good time, and that gave the RAF a chance to get in and wreck the plans to destroy London." Pause. "We also, I think, did quite a lot to prevent a German victory in the Battle of the Atlantic." Another pause, but "C" did not say how that was done.

Then I mentioned Philby. The mention of that name produced a three-word eruption that fortunately was not directed at me. H.A.R. "Kim" Philby was the son of H. St. John Philby, the Arabian explorer and adviser to King Ibn Saud of Saudi Arabia. He was also one of "C's" "honorable correspondents"—that is to say one of a number of well-placed men who, while pursuing their ordinary business, could be depended upon to undertake missions or provide the secret service with intelligence when the need arose. "C" used a number of "honorable correspondents," and the system had worked well. So well had it worked indeed that when St. John Philby wanted to place his son Kim in the secret service, Kim Philby was readily accepted.

In 1941 Kim Philby was seconded to "C's" service and had performed his duties with such ability that "C" appointed him first to the post of chief of the Iberian subsection, then chief of the Soviet section, then chief of station at Istanbul, and finally "C's" representative at Washington. Toward the end of his tour in Washington, "C" decided to promote Philby to the position of assistant chief of the secret service, an appointment that would have made Philby third in the line of succession to the post of "C." But then it was suspected—or discovered—that Philby was, and had been throughout his career in the British Secret Intelligence Service, a secret agent of the Soviet Union. That discovery provoked the greatest scandal in twentieth-century England.

The Philby scandal produced the greatest bullfrogs' chorus—as the Foreign Office called a press outcry, a term that derived from the fact that when one bullfrog croaks, all croak, producing a great chorus—in modern history. It was still reverberating even as we talked, and "C" had not emerged from the scandal very well. Because of the laws of secrets and libel in England, "C" had not as yet been shown to have been culpable in the disaster, a disaster in which, so it was said, the secret services of the entire Western alliance had been destroyed. But there had been a lot of hints.

"C" asked me whether I had known Philby, and I said that I had worked with him in Beirut and Cairo as a correspondent between 1959 and 1961. But the conversation did not develop very far, for "C" rose and exclaimed quietly, "The damned blackguard!" Since then I have thought often about the implications of that statement. Was it simply an expostulation? Or was it an admission that Philby had indeed outwitted "C"? For the moment it is sufficient only to recall that I formed the impression that "C" was angry, that his was a statement of a person who felt aggrieved, not an admission of culpability for what appeared to be a great disaster.

That impression has remained with me and explains why I have, in this volume, cast doubt upon the accepted version of the scandal. Morever, members of "C's" closest family assured me later that throughout the bullfrogs' chorus, which lasted for almost seventeen years from 1952 until 1969, "C" never showed any embarrassment, concern, or anxiety. Except in 1955, when "C" did suffer from prolonged nightmares in which Philby was the central character, Menzies had shown none of the signs associated with men who have been ruined—annoyance, anger, complaint, loquacity. Except for those three words—"the damned blackguard"—he made no attempt to discuss the affair with any member of his family. Throughout he remained silent and died without saying anything more about the affair.

Plainly, however, that afternoon "C" had no wish to discuss Philby further, and I did not press him. I had no wish to provoke "C" into another display of cold steel. Very agreeably he asked me whether I would like to see something of his house, of which he was proud and where he had lived since just after World War I. I accepted with interest and pleasure, for it had seemed to me that, although "C" was reputed to be very rich, he lived no more comfortably than a squire. His drawing room, once the stables, was, I recall, a beautiful room, with the old rafters exposed and large tapestries on the walls, a lovely medley of white, brown, and chrome yellow. There was some good Georgian silver—heavy forks with three prongs instead of the usual four, that sort of thing—and the windows gave out onto a pleasant, walled garden with a gate. It was here, I heard later, that "C" used to sit for hours watching a vixen with her cubs in the next field, occasionally tossing mutton bones to them over the wall.

"C" was interested in foxes, and although he was a lifelong hunting man he never revealed the existence of these foxes to his hunt.

From the dining room we went to his study. "C" took a book from the shelves that proved to be a copy of Churchill's war memoirs. The volume was inscribed "From W.S.C. to 'C.' " Here, Menzies said, he was writing a history of his term in the service and that he went to the headquarters of the secret service frequently to read the archives. The work was was already a document of some one hundred thousand words. Later, I asked the Cabinet Office if I might read it but received a message stating there was no such document in the Cabinet files. I understood completely: since the secret service did not exist, how could there be a report of its activities by its chief? Also, it was to emerge later, "C" was using this room to write some recollections of famous people such as King George V, King George VI, Churchill, Haig, Eisenhower. But he did not get beyond about 150 pages. It was for the family, and most of it was illegible. Eventually I saw part of this document, but only after "C's" daughter, Fiona Bell, had deciphered it for me.

The second hour had long since arrived when there was a knock at the door. "That's the taxi," said Menzies. "Tell him to come back at about six." I did.

Menzies did not put on any lights but sat there in the gloom of his parlor. He seemed to be quite willing to discuss anything. Unfortunately at that time I knew nothing of Ultra, Menzies's code-breaking operations, which were the greatest intelligence triumph of World War II, and perhaps of modern history. Nor did "C" venture anything about that operation. After nearly twenty years it was still a state secret.

However, I knew enough to ask intelligent questions about that other very secret matter of World War II: deception. Deception had been described by Allan Dulles as the most secret of all secret intelligence operations. It was the craft of the game of nations—the game involved in making your opponent do something disastrous in which he would lose the battle, if not the war. The British were supposed to be the masters at this game, and when I turned to the games "C" had played, I thought I was being too bold.

But no. Menzies made no bones about it. He admitted that a deception organization had existed, he told me what its name was (the London Controlling Section, which was then a tremendous state secret), and he said his service had been much involved in the deception operations from the Battle of Britain onward. He offered to put me in touch with the head of the organization. "C" warned me, however, that he thought the government would be opposed to any public discussion of such matters. Although I accepted his offer I heard no more about the meeting he had in mind. But perhaps "C" was as good as his word, for somewhat later I asked Sir Ronald Wingate, the deputy chief of the London Controlling Section and member of "C's" brotherhood, to act as my adviser in a book called *Bodyguard of Lies*, and Wingate agreed. He would not have done so without authority.

At the third hour, "C" rose, switched on the lights, went to a table, and poured one finger of exquisite malt into each of two exquisite glasses. "Ian Fleming tells me that I am James Bond's 'M,' " "C" announced with just a hint of pleasure and vanity, as if at last someone had recognized his work. Over the drinks I asked him if he had read John le Carré's *The Spy Who Came in from the Cold* and, if he had, what he thought of it.

"That fellow," declared "C," "knows something." What John le Carré knew "C" did not say. He cut some very thin slices of Dundee fruitcake, which were delicious with the malt. This was the Scots way of drinking malt, and he explained that it was of unusually good quality because he had connections with the Scotch whiskey industry, a claim that he phrased rather modestly in light of the nature of his connection—"C's" family had controlled most of the Scotch whiskey industry in the mid-1850s. There was no doubt about it, he was a most engaging, simple, straightforward fellow of the old school. I wondered how it was that an American friend had formed the impression that "C" was a "tough son of a bitch." I was to find out later.

In all it had been a pleasant and informative afternoon. It was to prove, indeed, one of those memorable meetings that occur all too infrequently. Thus, when twenty years later I was asked to write the biography of Stewart Menzies, I sprang to the task with enthusiasm and energy and labored at the book for four years. Yet for all the labor, the travel, the expense, the access to special recollections and documents, throughout that period I felt that there was an element to Stewart Menzies's life that I did not understand. What was it that I had found so attractive and interesting about him, his spying apart? "C" was certainly the denial of the proverb that the most cunning men are caught first. Stewart was caught only at the end, but that could not have been it, for it was not at all clear that "C" *was* ever caught. He was certainly very controversial, largely because it seemed to his colleagues in that curious artificial vivarium that he inhabited for so long that his triumph in World War II was due not to his own work, but to the labor of the industrious.

I slowly came to believe that "C" was a shadow. I was wrestling with a phantom. The reason for this was evident: the inner Menzies was a different man doing secret work who revealed himself rarely to few, if any, men or women of his generation. Yet such was his personality that most men and women thought they knew him, his strengths and weaknesses. But the reality was that he eluded them—as he had eluded me. *What*, therefore, was "C"? Sir James Easton, who worked with Menzies on clandestine affairs throughout World War II and who served under him as assistant chief of the secret service afterward, tried to sum him up for me. "Stewart," he declared, "appeared artless but was really sphinxlike and cunning." Yet that opinion did not encompass the range of Menzies's personality. There was something else.

There was the elegant little flourish of fine hands, the expensive handkerchief tucked into the breastpocket, the touch of scent, the cut of the coat, the breeches, and the riding boots. The breeding. The hint of wild nights at White's. The suggestion of the palace, garden parties, the King's Guard, countesses, and Boats Week on the Thames at Eton. The chase. "C" was by no means an ordinary bureaucrat, one of a group of men who wrote memos and wasted hours. There was his lack of bookishness, a hint of piety confined to Sundays. The Windsor-blue eyes.

Then it came to me. The officer who remarked that "C" reminded him of a character out of Buchan was in error. "C" was certainly of Buchan's period and spoke as Sir Richard Hannay would have. But he was really a Regency man, a throwback to that period just before the Victorians when, in 1811, George III became permanently incapacitated through porphyria and his eldest son, George, was appointed Prince Regent. The Prince Regent was noted for his gay and dissolute ways and was disliked by many for his attempts after his accession (1820) to divorce his wife, Caroline. A period ensued called "the Regency," one noted for its flowering in the arts, letters, and architecture, a period of style and elegance. Its poets were Byron, Keats, and Shelley; Eton, White's, the Beaufort Hunt, all the institutions to which "C" had belonged during his lifetime, had flourished. It was, all agreed (except the proletariat), a marvelous time in the affairs of men, despite the loss of the American colonies. It was the period in which the First British Empire ended and the Second Empire began, when England emerged triumphant from the

Napoleonic Wars. It was the last period of primacy before the aristocracy began its long, slow decline toward 1945 and the resumption of the ways of "Little England."

Then I had it. Stewart Menzies was, I realized, a queer combination typical of the Regency: the Platonic gentleman, supercrook, and paladin in the service of Imperial England. In a flash the phantom disappeared and "C" reappeared as the courtly secret servant of the state in Churchill's wartime. I understood what Churchill had seen in "C." His character was such that it would have baffled anybody who tried to take his measure. In particular, it would certainly have baffled an enemy.

CHAPTER

One

The Golden Lads
1890–1915

1 CHURCHILL v. MENZIES

Sixty-one days after the outbreak of World War II, on November 4, 1939, Admiral Sir Hugh Sinclair, chief of the British Secret Intelligence Service (SIS), died suddenly at King Edward VII Hospital for Officers in Beaumont Place, London. "C"—as chiefs of the British secret service were always known, for reasons of security and the need for anonymity in what was a dark trade—was sixty-six years of age.

Sinclair's death produced great anxiety within the War Cabinet of Prime Minister Neville Chamberlain. The office of "C" was one of the most powerful within the government, for he was the man who directed all espionage, sabotage, counterespionage, and much of the political warfare outside the British Empire. The post was so secret that it did not exist on any table of organization of the British government and was protected by a fortress of laws, rules, regulations, and customs to ensure that the identity of "C" was preserved as a secret of state. Foreign governments frequently regarded "C" as "the power behind the throne," as the Soviet government's prosecutor declared during an espionage trial of British subjects in Moscow in 1933. This was possibly an exaggeration of the powers of "C" in peacetime, but not in wartime or during great crises. Then "C" had exceedingly close connections in foreign affairs with the sovereign, the prime minister, and the foreign secretary. Indeed, "C" was the principal adviser to the government in matters of foreign intelligence and possessed the right of access to all three men at any hour. Who, therefore, was now to succeed in that high post at this grave hour?

The obvious choice was Sinclair's deputy, Colonel Stewart Graham Menzies. Now forty-nine, he was fit in mind, wind, and limb. He had been in the secret service since 1915, twenty-four years. Sinclair had regarded Menzies so highly that, in anticipation of his death, he had proposed Menzies as his successor in a letter addressed to the permanent head of the Foreign Office, Sir Alexander Cadogan. This letter was kept in a safe by Sinclair's secretary, Miss Kathleen Pettigrew, who had instructions to deliver the letter to the undersecretary upon his death.

Miss Pettigrew carried out her instructions immediately. Since Menzies and his record were well known to the king, the prime minister, the foreign secretary, and the members of the Cabinet, it was expected that Menzies's appointment would be approved almost as a routine matter at the next War Cabinet meeting. But Menzies was not approved. On the contrary, Winston S. Churchill, first lord of the Admiralty, opposed the appointment. He had known Menzies and his family from 1906, when Churchill had proposed marriage to one of Menzies's aunts, the then Miss Muriel Wilson, an exceedingly rich heiress. Instead, Churchill proposed the director of naval intelligence, Admiral John Godfrey, to the succession, although Godfrey was a battleship admiral who had been an intelligence officer for only ten months before the outbreak of war.

Churchill's nomination was resisted by the majority of the Cabinet, who favored Menzies as the obvious and, indeed, the only choice. In turn, Churchill proved obdurate and argumentative in his nomination of Godfrey and his opposition to Menzies. Although the war with Germany showed signs it would burst into major land, sea, and air operations, the arguments swayed back and forth for twenty-six days, an abnormally long period for a cabinet to make up its mind about an appointment at any time, and dangerously long in time of war. Throughout that period, Menzies acted as "C," and there was vigorous lobbying for and against him in most of the leading London clubs.

But Churchill refused to concede, and his objections began to take on the aspect of a personal, political, and professional antipathy for Menzies. That antagonism seemed to be mutual. Churchill's opposition stemmed from the peculiar social, political, and historical relationships of the British ruling class in the twilight years of its world power. Also, the relationship between Churchill and Menzies became of fundamental importance to the history of Churchill's conduct of office as prime minister during World War II. Indeed, despite Churchill's animus for Menzies at this time, Menzies subsequently became Churchill's most important adviser. He was therefore able to provide Churchill with intelligence that vitally affected the conduct of operations throughout the war—first, enabling England to survive the German onslaught and, ultimately, enabling the Grand Alliance to triumph.

Theirs became, in consequence, one of the most important—and the most intriguing—personal relationships of the twentieth century.

2 ORIGINS

Stewart Graham Menzies was born on January 30, 1890, at 46 Upper Grosvenor Street, London, a handsome house on a handsome street connecting Park Lane with Grosvenor Square. He was a Victorian born into the fifty-third year of the great queen's reign over the British Empire, the largest geopolitical entity in the history of the planet. His mother and father were on the fringes of the court of the Prince of Wales, and, consequently, there was much speculation about his paternity. By common report Stewart actually was believed to be the natural son of the prince, who in 1901 became King Edward VII.

The origin of that story lay in the curious fact that both had slightly red hair and "Windsor-blue" eyes, that there were pronounced physical differences between Stewart Menzies and his older brother, Keith Graham Menzies. Moreover, Menzies's mother, a great beauty, was a close friend of the prince's equerry; the prince was a lecher, and Menzies's mother climbed far too quickly into the highest reaches of society to have been anything other than the prince's paramour. Throughout his life Stewart Menzies enjoyed the royal favor in both his career and at court. Much of this proved undeniable. And it was certainly true that Stewart Menzies had a charmed life for a product of the meritocracy. For few, if any other, men of his class and generation did the system work as well as it did for Stewart Menzies.

But that theory simply reflects old speculations. Stewart's birth certificate shows that his father was John Graham Menzies, gentleman of independent means, and his mother Susannah West Menzies, née Wilson, also of independent means. Both were rich and well connected to the nobility through the wealth of their parents, who were "in trade" and therefore of a slightly lower order. What is clearly evident is that the source of Stewart Menzies's power and acceptability in society stemmed from his grandfather Graham Menzies's riches, ability, and presence rather than to princely dispensation. [1]

The owner of the Caledonian Distillery in Edinburgh, the second-largest distillery in Europe and the most modern in the world, Graham Menzies's wealth was relatively new. He was merely "comfortable" until about 1860, when the French brandy vines caught the pox and Scotch whiskey, which Graham Menzies manufactured in large quantities, became the world's favorite liquor. That misadventure across the Channel made Graham Menzies a solid-gold millionaire. With this wealth Graham Menzies did what all Britons did who aspired to a place within the nobility: he became a landowner. Land gave mere money respectability. It brought its possessor rank, and sometimes it earned him honors.

Around 1860, at about the time of the birth of Stewart Menzies's father, Graham Menzies bought Hallyburton, an ancient estate with a castle in the long, fertile valley known as the Strathmore. The nearest town stood a mile and a half away, its name was Coupar Angus, and it was on the railway between Perth and Aberdeen. The estate cost £300,000. An additional £135,000—a prince's ransom at that time—was spent to restore the castle, its twelve farms, and its church.

The purchase was made with a sharp eye for its position in society. Just to the north lay Queen Victoria's estate at Balmoral. Just to the east was Glamis, the seat of the earls of Strathmore, one of whose daughters, Elizabeth, became the queen consort of King George VI and the mother of the queen, Elizabeth II. Just to the south were the estates of the earls of Dundee, the family who entered Scottish history and legend through centuries of martial exploit against the

English and because a member took Robert Bruce's heart to Jerusalem. Not very far away stood the castle of Airlie, the home of the earl of Airlie, who was a special friend of Graham Menzies and of the court, for the Airlies had provided every sovereign since George III with a lord-in-waiting or a lord chamberlain. Moreover, Scotland's leading gentry and nobility lived all about that rich, black farming country. The Graham Menzies family was soon accepted.

They pronounced their name "Mingiss," as did Stewart Menzies, in the fashion of the nobler sept of the Menzies clan, the Menzies of Menzies of Dull Castle, Scotland. Graham Menzies adopted as the family motto "Vill God I Zall" (Will God I Shall). His family crest became a falcon preying upon a stork; and there was also the clan motto: "N'oublie pas"—"Do not forget." At Hallyburton there was keen observance of Scottish traditions, ceremonies, and feast days. They wore special tartan (red and green for hunting, red and white for the evening, and black and white for mourning). Their piper played their guests up the steps into the reception room. They held marvelous balls at which the orchestra played Highland reels from the minstrels' gallery. Great bonfires flared from the peaks of Macbeth's hills on the Sidlaws around the mansion, and the piper led the dancers in a single chain of red, gold, tartan, uniforms, and crinoline through the castle and out across the lawns and around the lake, on which were black swans from Australia.

On Sundays at breakfast the men of the castle always took their porridge standing up with their backs to the walls, a tradition, so they said, of Scotland in sterner times, when a man was liable to be stabbed in the back at breakfast time. The first stag of the season was always ceremonially gralloched.

There was much good malt—the best malt, in fact—on New Year's Day. Partridges were not shot after the second of February, and Graham Menzies always attended the rising of the Court of Session in March. One of the family was always present at the first day of the general assembly of the Church of Scotland in April. The family always assembled at Hallyburton for St. Swithins. The entire family came to the grouse and ptarmigan season on the "Glorious Twelfth" of August, when they went on to the Birnam Highland Games. They would appear at the opening day of the Ayr Races in September, wearing bowlers, capes, spats, and the grand air of the chosen. At Martinmas in October the Clan Bardess, Miss Menzies of Menzies, would recite the "Menzies Clan Poem" from the head of the great stairs at Hallyburton:

The first of Scottish Kings that Albion boasts,
Who oft to victory led the Scottish hosts,
Was Fergus, Ferchad's son, whose mighty
    shield
Bore a Red Lion on a yellow field;
Three hundred years and thirty was his
    reign,
Before Christ came to break sin's deadly
    chain.
Magnus the second son of King Fergus was,
Who on his shield emblazoned bore
A Red Chief on a white field. [2]

The Menzies's cipher and colors were the "red chief on a white field," as if the Graham Menzies sept came from antiquity, which they did not. There was always a great gathering of the estate and town workers on the tenth of December when the grouse, black cock, and ptarmigan shootings closed. And since Menzies had bought the distillery in London that produced Gordon's Gin, which was known as "Mother's Ruin," they owned a demimansion in Queen's Gate, London. The Menzies family used this house for the London season, which began in June and lasted until "society" departed for Scotland and Yorkshire for the grouse during the first week of August.

(By strange chance Mrs. May Philby, the wife of a tea planter in Ceylon and the daughter of the British army general commanding the garrison at Bombay in the Indian empire, obtained the lease on a house but a few doors from that of the Menzies's property. Since Mrs. Philby had separated from her husband and earned her own living, she ran a superior private hotel for imperial and colonial officials and officers on leave from their posts in the empire. May Philby was Kim Philby's grandmother. Thus we may have encountered the earliest proximity between the Menzies and Philby families.)

In all other matters, especially spiritual, the Graham Menzies family represented Victorian orthodoxy. They were Liberals by politics, Scots Presbyterians by religion, and members of the Scottish Order of Freemasons by association, most of which helped them to consolidate themselves within the Anglo-Scottish hierarchy. The only unorthodoxy tolerated was the "radical" politics of Graham Menzies's oldest son, Robert Stewart Graham Menzies. A member of Parliament and a masterful orator, Robert's politics were too radical for the Scots nobility. He advocated land and taxation reform, and he was suspected of being a "Little Englander." For a time Robert Graham Menzies was blackballed at most of the noble homes of Scotland; and he might have become prime minister but for his death from pneumonia at the age of thirty-one. Such a record casts important light upon the family, for without it the Graham Menzies sept might easily be dismissed, along with Stewart Menzies, as whiskey Gradgrinds. As it was, they were accepted as Christians who were more spiritual, more caring, than that grim old man of the dark, satanic mills.

By repute, Graham Menzies was a good landlord, employer, father, and citizen. He was, however, both ruthless and imaginative in business. Between 1879 and 1887 his distilleries produced an annual average of 1,710,000 gallons of excellent whiskey. He sold the whiskey to such blenders as Haig & Haig. But Graham Menzies was not content with mere riches. He wished to control the industry and proceeded to do so in 1856 when he and five other distillers established a trade association to limit production, control markets, and thereby create and maintain stable prices and profits. Through the elimination of small distilleries, sometimes by fair means, sometimes by foul (such as cutting off or buying up rivals' water supplies), Graham Menzies succeeded in his ambition. He himself obtained 41.5 percent of the interests of the trade association, against 15 percent to his nearest competitor, John Bald, 13.5 percent to Haig & Haig, and between 13 and 8 percent to the rest of his associates.

It was true that this domination did not last, for in 1865 a new agreement was negotiated in which he obtained only 28 percent. But it was a profitable business that returned dividends of between 8 and 14 percent. Some of the members made colossal profits, and the Graham Menzies family was one of them. Shortly the association became the Distillers Company Limited (DCL), the largest distilling combine in the world, and Graham Menzies's second son, William Dudgeon Graham Menzies, became chairman of DCL and remained on the board until 1944.

In all, therefore, Graham Menzies's record was, by the standards of the mercantile aristocracy, a triumph, for he had begun life with only one small distillery, the Saucel at Paisley with its weird Chinese-pagoda roof and golden spire amidst the ruins of the slums. He had persevered in what was a sharp-witted trade. Except for a single blemish on his record, he would have received a knighthood or peerage, the highest ambition of the Victorian merchant venturer. In the case of "the Queen v. Graham Menzies," it was alleged that Menzies had attempted to defraud the Excise on the tax due on 18,638 gallons of wort, the liquid formed in the early process of making whiskey.

He was found guilty on two of thirteen counts by a jury at the Court of the Exchequer in Edinburgh and was fined £400. That conviction proved sufficient to disqualify Graham Menzies from Queen Victoria's honors list, even though Menzies paid immense sums in taxes (in 1858, for example, he paid £1,040,000 duty on whiskey production totaling 2,080,000 gallons).

Graham Menzies died a commoner, of a hemorrhage in a lung brought on by an asthmatic attack. He was sixty and had worked himself to death. He was buried with Freemason ritual in the kirk at Kettins, a village lying about a mile from the castle. Having been deputy grand master of the East Perthshire Lodge of the Ancient and Accepted Order of Scotland, and a prince of Rose Croix, his coffin was carried from the hearse to the altar and then to the grave by the marquess of Breadalbane, the provincial grand master of Perthshire East, and seven other Masonic pallbearers all wearing the black bowlers, black suits, black ties, and white gloves and aprons of Masonic mourning. The Masonic Tyler carrying a drawn sword led the procession to the grave, accompanied by Stewards with the white rods, and the oldest member of the lodge carried a black cushion with the holy writings.

When the coffin was lowered into the rich black earth of Strathmore, the one hundred Masons present marched around the grave, and each dropped into it a sprig of cassia, intoning the dirge:

> What sounds of grief, in sadness, tell
> A Brother's earthly doom;
> No more in life's fair scenes to dwell,
> A tenant of the tomb.

3 JACK AND SUSANNAH

Stewart Menzies's father, John "Jack" Graham Menzies, was raised at Hallyburton as a Gladstonian Liberal. Baptised into the Church of Scotland, Jack became a Freemason and spent much of his boyhood and youth hunting, shooting, and fishing. At about the age of thirteen he was sent to Rugby, the school of Tom Brown, to learn how to become an English gentleman. Rugby was then noteworthy for such training, but, alas, it failed with Jack. He was a good sportsman, which counted for much at that time, but a poor scholar. Ever hopeful, Graham Menzies sent him to read law at Brasenose College, Oxford, but there again he was idle and left the university. Graham Menzies put him to work at Saucel Distillery, one of the family's interests, in order that he might learn the trade. At about the same time Jack obtained a commission in the Royal Scots Militia, becoming a captain. In 1881 he joined the Linlithgow and Stirlingshire Hunt, a meet whose emblem was a flying fox and whose founder was the twelfth Lord Elphinstone, of the First Battalion the Royal American Rifles.

It was a hunt that enjoyed numerous fames and infamies. It was hard riding, hearty, arrogant, clannish, and its pack was savage: its sires were said to have eaten their kennelman alive when he came drunk to the doghouse one night. The members were celebrated for their wild nights at the Star and Garter Hotel in Linlithgow, where they were required by article 7 of the rules of the hunt to meet each Wednesday nearest the full moon. And it was claimed that there was in the country a pure golden fox, one, according to the hunt's history, as "bright as a new guinea."

Jack became the master of the hunt, and he rode so furiously that he became known as "Hellfire Jack." Only rarely did he do any work in the distillery. He hunted between two and three times a week. When he was not hunting he was racing. He ran several horses. In 1885 he owned at least three racehorses: Melton, Busybody, and Lady Jane Grey. His only other interest was his regiment, where he was known as a great swell. But for all Jack's gasconading, Graham Menzies had confidence that Jack would do well once he had sown a few wild oats. That confidence was misplaced, for Jack never ceased to sow wild oats, and he died at it.

Nevertheless, such was his father's confidence that he left Jack a full one-third of his estate, which was probated at £432,823 (about £8.6 million by 1987 values). Under the terms of the will, Jack's share of the estate was put at about £144,000 (nearly £3 million). The will provided also that Jack should be made a full director of the Distillers Company Limited at the age of twenty-four, his task to watch over the handling of the Menzies family interests. That post produced directors' fees of at least £1,500, and together with his directorships in the Caledonian and his interest in Gordon's Gin, Jack had an income of about £14,000 a year. That made him devilishly rich, for this was a time when it was doubtful whether there was one young blade in a hundred thousand who had £10,000 a year. A cottager or a pitman earned £50 a year, a clerk £100, and a shopkeeper £250.

In August 1885, therefore, Jack joined the board of DCL. He was at first a good director, but his interest in the company declined quickly. The call of the fox, the fences, and the fields proved much stronger than that of the boardroom table. From 1886 onward he became virtually an absentee director. Then he went to Yorkshire to hunt with the Holderness, the leading meet in the county, where he met Miss Susannah West Wilson, who was at once one of the most gorgeous and the richest of the British heiresses. She was the second daughter of Arthur Wilson, who with his brother, Lord Nunburnholme, was the owner of England's largest privately owned shipping firm, the Wilson Line, of Hull.

By the time Jack met Susannah, the brothers Wilson were still "in trade," but they were rather more prominent than the Menzies family. Charles was a Liberal member of Parliament and in the process of being elevated to the peerage. Arthur was high sheriff of Yorkshire, sheriff of Hull, deputy lord lieutenant of Yorkshire, and a justice of the peace in the East Riding. In the light of all this wealth, position, and promise, both daughters were considered to be most eligible. It is here that we find the first known important connection between Winston Churchill and Stewart Menzies. In 1909, when Menzies was nineteen and Churchill a young and penniless politician and writer (but the grandson of a duke and the son of a baron), Churchill saw his future allied to that of Muriel, Arthur's other and younger daughter.* [3]

Muriel Wilson was to remember Winston Churchill walking up and down the drive at Tranby Croft repeating, to overcome a lisp, such phrases as "The Spanish ships I cannot see, for they are not in sight." But when he proposed marriage young Churchill did not prosper, for he was too much the Liberal radical for Arthur Wilson's taste. Was Churchill not the most determined opponent of temperance, a parliamentary cause close to the heart of Charles Wilson? His reputation at both Harrow and in the Fourth Hussars was that of a cad, an opinion that was held by King Edward VII, who wrote to the Prince of Wales in 1907 of young Churchill the politician: "He is *almost more* of a cad in office than he was in opposition." Giles St. Aubyn, whose family was close to Stewart Menzies later on, wrote a note about young Churchill that explains much about the antipathy

---

*Muriel Thetis Wilson (1875-1964). Married 1919 Major Richard Edward Warde (1884-1932), of the Scots Guards. Warde suffered multiple wounds and gassing in World War I and was not able to be either a husband or earn a living. Muriel remained a close friend of the Churchill family for life.

Churchill felt for Stewart Menzies when the question came before the Cabinet in 1939 about Menzies's suitability for the post of "C":

The ruling class in Edwardian England were slow to forgive Churchill, [for] . . . Winston's radicalism betrayed his family and friends. It was all very fine for him to affect the common touch, but when he wearied of the rough-and-tumble of the hustings, or found the stench of Oldham [his constituency] too obnoxious, he could always retire to the calm of Blenheim to contemplate a fresh assault on Dukes, or meet Lord Curzon at dinner.

Furthermore, had not one of Churchill's uncles been expelled from Eton for perversion?

Muriel rejected Winston, and he returned to London muttering ungallantly that this was the last time he would try to marry for money and complaining of Muriel's "tranquil *banalité*." [4] Conversely, Arthur Wilson had not rejected Jack, even though his record showed little promise as a son-in-law and despite the fact that, although the family's cause was temperance, Jack was a director of the leading distillers' in Scotland. But at least it was a genuine and charming love match. Accordingly their engagement was announced in the late autumn of 1886, when Susannah was twenty-one and known as "the pocket Venus." As *Modern Society* described her, she was "very small, very fair, with forget-me-not blue eyes and fluffy golden hair." Having made a marriage settlement worth between £40,000 and £50,000 in Wilson Line stock, Jack and Susannah were married at St. Peter's Church, Anlaby, near Arthur Wilson's new estate and mansion at Tranby Croft, on February 8, 1887. It was all a bride could wish for, a rich tradesman's wedding: ornate, high church, and binding in perpetuity.

Susannah left Wilson's mansion in a coach drawn by four handsome Galloways which passed under triumphal arches carrying such legends as "God Bless the Bridal Pair" and "Long Life & Happiness." Thousands of townspeople lined the bridal route. She was attended by six bridesmaids, each of whom had been given a diamond brooch presented by Jack and inscribed with the words "8th Feb., 1887." All the church bells of Anlaby and Hull rang merrily in honor of the marriage, and the ships in the port had been decorated with flags from stem to stern. In the evening a grand ball took place at Tranby Croft.[5]

Jack and Susannah began married life together at 46 Upper Grosvenor Street, opposite what was in 1987 the visa and passport section of the United States embassy. Their country home was Escrick Park in Yorkshire, which they had leased from Lord Wenlock, who had been appointed governor of Madras in the Indian empire. Here, in the pastoral splendors of East Riding, with an occasional visit to London for the season, Jack and Susannah began to spend most of their time producing boys, hunting the fox, and shooting large numbers of birds and animals. The first son, Keith Graham Menzies, was born in 1888; the second, Stewart Graham Menzies, followed in 1890; and the third and last, Ian Graham Menzies, was born in 1895.

The family rarely visited Hallyburton, for relations were bad between Jack and his brother, William. But Jack and Susannah did pay a visit in 1899, and then Stewart shot his first stag, which was gralloched in the traditional fashion. Stewart rarely if ever shot deer again. He learned to shoot partridge at Escrick Park and duck on the moors around Hull. But above all he learned to ride and hunt the fox. And in 1901 at the age of eleven he was blooded in the old fashion, with the brush of the dead fox across his cheeks.

4   GEORGE LINDSAY HOLFORD

When Stewart Menzies was born, his father and mother had not as yet entered the highest reaches of society. They were still known as "county." But their circle of acquaintances now included Captain George Lindsay Holford, equerry to the Prince of Wales, the heir to the throne. Holford was much taken with Susannah's beauty, vivacity, and the poise she displayed when she moved in society, where Holford was an important, if noiseless, personage. He held a commission in the First Life Guards and was distinguished and handsome in appearance. But although he was one of the most eligible bachelors in London, Holford had not married because, so it was said, Queen Victoria preferred her courtiers to be single men. Holford therefore lived what appeared to be a gorgeous albeit celibate existence.

Born in 1860, he was the son of an art collector and Gloucestershire squire who had suddenly grown very rich through a social and historical fluke: King James II of England and some courtiers and gentry, who included a Holford, formed an association in the mid-seventeenth century called the New River Company, the purpose of which was to corner London's water supply. The shares proved valueless until the Industrial Revolution, when London's population rose from 1.1 million in 1801 to 6.7 million a decade later. Having held the shares in trust from one generation to the next, the Holfords became rich almost beyond comprehension.

Being thrifty, viceless, and sensible, they held on to their money, and were accepted at court. When Susannah and George Holford met, Holford lived in vice-regal splendor at Dorchester House, his palace on Park Lane, on the site of what has become the Dorchester Hotel. He owned a second palace, Westonbirt, on an estate next door to the duke of Beaufort, the master of the king's horse, in Gloucestershire. The master of the king's horse was one of the most important appointments at court.

A prominent member of the Burlington Society, that most exclusive of all London art clubs, both his palaces were treasure troves of art. He owned a number of masterpieces such as Rembrandt's "Man with a Cleft Chin," Albert Cuyp's "Dordrecht on the Maas," portraits of Van Dyck and Justus Sustermans, and the famous "Portrait of La Marchese Caterina Durazzo." In all there were perhaps eighty or ninety masterpieces in Holford's collection, besides many ancient and valuable sculptures, manuscripts, and several libraries of the rarest and most valuable books. When the collections were sold in 1927, they fetched two million pounds sterling, perhaps fifty million dollars by 1987 money values, and established what was a single-day price record at Christie's.

Nor were Holford's talents confined to the collection of works of great art. Like his father, Robert Stayner Holford, he was perhaps the greatest gardener in the England of his time. Even as late as 1987, Westonbirt Arboretum was a testament to his skill in obtaining the rarest and most beautiful trees and shrubs in the world and making them thrive in Gloucestershire.

Holford was, therefore, no Edwardian vulgarian, but a man of exquisite instincts. Unusually handsome and well built, Holford had marvelous manners and charm, although it was to be said that there was a hint of narcissism about him. Yet his photographs give Holford the appearance of stiff-backed, military mustached masculinity. Above all he possessed what was considered to be the most admirable of all Edwardian virtues: a silent tongue. He never gossiped, and the palace's secrets—and especially the Prince of Wales's secrets—were safe with him. When the prince became king he engaged the War Office in a prolonged correspondence, written in the finest copperplate, to retain Holford's services. Here was an excellent example of the dis-

cretion by which Holford lived and survived at court. That correspondence remained a state secret even eighty-five years later, one
that could be seen only after special application and personal visit to
the Ministry of Defence in London.

Lieutenant Colonel Sir George Holford, knight grand cross of the
Indian empire, officer commanding the Reserve Regiment of Life
Guards, also was silver stick, a post that required Holford to wait
"next to His Majesty's person before all others, carrying in his hand
. . . an ebony staff with a silver head, engraved with His Majesty's
Cypher and Crown," his duty to "guard the very person of the King
from actual bodily injury, against a personal attack, and that to do so
with his own hands and body." Thus Holford became not only the
keeper of the prince's reputation, but also the protector of his person.
These were two powerful positions, ones made even more influential
through a series of marriages between members of the Holford family
and a group of the leading British landowners, bankers, and politicians. His was perhaps one of the most exclusive and most powerful
cousinhoods in the country in Edward's time. Certainly it was one of
the richest.

Because of his royal obligations and connections, it is impossible
to fathom how, or why, Holford permitted the relationship between
himself and Susannah Graham Menzies to mature, except that Holford
was genuinely besotted by Susannah. Some thought he suffered from
dementia erotica. Furthermore, the relationship seems even more
unlikely through the events of 1890, the year of Stewart Graham
Menzies's birth. In that year, there occurred one of the most unseemly
scandals of Victoria's reign. This scandal directly affected and embarrassed the heir to the throne at a time when he was already in
bad repute because he had been called into the divorce courts to give
evidence in a case where it was alleged that he had cuckolded a knight
of the realm. As a consequence of this new scandal, it seemed improbable that neither Susannah nor anyone around her would ever
be accepted at court.

The incident occurred at Arthur Wilson's home near Hull, Tranby
Croft, which had become rather famous because it was the first great
house in England to be equipped with electric lights and an early
form of water closet. The Prince of Wales was much interested in
these innovations, so he sought an invitation to spend the week of
the Doncaster races as the guest of Arthur Wilson and his wife, who
was a daughter of the postmaster of Hull. But since neither Jack nor

Susannah Menzies were present at that ill-starred house party, for reasons that have never been explained, it is necessary simply to sketch the events that occurred, if only because they were to reverberate throughout Stewart Menzies's life.

After the day's racing at Doncaster on September 8, the Prince of Wales and a party of friends arrived at Tranby Croft. The prince had not met any member of the Wilson family before, including, it is insisted, Susannah. Having bathed, dressed, and perfumed themselves, the party met for dinner at the gong. The dinner proved to be a memorable affair, partly because one of the prince's horses had won that day and partly because there were fourteen courses prepared by a French chef. The chef with his staff and equipment had been brought from Paris-Plage in a special carriage arranged by the London & North Eastern Railway, in which the Wilson brothers had major interests.

After dinner the ladies rose to permit the men to smoke and drink brandy. Then, upon rejoining the ladies, the party was first entertained by Ethel Lycett Green, the third of Arthur Wilson's daughters and therefore Stewart Menzies's aunt, who sang several songs. Then baccarat—a highly illegal game but one that the prince much enjoyed—was proposed. Arthur Wilson had been warned by Lord Coventry that this might occur. Although Wilson did not object, he did say to his wife in private that he thought such a game should not be played because junior officers and young people would be present, and he did not want to be held responsible for the corruption of their morals. It was therefore imperative that the rule of silence be observed, in both the interests of the prince and of the family's reputation.

About a dozen people gathered in the library. The servants were dismissed as the prince elected to become banker and croupier. The prince began to deal the cards. Before long, Arthur Wilson's son Stanley noticed irregularities in the way one of the prince's friends handled the counters, which were valued at £5 each. On some occasions after the prince had declared bank, his friend, Lieutenant Colonel Sir William Gordon-Cumming, of the Scots Guards, would slip extra counters onto his stake, and on others, when the cards were against him, he would take some of the counters away, apparently surreptitiously. When he won he was paid large sums by the prince. Afterward it would be asserted that Gordon-Cumming was cheating, using a sleight of hand known to gamblers as *la poussette*—the baby carriage—to increase or decrease his stakes when he had seen his cards.

This process was allowed to continue for three evenings when Lord Coventry, another of the prince's friends, challenged Gordon-Cumming. Gordon-Cumming then demanded an audience with the prince, in which the prince indicated rather than said that he accepted the allegation that the colonel had been cheating at cards. Appalled that a colonel of a household regiment should cheat his future sovereign at cards, the other guests then compelled Gordon-Cumming to sign a promise not to play cards for money again and to keep silent about the events that had occurred. All the other principal guests signed the document, which also bound them to silence. Gordon-Cumming then left Tranby Croft early in the morning while the rest of the house party was abed. Shortly afterward, the prince and his suite also departed, leaving Arthur Wilson and his wife in a state of severe chagrin at what had been a social disaster and a dangerous one, despite their extensive and expensive efforts to please the prince.

Notwithstanding the existence of the oath to silence, the story reached London, and Gordon-Cumming instituted actions for slander against Mrs. Wilson, Edward and Ethel Lycett Green (Wilson's son-in-law and daughter), Stanley Wilson, and Berkeley Levett, a subaltern in Gordon-Cumming's regiment and one who, with young Wilson, had drawn the attention of Lord Coventry to Gordon-Cumming's handling of the stakes. To make matters more serious, Gordon-Cumming's lawyers called the Prince of Wales to court to give evidence. Since this was the second time in recent years that the heir to the throne had been ordered before a common court, a scandal of large proportions followed.

The case was heard in June 1891. It lasted seven days, the manners and morals of the prince were scrutinized, and at length the jury found against Gordon-Cumming. He was then socially annihilated and asked to resign his commission. For weeks before, during, and after the hearing, the press was ferocious with all concerned, including the Wilsons in general and Arthur Wilson in particular. He returned to Tranby Croft a broken man, for as the *National Observer* put matters very bluntly:

As to the singular collection of persons generally spoken of as the Wilsons, they have passed, we hope, from the pages of contemporary history as suddenly as they appeared upon it, and if they never reemerge from their native obscurity, no one will regret it.

And that, exactly, was Arthur Wilson's fate. He resigned as master of the Holderness Hunt, and then he died in 1909, a plain mister, having spent the last years of his life in a state of what the *Dictionary of National Biography* called "undeserved obloquy." [6] Yet for all the magnitude of the scandal, the inability of certain members of the Wilson family to hold their tongue, and despite the embarrassment created for the throne and the prince, the Prince of Wales continued to accept Susannah in his circle. She marched onward and upward into the inner circle of the court, where she remained powerful and inviolate for the term of her life.

5 THE FAILURE OF HELLFIRE JACK

Stewart Graham Menzies was eleven and at Ludgrove, a preparatory school for Eton College, when Queen Victoria died on January 22, 1901, at the age of eighty-one, an epochal event in the history of the Crown and empire. She had been on the throne for sixty-four years, and she drew her last breath as her head lay cradled in the withered arm of her grandson, Kaiser Wilhelm II. The age of "Balmorality" ended, and she left one memorable warning. England must never become "subservient to Russia, for she would then fall down from her high place and become a second-rate power!"

Immediately upon her death, Edward went to Windsor Castle, where the princes of the world gathered for the obsequies. In a world where such matters were important, it was noteworthy that throughout, from the nineteenth of January when the queen began to die until the queen was interred at the royal mausoleum at Frogmore in February, Captain Holford was constantly at Edward's side. And while nowhere is either Jack or Susannah's name mentioned, we may be sure that they were within the phalanx of black and purple and ermine that constituted the new oligarchs. For with the queen's passing and Edward's accession, as the local newspaper at Hallyburton noted with pride, Jack and Susannah Graham Menzies were confirmed into "the highest circles in the land."

Yet if Jack and Susannah were rising socially by 1903, Jack's assets—his money, his health, his reputation—were all ebbing fast. Although he embarked upon a series of financial ventures, he succeeded at none. He made substantial investments in a diamond-mining corporation called St. Gerera, the name of a farm outside Salisbury, Rhodesia, which, so Jack believed along with several other prominent men about town, was rich in diamonds. Jack traveled to Salisbury to look over the property, although he knew nothing about mining, and returned impressed by what he saw, found, and heard. In 1899 he and his associates formed a public company called St. Gerera Development Company Limited. That promptly collapsed and cost somebody, probably Jack, a great deal of money. There was also much gambling at the table and on the racetrack; and Jack was present when his friend, Lord Edward Villiers, broke the bank at Monte Carlo, an episode that resulted in the song of that name.

When, in 1904, Jack left the Liberal party, became a Tory, and ran for the parliamentary seat of East Perthshire, his fortunes did not improve. There was much scathing comment in the press, and it appears that that was the way most of the electorate of East Perthshire felt about Jack's candidature. Before long the press announced that Jack had undergone "a somewhat serious operation" by Edward VII's surgeon, Sir Alfred Fripp, but that he had recovered and would open the Coupar Angus flower show on Tuesday.

But Jack did not open the flower show. He withdrew, and from the middle of 1904 onward he began to slip from the sight of his family and his friends. Jack and Susannah left Escrick Park and took up residence at Hall Place, Bexley, a great estate in Kent once the home of an archbishop of Canterbury. They went there to enable Susannah to attend to her social duties and, since their eldest son, Keith Graham Menzies, had entered Eton, and Stewart was soon to do so, to enable them to be closer to their boys. But there were other reasons for the move as well.

Jack Menzies's health was plainly failing, although he had not yet turned fifty, and the main cause of his decline proved to be alcoholism. In 1906 during a visit to Hallyburton Jack complained repeatedly that he had seen ghosts on the ministrels' gallery. But there was also another serious illness developing, tuberculosis, which was most likely discovered in the summer of 1906 when Susannah left Hall Place and returned to Tranby Croft. Where Jack went is not clear, but his next known address was Highcliffe, a small house overlooking the English Channel near Bournemouth, a city that was then well known as a center for the treatment of tuberculosis.

Thus it is possible that, having discovered that he had developed tuberculosis, a contagious disease, Jack took the honorable course.

So that he might not infect Susannah and the boys, and through them their friends, he left his home and went to a place of treatment. Nothing is known about his financial condition at this time, except that he had lost most of his money. Thus for all normal purposes the marriage was at an end, although there was no divorce or formal separation. If Balmorality had passed with Queen Victoria, divorce for any reason remained a social crime that led to an automatic loss of position at court. So in the eyes of the law at least Jack and Susannah remained man and wife.

That was fortunate, for by now Stewart Menzies faced what was not so much a school as a trial of strength, Eton College.

6 THE ROYAL COLLEGE OF ETON

Stewart Menzies entered Eton College, under the southern ramparts of Windsor Castle, at Michaelmas 1903. He was thirteen. Founded in the fifteenth century by Henry VI as a Catholic school for the poor, Eton had become, over the centuries, the leading Protestant college for the sons of the landed and titled aristocracy. The embodiment of the school was Menzies's headmaster, the Reverend Edmond Warre, the most formidable of all Eton's imperial headmasters, a man who, so it was said, had more to do with the soul of England than the archbishop of Canterbury. To the boys he appeared so massive that he looked as if he might be part of the battlements of the castle.

The singular quality about Warre was not his size but his educational background. There were seven colleges such as Eton at that time: Eton, Harrow, Westminster, Winchester, Rugby, Charterhouse, and Clifton. All seven headmasters, including Warre, were taught at the same school by the same man at the same time. All therefore had much the same philosophy as Warre. Their influence on what was to become the ruling generation of England in the period before, during, and after the two world wars were both similar and large. All were essentially classicists, as was Warre, and all held the view that superiority derived from elegant thought. Elegant thought produced elegant expression in both speech and writing; elegance of speech and writing produced the ability to command and lead. All believed to some degree in military or government service.

The difference between the seven headmasters was the depth of their militancy. Warre was the most military, establishing a curriculum that was a queer blend of God, Greek, and guns, his objective to create out of the sons of important men, who might otherwise become Philistines, the British equivalent of Plato's guardians of the state, a form of ideal man whom Plato chose "to defend the state in war when they are young and from whom, when they are older, he would choose the wisest to act as magistrates, rulers, and law givers." Plato's men were swift and strong, brave and high-spirited, "dangerous to their enemies but gentle to their friends." So therefore must be Etonians. They were to be trained in body and mind, not only in the use of their weapons and the control of troops in the field, but also "to admire what is beautiful and to display in everything they do a sense of harmony and proportion." This training in a sense of proportion would "make them virtuous and ensure that they do not try to overturn the state and become a danger to it." [7]

Warre was the ideologist, the distant figure on those long and haunted cloisters and alleys and playing fields. He did not succeed in making all his boys into gods, but he did produce a remarkable generation of Etonians at a time when British youth was itself regarded as the most remarkable produced, one that had not fought in a European war since Napoleon. They were called "the golden lads," and Stewart Menzies was one of them. Another of that generation, Reginald Pound, recorded, "No heirs of the ages had been granted a more triumphant sense of the human potential." His was the last of the English youth to be raised in a state of innocence. And it was one with which the "ironic gods never had more wicked sport with any generation."

Stewart Menzies's generation was the one for which there had been reserved the "transcendent excitement of seeing the first men fly." They had already witnessed the advent of the motorcar. They had seen the first moving pictures. They had heard the "first radio signals, cheeping like fledglings lost in outer space." It was a literate, perhaps poetic generation. Hitler, having fought its soldiers at Ypres in 1914, called it England's "heroic aristocracy" and sought to recreate its devotion and patriotism in the *Schutzstaffel.*

In producing the "golden lads," much was due to the quality of Warre's housemasters. Menzies's housemaster, Edward Impey, had a greater influence on Menzies's life than any other man. Dark, handsome, stocky, masculine (he had ridden with that most elegant regiment in the Indian empire, Skinner's Horse), Impey was dashing, an oak rather than an orchid, a full-blooded man and a classicist. He could be irritable, he was a disciplinarian and handy at floggings, but the boys liked him because, as Bernard Darwin, Charles Darwin's great-grandson, was to write, Impey was "the only beak who dresses decently and says 'Damn' like you or me." [8]

Also, Menzies admired Impey because he was the embodiment of imperialism. For generations the Impeys had been rulers of the British Indian empire. Impey himself had been born in India. A great-uncle, Lord Lawrence, had been a viceroy of India. Sir Henry Lawrence, another great-uncle, had been a defender at Lucknow, a hallowed episode of Victoria's reign. Impey's paternal grandfather, Colonel Eugene Clutterbuck Impey, of the Sikh Regiment, had become governor of Rajputana; Sir Elijah Impey had been chief justice of Bengal. Another forebear in India, General Sir Sam Browne, had had an arm shot off during the Indian Mutiny and had invented a special belt to carry his sword, pistol holster, compass, water bottle, rations, and map case. This came to be called the Sam Browne belt, that symbol of officers everywhere. The walls of Impey's study at Cotton Hall, Impey's house at Eton, were covered with the portraits of such men and the Indian princess through whom they ruled. No Victorian boy could have failed to be aware as he stood in that room that here was greatness personified.

Impey's teaching premise provided that those who wanted to rule and command must become gentlemen, that character was more important than intellect, that bearing should be considered as important as learning, that the first business of his house was the understanding of the Gospels, and that the purpose of the Gospels was to create men of courage, truth, honor, courtesy, chivalry, *manliness*. This was a very Edwardian word about which books were written explaining how manliness could be implanted and what it meant. A great deal of attention was paid to the Scriptures, psalms, and the now obscurer ceremonies of the church such as the Commination, that dread commitment to clean thought, conduct, and virtue.

As for the curriculum, there was Greek and Latin to sharpen the wits. Every boy was required to learn Thucydides' Speech of Pericles and especially the Funeral Oration, Lysias' Funeral Oration, and Plato's Menesenus, works that glorified Athenian imperialism. Hymns, poetry, music, feasts and holy days, the school rituals, sport. Every episode in the curriculum was calculated to confirm to the boys that England was first among nations, the royal throne of kings, the sceptered isle set in a silver sea. Much attention was paid to history, a subject that was intended to provoke an interest in, and a study of, the mechanisms by which the empire was established and maintained, the mechanism of power. A set of the questions put to Menzies at the First One Hundred Examination of 1908 has survived. It shows how political thought and responsibility were to be stimulated:

1. Sketch the history of the Jacobite rebellion of 1745 and compare it in general terms with that of 1715.
2. State precisely the grounds of Walpole's reputation as a statesman.
3. Illustrate and account for our early failure and eventual success in the Seven Years War. What did we gain at the end of it?
4. Point out the mistakes in the English policy towards America, and account for our failure in the War of American Independence.
5. Illustrate the characteristics and tactics of Wellington's generalship from the Peninsular War.
6. What are the chief merits and demerits of Pitt as a statesman?

Allied to this ideological concern was a considerable, enduring preoccupation with the United States and the revolt of the American colonies against the rule of George III, the sovereign who lived in the castle on hill above Eton College and became the college's most beloved patron. The school celebrated its greatest holiday on June 4, the king's birthday. It was not accidental that for two centuries the school's uniform was a tall black silk hat with mourning dress, the dress the school wore on the day George III died. Nor was the preoccupation with the United States mystical; it was political.

Since Eton was the *royal* college, the place to which, in general, went the sons of nobles, the clergy, the established oligarchy, it regarded all change as being for the worst, for it implied change in the established order. Thus it also deplored the American Revolution because it established republicanism, and the kings and the established order feared that republican ideas would spread to the lower classes in the empire, as they had spread to France and served to ignite the French Revolution less than twenty years after the colonists' secession.

As an expression of the underlying antipathy for America and Americans, in 1908—the year of the Root-Takahira Agreement in which the United States recognized Japan, not Britain, as a leading imperial power in the Pacific and thereby caused much irritation—this poem was published in the Eton College *Chronicle*, the school newspaper:

Russian, Yankee, and Prussian
Wherever you be,
That stand by the shores of our sea
And shake your fists over.
This is the castle of Dover,
You knaves!
That shall flog you over the waves
Of the world.

Menzies regarded America with reserve throughout his career. He believed as did most Etonians of his generation that America, for all her idealism, was bent upon world economic rule, that if she was to succeed, then she must at some stage set about the destruction of the British Empire of which she herself had once been the most important colony.

Yet perhaps to counterbalance Eton's influence, there was a strong connection between Holford and the United States. This derived from Holford's association with Whitelaw Reid, the American ambassador. Holford visited the United States on occasion, traveled widely, and invested heavily in the railroads. The Graham Menzies sept, too, had close connectons with Reid, based perhaps on the whiskey trade. Reid attended Menzies's family functions—he was a signatory at the weddings of Frederick Graham Menzies, one of Stewart's cousins— and his association with the two families provided early evidence of other associations between Stewart and his family and prominent Americans of the period 1917–1945. Those associations were to be of high importance later, the glimmerings of an alliance of Anglo-American capital.

In studies, Menzies did superbly well. In 1905 he was fifth in the First One Hundred Examinations; he won the Trials Prizes at Easter and Christmas in French and German; in 1907 he was awarded the King's Prizes for German. By Eton's standards these were creditable, although not outstanding, achievements. He might have done much better had he not been such a passionate huntsman. Toward the end of his stay at Eton Menzies hunted the beagles—hunting hares and foxes on foot with hounds, an exhausting sport—so frequently that, when his educational, social, and other sporting obligations are considered, it is surprising that he found any time for scholarship. Yet Menzies's hunting record was not regarded as idleness. Sir John Eardley-Wilmot, the fourth baronet who was at Eton a generation ahead

of Stewart Menzies and was by all accounts a great swell, contended
that the chase gave a boy

hardihood, and nerve, and intrepidity to our youth, while it confirms and
prolongs the strength and vigour of our manhood; it is the best corrective
to those habits of luxury and those concomitants of wealth which would
otherwise render our aristocracy effeminate and degenerate. . . .

(There was a certain truth in this statement, as a colleague in
secret service, Sir Dick Goldsmith White, wrote in his essay on Stewart Menzies in *The Dictionary of National Biography*. One of Stewart
Menzies's most important characteristics throughout his life was his
stamina and the excellence of his cardiovascular system, which, he
maintained, had been strengthened greatly by those almost unen-
durable hunts across the flat fields, streams, and hedges of the Thames
Valley.)

If Stewart Menzies proved superb at beagling, at staying the course,
he excelled at games and sport in general. That was important at
Eton, for this was a time when, so it was said, England won her wars
and kept her empire on the playing fields of Eton. In the ethos of
Eton, sport had become a definite part of the process of creating men
fitted to be guardians of the state. As early as June 1904, "Menzies,
Minor," as he was known until Ian Graham Menzies arrived, had
begun to impress his peers with what the Eton College *Chronicle*
called "his tremendous powers of endurance" in sport.

In his social and political life, however, he was less admired. His
family's money was "new" when the only money worth having was
"old." Given the "Royal Baccarat Scandal," his father's reputation,
his uncle Lord Nunburnholme's prominence in the antidrink movement, Robert Stewart Graham Menzies's advocacy of home rule for
Ireland and, worse, land reform, and the ruthless way Graham Menzies had made his money, Stewart would have encountered even
more savagery than he in fact experienced. What saved him was the
intervention of a boy who was accepted as one of the personifications
of the golden lad, Reginald Lindsay "Rex" Benson, a member of the
Holford cousinhood.

A year older than Stewart Menzies, Rex Benson was the son of
Robert H. Benson, a city merchant banker who lived in the grand
style at Buckhurst, an estate in Sussex. Benson's father had married
one of Holford's sisters, and Robert Benson was a magisterial figure
at the center of finance and politics for half a century. Rex was one
of the most popular boys at Eton, partly because he could play the

piano for four hours nonstop, but primarily for his conduct at that end of Eton's greatest sporting event of 1906, The Hurdles, an event that was still recalled and debated as late as 1984.

At the last hurdle, the most golden lad of Impey's, G.R.L. Anderson, son of the rector of St. George's, Hanover Square, was leading the field when he stumbled and fell. Benson was running second, and when he saw his rival fall Benson stopped in his tracks and waited until Anderson had recovered and resumed the race. Anderson then went on to defeat Benson. A great debate arose over Benson's gesture, one that broadened into a discussion about the purpose of Eton the echoes of which are still heard.

Well aware of Sir George Holford's great affection for Susannah Menzies, Rex Benson was powerful enough to demolish the antipathy for Stewart Menzies, which seems to have been centered on Julian Grenfell. A son of Lord and Lady Desborough, one of the most powerful families in London society, Julian Grenfell was not only a golden lad but also a swell. Most ordinary men might have found it very easy to dislike Grenfell, for he strode about those ancient cloisters cracking fifteen feet of Australian stockwhip at those he disliked, not the least of whom was Sir Phillip Sassoon, the Jewish banker's heir. Grenfell thought Sassoon was effeminate. Grenfell himself was a ruffian (he was known as "the Rough Man"), yet he was quite possibly the finest poet of his time. His difficulty was that he was too glorious, too gifted, too beautiful, too rich, too vital. Even Sassoon, when he became one of the richest men in England at a time when such men were very rich indeed, came to admire him, albeit posthumously.

It was not surprising that Grenfell disliked Menzies. When Menzies was sixteen, Rex Benson brought him into the *Club Nautique de Belges,* which seems to have had no purpose other than to talk, eat, and dress elegantly, although it did have a political purpose. The British had always regarded the neutrality and independence of Belgium as a first essential for British national security, and it was not accidental that whenever possible the Belgian ruling generation, too, sent its sons to Eton. (One who was there at Menzies's time was the future Leopold III, king of the Belgians, who came to regard Eton with as much affection as any Briton. Such connections, and others like them, were to prove useful when Menzies became "C." Whenever Leopold felt like surrendering to the Germans, "C" could always telephone him to remind the monarch that Etonians never surrendered.)

Benson succeeded in getting Menzies into the club, but when he was proposed for the club's Committee of Taste and Arrangement, Grenfell organized a blackball against Stewart's admission. It was a severe blackballing and was inflicted because, according to Laurence Impey, Edward Impey's son, he was "such a scruffy bugger." He rarely had his hair cut in the fashion, and sometimes he used pomade. His trousers often hung crumpled around his hips. His shoes were generally scuffed and unpolished. The flower he wore in his button-hole on George III's birthday and other feast days looked as if it had been plucked from a hedge.

At length, Menzies was admitted; and as one consequence he established himself socially and politically. As another he made friendships the memories of which were to have a lasting influence on his life. One was with Edward Horner, son of Sir John and Lady Horner, the latest in the line of Horners who had lived on an estate at Mells, Somerset, for four centuries. According to Lord Birkenhead, Churchill's great friend, to whom young Horner was articled as a law clerk in Temple Chambers, London, Horner was a typical golden lad. He was "six feet four in height, broad-shouldered and muscular, with a superbly shaped head and neck, a picture of radiant masculine beauty," and in mind he was "quick, polished, handsome, and intelligent" with a "rare and rich accumulation of gifts." He was also witty. On the morning Lady Cynthia Curzon was to be married to someone else Horner sent her a note: "For the last time, I am asking you to marry me."

With Horner came friendships with four other golden lads: Patrick Shaw-Stewart, Charles Lister, Ronald Knox, and Billy Grenfell, Julian's brother. Shaw-Stewart carried off the supreme prizes of Eton and Oxford, including the literary scholarship, the Newcastle Select, the Ireland and Hertford scholarships. He chose to be thought a Philistine, declaring frequently that "I have only worldly ambitions." Lister was the son of the last Lord Ribblesdale, who was fixed in the public mind as a magnifico by John Singer Sargent's portrait of him as master of the buckhounds, painted in 1902 and hung in the National Gallery. Although physically the epitome of the supreme aristocrat, he affected an interest in socialism, and as Ronald Knox recorded of his attitudes, he was:

> A rescue-the-poor young man,
> A waiter-look-sharp young man . . .

Knox's friendship was of high significance. One of the three sons of the bishop of Manchester—the others, both of whom were at Eton, were E. V., editor of *Punch* for seventeen years, and Arthur Dillwyn, who became Menzies's leading code breaker—Ronald Knox had doctrinaire differences with the church of his father, became a Catholic, was domestic prelate to the pope, produced a new Bible, and became a leading author of detective fiction. And above all there was Gerard Rupert Laurie "Twiggy" Anderson, who was quite possibly Menzies's inspiration.

Acknowledged as the best scholar-athlete of his generation, Anderson attained an extraordinary influence over his Etonian contemporaries. The consulting physician to the British Olympic Athletic Team that went to Stockholm for the games of 1912 wrote of Anderson:

Nature runs riot in her gifts on some occasions, and in an apparent desire to produce a very king of men, gives him beauty and health, grace, athletic ability, and intellect.

If Stewart Menzies's brain was not in the same class as these, his main friends at Eton, he did possess a quality of indomitability, of making the most of the gifts with which he was endowed. This indomitability became a political factor in his life. In 1907 Stewart Menzies intimated that he would like to join "Pop," the Eton College Society, the self-electing elite of Eton and perhaps the most influential of all British schoolboy institutions. Founded in 1811 by the marquess of Townshend's heir to "produce a love of reading and to encourage the study of history," Pop became in Menzies's time a sporting society and the school's main disciplinary body. It was a dandy institution, its members being "self-elected for their beauty, elegance, and charm, for their power to amuse and dazzle." [9]

Noted for its arrogance, exuberance, and daring, Pop, whose twenty-nine members had the power to beat or fine those who offended the code, was much concerned with dress and manners. Members ornamented the school uniform with silk facings, they wore black-and-white-checked trousers, flowers in buttonholes, and brilliant brocade. They alone were permitted to carry unfurled umbrellas in the street, to walk arm in arm, to wear patent-leather shoes in the spring and summer, Panama hats at cricket matches, and to "walk in front of the common herd when watching football matches." [10] To become a member of Pop was, therefore, to establish a special and lasting place not only in Etonian but also in British society. To know a member of Pop, or a man who had been a member, was like knowing a duke. It was enough.

In a world where Etonians were likely to dominate higher politics, higher administration, higher command, higher finance, higher church, and the court, members of Pop dominated the dominators. Consequently, to be considered and accepted as a member became overwhelmingly important, a test that worried all who tried. The English writer Cyril Connelly ran for Pop on a wit's ticket; he recalls: "At that time Pop were the rulers of Eton, fawned on by masters and the helpless sixth form. Such was their prestige that some boys who failed to get in never recovered; one was rumored to have procured his sister for the influential members."

When Benson nominated Menzies for Pop, his main assets consisted of his family's wealth, power, and connections, his prowess as a sportsman, and the fact that the chairman of Pop was Rex Benson. Another powerful friend was the president of Pop, Anderson, who admired Menzies's steeplechasing. Prowess proved another powerful friend. But even these important members could not make the committee accept Menzies at first. Old prejudice still hovered over his family. Thus at the first elections of 1907 Menzies received no less than eight blackballs—almost, it appeared, an insurmountable number.

But by 1908, five years after entering Eton, Stewart Menzies had overcome most, and perhaps all, of the prejudices against him. In that year he became prominent; his name appeared more frequently than any other in the little box on the front page of the Eton College *Chronicle*, which contained the names of schoolboy officers. He won the Prince Consort's Prize in French. His name was placed in the annals of the Eton College Hunt when, as master, the hunt made its greatest record, one that was still being talked about sixty years later. Menzies killed three foxes and ran two to ground, one of which was evicted and killed.

Then he won the hurdles again. He became first a team player and then keeper (or captain) of that most mysterious and unrewarding of Eton's sports, the wall game. Although the object was to score goals, to do so was rare, so rare that in the annual St. Andrew's Day match no goal was scored for sixteen years between 1950 and 1966. But such was Menzies's prowess that the Eton College *Chronicle* observed that "S. G. Menzies seems quite indefatigable." He knew "exactly when to use his pace and plays on the defensive as well as when on the offensive. He can always be relied upon for some brilliant runs."

All the old reserve about Menzies dissolved under a welter of schoolboy triumph. In his house he became head of library, a post responsible not for books, but for discipline. He became captain of his house and a member of the Debating Society, which also had the power to flog. And he appeared third in the First One Hundred Examination, having been awarded 550 marks against the 625 marks obtained by the man in first place.

He ran again for Pop. This time he succeeded. In turn he became a member in 1908, then auditor, and then chairman in that same year, largely because an unusually large number of officers of Pop left the school during 1908. And when in 1908 Rex Benson prepared to retire upon leaving Eton for Balliol, Benson proposed Stewart as his successor. Other factors may have played a part in the committee's deliberations. The press made mention of the presence at Windsor Castle of several of the Graham Menzies sept, including Susannah. In the circumstances, and at Benson's prodding, there could be one choice only, Menzies.

At Michaelmas 1909, the start of a period of danger in all affairs, Stewart Menzies departed Eton with his future established. He went not to Oxford, but into another of those English elite brotherhoods, the Grenadier Guards, who regarded themselves as being the finest soldiers in the world. He was commissioned as a probationary sub-lieutenant and began to appear in great parades of state wearing a tall black bearskin known as a busbee, scarlet tunic, black trousers, royal-gray greatcoat, and a sword at the present. Doubtless he adopted the swagger of the Grenadier Guards officer; and the world looked fair.

His peers felt he had more dash than talent, more vivacity than acumen, more common sense than learning. He appears to have been aware of the Etonian dictum "All men must count with you but none too much." And above all he possessed in the requisite degree that quality of "effortless superiority" and "unassailable primacy" that was, they said with pride, the hallmark of the Eton man. [11]

7 INTO THE LIFE GUARDS

King Edward VII died on May 5, 1910, just after his horse, Witch of the Air, won the 4:15 P.M. race at Kempton Park. The king was sixty-eight and had been nine years on the throne. His mistress, the Hon-

orable Mrs. George Keppel, a friend of the Holfords and of Susannah
Menzies, was invited to the death watch by the queen, Alexandra.
Edward's chief contribution to the safety and tranquillity of his reign
had been to smooth the way in France for the alliance of England
and France against Germany. He encouraged the Anglo-Japanese
Treaty of 1902, intended to secure the Indian empire against war
with Russia, but which irritated and worried the United States. And
he reached an understanding with the tsar. The effect of these treaties
proved grave: Germany felt surrounded by enemies, and in reaction
the kaiser created the largest and best-equipped army in Europe,
declaring that "there is no power in Europe, except God and my
twenty army corps."

With Edward's passing, it seemed that the *belle époque* was dead
and a period of perpetual revolution and war had begun. Yet there
were signs that the imperial dynasties might yet maintain the peace.
At the obsequies at Westminster Hall the German emperor, Wilhelm
II, laid a wreath of purple-and-white flowers on his uncle Edward's
coffin, although they had detested each other. Then, with the new
British sovereign, King George V, at his side and grasping his cousin's
hand, the British and German emperors knelt and said a prayer for
the soul of the departed prince.

For the Menzies family, the departure of Edward VII had little
effect upon their standing in society. As was the custom, George V
brought with him his own equerry, but Holford was not displaced at
court. His services as equerry were retained by Queen Alexandra,
who became the dowager queen with Edward's passing. Holford was
created a knight grand cross of the Indian empire and promoted in
his regiment; he was now styled Lieutenant Colonel Sir George Holford, First Life Guards. Shortly, Holford found a place for Stewart
in his regiment in curious circumstances that recalled the Tranby
Croft affair.

Evidently the Grenadier Guards did not suit Stewart Menzies,
probably because he was born in the saddle. What he wanted was a
commission in what was then the most romantic of all military formations, the Household Cavalry. However, not even Menzies could
find a place in the Horse Guards if there was no vacancy in the officers'
house. But then in the mysterious way of all tribes a place miraculously
opened for him. Arthur Wilson's son-in-law, Edward Lycett Green,
one of the defendants in the libel action brought against the Wilson
family by Gordon-Cumming, had managed to find a place in the

Second Life Guards as a probationary sublieutenant, despite the obloquy in which the family found itself after the Royal Baccarat Scandal.

But the regiment disliked Lycett Green for his part in the scandal and, happily for Stewart Menzies (and perhaps also for England), Green resigned his commission. On that same day Menzies took his place. He seemingly was uncontaminated by the Royal Baccarat Scandal, for neither Jack nor Susannah were present at Tranby Croft when it had occurred. Moreover, was not Holford, his mother's close friend, the colonel of the Reserve Regiment of the Life Guards? And was not the colonel of the Second Life Guards, Ferguson, not a member of the Holford cousinhood and a member of the cousinhood of the duke of Buccleuch, to which, again, Holford was related? And had Stewart himself not been president of Pop?

Stewart Menzies entered yet another highly exclusive brotherhood. One of the three regiments of Household Cavalry, he had joined a cabal so distinctive that its men called themselves not soldiers but "gentlemen of the Life Guards." The regiment's officers were drawn from what regimental standing orders called "the most select families of competent Noblemen and gentlemen of the Kingdom." Their main duty was to "guard the King's life, constantly and without intermission." [12]

As a group, the Life Guards suited Menzies's inclinations perfectly. They were conservative in politics and social attitudes, and they deplored all change. Although they were issued with khaki two or three years before the outbreak of World War I, they continued to wear their gorgeous raiment on all occasions despite king's regulations. They continued to call all machine guns "Maxims" long after Maxim guns had been taken out of service, and they were particular about such matters as the length of a sword, the cut of a pair of trousers, and whether a uniform coat should have six or five buttonholes. They guarded all tradition and custom with tribal pride and engaged all who would change anything in the regiment in a ferocious, interminable, and exhausting correspondence. As evidence, there is in the War Office files a massive correspondence written in beautiful copperplate insisting that they, and they alone, were entitled to bear arms in the royal palaces and in the presence of the blood royal.

They regarded themselves as being a race apart, men who acknowledged that they were subject to ordinary laws and conventions, but who did what they thought best or what suited them in most mortal pursuits. Most of the officers and troopers were Freemasons, since most of the blood royal were Freemasons, and there were lodges for both officers and men in all the Household Cavalry regiments. And it is assumed that Menzies was a Freemason, for he advanced too far too quickly not to have been one. Menzies's commanding officer, Algernon Holford Ferguson, was a Freemason. As a man, he was loyal, dependable, and brave: a praetor. His chief contribution to the military art was to perpetuate the tactic of the charge. Despite the general introduction of the machine gun, a regiment of 360 hur-rahing men and horse thundering at the guns was, he believed, mag-nificent and irresistible.

There was never any doubt that Menzies would be retained in the Life Guards. Nevertheless, king's regulations obliged Holford to go through the motions of estimating Menzies's suitability for his high tasks. Much attention was paid to Menzies's physique, his manners, his dress, and his bearing, what was called "the cut of his jib." A member of a *corps d'élite*, custom required him to dress and carry himself as such. To "fit" into the officers' house, Menzies was required to have several sets of uniforms made for him by the regimental tailor, all of which were expensive and were cut and decorated with the object of making it appear that the man under the serge appeared to be an immortal. He was required to have two chargers, two polo or riding horses, and between two and four servants, depending upon his equipage. He needed therefore an income of at least £2,000 a year. Where such a large private income came from is not clear, for it is almost certain that Stewart had no means of his own. Yet not only did he "fit," but he prospered in the regiment.

The system plainly worked well for Stewart Menzies. But it had not worked well for his father, Jack. Just before Menzies went to the Life Guards, he learned that Jack was dying, "having lived too well and too unwisely." [13] The truth proved otherwise, as Jack died of the tuberculosis that first struck him in 1906. He passed away on May 15, 1911. Only Stewart was present at his father's death. Jack was fifty. His death passed virtually unnoticed, even by the local press in Scotland. Where he was buried is not known. In death, as in life, he had left practically no record of his passage, except in one important respect, his money. Jack had not made a will when he died, so Stewart was appointed executor. After much delay and inquiry, Jack's estate was probated at just £163. [14]

In twenty-seven years he had squandered the equivalent of about £8 million by 1987 values. This was not impossible, of course, but nothing existed to show where or how Jack had spent his fortune, for he owned no property, having lived always on leased estates. He apparently disposed of all his securities, including his holdings in the Distillers Company Limited. Although she had the income from her holdings in the Wilsons' shipping, for Susannah Jack's estate was appalling. But her dismay was not prolonged, for upon Jack's death, George Holford proposed marriage to Susannah, and she accepted.

The ceremony took place in vice-regal circumstances on July 12, 1912, although by the social standards of the period and of court this was certainly an extraordinary union. Holford, one of the most important of the courtiers, was marrying the daughter of *parvenues* who had been excoriated throughout the realm for their part in the Tranby Croft affair. Susannah had been married to a man who, it was supposed, died in poverty and embarrassment. She was of an age when she could yet bear children to George, which would enable her to inherit Holford's enormous estate, a prospect that caused anxiety amongst Holford's trustees and beneficiaries. She possessed neither title nor position, and she was acceptable at court only because she was there, although nobody knew why.

Yet King George V set his seal of approval upon the marriage, for the king, the queen, the dowager queen, and Princess Victoria were all present at the wedding, which took place at the Chapel Royal. Stewart and Keith Graham Menzies, both wearing the full ceremonials of their regiments, escorted their mother to the altar. Noncommissioned officers of Holford's regiment, the First Life Guards, lined the aisle. The subdean of the Chapel Royal, Canon Edgar Sheppard, officiated. Colonel Sir Arthur Davidson, who had been a private secretary to King Edward VII, attended as Holford's best man.

Jewelry and presents of great value were showered upon the couple by the king, the queen, the court, the witnesses, and the guests. Such was Susannah's social power that even *The Ladies Pictorial*, known for its malice about the ruling class, had respectful things to say of the union:

Sir George looked very handsome and manly as he passed down the Chapel with his dainty, pretty bride. It was difficult to believe that the two good-looking, soldierly, well-set-up young men who walked on either side of her up the church were her sons. The relationship looked more like brothers. . . . She is a favourite with all who know her. That Sir George is goes without saying: he is so courteous, kind, and good. [15]

The journal took the opportunity to commiserate with Susannah at her previous misadventure by declaring that "Mrs. Menzies's first husband was a very wealthy man but had great money losses borne always by her with great cheerfulness." Many of the social luminaries attended the ceremony, among them the American ambassador, Whitelaw Reid, who was a Holford and Menzies family friend.

Dorchester House became Stewart's London home, Westonbirt his country estate. Holford adjusted his will so that Susannah would become one of the nine beneficiaries of his fortune. The other beneficiaries prayed fervently that George and Susannah would not produce children—a prayer that was to be answered. And as an immediate and tangible sign of his devotion, he gave her all his personal jewelry. Valued at some £200,000, (£4 million today), this treasure included "a row of superb pearls, very large and perfectly matched; a riviere of very fine diamonds; a ruby-and-diamond necklet fitted with fleur-de-lys points, which may be worn as a tiara; three superb diamond stars, which fit on a diamond necklet, also convertible into a tiara; a large corsage brooch of diamonds with one large pearl in the centre and three pearl-shaped pearl drops; a large diamond corsage ornament having one splendid diamond in the centre; and a diamond drop, a diamond bracelet, and a diamond pendant." [16]

Thus Susannah West Menzies was transformed into Lady Holford. After a honeymoon first at Paris-Plage and then at Monte Carlo, Sir George and Lady Susannah Holford were received in high style when they returned to Westonbirt. The staff and tenantry lined the long carriageway from the gatekeeper's lodge to the master's entrance of the mansion. In all they numbered 128 persons. There were pretty speeches and a good deal of curtseying and bowing. That night there was a grand dinner and ball at which Lady Holford was welcomed to Westonbirt and Sir George sat above the swaying squirearchy in one of the Medici's thrones, a benevolent figure in court dress. He wore the collar of gold of a Knight Grand Commander of the Most Eminent Order of the Indian Empire, with its little elephants, lotus flowers, peacocks in their pride, Indian roses, and the imperial crown bearing the legend "Imperatricis Auspiciis."

8 BACK TO BALMORALITY

More than any other factor, his mother's marriage elevated Stewart Menzies to the highest social circles in the land, including the court. This was a day and an age when to be acceptable at court was to be acceptable anywhere. Yet if court preferment assisted him in his career, it is only fair to state that Menzies possessed a natural ability to prosper in that ornate world. He certainly succeeded in the Life Guards, which were part of the court. He was exceedingly good-looking in the Hannay fashion of Edwardians. He walked and talked well. He had a boyish streak that the older officers found appealing and agreeable.

Although only five feet ten inches tall, his figure was excellent, and with a good chest and a fine curve to his waist and thighs, he looked well in uniform. He rode well, and at the hunt he was daring, riding at rather than over obstacles. He was neither "fast" nor a nancy. His mess manners were agreeable. He was what was known in the regiment as "a damm'd good chap." Excellent at swordplay, he could slice a candle from top to bottom with a single stroke of his sword. He could hold his own in that greatest trial of strength—which sub-altern could stand on his head and drink the quickest a glass of black-strap, a mixture of port and brandy peculiar to the regiment. He could ride with the best at the point to point. He cut an excellent figure when engaged in ceremonial soldiering, waiting in attendance upon the blood royal at such occasions as Royal Ascot, the state opening of Parliament, or the king's birthday parade at the Horse Guards. He was much sought after, as was usual with subalterns of the Household Cavalry, for the balls and dinners in the various London palaces and great houses. A good shot with pistol and carbine, in the laying of the Maxims and the preparation of the horse guns he was in the tournament class. He was neither idle nor arrogant. Above all, he was favorably known to his future sovereign, Edward, Prince of Wales, who lolled about the officers' house in Regent's Park and drank champagne cocktails on mess nights.

In his soldiering, Stewart Menzies constantly attended courses in musketry, machine guns, fieldcraft, map reading, compass reading, and veterinary surgery. In 1912 he also attended a school for adjutants, the officer in a regiment who assisted the commander by supervising the carrying out of the details of an order. Within the War Office, this course was considered to be significant: it was the first step toward high command. It separated the future staff officer from the fighting men. Again he did well, for in 1912 he was appointed assistant adjutant of the Second Life Guards. This appointment required a new set of uniforms, for on parade the adjutant wore a three-quarter-length frock coat much bedecked with black silk millinery. And in that same year Menzies found himself in personal attendance upon the new king, George V, as commander of the King's Guard at George's coronation.

On June 22, 1911, King George V was crowned king-emperor of the British Empire in a long ceremony at Westminster Abbey. Representatives of every country were present, and the German crown prince represented the German empire, that being the custom, and as a member of the blood royal he swore fidelity to the king during the ceremony. All London echoed to the sounds of martial music while every street glinted and flashed with swords and bayonets carried by troops from every corner of the empire—an empire that the *Daily Mail* noted with satisfaction was, with a population of 540 million people, nearly four times larger than America, and which in landmass—14,435,000 square miles—was almost five times as big.

It is one of the historical curiosities that in an age of deepening antagonisms between England and Germany, George V, in all sixteen quarterings of his origins, was a German prince educated in England. Yet this "High and Mighty Prince" was unquestioningly accepted as "our only lawful and rightful liege lord George the Fifth, by the Grace of God, King of the United Kingdom of Great Britain and Ireland, and of the British Dominions Beyond the Seas, Defender of the Faith, Emperor of India." Moreover, not only did he give style to a dangerous and restless epoch, but the people came to love him genuinely.

The king considered himself to be wholly an English gentleman, and as he remarked to Franklin D. Roosevelt at his coronation, "In all my life I have never met a German gentleman." Yet the tap of distant drums was heard even at his coronation. The apparition of the Shropshire Lad hung over the abbey as the prelates in hierophantic robes passed and repassed in the weak sunshine, in ceremonies that derived from Wotan:

> On the idle hill of summer
> Sleepy with the flow of streams,
> Far I hear the steady drummer
> Drumming like a noise in dreams.

On Coronation Day, and in the days that followed, Lieutenant Menzies assumed important duties with his regiment, the Second Life Guards. The regiment constantly attended upon the king throughout the coronation and afterward. At this time Stewart Menzies squired Monica Grenfell, Lord Desborough's daughter and Julian's sister, and as she recorded: "The summer of 1911 almost seems to have been the Fancy Dress Summer." Taplow Court, the Grenfells' house beside the Thames in Berkshire, hosted her own coming-out ball, a heavenly occasion that opened Coronation Year. Monica's ball and others that season were joyous affairs, but there was a sense everywhere that it was the joy experienced at the guards' ball on the eve of Waterloo: beyond the ballroom loomed the battle.

When at last the celebrations ended, and King George V and Queen Mary were returning to Windsor Castle on July 1, Menzies served as a member of the King's Guard on the occasion of the "Royal Progress" to Windsor. While men do many important things in life that excite the admiration of their peers, it was given to few men to appear before an entire college such as Eton in the full ceremonial uniform of a regiment such as the Life Guards in attendance upon a king-emperor. But that was Menzies's post that glorious first day of July in 1911.

The royal train arrived from London at Slough station. The King's Guard waited in the railway yard for the king and queen to enter their landaus. Proceeding at eight miles an hour, the line of landaus and the guard made their way out into the flat countryside of the Thames valley, halting at Eton College. The horses were tethered in the cobbled yard to the cannon captured by the Light Brigade at Sebastopol. Twelve hundred Etonians wearing their tails and toppers gathered in a dense mass as far as Baldwin's Bec and Tom Brown's, the school tailor. The school had been decorated in light and dark blue and evergreen, with hundreds of hanging baskets of flowers. Thousands of Venetian masts led the eye up the High Street to the castle on the hill.

The guard of honor of the Eton contingent of the Officers' Training Corps presented arms with a flash of bayonets. The King's Colour was dipped in salute. The band of the Royal Buckinghamshire Hussars played the National Anthem, and girls in pinafores approached, curtsied, and presented bouquets. The faculty, medieval in their black gowns and hoods, presented a loyal address.

Then the king and the queen, with Menzies and the King's Guard still in close attendance, rode on, down Eton High Street, past the low, old shops, across the Windsor Bridge over the Thames toward Curfew Tower. What a pretty sight it was! A procession of scarlet, black, and gold, with pennants flying and the glistening blacks prancing and snorting with the horse furniture jingling as the king "made his proceeding" under the battlements of the great, gray castle. The band played "Men of Harlech," the flags and bunting stood out in the light summer breeze, the men in the crowds doffed their bowlers, and the women curtsied as the procession moved up the hill and into the castle through Henry VIII's Gate. How good it was to be alive! What pride and pleasure there was to be in personal attendance upon the monarch and his consort! That night there was a band concert and fireworks in Windsor Great Park.

That night, too, Menzies and the Second Life Guards were ordered by the War Office with the army into a preliminary stance for war. The kaiser had sent a warship to seize the Moroccan port of Agadir, ostensibly to safeguard the lives and property of German residents in the port against sack by rioting Arabs. Whether that was true or not, the possession of Agadir would give the German emperor command of the sea lanes to British South Africa. For the first time, the Life Guards were brigaded as the Seventh Cavalry Brigade, Third Cavalry Division, First Cavalry Corps, British Expeditionary Force to France.

The Teuton furore between England and Germany had begun. It would last thirty-five years, for most of Menzies's career. Slowly but surely the cantilever of nations began to collapse. The general peace that had lasted since the Napoleonic Wars began to crumble. The distant tap of drums and the scream of fifes became louder.

9   "A STRANGE AND SCANDALOUS CULT"

On March 18, 1913, with the Balkan War rumbling savagely, the British ambassador at Athens, Sir F. Elliot, telegraphed the foreign secretary, Sir Edward Grey, in the stately fashion of British diplomatic telegrams:

Humble Duty. Terrible news has been received from Salonica of the assassination of the King of Greece, who was shot by a Greek and died almost immediately. Assassin, who is believed to be crazy, was seized, but an alleged accomplice escaped. Crown Prince, who is at Janina, has been asked to return to Athens as soon as possible. The Queen is on her way to Salonica. [17]

That telegram resulted in Lieutenant Stewart Graham Menzies's first foreign mission, his first personal experience of power politics in a dangerous world.

The king of Greece, George I, had been placed on the Greek throne by Edward VII, and he had been, therefore, an ally of England in the European power equation. Such was British power that, when King Otto, a prince of the German house of Wittelsbach, was expelled from Greece by the Greeks, Edward VII suggested to the Greek premier that his country might find his queen's brother, Prince Wilhelm of Schleswig-Holstein-Sonderburg-Glucksburg, who was eighteen and a naval cadet, an agreeable monarch. Such was the way the blood royal adjusted the cantilevers of power.

Before long, Prince William became King George I of the Hellenes and a loyal friend of the British throne. The British gave him a royal yacht and a small but useful navy, but with the assassination of George I a new factor entered the power balance. The heir, Constantine, was thought to be pro-German. If that was so, then the Greek army, of which, as king, Constantine would become commander-in-chief, might become an instrument of the kaiser. And so might the Greek navy. Moreover, Germany might obtain naval bases in Greek waters from which to challenge British naval supremacy in the Mediterranean. Therefore a strong British presence at the funeral was an indispensable matter of state.

A further consideration of state existed: England regarded herself as the most powerful nation in the world, with the most powerful navy, and here was an opportunity to display that power at a time of tension. It might serve to show the German emperor that, if the Prussians chose war, they would have to reckon with an invincible factor, the British fleet.

With these equations in mind, Lord Stamfordham, George V's private secretary, learned that an international squadron of German, Russian, Italian, and Austrian warships were gathering in the eastern Mediterranean to escort the Greek royal yacht, *Amphitrite*, which was to carry the embalmed corpse of the king to Athens. Stamfordham earnestly recommended to the first lord of the Admiralty, Winston Churchill, that a British force larger than the international squadron should be sent to join the escort. Attention should be paid to the size and age of the British warships to ensure that they were not smaller and less modern than the foreigners. Churchill agreed and ordered a combined force of battleships and cruisers to meet the international squadron. The commander of the British squadron took care to see to it that all ships' colors were half-masted and the Greek flag was hoisted at the dip on the mainmast.

In the same vein, the foreign secretary ensured that the rank of George V's representative going to Athens for the royal funeral would be at least the equivalent of any other representative. Accordingly the foreign secretary, in consultation with the secretary for war, decided that the British party should be led by His Serene Highness Lieutenant Colonel the Prince Alexander of Teck, Second Life Guards, younger brother of the dowager queen, Alexandra, and the nephew of the murdered king. It was decided also that he be accompanied by Major Lord Kenyon, also of the Second Life Guards, with Lieutenant Stewart Graham Menzies as aide-de-camp.

Thus began what was to prove to be a most important association for Stewart. Born in 1874, educated at Eton, nephew of George, duke of Cambridge, Teck became the earl of Athlone when German names became unfashionable. As such Athlone became, after Holford, Menzies's most powerful patron. In turn, Athlone became personal aide-de-camp to King George V and King George VI, governor of Windsor Castle, and governor-general of South Africa and then Canada, and he lived in great splendor at Kensington Palace, almost next door to Buckingham Palace.

As Teck's party traveled in a special coach attached to the rear of the London–Brindisi express, anxiety developed at the Admiralty. *Yarmouth*, the warship nearest to the Greek royal yacht, was older and slower than the German *Goeben*, the Russian *Uraletz*, the French *Bruix*, the Austrian *Maria Theresa*, and the Italian *San Giorgio*, all of which were converging. But then came better news. The royal yacht was immobilized in a great fogbank in the Aegean with her foreign escorts. Urgent signals flashed from the Admiralty's wireless station. Accordingly the British squadron made speed to eighteen knots so that, when *Amphitrite* emerged from the fog into the bright sunshine, those aboard would see a splendid British squadron with a few foreigners in attendance.

The king's body arrived at Athens on March 27. In a vast telegram to the Foreign Office, Sir F. Elliot noted with satisfaction that no foreign hands—particularly German hands—had touched the coffin between the time it was unloaded from the royal yacht and the moment it was placed in the royal grave at the home of the Greek kings, Tatoi. It was a fine point, perhaps, but that was the way power politics were made when Menzies was young. This was an age much preoccupied with precedence and protocol, when a nod meant something and a whisper in a chancery meant everything.

Elliot reported there had been some difficulty on the question of precedence in the cortege. The French and the Cubans insisted that they had the right to head the foreigners' procession. But King Constantine had been raised at 2:00 A.M. to settle the dispute, and he had agreed that foreign mourners should be placed in the funeral procession in alphabetical order, not in order of their importance to the Greek government. As Elliot went on in his telegram, the only disagreeable incident in the entire affair concerned the German cruiser, *Goeben,* which was allowed to anchor in Phalerum Bay. Alarmingly the Greek government had declined to accord the British squadron a similar courtesy. Also, the Greek battery had not fired the customary twenty-one-gun salute when the British squadron arrived; the commander of the Greek battery explained that there was "something wrong with the battery." A return salute was made, however, at 8:00 A.M. on the following day.

There was also an error on the part of the admiral commanding the British squadron, and this misjudgment had resulted in the Germans' success in placing twice as many seamen in one of the state processions as the British. On the other hand the Royal Navy's wreath appeared in a very prominent place at the cathedral during the lying-in-state. Moreover, Constantine had given Prince Alexander, Lord Kenyon, and Lieutenant Menzies a private supper to which the Germans were not invited. That had caused considerable satisfaction. Beyond all this, cordial connections were established with the new monarch. That was true. When he became "C" Menzies always enjoyed the closest connection with George II, whose throne Menzies succeeded in saving on a number of occasions, and it is noteworthy that when, forty years on, "C" retired from secret service, George II, king of the Hellenes, sent a personal telegram to Menzies through the British secret service chief in Athens, thanking "C" for "his many services to the Greek nation." That connection began here, and it was always an important one.

With the new king on the throne, Teck, Kenyon, and Menzies called at Tatoi to deliver their respects and hopes that Constantine's reign would be a long and happy one. (It was not, for the British forced him off the throne in 1917, restored him in 1920, and then deposed him again in 1922.) Then the British representatives returned to Brindisi, taking with them in their battleship, *Defence*, the Infante Don Carlos of Spain, who had no warship of his own to give him conveyance. Thus they had prevented the Germans from placing *Goeben* at his disposal.

From Menzies's viewpoint it had been a valuable journey. Although he never liked foreign parts, especially those east of Paris or west of Dublin, the Athens mission gave him insight into practical politics, protocol, and ceremony in a foreign capital at a time when knowledge of such matters could be important. It had enabled him to take the measure of the officers of the kaiser's Garde du Corps, who were in attendance upon the German princes. It had also given him practical experience in one other matter, the parsimony of the Treasury.

On their return to London, Teck's suite submitted their expenses for their journey, £18 5s. 11d., mostly for entertainment at Brindisi and Patros. Although that sum caused some surprise at the Treasury (a tot of whiskey in these days cost twopence), what really caused trouble was the 5s. 11d., which the party had paid for "washing bedding in the cabins occupied by H[is]S[erene]H[ighness] and Suite." The bedding in H.M.S. *Defence* was filthy, and Prince Alexander had demanded it be laundered before he would sleep in it. For that service the navy charged the suite the 5s. 11d., and submitted the bill before they left the warship at Portsmouth. When Menzies rendered the account there was much copperplate correspondence, given the size of the subject and amount, between government departments. Then it was decided that the bill could not be paid by the government because there was no provision in law for such expenditure. The 5s. 11d. was, therefore, sent to Stewart Menzies at Windsor Barracks for payment. Stewart never forgot the lesson.

Lieutenant Menzies returned to London in time for the start of the season. It was a period when, as a foreign member of society was to record, "a race of gods and goddesses descended from Olympus upon England" to live upon "a golden cloud, spending their riches as indolently and naturally as the leaves grow green." [18] It was the time when that "brilliant and powerful body," as Winston Churchill called the two hundred families of the oligarchy, came to the capital from their estates. It was a world where at the top everyone was related to everyone else. But in the mess, there was little talk of anything but the "German problem." War, they said, was coming.

While Menzies had gone to Athens, a fourth regiment of Horse Guards had been formed, its men being drawn from each of the three regiments. It was called the Composite Regiment, and its mission was to go to France with the British army immediately once war was declared. This development resulted in an important promotion for young Menzies. The adjutant of the Second Life Guards had gone to the Composite Regiment, thereby creating a position that Menzies had been trained to fill, and fill it he did. Although only twenty-three, Stewart Menzies was now the most powerful officer in the regiment after the commanding officer, Ferguson.

Under the new order of affairs within the regiment, Menzies was responsible under Ferguson for all matters of discipline. Among those duties was the requirement to ensure that the officers and men made desirable marriages. With King George V on the throne, the Life Guards wanted no divorcées, harlots, or hellcats in the regiment's baggage, for, on occasions, the regiment's women were required to meet the royal family. All officers and men were required, consequently, to advise the adjutant of their desire to marry and to provide the name, address, age, and antecedents of the woman concerned. If there was any suggestion that the woman might be undesirable, a check was made, and if the suspicions proved correct, the adjutant was required to call the man concerned to his officer and register the regiment's disapproval of the union—in the nicest way possible, of course.

In the light of the king's preoccupation with the proprieties, it was strange that Menzies sanctioned the marriage of his best friend in the regiment, Lieutenant David Euan Wallace, just twenty-one, to Lady Idina Sackville, the elder daughter of the eighth earl De La Warr, one of the oldest and most noble of families in England. And if Stewart Menzies had registered the regiment's reserve about the union, he would have saved himself and his friend a great deal of trouble later on.

A product of Harrow, one of the other six leading public schools, Wallace and Menzies had much in common. They were both from distinguished Perthshire families. They were both huntsmen and shots. They were about the same height, build, and appearance. They hunted with the same packs, danced with the same girls at the same balls, and both were members of the same club, the Bachelors' in Hamilton

Place near the corner of Piccadilly and Park Lane, a place described as a "modern club of fashion and distinction, much favoured by the *jeunesse dorée*"—the gilded youth—and which was made famous by P. G. Wodehouse as the Drones. [19] The chief difference between them was that whereas Menzies was "comfortable," Wallace had become extraordinarily rich in unusual circumstances. Wallace's uncle, William Weir, had made a great fortune when, being a bachelor of late years, he fell in love with an actress who returned his affections. So great did this passion become that Weir made the actress his sole beneficiary of an estate that was valued by *The Times* at £2 million (perhaps £50 million by 1987 values).

Weir's affections had changed abruptly when he found the actress locked in the embrace of her leading man. There were furious words, and Weir cut the actress out of his will, making Euan Wallace his sole beneficiary. Euan Wallace had inherited this fortune at Weir's death in about 1912 and thereby became one of the richest men of his generation. [9]

Before long, Wallace had met Lady Idina and had proposed marriage; and on the face of it, it was an excellent choice from the point of view of the regiment. Lady Idina came from a family that had served the Crown for over eight hundred years and had provided a governor for New York and one for the state of Delaware, which was named after the family. Her mother, Countess Muriel De La Warr, was a daughter of Lord Brassey, the great railroad builder, engineer, and one of the richest men in England. Although the Earl De La Warr and his wife had produced three children, Lord Buck De La Warr, Lady Idina, and Lady Avice, the marriage had foundered in 1901, when the earl abandoned the countess for an actress. There followed an unpleasant divorce action that, as usual, resulted in the participants being banned at court.

But beyond the De La Warrs' divorce there was another, perhaps more serious matter. After the divorce, Countess Muriel, the divorced wife of the earl, had embraced a strange and, at that time, scandalous cult, the Theosophical Society, the president of which was the female Marxist and professional reformer, Mrs. Annie Besant. Countess Muriel became a disciple of Mrs. Besant, as had a third woman of some importance to both Menzies and Wallace, Lady Emily Lutyens, wife of the imperial architect, Sir Edwin Lutyens. To make matters more bizarre, all three women were also involved with a certain Leadbeater, an official of the Theosophical Society and one who was wanted by several police forces in America and Britain for questioning concerning allegations that he had engaged in masturbation with young boys who were either members or sons of officials of the society. [20]

To escape the notoriety, Leadbeater had gone to Adyar, India, to establish a branch of the Theosophical Society there. In 1909 he had announced that he had discovered the "vehicle" for the Second Coming of Christ. This "vehicle" was a beautiful Brahmin boy named Krishnamurti.* By June 1909 Leadbeater had taken Krishnamurti, in his fifteenth year, under his protection to prepare him for the great moment in world history. Mrs. Besant visited Adyar to meet "the Messiah," as Krishnamurti was being called, and she agreed that he had the "correct aura." She then brought the boy to London, where he arrived on May 5, 1911. There, the Messiah was introduced to Countess Muriel, Idina, Avice, Lady Emily, and her daughters. Krishnamurti made Countess Muriel's home in the Ashdown Forest his own, and he became friendly with her daughters.

Krishnamurti's initiation as the Messiah took place at Taormina in Sicily in May 1912, with many of the world's forty-five thousand theosophists present. All this caused much uproar in the press, so that it was impossible that neither Wallace nor Menzies were aware of the De La Warrs' odd connections. However, the adjutant, Stewart Menzies, did not "express his reserve" when Wallace requested the regiment's permission to marry Lady Idina. On the contrary, Menzies accepted an invitation from David to be best man. The couple was married in July 1913, in a full-dress wedding at which the regiment provided an arch of swords. If King George V had restored Balmorality at his accession, it was evident from this queer tangle of unorthodoxy that, even with people of Menzies's and Wallace's generation and station, the age of conservative orthodoxy, on which the realm rested, had begun to crumble and give way to new, strange Oriental thoughts and passions.

These were to bring both England and Menzies no good. But the marriage itself, for the moment, seemed to have done Wallace's career no harm. As for Stewart Menzies, he was introduced at the ceremony into the De La Warr family, and for the first time he met Lady Avice, Idina's younger sister. She was seventeen or eighteen at the time, so

*Still leader of the Theosophical Society, Krishnamurti died in 1986. He had denounced the notion that he was the reincarnation of Christ in 1929. At the time of his death, Krishnamurti was regarded by his large following in England and California as a respectable divine and philosopher.

Stewart Menzies could hardly have taken much interest in her. But in fact he had met the woman he was to marry.

10   THE HOLLO OF BUGLES

The Household Cavalry brigade's levee of 1913 at Windsor Castle had never been a more agreeable affair. But the political fears that marked the end of the *belle époque* continued as the world moved from crisis to crisis, from assassination to assassination. In all there were four major political murders that year: George I, the commander in chief of the Turkish army, and the deposed president and vice-president of Mexico. And a month after Menzies returned from Athens, there was an attempt on the life of the king of Spain. War was in the air, although few people took serious notice. There had been so many disturbances in the past.

When Rex Benson left for India, only Keith Menzies and the Grenfell boys could be at the docks, for Stewart had not returned to England from Athens. Having assured his friends that he would return to his regiment, the Ninth Lancers, if war did break out between England and Germany, Rex sailed in the SS *Worcestershire* to become aide-de-camp to the viceroy of India, Lord Hardinge, a frequent guest of Robert Benson and George Holford during the shooting seasons of the past. The education of another member of the ruling caste had begun. That, again, was of importance in Stewart Menzies's career, for Rex became not only one of Menzies's "honourable correspondents," but also, at the time of Pearl Harbor, Menzies's secret representative at Washington. Also, Benson proved to be Menzies's most enduring friend and his closest confidant throughout his long career in secret service. [21]

On his arrival at Bombay, Benson, now twenty-three, became one of the "heaven born," as the Indians called their British rulers. A man of grace, wit, presence, and tact, Rex carried out his tasks with elegance and success that marked him as a coming man. For no task could be more difficult or treacherous. The Indian princes were as devious and intricate as any medieval Oriental court. His work required that he travel throughout the subcontinent in circumstances that were always uncomfortable and occasionally dangerous. Frequently he accompanied the viceroy in his grand proceedings, and the viceroy was himself an intricate man in a complex caravan.

Benson lived at Viceregal Lodge and was Hardinge's principal comfort in an isolated world. He believed absolutely in the dictum of a former viceroy, Lord Curzon, that "the sacredness of India haunts me like a passion. To me the message is carved in granite, hewn in the rock of doom: that our work is righteous, and that it shall endure." And when not in attendance upon the viceroy, Benson hunted tiger, played polo, raced his horses, and stuck pigs. This was a sport almost peculiar to British India. An outstanding polo player, Benson's team won the Beresford Tournament at Simla in 1913 by twenty goals to ten, delighting the viceroy, who presented the cup because it was the first time the Beresford had been won by his staff since the ground was made big enough for four-aside tourneys. At Christmas 1913 there was the Calcutta Championship Tournament. Benson played with the viceroy's aide-de-camp, the Honorable J. J. Astor, First Life Guards and future owner of *The Times*. Benson's opponents were a team drawn from the Indian princes and the cavalry. Again Benson's team won by eight goals to four. Then came the pig sticking at Meerut.

Benson recorded in his private diaries that, between March 16 and 18 of 1914, he had entered for the Kadir Cup at Meerut, the principal pig-sticking contest in British India. The object was to chase a wild pig on horseback and stick it with a spear not longer than eight feet. It was dangerous sport, for the pigs frequently fought back, and unhorsed riders had been stuck by the pigs' tusks and killed. The chase was run over about four miles of what was called "fair pig-sticking country" about thirty-five miles outside Meerut. There were generally three riders in each round, and it was usual to ride two rounds. To win it was necessary to wound the pig so that its blood could be seen on the spearhead by the umpire. Benson recorded that he got no blood, only fat, having chased and speared one small pig and then a big boar that succeeded in escaping into the bush.

In July Benson toured the northwest frontier between British India and Afghanistan, entering the mountain kingdom through the Khyber Pass to call upon the emir, Habibullah Khan, in the hope of inducing the Afghan army to march with the British Indian army if there was war with Germany. But although they took many presents to the emir, and paid him much courtesy, the emir declined to say yes—and he declined to say no. There was much dancing, feasting, and singing of Homeric poems. Then came word that the Archduke Ferdinand, heir to the throne of the Austro-Hungarian empire, and his consort, had been assassinated at a town in Yugoslavia called Sarajevo, a place so remote from British interests that Benson had to get a gazetteer to find out where it was. Few men in India gave a damn.

Yet suddenly, even before the corpses were cold, the cantilevers of world power began to collapse, inexplicably at first, but ever more rapidly as each arch of diplomacy, a diplomacy sustained by the 194 members of the British royal family, trembled, sagged, and then tumbled into the abyss. In what was the briefest chapter in diplomacy in modern European annals, the great powers mobilized for war, and the Gorgeous Age vanished forever.

Lieutenant and Adjutant Menzies was with the Second Life Guards at Windsor Barracks, about to leave for Wallace's estate at Dunblane for the grouse, when the wire from the War Office arrived during the evening of July 28. The message was not delivered immediately, for the duke of Althone had given a dinner party for the officers of the Household Cavalry brigade. About 120 officers were there, including Holford and Menzies. As mess etiquette required, there was no discussion of politics at the table and no discussion of business until after the loyal toast. But the subalterns were plainly beside themselves with excitement.

Having waited until the loyal toast had been given, the mess sergeant brought the signal to Teck, who then announced that the regiment should consider itself in a precautionary stance for war. Furthermore, Holford announced, the Life Guards would not have to provide a King's Guard for George V on the morrow since the king, in view of the situation, had canceled his annual visit to the Goodwood races.

At the War Office, the war book was taken from its special safe and then unlocked, and its provisions, drawn up to bring the empire in orderly progression from a state of peace to a state of war, were implemented. One hundred and sixty thousand men were prepared for continental service for the first time since Napoleon's Continental System was crushed at Waterloo in June 1815, nearly a century before. At Windsor, those officers away for the grouse flooded back to the officers' house. On the evening of July 30 it was rumored that the kaiser was about to declare war on Russia; the rumor was correct. On August 1 Menzies received a telegram from the War Office instructing

Ferguson to prepare his regiment for active service. When he asked for an elucidation, he was told that Russia and Germany were at war and that France was mobilizing against Germany.

In less than two weeks a general European war had broken out. On August 3 the German army invaded Belgium, and even as the first divisions of *feldgrauen* crossed the frontier, the alarm sounded in Whitehall. The Cabinet of H. H. Asquith went into secret session at which General Sir Douglas Haig, commander of the Cavalry Corps, called to give the prime minister advice on what sort of war could be expected. Haig declared that England and Germany would be fighting for their existence; therefore the war was bound to be long, for neither would acknowledge defeat after only a short struggle. The issue was primacy.

With that declaration, and with the invasion of Belgium, Britain must make up her mind, he concluded, whether she was to declare war on Germany. To make that decision, the Cabinet continued in secret session. There was opposition to British intervention, and the chief opponent was Lord Morley, lord president of the council and Holford's brother-in-law. At heart a pacifist, Morley argued that France and Germany should be left to fight it out without British involvement, that if Britain became involved, the empire would be ruined, as would be the Treasury.

But when the German armies crossed into Belgium and France, the Cabinet decided to send an ultimatum demanding that Germany respect Belgian neutrality. The kaiser ignored the ultimatum, which then expired at 11:00 P.M. London time on August 4. At the decision for war, Morley resigned from the government. The effect upon Sir George Holford of Morley's pacific protest was, for Morley, expensive. Morley had become the sole executor of Holford's will and one of the principal beneficiaries. Denouncing Morley for lack of patriotism, Holford wrote a codicil to the will, appointing Rex Benson principal executor and removing Lord Morley as a beneficiary. Morley's protest would, therefore, ultimately cost him around £70,000—about £1.4 million by modern values.

At the hour of 11:00 P.M., the War Office automatically sent out the mobilization telegram. It contained three words: *Mobilize stop Acknowledge.* At that hour, too, the foreign secretary, Sir Edward Grey, standing at the French windows overlooking St. James's Park, uttered the immortal words "The lamps are going out all over Europe, and we shall not see them lit again in our lifetime."

11 INTO BATTLE

With the receipt of the mobilization telegram, the regiment prepared
for active service in a joyous mood. At last, the Hun! At a ceremony
the standards were handed into the charge of the vicar of St. George's
Chapel at Windsor Castle for safekeeping. The ceremonial uniforms
were stored in camphor and mothballs with the quartermaster at the
cavalry barracks. The ornate horse furniture was placed in vats of oil
to protect it against rust. The regiment dressed now in khaki, with
dulled buttons so that they did not glint in the sunlight. The armorer
issued each man cotton bandoliers containing two hundred rounds of
.303 ball ammunition for the carbines. The blades of every sword
were dulled to prevent reflection. Each of the two squadrons drew
two .303 water-cooled machine guns. Medical kits were provided
each trooper with printed instructions on how to treat shock and stem
bleeding. Menzies and the assistant adjutant, Euan Wallace, worked
systematically through the regimental battle inventory:

Regimental headquarters, 4 officers, 3 warrant officers, 4 staff sergeants;
regimental war establishment, 380 men with first replacements of 46 men.
Of the 61 corporals, 10 might be lance sergeants; and of the troopers, 22
might be lance corporals. Bugles 4; frogs, cutter, wire, folding Mk. 1, 30;
knots, sword, brown, 377; strings, bugle and trumpet, royal, 11, cases,
horseshoe, P.M.G., modified, 6; needles, harness, size 2 (b), 45; machines,
mincing, small, 1; wallets, veterinary, 2; bits, bridoon, S. O., 26 . . .

For Menzies the inventory check was prolonged clerkly bondage.
But in three weeks every spring, bolt, hoof, pistol, water tank, rifle,
machine gun, thirteen-pounder artillery piece, nail, needle, and tooth
had been inspected. Everything had been replaced, signed for, signals
had been sent, letters written, sorted, double-checked, fired, exploded, tested, oiled, dulled, polished. In three weeks the Second
Life Guards had been transmuted from a splendid ceremonial force
to a splendid fighting force. That was certainly what the Life Guards
thought of themselves.

"I doubt if there was ever a better regiment to leave the shores
of England," wrote Trooper F. W. Buckley, Menzies's clerk. "All
lovely black horses 16 hands in height & over, each horse would have

had 18 months in the Young Horse Stables, a mere 'touch' with the leg, 'hands' on a good mouth, good jumpers all." The men were "all six-footers, strong, healthy, and young, good shots, swordsmen, and above all obedient." The officers were "all good leaders that the men would follow and gentlemen." [22]

At cock's crow on September 2 the regiment rode out from the old redbrick cavalry barracks. As they always did, the troopers' women gathered at the main gates to wave their men good-bye. There, too, was the barracks warden, "Whacker" Reynolds, standing at attention outside the guardroom, dressed in morning coat with spats, pin-striped trousers, canary-colored waistcoat, top hat, and primrose gloves and carrying an ebony riding crop with a gold knob. A street busker with a flute played "Good-Bye, Dolly Gray." The regiment proceeded in splendid order and carried everything it needed with it—every-thing except spades. What need had cavalry for spades? Digging was work for the infantry.

At the station "the gates closed on us, and there were our cattle trucks, loading platforms, and so on," Buckley recorded. "When all the horses had been boxed, would there be any chance of a drop of booze? A trooper who knew his way around had come back with two quart bottles; they both fitted excellently in either leg of his riding breeches, and it wasn't long before others thought it a good idea." There were more wives at the station, "faithful to the end of the day, waving handkerchiefs, some tears, but what lay ahead?"

At the declaration of war, Menzies and his regiment brigaded in Wiltshire as the Seventh Brigade of the Third Cavalry Division, which was commanded by General the Honorable Julian Byng. The Com-posite Regiment had gone to France and into action at a place called Mons. Rex Benson begged the viceroy to allow him to return to Europe and rejoin his regiment, the Ninth Lancers, and Lord Hardinge agreed only on condition that Benson send him a weekly letter about the military state of affairs in France. By the time of the retreat from Mons, Benson was with his regiment in command of a troop. In Menzies's regiment, his brother, Keith, was seconded from the Welsh Guards on "special duties" with the Second Life Guards, which awaited orders. Who arranged those "special duties," and what they were, is not known, but it was unusual, and it may have saved Keith's life, for most of the Welsh Guards officers were dead by Christmas.

August passed, and so did September. Menzies waited with

mounting impatience as the German juggernaut was repulsed at the Marne. When at last marching orders arrived, confidence was great. One officer's letter to his brother expressed the spirit of the regiment and the officer corps of the entire army:

The grand obstacle Hun hunt is now open. There is no charge for entry. At present we are sitting and looking dubiously at the first obstacle. It's a devilish stiff one and lots more like it to follow. However, if one does take a nasty toss, there's always the satisfaction of knowing that one could not do it in a better cause. I always feel that I am fighting for England—English fields, lanes, trees, good days in England, all that is synonymous with liberty.

When orders arrived they were from the first lord of the Admiralty, Winston Churchill. The Third Cavalry Division landed on the beaches and jetties at Zeebrugge, Belgium, on October 10, their mission to forestall the German capture of Antwerp. The division marched the following morning, a millipede of 12,000 men, 18,000 horses, 1,028 wagons, and 24 field guns that took five hours to pass. The cavalry was no more welcome now than it had been when Wellington marched on Waterloo. As the division approached, the peasants dismantled the pumps, forcing each of the nine regiments to purchase water for its horses and its water bottles.

Nor did the division get beyond Ghent before fresh orders were received. Antwerp had fallen when the first German secret weapon was deployed against the forts around the port. These were gigantic siege guns, the existence of which was unknown and the like of which had not been encountered before. A spy wrote to British GHQ, having seen the gun in Brussels:

. . . in the middle of German soldiers a piece of artillery so colossal that we could not believe our eyes. It was one of the eight giant cannon that the Germans call the "surprise of the war," the "420"! Their invention, known only to the Emperor and certain intimates, has been, one hears, totally secret. The metal monster advanced in two parts, pulled by 36 horses, if memory serves. The pavement trembled. The crowd remained mute with consternation. Slowly it crossed the Place Saint Lambert . . . attracting crowds of curious onlookers along its slow and heavy passage. Hannibal's elephants could not have astonished the Romans more! . . . The soldiers who accompanied it marched stiffly, with almost religious solemnity. It was the Belial of cannons!

At the end of the Boulevard d'Avroy . . . the monster was carefully mounted and scrupulously aimed. . . . Then came the frightful explosion! The crowd was flung back; the earth shook as if there had been an earthquake, and all the window-panes in the neighbourhood were shattered! [23]

The British General Staff, too, was mute with consternation at the appearance of the "Big Bertha," as the cannon was called, with no warning from the secret service. Menzies awakened suddenly to German armaments genius and never forgot the shock of surprise he experienced when he heard the Big Berthas thudding away at the Antwerp forts. Nor did he forget the clouds of Belgian infantry in their sky-blue uniforms, fleeing for their lives from the burning and stricken city along with the French heavy cavalry wearing curassiers, plumes, and mustard-yellow britches. The division was ordered to Ypres, a market town of Flanders and, in the opinion of the strategists, the outer keep to London.

There they arrived on October 14, after much sharp skirmishing with Uhlans, the German light cavalry scouts, among the copses and fields of dead sweet corn. A photograph of the division entering the city survives in the town hall of Ypres. A great crowd watched stunned as the first British cavalry since 1815 and Waterloo to enter the city clattered over the cobbles of the Grand Place. There were men in bowlers, urchins wearing clogs, peasant women in shawls and long, bulky dresses pushing wheelbarrows filled with vegetables. It was probably market day. There was little if any sign of flag or arm waving.

The Life Guards' stay was was brief, enlivened only by the appearance of a German scout plane that looked as flimsy as a dragonfly. It was shot down by rifle fire from the Second Life Guards. Menzies was far from pleased, however, for as he recorded in the war diary on that day, not only had the regiment wasted several hundred rounds of ammunition on the plane, but the rifle fire had frightened the horses, which had bolted down the side streets, causing damage, civilian casualties, and compensation claims from the mayor. [24]

Then orders arrived from the commander in chief, General Sir John French, who had conceived a grand scheme for demolishing the German advance and a counterstroke to push them back to the German frontier. Discovering that the enemy before him consisted of a single corps, French ordered his three corps of British, French, and Belgian infantry and cavalry to advance. The Second Life Guards and the Ninth Lancers, where Benson commanded a squadron, were selected as the spearheads of the advance of the army along either side of the arrow-straight road from Ypres to Menin, the Ninth Lancers on the left side of the road, the Second Life Guards on the right. The first objective was Menin, which, if taken, would cut the German railway communications in their advance upon the Channel ports and, thereby, end the war by Christmas.

During the march there occurred one of those minute, almost poetic episodes that excited the imagination and culminated in Stewart Menzies's entry into intelligence. Menzies had received several bulletins about the need for vigilance for German espionage, including one that reflected ingenuity, a quality he admired. It had been found that the reverse side of some of the metal Maggi soup advertisements nailed to telephone poles and *estaminet* walls throughout northern France had what appeared to be German route maps painted on them. The regiment was to tear down every Maggi advertisement they encountered, therefore, and report. Since there were scores if not hundreds of such advertisements, this proved so large and irritating a task that Menzies formed a special section to do it lest the advance be stopped each time a Maggi soup sign was encountered. [25]

In looking for soup signs, however, the section discovered other suspicious signs on telegraph poles, the corners of walls, and places that stood out on the low, undulating landscape. These were colored red, blue, and green, and, as the intelligence section at Cavalry Corps headquarters recorded, there was "nothing to show who put them there or why, but it seems possible that they conform to some route plan or serve as cache signs. French can offer no explanation, and in the case of telephone poles they are usually on the side away from the road." Was every telephone pole to be inspected for the marks? Menzies thought not, and corps agreed, believing them to be "wood merchants' marks."

Perhaps they were, perhaps not. But nobody had the time for such a task, at least for the moment. At first, the advance succeeded. The Second Life Guards entered Menin on or about the twentieth and might have held the city if there had been greater strength. As it was, Colonel Ferguson's scouts warned that the Germans were in strength in the side streets and that the regiment might be running into an ambush. Ferguson then withdrew the regiment back down the Menin–Ypres road, leaving Menin to the Germans. It remained in their hands for the next four years, and many tens of thousands of men were killed or wounded in an uncountable number of actions to capture that *Flamand* pimple on the Franco-Belgian border.

As for the rest of the army, its advance produced a huge bulge before the Germans brought up powerful reinforcements, stopped French's march, and then began a gigantic offensive calculated to throw the British army into the English Channel. That bulge would go down in military history as "the Ypres Salient," which became the most blood-soaked area in military record, before or later. Over three million men fought there, and a million of them were killed or wounded. The First Battle of Ypres then began. It proved to be at least the largest and most violent battle between dynasties so far recorded. In that confrontation, the Second Life Guards played a vital, even Homeric part.

By about 2:00 P.M. on October 22, the regiment arrived back on the western side of the Messines ridge, under a village close to the Ypres–Menin road. The village was called Zandvoorde, and its chief purpose until now had been to raise pigs and sell them at Ypres's market. It had a shuttered, silent, suspicious, deserted air like so many of the Belgian villages. Here the regiment was ordered to dismount, assume the role of infantry, and defend the crest of a section of ridge just outside Zandvoorde that faced in the direction of Lille. These trenches had been dug originally by Wurttemburgers and Bavarians. The troopers reached them along the pathway between 2 and 4 Komenstraat, close to the shrine of Ste. Theresa.* For Stewart Menzies, it was here that all the folly and joys of the past were swept away forever. Menzies and the regiment would experience for the first time the full wrath of the Teuton furore. For Menzies especially, the events of the next few weeks would be traumatic enough to mark him for life.

Menzies's headquarters were located in an abandoned cottage with an earthen floor. It had been fouled and looted by Wurttemburgers when they had occupied Zandvoorde during their advance. Partly burned, the cottage had half a roof, and the windows were blasted out and patched up with tar paper. Menzies shared the ruin with Ferguson, the commanding officer, a man of great presence but few words whose nerves, they said, were much stronger than his imagination.

The moment they arrived the area came under shell and mortar fire, what the troopers called "flying pigs," for the German line was not more than seven hundred yards away down the eastern side of the ridge. Menzies soon discovered that A1 Amber, his horse, which

---

*At Zandvoorde, there remains an oddly shaped, brick-built shrine to St. Theresa, the French Carmelite nun whose name in religion was Ste. Theresa of the Child Jesus. She died of tuberculosis in 1897 and had become one of the most beloved saints in the Roman Catholic church. There was a shrine to her on Komenstraat because she is said to have stopped here on her way to the Catholic center of learning at Louvain near Brussels. Inside the shrine was the illuminated imprecation, *Regardez nous que Pluie de Roses*, which nobody could understand except one learned trooper. He explained that Ste. Theresa was often represented in art with an armful of roses because of her cryptic promise: "After my death, I will let fall a shower of roses."

he loved, was like all horses: he could not withstand the noise of gunfire, nor continuous wind, as easily as humans. A1 became terrified, disconsolate, and lost weight so rapidly that unless care was taken he would have to be knackered. Menzies carried the usual personal weapons, a .38 Smith & Wesson service revolver, a new Lee Enfield cavalry carbine, a haversack of Mills fragmentation grenades. His only reading matter, apart from official documents, was a paper called *Du Role Strategique de la Cavalerie*, which the French liaison officer at Cavalry Corps headquarters had given him, and part of a book called *With General French and the Cavalry in South Africa*. The regimental map hung in its leather case from the back of one of the room doors.

It was dark when the squadrons arrived. The squadron leaders' orders were to take over the trenches on the easterly slope of the Messines Ridge, the side of the ridge overlooking the Germans, Menin, and Lille. The guides met the troopers at the foot of the ridge, near Menzies's cottage. Then the march began in single file up along the hedgerows to the lip of the ridge. There was occasional firing, the rasp of flares, the thump of a flying pig. But all went well until the guides got to Ste. Theresa's shrine. There they would go no farther, for, they said, the Bedfordshires did not know the Life Guards. Because they were not familiar with the Life Guards' riding cloaks, they might think they were Huns and would almost certainly open fire. The Life Guards would have to make their own way into the Bedfordshires' trenches. A map was drawn, and then the guides vanished, explaining that they did not propose to get shot by Bedfordshire peasants mad with rum.

"Soon we were climbing up the back of the low, broad ridge," Trooper Lloyd, one of Menzies's messengers, would write. "The night was as black as the pit." There was a strong stench of burned explosives and rotting black-and-white cows. The group wore their long cavalrymen's cloaks, so that when they appeared on the skyline they presented a bulky target. The Germans "immediately let fly at us with machine gun and rifle fire," and they "straightway fell flat among the vegetables and listened to the bullets clipping the turnip tops." Trooper Franklin discovered later that a "machine gun had fired a spurt right underneath him, between his stomach and the ground. His cloak was torn in shreds just as if it had been slashed across with a very sharp knife." [14] The Life Guards found it difficult to crawl wearing cloaks, and when they did they came under fire at point-blank range from the Bedfordshires, just as the guides had warned. Then they discovered the trenches were "chockful of men who absolutely refused to admit us into their already cramped space." In the event they found sanctuary only "when I let it be known I had a cargo of Woodbines [cigarettes] on my person." Their colleague, Harry Pudney, came in much later, "about done up and bubbling with indignation." He had been crawling about for half an hour in a spray of bullets, "seeking an opportunity to hold a portion of the line for his King and country and being grossly insulted everywhere he showed his nose." [26]

At daybreak on October 23, Menzies and two or three officers came up to the ridge to look at the trenches, for he was concerned by the complaint of Major Lord Tweedmouth that the earthworks were very primitive, "a perfect example of what trenches should not be, being on the forward slope and in full view of the enemy's trenches and observation posts." [27] Once occupied it was "impossible to reinforce them in daylight or to take ammunition up or to communicate between the trenches." Menzies agreed, stating that "one was much too deep to allow of the occupants seeing over the top, and the troops [in that trench] would hardly be in a position to offer any effective resistance."

At about 7:00 A.M. that day, Menzies reported back to Ferguson at regimental headquarters about his concerns. Ferguson decided to go and see for himself and left immediately with the brigadier, General Kavanagh, and Kavanagh's staff. On the way Ferguson collected Lieutenant Colonel Edgar Brassey, commanding First Life Guards, Lieutenant Lord Tweeddale, First Life Guards, and four other officers, one of whom was referred to in Tweedmouth's diary as "Stewart." [28] It can only be assumed that this was Menzies, for there was no officer with the surname "Stewart" in the Household Cavalry brigade. It was then that the regiment learned forcibly what those little red, green, and blue markers on telephone poles and other such prominent points might be. They were aiming points for German guns and mortars placed there during the first German march on Ypres.

Some were found in Zandvoorde, and when the trench inspection party appeared in the German line of sight, the Germans opened fire with 5.9s and flying pigs. One of them burst just above the inspection party, which was clustered in a tight group because the wind made it difficult to hear Kavanagh's and Ferguson's orders. Ferguson was hit by shrapnel in four places; one leg injury was severe enough to put him in the hospital. Tweeddale was hit in the lip, Brassey in the ear, and the other officers, including Kavanagh, were all slightly injured in the blast. According to Tweedmouth, "Stewart" was hit in a place that he called in his diary "Xth," which indicated that he did not know where "Stewart" was hit or, if he did, he preferred not to say.

Menzies's service records reveal no sign of a wound, although the war diary during the next sixty hours was in the hands of another. This suggests Menzies might have been away at a casualty station. When Menzies resumed the keeping of the diary, the regiment had a new, acting commanding officer, Major the Honorable Hugh Dawnay, while Ferguson was in hospital. A member of the Cavalry Corps staff, Dawnay was regarded by Menzies among others as one of the best officers not only in the British Expeditionary Force, but in the entire British army. His was a very illustrious family at court (Dawnay's wife was Lady Katherine de la Poer Beresford, a daughter of the sixth marquess of Waterford); they owned financial trusts and, besides, a great chain of hotels, the *Financial Times* and *The Economist*, and Hugh Dawnay's branch had been in the Royal Horse Guards since Cromwell's time. The entire army command was, in Menzies's view, like Dawnay. In his attitudes, Dawnay resembled the medieval chivalric knight or the Athenian freeman.

In these circumstances, nothing was or could be done to improve the trenches. Even if there had been someone to give the orders, it seems improbable that the regiment could have done more than it did. It had no spades, for it had not been foreseen that the regiment might have to act as infantry, which had in fact become their role. There were no sappers available, and if there had been, they would not have been able to get to the trenches during daylight, for every move provoked German fire from the willow line at the foot of the ridge. The Hun watched through glasses from the spire of a church about three-quarters of a mile to the southeast. Before he was hit, Kavanagh had told the horse gunners to knock down the spire, and that had been done. But the Germans were still in the rubble of the spire. The only digging tools the men in the trenches had were their bayonets, hands, knives, and swords.

Ferguson and Menzies's responsibility for ordering the Life Guards into the trenches was debated from time to time afterward. But Menzies's case was a good one. He had directed the attention of the command at brigade and divisional level to the dangerous location of the regimental trenchline. Nor was there very much that could be done in the time available before the German offensive opened—at least not with the tools available. At all events, Haig himself did not blame the command of the Second Life Guards.

Nevertheless, that small sector of the front caused anxiety. During the evening of the twenty-eighth, the British commander in chief, General French, warned all field commanders that "the enemy's XXVll Corps opposite us would attack at 5:30 A.M. on the line Zandvoorde-Kruiseik." [29] The British were reading the German command cipher, and not for the last time in history, either. That intercept proved to be the harbinger of a gigantic German attack that produced what the official British historian later called "one of the most critical days in the history of the British Expeditionary Force, if not the British Empire."

By a chance of military decision and history, the German units assembling in the sector were First Company, Sixteenth Bavarian Reserve Infantry Regiment, Sixth Bavarian Reserve Division, Fourth Army. In that company, about to experience his first battle, was a young messenger by the name of Adolf Hitler. Born in 1889 at Braunau, Austria, the son of a customs officer, Hitler wrote years later that he fell on his knees to thank God for the opportunity to take part in this war. Years later a photograph was published of him among thousands of others listening to the declaration of war in the Odeonsplatz in Munich. He stood enraptured, a broad smile on his face, waving his hat in a fervent display of patriotic excitement. He was on his way to offer his services to Ludwig III, king of Bavaria. Now he was at the front. As he wrote of that dawn twilight before the battle:

A damp cold night came on, and we marched silently through it; then, as the light began to appear through the mists an iron hail suddenly whistled over our heads, the sharp detonations scattering their shrapnel among our ranks, and whipping up the sodden ground. Even before the little cloud had vanished, a shout of hurra had roared out two hundred throats to greet this first messenger of death. Then the enemy fire began to chatter and rumble and we to sing and shout, and with excited eyes we pressed forwards, always faster, until away over root fields and hedges the fight began. The fight of men against men. Then from a long way off the sound of a song reached our ears, and came steadily nearer and nearer, as company after company joined in. Then, as death began to work in our ranks, that song reached us and we passed it on: Deutschland, Deutschland uber alles. . . . [30]

The German attack opened as predicted at 5:30 A.M. on October 29. It was a preliminary attack to eject the Horse Guards from Zandvoorde and thereby gain the ground needed to control the Ypres–

Menin road during the main attack, which would follow on the thirtieth. The Germans attacked through thick fog, and very severe fighting developed that resulted in heavy casualties. Hitler's commanding officer, Colonel List, was shot dead in the charge from behind the willow line. The British line was dented near Kruiseeke, a hamlet near Zandvoorde, but with the arrival of a heavy rainstorm in the early evening, the Germans paused, and the Life Guards remained in possession of Zandvoorde.

The battle reopened at 6:30 A.M. the next day with simultaneous assaults around the entire forty miles of front to the east of Ypres. As eighteen German divisions hurled themselves at the eighteen British brigades straddling the Ypres–Menin road, some 260 German artillery pieces and mortars, including heavy cannon, began to fire on the horseshoe-shaped trenches occupied by the Second Life Guards. Menzies and his men were backed by the machine guns of the Royal Horse Guards. Each squadron was understrength at about eighty rifles, and the entire formation had two machine guns, one of which did not work because it lacked oil and had been clogged by slime. Six field pieces and one section of old six-inch howitzers supported the regiment. Behind them two cavalry brigades, both badly weakened, were in reserve on the Zillebeke Ridge, the last line before Ypres.

The bombardment lasted for seventy-five minutes and devastated the Household Cavalry trenches, burying alive many men and killing and wounding many more. The fire was heaviest in the sector of the Second Life Guards and the squadron of the First Life Guards next to it. Indeed it was so heavy that no coherent picture of what occurred up on the ridge was ever obtained by Menzies or anyone else. The two squadrons were annihilated or, if any survived, were executed later. Among the dead was "Pickles" Lambton, who used to wear pink silk underclothes. He was first buried alive with five of his men, and then, as he clawed himself out of the clay, he was shot through the head and killed. Captain Lord Hugh Grosvenor, the heir of the duke of Westminster, the richest man in the empire, was killed at the side of his brother-in-law, Lieutenant the Honorable G.E.F. Ward, the earl of Dudley's heir. So, too, was a scion of the leading British army family, Captain Alexander M. Vandeleur, and his friend, Lieutenant Lord Worsley, the earl of Yarborough's heir. All were at Eton at about the same time as Menzies.

At 8:00 A.M. the bombardment lifted, and the German infantry attacked. First came three battalions of *Jaguar* light infantry, heroes of the Seven Weeks War, prancing forward with their odd little steps when possible at 140 paces a minute, their left arms pumping jerkily as puppets. Then came the rifles of the Thirty-ninth Division, some of them looking and sounding like Wallenstein knights as they clanked across the fields in their body armor. Several German battalions carried their regimental colors. They blew horns, waved rattles, and sang heroic patriotic marching songs:

> Lieb Vaterland, kannst ruhig sein,
> Fest steht und treu dei Wacht,
> De wacht am Rhein . . .

With houses and farm buildings in flames all across the valley, the remaining Household Cavalry troops opened what was the most prolonged "mad minute"—a minimum of eighteen aimed rounds—of their career. Their fire was so intense and prolonged that over every bush, hedge, and wall floated a haze of blue gunsmoke. It was fire so rapid that the Germans came to believe that the troops were part of a "machine-gun army," when in reality there were only two machine guns to each regiment. These fired so rapidly and so long that the water boiled in their cooling jackets.

But still the Germans came on across the fields of dead beet. They then gained an enfilading position on the trenches. That, combined with the unexpected retirement of a battalion to the left of the Household Cavalry troops, forced the survivors to withdraw into the second line of defenses. Only one officer and three men of the original 205 officers and troopers appear to have survived.

By 10:00 A.M. the Germans had captured Zandvoorde, but they came on only cautiously. They had taken very severe casualties themselves. The German official history would show that in Hitler's regiment of 3,600 men, 722 fell during the four days between October 29 and November 2. [31] And by their conduct it seemed to Menzies afterward that they intended not merely the military defeat of George V's Household Cavalry, but also their physical extermination. Siegfried Sassoon, an Etonian of Menzies's generation and one who was present in the battle, wrote the lines:

> Pray you'll never know
> The hell where youth and laughter go.

When the Germans got into the British trenches, they appear to have behaved atrociously. One of the few survivors, Surgeon-Major Pares, brought back to Menzies evidence that the Germans executed wounded Household Cavalry troops. When the mother of Lord Worsley, who had entertained the kaiser when he was in England for Queen Victoria's funeral, asked for information about her son through the U.S. embassy, London, she received what the Household Cavalry historian called "a callous and unmannerly reply." [32]

Worsley's corpse was never recovered, so that it was never established whether he was executed or whether he died of battle wounds. Nor were any other corpses recovered from the trenches, for they remained in German hands for the next four years and with them the Household Cavalry's graves. Nevertheless, Menzies, too, came to believe that those colleagues who had not been killed in the assault had been executed, for he wrote in a report of the action:

I fear that one must assume that the Germans behaved in an ultra-Hunlike manner and gave no quarter. According to one NCO, they did not trouble to remove the wounded who were left out, and he attributed his being taken to the German dressing station to the fact that he was wearing a pair of leather gloves and may therefore have been mistaken for an officer. [33]

By the end of the fighting of the thirtieth, Menzies's regiment had received severe casualties and had been forced off the ridge. Yet, despite the vast superiority of the enemy in numbers of men and artillery, the line had not broken. Ypres remained in British hands, and the British army remained on the continent of Europe. That fact produced a strategic crisis at German headquarters. The imperial Russian army appeared to be about to occupy the eastern provinces of Germany, and the kaiser regarded it as imperative to obtain a final, complete victory in the West in order to release troops to repel the ancient foe, the Russians.

With that decision, Kaiser Wilhelm II came forward to German supreme headquarters on the Ypres front, arriving there at noon on October 31. From his train, the kaiser issued an order of the day, exhorting his army to settle "forever with the centuries-long struggle" with France and declaring that "we will finish with the British, Indians, Moroccans, and other trash, feeble adversaries who surrender in great numbers if they are attacked with vigor." There is no reason to doubt, as the Household Cavalry's official historian later maintained, that the kaiser intended revenge upon the Household Cavalry regiments for their "arrogances," that he wished to teach the English aristocracy a personal lesson about German power that they would not forget. [34]

Beyond the kaiser's desire, however, there were geopolitical designs. The leading German gunsmith, Gustav Krupp, came to the front to watch his Big Berthas performing, and he spoke of the German desire for a Prussian empire in Africa ringed by coaling stations and naval bases. That ambition could be realized only if Ypres fell and Germany stood on the English Channel. If Ypres fell, then "German culture and civilization will direct the progress of humanity." To fight and conquer for such a goal was "worth the price of noble blood!" For on the Channel, he stated, "we should be lying at the very marrow of England's world power, a position—perhaps the only one—which would bring us England's lasting friendship. For only if we are able to hurt England badly at this moment will she really leave us un-molested, perhaps even become our 'friend,' insofar as England is capable of friendship at all." [35]

When those words were uttered, the Life Guards had been march-ing and fighting for twenty days. For the last ten days they had been almost continuously in action in snow, sleet, hail, rain, gales, and frost. Their horses were being knackered through exhaustion and terror. The replacements of men and horses were only dribbling out from Windsor, which had long since ceased to send blacks out, for to do so might imperil the line. The horse and wagon lines had been destroyed by shellfire in which one flying pig blew to pieces thirty-two of the blacks, which had once been the pride of the regiment. Now the Household Cavalry rode only browns, and not the best ones at that.

The men were saddle sore, bearded, and filthy. Their boots were disintegrating through the effect of alternatively getting them sodden and then drying them out. Some troopers wrapped puttees around them to keep them together. Through the hard riding, some of the men had lost the seat of their riding britches. Most men, including Menzies, had not been able to change their underclothing. All were badly constipated, one of the curious physical consequences of being under continual shelling. They were living off hardtack and hares shot in the corn stubble. The thimbleful of SRD (service rum diluted) was the greatest restorative at stand-down. One of the troopers termed it "sunshine administered internally"; and so it was. And as Trooper Lloyd wrote of those last days of October and the first of November 1914:

The battle had developed the appearance of an ugly dream. Several features stand out vividly, but the whole is so blurred as to defy any attempt at grasping it and presenting it as a correct and ordered sequence of events.

All idea of time was lost. Nobody could have named the date or the day of the week, and nobody cared. The only factors which reminded us of the passing of time were daylight and darkness. In the line we fought for our lives, and when we were out of it we lived the life of a water rat in a swamp. [36]

Yet the regiment and the army continued to fight. Not a single case of mutiny, desertion, cowardice, or a refusal to obey orders occurred during this period, although all troops in the Ypres salient were aware that if they remained, they had no other choice but to stand and fight and, very likely, die. And the Germans came on and on like robots, relentless, massive, careless, gibbering with schnapps, pain, and fear. It was a heroic madness fought out in dark swamps, without purpose, without supply, without order, and without direction except for the order "There is the enemy line. Take it and kill him."

In that murderous spirit, the First Battle of Ypres, the first great contest of will between the British and the German nations, entered what was its last and most ferocious phase. On November 1, thirteen German battalions attacked down the Ypres–Menin road and captured the British fortified village of Gheluvelt, the gateway to Ypres. That action produced the gravest crisis of the career of the corps commander, General Sir John Haig, who was later to command all six British armies in France. If the Germans were not held, and if Gheluvelt was not recaptured, Ypres would fall, the roads to the Channel ports would be open, and the kaiser would then be able to attempt the invasion of England.

In a charge so brave that it defied the laws of human rationality, Gheluvelt was recaptured that day by a single battalion of the Worcestershire Regiment, with the Second Life Guards attacking along the right-hand side of the road to divert some of the German battalions from the main attack. The battle swayed backward and forward until November 5. On that day Stewart wrote to his mother:

Dearest Mother,
    I write again to let you know that Keith and I are still unhurt—naturally every day one has many scrapes. For the moment the fighting is less desperate, as both sides are somewhat tired. We have inflicted enormous losses on the Germans—in front of this portion of the battlefield they have lost 20,000 in the last 4 days. Today they are said to have lost 4,000, so you can guess what sort of a time we are having. . . . Someone said to me today: "I believe, Stewart, you are enjoying this life and seem to revel in the

fighting." If only they could see my inner feelings—I never want to fight again and would give everything to be back. Still it pleased me enormously not to show my feelings, for that is what matters above all else—one's outward appearances when facing death. I hope for a rest shortly, as things are improving at last. [Menzies's horse] Amber was hit again by a shell, but it is not bad.

Best love,
Stewart

This hour was Menzies's finest moment as a combat soldier. By now the man who was once regarded as the pride of the Trocadero and the envy of the yeomanry in his lovely millinery and exquisite tailoring looked like the hedge dweller he had become. He had given up shaving because, his friend James Marshall-Cornwall remembered, "the razor blades did not come through from Harrods, and in any case the matches were usually too wet to light the fire to boil the water which in any case was almost liquid mud." [37]

As intelligence reported through their reading of German wireless messages, on November 6, two brigades of Prussian Guard came into the line at Klein Zillebeke and made what Menzies called "a most determined attack." By 3:00 P.M. another major emergency had developed in which all that stood between the Prussian Guard and the Cloth Hall of Ypres, now a semiruin less than three thousand yards away, was a line of defensive works dug on the western side of the Comines Canal, the ramparts of the city, and the remnants of "French's Fire Fire Brigade" hidden in woods at Verbrandenmolen. There, as one of Menzies's troopers recorded anonymously, "the morning passed most peacefully, hardly any artillery fire being audible in our immediate neighbourhood."

The call came shortly after 3:00 P.M. from Lord Cavan, commanding the Guards Brigade. It had in it "a note much deeper than alarm." And as the anonymous corporal-of-horse in Menzies's regiment wrote: "Quite of a sudden we got the order to mount, and on emerging from the shelter of the trees we galloped in quite cross-country style toward that unhallowed spot known to Fame later on in the War as 'Hill 60.' My horse, who always enjoyed anything that reminded him of the hunting field, got away in great style until we came to a boggy piece of ground, into which he almost went head over heels, and we temporarily parted company, as I felt irresistibly compelled to 'take a toss'! Gray, who was close behind, very decently pulled up and helped me to catch my now thoroughly excited animal, a circumstance that I was the more grateful for in that we were then under rifle or machine-gun fire, perhaps both." [38]

It was now about 4:00 P.M., and dusk had begun to gather. Unless the gap was sealed shortly, and the Germans forced back to their own lines, the enemy would have the night in which to exploit the breakthrough. It was imperative, therefore, that the Household Cavalry restore the line. The cavalry troops dismounted and then began to counterattack to take Zwartelen. The brigade major was shot from his horse, dying shortly afterward, and as the corporal-of-horse recorded: "The place got decidedly warm the further we advanced, for in addition to incessant small arms fire there was a lot of shrapnel flying about." With the light failing, the remnants of the Household Cavalry troops were mown down, but the survivors pressed on with the counterattack across a turnip field that made an open gap between a wood and the Ypres–Menin railway.

Shortly most officers were killed or wounded, and at least one of the Second Life Guards' squadrons was without officers. Its last officer, a young fellow called Petersen, was first wounded and then killed with a second shot as he tried to find cover from which to direct the battle. In what had become a frenzied melee, the object of which was to regain Zwartelen, Menzies took command of the squadron that had lost the last of its officers. He then led it, pistol in one hand and a rifle and bayonet in the other, across open fields and through a small copse.

The Germans began to retreat through the village of Zwartelen, followed by Major Dawnay, commanding Second Life Guards, and Colonel Wilson, commanding the Royal Horse Guards. As both commanding officers approached the village, both were killed. Captain Lord Gerard, Captain the Marquess of Northampton, Colonel Brassey yet again, all were wounded in the cut and thrust of what may have been one of history's last sword-and-pistol charges. Captain the Honorable A.E.B. O'Neill, a member of Parliament and a son-in-law of the first marquess of Crewe, the secretary of state for India, was shot dead, sword in one hand, pistol in the other, as he led his squadron into the copse. The regimental interpreter, Lieutenant Alexis de Gunsberg, was machine-gunned to death.

But the charge continued. Lord Tweedmouth took command of the Royal Horse Guards and Menzies the command of the Second Life Guards. The village of Zwartelen was retaken. The defeat at Zandvoorde a few days earlier was avenged, and the line was restored.

The Prussians counterattacked as teeming sleet came in dark gray clouds direct from the sea. There were no rations save the rum and biscuits that Menzies and his men had brought with them. The cold bit through the thick cavalry cloaks.

As he was trying to link up with the cavalry squadron to his right, Menzies himself was almost killed and had a "remarkable escape." As darkness fell, he had leapt into a trench that he thought was empty but proved to be filled with Prussians. As a Prussian came lunging at him with a sword, he cried—why, he would never be able to fathom—"*Ne tirez pas! Je suis français!*" ("Do not shoot! I am French!") [39] Perhaps he meant to say that he was a German. We shall not know. But in any case the Prussian stopped, and with a look of surprise on his face, he lowered his sword. In that moment Menzies hopped out of the trench and disappeared into the dark copse.

The fighting continued between sleet storms throughout the night. When the torrents stopped the Germans attacked again. Captain the Honorable W. R. Wyndham was shot dead, and Second Lieutenants Jobson, Hobson, and Sandys were wounded. But the Prussian attack was defeated; and with that defeat the German plan for the conquest of Western Europe was itself defeated. With the Prussian Guard's failure to open the road to Ypres between November 6 and 11, the Germans were compelled by their situation on the eastern front to go over to the defensive in the west, transferring every man they could spare to fight the Russians. The British troops handed the salient over to the French, and the campaign of 1914 came to an end.

On the afternoon of November 7 all Household Cavalry troops were withdrawn from the sector and went into billets. By now there was very little of the regiment left. Menzies commanded the few who survived. Forty years on he was to remember that first night alone in his headquarters. He was almost heartbroken. He had triumphed, but almost all his friends were now dead, wounded, or missing. Of the dead and wounded Wilson (who had saved Queen Victoria from an assassin's attack at Windsor by beating the gunman to the ground with his umbrella), Dawnay, O'Neill, Northampton, Wyndham, and Hobson (who returned to the battlefield after his wound and was then killed)—all were at Eton.

The gallant nature of the charge did not escape the General Staff. A despatch arrived from the Cavalry Corps commander, Sir Douglas Haig, addressed to Dawnay, now dead. It was read to the survivors of the charge by Menzies:

(1) From Sir Douglas Haig to GOC 3rd Cavalry Division 6.11.14 8.25 P.M. Begins aaa Sir Douglas Haig wishes to thank General Kavanagh's Brigade for the splendid support given to the Infantry at a very critical moment aaa ends aaa Sir Douglas Haig aaa adds that he deeply regrets the heavy loss incurred aaa [40]

Then came further despatches. Such was Menzies's conduct during the charge that he was recommended for the Distinguished Service Order, Britain's second-highest award for gallantry in battle. It was said at the time that, but for the death of Dawnay, he would have received the highest award, the Victoria Cross. In a despatch from Kavanagh, the brigadier, to Byng, commander of the Third Cavalry Division, Kavanagh reviewed the operations of November 6. He wrote that "while having the pleasure to report the splendid manner with which all ranks behaved," he wished especially to mention the parts played in defeating the Prussian attack by four officers. The fourth officer was Menzies, who, wrote Kavanagh, "showed the greatest coolness during the evening." [41]

And on November 8, a family friend, Lieutenant Colonel J. C. Brinton, a gentleman usher to the king, wrote to assure Susannah that he had just seen Stewart and Keith, and that he had "found them none the worse for the terrible and tragic experiences of the last ten or fifteen days." The way in which the brigade had fought, and "in particular the Second Life Guards," Colonel Brinton advised Lady Holford, had "saved a very critical situation but suffered, in doing so, much heartbreaking casualties." Their exploits would "be recognized hereafter as one of the most brilliant and gallant achievements during the war." How Stewart escaped death, injury, or capture in the German trench was "a miracle." Brinton emphasized that "you ought to be proud of him," for "life in the trenches under this heavy shellfire has been almost more than human nature can stand." It was "quite wonderful how your boys have stuck it," for as Brinton confessed, "the loss of my old friends has knocked the heart out of me." Brinton's grief was shared by Stewart Menzies, for the families that had lost the most men were those with titles. At one count the dead included six peers, sixteen baronets, six knights, ninety-five sons of peers, eighty-two sons of baronets, and eighty-four knights' sons.

Menzies's grief became the greater when, as the remnants of his regiment marched out, the Cheshire Regiment marched in to take its place. One of the platoon commanders was Lieutenant G.R.L. Anderson, the golden lad of Menzies's house at Eton. They had a brief talk about fields of fire, the whereabouts of the Prussians, the likelihood of a German counterattack, the state of the artillery. They shook hands and said good-bye, promising to meet at the casino at Paris-Plage. That same day—November 8, 1914—Anderson was killed in action against the Prussians near Zillebeke Wood.

In all, when the First Battle of Ypres ended on or about November 11, the army had lost 2,298 officers and 51,817 other ranks. The flower of fighting England, the candidates as Plato's guardians, were perishing. As Menzies wrote to his mother:

Dearest Mother,

 I know that you will be pleased to hear that Keith and I are still, thank God, safe. We are the only two survivors among the officers of the Regt. We made a desperate and I think glorious charge yesterday. . . . How I am alive I do not know. Go and ask Euan Wallace about my escape in the German trenches. It was thrilling! Oh, no one will realize what a problem I have before me, and I only pray that I may be able to pull the Regt. through, but it is a terrible strain seeing all one's friends fall before one. Dawnay's death is irreparable—the army has lost one of the most brilliant soldiers of modern times—he died gallantly. . . . *Private.* I want you to know that [General Kavanagh] said this morning that he had never seen anyone cooler under fire than I was yesterday, and he was v. pleased with me, so anyway I have not disgraced the family.

Best love to everyone,
Stewart

12   DEATH OF THE SECOND REGIMENT

Captain Menzies, as he had become on November 14, received his Distinguished Service Order from King George V on December 2, 1914, while the regiment rested and refitted in a brewery at the small *Flamand* village behind Ypres. Afterward Menzies drove to Mr. Rentegem's farm at Fontaine Houck to give Captain Rex Benson a hand laying out the two-mile course for the second Cavalry Brigade point-to-point races, in which Menzies rode on December 14. There were four races, each over a two-mile course of mainly grass with "fair" hunting fences, and the prize for each race was a gold sovereign. This was Menzies's only leave, for he was heavily engaged in helping to rebuild the regiment after the First Battle of Ypres. [42]

On New Year's Day, Stewart Menzies's first cousin, Lieutenant Alistair Graham Menzies, heir to the Hallyburton estate, was killed by a sniper. He was twenty-one and with the Scots Guards. Two days later, Alistair's brother, Lieutenant Victor Wombwell, adjutant of a battalion of the Cameron Highlanders, was buried alive when a flying pig hit his dugout. He was the heir to Newburgh Priory, the family's great estate in Yorkshire.*

The frost remained biting throughout Christmas and the New Year. The troopers were quartered in what had been the barrel room of the drafty old brewery or in the barns where the hops were stored. Almost all were new to France and the front. By the end of January 1915, the regiment was restored and ready for active service. At parade on February 1, without warning, the squadrons found themselves confined to camp and under orders to be ready to move without horses but with full equipment at 6:00 P.M. that same day. Menzies and the 380 troopers were now in the hands of "higher authority," General Sir Douglas Haig, commander of the new First Army, a son of the great whiskey family Haig & Haig and a close friend of Holford and King George V. The regiment was not told where it was going, but Menzies knew and the troopers knew that they were going into the line. Nobody was permitted to write or post a letter, but each trooper was given a postcard on which had been printed a number of one-line statements such as "I am well and happy, and I send my love." The troopers crossed out all but the one statement they felt said best what they wished to say, addressed the card, and then gave it to their troop leaders for postage through the army censor.

The rest of the day was spent in preparation. Each man's personal equipment, which included his rifle and one hundred rounds of ammunition, weighed over fifty-five pounds. Each man was permitted to take one haversack with him, which was packed with as much care

*William Dudgeon Graham Menzies succeeded his brother, Robert Stewart Graham Menzies, as laird of Hallyburton. William married a daughter of Sir George Wombwell, of Newburgh Priory, a friend of Edward VIII, a survivor of the Charge of the Light Brigade during the Crimean War and "the first squire of England." When Sir George's two sons both died in active service at the turn of the century, one in India the other in the Boer War, George was left without heir to what was one of the largest and most famous estates in the United Kingdom. In 1920, Newburgh Priory was offered to Stewart Menzies, by that time an authentic war hero. He declined the offer in favor of the secret service. The estate was then offered to W. D. Graham Menzies's second son, Malcolm, on condition he assumed the surname Wombwell. He did and thereby became lord of the manor of Newburgh Priory. With the death in action of Alistair, Hallyburton then passed to W. D. Graham Menzies's third son, Neil. To an extent this tangle reflected the havoc caused within the landed aristocracy by the cropping of the heirs at Ypres.

as explorers going to Tibet: chocolate, tobacco, candles, bolt cutters, saws, sandbags, four-by-twos, mittens, cardigans, face masks. The squadron leaders inspected each rifle barrel to ensure it was cleaned and not pitted. The 131 moving parts of each rifle were checked and tested with a rattle of bolts. Then each trooper bound his muzzle with an old oiled sock and the bolts with oiled rags. Feet were inspected. The padre hung about in the background to take confessions or say prayers with the faithful, and equally in the background stood the "vicar of the regiment," Stewart Menzies. The men regarded Stewart Menzies as an unobtrusive, high-minded, conscientious, uncompli-cated, and unaffected young buck of a captain. These, by the standards of the times, were almost tributes when compared to the dissaffection and even contempt they displayed whenever "the Sardine," Edward, Prince of Wales, heir to the throne, came calling.

At 6:00 P.M. the long convoy of double-decker, roofless buses, in the red-and-gold livery of the London General Omnibus Company, their destination boards and theater bills still showing, arrived at the brewery. Then, with all men aboard, the solid-tred buses rumbled off down the *pave* to Ypres. If there was singing then, as like as not it was the hit of the year, "Any old night is a wonderful night if you're out with a wonderful girl. . . ." Still nobody knew where they were going, except the acting commanding officer, Torrie, and his adjutant, Menzies, who led the way in the staff car. All the men knew that they were about to join what Menzies called "that very small club," men who had served at the firing line.

The convoy skirted the center of Ypres, taking the side streets near the prison to the Plaine d'Amour. There the convoy stopped to enable the men to use the latrines. When the NCO in charge of each bus reported that his complement of men had returned, the journey resumed across the dark countryside until at a point about seven miles from Ypres a light shone briefly at the staff car. The regiment had reached the point where they were to leave the transport and march to the front line. By dawn twilight the regiment had taken over from a French regiment a section of the line near Bixschoote, at a place where the front-line trenches were so close together that the troops could hear the gramophones playing in the German trenches.

At the regiment's first stand-to before dawn, one of the two periods in the day when it was thought the enemy would most likely attack, there occurred one of those small incidents that remain undying in the memory and one that had peculiar importance for Stewart Men-zies personally. At that stage in the war, spirits remained high enough on both sides of the line for adversaries to greet each other when a fresh unit arrived in the trenches opposite. The replacement of the French regiment by the Life Guards on February 2 illuminated that practice, for on this occasion out of the German line hurtled a peculiar missile. By one account the object was a matchbox; by another it was a bottle. Most likely it was the latter. But in any case, the bottle contained a note, which read: "We are a battalion of an Alsace regiment; don't shoot us, and we won't shoot you. *Vive la France*, but Germany comes first." [43] The note then made insulting remarks about "the English cavalry" who had come into the line to replace the French.

The report of the incident caught Menzies's attention, for as adjutant he was also responsible for intelligence and security. Since all military movements were conducted in the greatest secrecy, how had the Germans known that the French were about to be replaced by "the English cavalry"? They could not have obtained such information from a prisoner, for the Germans had taken no prisoners from the regiment or brigade. Nor could they have made the identification visually. The brigade had taken over the line during darkness, and they had come up to the front in buses. They had not stopped in Ypres. All identifying badges had been removed. The information could have come, therefore, only if the Germans were tapping the telephone lines into the brigade area or if they had a spy either in Ypres or elsewhere on the line of march up to the trenches.

The incident tickled Menzies's concerns. He discussed the matter with Major T.G.J.Torrie, lately of the Seventeenth Light Cavalry of the Indian army, who had been with GHQ intelligence at the outbreak of the war but had resigned to join the Life Guards at the front. Torrie had then been appointed acting commander officer of the regiment in the absence of Ferguson, who was still in the hospital recovering from his wounds. Torrie decided to report the incident to a friend, Major Walter Kirke, chief of the intelligence branch of general headquarters. If the Germans knew that an "English cavalry" unit had replaced the French regiment, how much else did they know? A report of the "matchbox incident" arrived on the desk of Major Kirke, who, as his diary shows, had been examining the persistent indications that the Germans were getting intelligence of British military movements in and around Ypres. Kirke recorded in his diary on February 15: "Torrie reports that when they relieved French near Ypres, the Germans had thrown over a bottle into French trenches saying they were about to be relieved by the English cavalry, with some abuse of the latter."

An investigation followed, but at first no answer could be found to the mystery. Two days later, as Kirke's diary again shows, the First Cavalry Division in the line near Ypres reported that it had found its telephone line "had been cut & a telephone apparently tapped in." That pointed to the "existence of a highly organised service of espionage communicating by rockets, lamp signalling, & possibly telephones." It was fifteen months before it was discovered that the Germans had developed a listening apparatus that acquired the ground waves created by the Fullerphone, the British military telephone system. As Kirke was to record of that discovery, an enameled wire attached to British telephone wire led back across the front line into the German trenches. The German apparatus, which was captured, showed that British telephone conversations had been audible to the Germans on the apparatus at least to five hundred feet and under certain circumstances to one thousand feet, and there was no doubt in his mind that "there has been a very great leakage of information due to earthed telephone returns." [44]

The age of innocence about wire and telegraphic communications was at an end. The age of cunning in the use of such communications had begun. Menzies was brought into contact with Kirke over the matchbox incident, and in due course Kirke, who was looking for men of good background with languages, seems to have offered him a post at GHQ intelligence. As Menzies told his mother in a letter dated April 14, 1915:

There is just an outside chance that I might go on to the Staff later on, but *on no account* is this to be mentioned to *a soul*, as if it leaked out there would be an awful fuss. I shall not go unless I get a good post & of course if there is not much probability of the Regiment doing much fighting. I simply loathe the idea, & yet it is obvious that to get on one must go on the Staff for a while. Anyway nothing will happen for many weeks, so please be very careful not to breathe this. If anyone gets to know, I am done.

But whatever course Menzies's ambitions were to take him, nothing could happen immediately, for eight days after writing that letter the Second Battle of Ypres erupted with, again, evidence that there had been an information leak concerning British intentions. The army commander, General Sir Douglas Haig, had just prepared an offensive to free the North Sea ports of German submarine bases from which U-boats were sailing to blockade England. But the German commander had got wind of the attack, probably through telephone conversations in the British trenches. The German commander then launched a spoiling attack preceded by a cloud of chlorine gas emitted from some five-thousand cylinders. This was the first use of poison gas on the Western front. This had been foreshadowed, and chlorine was regarded as an inefficient weapon. It could be seen, and the killer clouds could be avoided. One thousand parts of gas in a million of air were required to destroy the alveoli of the lungs and the smaller bronchial tubes. If that concentration was obtained, then the victim drowned in the mucus of his tortured lungs. The gas terrorized the two French divisions holding the line. They broke, exposing the flank of a Canadian division. Overcome by the gas cloud, sixty percent of the Canadians had to be returned home, and 40 percent of these were still fully disabled at the end of the war. The front broke, and Menzies and the regiment found themselves being used once again as "a fire brigade," being rushed hither and thither to the points of actual or threatened penetration.

By April 30 the regiment again fought for its life in the waterlogged fields and copses to the east of Ypres. Despite the appearance of this new, diabolical weapon, Menzies reflected only calm when he wrote to Lady Holford from the old trenches in the area of Klein Zillebeke that day:

My dear Mother,

I have been very busy of late, hence the delay in writing. Well, I suppose this 2nd Battle of Ypres has been the fiercest of the war. It lasted (unless resumed today) 6 days, and there must have been close on 100,000 casualties including British, French, Belgian & German. Unquestionably our fellows fought better than they ever have done & saved a most critical position. Of course we lost very heavily, about 28,000 I believe, but many wounds are very slight. Still those figures give you an idea.

Then the artillery fire was something astounding—it fairly took our breath away as it never ceased day & night—one continuous roar of the loudest thunder.

All the cavalry went up to support & we had little sleep or food for several days. . . . Unquestionably our air superiority is established—we seem to be able to do absolutely anything & keep on bringing their machines down. . . . Will you please send me some small tins of potted meat & jam? Also a linen bag to put my food into. . . . It is frightfully hot out here & very nice sleeping out.

We may be off to the trenches this morning but not very likely.

Best love
Stewart

By May 10 Menzies and his regiment were deeply involved in the fighting at Hooge, near the place where he had won his D.S.O., and in a note to his mother from the trenches on that day, he spoke of being in "desperate fighting." What Menzies did not tell his mother was that on May 13 and 14, over half the fighting strength of the regiment—about 150 men—had been killed, wounded, or were missing. The regiment's commander, Ferguson, who had returned from the hospital in March, was again badly wounded and had gone back for treatment. Again Menzies had taken command. Such was his part in the fighting that later it was announced in the *London Gazette,* the official newspaper, that when Ferguson was wounded Menzies had "displayed conspicuous ability, coolness, and resource in controlling the actions of his regiment and rallying his men." He was awarded the Military Cross, Britain's third-highest award for heroism. In only six months Menzies had received the second- and third-highest awards for bravery in the field.

Moreover, at no time did he tell his mother that on May 25 he had been caught by a gas cloud. The regiment had not as yet been issued gas masks—what Menzies called "smoke helmets"—and although he inhaled some of the gas, he was saved from asphyxiation, probably by a pad of gauze and flannel steeped either in a solution of hyposulphite of soda and kept moist with water and glycerine or in urine. But there were many others in the regiment (and in Rex's just to Menzies's left) who were not so fortunate. As the report on the gas attack stated: "The casualties resulting from the gas attack of the 24.5.15 were heavy. The number of gas cases passing through our [casualty stations] as a result thereof amounted to 3,284, of which 53 died; but in addition large numbers of dead bodies and gassed men were left behind and fell into the enemy's hands." [45]

In these same actions, Rex Benson was badly wounded by a bullet in Zouave Wood. Unable to fight further, he left the field in serious condition. The brachial artery and the central nervous system of his right arm had been destroyed. He was also badly gassed. Taken to No. 7 General Hospital at Boulogne, Rex found that two other golden lads at Eton, Teddy Horner and Julian Grenfell, were there. Shot in the stomach at the Battle of Neuve Chapelle in March while with the Eighteenth Hussars, Horner had lost a kidney and was hovering between life and death. But Horner would survive, be offered a position on the General Staff, refuse it, return to his regiment, and then be shot again in the stomach. There would be no hope for him this time, and with him perished the last hope of direct male succession in the ancient and honorable English house of Horner of Mells, Somerset.

Benson found out there was no hope, too, for Julian Grenfell. On May 13, while with the First Royal Dragoons and having that day made no less than three highly dangerous reconnaissance missions, he went to hill 60, a mining spoil heap near the Ypres–Menin road, with his brigadier, General Campbell. As he climbed back up the side of the hill, a splinter from a flying pig struck him in the head. "Go down, sir," he shouted to Campbell. "Don't bother about me. I'm done." Taken to No. 7 General Hospital, which was administered by the duchess of Westminster, he was received by his sister, Monica Grenfell, whom Stewart Menzies had squired during Coronation Year in 1911 and who was now nursing at the hospital.

At the hospital, X-ray examination showed a fracture of the skull and laceration of the brain; a splinter from the flying pig had penetrated about one and a half inches into his brain. After the operation, the surgeon expressed the hope that he would survive, but the wound turned septic. "Better come," read Monica's ominous telegram to their parents, Lord and Lady Desborough. They did, making the Channel crossing in an army ammunition ship. Grenfell received them with a "most radiant smile" and then died. He was buried in the soldiers' cemetery on a hill at Boulogne, his parents in attendance. After the funeral, Lord and Lady Desborough went to rest in the Forêt de Hardelot for a short time. While there, their second son, Billy, another of the golden lads, appeared before them like an apparition. Billy had been given three hours' leave from his regiment, the Rifle Brigade. Billy returned to the front after trying to comfort his parents. They never saw him again, for he, too, was killed in action.

Julian's death, and Billy's after him, produced a great wave of despair through British society, a wave made all the worse by the discovery in Julian's effects of a poem he had completed on the morning of the day on which he was wounded. Called "Into Battle," this poem was widely regarded as the perfect expression for the times. As the *Morning Post* said of the poem in publishing it, it was "the one incorruptible and incomparable poem which the war has yet given us in any language." With his "long dogs" around him—he had six greyhounds with him in France: Now, Dawn, Dusk, Hammer, Tongs, and Toby—Julian Grenfell lay in the sunshine amidst straw bales writing the poem, creating a scene that resembled what another golden lad called "a freshly woven Gobelins." The poem contained these lines:

> The naked earth is warm with Spring,
> And with Green grass and bursting trees
> Leans to the sun's gaze glorying
> And quivers in the sunny breeze;
> And Life is Colour and Warmth and Light,
> And a striving evermore for these;
> And he is dead who will not fight;
> And who dies fighting has increase.
>
> The fighting man shall from the sun
> Take warmth, and life from the glowing earth;
> Speed with the light-foot winds to run,
> And with the trees to newer birth;
> And find, when fighting shall be done,
> Great rest, and fullness after dearth.
>
> All the bright company of Heaven
> Hold him in their high comradeship,
> The Dog-Star, and the Sisters Seven,
> Orion's belt and sworded hip.

The poem continued:

> In dreary doubtful waiting hours,
> Before the brazen frenzy starts,
> The horses show him nobler powers;
> O patient eyes, courageous hearts!

And it ended:

> The thundering line of battle stands,
> And in the air Death moans and sings;
> But Day shall clasp him with strong hands,
> And Night shall fold him in soft wings.*

Grenfell's death was the ultimate testimony to the efficacy of Warre's doctrine. As for Benson, his life was saved, and he took three months "getting my wind back and my tubes reknitted." When Benson's war

---

*This poem was published in full—it was long and exquisite throughout—in the front of a privately printed book entitled *List of Etonians Who Fought in the Great War, 1914–1919.* Stewart Menzies was an adviser to the committee that published the work, which was beautifully printed. The committee consisted of the provost, vice-provost, the headmaster and lower master of the college.

ended, he was awarded the Distinguished Service Order and was mentioned in despatches three times. He was then sent to a cavalry division on pacification duties in Ireland. Disgusted with the work in Ireland, he had his father write to the prime minister to get him back to his regiment, the Ninth Lancers, and then, after the Second Battle of Ypres, he was transferred as Menzies's representative to *Bureau Interallie*, the headquarters of the Allied counterespionage service. There he distinguished himself by arranging the capture of the famous German female spy, Mata Hari.

At Second Life Guards' headquarters, meanwhile, Menzies had survived the war's first mustard-gas attack, this time because the regiment had been issued with gas masks. He emerged from the dust and yellow fog of the gas-shell bombardment a spectral figure with most of his regiment casualties. Yet for all the bloodshed, for all the termination in the male line of families famous for five hundred years and more, when the Second Battle of Ypres ended the Germans had been stopped again. Ypres remained in Anglo-French hands, although sixty thousand Britons and ten thousand Frenchmen had fallen.

And for all the demands and dangers of the battle, the Etonians with the brigade, or their remnants, maintained the traditions of the college. At Menzies's headquarters in an almost shattered cottage, the war stopped for five minutes on June 4, the birthday of their patron, George III, and one of the greatest of Eton's feast days, so that all present might toast the school with blackstrap drunk from tea mugs. Then the war resumed until it was brought to a stop by the autumnal rains in October.

Throughout the fighting Menzies made no mention again of his prospects with the staff, but with the end of the campaign he returned to the matter in a letter to his mother on October 15, declaring that he was "heartily sick of our present existence & am contemplating trying to go on the Staff." But he added, "I loathe the idea of leaving the Regiment which has been everything to me."

He never forgot the First and Second Battle of Ypres in which, by the end of 1915, British casualties totaled 381,982—75,957 killed, 251,058 wounded, and 54,967 missing. G.R.L. Anderson, Julian Grenfell, Billy Grenfell, Teddy Horner—four of the seven golden lads were dead. Rex Benson was badly wounded. That left only Stewart Menzies, Patrick Shaw-Stewart, Ronald Knox, and Charles Lister. Lister was the next to die. Having declined a job in the secret service, Lister was wounded at Gallipoli in May, recovered in August, returned to Cape Hellas, and in an action on August 28 was killed. He was shortly followed into the grave by Patrick Shaw-Stewart. The loss of these friends presented Menzies with *the* decisive physical and moral experience of his life. He came to dread leave, avoiding so far as possible the group's "joy places" in fear of their ghosts. He began to experience guilt that he alone had survived. And that was why he stayed as long as he did in the firing line. But now the time had come to leave.

With Ferguson's return from the hospital on December 10, 1915, either GHQ spoke to Ferguson or Menzies did, and Ferguson did not resist Menzies's appointment to the staff. He had had an outstanding career with his regiment. If he had remained, and provided he lived, he might well have become its commanding officer. He had displayed great gallantry and ability in action, and he had been in the fighting for thirteen months. Nobody could say, therefore, that he had funked the firing line, which was what was usually said about people who sought staff appointments.

On December 15 Menzies was succeeded as adjutant by Captain Euan Wallace. Menzies, Ferguson, and Wallace had a final glass of blackstrap, and then Menzies drove off to join the Grand Staff at St. Omer, just behind the Ypres front on the old post road from Calais to Paris. There Menzies entered the secret world from which he was not to emerge for the next thirty-seven years.

TWO

On Secret Service

1915–1933

1 AT GHQ

Captain Menzies reported for duty to the intelligence section of the Grand Staff of the British armies in France on December 16, 1915, shortly before his twenty-sixth birthday. He spent Christmas at general headquarters at St. Omer, and from then until the end of the war in November 1918 the secretive side of his personality emerged. He began to live and work with the silence and devotion of a cenobite at a monastery, which general headquarters closely resembled.

That way had been made for him is evident. He held the post of chief of counterespionage and security to the British armies in France, although he had had no training for such work. As he moved in, his predecessor, a Captain Campbell, moved out. Plainly, therefore, the same influences had been at work to get him to GHQ as had got him into Ludgrove and Eton, the places where Menzies began his climb into the ruling generation.

At GHQ there was some speculation when Menzies, the apprentice, replaced Campbell, the journeyman, in a task so important and demanding as securing the "safety and dignity of the British armies in France." Since the new commander in chief of the armies was General Sir Douglas Haig, who had commanded at Ypres, it was considered to be not at all unlikely that Menzies owed his appointment to Haig.

The son of John Haig, head of the family that owned the Haig & Haig whiskey company, co-founders with Graham Menzies of the Distillers Company Limited, both General Haig and Sir George Holford were members of the circle around King Edward VII, whom General Haig had served as aide-de-camp, and the Prince of Wales, who became King George V. It was George V who ensured that Haig obtained the appointment of commander in chief of the British armies in France. Since it was the custom for commanders in chief to select their staffs from within their own circle, there was no reason at all why Haig should not have appointed young Menzies.

The reason was simple. Had he not played an important role in holding the line during those calamitous days at Zandvoorde, when Haig was confronted with the greatest crisis of his career? Was Menzies not well connected? Had he not been president of Pop? Yet there remained unpleasant rumor that Menzies had obtained the appointment because, obedient to a dictate from the Freemasons, the ruling generation had been instructed to arrange the removal of at least one son from the firing line in order that the established power might be perpetuated. It was one of the characteristics of Menzies's career that his rivals and critics could always find a reason other than the real one to explain why he had obtained a desirable appointment. The real one in this case was that he had earned it and because the system was training him for a position of high responsibility.

Such was the intensely political and intricate world that Menzies now joined that in his work and personal life he was little more than a shadow. He left very few papers of his activity at this time. A letter did survive from Menzies to his mother and stepfather. It was written on December 23, 1915, on notepaper bearing the royal coat of arms of GHQ. In it Menzies revealed something of his attitude toward the war when he wrote: "My Christmas greeting to you & Uncle George & [illegible] hope & pray that 1916 will see the end of this nightmare." But such was the need for censorship, discretion, and secrecy that he did not say what his work was and confined himself to pleasantries, like a boy entering a new school. "Needless to say the Christmas post

& the change of address proved fatal to the Turkey," he told his parents, and it arrived "in a horrible condition which nearly caused me to don my smoke helmet!" Menzies added that a friend at Eton, Archibald Sinclair, who was to become the leader of the Liberal party, had taken him to lunch with Winston Churchill. Churchill was, Menzies declared, "an entertainment, I assure you!" But as Stewart also wrote, he could say nothing about the discussion at lunch, for there were "doings on this front to relate," and Menzies did not wish to say anything that "might offend the censor's eye."

Menzies and Churchill did not know each other well at this stage in their lives, although their paths had crossed at Tranby Croft and at the Bachelors' Club. One senses that Menzies's attitude, like that of so many of his class, reflected mistrust of Churchill's political opportunism and ebullient personality, that Churchill was "too clever for his own good." It is unlikely that they were friends, for there were fourteen years between them. Given Holford's sense of probity, Menzies's attitude toward Churchill may well have been influenced by the scandalous charges laid against Churchill by a man called Bryce in 1896. This affair had culminated in a writ for libel by Churchill against Bryce, at which the jury looked into allegations that while with the Fourth Hussars Churchill had engaged in "gross immorality of the Oscar Wilde type," the ringing of horses, the horse troughing of subalterns, and the blackballing of officers to the point where they were forced to leave the regiment because they did not have large-enough private incomes and were not of the "correct" class. All these charges had been aired in court, by the War Office, and in Parliament, and Churchill had been cleared of them.

Yet these and other matters of an unseemly nature may well have put Churchill, in Stewart's estimation, beyond the pale. Nonetheless, Churchill could not be disregarded. At thirty-six he had been president of the Board of Trade, at thirty-eight the home secretary, at forty and the outbreak of war the first lord of the Admiralty and one of the four most influential members of the Cabinet. Until the Dardanelles campaign, a stroke of Churchill's strategical genius that went wrong, it had seemed sure that Churchill would become prime minister one day, perhaps soon. But Churchill, forced to resign over the Dardanelles business, had volunteered for firing-line work as commander of a fighting battalion in France with Sinclair as his deputy.

We do not know what Churchill thought of Menzies. Nor does it matter much. Although they may have seen each other at the Casino at Paris-Plage, the highly fashionable resort near Boulogne kept open for officers during the war, there is no evidence that they came to know each other better until the thirties. Then the hunting book at Thurso, Sinclair's estate in Scotland, shows that they shot the grouse together. For the moment, therefore, Menzies seems to have regarded Churchill with little more than levity. Certainly he was cautious about what was said over the lunch table, for Churchill could be both indiscreet and explosive in his remarks. He was a man who was not at his best when he was young.

Yet for all the secrecy with which he now began to enshroud his work, it is clear that Menzies continued to make a good impression. Upon meeting Menzies at GHQ on New Year's Eve of 1915, the chief of the secret service section at GHQ, Major Walter Mervyn St. George Kirke, recorded in his diary: "Charming fellow," adding, "He'll do well." So he did. But it is far from clear what it was that he did do well. Perhaps this was because of the savage laws that existed to protect the secrecy of intelligence operations and the anonymity of its personnel. It was even unclear whom Menzies worked for.

On the one hand he had responsibilities to Haig's chief of intelligence, General John Charteris, and to Charteris's deputy for secret service, Kirke. On the other, as Rex Benson states, he worked for "C," the chief of the secret service and an official responsible for keeping the prime minister informed about Haig's conduct of the battle. If Menzies was "C's" representative at GHQ, then he had a very dangerous job indeed. Vast casualties resulted through Haig's policy of "stupendous and incessant" offensives against the German line. Consequently Haig's personal position as commander in chief became ever more uncertain as the war and its casualties reached the proportions of a national disaster.

Moreover, not only were the British military and secret intelligence services bitter rivals, but also the chief characteristics of Charteris as intelligence master to the commander in chief were (a) that he tended to send Haig only favorable news, not bad, and (b) on occasions when the slaughter became large he rigged intelligence reports to sustain Haig's nerve. It followed therefore that if Menzies's work was that of the secret service's liaison officer at GHQ, then he must have been informing "C." In other words, Menzies was spying on Haig and Charteris while acting as their security officer. What was more, in light of what happened to him later in his career, we must assume that Menzies was dutiful, for his fitness reports were uniformly good to excellent.

Certainly there was considerable evidence of Charteris's unprofessional conduct in his handling of intelligence reports to the commander in chief. James Marshall-Cornwall headed the intelligence branch in charge of its most important section, 1a, where enemy strengths, capabilities, and intentions were estimated. He wrote in his memoirs in 1984 that upon his arrival at GHQ:

[He] soon discovered that the views held by Charteris, and reported by him to Sir Douglas Haig, regarding Germany's manpower reserves, morale, and economic resources differed widely from the estimates made by the Director of Military Intelligence at the War Office. . . . Charteris . . . with breezy optimism, disregarded the sounder and more cautious forecasts which emanated from the War Office and were submitted to the War Cabinet. Consequently the GHQ Intelligence Summaries seemed designed to bolster up our own morale rather than to present a true picture of the enemy's strength and fighting qualities. This divergence of views led to constant friction between GHQ and the War Office; worse still, it misled the C-in-C in the field, who placed implicit confidence in his Chief Intelligence Officer. [1]

At the beginning of April 1916, Charteris became ill with pneumonia and was away for four weeks. By then Marshall-Cornwall had become a close friend of Stewart Menzies and remained so for the rest of their careers. Marshall-Cornwall became the senior general of the British army and served, for a time, as one of Menzies's deputies when he became "C." During Charteris's absence:

It fell to me to report personally to Douglas Haig each morning on the Intelligence situation. I was appalled to find what a mistaken view he held about the German troops confronting us. He seemed to think that they were on the verge of collapse and that only one more push was wanted to create a gap for the Cavalry to break through. I tried tactfully to give him a more realistic view but found that his ideas on the subject were obstinately fixed. . . . There was no doubt of his determination to pursue these to the end.

As a consequence of Charteris's dishonesty and ill-founded optimism, and the need of some the younger officers to do what they could to bring realism into GHQ before a generation of Britons was lost, Menzies and Marshall-Cornwall formed a close association with two other members of the intelligence officers' mess, which was dominated by Charteris and in which he was an omnipresent figure. These men were Major E. M. Jack, head of Field Survey and Map Department, and Major John Dunnington-Jefferson, commandant of the Intelligence Corps in France. That association resulted in the formation of what Marshall-Cornwall was to call "a small dining club," which "foregathered once a week in a private room at a local *estaminet*, where we could exchange views more intimately than in the Mess."

But through Charteris's influence on Haig's thinking, through Haig's moral dependence upon Charteris, and King George V's absolute confidence in Haig, Charteris's position at GHQ remained impregnable until late 1917. By that time, largely upon the basis of Charteris's reports, Haig had undertaken a series of gigantic offensives and had suffered very nearly two million casualties without seriously discommoding the enemy. Then Charteris made a mistake. Marshall-Cornwall found irrefutable evidence of Charteris's rigging of the order-of-battle estimates in order to maintain Haig's morale and nerve.

Then, for reasons known only to himself, in November 1917, Menzies did what he rarely did throughout the war—he obtained leave and went to London. Whom Menzies saw while he was there we do not know, although he took Euan Wallace with him, and, as a letter shows, he stayed with Holford at Dorchester House. Almost immediately after Menzies's return from leave, on December 12, *The Times*, then the most powerful newspaper in the world, published a first leader entitled "A Case for Inquiry," which contained this criticism of Charteris, without actually naming him:

We can no longer rest satisfied with the fatuous estimates, *e.g.* of German losses in men and *morale*, which have inspired too many of the published messages from France. It is high time that this mass of partial information should be placed in true perspective, that the charges of blundering should be sifted and that the blame should take shape in the prompt removal of every blunderer. . . . Sir Douglas Haig's position cannot but depend in large measure on his choice of subordinates. His weakness is his inveterate devotion to those who have served him the longest—some of them perhaps too long.

In January 1918, Charteris was replaced as chief of intelligence, although Haig was retained as commander in chief. In later years Marshall-Cornwall was inclined to believe that during his leave, Menzies showed the evidence discovered by Marshall-Cornwall to Holford and Lord Derby, the war minister, and that they in turn showed it to other high personages in London, the result being strong political pressure upon Haig to get rid of Charteris. If Marshall-Cornwall's belief has substance, then this was Menzies's first major intrigue, although it must be stated that there is no other evidence that Menzies showed any signs or acquired a reputation of being an intriguer. But the "Charteris Affair" was certainly Menzies's most important experience at GHQ, for if nothing else it taught him what an intelligence master should *not* do if he wished to keep his job.

During this period, Menzies was promoted to brevet major, a rank created by the British to give an officer the authority he needed for the job without incurring the need to pay him the rate for the work. He was also admitted into the lowest rank of the Ordre de la Croix de Guerre, the preeminent order for gallantry in France. It is evident, therefore, that Menzies's masters were pleased with his work and that he showed ability in it. By late 1917, moreover, the nature of his relationship with "C" became more evident. Kirke departed, worn out by the endless intrigues at GHQ, and was replaced by Major Reginald G. Drake, one of the founders of the Security Service, the counterespionage organization of the British government. Drake was one of the few professional spy catchers, work that he did with ability and success. Through Drake, Menzies came into more intimate contact with "C," and an association between "C" and Menzies developed that greatly advanced Menzies's prospects and career.

Captain Sir Mansfield Cumming stood at the top of the hierarchy of the secret world as the first "C." A naval officer, Cumming had been chief since the reformation of the secret service in 1909. A clubby, agreeable eccentric who had had to leave the navy through incurable seasickness, his real name was Smith, but he had married a Scots heiress named Cumming, so he called himself, first, Smith-Cumming, and then dropped the Smith and simply became Cumming. He always wrote official papers in green ink and he signed himself with his own cipher, "C."

Born in 1859, "C's" naval record described him as "a clever officer with great taste for electricity" and "a knowledge of photography." He was noted for the high speed at which he drove his Rolls-Royce "Ghost" in Whitehall, and he was one of the earliest aviators. The Scots novelist Compton Mackenzie worked for "C" in Athens and played a part in the removal of King Constantine of Greece, whose accession Menzies attended with Teck and Kenyon in 1913. Mackenzie found "C" to be "a pale, clean-shaven man" with a "Punch-like chin, a small and beautifully fine bow of a mouth, and a pair of very bright eyes." He wore a gold monocle, and Sir Paul Dukes, when he returned from Russia after attempting to overthrow Lenin, wrote:

At first encounter he appeared very severe. His manner of speech was abrupt. Woe betide the unfortunate individual who ever incured his ire! Yet

the stern countenance could melt into the kindliest of smiles, and the soft-
ened eyes and lips revealed a heart that was big and generous. Awe-inspired
as I was by my first encounter, I soon learned to regard "the Chief" with
feelings of the deepest personal admiration and affection. [2]

Cumming regarded himself first and foremost as a servant not of
the prime minister, the foreign secretary, or the Cabinet, but of the
sovereign, King George V. Somewhat oddly he kept extensive diaries,
which years later vanished from the archives of the secret service.
Cumming announced his intention of writing his memoirs upon his
retirement, declaring, "I shall call them *The Indiscretions of a Secret
Service Chief.* It will be a splendid-looking publication bound in red
with the title and my name embossed in gold and consisting of four
hundred pages—every one of which will be blank!" He habitually
wore disguises and went on mysterious journeys. He remarked to
Mackenzie that he regarded secret service as "a capital sport."

Unlike all other hierarchs of the British administration, Cumming's organization was not so much a government department as a
league of gentlemen, one bound, like Eton and the Life Guards, by
a code of its own. It conducted all manner of secret works that the
government might have to disavow. These ranged in scope from political warfare, including assassination, rumormongering, secret support for politicians favorable to British interests, and the establishment
of puppet governments. Its archives were kept secret in perpetuity
in the custody of the secret service. Exceptional laws existed to protect
the anonymity of all members of the service, past and present. Its
papers were always returned after reading and could never be included in official files. Its maxim, that to be effective a secret service
must be secret. That maxim was carried to such lengths that all personnel were employed by "C" personally, not by the government.
Its finances were called "the secret vote," the service paid no pensions
because they left a trail of paper, and all members were bound to
secrecy for life. Even the whereabouts of Cumming's headquarters
was a secret, although the average taxi driver knew well that they
were at Whitehall Court, next door to what was, in 1987, the Royal
Horse Guards Hotel.

Part of "C's" work involved spy catching, the most convoluted of
intelligence activity, and it was on that work that Menzies concentrated his principal efforts while at GHQ. He became part of an
organization or a concept known as the National Preventive Intelligence Service. This organization existed throughout the world. It

controlled all human movement in the ports and shipping lanes that Britain's enemies had to use in order to travel, and it was one of the main instruments by which England controlled a world empire.

In this work, the word "procedure" dominated all others. To enforce that procedure, Menzies developed a large staff. At GHQ he had four officers and thirty clerks working on a large card index system of known and suspected enemy spies and political and religious extremists and deviationists of all kinds. The Theosophical Society became an object of constant interest because its teachings were considered to be inimical by the established church and therefore to the established order, and also because of its links to Bolsheviks and pacifists throughout the empire. The object of all that clerkly bondage was to group humanity into classifications that would enable Menzies to decide whether they were friend or foe, hostile or neutral. All this vigorous procedure produced derisive comments and at least one poem that illuminated the absurd aspects of the procedure:

> A Minute came to P.M.1,
> To tell him something should be done,
> He passed it on to B.M.2,
> And told him what he ought to do.
> From him it went to A.M.3
> Who said "It is not meant for me,"
> So sent it on to B.M.4,
> Who lost it for a week or more.
> It next appeared in A.M.5
> Who tried to
> keep the thing alive
> By sending it in quick succession,
> In alphabetical procession,
> To B.M.1 and D.D.G.,
> And thence by way of D.M.G.
> To C.M.1,2,3 and 4
> Until it reached the panelled door
> Of D.M.P. who thought it wrong
> To stop it, so it passed along
> To D.A.O. till very late
> It reached the home of C.M.8
> Who, just to have a bit of fun,
> Sent it straight to P.M.1.
> It now approached its final doom,
> For, when it reached P.M.'s room,

He, thinking there was nothing in it,
Crossed out his name, which killed that Minute. [3]

Yet it was a necessary procedure, as all nations found. Under it suspects were indexed according to a civil classification: BS (British), AS (Allied), NS (Neutral), or ES (Enemy) subjects. Then followed their intelligence classification ranging. Here the code ranged from AA to BB:

AA: "Absolutely Anglicised" or "Absolutely Allied"—undoubt-
     edly friendly.
 A: "Anglicised" or "Allied"—friendly.
AB: "Anglo-Boche"—doubtful, but probably friendly.
BA: "Boche-Anglo"—doubtful, but probably hostile.
 B: "Boche"—hostile.
BB: "Bad Boche"—undoubtedly hostile. [4]

The categories were further broken down into yet more subsections:

A. "Antecedents" in a civil, police, or judicial sense so bad that
    patriotism may not be the dominant factor, and sympa-
    thies not corruptible.
B. "Banished" during the war from, or forbidden to enter, one
    or more of the Allied states.
C. "Courier," letter carrier, intermediary or auxiliary to enemy
    agents.
D. "Detained," interned or prevented from leaving an Allied
    state for SI reasons.
E. "Espion." Enemy spy or agent engaged in active mischief
    (not necessarily confined to espionage).
F. "False" or irregular papers of identity or credential.
G. "Guarded," suspected, under special surveillance, and not
    yet otherwise classified.
H. "Hawker," hostile by reason of trade or commerce with or
    for the enemy.
I. "Instigator" of hostile, pacifist, seditious, or dangerous prop-
    aganda.
J. "Junction" wanted. The person, or information concerning
    him, wanted urgently by SI or an Allied Service.
K. "Kaiser's" man. Enemy officer or official or ex-officer or
    official.

If the terminology seemed antique to the point of absurdity, that document nonetheless became the model for all population control everywhere. It served as the basis of the systems for checking on the identities and allegiances of persons on the move at all international airports even as late as the second half of the twentieth century. By the age of twenty-seven, therefore, Menzies sat at one of the centers of an interlocking system of counterespionage bureaus operating virtually throughout the world. He was a superclerk operating a formidable procedure, one tested by time and experience throughout the world, its political and social purpose to defend the established order. He was a born counterespionage officer.

By all accounts, the discipline that Menzies imposed on the rear areas of the five British armies in the field was exceptionally severe. Operating through a large number of British officers and Scotland Yard detectives sent from London for the purpose, Menzies had a man or men in every town, village, port, and headquarters and on every train. All mail, telephones, telegrams, French as well as British, were liable to interception. All newspapers, British as well as French, were under censorship. All correspondents and reporters were liable to military discipline and law. Nobody could enter or leave the zones of operations without permission. Owners of all hotels and lodging houses, and all persons giving bed and board to visitors in their homes, were required to deposit the papers of those individuals with the French police. All ordinary law was set aside, especially the law of habeas corpus. Suspects could be arrested on suspicion and, by edict from GHQ 1b, could be "badgered till you get something out of him to incriminate others," and they could be watched "until they incriminate themselves."

An officer called Woolrych, who worked for Menzies, remembered that he took over population control in a "pretty big area that ran back to the coast." To maintain control, he ran "several subalterns" and "roughly fifty intelligence police." These men were taught to "use their eyes" and to "get to know *everybody* and *everything* in their area." They were required to list every living person in their areas, and all males, and most females, were required to complete questionnaires about themselves and their attitudes. As Woolrych was also to record:

Unfortunately one of these questionnaires got into the hands of the local paper, the *Gazette du Nord*, of Boulogne, who made great play with the suggestion that the British wanted all this information because they proposed to annex the area after the war. I reported the matter to Major Menzies at GHQ, who took [the stories of annexation] up immediately and put a stop to the campaign. The *Gazette* was informed that, if there was further nonsense of the kind, all *permis* to circulate in the area and therefore to sell their newspaper would immediately be withdrawn. [5]

Later, Menzies remarked that his three years in this work gave him thirty years of experience in the ways of humanity. No matter what the seasons, regardless of time or the harvests, his control was absolute. Every human crime appeared in the reports that crossed his desk, including treachery. He supervened in three cases of alleged treachery involving British other ranks at GHQ, one of whom was in the signals section. The fates of these men are not known, but Menzies did gain the reputation of not being in favor of execution for any crime. His reason: A corpse had no utility. A live spy or traitor could always be used and *always* knew something more.

Nor was Menzies's experience confined to British affairs. Through Rex Benson, who served as a counterespionage officer on the inter-Allied commission, or through "C," he communicated with the entire alliance, including Russia. Stewart Menzies was the earliest Allied intelligence officer to detect that a "nebulous Russian organization was at work, with the secrecy which one might expect, in Paris, and it is believed in Holland." It was not known at first how that service worked, and as Drake reported to London in 1917, "the possibility of their entering the field in Belgium as bidders for our own & other Allied services is not excluded." In other words, Drake expected penetration of Allied networks. If that occurred, he warned also, it was not at that time "possible to say in whose interests these services, if purchased, were bought; or how much such purchase, if it occurs, will contribute to the dislocation of our [secret service] organizations." In the event, this proved to be the first glint of the earliest Soviet service, the Cheka. [6]

Then came the Americans. With the American declaration of war in 1917, the first American staff officers came calling in June. General Charteris, chief of GHQ intelligence branch, a man who was surprisingly pro-American in a staff where such men were rare, wrote in his diary on June 26:

To-day I have had with me General Nolan, who is to run the American Intelligence. He is here picking up wrinkles. If all the American Staff is of his type, they will do very well. He is precisely the man for the job, clearheaded, and very penetrating in his criticisms and questions. He is the exact opposite of the usual British conception of the American. Very courteous, not in the least assertive, genuinely anxious to learn and not to teach, and very appreciative of the part we have played in the war. [7]

Nolan brought with him his counterespionage adviser, First Lieutenant Eugene C. Pomeroy. Menzies spent five days with Pomeroy at GHQ and at his villa near Dieppe, where the archives were housed and serviced by the clerks. As Pomeroy reported to Washington, he was well content with his reception, having encountered nothing but courtesy and cooperation from Major Menzies. But as Pomeroy also observed, there seemed to him to be in Menzies's office "just a little too much of rules and schedules and an attempt at exactitude." When asked by Pomeroy about the need for such rigidity, Menzies replied not without some pride that "the capture of a spy in one of our areas would not be regarded as a triumph." It would be regarded as "evidence of [our] inefficiency."

It does not seem that Menzies was boasting; in 1918, according to Pomeroy's records, the British promulgated a document entitled "Chart No. 8 prepared by the British counterespionage service," which showed that between 1917–1918, Menzies's section had captured three German spymasters, Friedrich Pipo, Hermann Rehm, and Theodore Schloss. Through these arrests, some eighty of Pipo's agents and forty-eight of Rehm's were arrested. Some "100 to 200" controlled by Schloss were under investigation.

Unfortunately, Menzies's experience with the Americans was not uniformly auspicious. On October 20, 1917, Charteris and his staff, including Menzies, visited the American headquarters at Chaumont in the Marne, and Charteris recorded:

American GHQ is more than satisfactory. Everyone from Pershing downwards is confident and sound and tremendously in earnest. Their Intelligence show has prospered quite marvellously and will be excellent within a few months. They are working independently of both of us and of the French in all deductive work, which is all to the good. They bring fresh minds, and very competent minds, to the Intelligence problems. They will be very valuable next year. They have adopted throughout our system and organization as regards "I," after careful study of both ours and of the French.

Charteris added of the men he had encountered, exuding that spirit of a brotherhood-in-arms that marked most early Anglo-American intelligence encounters:

I saw some of the American troops, which are first-class material, very serious-looking men, of excellent physique, well found and apparently very keen. The discipline is exceedingly strict. Their weak point will be inexperience of regimental officers and of the staff in lower formations. There is a marked change in their outlook as regards the British Army. They have been following events very closely and are very genuinely appreciative now of the British.

Only two days after the visit to Chaumont, Drake and Menzies were responsible for an incident that cast the first shadow upon the Anglo-American intelligence alliance and gave Menzies in particular a reputation for anti-Americanism that he deserved no more than the average officer at GHQ. Menzies arrested not just any American general, but General James Franklin Bell, one of the most distinguished officers of the U.S. Army, and one of its most voluble and volatile men. [8]

During Charteris's visit to Chaumont, General Bell, who was on an inspection tour of the front for the War Department in Washington, asked Charteris for permission to visit the British First Army zone of operations in the area of that village of grim repute, Passchendaele. Lost in the First Battle of Ypres, on a clear day the village commanded a view of the Belgian plain as far as Bruges and Ostend. In consequence, it gave its name to the gigantic offensive operation that, culminating in an assault by Canadian brigades on November 6, 1917, made that small village into a symbol of heroic and almost superhuman effort. It also came to symbolize the strategic failure and terrific endurance of the British army in the field.

Also known as the Third Battle of Ypres, the fight for Passchendaele lasted for three and a half months. Its object was to relieve German pressure on the French army, which had mutinied through their vast casualties, and to deepen the Ypres salient. That relief and deepening was obtained, but only at vast cost. Some 300,000 Britons and 8,500 Frenchmen fell in return for some five miles of terrain. Given the extreme secrecy and iron discipline that Drake and Menzies always imposed on movement into and from the zone of operations, that was no time for sight-seeing by an American general in a uniform that was unfamiliar to most Britons. Still less was it a prudent time for General Bell to attempt to take into the zone of operations a car of unfamiliar make driven by a chauffeur of very uncertain origins.

Charteris, who should have counseled against such a visit at such a desperate time, sanctioned Bell's visit verbally and without giving the American the *laissez-passer* that might have spared him the embarrassment that was visited upon him. Bell then set out in a car driven by a Greek chauffeur, Angelo Damoulakis. Inevitably, on approaching the zone of operations, British military policemen stopped Bell's car for a security check. The sergeant did not like the accent or look of the chauffeur, and when asked for his papers Damoulakis produced a pass permitting him to drive an ambulance, not a staff car. Since his papers were not in order, Damoulakis was arrested while a check was made on him in Menzies's indexes. This took many hours, and General Bell fumed throughout.

At length, word came back from Menzies's office at GHQ that Damoulakis was a suspected enemy agent known as Anton Babel. That was a firing squad matter, which was resolved only after fifty hours of enforced immobility for General Bell while Damoulakis was investigated further. Damoulakis was then exonerated and provided with the correct travel documents, and Bell was allowed to go about his business. There had been an error in the procedure.

However, there was no indication that Menzies was contrite or inclined to apologize for the severe inconvenience suffered by an important general of an Allied army. On the contrary, when he received the American protest at the manner in which Bell had been treated, Menzies wrote the sharpest note to the U.S. liaison officer at Haig's headquarters, Captain J. G. Quekemeyer:

I shall be glad if you will take up the question with the American HQ, and point out that the British Intelligence view with considerable concern this Greek chauffeur being brought into the British Forward Zone where he had unique opportunities of acquiring valuable information.

Plainly, as the record shows, the security control was justified in stopping vehicles entering a zone of military operations. And if no discourtesy was intended, none was experienced by General Bell. Nonetheless, in the U.S. Army General Staff the episode earned for Menzies the reputation of being an officer who needed watching. Menzies sought to lay that ghost to rest by accepting work that entailed meetings with American officers and by training their counterespionage officers in British procedures. He himself took charge of liaison in counterespionage matters between American and British general headquarters, but here he found little inclination to collaborate, perhaps because of the origins and attitudes of his American counterpart.

Colonel Aristides Moreno was an officer of about Menzies's age who was of New York Puerto Rican origins. He was also a confirmed republican. Such men did not often entertain much regard for either the British or their empire. The liaison was not, therefore, a success. Whether the quality of *superbia Brittanorum* in Stewart Menzies's bearing and manner played any part in this unfortunate antipathy we do not know; it is not unlikely, for in the American opinion that quality was among the more unpleasant of the characteristics of the British ruling class.

Against the background of the Bell incident, and the Moreno-Menzies relationship, Menzies traveled to U.S. GHQ at Chaumont in the Haute Marne to see Moreno only once. He had two purposes. First he desired that British and American GHQs should work together in the common interest to neutralize German propaganda, which was intended to make enemies out of allies. As Menzies's paper showed, there was a "fertile field" for such propaganda due to the "inherited and almost instinctive antagonism" between the two armies. He recommended a program to develop "a positively friendly feeling" between the Americans and the British, one that would combat German propaganda and "American ignorance and baseless antipathy." What Menzies recommended were pro-British articles in the American press, "cinematograph representations" about the achievements of the British army in the field, and "constant effort on the part of company officers to instruct their men" in the amount of assistance the Americans had received from the British "and the danger of subtle calumny." Menzies invited Moreno to direct all U.S. officers to read to the troops "an occasional order or bulletin" on parade and in "observation of British holidays and victories."

Menzies's second proposal called for closer working between U.S. and British intelligence. He warned that Japanese agents were at work in France in hostile fashion and intimated—and here we find him entering the field of high politics for the first time—that the British intended to abandon the Anglo-Japanese treaty after the war, a treaty that had been the cause of much irritation to the United States. Menzies also provided Moreno with a number of CX reports (the codification for reports of the British secret service ordinarily shown only to the prime minister and the foreign secretary) identifying the agents concerned.

In retrospect, Menzies's representations were soundly based, for there were serious antagonisms in the U.S. Army against the British, although there was not the same sort of antagonism within the British army against the Americans. But young men say and do all manner of tactless things, even Etonians, and Menzies was not exceptional. It would have been much better had Menzies advised not Moreno but his chief, General Nolan, of the dangers being detected by British intelligence. As it was, the paper demonstrated that Menzies had not as yet learned the basic lesson of all contact between the two armies, that the Americans were quite prepared to learn from the British but were not prepared to be taught by them.

With memories of the Bell incident still fresh, and at any rate in the belief that the army of a nation that disliked George III would not be likely to commemorate the birthday of George V, Menzies's proposals did not sit well with Moreno. Moreno did nothing with Menzies's note, although Pershing's G2, General Nolan, who saw the dangers, did. Later that same month a prominent U.S. author, Owen Wister, visited British GHQ and was well received. Soon after that an article by Wister appeared in the *Philadelphia Inquirer*, which was not only syndicated throughout the United States, but was also circulated in battalion orders to all American units with the expeditionary force. Called "The Ancient Grudge," it was a handsome account of the high courage and sacrifice of England, and it contained an appeal for a better understanding with England in a deeply troubled period. The article was republished in all U.S. company orders under the headline STOP HATING ENGLAND!

Yet for all the generosity of that handsome tribute, Menzies's basic attitude toward the United States did not change, although there were to be a few examples of close relationships developing, first with General R. H. Van Deman, who was regarded as the "father" of the modern American intelligence system. There was, however, one important collaboration that involved Stewart Menzies and the U.S. intelligence staff in each other's affairs. In the light of future events in Menzies's career, that collaboration proved important. This was a strategic deception operation that at the time was called Document "X." [9]

Part of an operation to conceal American military weakness in France and America during the period 1917–1918, this deception began in Washington, where a document known as "The 'X' Report" was played into German hands. It was played also into those same hands in Mexico City and Madrid and was confirmed by fragments of information disseminated by the British service and the Office of the Counsellor, the State Department's secret service, and throughout Europe, including Menzies at GHQ. By indirection, "The 'X' Report" was intended to demonstrate to the Germans that the United States was marshaling gigantic industrial, financial, and manpower resources for the French front, and that the first major forces were already reaching France.

In France both Menzies and his French and American colleagues had parts to play. Since the Anglo-French counterespionage services had created what was virtually a wall around the two armies, one that was impenetrable to German agents, it proved possible to inflate the numbers of Americans arriving by a factor of ten. An American platoon became a company, a company became a battalion, a battalion became a regiment, a regiment became a division, a division became an army, and an army eventually became an army group. Much was claimed for the effectiveness of Document "X," for as an anonymous officer high on Haig's staff wrote:

There was a very elaborate and very successful mystification over the time, the extent, and the equipment of the American arrivals on the Western Front. The American "Intelligence," in co-operation with our own and the French Intelligence branches, managed to surround these matters with so much mystery that some of our own high Staff Officers never knew the exact position, and strangely over-estimated the strength of the American Force on the Western Front. There is good reason to believe that the German High Command was completely deceived and found its difficulties increased accordingly. [10]

By the end of the war, therefore, Menzies had had almost three years' experience in the stern school of secret service on a major battlefront. He had been introduced at a central place in the conduct of the war to high strategy and low tactics, to the interaction of strategy and intelligence, and if his fitness reports were a true reflection of his ability and conduct, then he had emerged as perhaps the most promising man in intelligence of his generation. He had taken to the game almost instinctively, even though it promised little promotion, and he was regarded as a reliable professional with few vices. But in one respect his conduct caused comment among those who interested themselves in his affairs.

As the end of World War I drew near, Menzies was subjected to the first in a series of periodic official reckonings that marked his career. Menzies's fitness reports, written by his superior officers in the Grand Staff for the War Office at the end of the war, were uniformly good. All his superior officers appeared to be satisfied with his performance of his duties.

Haig's former chief of intelligence, General John Charteris, felt able to record that Menzies had "great tact, energy, and is a good linguist" and that he had showed "considerable powers of organisation." [7] The head of the secret service section, Kirke, wrote on the same report—the report on which the War Office took the decision whether to promote a man—that he had "the highest opinion of

[Menzies's] abilities," in addition to which "he possesses the tact necessary for intelligence work and untiring energy." The organization of the "contre-espionage branch of Ib owed its success mainly to him, and the happy relations which existed between the British, French, and Belgian services were largely due to the same cause."

But the most important report on Menzies came from Lieutenant Colonel Drake. As Kirke's successor, Drake had led Menzies's section during the last year of the war and during the "X" operation. Drake was one of the men who had established the British security service and was therefore a man of power and influence, but not one who was either a lover of mankind or an admirer of Menzies. As Drake wrote on Stewart Menzies's official report:

For his years, Major Menzies is one of the best officers I have ever met. Extremely capable, hardworking, and talented, his personal qualities, tact, and charm endear him to all. A good organiser and administrator, he should guard against over-centralization in his own hands—a fault due to keenness and zeal but apt to lead to his getting overworked. He has good judgment —better, I think, of things than of persons, speaks French excellently and fluently, and is able and willing to take responsibility. [11]

The telling remark concerned Menzies's judgment that he understood *things* better than *people*. This proved an enduring characteristic. In intelligence such a weakness was considered to be serious and dangerous, for it was people who made events, and a faulty judgment of people made for an equally poor appreciation of events.

Later Drake revised his opinion of Menzies as a man and as an intelligence officer, declaring in a private letter written in 1947 that he had "always thought" Menzies was a "Pretty Boy" and "very much overrated in nearly every way, as regards capacity, soundness of judgment, loyalty (in the *real* sense of the word), truth, and all the solid qualities that really matter, but which one so rarely finds." Menzies was "clever enough never to say a bad or unkind word to or about anybody but he is nonetheless insincere." Menzies possessed physical courage "to a marked degree: when the [Life Guards] were put into the line [at Ypres in 1914] he earned, but like so many people did not get, the V[ictoria] C[ross], so I am told."

The earl of Athlone, the former Prince Alexander of Teck and a member of the royal family, was now governor-general of Canada. Athlone "thought a lot of" Menzies, and, Drake conceded, Menzies "was and is generally popular." But Drake felt that was "not difficult if you exude charm and agree with superiors: it is the way to get on, to establish a reputation." As a result, Drake continued, there were many at GHQ who "thought it was [Menzies] who really did the work whilst I idled, whoremongered, dissipated, and drank deep" and "rushed others to the front to claim the credit!" Drake continued: "I! Who did not give a damn for what people thought, so long as they did not interfere with me in trying to do my job, didn't care a d— about my career and all the Orders and Decorations in Christendom. . . . What good is a [knighthood] to [Stewart] or anyone else? It won't help him to pass his water when he's 80, nor even possibly to retain it."* [12]

Other survivors of the Great War were, however, greatly impressed. General Sir James Marshall-Cornwall held that everyone "from the C-in-C and 'C' downwards, including everyone in the Intelligence Officers Mess, thought that technically Menzies's work was superb." Between them, Marshall-Cornwall declared, Kirke, Drake, and Menzies created what amounted to a revolution in British intelligence. It was GHQ that introduced aerial reconnaissance and photography. They manipulated captured agents for deception purposes. They created a deception doctrine. From the first to the last days of the war, they broke the highest to the lowest German codes and ciphers as a matter of routine. They became proficient in "Y" intelligence, the craft of estimating enemy strengths, locations, and intentions from the volume, pattern, and nature of his wireless communications. They introduced the parachute (the "guardian angel") as a means of inserting agents into hostile territory. Menzies developed field security, population control, large-scale censorship of telegrams and mail.

If Haig's campaign was not marked by any quality other than a gigantic butcher's bill, Marshall-Cornwall maintained, that was the fault not of intelligence, but of the use to which the intelligence was put in the formulation of Haig's strategy and tactics. As for Stewart

---

*This letter was written in 1947 to R. Payne Best, a senior British secret agent who had been captured by the Germans in 1939 and who had a financial claim against the secret service. Drake had been Best's commanding officer during World War I, and Best sought advice on how to pursue the claim. Drake was a very sick, disillusioned man who died soon after writing this letter. In other correspondence Drake showed not only that he was jealous of Menzies's enormous success, but also that he held Menzies personally responsible for the nonrealization of his greatest ambition—to appear before his school as a knight of the realm. Menzies was not in fact responsible for the failure of the secret service to secure a knighthood for Drake. Drake was a member of another service, the Security Service, not the British Secret Intelligence Service. Menzies therefore had no say in the process by which Drake was passed over for an honor. Moreover, not to put too fine a point on the Best-Drake correspondence, what the letters amounted to was a conspiracy to blackmail Menzies into granting Best £15,000 from his secret funds, a fortune at that time.

Menzies himself, the only mention he made of his attitude toward his work was in a letter to his mother on March 21, 1916, when he said he found his work "extraordinarily interesting."

2 GRIEF AND MARRIAGE

Four weeks before World War I ended, Menzies was recalled to London to familiarize himself with a new and urgent task. The sheer magnitude of the butchery had produced the first glints of Russian-type revolution. Everybody knew that there had been a catastrophe. Nobody, not even the War Office, could be sure of the number of dead, missing, and wounded. As late as 1974, a body of a soldier in The Buffs was revealed by a plough. Still later, in 1985, Denis Winter in his masterful social history, *Death's Men*, could only estimate the number of dead at 1,104,890, the number of missing at 517,773. The number of wounded was just under two million, the number of men treated in the hospital for one reason or another at nine million. A new generation had been created, of whom Stewart Menzies was a member. It was known as "the separate generation," those who had either fought and survived or the far larger proportion of the population that had not fought but had suffered, usually through grief.

In four years of Haig's "stupendous and incessant" offensives, the German nation had finally collapsed in a welter of Red revolutions, as had Russia. But the victory was pyrrhic, an epic instance of what the king of Epirus, Pyrrhus, had meant when, having defeated the Romans at Heraclea, he himself suffered so many casualties that he declared: "One more such victory, and I am lost." An avalanche of suffering and grief embraced every family in England. In many families, in the working and agricultural as in the noble classes, all the men had been killed or maimed. As a consequence the country came close to revolution against the established order.

Winston Churchill, minister of munitions and about to become war minister, spoke of "a very anxious period, marked by many ugly and dangerous episodes" in which "not only the armies but the peoples were profoundly affected." The poise and balance "even of Britain was deranged." So many "frightful things had happened, and such tremendous collapses of established structures had been witnessed, that a tremor, and indeed a spasm, shook the foundations of every state." [13] Such were the casualties, such was the strength of the spasm, that when Menzies visited his tutor at Eton, Edward Impey, he found that even the Royal College had produced its first serious defector since the Jacobites.

Impey had grown old through all the casualties the school had suffered. He himself had had one son killed and another gassed and invalided for life. At the college, five generations of Etonians, 5,768 men, had joined the colors. Of those 1,160 had been killed, 1,467 had been wounded, 130 had been prisoners. Thirteen had won the Victoria Cross, 548 the Distinguished Service Order, 744 the Military Cross, 1,669 had been mentioned in despatches. Eton had provided 2 admirals, 2 field marshals, 209 generals, 90 colonels, 666 lieutenant colonels. All but 798 had served overseas, and all but 467 of them had served in the army, 2,648 of them in the infantry, 1,374 in the cavalry. These casualties demonstrated what had occurred throughout England.

It was a remarkable testament to the effect of Warre's teachings that of the twenty-eight members of Pop when Menzies was president, twenty-seven saw active service. G.R.L. Anderson and his brother, R. G., the outstanding scholars of their generation, were dead. So, too, were the Hon. V. D. Boscawen, F. L. Harvey, D. B. Lansdale, the Hon. A. Windsor-Clive, K. F. Granville-Smith. W. H. Thomas had been wounded three times and had then died of his wounds. The wounded included G. Babington, J. C. Craigie (four times), R. O. Kenyon-Slaney, W. S. Scholfield, C. Sutton-Nelthorpe (three times), R. H. Twining, W. A. Worsley, and J. H. Nettlefold.

When he learned what had befallen his own small, exquisite world, Menzies's limitless calm for a time was broken, and for the rest of his life he was haunted by what Nurse Millard called "the dark caravan that winds endlessly through the memory of my youth." He declared to his tutor that if he had anything to do with the central direction of war in the future, he would see to it that it was fought in a very different way from Haig's. He felt profoundly—in fact, it may well have been the deepest experience of his life—the guilt that he alone had survived. For the rest of his days he was haunted by the poem of Leonard Barnes, "Youth at Arms," which summed up exactly his own moral disquiet:

> But roll-call works a change. Name after name
> Of comrades gone recaptures bit by bit

The battle for minds which thus can pause on it
With infinite compassion and no shame.
Thus do they focus sense diffused of grief
On the particular dead, and thus derive
From pity and envy mixed a child's relief
That they themselves incredibly survive.

Reactions to the slaughter took many forms. Paradoxically J.B.S. Haldane, the King's Scholar who had pledged the school to fealty "even unto death" when the king visited there on his return to Windsor Castle after his coronation in 1911, reacted politically. He became Eton's first Marxist defector. Having served as a captain in the Black Watch for six years, Haldane was wounded twice with his regiment in France and Mesopotamia. Nor was Haldane's a passing apostasy. Menzies considered it to be a permanent derangement when Haldane became in turn chairman of the editorial board of the London *Daily Worker* and an honorary member of the Moscow Academy of Sciences. And the reason for his repudiation of the canons in which he was raised was that through aristocratic incompetence England had suffered a genetic disaster from which she would not recover. As Menzies discovered to his personal cost, Haldane was not the only turncoat. He was just the first.

On the wider scale, the country seethed with a political undercurrent that resembled prerevolutionary Petrograd. To meet the menaces implicit in the situation, the War Office formed a secret service called MO4x, to which Stewart Menzies was attached. One of the functions of MO4x was to provide intelligence on the internal situation to the king, George V, and the Cabinet of Prime Minister David Lloyd George. Another function was to estimate the extent to which the armed forces had become disaffected through the combination of the end of the war and the Bolshevik counterrevolution in Russia.

Yet even as Menzies began this dangerous and intricate work, and as Bolshevik-type mutinies occurred in the army, navy, and throughout industry, he took a personal step that could hardly be reconciled with the fierce anti-Red attitude of some of his masters. Nor did it fit with the countersubversive nature of his work. Young Menzies, the ideological watchdog, proposed marriage to Lady Avice Sackville, a daughter of a known subversive.

In the first place, Lady Avice's father, the eighth earl De La Warr, was an adulterer who could have found himself in the divorce courts. But for his death while on active service in a motor torpedo boat in the Sicilian Narrows in 1916, there might have been yet another unsavory action that would have resulted in yet more disgrace. Still more troubling were the attitudes of Countess Muriel De La Warr, whom the earl had abandoned for an actress before the war. According to the very intelligence bulletins that Menzies received each week from the Home Office, the countess, his future mother-in-law, subscribed to all manner of causes that were regarded as being seditious or very nearly so. These ranged from theosophism to pacifism, from a mild attack of bolshevism to her more serious devotion to various movements supporting freedom for British India. Nor were those aberrant interests confined to the countess.

The earl's successor, the former Lord Buckhurst, had been a pacifist and a conscientious objector and would have gone to prison had he not volunteered for work in a minesweeper in the English Channel as an ordinary seaman. Furthermore, there were rumors (which ultimately proved true) that Stewart Menzies's best friend, Euan Wallace, was about to sue his wife, Lady Idina, Avice's sister, for divorce on the grounds of her adultery while he was on active service in France.

To make the marriage appear to be still less desirable, at least for the moment, only a few months before the country had been badly shaken by extensive allegations of aristocratic excess, sexual perversion, and financial misconduct even as a generation of Britons was perishing in France. The Pemberton Billings case of criminal libel was heard in June 1918 and was directed at the conduct of the first British wartime prime minister, H. H. Asquith, his successor, David Lloyd George, and their foreign secretaries, Lord Grey and Lord Reading. Many famous society women, some of whom were at the Holfords' wedding, were named as being in the lesbian thralldom of an erotic dancer, Maud Allen, who, it was alleged at the trial, had connections to the German intelligence service. They included the duchess of Rutland, Lady Diana Manners, Lady Tree, and Lady Constance Stewart Richardson. Miss Allen, it was claimed, became a regular visitor to the home of Prime Minister Lloyd George. [14]

And if sensible men regarded the allegations as feverish inventions of minds unbalanced by the war itself, there were many Britons who were prepared to believe them. From the evidence it appeared that the ruling class had danced and misbehaved on the graveyards of the generation of the dead, especially after the jury found that the man who had made the allegations in his scandal sheet, Pemberton Billings, was *not* guilty of criminal libel. In other words, Billings had written the truth. With all the allegations of aristocratic incompetence in the direction of the war, the assertions made in the high courts of justice served to undermine further the almost absolute confidence and primacy that the oligarchy had enjoyed. It played its part in the awakening of the specter of Petrograd in England—indeed, ten thousand British soldiers mutinied at Victoria Station as they were on their way back to France from leave and, being fully armed, marched on Buckingham Palace. They were easily deflected by the Horse Guards, but the series of events revived the warning of Queen Victoria in 1868:

Danger [to the monarchy] lies *not* in the power given to the Lower Orders, who are daily becoming more well-informed and more intelligent, and who will *deservedly* work themselves up to the top by their own merits, labour, and good conduct, but in the conduct of the *Higher Classes* and of the *Aristocracy.*

Yet if Lady Holford was made cautious by the trial, and the reputation of the De La Warrs, she did not prevail. Menzies's engagement to Lady Avice was announced on October 13, 1918, just under a month before the end of World War I, when *The Ladies Pictorial* noticed:

The engagement of Major Stewart Menzies, Life Guards, to Lady Avice Sackville is interesting. He is the elder son of Lady Holford by her first marriage with the late Mr. J. Graham Menzies. When she married Sir George Holford her son gave her away. It is difficult to realise that he is now a Major in a crack cavalry regiment and a bridegroom shortly to be. He was such a boy at the wedding, and it was only six years ago. . . .

Such was the social prominence of the couple that the notices filled no less than eleven pages of Lady Avice's photographic album, perhaps because Menzieses' would be the first large society marriage of the peace. All the entries about Avice were much the same as this one:

Lady Avice . . . is built on a larger scale than her sister, Lady Idina Wallace, who is rather petite and pretty. She has darker hair and eyes and is certainly a very pretty and attractive girl. I hear the young people are tremendously in love and very happy . . . Major Menzies has inherited a great deal of the good looks of his wonderful mother, Lady Holford, who really might be taken for her son's younger sister.

Yet Menzies did make one concession to the mood of the times. There was to be no ostentation at the wedding. It must be a plain, simple, wholesome affair. Accordingly, at two o'clock on Thursday, November 29, 1918, eighteen days after the German surrender, Stewart Menzies's wedding bells rang out from St. Martin-in-the-Fields over Trafalgar Square. Menzies and his best man, Euan Wallace, waited in uniform at the altar, the only color in Menzies's uniform being the single line of medal ribbons, including the blue and red of the Distinguished Service Order and the white and black of the Military Cross. Captain Adrian Bethell, Captain Ralph Burton, and Captain Julian Symons, all of the Second Life Guards, were ushers, thus demonstrating that the regiment approved of the union. Indeed, the regiment commissioned the court silvermaster to make a magnificent silver statue from the photograph taken of him with the King's Guard in July 1911. It was eighteen inches high and made of solid silver.

Lady Avice appeared on the arm of her brother, the ninth earl De La Warr, who wore the bellbottomed uniform of an able seaman of the lower decks. As the press recorded, she was "delightfully dressed in silver brocade with a slender train and a tulle veil," her bouquet being of mauve orchids raised by Holford at Westonbirt. The bridesmaids were Lady Diana Somerset (of the family of the duke of Beaufort), Lady Morvyth Ward (of the family of the earl of Dudley), Miss Sadie Greenwood (a daughter of Sir Hamar Greenwood, who was becoming chief secretary for Ireland), Lady Cynthia Curzon (Lord Curzon's daughter, who was engaged to Sir Oswald Mosley), and Miss Diana Leigh (of the family of Lord Leigh).

A reporter recorded that, as Lady Avice advanced down the aisle to her groom, Lady Cynthia Curzon stepped forward to give the bride "a sprig of lucky white heather as she arrived at the church, an attention which Lady Avice received with a beaming smile." Passing between lines of noncommissioned officers of the Second Life Guards, Lady Avice arrived at the altar, which was decorated with chrysanthemums again brought from Westonbirt, another innovation since hitherto such flowers had been associated with funerals. Lord De La Warr formally handed his sister to the care of Stewart Menzies. The congregation rose for the service to begin.

The vows were the old-fashioned ones, in which Lady Avice swore to "have this man to thy wedded husband, to live together after God's ordinance in the holy estate of Matrimony," and to "obey him, and serve him, love, honour, and keep him, in sickness in health; and, forsaking all others, keep thee only unto him, so long as ye both shall live." They then took holy communion, as was the custom, including the collect, in which Stewart and Avice promised to honor God's name, keep the Sabbath, not to commit murder, theft or adultery, nor to bear false witness, covet a neighbor's house, wife, servant, maid, ox, or ass, "nor anything that is his."

The ceremony over, Stewart gave each of the bridesmaids a signed portrait of the couple, unlike his father, who had scattered diamond brooches far and wide at his marriage. The register was signed by Lady Holford and Earl Brassey, uncle of the bride and the great industrialist whose estate would pass in part to Lady Avice. Then the couple passed into the wet and windy afternoon beneath an arch of the drawn swords of men of the Second Life Guards. They motored to Walmer Castle, the coastal fortress on the English Channel near Dover that was the official residence of the Lord Warden of the Cinque Ports, the seventh earl of Beauchamp, a friend of Holford's who had been Lord Steward of the Households of King Edward VII and King George V. Avice and Stewart spent their honeymoon at the castle and then, after a week, returned to Dorchester House, for the "khaki" election was on.

Sir George Holford gave them a large flat in Dorchester House and an apartment at Westonbirt for weekends. These were their first homes together, and it was an arrangement that lasted until 1924. After that generous act—for neither Stewart Menzies nor Avice Sackville were able to buy their own home at that time—Menzies reported for duty at Whitehall Court, headquarters of the British secret service. At some stage after his return from GHQ, he had advised his regiment and the War Office that he wished to make a career in secret service—partly, at least, because he was genuinely interested in and fascinated by the work.

But there was another reason advanced for that decision, for a career in intelligence offered little chance of promotion into the highest ranks of the army. That explanation, offered by Robert Cecil, one of Menzies's personal assistants in World War II, concerned Menzies's character:

Despite all the assets that would have enabled him to lead an extrovert life and win popular acclaim, Menzies was by nature very reserved—even at times diffident. To remain in the shadows and exert covert influence was more congenial. [15]

At his meeting with "C," Menzies received instructions to report to the Hotel Astoria in Paris on January 2 as the secret service representative on the staff of Sir Basil Thomson, chief of security of the

British delegation to the Versailles peace conference. In a dangerous age, the British prime minister, David Lloyd George, required protection, as did the entire British delegation. Judging by Menzies's statements later, "C" had also seen the writing on the wall. If the peace was to be kept, then in "C's" opinion there must be a continuation of the Anglo-American "association" into the peace, for England no longer possessed the power to keep the peace by herself. The facts spoke for themselves. U.S. coal production per annum was 645.5 million tons, England's 229.5. The United States produced 443 million barrels of petroleum products, Britain (in Persia) only 12 million. The number of motor vehicle licenses taken out in the United States in 1918 was 8.9 million, the United Kingdom 663,000. The population of Russia was 136 million, Japan 78 million, Germany 60 million, the United Kingdom 42.7 million, France, 39.2 million, Italy, 38.7 million.

"C" therefore enjoined Stewart Menzies to enter into the closest relationship with his American counterpart, Colonel Ralph H. Van Deman, and to broach the question of an Anglo-American intelligence relationship that would continue into the peace, one directed mainly against the Bolsheviks but also to ensure that Germany observed whatever terms were imposed upon her and, in particular, that she demobilized her army and kept it, and her military-industrial production, demobilized.

With these instructions, Menzies then left London for Paris. There, as the triumvirs gathered in the clock room of the French Foreign Office on the Quai d'Orsay on January 18, 1919, to write a peace treaty that would prevent Germany from again making war, one of Menzies's first calls was upon Van Deman, who had just taken up similar duties nearby at 4 Place de la Concorde. The first meeting took place at the Traveller's Club on January 13, and as Van Deman recorded in his diary, he had had

a long talk with Colonel Menzies, of the British Intelligence Service, on the possibility of cooperation between British and United States military intelligence services after the war. Menzies was very much in favour of such cooperation in order that tab might be kept particularly on the activities of the Soviet Government in all parts of the world.

Van Deman, too, favored such a relationship, for he regarded the Bolsheviks as being the main danger of the postwar period.

The prospect of a more enduring relationship in intelligence between the Americans and the British moved forward again when, on January 23, Menzies attended a dinner given by "C" for Edward Bell, the U.S. intelligence liaison officer in London, and Captain Bronson Cumming, the London representative of the U.S. military intelligence service in London. Cumming was certain that the alliance would work well, especially if Van Deman were placed in charge because, as Cumming remarked, "not only had Van Deman been at [secret service] work longer than he or anybody in England, but his knowledge was profound and on the whole he thought he was about the soundest S.S. officer he had ever met or dealt with." [16]

As for Winston Churchill, he had become war minister and was therefore Menzies's political chief, and he, too, favored the closest association with the operational and intelligence staffs of the United States fighting services. At a dinner for General John J. Pershing, the U.S. commander in Europe, and Walter Hines Page, the U.S. ambassador in London, at which were present Van Deman, Bell, and Cumming, Churchill declared that another great war would come sooner or later, and that it would "without doubt find the Germans, the Russians, and very probably also the Japanese, on one side, and the French, British, and the Americans on the other." [17]

Bell advised his chief that Churchill might well be prime minister in such a future war and felt that the general staffs of England and her friends should "make their plans for the future with this possibility clearly in mind." Churchill had then indicated that secret talks were afoot for the creation of what Bell called "the proposed three-cornered defensive alliance between France, Great Britain, and the United States," and that when this alliance "came into force we should in fact be allies," not "associated powers," as they were at the moment, and that "the three General Staffs should remain in constant and close communication with a view to the eventualities he had indicated."

To that end, Churchill intended to send to Washington a mission with the rank of ambassador. Lord Reading, the former foreign secretary, would present the political aspects of Britain's case, General Keppel Bethel the military. Captain Euan Wallace would have a proposal relating to an exchange of intelligence and counterespionage information. The mission would sail for the United States in June 1919. Would the United States have representatives of an equivalent rank to discuss the basis for a perpetuation of the "association of powers"? That letter produced a reply that was hardly encouraging.

In 1919, at the height of victory and with a prestige and power in the world that she had never previously attained, the United States was undergoing an especially severe form of disillusionment with war, even successful war, which affected all the nation. She had not, it was true, suffered as severely as her allies, but she felt even more acutely that the suffering had not been worthwhile, and many of her citizens were repudiating Woodrow Wilson's League of Nations in the belief that American entry into world affairs had been a grave error in the first place. Many suspected that America had been tricked into the war by the British intelligence services through the Zimmerman telegram episode, and that her representatives at Versailles were being tricked all over again as England and France scrambled for possessions in the old Ottoman empire in Arabia.

America wished only for a rapid return to what was being called "normalcy"—isolationism. At the same time the Hearst press began to publish allegations that British secret service agents were financing Warren Harding's Democratic opponent in the elections, Governor James M. Cox of Ohio, who advocated that the United States should become a member of the League of Nations. The Hearst press also alleged that there were an estimated five thousand British agents in the United States, and that a huge propaganda bureau was beginning to flower in New York and elsewhere for the purpose of influencing the American elections and capturing American trade.

There was trouble over the Anglo-Japanese treaty, through which the United States suspected that the British were negotiating in Tokyo to enable the Japanese to establish a naval air arm equipped with British aircraft. There was a suspicion, not unjustified, that the British intended to annex north Russia and the Siberian gold fields, using U.S. troops to help them. There was a flood of allegation that the British secret services had entered into relations with the ex-enemy services in South America with the object of excluding the United States from trade in the region. Furthermore, the Americans thought the British were carving up Arabia with the French and bribing the princes to prevent American oil companies from doing likewise. The Irish independence question further inflamed the antagonisms.

Although numerous powerful men within the U.S. political, military, and financial worlds did support a continuation of the association, American suspicions of the British secret service were not easily overcome. In June 1918, General Marlborough Churchill, chief of the U.S. military intelligence service, reflected those suspicions when he telegraphed all his stations to request information on activities concerning the British Passport Control Office, the worldwide organization through which the British Secret Intelligence Service went about its business. As Marlborough Churchill's message read:

Information is desired on the subject of the workings of Military Passport Control officers of Great Britain, and following is desired: 1. What are the points throughout the world at which British Passport Control officers are stationed? 2. What is the system whereby they are accredited to the various neutral countries? What is their exact status? Send cable report supplemented by full report by Mail. [18]

The replies of the American military attachés reflected that they knew *nothing* about the organization, its officers, composition, and finances, other than the fact that it was closely related not only to political, but also to military and economic espionage.

Then came the matter of David Boyle, a relative of the earl of Glasgow, one of Menzies's closest friends, and a member of the British secret service in New York. Accused of plotting to kidnap Eamon de Valera, president of the *Sinn Fein*, who was living in the city, the State Department compelled the Foreign Office to withdraw Boyle's mission. The Boyle mission was liquidated, and Boyle was sent to the staff of Edward, Prince of Wales, who was visiting Canada.

Such was the absence of enthusiasm for such an association that Reading was not allowed to present his credentials, largely through the Irish question. When Reading announced that he was leaving the American capital, he had to insist that a sixteen-gun salute be fired as his Cunarder departed New York, the salute usually accorded ambassadors of foreign powers. Only after much deliberation did the State Department authorize the salute. But before returning home —to divorce and resignation from his regiment—Euan Wallace did, it appears, succeed in persuading J. Edgar Hoover to arrange for one representative of the British secret service to remain in New York as liaison with the Federal Bureau of Investigation. But that was all. All other representatives were ordered to leave the country or cease their activities.

The ancient grudge had returned. Anglo-American official relations became as hostile as ever and remained so throughout the twenties and thirties, worsening progressively to such an extent that both powers resumed war planning against the other.*

---

*The U.S. plan for war with England has survived, and it is in the National Archives. Written by the U.S. War Department, it visualized a war between the United States and a coalition led by Britain that included Japan, Mexico, and Canada. The United States proposed

As Sir J. W. Wheeler-Bennett, the royal historian, noted in his biography of King George VI: "It may well have been forgotten that, in the late twenties and early thirties of this century, unofficial committees were formed in both Britain and the United States for the study of possible means of mitigating the existing Anglo-American hostility; while British statesmen were at pains to emphasize that war between the two countries was 'unthinkable'—a sure sign that it had indeed been thought about." [19]

Indeed, Britain did not abandon war planning against the United States until 1933. Then a representative of the War Office advised the U.S. military attaché in London that the possibility of war between the United States and the British Empire was no longer considered a factor in British military calculations, adding that the American section of the War Office had been liquidated and placed within the section that dealt with Russian, Asiatic, and Pacific affairs.

Despite the revival of the ancient grudge, however, there remained the small but important group of Americans, and a larger group of Britons, who believed that an Anglo-American understanding was fundamental to the containment and perhaps the liquidation of bolshevism. That group included Vincent Astor, a member of the American branch of the British family; Kermit Roosevelt, who had fought in the British army during the war; David Bruce, Andrew Mellon's son-in-law; Nelson Doubleday, the New York publisher; Winthrop Aldrich, the banker; Henry Gray, the New York lawyer; Judge Frederick Kernochan; and what has been described as "a distinguished selection of stockbrokers, philanthropists, and academics."

The group met monthly at 34 East 62nd Street, New York City, in an apartment "with an unlisted telephone number and no apparent occupant." Known as "The Room," the group was essentially a private intelligence service that worked in collaboration with the British secret service. Later, The Room seems either to have been superceded by, or to have had contact with, the Walrus Club in New York, a dining club whose members consisted exclusively of leading citizens who were Anglophiles. The principal point of contact with that service was Sir William Wiseman, chief of the British secret service in New York during World War I, who had remained in New York and become

---

to fight a defensive war with the U.S. Navy in the Atlantic and Pacific oceans, while the U.S. Army and Army Air Corps defended the frontiers with Canada and Mexico. Curiously, unlike the plans for war with Russia, the Anglo-American war plan did not forecast the outcome of the war and did not visualize an American victory.

a partner in Kuhn, Loeb, the New York merchant bankers. He became a member both of The Room and the Walrus Club. "Wild Bill" Donovan, a leading Wall Street lawyer and the founder of the OSS, the U.S. secret service during World War II, was certainly a member of the Walrus and was probably also a member of The Room.

These institutions had the closest links with two similar British organizations in London. One was the Ends of the Earth Club, the other the 1b Club. Stewart Menzies, Wiseman, and Rex Benson were members of both, and both had close links to the British secret service. The Ends of the Earth Club was Anglo-American in its composition, and its main social function was a white-tie dinner each year at Claridge's Hotel in London during Royal Ascot race week. The 1b Club consisted almost exclusively of members of the old GHQ intelligence service, with Americans such as General Nolan, chief of the old U.S. service in France, and Van Deman as regular visitors.

In all this intermingling of politics and capital, the main force was the threat of bolshevism. And a further key figure was Rex Benson, who became one of Stewart Menzies's "honourable correspondents" and chairman of his father's merchant bank in the city of London, Robert Benson and Company, Limited. In that work, and as a champion international polo player and chairman of the English Speaking Union in London, Benson became associated with all the leading U.S. bankers of the period. Indeed, he almost married Miss Bee Patterson, a daughter of the leading Philadelphian moneybags and publisher.

The French end of these interconnections was centered in the Traveller's Club on the Champs-Elysées in Paris, where there foregathered each lunchtime for years most and often all the executives of the French service and some members of the British and American services. Stewart Menzies appeared there regularly and was extremely popular, being known throughout the club as "le Kernel Ming-eez." He and his French and Belgian associates drank liberally of Scotch and champagne, ate hare, and thereby, while the politicians quarreled over the spoils of the war, kept alive the spirit of the old intelligence alliance.

3   A "GIGANTIC CAMPAIGN" AGAINST RUSSIA

Stewart Menzies was recalled from Versailles after less than ninety days in the belief that the vengeful nature of the treaty the Allies intended to impose upon Germany would produce an armistice lasting only ten or twenty years, at which time the war would resume between England and Germany. The hobgoblins created when Menzies arrested General Bell had been revived with the appearance in Paris of Colonel Moreno on the staff of Van Deman. "C" felt that Colonel Claude Dansey would be able to achieve a better relationship with the Americans than Menzies, so he handed over his post to Dansey. Assistant military attaché in Washington between 1915 and 1917, Dansey had worked closely with Van Deman in the establishment of an American intelligence service, and "C" considered Dansey more likely to be able to form a close relationship with Van Deman than Menzies.

Menzies was not without some apprehension about his sudden succession, for this was not the first time that he had heard Dansey's name, and it was not by any means to be the last. Dansey was to become a key man in Stewart Menzies's career, and there was to be much debate about the nature of the relationship between the two men. Since several secret services had a front man as chief and another who was "in charge of all that was ultrasecret," the "man who made the most important decisions," who was "probably the most feared man in the world," some high officers of the French service thought "the Old Colonel," as Dansey was called in Paris, was the real chief of the secret service.

That opinion was even expressed in Dansey's biography, *Colonel Z.* As the authors of that biography declared: "Unfortunately Menzies was neither liked nor respected in the service. Many of his contemporaries . . . considered him a lightweight, a social butterfly who had drifted into intelligence work because it provided him with a pleasant adjunct to his social life. They regarded him with contempt, knowing that he lacked vital practical experience in the field and thus knew little of the harsh realities of espionage."

After Menzies became "C" and Dansey his deputy, the authors of that volume continued, it was soon noticed that [Dansey's] domination of the younger man now seemed total. It became almost impossible to see Menzies, even in his own office, without Dansey being present; most operational decisions were made with Dansey at his elbow. In due course, thanks to his hold on Menzies, Dansey . . . thus became the single most powerful figure in British Intelligence.

Although there was some truth in these claims, Dansey's experience of secret service was no greater and, in the higher levels of the game, much less than Stewart's. But it was a peculiar characteristic of Stewart's life that there were lesser men always ready to claim credit for Menzies's work and, still more strange, given the sort of man he was, protagonists of Dansey who were ready to confer on him the laurels of omniscience and ubiquity. In its sum, the complete truth was very different.

Menzies always regarded Dansey as *the* most professional officer in the British service, except for himself. He always treated Dansey with extreme reserve for two reasons: (a) Dansey was a rival who would stop at nothing to get what he wanted, which was the post of "C," an appointment that Menzies intended for himself, and (b) Dansey was a dangerous man. Not even the regius professor of modern history at Oxford, Professor Hugh Trevor-Roper, felt no need to confer credit upon Dansey where credit was not due. "Claude Dansey was an utter shit," declared the professor, adding that Dansey was "corrupt, incompetent, but with a certain low cunning." Edward Crankshaw, the English specialist on Russia who had had much business with Dansey, agreed, declaring that Dansey was "the sort of man who gives spying a bad name." [20]

Nor was Dansey's reputation any better at Versailles. It was said that Dansey's unhappier tendencies—he was a rugged, bearlike man with a bitter tongue—developed through several unhappy youthful experiences. Born in London in 1876, Claude Edward Marjoribanks Dansey was the first son of Captain Edward Mashiter Dansey, First Life Guards, the regiment that Holford had commanded. Neither Dansey's father nor his mother were rich or remarkable, except as worthies, and Dansey was educated at the English College in Bruges, Belgium. While there, according to his biographers, at the age of sixteen he was seduced by Robert Baldwin Ross, twenty-four, who claimed to have been Oscar Wilde's first lover. Captain Dansey discovered the association. It destroyed young Dansey's prospects with the Life Guards, on which his father had set high hopes. Claude was then sent out to the African empire and spent the next nineteen years there as the representative of Thomas Fortune Ryan, the Wall Street financier. As reward for poor pay Ryan made him a director of the Sleepy Hollow Country Club at Scarborough-on-Hudson, about thirty miles north of New York City, leaving that post at the outbreak of war in 1914 to join the colors.

Having joined the Security Service, he was by 1915 with the National Preventive Intelligence Service in charge of Boulogne, the principal port of entry for the British army into France. While in that work, he married Mrs. Pauline Monroe Cory Ulman, a divorcée of New York, at Hanover Square Registrar's Office. This marriage collapsed, it was said, because Dansey was a misogynist given to pederasty. But the effect of his association with Ryan and Mrs. Ulman, combined with his experience at Bruges and the ancient grudge that so many Englishmen of Dansey's kind held for Americans and America, left Dansey disenchanted with both Americans and women in general. Add to this an intense sense of patriotism, an admiration for British institutions, a detestation of "the Huns," a formidable ambition, and Dansey became (as Menzies was to discover) a man who could commit murder easily, so long as he was not caught—in short, a man capable of anything, and therefore exactly the sort who could rise to great heights in the secret service of post-Edwardian England.

Menzies arrived back in London on March 19, 1919. There proved to be little in Dansey's appointment to concern Menzies, for "C" intended to pay Dansey off at the end of the Paris mission, which he did. Dansey became a contract man until 1933. Then the theft of the tiara of the ambassador's wife from a safe at the Rome embassy made it certain that the Italian secret service was at work inside the chancellery and opened up possibilities that, it was considered, Dansey could deal with better than most others. He was brought back into the service, therefore, as passport control officer, Rome.

Menzies, on the other hand, was to be promoted still further. Now, at a time of crisis over Bolshevik activities against Britain and the empire, he was made chief of the War Office secret service, a large wartime organization that had been reduced to a small bureau, the main purpose of which was to carry out military-type espionage primarily in Russia, Germany, Austria, and Turkey. His title was assistant director for special intelligence, and he was promoted to the rank of lieutenant colonel of the Imperial General Staff in the rank of General Staff officer, first grade, a rank within a rank that was envied and respected by professional army officers, although in Menzies's case the need to sit for a special examination was waived.

Stewart Menzies was perfectly aware that he was a fortunate man to be able to pursue any career at that time, and every day he must have uttered thanks to his Creator, for there were few jobs like this available, everybody wanted them, and every day *The Times*'s personal column was filled with the advertisements of those who had failed to get them:

Will patriot give wounded officer £50 to enable him to start civilian life unencumbered. . . . Old Etonian (twenty-seven) married and suffering from neurasthenia but in no way really incapacitated in urgent need of outdoor work. . . . Would be glad to accept the post of head gamekeeper at nominal salary. . . . Will any Mason help brother Mason to obtain an engagement? . . . Major. Served in France. Public-school man aged thirty. Married. Has handled Chinese labour in British Columbia. Do anything. ˙Go anywhere. . . . Will lady or gentleman finance subaltern £100. Five children. Wife seriously ill. No means. Urgent. . . . Linguist with French, Russian, German. Used to managing foreigners. Not afraid of hard work. Russia preferred. Waiting demobilization.

Stewart, however, had landed on his feet, as always. And the fact that his appointment had to be confirmed by the war minister, Winston Churchill, suggests that Churchill knew enough about Menzies to be satisfied with him. That was an important attitude, for at that time Churchill was in a highly operational mood regarding Russia. Such indeed was his desire to exterminate Bolsheviks that the *Daily Express* reported there were "ominous signs" that the government was about to commit Britain to a "gigantic campaign" against the Russian Bolsheviks. Although Britain had only just spent a treasure in blood and gold to destroy German militarism, Churchill had actually proposed that "we might build up the German army, as it was important to get Germany on her legs again for fear of the spread of bolshevism." He warned, too, how in Russia the Bolsheviks were extinguishing civilization over vast areas as they "hop and caper like troops of ferocious baboons amid the ruins of cities and the corpses of their victims." [21]

To prevent the spread of this "animal form of Barbarism" Churchill proposed, and Lloyd George accepted, that the secret services be centralized. There would be more punch for the pound that way. Within a few months of Menzies's appointment as chief of the War Office secret service, therefore, Lloyd George reestablished the British Secret Intelligence Service (SIS inside the organization, MI6 outside it) as an interservice organization responsible to the Foreign Office. This organization came to be called "The Firm."

Cumming remained the chief, and the executive was recruited from the three wartime secret services. Cumming was made solely responsible for all espionage operations conducted against foreign territory and was prohibited by mandate from conducting any such operations within British territory. These operations became the responsibility of the Security Service (MI5), which was separate from SIS but worked closely to it, at least in theory.

Also, a third service was formed as part of SIS, the Government Code and Cypher School (GC&CS). Although its overt purpose was to advise the government about the security of its cipher systems and to devise and introduce new code and cipher systems, the covert purpose was to "study" the code and cipher systems of foreign powers, principally Germany, Russia, Japan, the United States, and France. Thus Cumming became chief of the secret service (CSS) and director of GC&CS.

At the amalgamation, Menzies's organization at the War Office was liquidated (although for cover and security reasons Menzies's name, that of his principal assistant, a certain Haddon-Hall, and the name of the office remained on the War Office list), and its assets were transferred to Cumming's control. At that point Menzies became "military representative" of the War Office at Cumming's headquarters. His work remained the same: the conduct of military espionage operations. Headquarters were located at 24 Queen Anne's Gate, a row of lovely William and Mary houses between between Buckingham Palace to the left and the Foreign Office to the right.

The new service thought of itself as had the old one, that it was a "league of gentlemen" devoted to the task of protecting the established order. The chief characteristic of the members of the service was homogeneity combined with marked conservatism. Almost all the personnel were ex-officers of the armed forces who had private means. They tended to be patriots who were uniformly hostile to any power that threatened England's. Thus at this time the service was generally intensely hostile to Bolsheviks and anti-American, anti-Japanese, and anti-French. But while all were targets, until the mid-1930s focus centered on Soviet Russia.

For operations against Russia, the service consisted in 1920–1921 (remaining so constituted until 1940, when there were slight reforms) of a "general headquarters," which included the chief and his personal staff, and the staff responsible for conducting and supervising operations. These operations were divided (by 1939) into ten sections: I

Political, II Military, III Naval, IV Air, V Counterespionage, VI Industrial, VII Financial, VIII Communications, IX Ciphers, X Press. To carry out the operations SIS maintained "stations" at Vienna, Tallinn, Riga, Brussels, Sofia, Prague, Copenhagen, Helsinki, Paris, Berlin, Athens, Rome, Japan, Rotterdam, Oslo, Warsaw, Lisbon, Bucharest, Madrid, Stockholm, Berne, Vladivostok, Beirut, New York, and Buenos Aires.

As for the main adversary, Bolshevik Russia, the peacetime SIS was considered to be adequate to defeat what men such as Cumming and Menzies thought were "mere rabble." Yet even as he found his way inside the new secret service, Menzies received an unpleasant reminder that treason and its handmaiden, sedition, were omnipresent, that nobody was immune to the siren call of communism, that it was liable to infect even the best families in the land, including his own.

In July 1919 Sir Basil Thomson, chief of the Home Office's Special Intelligence Bureau, circulated a special Cabinet paper entitled "Indian and Egyptian Conspirators in England, and the Remedy" at almost the same time Menzies was appointed chief of the War Office service. This report contended that small but powerful political movements had developed in both India and Egypt that were determined by all means, including assassination, to obtain complete political independence from Britain. Thomson warned that *fedais*, religious assassins, could be expected to appear in London and attack prominent people. He also pointed out that the Indian freedom movements were closely identified with the Russian Bolsheviks.

Thomson asserted that prominent Britons in London were assisting the terroristic wings of the conspiracies by "conducting agitation for home rule for India and imbuing the Indians with the idea that there is a large body of support for their extreme views in this country." Indian and Egyptian visitors to Britain "formed the backbone of the 'politically-minded' classes in India, and the lamentable conclusion must be drawn that the source of the movement for the secession of India from the British Empire is to be found in the metropolis of that Empire itself." Some of those collaborating with the terrorists were British citizens of the empire. [22]

Thomson then named and described the activities of some of those prominent Britons, Indians, and Egyptians known to his service to be involved in the movements. Among the twenty-seven "more prominent British Subjects of the United Kingdom who are in close touch" with the Indian seditionists was Menzies's mother-in-law, Countess Muriel De La Warr. Since sedition was in the British mind akin to treason, and finding treason even within his own domestic circle, Stewart Menzies offered his resignation "for the good of the service." That was undoubtedly the correct thing to do, for how could the War Office have confidence in a high officer of secret service whose mother-in-law was a seditionist, one who by "conduct or language incites to rebellion against the constituted authority in a state"?

Menzies's record shows that the War Office did not accept his resignation, but the fact remained that this incident taught him, as had no others, that treason affected all classes, not only the proletariat, a lesson he seems not to have fully appreciated. Much later, when a member of Menzies's staff came to see him to confess that while at Cambridge he had toyed with bolshevism (but that subsequently he had seen the true path and had returned to the ways of capitalism), Menzies became very irritated and uneasy and erupted: "I don't know why you are telling me all this. Only people with foreign names commit treason." [23]

Thomson's warning was not, however, an idle one, for the times were dangerous. Just as the warning was uttered, two Irish gunmen killed Field Marshal Sir Henry Wilson, lately chief of the Imperial General Staff, first soldier of the empire, as, in full dress uniform with sword and pistol, he alighted from a taxi at the steps of his home just off Eaton Square, London. Next, Irish gunmen shot and killed twenty-two British agents and intelligence officers and agents (including one major of the Grenadier Guards who was well known to Menzies) in their beds in a Sunday-morning sweep of Dublin. And then the *fedais* assassinated Sir Lee Stack, governor of the Sudan, while on a visit to London.

Countess De La Warr was not, however, indicted for conspiracy, although Thomson tried to bring a charge against her on several occasions. But if this episode caused Menzies any serious embarrassment, as it would anyone else, it was not reflected in his annual fitness report. In 1920 General Sir William Thwaites, director of military intelligence, made his last fitness report on Menzies before Thwaites moved to other duties. Declaring that Menzies had maintained a "high standard in his control of the Secret Service abroad" and that "as a specialist in this line he is invaluable," Thwaites added that Menzies's "forcible personality, tact, good temper, and sound judgment mark him as a leader." Menzies was a "first class staff officer" and one "much above average in those qualities connected with his work, organising capacity, ability, power of arriving at logical and sound conclusions, and shrewdness."

Winston Churchill, meanwhile, continued his antibolshevik campaign throughout 1919-1920, warning Lloyd George that "one might as well legalize sodomy as recognize the Bolsheviks." He called upon the triumvirs meeting at Paris to declare war on Bolshevik Russia and set the General Staff the task of preparing what Churchill called "a complete military plan" for the destruction of the Soviet government and party, which he sent to Paris for tripartite consideration, although the Americans had declined to intervene in Russia. Lloyd George, too, spoke against such operations, declaring that "the reconquest of Russia would cost hundreds of millions" and that it would "cost hundreds of millions more to maintain the new Government until it had established itself." Lloyd George advised Churchill that the country could not afford to spend that much money on a such an operation. However, he did agree to the arming of the White Russian counterrevolutionary armies with equipment to a total value of £14.5 million and to the despatch of military missions to various parts of the Russian continent. At the same time, in February 1920 Lloyd George made a strong appeal for peace and trade with the Bolsheviks.

By that time the Russian civil war had spread to Poland, and it seemed to Churchill that the Bolshevik revolution would spread to England if the Russians were not diverted. During this period, Menzies spent some time with the small British army in Murmansk and Archangel, establishing a Russian intelligence service based upon the British puppet government, which was called the Supreme Administration of the North. Headed by a moderate Socialist, Nikolai Tchaikovsky, the administration had its own flag (the royal blue of Catherine the Great) and established a separate currency, its notes being manufactured by the Bank of England, which also backed the currency.

In these operations Menzies was assisted by two family friends. The first was Lord Dynevor's heir, Charles A. U. Rhys, an intelligence officer with the British North Russian Expeditionary Force. The second was Prince Alexis Dolgorouki, who was reputed to be one of the richest men in Russia. In 1896 Dolgorouki married Miss Fleetwood Wilson, the only daughter of a rich recluse and a member of the Wilson cousinhood. Upon her father's death, Princess Dolgorouki inherited her father's estate, estimated by *The Tatler* to produce an annual income of £40,000 a year, a huge sum by the standards of the times. One of Miss Wilson's "social godmothers" was Lady Julia

Wombwell, a daughter of the earl of Jersey, a major London banker and a member of the Holford-Menzies sect. Lady Julia's daughter married William Dudgeon Graham Menzies, laird of Hallyburton and chairman of the Distillers Company Limited. Thus arose an alliance of Anglo-Russian-Scottish capital.

Now that alliance linked up with Holford's set. The princess became a familiar figure at Hallyburton and a close friend of Lady Holford, Stewart's mother. The prince and princess were the house guests of the Holfords at Dorchester House and Westonbirt, where they met Stewart Menzies. The Dolgoroukis lived in great style; their town house was in Upper Grosvenor Street, their Scottish house was Braemar Castle near Balmoral, their English country house was "Nashdom," a Russian oasis in the Thames valley near the Astors' home at Cliveden. They had also leased a villa on the Riviera. Before the war they traveled frequently to the prince's estates in south Russia, the main area of British army activity in Russia, and they were received at the court of Tsar Nicholas II. Menzies's relationship with Prince Dolgorouki was well established when, with the murder of the tsar, Dolgorouki and his wife resolved to use their fortunes to overthrow Lenin to restore tsardom to Russia.

Whether the Dolgoroukis played any part in the near-successful attempt to assassinate Lenin in Moscow in 1918 is not clear, but they had political ties with the Right Social Revolutionaries, and it was one of the RSR, Miss Fanny Kaplan, who shot and almost killed Lenin at the Mihelson Factory in Moscow in June 1918, almost exactly when the main force of the British North Russian Expeditionary Force landed at Murmansk and Archangel. What is known is that they were strong advocates of the restoration of the monarchy in Russia in the person of Grand Duke Nikolai Nikolayevich, grandson of Tsar Nicholas I of Russia and one of the Russian imperial family to survive the Bolshevik revolution. Although the Dolgoroukis disappeared from the scene in 1927, their intervention on behalf of the grand duke was of importance, for anti-Bolshevik secret societies were established that survived not only all Soviet purges in the twenties and thirties, but also German purges in World War II. Consequently, their remnants were still to be found in Soviet-occupied Eastern Europe and within the Soviet Union itself as late as the fifties.

With the end of Allied military operations against the new Soviet state, negotiations began from May 1920 onward between British and Soviet representatives in London. The Soviet agents were Leonid Krassin and Lev Kamenev, and agreement was struck in which, as part of any trade agreement between the two powers and the restoration of normal relations, the Bolsheviks would stop their anti-British, anti-imperialist propaganda. Now back in London, Menzies found that the Government Code and Cypher School had broken into the Soviet agents' diplomatic cipher. These intercepts showed plainly that, despite the agreement to stop subversion, Soviet representatives were, if anything, intensifying it, especially in London.

Displaying vitality despite the weakness of Russia in general, Soviet agents, some of whom were British, smuggled gemstones in large quantities into London, which they used to purchase British banknotes. With that currency they sought to establish a major Socialist newspaper, to obtain control or at least a measure of strong influence within the Trades Union Council, to create tensions between England and France, and to create ferment in the industrial centers. One intercept in particular provoked great anxiety at 10 Downing Street. It showed that Kamenev had telegraphed the Soviet foreign minister, Chicherin, regarding his plans to arm some fifty thousand British workmen and perhaps many more. These were sent to Churchill, who was still war minister, and as Churchill wrote to the director of military intelligence, General Thwaites, on August 19, 1920: "The more evidence you can secure to compromise Kameneff and Krassin the better. Pray keep me constantly informed." [24] Against a general background of covert rather than military responses to the activities of Soviet agents, Stewart Menzies became involved in what was one of the most curious operations of his career.

Churchill's favorite first cousin, Clare Consuelo Frewen Sheridan, was the granddaughter of the American financier and sportsman Leonard Walter Jerome of New York. One of Jerome's daughters, Clara, married an Anglo-Irish merchant banker, Moreton Frewen, to whom Clare was born. Another Jerome daughter, Jennie, married Lord Randolph Churchill, Winston's father. Clare Sheridan was an exceptionally beautiful and talented woman who, being a war widow, earned her living as a successful sculptress, "doing" the heads of Marconi, the inventor of wireless telegraphy, and of Winston Churchill himself as the young statesman. [25]

In the summer of 1920, she decided to see whether she might be allowed to sculpt the head of Leonid Krassin, the senior of the two Soviet representatives in London, and just before the outbreak of the Russo-Polish war, she mentioned her desire to a friend who was named by her only as "Fisher." He may have been H.A.L. Fisher, a close political friend of Churchill's, but in any case "Fisher" plainly had connections with the British secret service. "Fisher" agreed to help, and an appointment was made for her to see Krassin in August around the time that her cousin, Churchill, was inviting General Thwaites to do all that he could to compromise Krassin and Kamenev.

When Clare Sheridan arrived at the Soviet trade offices, she found not Krassin but his colleague, Kamenev, whom the British service regarded as being one of Lenin's "phantomas," Lenin's term for a Soviet secret agent. Krassin apparently did not have the time to sit for her, but Kamenev would be pleased to do so. Clare Sheridan was much taken with Kamenev's appearance and personality. As she wrote of him, "he had a neatly trimmed beard and pince-nez and an amiable smile. He might have been mistaken for a bourgeois French banker." That Kamenev was not. He was a senior official of the Communist International, which had been formed in March 1919 by Lenin as "the general staff of the world revolution of the proletariat."

Although Clare Sheridan was at the time engaged to be married to one of England's leading aristocrats, the earl of Wilton, she and Kamenev (who was married to Leon Trotsky's sister) soon became such constant companions that London society hummed with speculation that they were lovers, which may well have been true. Certainly the political staff of the U.S. embassy reported that was so when they referred Mrs. Sheridan's application for a visa to Washington for approval.

By her own account, they saw each other every day during August, the time when Anglo-Russian relations were in severe crisis over the Russo-Polish war. In the process, as Mrs. Sheridan herself recorded in her memoirs, Clare learned "a good deal about the new Russian regime, its aims, its methods, and the lies that were misrepresenting it abroad." At the same time, Clare Sheridan also saw a good deal of a man whom she identified in her memoirs only as "Melbourne," and it was thought in London society that this man was Stewart Menzies.

"Melbourne" proved to be intensely interested in Kamenev's activities, his movements, his associates, his meetings. Consequently, Clare recorded, "a Russian atmosphere began to pervade my studio." [I] felt myself beginning to be entangled in a web." But although clearly fascinated with Kamenev, and perhaps in love with him, she defended her reporting on him to "Melbourne" on the grounds that it was "better for him that I were substituted in the place of some importunate third person."

The relationship was just over a month old when the Lloyd George Cabinet decided that Kamenev's activities in England were prejudicing good relations between the British and Soviet governments. Lloyd George called him to 10 Downing Street and suggested that he return to Russia on leave and not return, a course of action that would spare the British government the embarrassment of expelling him. Kamenev accepted that suggestion, and in preparing to leave London, he invited Clare Sheridan to Moscow as the guest of the Soviet government. There, he persuaded her, she would be able to sculpt the heads of the Soviet leaders, including Lenin and Trotsky. By her own account, "Melbourne," who was plainly a British secret service officer, encouraged her to accept and offered her the sum of £100, at that time a great deal of money, toward her expenses. He also, it appears, encouraged her to keep a diary.

With relations between England and Russia still in a state of near war, the couple left England in September 1920, "Melbourne" escorting Clare as far as the ship at Newcastle. On their arrival in Moscow, Clare was accommodated in Kamenev's private apartment in the Kremlin. But there she ran afoul of Madame Kamenev, who insisted that Kamenev terminate the relationship. Clare then moved out of the Kremlin and into the "Sugar King's Palace," a great mansion that in 1920 was used as quarters for official guests of the Soviet government. Here she met several of Lenin's most important "phantomas," including Louis Fraina, Mikhail Borodin, and John Reed, Lenin's principal representative in the United States. She had particularly intimate talks with Borodin, the phantoma who injected bolshevism into China in the 1920s and very nearly succeeded in making China into a Soviet convert.

Possessing as she did the sculptress's keen eye for human detail, she was able to confide to her diary a remarkable series of word and pen portraits of her companions in the mansion. True to his word, Kamenev arranged for her to sculpt Lenin (who had yet to recover from the effects of an assassin's bullets in his chest), Leon Trotsky (who replaced Kamenev as her constant companion), Georgi Chicherin (the Soviet foreign minister, who was not able to sit for her because of pressure of work), and Feliks Derzhinsky (head of the first Soviet secret service, the Cheka). Her escort during these visits was Maxim Litvinov, another of Lenin's phantomas and one who later became Soviet ambassador in both London and Washington. From the point of view of "Melbourne," therefore, this was a brilliant operation, for his informant met and talked at length with a constellation of the leading Soviet clandestines, about whom little was known in London at that time.

If London understood little about the leading personalities in Moscow at that time, however, Litvinov seems to have known more than was desirable about "Melbourne." When Clare Sheridan prepared to return home after about eight weeks in Moscow, she found, as she wrote, "to get out of Russia was far more complicated than to get in." Inquiring about her passport, which had been taken from her on her arrival, she learned that she would have to wait for it until her sponsor, Kamenev, returned from a visit to the front. A visit from Litvinov contributed to a growing uneasiness. Although she was taken to a cavelike building and invited to take her pick from a collection of hundreds of the rarest and richest furs, when Mrs. Sheridan began to thank Litvinov for his courtesy, he cut her short and asked her whether she knew "a certain person in England called—Melbourne?"

As Mrs. Sheridan wrote in her memoirs, the way Litvinov asked the question "produced a shiver down my spine." And did she know, Litvinov continued, "that he is in the Intelligence Service?" Clare said she knew only that he worked in "a City office." Litvinov persisted: "But he *was* in the Intelligence Service." When she admitted that he may have been during the war, Litvinov smoked a cigarette in silence, his "small eyes" scrutinizing her until she felt she was "the author of a murder." Soon Litvinov was followed by Kamenev, and when Clare Sheridan attempted to thank him for the arrangements he had made, he, too, cut her short, declaring, "We are glad to have amongst us *une femme artiste*," but "your nationality and your relations are nothing to us." There was "only one thing we cannot stand." That was, Kamenev declared, "*l'espionnage!*" Nothing further occurred or was said. Clare's passport was returned to her, and with her sculptures and furs with her, she left Moscow by train for Helsinki on or about November 6, 1920. When she offered the £100 as part payment at least for her expenses, it was refused by Litvinov.

On her arrival at Newcastle docks, Mrs. Sheridan was met by "Melbourne," who escorted her to London. When Mrs. Sheridan handed her diary over together with the £100, Melbourne took the diary but insisted she keep the money. On her arrival in London she visited the Foreign Office, where presumably she was questioned about the persons she had met in Moscow, and in due course the diary was returned to her. Whether it was complete is not known, but the Foreign Office did sanction its publication. It appeared in both the London *Times* and *The New York Times* newspapers at great length, and it caused such a great sensation that it was also published as a book entitled *The Naked Truth*. Mrs. Sheridan, the author, became a celebrity.

But inside herself, as she wrote in *The Naked Truth*, she was "in a very unsettled and tormented state," for "Russia with her mysticism, her art, her romance, her martyrdom," had "seized my imagination." Her reaction to Russia was "sensual but artistic also, and almost religious." To the consternation of London society, and no doubt to Winston Churchill, Clare Sheridan had returned a Bolshevik. In time, bolshevism consumed her entire interest, and as an escape she became addicted to cocaine and did not recover.

Plainly Clare Sheridan had become entangled in an intelligence net, and if "Melbourne" was not Menzies, then Menzies surely was involved, for this was clearly a War Office undertaking, and Menzies was chief of the military secret intelligence section. At the very least he would have known about the operation and either approved it himself or obtained approval for it. Only one person could have had such authority, and that was the war minister, Churchill.

4 ENTER "QUEX"

With the death of "C" on June 14, 1923, at his official residence in Queen Anne's Gate, Admiral Sir Hugh Sinclair became chief of the secret service and retained the service and its personnel in the same state as he found it. Known throughout Whitehall as "Quex," the nickname derived from Sir Arthur Pinero's play, *The Gay Lord Quex*, first performed in 1900, about "the wickedest man in London." By several accounts, "Quex" had had a stormy married life, and the quarterdeck of his battleship, HMS *Renown*, was said to have vibrated with anger and noise when his wife came visiting him in his cabin. They were divorced in 1920, just after Sinclair was made naval aide-de-camp to King George V. The sovereign, however, liked Sinclair, and for the first time George allowed a divorced officer into his court, although Sinclair was never allowed to be seen with the king at Royal Ascot.

Like Cumming, Sinclair was "a terrific anti-Bolshevik" [26] and very secretive about his movements, for 1923 was a time when Bolshevik and Irish assassins were said to be lurking about every street corner in Westminster. But he was very identifiable, for he rode about London in an enormous, ancient Lancia Landau. As did most men, Sinclair took a great liking to young Menzies, and "11a," as Menzies was known within the brotherhood, was devoted to "the chief."

As a security and economy measure, the British Secret Intelligence Service was moved from Whitehall Court to Melbury Road, off Kensington High Street, a better area of London than it became. Although the house in Queen Anne's Gate was kept by the new "C" as his official residence, the SIS staff, including Menzies, found themselves occupying part of Sinclair's semipalatial villa, which was said to have been the home of William Holman Hunt, the English painter and founder of the pre-Raphaelite brotherhood. It was an area celebrated for its high Victorian art, and the house and its location were in keeping with Sinclair's character and personality. His severity of manner was tempered by a clubby, avuncular quality that "his ruffians" found agreeable.

Sinclair was very popular with the Tories and played a leading part in the "Zinoviev Letter" conspiracy that led to the downfall of the first Socialist government of J. Ramsay MacDonald in 1924, thereby wrecking for good SIS's reputation of being a nonparty organization that provided exactly the same intelligence to all governments, whatever party they represented. The new "C's" chief weakness was that he did not fight the fiscal repressions that the Treasury imposed on all departments, with the result that by 1939 SIS became little more than a cadre upon which the World War II service of Stewart Menzies could form.

Sinclair was otherwise a great patriot and was much loved by his colleagues within the service, including Menzies, who always kept a portrait of "Quex" in his office, even after Menzies himself became "C." Their personal relationships were undoubtedly excellent, for when Commander Wilfred Dunderdale, who was reputed to be the model for Ian Fleming's James Bond 007, joined SIS from naval intelligence at Constantinople in 1924, he found that "Stewart Menzies was for all practical purposes 'C's' deputy, although at that time there was no such position. He was, therefore, personal assistant to the chief, as well as doing his own work. Stewart Menzies seemed to attend every meeting, usually standing in the shadows near the French windows which opened to 'C's' garden. Dunderdale quite missed out. Stewart was very reserved and quiet but, I thought, the office worked well, despite its isolation from Whitehall. If we were short of money, so was everyone else, and when I went on in 1924 to become chief of the Paris station it always seemed to me that our communications worked well. That was the most important thing."

Dunderdale recalled that in all the years he worked for SIS, first as its Paris representative between 1925 and 1939 and then as head of the French section in London, he was never required to organize an act of assassination, "although on one occasion when I was going back to Paris in the night train it was suggested that I would render the country a great service if I nudged a certain individual into the English Channel. Unhappily the man concerned was not on the train so there was nobody to nudge." [27]

As for men anxious to obtain employment in the service, which had a supernatural reputation in the twenties, the secret service was a world apart, one that was neither seen nor heard by ordinary people. But occasionally there were glimpses to be had in the twilight of Melbury Road. In about 1923 Guy Vansittart, brother of Sir Robert Vansittart, who became permanent head of the Foreign Office and a close friend of Menzies, attempted to get a job with SIS in the early 1920s. He recalled:

I was in White's billiards room when Stewart came in. I asked him if I might have a word with him and we went and sat by the fireplace. He told me to say nothing for the moment and I noticed that the man with the chalk on the table left the room. Then I said to Stewart that I wanted a job in the secret service. He said he would see what he could do for me and told me to be at White's at 5:00 P.M. the next day. At that hour I waited and a man came up to me and asked me if I was Guy Vansittart and when I said I was no other he asked me to accompany him. He got into the back of a car which had blinds drawn. He then drove for about an hour or so [Melbury Road is about twenty minutes by taxi from White's] and then I found myself outside a large Victorian house but in a district I had not visited before.

We went up to the front door and a burly man opened it and I was shown into a room that was bare except for a table and three chairs. I heard a good deal of clumping about on bare floors and then two men came in. I had not met either before, although I think I saw one of them later at Boodle's. They asked me a lot of questions about my politics, money, whether I was "queer," said they would get in touch with me, and then I found myself back in the car being driven around London until, presently, I found myself back at White's.

Stewart told me next day that everyone was impressed but they were tight for money and it might be some time before they could take me on.

So I went off and got a job as European representative of General Motors. Sixteen years later, Stewart asked me to come into the billiards room, and he asked me what I knew about explosives and Rumania. I said I knew nothing about either but later I learned that a group had gone out to the Baku oil fields to blow up the power houses to stop the pumping of oil to the Hun. [28]

Sinclair did not remain long at Melbury Road, largely because it was remote from his club, the Army and Navy, where he spent most afternoons at teatime quaffing brandy and soda under the great portrait of Nell Gwynne, the orange seller at the Theater Royal who became the mistress of King Charles II. With the return of the Conservative government in 1924, Sinclair secured the necessary funds from the new chancellor of the Exchequer, Winston Churchill, and moved SIS and the code breakers back to the seat of government. He leased the third and fourth floors of 54 Broadway, a large office block just off Parliament Square. The premises were guarded by men of the sergeant-major type belonging to the Corps of Commissionaires, who wore blue uniforms with black patent-leather pouch belts across their chests. These men were brisk, efficient, and diligent, and their duty was to keep strangers out and to record the comings and goings of secret service officers and the staff.

Also in the building were a quarry merchant, a canteen run by the Misses Hatton, some offices of the British and Foreign Bible Society, and the Broadway Press, publishers of the magazine *Our Empire*. Owned by the British Empire Service League, the magazine described itself as "an Imperial Magazine with an Empire-wide influence." This move led to greater intimacy between SIS and GC&CS, a step that was desirable and necessary because it was part of SIS's work to procure—by theft, blackmail, burglary, or subornation—documents that would enable the code breakers to "unbutton" foreign ciphers. In that work David Boyle, whom we last saw escaping toward Canada after an attempt to kidnap Eamon de Valera in New York, had become head of "N" section and had an important part to play, waylaying and diverting diplomatic couriers so that their pouches might be opened and the contents examined without their knowledge.

By 1925 Menzies had arrived at the address he was to occupy for the next twenty-seven years, including the six years that he served as Winston Churchill's spymaster. He was, they said, a natural—he had what was called "flair" for the great game. Menzies's annual fitness report for 1925 reflected this ability. Brigadier A. C. Temperley, who became director of military intelligence at this time, wrote:

Lieut. Col. Menzies is employed in a special appointment not directly under me. I understand Menzies's work is characterized by a singular capacity and devotion to duty. From what I can see of it, I can bear this out. Lieut. Col. Menzies is a very able officer and does work of great service to the country. [29]

In that estimate, Temperley did not exaggerate. Although Menzies would have been the first to agree that the main purpose of the SIS at this time was to survive against the day of the next big war, and was hardly larger than a professional cadre around which the wartime service could form when the emergency came, Stewart Menzies was nonetheless responsible for a number of espionage operations of consequence. The first of these was against the German General Staff's work to maintain at least a cadre of the German army in readiness for the next round of the Great War. Also, that operation concerned surveillance of the German armaments industry to ensure that the disarmament provisions of the Versailles Treaty were honored. These operations were noteworthy not for intelligence on the epic scale, but for small engagements, dangerous ones in grim, damp, hate-ridden little German industrial towns of the Ruhr and Silesia, places a world apart from Menzies's natural habitat, the slink and mink set of ragtime London.

The probability is that their early intelligence tradecraft was no more elementary than the basic tradecraft of the CIA, KGB, or the SIS in the second half of the twentieth century. The principles remained the same. They were certainly effective at the time. Through them Menzies's agents in the Rhineland succeeded in infiltrating a nationalist secret society known as the German Workers' party, the slogan of which was "Good work, a full cookpot, and a fair chance for the children." This was the party that Adolf Hitler took over and which became the National Socialist German Workers' party, the original Nazi party. The official who was suborned was a small-time beerhall Nazi who, with the money he received from the British, was able to rise into the Party's highest ranks. He was still in place at the outbreak of World War II. There were also infiltrations of the Abwehr, the German counterespionage service. Also, Menzies discovered that the Germans were violating almost every clause written into the Versailles Treaty to keep them disarmed.

At the same time, Menzies conducted two long, witty operations against the Russian government that lasted throughout the twenties and for much of the thirties, with a remnant of activity still to be found as late as the fifties. With Prince Dolgorouki's cash assistance,

Grand Duke Nikolai established the Supreme Monarchist Council. This group lived in isolation near Paris. Commander Dunderdale, who was born in Odessa of British parents and spoke Russian as a native, was sent to Paris by Sinclair to handle relationships with the grand duke, which he did through a series of intermediaries. The best of the White Russian generals served under the grand duke. His name was General Petr Nikolayevich Baron Wrangel. He possessed what a CIA historical study of the organization was to call a "breadth of vision not normally found in the old school of Russian generals." He created the Russian Armed Services Union. His headquarters were in Yugoslavia, and as a policy he eschewed violence against Russia as being as valueless as pinpricks.

Wrangel's Paris representative, General Aleksandr Pavlovich Kutepov, on the other hand, had seen how Lenin had come to power through a combination of force and subversion and concluded that only by the use of similar methods could the Bolsheviks be dislodged. Terrorism on a large scale was needed. For this purpose Kutepov formed what he called "the Combat Organization." Kutepov trained "the CO" in terrorism and sabotage, and for their protection he established a counterintelligence organization that came to be called "the Inner Line." This, too, was financed by people such as the Dolgoroukis, acting through Menzies. The Americans never thought much of the counterrevolution, however, and as a CIA estimate of Kutepov's organizations was to state:

In theory, the emigres appeared to be organized for some kind of effective action [to bring down the Bolsheviks], but in reality they floundered. Eking out a living took precedence over patriotic service, and the emigres mulled over paper plans as a spare-time activity. As a whole they were divided by internal friction, geographical divisions and a lack of funds. Lack of funds was both a psychological and operational handicap because it forced the emigre organizations to depend on hand-outs from Western intelligence services. The latter, concerned with their own particular interests, often rode rough-shod over the idealism of emigre activities, and provided food for Soviet propaganda which claimed the emigres were simply hirelings of hostile Western intelligence. [30]

Whatever the accuracy of that estimate, the CO existed as a major political irritant that, at critical times throughout the period from 1925 until the mid-1950s, nourished Soviet insecurity. During the period immediately before World War II the CO cells inside Russia—they were known by such code names as the Prometheus Network, the Inter-Marium Programme, the Abramtchik Faction, and the Russian Army of Liberation, were redolent of the Pale of the Settlement or places with names like Byeloroossia, and their members were said to be handy with revolvers—were taken over by the German military intelligence service of Admiral Wilhelm Canaris as the embryo of a reporting service that stretched, so it was claimed, into the Kremlin itself.

There is some evidence that Canaris's acquisition of these services was not done without Sinclair's and Menzies's knowledge and encouragement, as they, on the other hand, began to take the measure of Canaris's organization and, in the Rhineland, to penetrate it at quite a high level. After World War II, when Canaris's men were all in jail, Menzies reacquired interest in these organizations until, at last, he passed them to the American intelligence services. Such complex tangles were not uncommon even in the twenties, although they had not yet become the infinity of complication, the wilderness of mirrors, where, as the good wizard said of the bad ones in J.R.R. Tolkien's epic, *The Lord of the Rings*, "It is difficult with these evil folk to know when they are in league, and when they are cheating one another."

At the same time, Menzies ran an intelligence operation to report on Soviet industrialization and electrification. This organization received the unwitting assistance of representatives in Russia of Vickers, the big British industrial combine, which had large contracts with the Soviet government established through the trade arrangements made between the two countries in the early twenties. The numerous representatives of Vickers inside Russia made progress reports on their work and, for the purposes of keeping themselves informed about Russian creditworthiness, political, economic, industrial, and military developments and plans. [31]

These reports found their way onto Menzies's desk through the agency of David Boyle's Section "N," which was responsible for diplomatic mail interception. The arrangement worked well between about 1924 and 1933, when the Soviet secret service, the NKVD, *thought* it had discovered the system. It had not, but in arresting several of Vickers' employees in Russia, who were being used for the purposes of intelligence without their knowledge, they neutralized SIS's sources. There can be little doubt that the loss of Vickers as a source was, for Menzies, a serious defeat, for it came at a time when SIS had just lost its most important source of secret intelligence about Soviet intentions, the ability to read the diplomatic cipher that had been an open book to the Government Code and Cypher School ever since the establishment of that agency.

In April 1927, the Chinese warlord Chang Tso-lin sent some three hundred policemen and soldiers over the walls of the Soviet embassy compound in Peking in what was, as an American military intelligence report noted, a "carefully planned and well-executed" operation intended to establish the extent of the Communist International's penetration of China. That phrase suggested British involvement, and, indeed, there was a British secret agent not far away, a certain H. R. Steptoe, a reporter with the English-language newspaper in Shanghai. Through the intelligence gathered in that raid, so it was claimed, Chiang Kai-shek was able to turn the Chinese revolution "from Red to right" and the Comintern's organizer, Mikhail Borodin, was compelled to flee back to Moscow, where, subsequently, he was shot.

In the course of the raid, evidence was uncovered and sent to London that revealed that Arcos, the Soviet official trading organization in London, was a center of Soviet espionage in Great Britain. On May 12, 1927, several hundred London police raided Arcos's offices in "Soviet House," at 49 Moorgate, London, in the heart of the city. They occupied these offices for four days, along with several other premises leased by the Russians. During the occupations, police and intelligence authorities removed several truckloads of Soviet filing cabinets and safes.

The Arcos operation was a major development in the history of Anglo-Soviet relations; at the same time, it also affected the relationship between America and Britain. In the course of the British police search of Arcos, much intelligence was uncovered that illuminated a major Soviet revolutionary substructure throughout the arc of Asia between Teheran and Hong Kong and an important intelligence substructure in both England and the United States. That intelligence proved of substantial interest to J. Edgar Hoover, thus providing Menzies, who had responsibility within SIS for maintaining contact with foreign intelligence and security services, with the opportunity to refresh relationships after the troubles of 1919–1921.

Yet in immediate terms the Arcos raid had another, more immediate effect of importance. For the first time, a British government publicly revealed a secret source of intelligence in Parliament in order to justify politically the decision to launch the raid at all. Until this time, all governments had refrained making such revelations without first consulting the secret service. But on this occasion, the government was challenged in the Cabinet on May 23, 1927, and in the House of Commons afterward; thus it felt compelled to show that the intelligence taken from Soviet House revealed such hostile intentions that in itself the intelligence was sufficient to justify a complete break in diplomatic and trade relations with Russia, an action considered at that time to be only one step short of war.

The opposition, however, demanded proof of the accuracy of the intelligence upon which the decision to stage the raid on Arcos was taken. The only way such proof could be offered was to produce the documents. In turn this would reveal publicly that the British government could read the most secret Soviet cipher traffic. In short, was the prime minister prepared to reveal the existence of these supersecret sources of intelligence in order to justify the raids and the diplomatic action?

Immediately, "C," Menzies, and A. G. Denniston, chief of GC&CS, began to lobby furiously, pointing to the value of the source and the dangers that would certainly develop if Britain lost that source through any parliamentary revelation. The protests and warnings did not, however, persuade Prime Minister Stanley Baldwin that the source was more important than the life of his government. Baldwin went before the Commons and produced evidence to placate Parliament that could only have been obtained by cryptanalysis.

Predictably, the evidence did not placate Parliament, although it did alert the Russian coding experts that the Soviet trade, diplomatic, and clandestine ciphers were an open book to the British and had been since 1919. As Commander Denniston stated in a 1944 memo: "HMG found it necessary to compromise our work beyond any question." The consequences of the compromise were disastrous. GC&CS could not again read Soviet ciphers on such a large scale until the late forties and early fifties. As Denniston recorded: "From that time the Soviet government introduced O[ne] T[ime] P[ad] for their diplomatic and commercial traffic to all capitals where they had diplomatic representatives." [32]

These revelations were followed by a suspension of diplomatic and trade relations between England and Russia, which produced little beyond excited Soviet proclamations that war was imminent. The relationship was patched up in circumstances that suggested England needed Russia more than Russia needed England. The episode did, however, yield one important lesson which Menzies employed when a new major source opened a little later on, and which had fundamental consequences upon the outcome of World War II. Nobody in government understood the importance of sources as much as the professionals; such knowledge, therefore, must be confined to the fewest-possible persons in the highest-possible places in the state. As for the relationship with Hoover, the United States and Britain embarked upon a small but steady exchange of intelligence, mainly to do with Soviet work in the English-speaking world. By 1938 and the German emergency, it was to become an important source.

The Arcos raid was undoubtedly one of Menzies's greatest successes, for if it did not result in the elimination of Comintern activities in China and Asia, it at least stemmed the onrush of Marxism there for two decades. It also enabled the Indian and Malayan intelligence services to eliminate, if only for the time being, Soviet subversion in those countries.

By the conclusion of the 1920s, Menzies had plainly emerged as a major figure in world intelligence. The extent to which the Soviet service was aware of his identity cannot be established, but if Menzies was "Melbourne," then certainly they knew who he was. If that was the case, then he was an obvious Soviet target. Furthermore, he was a target about whom much could be learned simply from turning to his entry in *Kelly's Handbook to the Titled, Landed and Official Classes*. This would have provided a spy with his address, telephone number, and a biography. But that was all such a spy was likely to learn about Stewart Menzies, unless the Soviet service had penetrated SIS. For during the twenties Menzies submerged himself into what was a social fortress, places so exclusive that, it was hoped fervently, a phantoma would never get through the front door and where he would be spotted for what he was the moment he stepped off the train.

5 THE PRIVATE MAN

Stewart Menzies was well aware of the dangers: a secret service was an obvious first target for a hostile competitor. He was also aware of the need to protect himself. Indeed, after the assassination of Field Marshal Wilson and the twenty-two intelligence officers in Dublin, the government issued an order—and in some cases pistols—to all senior government officials requiring them to take precautions. In the case of Menzies, it was barely necessary to conceal himself, for as one of his staff officers remarked, Menzies "posed as himself." He was protected by the almost impregnable nature of the institutions that he joined after World War I and to which he belonged for the rest of his life.

To the world beyond the secret circle, Menzies appeared to be still with his regiment, a gorgeous figure in scarlet and gold riding under the plane trees of St. James's Park with the standard, or at the King's Birthday Parade on the Horse Guards at the head of a squadron. When he was not riding with the regiment he was working in the War Office or riding with his hunt. What he actually did nobody knew, and few men cared, except, as he was well aware, the enemy.

Of all the institutions that provided him with cover, the most important was White's, which he joined in 1921 or 1922. White's was the most exclusive club in London, and when he became a member he had entered the inner circle of the ruling generation. The fact that he was proposed, seconded, and admitted immediately was testament in itself to the power of the secret service and the influence and popularity of the man, for as one of the club's historians wrote of the process whereby a man became a member, White's was

a place of probation where one waited, with what patience one could muster, for admittance to the Holy of Holies. And on the extent of your personal popularity and the amount of influence you could exert depended the length of your probation. Fox had only to wait a few months; other distinguished people waited for years, and some waited forever. [33]

White's did not serve as the secret service club (which was its rival, Boodles, just down St. James's Street), but it was used by "C" and the executive of SIS. It was probably Holford and people at court who proposed him, but we do not know, for White's history was, as it remains, as closely guarded a volume as the war book in Whitehall. Nor does it matter, for White's was the most famous club, if not the most notorious, having been satirized by Pope in verse, Swift in prose, and Hogarth in paint.

Founded in 1693, a year before the establishment of the Bank of England and long before the union with Scotland, White's had been a legend for centuries. It was undoubtedly a secure place, for several members of the staff spent their time keeping out those who wanted to get in, and its membership showed the sort of place it was—a sanctuary where only men with money, position, and discretion could remain comfortably for very long. Most of the royals were, or had been, members at some time, and everybody was somebody at White's, but being somebody did not guarantee membership.

Closely connected to Eton and the Life Guards, White's was a very political place, one much concerned with bloodlines, mares, and heirs. Lord Castlereagh was blackballed thrice because he had protested in Parliament when George III refused to allow Catholic emancipation. When he did get in it was from White's bar that he set out to fight his duel with Canning over an early disaster in the Peninsula Wars. Canning was wounded, and Castlereagh was expelled, only to be proposed and readmitted when he successfully established the Quadruple Alliance against Napoleon through the Treaty of Chaumont. A member of the proletariat would not survive a minute in such a place.

The climb was still wild and exclusive (those in "trade" were then rarely admitted, no matter how rich they were) in the twenties, but less Philistine than it had been, for like all other such feudal institutions it reflected the national loss of confidence that followed (and was caused by) the casualties during World War I. The survivors still resisted all change, as had one of its greatest members, George, duke of Cambridge.

Beyond all else it was known as the place where no bottle of nonvintage wine was *ever* served, not even in the midst of two world wars. It was famous for its Hine '28 and its Wolfschmidt Kummel, supplies of which *never* ran out, although it was a German wine. "White's, one can only repeat feebly," wrote Charles Graves, "is unique." And so it was to Stewart Menzies. On most days he lunched on *coujon de sole*, a club specialty. Menzies felt so much at home that he made it a sort of annex to Broadway. He had much of his most secret (or his most ticklish) mail sent there, in the belief that it was more likely to be safe in the hands of Groom, the hall porter, than the mail room of the secret service. He was often to be seen during the week reading papers by the fireplace in the billiards room, which was almost always empty and over which hung a bust of Edward VII and the "Champion of England" boxing belt presented only God knew when to J. C. Heenan by the referee and editor of *Bell's Life of London*. Remembering the fate of his father, Menzies was very careful with spirits, although it was rumored that, late at night after the dinner guests had left the building and only members were left, there were some very wild nights. Also, it may be noted, *females* were never admitted even to the waiting room of the club. The only known exception to that rule was Menzies's daughter, Fiona, who used to call to collect Menzies's mail, but even she was never allowed in after she passed puberty.

Although everyone at White's knew who Stewart was, and what he was doing, including the staff, there was never gossip, and the higher he rose, the more difficult it became for anyone to see him. When important messengers arrived from Broadway, they were always intercepted by the porters and made to wait in the anteroom with the words, courteously uttered, "Please wait here, sir, and I will see whether the colonel can see you at the moment." If Menzies could see them, they were invariably seen in the billiards room, where Menzies could talk without having to lower his voice.

The other institution in Menzies's life was at least as impenetrable and as glorious (to everyone except the Marxists) as White's. Each Thursday evening, when possible, he would catch the Spa Express from Paddington to Bath. By prior arrangement, the express would make a special stop at the duke of Beaufort's private railway station, where Menzies and other friends of the duke would alight. He would then be driven to Westonbirt. There Stewart Menzies became a fox-hunting man with that most famous of all hunts, the Beaufort.

Here, at the start of the fox-hunting season of 1921-1922, Stewart Menzies received what was regarded as being the highest honor after the DSO, one even higher than membership at White's. He was invited by the marquess of Worcester, the duke of Beaufort's heir and master of the Beaufort Hunt, to wear the blue-and-buff riding coat, an invitation that was rarely extended and which was more important than it sounds, for the wearing of the coat showed that Menzies had become accepted in a little world that was not only a sporting fraternity, but also a political and social cabal of great influence.

Menzies now put aside the traditional scarlet and black of the huntsmen and became a Regency figure in a tall black silk hat, riding coat, pure white riding breeches, riding boots with pink tops, and brass buttons engraved with the initials "GPR," which stood for George, Prince Regent, "first gentleman of Europe." The Prince Regent was admired greatly by "Master," as he had been by his predecessors.*

---

*In 1811, when George III became permanently incapacitated through porphyria, his eldest son was appointed Prince Regent. The Prince Regent was noted for his gay and dissolute ways and was disliked by many for his attempts after his accession (1820) to divorce his wife, Caroline. As with the late Edwardians, however, "the Regency" was noted for a flowering in arts, letters, and architecture. Eton, White's, and the Beaufort all regarded the Regency as being a marvelous time, despite the loss of the American colonies, and was widely regarded as the period in which the First British Empire ended and the Second Empire began.

Almost always Menzies was accompanied by Lady Avice, who *always* rode sidesaddle and wore a bowler hat and black hunting habit with a skirt that reached to her spurs. Both Avice and Menzies were friends of the marquess of Worcester, who was about the same age as Avice. Avice's friendship with "Master" caused much comment, it being said that the marquess was in love with her and she with him. But the relationship may have been a mutual devotion created by the salmon and trout fly, for both the marquess and Avice were the keenest fishermen and spent much time together even from the earliest days of Stewart's marriage, fishing the Scottish, Hampshire, Wiltshire, and Yorkshire streams.

In the end there was certainly little to the association that concerned him, for in 1923 the marquess married Lady Victoria Constance Mary, a niece of Queen Mary. "Master" then "succeeded to the dignity" of the dukedom upon the death of his father. And when he succeeded he also inherited perhaps the greatest estate in England except for the Crown's, sixty thousand acres of the best agricultural land of Wiltshire, Gloucestershire, and Somersetshire. This "Master" ran almost as a principality.

Stewart Menzies remained a close friend of the duke throughout his life, and he hunted with passion as frequently as his secret duties would allow. And the frequency with which he hunted was, in a sense, a barometer of politics. When the world situation became serious, Menzies did not appear at all. When he appeared frequently the realm was secure. Thus, according to Lady Avice's hunting diary for 1921, Menzies hunted only seven times, all in December. In January 1922 he hunted seven times, in February five times, in March seven times, in November six times, and in December eight times.

During the week he was to be found living at Dorchester House and collecting the secrets of princes and proles. At the weekends he was at Westonbirt, thundering after foxes. He was popular and trusted, for he was almost famous for his sense of discretion and his dry wit. Nobody could get out of Stewart the inner secrets of the service, not even the king, for in 1923 this exchange took place across the dinner table at Dorchester House between Menzies and King George V, who was there dining with Sir George and Lady Holford:

THE KING: Menzies, who is our man in Berlin?

MENZIES: Sire, if my service has a man in Berlin, I may not divulge his identity.

THE KING: Menzies, what would you say if I said, "Menzies, give me the name of our man in Berlin, or off with your head?"

MENZIES: Sire, were you to give such an order, and when your order was carried out, my head would roll with my lips still sealed. [34]

Like his father and his brothers, Stewart Menzies remained a passionate huntsman, for, as he explained, it brought color, vigor, and fresh air into his life. In an age when all else was crumbling—death duties were now 40 percent on estates worth over £2 million—"hunting was the last vivacity." At Westonbirt, George Holford had six thousand acres while the duke's estate was so large that he had six hunting "countries" stretched over three counties, one for each day of the week except the Sabbath.

The little silver tankard of blackstrap served from a silver jug and salver by a servant in green serge as the horses snorted and the hounds bayed and yelped on the greensward outside Badminton, the lifting of the tall hats in salute, the sound of the master's horn, the canter out to Silkwood, the viewing of the fox, the speed and excitement of the chase over hills, valleys, and through the woods, the beauty of the countryside, the challenge of jumps over stone walls, over hedges and gates—all this created, as Menzies was to state, a sense of supervigor and physical well-being that no other sport could produce. It sharpened the wits, honed the will, toned the muscles, and kept the bowels open.

There can be no doubt that hunting kept Menzies fit, both mentally and physically, for when World War II came and he turned fifty, he was in superb condition—his blood pressure was still that of a long-distance runner at 120 over 80. He once declared that "the chase" was the best antidote for arteriosclerosis.

Nor was there any better companionship, either male or female or animal. Afterward there were drinks, songs, and beef in the Leat Kitchen of Badminton, with all the original copper pots and pans hanging from the walls. The Prince of Wales, George V's heir, rented a house at Easton Grey next door to Keith Graham Menzies, with whom the prince stabled his horses. Rex Benson, who was just home from having been military secretary to the governor of Bombay and was now a merchant banker, adored the hunt. In turn, the inner circle of the hunt trusted Menzies because they knew that their *affaires* were safe with him, that he would not go gossiping about them in White's, Whitehall, Westminster, and Windsor. Also, it was thought correctly that he was running some sort of war against Lenin, who was trying to bolshevize England and the empire.

So congenial was "Beaufortshire" that it was natural Menzies should make his home there. He found Bridges Court, a working farm of about forty acres not far from Badminton and Westonbirt. To buy it Stewart used his share of a gift from his mother to each of her three sons: one exquisite bejeweled tiara broken precisely into thirds. Bridges Court became known in the family as "the Topaz House." It was not a stately home, just two or three cottages and some stables surrounded by a walled garden of about an acre at the back and a small walled front garden. But when the restoration was completed in 1924, Menzies owned the residence of "a country gent." Its chief feature was "the Long Room," the dining room, which Menzies had converted from a barn attached to the main house. In the conversion he kept the old, heavy oaken rafters; the small windows gave out onto the tulip and rose gardens and the lawns, which were small but laid with thick and expensive sod mown precisely in parallel lines.

The walls of "the Long Room" were hung with old, glowing tapestries. The furniture was English antique, and the silverware was Georgian. There were some stables for Menzies's horses—he kept two or three throughout his life. The gardens were laid with lawns and flower beds preserved by a gardener working under Lady Avice's direction. A rose garden and a small pond was put in.

Lady Avice appears to have liked the house at first, but by 1923 her discontent had become evident for two reasons: their failure to produce a family, which may have been the result of Menzies's "Xth" injury on Windy Ridge in 1914 (if he was indeed the Stewart who had caught the shrapnel), and Avice's aspirations to grander living than Bridges Court. The court in no way compared with the great houses and estates of their closest friends. Yet the troubles that beset the couple were not wholly Lady Avice's fault, for Menzies himself was not beyond criticism.

Adoring lively women as he did, and especially those outside the mink and manure set of his hunt, Menzies first met Ursula Lutyens, who was in her early twenties, in August 1921 at Euan Wallace's estate at Kildonan, near Barrhill in Ayrshire. Ursula was the daughter of Sir Edwin Lutyens, the imperial architect, and Lady Lutyens, a devotee of Krishnamurti and a sister of Barbara Wallace. When Euan Wallace had divorced Lady Avice's sister, Idina, on the grounds of her adultery, Lady Idina had married the twenty-third earl of Erroll, hereditary lord high constable of Scotland, and Wallace had then married Barbara Lutyens.*

---

*Lady Idina's marriage to the earl of Erroll did not prosper, and she soon abandoned him for a man named Haldemann. In all Lady Idina had five husbands before dying at an early

As Ursula's sister, Mary Lutyens, the novelist and biographer of Krishnamurti, remembered (and Ursula's diaries were to show), Ursula fell seriously in love with Stewart. The association lasted about a year, from 1922 to 1923, and Ursula wanted marriage, but Menzies refused to leave Lady Avice, perhaps because of the lesson he had learned from Euan Wallace's predicament, that while the old Victorian morality had been shattered by the war, a man who found himself involved in a divorce action had nevertheless to resign from his regiment. Euan was still not acceptable at court, and he still found it difficult to obtain public or even political office. Never one to change horses without a good deal of thought, Menzies remained with Lady Avice, his friendship—love affair would be a more accurate term— with Ursula Lutyens came to an end, and on October 13, 1924, with the full panoply of St. Margaret's, Westminster, Ursula married another old Etonian, Lord Ridley, who owned 10,200 acres in Northumberland.

As for Lady Avice, who did learn about Ursula Lutyens, that episode came as a greater shock than might otherwise have been the case because it made her realize that she was, according to her aunt, the Dowager Countess Sylvia De La Warr,

no more than an ornament in Stewart's life and not being very political herself she really did not understand what it was Stewart was doing. She did not particularly like his friends, who seemed to her to be agreeable but close-mouthed fellows of the retired military or naval type. Nor did she believe that there was some reason for the secrecy, that she ought not to know and was better off not knowing. After the Ursula business she felt that there must be a string of Ursulas as, perhaps, Stewart being Stewart, there were. [35]

By 1926 rumors began to be heard in Beaufortshire that Avice was unhappy and that having failed to capture the duke of Beaufort, she was now interested in Captain Frank Spicer, of Spye Park, a large and beautiful estate not far from Bridges Court. Spicer was thirty-three, unmarried, and the third son of Captain John Edmund Phillip Spicer and Lady Margaret, daughter of the twelfth earl of Westmor-

---

age, leaving a daughter, the present countess of Erroll. The earl of Erroll was murdered in Kenya in 1941, execution style, and his killer was never found. "Barbie" Wallace became one of the most famous political hostesses of her time. She also became one of the most tragic figures in London society when all the male members of her family, including Euan Wallace, died during World War II either from cancer or on active service. Her last son, Billy Wallace, who was said to have been Princess Elizabeth's first love, died of cancer in the 1950s.

land. Spicer had served in the Twelfth Lancers in the Great War from 1914 until 1919. He was a tall, lanky, and handsome man who sat well on a horse and had no occupation other than that of "gentleman of private means," although this title was too grand both for his income and his expectations, which were negligible. His father made Frank an allowance of £400, with free board and lodgings at Spye Park. By nature Spicer was an agreeable hunting man who had few if any interests other than blood sports and would have been quite hopeless at any job.

At first Avice was merely attracted to him. There was no question of leaving Stewart for Frank, for how would they live? It was true that Avice herself had large expectations, but these would not be realized until her mother's death, and even then it might emerge that her mother had spent most of her money on the Theosophical Society. The question of finance apart, Frank and Avice began to appear ever more frequently together. It seems that Stewart knew of and protested against the association, which embarrassed him. If it went too far, they would have to be divorced, and that could ruin Stewart. But Stewart's protestations went largely ignored.

Thus far Menzies, who was now thirty-six, had emerged as a brave, able, loyal man fighting constantly with the errantry that had marked his father's life and continued to mark the life of his older brother, Keith Graham Menzies. He had advanced quickly in British life, most probably because of his wit, his mother's ambitions for him, the high patronage of Sir George Holford, his handsome visage, and the gaze of those steady blue eyes that were, strangely, so much the same shade of blue as those of the Prince of Wales. Whether he had the inner stature required for the highest office inside his trade remained to be seen. But then suddenly he lost one of the three high cards in hand.

As Lady Avice's *affaire* wended its troubled course, family gossip disclosed the occurrence of one of those near disasters peculiar to English country houses. In February 1926 Sir George Holford decided to sell part of his collection of 114 Italian paintings, which were believed to be the finest in England and worth at least £1 million by the standards of the times and perhaps £20 million by those of 1987. A platoon of art specialists moved in to transfer the collection into "the Great Hall," where, so that they might receive the best light, they were laid out on the floor ready for the inspection of Duveen, the art dealer.

As the cataloger began his work, there was an outcry from outside the mansion. A fox had been viewed in Silkwood by the Beaufort Hunt's pack of what the duke called his piebald lovelies; they had hunted it into the parkland around Westonbirt, it had made for the house, and, closely pursued by the pack, it then entered the house through an open door. The fox came hurtling down one of the passages and flew across the pictures, but before the hounds could enter the Great Hall, where they would surely have at least damaged some of the paintings, the butler managed to slam shut the doors from the entrance hall. The pack and the fox were then evicted by the servants. (The collection was sold to Duveen for £4 million, perhaps £80 million in 1987 values.)

But such was Holford's fright that, suffering from emphysema, he collapsed. He did not recover. On or about September 14, 1926, Sir George Holford called his servants, workers, and tenants to the French windows of a room on the ground floor of Westonbirt, which looked out upon the square mile of parkland with its Japanese maples and Javanese rhododendrons. The next day, he passed away quietly. He was sixty-six, and Susannah Holford, Stewart Menzies, and Stewart's brothers Keith and Ian were present during his last hours.

With him, it seemed, had passed an epoch in English life, the age of the great Edwardians. George Holford was given a traditional funeral at Westonbirt. The coffin was fashioned without ornament from an oak taken from the estate. The tenants carried it from the great house across the lawns to St Catherine's Church, the Holfords' private chapel within the grounds of the mansion. There Holford's remains lay in state for three days under the catafalque of his father, who was attended by clouds of alabaster angels and cherubs with cheeks puffed as they blew alabaster flutes. The residents of Holford's estates came to pay their respects, for he was much loved, although the wages he had paid were very low.

At the funeral only the family and Sir George's personal retainers were present, together with his closest friends. Sir George was then carried to his last resting place by tenants and servants. His grave lay within the common churchyard, amidst those of generations of the family's retainers. It stood on a knoll slightly above all others. Eventually the grave was marked by a stone cross eighteen feet high—the same height, shape, and stone as the Life Guards' memorial on Windy Ridge at Zandvoorde in Belgium where so many of Holford's men had been killed or executed by the Germans.

As was to be expected, George Holford left his affairs in good order. The determining factor behind his will involved that of his

father, Robert Stayner Holford. The elder Holford's will decreed that
the estate would pass to Sir George's heirs, but if Sir George did not
have what the will called "issue of his body," it was to be sold and
the proceeds passed to surviving members of the Holford family. [36]
Nobody knew why Holford had made this provision, and no one could
understand it, for it meant the dissolution of one of the great English
estates, one rich in art treasures of all kinds.

Since Holford had married but had produced no children, there
was no "issue of his body." Holford could, and did, make provision
for Susannah, Stewart, and the latter's two brothers, but the proceeds
could not and did not pass to them but to his nine blood relatives.
Thus Susannah and her boys missed becoming extremely rich, for
when probate was granted on March 17, 1927, Holford had left an
estate worth in all about £3 million (by 1987 purchasing power, perhaps £60 million).

In the will Sir George confirmed the gift he had made at the time
of his marriage to "my dear wife Susannah West" of all "the jewellery
which I possessed other than that worn by me personally." Moreover,
Susannah should have "such of my household furniture, plated articles, and articles of personal or household use (but not including any
of my picture books, china, statuary, and works of art) as she shall
select for the furnishing of a suitable residence for her own occupation."

Sir George also bequeathed to Susannah an annuity of £10,000
per annum, a large sum at a time when £100 a year was a good wage.
At the same time he bequeathed "free of legacy duty to my three
stepsons, Keith Graham Menzies, Stewart Graham Menzies, and Ian
Graham Menzies in equal shares such a sum as will be required to
make up the value at the date of my death of the Shares which they
or their mother purchased in Messina (Transvaal) Development Company Limited to twenty thousand pounds." The will provided that
£75,000 should be invested to pay the income for Susannah's annuity,
and that after her death the capital and income of that legacy could
pass to Keith, Stewart, and Ian.

With these important legacies, the rest of the estate, including
the palaces, lands, art collections, and investments were sold or auc-
tioned and the proceeds distributed according to the terms of the
will. Of the last day of the sale, which took place at Christie's on May
17, 1928, *The Times* noted that "apart from anything else, the sale of
the final portion of the Holford collection of pictures which began
yesterday at Christie's is a striking revelation of artistic resources in

this country unsuspected by the majority." The proceeds of the first day's sale—£364,094 7s. for seven lots consisting exclusively of work by Dutch and Flemish artists—constituted a world record for one day's auction of pictures or any other collection of works of art.

As late as 1984 the sale of the Holford collection was still regarded as one of the epic events in the history of auction houses. The total realized in cash was very great: in excess of £2 million—perhaps £40 million by 1987 standards. Westonbirt then became a girls' school, and Dorchester House was demolished by an American syndicate and rebuilt as the Dorchester Hotel. Having been constructed to endure the centuries, it had lasted just eighty years, the span of the heyday of the Second British Empire. Rex Benson and the chancellor of the Exchequer, Winston, "did a deal," according to Rex's son David, in order to preserve their capital.

Shortly after the loss of his main patron, Stewart Menzies faced the very real perils of a divorce action—for this was still a day and age when divorce could mean social annihilation. With Holford's passing, Stewart Menzies became somewhat richer than he had been. He was now worth about £6,000 a year from all sources, an excellent income and one decidedly superior to that of his rival, Frank Spicer, who still had only £400 a year. With the sale of Dorchester House and Westonbirt, Stewart moved out of both apartments permanently. His London home became a mansion flat in Mayfair. Stewart's friend, Euan Wallace, now a Tory M.P. and parliamentary secretary to Leo Amery, secretary of state for the colonies, had his London home in the same building.

But by the autumn of 1928 Frank Spicer and Lady Avice appeared everywhere together, careless of gossip and discretion alike. As usual everyone asked them either to be careful in what they were doing or to think carefully about the implications of their actions, on the grounds that Stewart was engaged in work of national importance, and the dangers to his ability to remain in that work were great if there was any form of scandal.

Then, through the machinations of the gods, Spicer became richer than Stewart Menzies. In April 1928 Captain John Spicer, head of the Spicer family at Spye Park, died and left an estate of about £650,000. His eldest son, Anthony, also of the First Life Guards, was his sole heir—as was the custom where great estates were concerned, Frank benefited by his father's death not at all; his annual income remained at about £400. It seemed, therefore, that since Anthony Spicer was only in his early forties, there was no chance that Frank could succeed to the family fortune and little chance at all of his marrying Lady Avice.

But now the fates intervened, and Avice found herself able to change horses. In November 1928, only six months after John Spicer's death, a violent gale swept through Spye Park; Anthony took shelter under a large tree, the tree was struck by lightning, and a limb fell and killed him. Frank thereupon inherited the family fortunes, including the great mansion, the fine park, and the enormous estate, although the fortune was reduced greatly by the need to pay a second set of death duties on the original £650,000. There was, therefore, barely enough cash left over to maintain the estate, although there would be if Lady Avice inherited her fortune. [37]

In August 1931, Lady Avice's mother, Countess De La Warr, died having exhibited one final eccentricity. She invited Lady Cunard to dinner, and their meal, consumed by the countess in bed, consisted of pâté de foie gras eaten with shoe horns. Despite her generosity with the theosophists, she left a substantial estate to Avice and Idina. Now wealthy, Avice left Bridges Court to live at Spye Park with Frank Spicer. It would be said that since Spicer was short of cash, she helped out in the maintenance of the estate. Whether true or not, a major scandal evolved, one that had the potential to ruin Menzies. There were attempts to intervene and prevent this ruin, and one of the attempts may well have involved the king and the queen, for between November 12 and 18, 1928—three months after the death of Anthony Spicer—both Stewart and Lady Avice were the guests of King George V and Queen Mary at Sandringham, the royal shooting lodge in Norfolk.

There was a great deal of gunfire over three days in which the party killed 749 pheasants, 60 partridges, 20 hares, 6 rabbits, 13 woodcock, 10 wood pigeon, and 5 "miscellaneous," for a total bag of 863 birds and animals. But if the king or the queen had words with Stewart or Avice, nothing prospered. On June 20, 1929, it was announced that Menzies had resigned from the Life Guards, a necessary first step before a divorce. At the same time it was announced that Menzies had been placed on half pay and confirmed on the staff as a lieutenant colonel, all with effect from that date. While Menzies's resignation from the regiment was plainly connected with his intention to divorce Avice—just as Euan Wallace had resigned his commission to divorce Lady Idina—it is not likely that being placed on half pay was any form of sanction on the part of the General Staff, for Stewart received tenure at a time of substantial retrenchment.

Thus the hierarchs at the War Office took with one hand and gave away with the other, preserving the appearance of confidence in his future.

Shortly Lady Avice left Bridges Court for Spye Park, taking Menzies's cook and chauffeur with her. Menzies remained alone at Bridges Court. And as Rex Benson recorded in his diary after having visited Beaufortshire to look at his polo ponies: "Stewart is separating from Avice & Avice is to marry her new young man, Frank Spicer. I think Stewart is lucky, though it will be difficult for the next year or two."

Stewart Menzies then filed for divorce. This was a long and complicated task involving the king's proctor, who would ensure that no conspiracy existed between the couple to procure an annulment. Evidently the king's proctor was satisfied and the papers were forwarded to the divorce court. There was much communication between Stewart's lawyer and those of Avice and Frank Spicer. They intended to dissolve the marriage as quietly as possible so that Stewart Menzies's career would not be further damaged, at the same time making it evident that he was not the guilty party.

Also, the lawyers intended to dissolve the marriage in such a fashion as to preclude any gossip. Further, an absolute agreement was reached between the parties that whatever Avice or Frank Spicer had learned about Stewart's work during the marriage was to be regarded as a permanent confidence. For the rest of their lives both avoided all discussion about the marriage with any third parties. Frank Spicer went to his grave having said nothing about it, and throughout Lady Avice's long life—she died in 1985—she "acted and talked as if she had never known Stewart Menzies. It was as if the only man she had ever been married to was Frank Spicer. It was as if she had wiped her mind clear of all remembrances about the marriage." [38] The most significant arrangement reached by the lawyers under the divorce settlement was Stewart's right to insert this formula in his entries in works of reference:

Menzies, Col. Stewart Graham, D.S.O. (1914), M.C. s. of late John G. Menzies; b. 1890, m. 1918, Lady Avice Ela Muriel (*from whom he obtained a div.* 1931) . . . [39]

That formula meant Avice, *not* Stewart, was the guilty party in the divorce. Indeed, the grounds for the divorce were that Lady Avice committed adultery with Captain Spicer at a hotel in Paris, and that they continued to maintain an adulterous association despite Colonel

Menzies's protestations. So effectively was the action conducted by Stewart's lawyers that the divorce went through almost without notice, despite the social prominence of the parties that would ordinarily have meant sensational press coverage. Certainly there was no reference to Menzies's work in the secret service, for his anonymity, position, and work were protected by the Official Secrets Act. Indeed, the case passed so rapidly before the court that the only publicity was a single paragraph buried deep inside the *News of the World*, the leading London scandal sheet.

Lady Avice and Frank Spicer were married almost immediately and spent the rest of their lives together. Lady Avice's principal contribution to Stewart Menzies's life was not marital tranquillity but literary notoriety. She provided John le Carré, the espionage novelist, with the model for Lady Anne, George Smiley's aristocratic and errant wife who, knowing nothing of her husband's work, betrayed him for an orchid while Smiley was in India interrogating Karla, the Comintern ideologue.

As for Stewart Menzies, he was not without a wife for long. In November 1932, as the world storm began, there appeared a small announcement in a gossip column:

Among recent interesting engagements is that of Mrs. Garton, the youngest of Mr. and Mrs. Rupert Beckett's daughters, who is to marry Colonel S. G. Menzies, of Bridges Court, Luckington, Wiltshire. Mrs. Garton is very attractive, charming, and intellectual. These days Mrs. Rupert Beckett is not so much in evidence as when she was taking her girls about, but she is as intellectual as any woman in the social world and has every topic almost at her finger ends—music, language, literature, yachting, and politics. [40]

Menzies's marriage followed at Prince's Row Registrar's Office, London, on December 12. The ceremony was attended by Euan and Barbara Wallace and Sir Archibald Sinclair, who was becoming leader of the Liberal party. Rex Benson could not be there. He, too, had just married, for the first time, at the age of forty-three. His bride was Leslie Nast, the ex-wife of Condé Nast, the New York magazine publisher. The couple were on their way to India to spend their honeymoon as guests of the viceroy, the marquess of Willingdon.

Stewart and Pamela Menzies spent a brief honeymoon at the villa in the south of France of W. Somerset Maugham, the novelist and ex-spy. They then returned to Bridges Court. Although the family was one of the richest in the north country, Pamela brought no money to her marriage with Stewart Menzies. But she did have much style and a sense of dress, and she was a darkly beautiful woman with an intense air. At the start, they seemed happy enough. But it soon became evident that Pamela was suffering from some mental illness that defied diagnosis. Most of the time she was lucid, calm, and enchanting. But there were occasions when—and these increased in frequency, duration, and severity as time went by—she became despondent and would take to her bed for long periods, emerging only as a wraith. For all the medical attention she had received by 1939 and after the outbreak of World War II, she became not better but worse as each year passed.

Her illness appears to have been complicated by the special problem of a spymaster's wife, the fact that she was totally excluded by Stewart Menzies from that most important part of his life, his work. She did not know that he was a high officer of the British secret service. Rather, she believed that her husband was engaged in confidential work for the War Office that required considerable liaison with the Foreign Office, and that the work itself was routine. That mystery troubled her, as it had troubled Lady Avice. and she came to suspect and fear that Menzies had a mistress, a suspicion that was unfounded. Even so, Stewart and Pamela appeared to have been happy together.

Although Stewart Menzies detested "foreign parts," he began to do what he had not done before, take his wife on foreign holidays, usually a winter cruise to Egypt. These holidays may well have been cover for something else, for that was a time when SIME (Security Intelligence Middle East) was being established. But if it was, Pamela neither knew nor guessed. In any case, in 1934 Pamela produced a daughter, Fiona, who became, as they said in the language of the times, the apple of her father's eye. Although Menzies wished for a larger family, this was to be denied him. Fiona would remain the only child.

Menzies's career had not suffered at all from the divorce. Even as he was remarrying, he was also being promoted in his trade. In July 1932 Stewart Menzies was made a full colonel and became Sinclair's deputy in title as well as fact. Nor was there any displeasure with him at the War Office. In what was Menzies's last fitness report uttered by the War Office, General W. H. Bartholomew, director of military intelligence, noted on Menzies's record:

I have known L'Colonel [sic] Menzies for many years and cannot speak too highly of the quality of his work or of his sound common sense and balanced perspective. He is excellent in his present capacity, and has my complete confidence.

In all, therefore, far from being disgraced, he had emerged as a member of the War Office establishment, one of the mandarins, although still only in his early forties. He remained perfectly acceptable at the royal enclosure at Ascot. And as they said admiringly as Menzies strode down Whitehall: "Lucky, *lucky* Stewart." Whether Stewart's "impervious" professional existence would endure remained to be seen as the world entered a period of severe political disturbance in which the moles began to burrow.

Three

To the Outbreak of War

1932–1939

1 ENTER A PHANTOMA

As Stewart Menzies passed through the divorce court in 1931, a phenomenon took place in his stars: the Great Depression struck England. The effect was to make him personally a marked man. Although he remained as he was created, an admirable, able, brave, attractive man, his fortune proved the source of the misadventure that would befall him. He was a member, indeed a living symbol, of a class that had been condemned to death. And the cause and effect of his fate, his traducement, can be seen only in the political and social terms of the thirties, not in anything that he did personally.

With the Depression, the widespread disillusionment and dissatisfaction with the British system produced by World War I intensified, especially within the intellectual elite of England at Oxford and Cambridge. There, the monarchy, state, church, banks, private enterprise, imperialism, the family, the civil service, Parliament, the political parties, the press, the radio, the publishing industry—all were widely repudiated as Victorian or Edwardian anachronisms.

As vigorously as the English faithful demolished the icons of the Eastern churches in the sixteenth and seventeenth centuries, many of the intellectual elite of England looked east to Russia—and to a lesser extent to America—for inspiration and for solutions to the problem of England's decline. The Oxford Union, a leading debating society in England, decided by 275 votes to 153 that "this House refuses in any circumstances to fight for King and Country," a decision that was denounced by Churchill as "a very disquieting and disgusting symptom." But the iconoclasm of the period was not peculiar to Oxford. It emerged still more vigorously at Cambridge University, and particularly within a small, exquisite group called the Apostles.

That group regarded itself, as did the Soviet intelligence service, as masters of the English future. And it was within that group, almost exclusively, that the worm of revolutionary Marxism entered the British apple. The political response to the Depression, together with that to the conduct of the Prince of Wales, the rise of nazism and fascism, the emergence of Soviet power, the deterioration of British power, the smugness of the middle class, the isolation of the United States, the collapse of its economic system—all served to persuade the Apostles, tutored as they were by Soviet clandestines, that they possessed the answers for the future. Among those answers was the requirement to make *a target* of men such as Stewart Menzies.

The immediate cause of the Apostles' swing to the militant left was the conduct of the Socialist government of J. Ramsay MacDonald. To prevent a collapse of British civilization, MacDonald's government decided that the value of the pound sterling had to be preserved, and that it could be saved only by obtaining large credits in Paris and New York. But in making applications for credit, they found that the foreign bankers would lend money only if the British government balanced its budget. That could only be done through heavy increases in taxation and cuts in expenditure. Among the cuts that the bankers wanted was a 10 percent reduction in unemployment benefits. Here was the issue. If the Labour government did not make that cut, they would get no loans. If they did, they would be accused of betraying the working class that had brought them to power. But MacDonald had no choice: he decided to cut the dole (often the sole means of livelihood for over two million unemployed) and reduce government spending—one of the reasons why Stewart Menzies was put on half pay.

The decrease in the dole produced the bitterest reaction from the Socialists and many of the intellectuals. Inspired by alternatives offered by fresh revolutionary forces—nazism, fascism, and Stalinism —an important group of Oxford and Cambridge men and women began what amounted to a revolt against the established order. In that group was a young Cambridge historian and economist, Harold Adrian Russell "Kim" Philby.

Young Philby was born in Ambala, India, in 1911. Sir Ronald Wingate, a son of a hero of empire, Wingate Pasha of the Anglo-Egyptian Sudan, remarked later: "If you want to understand Kim Philby, you must first try to understand his father." Harry St. John Bridger Philby belonged to Stewart Menzies's generation, although he was not of Menzies's class. Born in 1885, St. John Philby was the son of a British tea planter in Ceylon who had married May Duncan, a daughter of the commanding officer of the Colombo Rifles, Colonel John Duncan, who was in the process of rising into the hierarchy of the British army. Recommended for a Victoria Cross at the Relief of Lucknow, he was in the 1870s an instructor at the Staff College at Camberley. By the eighties he commanded in Ceylon and had held high office in the adjutant-general's department of the Irish Command. In the nineties he became deputy adjutant-general at the War Office. And he died in 1898 while commanding at Bombay.

May Philby returned to London, and with money borrowed from her family in about 1902–1903 she bought 102A Queen's Gate, a house that she turned into a residential hotel for persons of the officer class on leave in England. The Menzies clan book shows that Beatrice Graham Menzies, wife of Graham Menzies's second son and heir, William Dudgeon Graham Menzies, had her London home at 88 Queen's Gate. This suggests at least neighborly association between the two families at that time. May Philby's favorite and most famous son, St. John Philby, the father of Kim Philby, became a Queen's Scholar at Westminster School, one of the six major public schools in England. Located around the corner from Westminster Abbey, it was closely associated with the business and rituals of government. Its choir, of which St. John Philby was a member, sang at those great occasions of monarchy, coronations, royal weddings, and royal funerals.

St. John Philby became captain of the school and excelled at most things he did. His labors were rewarded with an exhibition in classics to Trinity College, Cambridge, which was then passing through what was called "an extraordinary outburst of philosophical brilliance." But before he left Westminster, "declamations" were held. Being a very democratic institution, Westminster permitted the general body to say what they thought of St. John Philby as captain. His successor recorded what was an exceedingly revealing psychological study of that strange and able man. Philby intended not just to succeed, but also to *rule*. Philby's reign was a "mixture of good and evil":

That [Philby] raised morals from the low estate into which they had fallen; that he restored order and discipline where before had been little less than chaos, I do not deny. Neverthless, although his system will I trust bring forth good fruit, at the moment it was not a success. Autocracy was his aim and autocratic rule his avowed intention. He meant to rule with an iron hand and he had not the good sense to conceal it in a velvet glove. The result was that his year was conspicuous for internal dissension. [1]

Father and son were alike in that respect, and what made them so dangerous to the established order was that both were endowed with the high ability required to realize that intention. Father and son had the charm, tact, and good bearing—both were handsome men—necessary to achieve their ends. And what they meant by "rule" was not merely command of a regiment or the management of a factory, *but absolute political power*. In that ambition, in fact, the son was to prove abler than the father.

At Cambridge, Philby graduated in classics with distinction. Here, then, was a golden lad of the empire. Yet St. John Philby was not twenty when he began to experience his first transformation. Since British universities existed not only to teach, but also to show men how to think—this was their great gift, and also their great danger, for some scholars began to think wrong things and experiment with dangerous causes—St. John Philby began a conversion from sincere Christianity to what he called "agnosticism, atheism, anti-imperialism, socialism, and general progressive revolt against the philosophical and political canons in which I was brought up," Queen Victoria's imperialism. St. John Philby became a Fabian Socialist, a growth from an organization founded in 1883 and called the Fellowship of the New Life. The Fabians were opposed to the revolutionary theory of Marxism and specifically repudiated the necessity for violent class struggle.

St. John Philby found the Fabians to be little more than a sleepy debating group whose members were more interested in free love and philosophical argument than in reading *Das Kapital* to each other under the chestnut trees. As a result St. John Philby passed from the

Fabians through an extreme form of fascism—so extreme, indeed, that he was arrested as a potential enemy of the British state during World War II—into the ranks, during his old age, of the revolutionary Marxists.

As a man St. John Philby was brilliant, arrogant, opinionated, licentious. Like father like son. After Cambridge, St. John Philby sat for the Indian civil service examination. He did well, earned golden opinions, and became an assistant commissioner—tax collector and magistrate—in the Punjab in 1908. In 1910 Philby met Dora Johnston, the toast of the Cavalry Brigade at Rawalpindi. They were married with full choir at Murree Church in September 1910, and the best man was a cousin of Dora Philby, Lieutenant Bernard Montgomery, then of the Royal Warwickshire Regiment in India, later General Sir Bernard Montgomery, commander in chief of the Allied armies on D-Day in Normandy and, later still, chief of the Imperial General Staff.

In 1912, while St. John Philby was stationed at Ambala, Dora produced the first of four children, a boy they named Harold Adrian Russell Philby. He came to be nicknamed "Kim," the hero in Kipling's story of espionage and counterespionage between England and Russia in Afghanistan and northern India during Victoria's reign. This work contained lines expressing the ambivalence that many Englishmen (including young Philby) who were born or had spent long periods of their lives in India felt toward "home":

> Something I owe to the soil that grew—
> More to the life that fed—
> But most to Allah, Who gave me two
> Separate sides to my head.

Indeed, as life progressed Kim Philby found that he did have two separate sides to his head. One lured him powerfully to things British, the other to things Russian.

By now St. John Philby was a linguist, scholar, ornithologist, archeologist, botanist, and explorer, an outstanding man. If he was too vigorous to respect the Christian laws of marriage, at least he tried to be a good father. But time, distance, and events made it difficult for him to exercise direct paternal influence over Kim Philby, who was sent to England at an early age to begin his education. At the outbreak of World War I Philby joined the British army expedition to Mesopotamia, now part of Iraq but then an ancient country ruled by Germany's ally, Turkey. "Mespot," as the place was always called by English colonial servants, extended from the Persian Gulf north to the mountains of Armenia and from the Zagros and Kurdish mountains in the east to the Syrian Desert.

With the British army, Philby served as a member of the staff of Sir Percy Cox, an Arabist and explorer of note and the British military intelligence service's representative with the expeditionary force. This was St. John Philby's introduction to the British intelligence system. After much work connected mainly with the raising of taxes from the tribes, a task that gave him great practical experience in haggling with Arab chieftains, he was given a job in 1917 that brought him to the forefront of imperial politics in Arabia, much of which England proposed to annex after the war. Cox appointed Philby head of an intelligence mission to raise the tribes of Ibn Saud of Saudi Arabia, who tended to be pro-British, against those supporting the Turks. Subsequently he made a great name for himself when he became the first foreigner to chart the empty quarter of the Rub-al-Khali, for which he received the Founder's Medal of the Royal Society, perhaps the greatest of all such honors.

By the end of World War I, Philby had emerged as a personality at least as great a hero as Lawrence of Arabia and almost as well known. He was well received by two mandarins of Arabian intelligence, Wingate Pasha of the Arab Bureau at Cairo, and D. G. Hogarth, the keeper of the Ashmolean Museum at Oxford, Wingate's assistant. And from this time until about 1930 St. John remained a pendant of the British military intelligence service in Arabia, which was a term invented to conceal the existence of the secret service of Captain Mansfield Cumming and Admiral Sinclair.

In 1919 he is supposed to have stained his skin nut brown and, wearing Arab habit, infiltrated the Communist International's First Congress of the Asian People at Baku, the capital of Soviet Azerbaijan on the Caspian Sea. The purpose of this congress was, as the head of the Comintern told the congress, to strike at imperial London through Delhi and the other great capitals of the raj.

When the Versailles powers conceded to Britain the mandate on certain of the former countries in Arabia of the old Turkish empire, Philby became adviser to the minister of the interior in the first Iraqi government between 1920 and 1921. Between 1921 and 1924 he was chief British representative in the old Turkish province of Transjordan, which included most of what in 1985 was Israel and Jordan.

But in 1925 Philby appeared to have experienced another trans-formation. He confessed to a sharp political revulsion against the British government, largely, he declared to all who would listen, because of that government's failure to concede to the Arabs the absolute freedom they had been promised in return for their assis-tance against the Turks during World War I. Also, he was deeply opposed to Churchill's dalliance with the Zionists, which, he declared loudly and at length while in Jerusalem with the British political mission, would wreck Britain's position in Arabia and inevitably pro-duce what was, even then, a dangerous Muslim fundamentalism.

Philby resigned from the Indian and British civil services in 1925 and, parking his wife and family in Maida Vale in London, went to Riyadh, the Saudi capital. There he became confidential adviser and the only foreign friend of the king and founder of Saudi Arabia, Ibn Saud, the leader of the ultraorthodox Wahabi tribe. St. John Philby arranged the king's coronation, advised him about his investments, taught him the importance of the oil pools. Since he was an exceed-ingly interesting and witty conversationalist even in Wahabi, the king formed a lifelong trust in Philby. As an old man, whenever the king felt tired he would call his physician and instruct him to "give me a pint of *Feel-bee*'s blood—he's got plenty."

While Ibn Saud's court accepted that Philby was a British spy, the king trusted Philby absolutely. They became lifelong friends, and eventually Philby stunned orthodox London society by announcing his third transformation. Just as the intellectual revolt was beginning in England, St. John Philby felt what he called "dissociation from British ideals" and declared that he had "felt increasingly cut off from things British and drawn to things Arabian." He announced that he had decided to become a Muslim, a statement that produced con-sternation in London's learned and political worlds, which were bound by the liturgy of Canterbury, the established religion of the state.

On August 7, 1930, Philby set out for Mecca. At Hadda he was met by Ibn Saud's finance minister, the deputy foreign minister, and by the editor of the Mecca newspaper, *Umm al Qura*, who supervised the lengthy rituals through which Philby passed. The ceremony took place by moonlight. In these, St. John Philby experienced the sort of exaltation he felt when he used to sing the Latin service by can-dlelight around the tomb of Queen Elizabeth I, who reestablished Westminster School in 1560, or when the choir shouted the famous *vivats* on royal days. By moonlight "Feel-bee" prostrated himself at

Abraham's station, prayed constantly, chanted incantations, had his hair shaved, drank from the holy well of Zamzam, and kissed the black stone of the sacred *Kaba*.

With that last rite he abandoned Christianity and became a Muslim. The king bestowed upon him the name of Abdullah, slave of God; he was given the right to visit the royal concubines, which he did frequently, and in due course his *bhint*, Muriel, arrived at his house, ready to bear his children, which she did. There was, however, much whispering at court about Philby's sincerity. "Do you know what people here say about you?" asked Fuad Hamza, Ibn Saud's foreign secretary. "They say they cannot explain you at all except on the assumption that you are in the Secret Service of the British Government."

Cumming may have done so, and so would Sinclair, but Menzies did not, for Menzies would never have employed a man who could (as Philby did on August 15, 1930) utter this statement in the *Umm al Qura*: "Allah has opened my heart to the acceptance of Islam and has guided me to accept this religion in the rooted belief and full conviction of my conscience."

Nor was he likely to appreciate Philby's statement to London and Cairene newspapers that he felt drawn to Islam for much the same reason that the Roundheads had been drawn to Cromwell. Islam's puritanism was the source of Arabia's strength, he said, as Cromwell's puritanism had been the source of England's strength. And he avowed:

I believe that the present Arabian puritan movement harbingers an epoch of future political greatness based on strong moral and spiritual foundations. Also I regard the Islamic ethical system as a real democratic fraternity, and the general conduct of life, including marriage, divorce, and the absence of the unjust stigma of bastardy, resulting in a high standard of Arabian public morality, as definitely superior to the European ethical code based on Christianity. . . . I consider an open declaration of my sympathy with Arabian religion and political ideals as the best methods of assisting the development of Arabian greatness.

Philby's defection from British ideals was now complete. A golden lad of the empire had changed his religion and his allegiances from Christianity and the empire to Islam and Arabia. This was a remarkable if not sensational occurrence. It was certainly held to be symbolic of the uncertainty of purpose and loss of interest to "the Cause" that had beset British social and political life since the end of World War

I. Moreover, St. John Philby's apostasy became the more remarkable because at the same time at Cambridge, Kim Philby underwent a similar conversion for reasons similar to those of his father. The difference was that, whereas Harry Philby had turned to Mecca, Kim Philby had turned to Moscow.

Having attended Westminster School like his father before him, Kim Philby had entered Trinity College, Cambridge, in 1929, as one of Westminster's three best scholars of his year, exactly as St. John Philby had done, on an exhibition. Kim Philby's subject was history, but halfway through his stay at Trinity he changed to economics, his intention to become, as his father had decided, a proconsul in the empire. By all accounts a highly intelligent man, a good scholar, and a personable fellow, Kim Philby's conversion from capitalism to communism had a philosophic origin somewhat similar to that of his father. Kim Philby believed—as his father had believed, evidently—that Mecca was better than Canterbury, that British capitalism and MacDonald's socialism had failed.

At Trinity, Philby met Guy Francis de Moncey Burgess. Born in 1911, the son of a naval officer, Burgess went to Eton College in 1924. But as suddenly as he left Eton to go to Dartmouth Naval College, he left Dartmouth to return to Eton. At Eton, he proved to be a brilliant if erratic student, widely disliked for his effeminacy. He failed to get into Pop on that account, but he did win the Gladstone and Rosebery prizes for history in 1929 and a scholarship in history to Trinity. Sir Steven Runciman, who became a leading expert in Byzantine and Greek art, was at Eton and Trinity with Burgess and found him "a bit grubby" but bright and charming. As Burgess got older "the charm got muddier, he became more and more drunk, and after he became a Communist he never washed."

Philby regarded Burgess as being, potentially, the finest historian of his generation. Philby was not repelled when he discovered that Burgess was an aggressive homosexual, although Philby himself suffered from the same satyriasis as his father. Through Anthony Blunt, a student of philosophy and mathematics and, later, an art specialist and British counterespionage officer, Burgess was introduced into the Apostles. In his turn, Burgess introduced Philby.

A secret society and a self-elected elite, the Apostles were associated by tradition with the Cambridge secret societies that, in another century, had opposed the church and the ruling generation. The object of the Society, as the Apostles also called themselves, was "to put all in question," to engage in what was called "the ethereal atmosphere of free and audacious inquiry." John Maynard Keynes, the economist, declared of the Society, in which he was prominent:

We repudiated entirely customary morals, conventions, and traditional wisdom. We were, that is to say, in the strict sense of the term, immoralists. The consequences of being found out had, of course, to be considered for what they were worth. But we recognized no moral obligation on us, no inner sanction, to conform or obey.

In Philby's time, the Apostles had come under the influence of the chief Soviet secret agent in London, Samuel Borisovich Cahan. He made agents of Marxism out of some, but by no means all, the Apostles. Compelled as they were by "a fearful oath," they were bound together still further by that queer trinity of the thirties, communism, catholicism, and sodomy. Hence the need for a continuation of circumspection and secrecy, for the establishment had outlawed all three. As the thirties progressed, the Apostles developed the philosophy that, if a student loved mankind enough to want to change a bad society, it was necessary to become a Marxist. That required even more secrecy, for a man's career could still be doomed, no matter how able he was, if the codification "KCA"—"known Communist affiliations"—appeared on his college record.

Godless, pro-Stalin, contemptuous of the British ruling generation, the Apostles argued that Stalin's purges were trivial compared to the sufferings of the tens of millions who were unemployed through European and American capitalism. The Apostles, too, were inclined to treason if they thought the cause was just. One earlier Apostle, the novelist E. M. Forster, declared that if an Apostle was "forced to choose between betraying a friend and betraying his country, he hoped he would betray his country." [2]

It was a phenomenon of the period that almost all the pro-Soviet traitors of the forties and fifties—Philby, Burgess, Maclean, Blunt, and others—were Apostles. And it was the Soviet intelligence service's greatest triumph of the thirties in England that, recognizing that the Apostles were likely to occupy the future, it controlled the group physically and philosophically. It was extremely odd that the head of counterespionage in England at that time, Guy Liddell—who preferred homosexual company, although it was claimed that he himself was not a homosexual—paid little if any attention to the politics of the Apostles. Nor was much, if any, attention paid to the link between the Apostles and the Cambridge University Socialist Society, into which Philby was introduced again by Burgess and of which

Philby became treasurer. As a result there was little in the records of the Apostles' affiliations, so that when Burgess left Cambridge he readily obtained a post in the BBC Talks Department, an "establishment" post from which, assisted by his charm and wit, he was able to contact, and in some cases to seduce, many persons of influence.

Through his connections with the Apostles, Philby joined the clandestine wing of the Comintern, his desire to make a sad world a better one, at precisely the time that the Communist International, having failed to revolutionize the British proletariat, began a policy of using Englishmen of good birth and education who were sympathetic to Soviet causes to penetrate the main organs of the British administration. Once they were in, they were to work in the Soviet interest. Here lay the only important difference between father and son. As St. John Philby stated, while he often found himself in violent opposition to the policies of the British government, when he found himself thinking disloyally he resigned from its service. Kim Philby, on the other hand, had no such scruples. From the moment he left Cambridge he intended to destroy the establishment in true Apostles fashion, which meant the destruction not of the man, but of his reputation, which in England amounted to very much the same thing.

Shortly Philby was approached by his Russian controller and given the main task of his life and career: Burrow into the secret service and then control it in the Soviet interest. He would be protected. No Apostles would betray his Marxism, no matter how high he rose in the administration. There is evidence of this: when another economics student, Sir Richard Clarke, by then permanent head at the Ministries of Aviation and Technology, was asked about Kim Philby's politics, Clarke declared that Philby was "a calm, dependable Social Democrat."

In February 1934, Kim Philby decided on a career in the foreign service. Since the post he had in mind required a knowledge of German, he went to Vienna, where he found a cheap room through the Austrian Relief Fund for the Victims of German Fascism, a known Communist-front organization. Then he made what was really his only false step: he fell in love with his landlady, Frau Lizzy Friedman, who was well known to the Austrian security service as a Marxist revolutionary and therefore subject to police supervision, denied a passport, and not allowed to change her address without police permission.

Philby's marriage to her left traces of Communist affiliations; and when Philby took his wife to England on his passport, he left still more traces. Nonetheless, on his return to London he applied for and received the application form to sit for the British Civil Service examination. This form required three referees, one of whom had to be his tutor at Cambridge. One of the referees, his tutor in history, knew nothing of his Communist associations, for he gave Kim a clean bill of political health. But the other two referees declined to do so. Philby's tutor in economics, Dennis Robertson, an Etonian and a fellow of Trinity College, and St. John Philby's old friend, Donald Robertson, who became regius professor of Greek and a member of the governing body of Westminster School, consulted and declined to give him a reference.

Bound as they were to be frank in their letters to the Civil Service Commission, for to be otherwise would jeopardize the careers of others, Dennis Roberston wrote to Kim Philby personally to state that while they were both "pleased to vouch for his intelligence, industry, and personal qualities, [they felt] bound to add that his 'sense of political injustice might well unfit him for administrative work.' " At that damning statement, Kim withdrew his application to sit for the examination.

Philby became a journalist, and, doubtless to cover his spoor in the Communist underground and to provide evidence that he had seen the error of his ways and had returned to the true path of capitalism, he began to associate openly with extreme right-wing causes. Through his father, Philby then joined the staff of *The Times* and with that appointment entered the newspaper branch of the establishment. As Robin Barrington-Ward, deputy editor of *The Times*, who was at Westminster with St. John Philby, recorded on May 20, 1937:

[St. John] Philby lunched with me. I suggested . . . that his son, also an Old Westminster, should become our special correspondent with Franco's force in Spain. He jumped at it. . . . His son duly came to see me. He looks good. We fixed him up.

Through Barrington-Ward's need of a correspondent in Spain, and his ignorance of the record at Cambridge and Vienna, Kim Philby was restored to respectability. Kim joined The Athenaeum, a place founded for "the association of individuals known for their scientific and literary attainments, artists of eminence in any class of the fine arts and noblemen and gentlemen distinguished as liberal patrons of science, literature, or the arts." It was a place so brainy and so respectable that an early member, Sir Humphrey Davy, the illustrious secretary of the Admiralty, wrote of it:

> There's first the Athenaeum Club;
> so wise there's not a man of it
> That has not sense enough for six—
> in fact that is the plan of it;
> The very waiters answer you with eloquence Socratical,
> And always place the knives and forks in order mathematical.

Yet if Philby's controller was influential and adroit in the steerage of his nominee for greatness, he could not control Philby's every action. For it was about this time that Philby met a certain Mrs. Flora Solomon. Mrs. Solomon was a lady of Russian origins who had been close to Alexander Kerensky, prime minister of the government that followed the overthrow of Tsar Nicholas II. Making her home in London when Lenin overthrew Kerensky, she established the famous welfare department store of Marks and Spencers, which became the model for all others. In some fashion Mrs. Solomon became friendly with Philby, and while he was on leave from Spain in, perhaps, 1938, Philby told her that he was doing "a very dangerous job for peace, working for the Comintern" while using his *Times* post as camouflage. He said he needed assistance in his Comintern work and asked Mrs. Solomon to join "the cause." This she refused to do, although she did tell him that "he could always come to her for help if ever he was desperate, and that she would keep his secret."

In Mrs. Solomon there was, at the least, the sixth person who, before Philby was recruited into the British secret service, knew that he was either a Communist clandestine or a Comintern spy. None, so far, had decided his statement was important enough to report to the authorities. When at length Philby found himself in the small, bare room of an SIS safe house off Victoria Street, being interviewed by his British recruiting officer, there were a few vague entries regarding left-wing associations on his card at the Security Service, but these could not have been damaging, for when the service was asked by the head of personnel at Broadway whether there was anything derogatory known about Philby, Broadway received a card stating "NRA"—"nothing recorded against."

2 THE PRINCE AND MRS. SIMPSON

In 1936 a fresh face appeared in Luckington, the village where Menzies had his country home. Baron Robert Treeck leased Luckington Manor, the next house to Menzies's, and then arrived at the manor accompanied by a caravan of pantechnicons and horse boxes and a mistress, Baroness Violetta de Schroeders, a Chilean. With the couple came a chef, a stud groom, a butler, and a valet, and Treeck employed locally a footman, a housekeeper, two undercooks, three maids, two grooms, and three gardeners. Treeck announced that he was a German Balt born in Latvia and had served with the Uhlan light cavalry during the First World War. He declared a profound dislike for Russia and communism, telling all who would listen that the Bolsheviks had expropriated his family's estates during the Russian revolution. He claimed, too, that during his escape to Germany he had been shot by the Bolsheviks in the throat, which, he said, accounted for his pronounced scar.

Menzies did not doubt for a moment that Treeck was a German secret agent. Almost certainly Treeck was an agent of Admiral Canaris's service, the Abwehr, the intelligence and counterespionage service of the German General Staff. Treeck's business in Luckington, however, almost certainly had to do with political intelligence. For, as we have seen, the Beaufort Hunt was not only a sporting, but also a political, cabal of great power and influence, the more so since the Prince of Wales, heir to the throne, took a house at Sherston Magna a few miles from Menzies in order to ride with the hunt.

Although Menzies declared that he had no contact with Treeck, either publicly or privately, Treeck was not misplaced in Luckington. In discussing Treeck and the prewar political attitudes of the Beaufort Hunt, Major Gerald A. Gundry, the hunt secretary, went through the list of the twenty-one members of the hunt committee between 1936 and 1937. All proved to be men who were prominent either in county or London society, all were high Tories, all were landowners, some were in one way or another associated with the court, all were influential in politics or finance, most had fought against Germany during World War I, and all were, like Menzies, "terrific anti-Bolsheviks." In each case, Gundry pronounced, in 1936 the committeeman concerned would have supported an alliance of England and

Germany against Russia, especially if the Prince of Wales became a protagonist, as he did.

Consequently, Treeck was not inconvenienced when he wished to ride with the hunt, as he did frequently. Certainly Menzies did not object to Treeck either as his neighbor or as a member of the hunt, although he was in a position to do both. Although Treeck seems not to have been a popular man, he was a generous one. Whereas for the 1937-1938 hunting season Treeck contributed £150 to hunt funds, Menzies paid only £35. Furthermore, it seems that Treeck must have had some form of official status in England, for he made no secret of his name or his activities.

He had other expensive addresses, including 12 Cheyne Place, London, a quarter much favored by British politicians, editors, and wealthy members of the squirearchy, and Guilsborough House, a small estate with a master's house of twenty-one rooms in the heart of the Northamptonshire hunt country. There he had joined the Pytcheley, a hunt that was only a shade less exclusive than the Beaufort. He married the baroness de Schroeders openly but quietly on April 27, 1938, at the Chelsea Registry Office, declaring on his wedding lines that he was forty-one and a "gentleman of private means." His bride declared herself to be thirty-eight, also of private means, and she identified herself as "Violetta Cousino, otherwise de Schroeders." Their witnesses were two friends, Connor Carrigan, an Anglo-Irish sportsman, and Mrs. Pearl Balfour, a society woman, of Smith Street, Chelsea.

Treeck remained at Luckington Manor at Guilsborough House until the late summer of 1939, at which time he disappeared, leaving behind valuables that were placed in the care of the Custodian for Enemy Property. Whom he saw, what he did, whom he knew—all were obscure, although he entertained well and often. As with Menzies, so with the Prince of Wales: There was no evidence that they met, but most people in Luckington assumed that the baron and the prince did so when it suited them. Nor was this unlikely, for the prince was greatly interested in Germany and nazism. Indeed, Hitler came to regard the Prince of Wales as his most important ally in England.

By 1936 it was evident that the prince had become deeply enamored of Mrs. Wallis Warfield Simpson, an American woman born in Baltimore in 1896. Mrs. Simpson had married a U.S. naval officer in 1916, divorced him in 1927, and in 1928 had married an American businessman resident in London, Ernest Aldrich Simpson. The fact that the prince associated with Mrs. Simpson caused anxiety for several reasons. First, being a divorcée, Mrs. Simpson was not regarded as a suitable companion for the heir to the throne. Second, whether justified or not, there was concern that she might be in contact with Hitler's adviser on British affairs, Joachim Von Ribbentrop. Third, there was evidence that both the prince and his mistress had developed a strong admiration for the dynamics and discipline of the Third Reich, despite the constitutional principle that the royal family, and particularly the king and his heir, must remain above politics.

All this bore personally upon Menzies, for the Prince of Wales had been a friend of the Graham Menzies family since 1911. At Oxford University the prince was close to Alastair Graham Menzies, the master of Hallyburton, who was killed in action on New Year's Day of 1915. Stewart Menzies and the prince had become messmates when the prince was attached to GHQ intelligence in 1915. Menzies's wife, Pamela, had been one of the prince's dancing partners. He had become a close friend of Keith Graham Menzies, stabling his horses with Keith at Easton Town Farm. The prince made Rex Benson a member of the Royal Victorian Order for "extraordinary, important, or personal services" to the prince during his visit to India as emperor-apparent in 1921, and one of Menzies's closest friends, David Boyle, had been the prince's aide-de-camp during his state visit to Canada in 1919.

Both Stewart and his two brothers had been officers in Household Cavalry regiments, had taken the king's shilling, and had sworn fidelity to the blood royal for life. Stewart Menzies in particular had undertaken on several occasions to defend the person of the sovereign, his heir, and the blood royal even unto death. But Stewart was also an officer of the secret service, and he had taken certain oaths in that position as well, so that as the political contacts developed between German representatives and the prince and Mrs. Simpson grew politically dangerous, the questions arose: What was Stewart Menzies's first duty? Was it to the person of the heir to the throne, or was it to the secret service? What position would Stewart Menzies have to take if the state decided to act against the prince? Since Menzies and the prince were so close, was it his duty to keep the government advised of the prince's private utterances?

By 1936, Stewart Menzies's dilemma was resolved for him. Although the official attitude of the government was becoming one of extreme reserve toward Hitler, such was Mrs. Simpson's association with Joachim von Ribbentrop, Hitler's foreign adviser, that Menzies felt obliged to have inquiries made about Mrs. Simpson in both Berlin and Washington. As distasteful as such inquiries may have been, they were necessary because it was feared that Mrs. Simpson was being manipulated by Ribbentrop, who was then regarded as "the arch-Hitler spy of Europe," as Sir Henry "Chips" Channon recorded in his diary. [3] The historian J. W. Wheeler-Bennett, who had friends at Broadway, asserted later that "Ribbentrop *used* Mrs. Simpson," and that *The Times* had proofs but had not published them because of the agreement between the newspaper proprietors to keep silent about the affair. [4]

At about the same time, Robert Bruce Lockhart, a journalist with close ties to the secret service, recorded in his personal diary that Edward had remarked to Prince Louis Ferdinand, the kaiser's grandson, that "it was no business of ours to interfere in German internal affairs either *re* Jews or *re* anything else," and that Edward had added that "dictators were very popular these days and that we might want one in England before long." Lockhart added that Edward had seemed "quite pro-Hitler" and intimated also that he was being influenced in these dangerous opinions by Mrs. Simpson. [5]

These attitudes were not ignored by the government, and as Frances Donaldson, the prince's biographer, stated, Edward was "often" under the "surveillance of security officers," and that "Mrs. Simpson was the primary object of these attentions" because of "her unrivalled opportunities for securing information." As a result, the prince's state papers were screened "in the Foreign Office," recorded Lady Donaldson, "before the red boxes went off to [Edward]." Further, as Menzies discovered, Edward was in correspondence on political matters with Hitler and the ex-kaiser, Wilhelm II, who had been in exile in Holland since he had been deposed at the end of World War I. Menzies made extraordinary efforts to intercept the letters but was largely unsuccessful, and it was not until immediately after World War II that they were found. Then they gave the Churchill government and its successor a severe shock when evidence was received that laid Edward open to charges of having committed treason.

To make the case more serious, in 1936 it became evident that the prince was in love with Mrs. Simpson and that he intended, when he became king, to make her the queen. On New Year's Day of 1936 Rex Benson gave a dinner at his house in Belgravia. By now Benson was chairman of Robert Benson and Company Limited, the leading merchant banking house in the city. Benson's guests included the Prince of Wales, Mrs. Simpson, Sir Duff and Lady Diana Cooper (he was the new war minister, she a leading personality in Anglo-French society), Sir Robert Vansittart (permanent head of the Foreign Office) and his wife, "Foxy" Gwynne (a rich man-about-town), and Johnny McMullen, a writer for *Vogue* and close friend both to Mrs. Simpson and Benson's wife, the former Mrs. Condé Nast.

Although the party was overshadowed by the illness of King George V, the reigning monarch, and the realization that he could not last much longer and that Edward would then become king, the gathering was a great success. The Prince of Wales and Mrs. Simpson stayed until 1:45 A.M., and, as Benson recorded in his diary, he "must have played [on his piano] all the popular airs from 1900 until today." The prince "sang and danced & was in great form." He was "very devoted" to Mrs. Simpson, whom Benson found to be "charming and much more woman than Lady Furness," Mrs. Simpson's predecessor in the prince's affections.

Within sixteen days of the party, the omens were realized. At about 11:40 P.M. on January 20, the king died at the age of seventy. At that moment, the Prince of Wales became King Edward VIII. To make the manner of the ending of the king's life politically sinister, in the wings at Sandringham waited a Nazi agent of influence, the duke of Coburg, who was born in England, educated at Eton, and related by blood to both the old and new kings through his grandfather, Prince Albert, Queen Victoria's consort. The presence of the duke of Coburg in the vicinity of Sandringham lent a Gothic note to the death watch, although there is no evidence that he had contact with either Queen Mary, the Prince of Wales, or Lord Dawson of Penn, the attending physician, until after the king's death.

Later, Coburg's report was to fall into Menzies's hands. It was addressed "Only for the Führer and Party Member v. Ribbentrop," and it contained the phrase "on the occasion of carrying out the Führer's commission," he talked with King Edward VIII at Sandringham on the morning after the death of King George V, "with pipe at fireside" for "a little more than half an hour." [6] The duke then accompanied the king to Buckingham Palace, where he took tea with Queen Mary and had a second conversation with the new king. Later that day, the duke claimed to have had a third conversation with Edward "between State dinner and reception at Buckingham Palace." Coburg reported that "the conversations took place in the same way as before in familiar frankness." As to the content of these conversations, the duke of Coburg reported that, for the king, "an alliance Germany-Britain is . . . an urgent necessity and a guiding principle for British foreign policy. Not, of course, against France, but, of necessity, including her. In this way safeguarding a lasting European peace."

Although the king had been warned against making political statements to anyone, and that to do so would leave him liable to charges of unconstitutional conduct, Edward then began to discuss that most troubling matter, relations between England and the Nazis. When Coburg mentioned that a meeting between Prime Minister Stanley Baldwin and Hitler might prove fruitful, the king responded: "Who is king here? Baldwin or I? I myself wish to talk to Hitler, and will do so here or in Germany. Tell him that, please." The king "spoke well" of Rudolf Hess, the deputy führer of the German Reich, and said that he was looking forward to Hess's visit to England "with pleasure," and that the king would "receive him at any time, as he is interested in him as a personality." The king spoke "appreciatively" of Joachim von Ribbentrop, who, while not yet the German foreign minister, was the most dangerous of Hitler's main foreign policy advisers.

The king made it evident that he preferred Ribbentrop to the present German ambassador to London, Leopold von Hoesch, whom the king thought was "a diplomat as industrious as he is oily" and a man who, if he was "a good diplomatic representative of the German Reich," was a "bad representative of the Third Reich." The king encouraged Hitler to replace Hoesch with Ribbentrop, with the words that he "wished to have a representative National Socialist from Germany as an ambassador," one who "through his personal rank in society belongs naturally to the 'gentry,' " but who "could be regarded as the representative of the official policy and as the confidant of Hitler." And, the duke of Coburg went on to claim, Edward VIII declared that he was "resolved to concentrate the business of government on himself."

In a state where the monarch had only the powers to advise and consent, these were dangerous statements. As the king became ever more admiring of the Nazi system, his conviction being that British Marxists would try to overthrow the monarchy as they had murdered the tsar, a blood relation of the English Crown, in 1918, he placed Stewart Menzies in what was the greatest dilemma of his career in two different but interrelated directions: the monarch's desire to become a political king and Edward's *affaire* with Mrs. Simpson. As the U.S. ambassador to London reported home, Mrs. Simpson was a woman with great influence over the king's actions, and, also, there were those reports that Mrs. Simpson was altogether too close to Ribbentrop.

In these circumstances, the old king was buried in the Royal Mausoleum at Frogmore, and preparations were then begun for Edward's coronation, which was to take place after the end of the prolonged period of court mourning, on May 12, 1937. Hitler was not prepared to wait so long before he took advantage of Edward's pro-Germanism. Six weeks after the funeral, the German army suddenly reoccupied the Rhineland, which had been demilitarized under the terms of the Versailles Treaty.

Menzies possessed foreknowledge of the operation, although he could not be precise as to the date on which it would occur, nor could he advise the government concerning the strength of the forces that Hitler intended to deploy. In the event Hitler could find only one brigade for the operation, a force that could easily have been ejected, provided the Anglo-French governments acted together. But if there was any possibility that the British might join the French army and eject the German army from the Rhineland, this hope was demolished partly at least by the intervention of the king. Fritz Hesse, a German official news agency reporter in London, recorded Edward VIII's telephone statement to the German ambassador, von Hoesch, soon after news of the Rhineland reoccupation reached London:

Hoesch whispered to me: "The King!" and handed the second receiver to me, so that I could listen to the conversation. The voice on the line said: "David* speaking. Do you know who's speaking?" To which Hoesch replied: "Of course I do." The voice continued: "I sent for the Prime Minister and gave him a piece of my mind. I told the old so-and-so that I would abdicate if he made war. There was a frightful scene. But you needn't worry. There won't be war." Putting down the receiver, Hoesch jumped up and danced round the room. "I've done it!" he cried. "I've outwitted them all; there won't be a war! Herr Hesse, we've done it!" [7]

At the same time, according to the Foreign Office, the London correspondent of the *Berliner Tageblatt* telephoned his editor: "The king has taken an extraordinarily active part in the whole affair; he has caused a number of important people in the government to come and see him and has said to them, 'This is a nice way to start my reign.' The king won't hear of there being a war." The reporter added: "In view of the tremendous influence possessed by the king and his

---

*Although the king's official name was Edward, he was usually known as David, the last of his seven Christian names, and he usually referred to himself as David.

immense energy, due importance must be attached to this where Germany is concerned." [10] Ambassador von Hoesch telegraphed Ribbentrop on March 11, 1936: "Today I got into direct touch with the Court." He found not "just understanding for the German point of view" in the crisis, but also that "the directive given to the Government" by the court was "to the effect that, no matter how the details of the affair are dealt with, complications of a serious nature are in no circumstances to be allowed to develop." [11] On receiving that telegram, as Albert Speer recorded, "I can recall that in Hitler's entourage the peaceful conclusion was attributable to the influence of the King of England. 'At last!' exclaimed Hitler. 'The King of England will not intervene. He is keeping his promise. That means that it can all go well.' " [8]

All did go well for Hitler. The reoccupation of the Rhineland and the personal intervention of Edward VIII sent a signal to Hitler that he could, when he chose, march against the source of Edward's political fears, Soviet Russia. Also, Hitler could confront his doubting generals with a clear triumph of his judgment over their fears and hesitations, for the German General Staff had predicted that the Anglo-French governments would react by sending a powerful expeditionary force into the Rhineland to force the German army back onto the east bank of the Rhine and, probably, occupy the bridgehead permanently. As for the British government, it was aware of the king's intervention, for the foreign secretary, Anthony Eden, told Jan Masaryk, the Czechoslovak ambassador in London, that the Foreign Office was "worried" over the king's "increasing and disturbing intervention in foreign affairs," and that if it continued, there were "ways and means of compelling him to abdicate." [9]

No sooner was that ominous statement made than, in accordance with the suggestions put by Edward VIII to Coburg, there were changes at the German embassy in London. Ambassador von Hoesch died suddenly, and Ribbentrop left Berlin for London on October 26, 1936, to become ambassador at the court of St. James's. As Ribbentrop declared later, his great hope for Anglo-German "understanding" was the attitude of King Edward VIII. The king's admiration for the Third Reich, nourished as it was by his intense animus for Bolshevik Russia, had been a "factor in the British situation which had contributed to my having been sent to London." [10] Ribbentrop duly presented his credentials to Edward VIII soon afterward, wearing a dove-gray uniform on the epaulets of which were the insignia of the German Foreign Ministry, an eagle with the world in its claws.

But Ribbentrop had come too late: England was in the process of sacking its king.

The prime minister, Stanley Baldwin, had confronted the king on several occasions and on several aspects of his relationship with Mrs. Simpson. The overt issue was not, therefore, political. It was personal, although the king's interference in state matters played its part in Baldwin's representations. When the king announced his intention to marry Mrs. Simpson after her second divorce became final, Baldwin opposed the marriage, and the issue developed into a struggle between monarch and Cabinet. Edward insisted on his right to marry the woman of his choice, even though her marital background made her unacceptable as queen to both the public and the government. The government saw in his challenge to its wishes a threat to constitutional procedure. A proposal that there should be some kind of morganatic marriage came to nothing. And so at last Edward advised the prime minister: "I want you to be the first to know that I have made up my mind, and nothing will alter it—I have looked at it from all sides—and I mean to abdicate and marry Mrs. Simpson." [11]

The dispute was resolved. The instrument of abdication was prepared in nine copies and was ready for signature by Wednesday, December 10, 1936:

I, Edward the Eighth, of Great Britain, Ireland, and the British Dominions beyond the Seas, King Emperor of India, do hereby declare my irrevocable determination to renounce the Throne for Myself and for My descendants, and My desire that effect should be given to this Instrument of Abdication immediately.

All nine copies were signed, and the act of abdication was then taken to the House of Commons, where the clerk of the house rose to read the royal assent. He spoke the last phrase of the assent at 1:52 P.M.: "Le Roi le veult." And at that moment Edward's younger brother succeeded to the throne as King George VI.

Edward had reigned for 325 days. A few days later, Edward was created duke of Windsor by the new king. Then he went into exile. There the security problem, hitherto the responsibility of the Security Service, now became the province of the Secret Intelligence Service. Menzies's embarrassment created by Edward's associations did not end there. On the contrary, for Stewart Menzies they became more serious almost immediately.

Rex Benson, Menzies's principal direct contact with the duke throughout the next four years, suddenly and without explanation abandoned an expensive duck- and goose-shooting expedition on the estates in Hungary of Count Czernin, son of Archduke Karl's foreign secretary during World War I. Accompanied by the count, Rex hastened to Vienna, arriving there on the eve of the duke of Windsor's own arrival from London. Benson appears to have met the duke at the Hotel Bristol, to arrange his residence at Castle Wasserleonburg, the sumptuous establishment in Carinthia, Austria, of Count Paul Munster. This became the duke's first place of exile. Benson may also have have arranged with the Austrians to guard the person of the duke while he was in Austria, for the Austrian Nazi party was active and would shortly seize the power of the state.

Whatever was said, Windsor did not remain long at Castle Wasserleonburg. He turned about and took up residence in the Château de Cande near Tours in France, the French residence of a Franco-American Fascist, Charles Eugene Bedaux, a time-and-motion study expert and model for Charlie Chaplin's 1936 satire, *Modern Times.* Bedaux was a Nazi agent of influence much obligated to Hitler's aide, Fritz Weidemann, who himself ran a private secret service operating in the Führer's interest. The duke married Mrs. Simpson at the château, at which time she became the duchess of Windsor, although King George VI would not permit the duchess to be styled "Her Royal Highness." She remained a commoner, and this royal refusal to acknowledge the marriage caused bad blood between the new duke and the new queen. Not long after the marriage, Bedaux arranged with Weidemann for the duke and duchess to pay a state visit to the Third Reich. The duke undertook the journey despite the entreaties of the Foreign Office not to do so.

On October 11, 1937, the duke and duchess of Windsor arrived at the Friedrichstrasse Station in Berlin as Hitler's guests, ostensibly to examine Nazi slum clearance and rehousing projects. *The New York Times* noted that on two occasions the duke gave the stiff-armed Roman salute, on one occasion to Hitler personally. And as Britain and Germany came close to war again, the British government, including Menzies and the secret service, had to give thought to the possibility that Hitler might use the duke of Windsor as the French had tried to use James II and James III, and the house of Stuart, during the Jacobite rebellion—as puppets.

3 MATTERS OF "DEADLY SECRECY"

In 1937 Menzies found himself with a new king, George VI, a new queen, Elizabeth, and a new prime minister, Neville Chamberlain. Born in 1869, Chamberlain was a man of property, a son of a famous political family, and, so it seemed, he was as solid as his silver. Part of his foreign policy came to be called "appeasement," to be used by the extreme right and left, wrongly, as a euphemism for profascism, antibolshevism, and British moral weakness. In reality Chamberlain followed the same strategy as did Stalin and Roosevelt when they found themselves menaced by the great dictators: he played for time in which to rearm with the only weapon at hand, concessions to Hitler.

Yet as the world crisis deepened after the German occupation of Austria in March 1938, and as Hitler then began to threaten the sovereignty of Czechoslovakia, another secret policy began to unfold, one calculated to overthrow Hitler and his regime and replace it with a military government constituted from conservative civilian elements, the German secret service of Canaris, and high officers of the German General Staff.

The principle ingredient of Chamberlain's two policies was that under no circumstances was there to be any agreement, written or spoken, with the Soviet Union. She remained *the* enemy. A second but no less important aspect of the policy was that under no circumstances should England fight Germany again. Since there was little or no prospect of an Anglo-American front to restrain Hitler, a way other than war *must* be found *without* embrangling British policy with that of Russia, which in the short and the long terms was hostile to British interests. As Chamberlain suspected, Russia was seeking to precipitate a war between England and Germany that would leave Russia the most powerful nation in Eurasia, and as he declared in a letter to his sister on March 20, 1938, just before the world crisis began: "With the Russians stealthily and cunningly pulling the strings behind the scenes to get us involved in war with Germany our Secret Service doesn't spend all its time looking out of the window."

With the German army's occupation of Austria, an event that made it clear to Whitehall that war with Germany was inevitable before the end of the decade unless there was an act of God, Chamberlain arranged for increases in the secret vote to enable Sinclair to create the secret departments necessary for the execution of his secret policy. Section V was reestablished as the counterespionage branch of the service, but, significantly, the new branch's operations were not directed against Germany. They were directed against Russia. The chief of Section V was Colonel Valentine Vivian. Felix Cowgill, a high officer of the Special Branch of the Indian Police and a specialist in anti-Marxist activities, was brought to London to build up the Soviet subsection of Section V.

At the same time, Sinclair created Section "D," for Destruction, an organization responsible for political warfare, sabotage, and the creation of guerrilla forces. The chief of the organization was Colonel Laurence Grand, a tall, thin, dark man who chain-smoked and wore a rose in his buttonhole. Charged with investigating "every possibility of attacking potential enemies by means other than force," Grand's first important meeting was held ten days after the German army entered Austria and Hitler declared his homeland to be part of the "Greater German Reich." At the meeting were the new foreign secretary, Lord Halifax, the new permanent head of the Foreign Office, Sir Alexander Cadogan, the chief of the Imperial General Staff, Grand, and Menzies. The meeting agreed that, subject to the prime minister's approval, which was forthcoming, "a few active preparatory steps could now be taken in deadly secrecy by Section D, to counter Nazi predominance in small countries Germany had just conquered or was plainly threatening." [12]

For security reasons, Section D was controlled indirectly from Broadway by Menzies, and its appointments were made, again for security reasons, by Grand personally without necessarily consulting Broadway. Menzies strengthened his organization at The Hague, which became the forward base for operations against Germany. Selecting a man not known to the German security service, Menzies made (or so it seemed at the time) an excellent choice in Major Richard H. Stevens. Aged forty-four, Stevens came at the recommendation of General Sir Claude Auchinleck, Stevens's commanding officer in India. Born in Athens, Greece, the son of a British Merchant Navy captain and a Greek mother, Stevens had joined the British Malay States Police in 1913 as an officer aspirant. At the outbreak of World War I he was commissioned into the Indian army as a lieutenant with the Rajput Rifles. In March 1933 he joined the British-Indian army's intelligence service, where for two years he translated decodes of Russian radio messages. During that assignment, Stevens was promoted from captain to major. Between 1935–1937 he was engaged in war mobilization planning under Auchinleck and was then called to London in April 1938 to join SIS. After introduction to "C," Stevens was sent to each of the SIS sections to familiarize himself with the work going on there. Having acquainted himself with the range of the Anglo-French secret intelligence relationship, he then returned to London to meet the head of the Dutch intelligence service, General van Oorschot, who was visiting Broadway and undertook to give Stevens protection in Holland. At that time Stevens was proposed to van Oorschot as the new passport control officer at The Hague; he was accepted and took up his duties there on July 19, 1938, his orders to intensify the recruitment of agents and to expand his predecessors' connections with the Dutch government. [13]

Stevens claimed later that he was unfitted to the duties at The Hague because "I had never been a spy, much less a spymaster. My intelligence work, mainly the evaluation of military reports on the deployment of armed native tribesmen, was done solely on the Northwest Frontier. I agreed to go to The Hague as long as my superiors realised that I thought myself to be lacking in experience and training for the assignment and was, in my own opinion, altogether the wrong sort of man for such work."

Stevens may well have been unsuited to his trade, but untrained he was not. He had been unusually well trained and had been so instructed that he was familiar with all branches of the British and British-Indian intelligence services. When he arrived at The Hague he still had about fifteen months in which to acquaint himself with his work and with operating conditions in northwest Europe. Furthermore, as war approached Stevens received substantial reinforcements from both Broadway and the Czech intelligence service, which, at the time of the Munich crisis, had entered into an alliance with the British against the German services.

With Stevens and his assistants in place, Menzies began what were his first operations of World War II. Following the German occupation of Austria and the intensification of the world crisis after Munich, Chamberlain gave Sinclair authority to undertake two separate but interlocking operations. Menzies was in charge of both under Sinclair's direction, and the first concerned Austria. Through his seizure of Austria, Hitler had unleashed a substream of underground politics that Menzies was now, and for the first time, authorized to exploit. Through intermediaries, Menzies succeeded in establishing clandestine relations with the pretender to the throne of the Austro-Hungarian empire, Archduke Otto, who lived with his mother, Empress Zita, at the Château Sternockezeele, near Brussels.

The archduke enjoyed considerable support through the Austrian Legitimists, who supported the restoration of the monarchy and were influential in some ten thousand communes of Austria, mainly in the Tyrol. Menzies arranged that a subsidy be paid to Archduke Otto, one that was "not far short of" £50,000 *a month* (about $250,000) toward the end of 1939. But from the outset the operation was deeply troubled through the inability of certain of the Legitimists to obey the first law of the survival of the clandestine: silence. The movement was soon exposed, with heavy casualties, by the Sicherheitsdienst, the Nazi party's intelligence and security service, and played little effective part in the conspiracy against Hitler. [14]

When it became evident that Hitler was planning to do to Czechoslovakia what he had just done to Austria, Chamberlain set forth the second operation by asking Admiral Sinclair for a paper on what Britain should or could do to restrain Hitler without war. The paper, entitled "What Should We Do?", was sent to the prime minister on September 18, eleven days before the culmination of the Munich crisis. By its very existence the paper was important, for such documents were, as they remain, as rare as rubies in British official records. This document was of additional importance because (a) it demonstrated the proximity between Chamberlain and the secret service, and (b) to a large degree Chamberlain's policy during the last phase of "appeasement" rarely departed from Sinclair's recommendation, thus lending some substance to the Soviet belief that the office of "C" constituted the "power behind the throne."

Although unsigned, as the custom dictated, the paper was almost certainly drafted by Sinclair, Menzies, Major Malcolm L. Woollcombe, head of the political section, and perhaps also Woollcombe's deputy, David Footman. If Footman was involved, there could have been a leakage, for at this time Footman was involved with Guy Burgess, the homosexual Apostle. The document advised Chamberlain that, in the view of the Secret Intelligence Service, the Germans were bent upon the establishment of "supremacy" in central and southeastern Europe, Belgium, Holland, the Baltic states, and Scandinavia, while promoting the disintegration of Soviet Russia. They wished for "a deal" with the British, "in return for which, at any rate to start with, there would be recognition of Britain's supremacy overseas," and under certain circumstances a deal might not prove uncongenial. The Germans expected, however, that they would in due course attempt to recover their overseas empire. In that event, while not conceding too much, they should be accommodated. The secret service also predicted that the Germans would attempt to penetrate into the Middle East and increase Britain's difficulties there and also seek to foment trouble wherever possible in the British Empire— and particularly in India, Ireland, Egypt, Palestine, and South Africa.

In attaining these objectives, the Germans were creating "the strongest possible Armed Forces, sufficient to overcome any combination of Powers and emerge victoriously in any conflagration." The Germans were also creating a "superlatively strong disciplined Reich" coupled with economic self-sufficiency and "an impregnable international position, with adequate external support and resources—the Berlin-Rome-Tokyo Axis being the foundation—and safeguards against the formation of dangerous hostile combinations." Menzies and his colleagues recommended that to gain the time needed to rebuild British military power, part of, and under certain circumstances all of, Czechoslovakia should be conceded to Germany, leaving no more than "a State which would be literally Czechoslovak—a compact, homogenous, neutralised State under international guarantee."

Without actually using the words "covert diplomacy," the paper also advocated as an "immediate step" a program calculated to make the Axis partnership "much more artificial" while not being seen to be trying to do so. To forestall the expected German penetration of the Near East, the demands of the Arab world should be satisfied by the construction of "a mere token State for the Jews, with rigid safeguards against Jewish expansion." Better still, the paper argued, would be "Jewish cantonisation in an Arab state." At the same time, and above all, "*we should unremittingly build up our armaments* and defensive measures and maintain them at the highest possible level, never relaxing."

As to Allies, the British intelligence masters felt "we cannot really trust any foreign country." France was "bound to us (as we are to her) by ties of necessity, and we should maintain these ties on the firmest possible basis—*a permanent defensive alliance.*" Britain could "never really rely in an emergency on the fickle and unscrupulous Italians." Italy would "never be a stable factor in any 'defensive front,' " even if "such were desirable." But "we can at least always work to keep them on the right side, treating them, above all, as equals, playing up to their pride, and always being quick to remove any suspicions which they may entertain as to our motives—at the same time never relaxing our vigilance over them." As to Japan, that country was "a more difficult proposition," but "we might at least go some way, even at the sacrifice of some principle, in recognizing . . . Japan's special position in East Asia." Even "gestures on our part, which cost us nothing, may go some way psychologically."

Touching lightly and briefly on Chamberlain's secret policy, for the paper was intended for eyes that knew nothing of Chamberlain's covert intentions, the authors recommended that "we should inject resisting power" into those countries which Germany had earmarked as vassal states, by "(a) helping them financially and economically and making them less dependent on Germany for trade; and (b) making them realize that we and the French are strong and united; encouraging them as far as possible to look to us, short of committing ourselves to supporting them actively."

Since the Spanish civil war was as yet undecided, and since "we cannot spot the winner yet," Britain should "keep the way open for good relations with whatever Spain emerges." Also, Britain should "almost get on alliance terms" with Turkey, for Turkey was a "powerful factor in Balkan resistance to the German drive Eastwards and can herself be a bulwark in the Middle East." In the case of the United States, Britain should maintain "the closest possible relations" and "utilize" the present crisis "to strengthen the ties." There should be no encirclement of, or defensive front against, Germany, for it "seems undesirable to give Hitler any pretext for saying Germany is being encircled or that hostile combinations are being built up against her; for if he has that pretext it is a rallying cry and, in his eyes, a justification for various dynamic and dangerous measures."

In short, Britain must ensure everywhere that "Germany's style is cramped in every way possible, but with the minimum of provocation." Nor should friendship with Germany be ruled out. On the contrary, friendship should be cultivated "as far as we can, and without sacrifice of our principles and vital interests." As to Germany's grievances and claims in general:

We should not wait till these become, in regular sequence, critical. International steps of some sort should be taken, without undue delay, to see what *really legitimate* grievances Germany has and what surgical operations are necessary to rectify them. Potential sores should be discovered and treated quickly. If there are genuine cases for self-determination they should be established and remedied. . . . It may be argued that this would by giving in to Germany, strengthening Hitler's position and encouraging him to go to extremes. Better, however, that realities be faced and that wrongs, if they do exist, be righted, than leave it to Hitler to do the righting in his own way and time. . . .

Little store, however, could be set by anything that the Russians did or promised. As the authors of the paper noted, "We can never bank on this country," although "to keep on the right side of this devil, we must sup with him to some extent, adapting the length of our spoon to circumstances at any given moment."

With the promulgation of that neat and devious document, and with the Anglo-German crisis deepening, it seemed by the hour, Broadway appeared to be committed firmly to Chamberlain's policy of "appeasement." At his meeting with Hitler at Munich on September 29 Chamberlain went further than Sinclair would have recommended in regard to Czechoslovakia, for he permitted the immediate occupation by Germany of the Sudetenland in return for a document that enabled Chamberlain to announce on his return to London that he had secured "peace in our time." The reality was different but important. He had secured peace for twelve months, just time to enable the Air Ministry to introduce the fast, eight-gun Spitfire fighter into squadron service. That stay of war proved to be decisive in the defense of the United Kingdom.

In that situation of near war, during the Munich crisis Menzies's agents in Berlin and other key centers of Germany reported that there had been severe tensions between the General Staff and the leaders of the Nazi party. Although deputy chief of the secret service, Menzies was still chief of the military section, and as he reported on November 15, throughout the crisis the German army chiefs "strove unremittingly and courageously to restrain Herr Hitler, and were instrumental on at least one occasion in averting an order to march." General Ludwig Beck had resigned as chief of the German General Staff on the grounds that he thought Hitler would land Germany in a disastrous war that it could not win.

Beck had indeed warned Hitler that an attack upon Czechoslovakia would provoke war on several fronts and bring in not only France and England, but also, eventually, the United States. Hitler was not, however, dissuaded. He declared to his generals his "unshakeable determination" to eliminate the "threat" of Czechoslovakia; and when Beck demanded "specific guarantees" that Hitler would desist from military action, guarantees that Hitler would not give, Beck resigned with the further warning that "a war begun by Germany will immediately call into the field other states than the one she has attacked, and in a war against a world coalition she will succumb and for good or evil be put at that coalition's mercy." As Hitler accepted Beck's resignation, he remarked to an assistant: "The only one of [my generals] whom I fear is Beck. That man would be capable of something."

In the other aspects of his assessment, Menzies proved equally correct. After Chamberlain broke his guarantee of Czechoslovakia's sovereignty, Beck lost the support of the other members of the General Staff, who, Menzies reported, argued against military action "solely on the military aspects, i.e. Germany's unreadiness to engage in a general war of long duration." It seemed clear, too, that, "had the advice of the Generals been overruled, they would have loyally carried out their orders." Nevertheless:

In certain high Army quarters secret approaches were made abroad, and there was a hope that an outbreak of war might lead to the overthrowing of the regime. But there was evidently no [popular] willingness to take the risk of leading a movement. There is no doubt as to General Beck's anti-Nazi feelings; he even hopes that Colonies will not be returned so long as the Nazi regime lasts, believing that that would bring a "Napoleonic" trend with similar consequences to Germany. [15]

There were, too, indications that the attitude of the army reservists had been opposed to war, although whether this would have "affected the fighting efficiency of the Army, at any rate for some time, is perhaps questionable." The same report also noted that "we had an abundance of evidence that opposition to, and fear of, war were widespread in Germany and became particularly marked when in about the last week it was realized that Germany was on the brink of a real conflagration." Had there been a conflagration, Menzies went on:

the morale of the people, and particularly of the working classes, would not have been good. But although there was much anti-Nazi sentiment, which was finding certain sporadic forms of manifestation, and although General Beck now says that Germany before Munich was in great danger of revolution, we had no sure evidence of the existence of any cohesive opposition movement which could have shaken the regime, whatever might have happened had serious reverses come at a later stage. The indications seem on the whole to have been that, while the Gestapo would have had to deal with some 20,000–30,000 saboteurs, the bulk of the nation, largely unwillingly but resignedly, would have followed the Fuhrer into war. [16]

In short, Menzies estimated, the internal German political situation favored the operation to overthrow Hitler, although the German conspiracy against Hitler was greatly weakened when Chamberlain conceded Czechoslovakia, a fact that Menzies did not report until after the preliminary steps had been taken toward British official encouragement to the plotters around Canaris, a group whose members may well have included Menzies's mysterious neighbor at Luckington, Baron Robert Treeck. On the basis of these reports, Menzies displayed cautious interest in two proposals to assassinate Hitler. The British military attaché at Berlin, Colonel F. N. Mason-Macfarlane, and William S. Stephenson, a Canadian-born industrialist closely associated with Churchill, both offered to shoot Hitler with high-powered sporting rifles. Alas, the proposals were rejected by the foreign secretary, Halifax, with the pronouncement that "we have not reached that stage in our diplomacy when we have to use assassination as a substitute for diplomacy."

At that declaration, Menzies gave no further thought to the murder of Hitler, and Sinclair and Menzies concentrated instead on what became a main preliminary operation in the immediate prewar period: To establish whether the anti-Hitler group in Germany was powerful enough to establish an alternative government to that of nazism. That operation was not, however, entrusted to Menzies—not at first, at least. Believing that SIS might have been penetrated by the Germans, as indeed it had been, particularly at The Hague, Sinclair established a third new service, one called Section "Z."

Lieutenant Colonel Claude Dansey was recalled from Rome, where he was passport control officer, and put in charge of "Z" with instructions that he was to operate throughout Europe in parallel to SIS but with neither organization being aware of the existence of the other until the outbreak of war. At that time "Z" officers were to report to the passport control officers and place themselves under their control. Dansey's headquarters were not at Broadway but at Bush House in The Strand. His chief of staff was a sensitive, able, and experienced naval officer, Commander Kenneth H.S. Cohen, a son of a barrister of the Inner Temple. "Z" possessed a structure independent of that of Broadway, and it existed not only to conduct espionage, but also to undertake what the Germans called "higher political tasks." [17]

Dansey's first major appointment was Captain S. Payne Best, who was made "Z" representative at The Hague in parallel to Major Stevens. Born in April 1885 at Cheltenham, Best was the son of a doctor.

Before World War I he had graduated from the London School of Economics in accountancy, and at war's outbreak he volunteered for intelligence, having a good command of German. He had done well in World War I, but he had tried to do too much in dangerous circumstances (two of his agents were electrocuted while trying to pass through the German electric fence along the Dutch-Belgian border without benefit of rubber boots), and he had had a nervous breakdown. In April 1919, while GHQ representative at Interallie Brussels, Best resigned from the secret service, although he remained a captain on the reserve of officers. He moved to The Hague in 1919, remaining there until November 1939, and he became first an advertising agent and then a manufacturer and merchant of pharmaceutical products, probably with the help of Broadway.

Monocled, spatted, tall, slender, in his prime Best personified the European vision of *superbia Brittanorum*, despite a vague air of disrepute that surrounded his name at the British legation over a matter of bounced checks in Amsterdam in the early twenties. By repute if any man was capable of assassination, it was Best. And in business he had a reputation for being exceptionally ruthless and probably dishonest. Nevertheless, Best was acceptable in the Dutch court and the coteries around the north German grand duchies of Mecklenburg and Oldenburg. Through his second wife, the Dutch painter Maria Margareta Van Rood, Best became a familiar figure at the court of Queen Wilhelmina of the Netherlands. Through that court Best met the heads of several of the leading noble families of north Germany, families that, it was estimated, would support the overthrow of Hitler. One was the grand duchess of Oldenburg, head of the remnants of the old German royal families of Oldenburg and Mecklenberg and a sister of Prince Heinrich, consort of Queen Wilhelmina.

Best stayed at least once every year at the grand duchess's home, Rabensteinfel, near Schwerin. He was on equally friendly terms with Grand Duke Niklaus of Oldenburg, at whose castle (Lensahn in Holstein) he spent Christmas 1938. As Best advised Dansey in a letter, "To the Grand Duchess Elisabeth, the Grand Duke Niklaus, and his wife the Princess Helene, I made no secret of the fact that I was engaged on intelligence work as I felt I could count upon their assistance in the event of war." [18] He smuggled letters from Grand Duchess Oldenburg to Queen Wilhelmina of the Netherlands, which he read and which gave him a keen insight into the attitudes toward Hitler within the north German aristocracies. Best also became friendly with the grand duchess of Mecklenburg. Through her brother, a high official of the Colonial Office, and cousin, a high officer of the General Staff, Best acquainted himself with the inner politics of those organizations.

Best was extremely well informed also about north German politics, and possibly it was through Best that Menzies personally saw an emissary of General Beck. Karl Goerdeler, the former lord mayor of Leipzig and price controller of the Third Reich, was the head of the civil side of what proved to be an important group of military conspirators that included Admiral Canaris, Colonel Hans Oster (Canaris's deputy and head of the administrative section of the Abwehr), General Beck, and General Franz Halder, Beck's successor, who was to remain in that post until 1942.

As the permanent head of the Foreign Office, Felix Cadogan recorded in his diary that Goerdeler proposed that Britain and France should suggest to Germany a negotiation for the settlement of outstanding issues, on the condition that Hitler cease his policy of internal and external violence. If Hitler rejected this suggestion, Britain and France would break diplomatic relations with Germany, "in which event Dr. Goerdeler undertook that appropriate action would begin in Germany to produce an administration prepared to talk on these terms." [19] Goerdeler required that Britain should "liquidate" the Danzig corridor between Poland and Germany, which the Germans regarded as a serious irritant arising from the Versailles Treaty. Also, Germany should be given a block of colonial territories and receive an interest-free loan of £400–£500 million. That sum, so it was rumored later, was increased to £1 billion ($4.6 billion) at 2 percent.

In return Germany would restore a free exchange system, eschew hegemony in southeastern Europe, guarantee the *status quo* in the Mediterranean, and promise to cooperate in the Far East. Cadogan's reaction to this message reflected Chamberlain's attitude toward these unusual propositions. In his diary entry of December 10, 1938, as the world prepared for war, Cadogan recorded that

a message from Goerdeler outlining plan of a (army) revolution in Germany, to take place before the end of the month. G wants a "message" from us. He had already sent us a "programme," which we couldn't subscribe to— too much like "Mein Kampf"—and that rather put me off him. But he *may* want something merely to show his fellow conspirators that we shan't fall upon a divided Germany, and would want to work with any decent regime that might come out of the mess. I drafted hurriedly the kind of message (very non-committal) that we might send him, and sent it up to H[alifax]. I don't believe much in this, but if there *is* anything in it, it's the biggest thing for centuries. . . .

There lay the danger. It was the "biggest thing," at least since Napoleon, in several directions. It was evident to the Russians that an Anglo-German military coalition might arise from the tumult as Hitler conquered country after country by diplomacy to clear the way to the Soviet frontier. Aware, too, that Chamberlain might have a covert policy to deflect Hitler from France on to Russia, the Soviet intelligence services sought to obtain knowledge of Broadway's activities. Broadway, too, was aware that this would be the policy of the Soviet service and was vigilant for attempts at Soviet infiltration, hence the creation of the Section V as an anti-Soviet counterespionage service. Section V may not, however, have been vigilant enough. For into the service came Guy Burgess.

On leaving Cambridge, Burgess joined the BBC Talks Department, where he met David Footman, a member of Broadway's political section. Born in 1895, educated at Marlborough and exhibitioner in modern history at New College, Oxford, Footman had married a girl also named Footman in 1927. The marriage was dissolved in 1936, there were no children, Footman never remarried, and he was rather dandified in dress and speech. Recruited into the British Secret Intelligence Service from the Levant Consular Service, Footman was in a position where he could learn much about the inner politics of Broadway. The chief of the political section, Major Woollcombe, was soon to retire, to be succeeded by Footman. Intellectually tough but morally weak, Footman was a man who by birth, education, and politics would not find an Apostle uninteresting. By chance Footman met Burgess in 1937, and Burgess persuaded him to give a radio talk on Albania. The two men became friendly, largely through their mutual interest in history.

When Section D was formed, Footman put forward Burgess's name as a likely lad, and the proposal was seconded by Guy Liddell, chief of the counterespionage branch of MI5. While an MI5 informant Burgess had seduced a junior German diplomat in Ribbentrop's embassy in London, Baron Wolfgang zu Putlitz, who provided excellent information about German activities in London and The Hague, especially concerning the duke and duchess of Windsor's association with Ribbentrop and then with the ex-kaiser, Wilhelm II, who was in exile at Doorn in Holland. Burgess attended an interview with Grand, chief of Section D, at St. Ermyn's Hotel, the section's headquarters. Grand was looking for unorthodox people with good brains, and Burgess was amply endowed with the qualities that Grand desired. Backed as he was by excellent references from the BBC and MI5, Burgess was offered the job of deputy chief at Section D's training center, Brickendonbury Hall, a large country house at Hertford, about thirty-five miles north of London.

Inexplicably, given the close links between SIS and Eton, Menzies's security section made no attempt to speak with the headmaster of Eton, Robert Birley, who knew Burgess to be both a Marxist and a sodomite. As Birley himself related after visiting Burgess at Trinity College:

Of course Guy wasn't in when I arrived, so I entered his room in New Court and waited. There were many books on his shelves, and I'm always drawn to other people's taste in reading. As I expected, his taste was fairly wide and interesting. I noticed a number of Marxist tracts and text-books, but that's not what really shocked and depressed me. I realized that something must have gone terribly wrong when I came across an extraordinary array of explicit and extremely unpleasant pornographic literature. He bustled in finally, full of cheerful apologies for being late as usual, and we talked happily enough over the tea-cups. [20]

On his arrival at Brickendonbury Hall, the Soviet mole began his burrow.

Philby was soon to follow.

4 FOXES AND ENIGMA

Just before Christmas 1938, Admiral Sinclair, chief of the secret service, told Menzies in confidence that he was suffering from cancer of the colon. Since Menzies might have to take command of the service at short notice, and since war might come in the spring, Sinclair advised Menzies to take three months' leave, as he might not get any more for a very long time. In view of his illness, Sinclair declared, it was essential that Menzies be fit and ready for his great trial.

Menzies went home to Bridges Court, where he planned to do nothing but hunt and attend to family business, including his wife's health, which was not improved. But that winter was one of the worst for years. Blizzards, high winds, snow, floods, sleet storms, frost, and foot-and-mouth disease—all served to make hunting impossible. Much of the time the telephones were down, so that Menzies found it difficult and sometimes impossible to maintain contact with Sinclair and Broadway. Neither mail nor telegrams got through. The roads were often impassable and the rails uncertain.

As December gave way to January, the reports that came to Menzies in a pouch brought from Broadway became increasingly ominous. It seemed that Hitler intended to launch a surprise attack against Holland. Once occupied, the reports warned, Hitler intended to use the Dutch airfields as a base from which to launch the German air force against London without declaring war. That warning resulted in a survey of all intelligence reports received during December by Gladwyn Jebb, in Cadogan's office. Jebb's report was of importance to Menzies in his evolving plot against Hitler, for Jebb described Hitler as "a blend of fanatic, madman and clear-visioned realist" who was supreme in Germany. To make him the more dangerous, he was embittered and exasperated by Britain's cold shoulder to his proposals over the years for an Anglo-German front against Russia; he was incalculable even to his intimates, and he was capable of throwing the machine he had created in any direction at short notice. [21]

These and other such reports played a substantial part in the acceleration of British rearmament, the decision to create an army for continental operations, and intimations to Germany that Britain would regard an invasion of Holland as cause for war. Menzies abandoned his leave, as he was well aware that the government feared greatly the "bolt from the blue" that the reports foreshadowed. Although this was not known at the time, that fear was largely the result of the air section's exaggerated reporting of the offensive power of the German air force. There, Squadron Leader F. W. Winterbotham was chief, and through Winterbotham's close contact with the chiefs of the German air force, he was persuaded that London would be knocked out in the first blows. His information suggested that German bomber strength in September 1938 consisted of 927 long-range aircraft, and that the German air force would be capable of launching 720 sorties a day to deliver 945 tons of bombs. Since it was also estimated that there would be fifty casualties for each ton of bombs, fifty thousand casualties would result in any one twenty-four-hour period.

But then—such was the war of nerves and deception being waged by Hitler, to confuse and confound Chamberlain—there was no invasion of Holland. Instead Romania was to be occupied for its oil. Then the Ukraine for its wheat. Then Denmark for its access to the Atlantic. Then Norway for its iron ore. Then Hungary. Then Poland. Every gunroom in Europe held a different story. Menzies saw a consistent deception campaign and with it a decline in the standing of his espionage sections. Lacking both documentary and cryptanalytical intelligence in volume sufficiently large to be able to make an accurate evaluation of the reports received, Broadway and hence the government was prey to every rumor. Only 20 percent of Broadway's reports were assessed as true, and the British ambassadors at both Berlin and Moscow complained about the value and veracity of the reports they received from SIS.

By the end of February 1939 the complaints had become so severe that, as the government official with departmental responsibility for Broadway and the permanent head of the Foreign Office, Cadogan felt compelled to come to its defense. Writing to Sir Neville Henderson, the British ambassador at Berlin, Cadogan declared:

Our agents are, of course, bound to report rumours or items of information which come into their possession; they exercise a certain amount of discrimination themselves, but naturally do not take responsibility of too much selection, and it is our job here to weigh up the information which we receive and to try to draw more or less reasonable conclusions from it. In that we may fail, and if so it is our fault, but I do not think it fair to blame the S.I.S. Moreover, it is true to say that the recent scares have not originated principally with the S.I.S. agents in Germany, but have come to us from other sources. [22]

Cadogan's observations were not less than accurate. Although the German stations were under the constant observation of what was proving to be a ruthless, able, and omnipresent security service— the Gestapo—Broadway was well informed throughout the crises that led to war except in one direction: Moscow. The British ambassador to Moscow in October 1938 complained it was "impossible to obtain even an inkling of what is discussed within [the Kremlin's] walls." [23] Early in 1939, the secrecy of the Soviet government was lifted slightly as Stalin, feeling the menace of Hitler's glare, made signs that suggested he desired a rapprochement, an Anglo-Russian front against Germany. That overture received no more than a frigid response from Chamberlain, who maintained his policy of attempting to deflect Hitler eastward toward Stalin.

The crisis over the reliability of Broadway was, therefore, just beginning when the weather changed for the better; Menzies decided to resume his leave, returning to Luckington in time for the hunt ball. The ball that year was held at the pump room in Bath, the Georgian assembly rooms over the Roman Baths, and under the Abbey towers—it was usually held at Badminton, but that year the palace was being prepared as an evacuation center for the royal family should Buckingham Palace and Windsor Castle become bombing targets. Jack Jackson's string orchestra played, and the dancing went on until 4:30 A.M. on Friday, February 4. Six hundred people danced until the wee hours, including at least one Nazi spy, a certain Bales, who had bought a farm in Beaufortshire that he used as a base from which to conduct military espionage. He was well placed to obtain such intelligence, for many cavalry officers were members of the hunt, and from his contact with these men it was a relatively simple task for Bales to establish the key secret of the times: Was Britain about to send, as she had done in World War I, an army and an air force to France?

The hunt ball was followed by a hunt, which began at noon and was the best of the season so far. The wind was in the southeast for the first time, and that was the quarter that invariably produced a scent. Sure enough, a fox was soon holloaed away from Bath Verge. He ran by the Slaits, the Deer Park to Cherry Orchard, where hounds caught him. Going quickly on to draw Allengrove, the hunt was soon away with another fox, and the scent proved first rate. This was an excellent hunt, as *The Field* reported, one "reminiscent of the old days and the straight-necked foxes." It lasted two hours, with a point of just over six miles. On the way back there was more excitement over stone-wall country. But the hounds divided between Ragged Castle and Swangrove, and "Master" stopped the hunt at dusk.

That was Stewart Menzies's last hunt for nearly six years, for the duke of Beaufort decided that war was inevitable and close, and because of their great value as breeding stock, he decided to send his "piebald lovelies" to Canada "for the duration." The hunt was closed down, and the secretary, Major Gerald Gundry, rejoined his regiment, the Sixteen Fifth Lancers, which had been reequipped with armored cars. He met Menzies by chance at the duke of Beaufort's railway station while waiting for the London train. Gundry and Menzies were on good terms, perhaps because Gundry had been master of the Eton College Beagles, just as Menzies had been in 1907. "It's like old times, sir," Gundrey declared as they boarded the train, which was filled with men in khaki. Menzies replied, "Yes it is. Do you realise that I have spent almost my entire adult life either preparing to fight or fighting Germany?"

By the middle of March Stewart Menzies was back at his desk at Broadway to find that consideration was being given to a revolutionary proposal from Brigadier F. G. Beaumont-Nesbitt, deputy director of military intelligence at the War Office. The British intelligence system had proven inadequate to the task of sifting the true from the false in the overwhelming mass of intelligence reaching it from all quarters. To modernize the machine to meet the conditions for both total war and armed truce, Nesbitt had proposed what amounted to a revolution in British intelligence, the establishment of a "Central Intelligence Bureau" as a point at which all intelligence relating to given problems should be collated and analyzed.

To the surprise of all the departments involved in Nesbitt's proposal, Broadway did not resist. Hitherto, the Secret Intelligence Service had always resisted membership of any of Whitehall's committee on the grounds that such membership would compromise the security of the organization and the identity of its personnel. But as Menzies wrote to Beaumont-Nesbitt, he was "confident that the basic idea underlying this scheme is sound and necessary." Broadway's "own constantly recurring experience of being called upon for ad hoc notes on various aspects—which can only be one-sided—is our strongest proof that such machinery is badly needed."

Menzies then requested that the Secret Intelligence Service be represented at any interdepartmental discussions and recommended that the SIS become a member of the Joint Intelligence Committee (JIC). That request marked the end of SIS's isolation from the government machine. Shortly the Joint Intelligence Committee, which until now had been little more than a growth in the side of the Foreign Office, was placed under the chairmanship of a Foreign Office man, Victor Cavendish-Bentinck, heir to the duke of Portland. Under Bentinck the new organization acquired fresh vitality and significance. Menzies represented his services on the committee, a position he occupied at least until 1952, and the JIC became a subcommittee of the chiefs of staff.

It established the Joint Intelligence Service (JIS) and made it responsible for analyzing and collating all intelligence on issues of interest for presentation to the Joint Intelligence Committee, who, in turn, debated the findings before passing them to the king, the Cabinet, and the chiefs of staff. Yet no piece of machinery could quickly make good the lack of resources that had afflicted the intelligence services for so long, nor could they alter some of the long-established practices and attitudes that inhibited change. Certainly they could not expand overnight the sources available to Broadway. As Sinclair told the Treasury, that could only be accomplished by money, more money, and still more money.

But the new organization was in place by March 15, when the German army occupied the rest of Czechoslovakia and Hitler proclaimed the establishment of the "Protectorate of Bohemia and Moravia." From that day forward, under Sinclair's overall direction and according to the procedures laid down in the war book, Menzies began to expand the secret services to war establishment as reports arrived that Hitler would invade Poland in the autumn. As a consequence of those reports, at the end of March Chamberlain announced British and French guarantees to Poland, Romania, and Greece. And one of the consequences was an intelligence alliance of high importance between the British, Poles, and French—Enigma.

Since the Versailles conference, Menzies had remained in close and friendly association with Alexander Denniston, the head of the Government Code and Cypher School (GC&CS); Colonel John Tiltman, the chief War Office cryptanalyst; and with those in charge of the range of technical methods of code breaking. By 1928, Menzies was well aware that the German General Staff was converting to a new system that would produce ciphers in great abundance, a small machine called Enigma. About the size of a large portable typewriter, Enigma could produce almost an infinity of ciphers. One variant could make no less than one hundred and fifty million, million, million different encoding positions for each letter of the alphabet. Another variant could produce up to two hundred quintillion* settings.

Believing each cipher thus produced to be absolutely unbreakable, the German government began to employ Enigma to conceal almost all their secret communications up to the level of armies. From armies to the supreme command they intended to employ a second machine, one known as the Geheimschreiber. But neither Enigman nor Geheimschreiber remained as secure as the German signalmasters believed them to be. The nature of Geheimschreiber was deduced from

---

*In Great Britain a quintillion is defined as the fifth power of a million (1 followed by thirty ciphers, i.e. 1,000,000,000,000,000,000,000,000,000,000). In the United States it is the cube of a million (1 followed by eighteen ciphers, i.e. 1,000,000,000,000,000,000). In this context, the term is used in the British meaning.

its trial transmissions in 1936; Enigma was broken into by a young Pole, Marian Rejewski, as early as 1933.

Working against information procured by the chief of the technical section of the French secret service, Colonel Gustav Bertrand, and with his own native mathematical genius, Rejewski broke into the German army's Enigma for two months in 1933. The intelligence was purchased by Bertrand from a German traitor, Hans Thilo-Schmidt, an employee of a German cipher service, B-Dienst. The brother of a German general, Schmidt worked as a courier of secret crypto-graphic materials by the "Cipher Bureau of the Ministry of Defense" in Berlin. [24]

In all, Schmidt sold seven sets of Enigma documentation, his motive being not ideological but sexual. "He liked money," Bertrand related, adding, "He needed money, for he liked still more women." [25] But if Bertrand regarded Schmidt's documentation as being of epic importance to the safety of France, that belief was not shared by the French code breakers. They believed, as did the Denniston group in England, that Enigma was impenetrable. Since his own cryptographers were not prepared even to try to get into Enigma, Bertrand gave his information to the Polish intelligence service. As Rejewski stated, with only brain power it might have taken forever to penetrate Enigma. With Bertrand's documents, decipherment of German traffic became possible within days and, sometimes during those two months, within hours.

After the first, decisive success, Rejewski was joined in the attack against Enigma by two other cryptanalysts, Jerzy Rozycki and Henryk Zygalski. Employing new mathematical methods, in particular certain fresh theories regarding permutations, these three men devised meth-ods of finding the Enigma keys faster than previously. By the first half of 1938, they were able to decipher the intercepted Enigma traffic, as Rejewski recorded, "practically every day, and often at a record speed." Their key invention was a machine called the bomba, a word invented for the purpose. The bomba proved to be a numbers counter that facilitated the scanning of the Enigma "period"—all the permutations of a three-letter code possible on three rotors—at very high speeds. [26]

The Polish triumph ended in the second half of 1938 when the Germans, as part of their security procedures, introduced two major changes to their enciphering procedures that defeated the Poles, although their theoretical solutions remained valid. With Hitler turning his army against Poland, that failure constituted a political calamity, one that could be overcome only if the Poles gained the technological support of the British and French, neither of whom had succeeded in making any substantial penetration of the Enigma secret.

At Bertrand's initiative, therefore, a Franco-British-Polish conference met in Paris between January 7 and 9, 1939. There was "a useful exchange of technical ideas," but the Poles would contribute little regarding their technical knowledge because they were under instructions not to disclose their achievements unless the other participants did so. The Poles "formed the impression that the French and British had nothing to offer." [27] Here they were almost correct, for Denniston's team at Broadway still preferred the paper-and-pencil approach to the problem and rejected the proposition that a machine invented by man could best be defeated by another machine invented by man.

However, under the emergency of looming war, they were coming to accept the notion that machines would probably be necessary. Contacts had been made with a number of Cambridge men, notably Alan Mathison Turing, a pure mathematician of King's College, Cambridge, who had recently published a paper of fundamental interest to cryptologists, "On Computable Numbers," the philosophy of which was that a sonnet created by a machine could best be understood by a machine.

The second man of importance, C. E. Wynn-Williams, a Cambridge physicist, had devised a machine that would count electron particles at very high speeds. In theory and practice the Wynn-Williams machine did much the same work as the Polish bomba, but at far greater speeds—speeds sufficient to break into the more advanced Enigma procedures that had defeated the Poles. Wynn-Williams's achievement appears to have been known to Rejewski and his colleagues, for in July Denniston and Bertrand received invitations to a further meeting with the Poles.

That meeting took place at Polish cryptanalytical headquarters in the Pyry Forest outside Warsaw on July 24–25, 1939. Present were Denniston and Arthur Dillwyn Knox, classical scholar and GC&CS's chief cryptographer. At the meeting the Poles announced that they had again broken into Enigma, if only sporadically, and proposed full collaboration in exploiting the breach. Their technical work was of interest to the British and French programs. Both Denniston and Bertrand eagerly accepted the Polish offer of a Polish-built copy of

Enigma and technical drawings of the latest bomba. The British, as always, revealed virtually nothing of their work or results and certainly not the fact that a contract had been placed for a bomba of their own design. Nor did they reveal that they had broken into some variants of Enigma, albeit only occasionally.

The Polish offer was accepted with enthusiasm, and so began what Peter Calvocoressi, an officer responsible for the circulation of Enigma decodes later, called such a degree of secrecy that it was "a phenomenon that may well be unparalleled in history." [28] The man who devised that security screen was Stewart Menzies. And if Menzies achieved nothing else during the coming war, he so secured the secret of the penetration of Enigma that, in the public world, at least, the secret was kept for thirty-seven years. Certain key elements of Enigma, indeed, remained a secret in perpetuity as late as 1987, despite the involvement of tens of thousands of people of several nationalities throughout the world. Never was a secret better kept for so long.

At the July meeting the representatives of the three powers agreed that the British should concentrate on devising the technology required to break Enigma totally, the French and the Poles on breaking the daily keys of the German army Enigma. Arrangements were made that the results of the two tasks should be exchanged between the French and British code-breaking headquarters; and the Poles proved to be as good as their word. As Sinclair ordered his secret services into a state of "preliminary stance for war" on August 1, 1939, the Poles delivered to Bertrand in Paris the two Polish-built copies of Enigma and two sets of technical papers on their bomba. In turn Bertrand delivered one set to Commander Dunderdale, the chief of the SIS division in Paris, for delivery to London. [29]

The bulky and heavy equipment was packed into the largest diplomatic bags that Dunderdale could find at the British embassy. The bag was sealed, and Dunderdale's *chef de cabinet*, "Uncle" Tom Greene, the owner of Greene's Whisky of Ulster, a large, rich man who worked for Dunderdale without pay, was appointed king's messenger to enable him to get the equipment through the various customs checkpoints without questions in order to maintain strictest secrecy. He was escorted by Archibald and Archibald, the two senior partners in a British firm of solicitors of that name long practicing in Paris and who also worked for Dunderdale for "the honour of the flag." Greene and the Archibalds set out for the Gare St. Lazare and the Golden Arrow boat train to London, accompanied by Dunderdale and Bertrand, who was present to pay his respects to "le Colonel Mingeese."

At Dover Customs and Immigration the British party followed in the wake of Sacha Guitry, the French playwright, and his wife, actress Yvonne Printemps, whose baggage seemed mountainous. On their way to London for a performance of Guitry's latest hit, *Pearls in the Crown*, Dunderdale arranged with customs that the Guitrys' baggage should act as camouflage for the diplomatic bags, lest there was anyone present who might be interested in such a large diplomatic consignment. To the gratitude of the Guitrys, who were neighbors of Dunderdale in Paris and heavily laden with dutiable goods such as Chanel No. 5 and cognac, the entire party was waved through control. The Golden Arrow then set out for Victoria Station, London, where Dunderdale and his group arrived toward the end of the rush hour on August 16, seventeen days before the outbreak of World War II.

Awaiting them was Menzies, who was embraced and kissed on both cheeks by Bertrand. And as Bertrand recorded admiringly, Menzies was *"en smoking, avec rosette de la Legion d'Honneur à la boutonniere,"* and, Bertrand exclaimed, *"accueil triomphal!"* [30]

5   THE VENLO INCIDENT

Although Menzies's agents warned leading members of Parliament as early as June 19, 1939, that a Nazi-Soviet pact might develop from Russo-German trade talks in Berlin and Moscow, on August 22 Menzies received one of the most smashing blows of his career. As a British mission to Moscow sought in halfhearted fashion to establish an alliance between England, France, and Russia, on that day Ribbentrop and the new Soviet foreign minister, Vyascheslav Molotov, signed a pact in which both powers undertook not to attack the other or support a third power against the other. In a secret protocol Hitler conceded to Stalin all Latvia and Poland up to the river Vistula as lying within "the Russian sphere of influence." In return, Stalin promised not only to refuse to assist Poland against German attack, but also to join in her dismemberment. England now had not one but two powerful enemies united, so it seemed, in a pact of steel that extended from the Rhine to Vladivostok. That nightmare of the English geopoliticians—the Mackinder Theory—had come to pass.*

Parliament was in a savage mood with the secret service when it convened in emergency session on August 24. Chamberlain felt compelled to offer his resignation, an offer that the king rejected, and as Harold Nicolson recorded, the House of Commons, unlike the ecstatic days before the outbreak of World War I, was in the "depths of gloom." Members "scarcely spoke to each other above a whisper, as if some close relation was dying upstairs." [31] In the lobby Menzies and his colleagues faced their most severe criticism, although their failure to predict the imminence of the pact, and therefore the inevitability of war, was in reality the culmination of the loss of the ability to read the Soviet diplomatic cipher in 1927 and of the severe cuts in government expenditure in 1931. As R. A. Butler, the Foreign Office representative to Parliament, reported to Cadogan on August 25, "In the Commons last night everyone was asking me what 'our intelligence was up to.' "

Much the same question was presented to the Foreign Office by every government department in London affected by the treaty, and Laurence Collier, head of the northern section, presented a paper entitled "German-Soviet Intrigue," in which he stated the predicament of the intelligence authorities in piquant terms: "In general, we find ourselves, when attempting to assess the value of these secret reports, somewhat in the position of the Captain of the Forty Thieves when, having put a chalk mark on Ali Baba's door, he found that Morgiana had put similar marks on all the doors in the street and had no indication to show which mark was the true one." [32]

Yet the criticism of Sinclair and Menzies in this affair was not wholly justified, for as Butler advised Cadogan on September 5, he understood that "the outline terms" of the Nazi-Soviet Pact "were known to our intelligence, and reached this office." But it appeared that Sinclair did not give sufficient weight to the report when he presented it to the Foreign Office.

*Sir Halford Mackinder (1861–1947), an Oxford man who became director of the London School of Economics and a member of Parliament in 1904, wrote *Democratic Ideals and Reality.* Propounding the view that Eurasia was the historical and geographical pivot or "heartland" of the world, Mackinder held also that the man who controlled Russo-Germany would also come to control the world. He argued that German industry combined with Russian manpower would create a world-invincible force. While the Mackinder Theory received little attention in Great Britain and the United States before World War II, it was adopted by Hitler's geopolitical adviser, Kaul Haushofer, and became the basis of the theory of Nazi geopolitics.

In that situation, the secret services went to war stations through-out the world. In the expectation that Westminster would be attacked and devastated immediately after the declaration of war, "Captain Ridley's Hunting Party"—code name for the GC&CS headquarters group—left Broadway in three motor coaches and proceeded up to Marble Arch and the A1 road to the north. The coaches were then driven about forty miles to a village on the road called Heath and Reach. There they had turned off and entered the lovely rolling countryside of Buckinghamshire. Outside the railway town of Bletchley, they entered the drive of a large estate. At the center stood the main house, a mass of imitation Victorian-Gothic-Tudor brick and timber called Bletchley Park, built originally for the peace and comfort of a boot and shoe manufacturer. "Captain Ridley's Hunting Party" had arrived at its war station and began work on the Polish consignment in "The Laboratory," a small cottage adjoining the stables.

Menzies, too, went to his war station, a country house in its own grounds outside Markyate, a large village on the A1 highway about thirty miles from Broadway. The house was said to be haunted by the ghost of Lady Jane Grey, the sixteen-year-old queen of England who ruled for only nine days, and who was later beheaded for high treason. But although the house was comfortably appointed and at-tractive, Menzies soon felt the languor of Bedfordshire and stayed at Markyate no longer than Lady Jane was queen. Feeling isolated and remote from the seat of power, and in any case unable to advise and control at a time when Sinclair plainly would not live much longer, he returned to Broadway and White's and his conspiracy against Hitler.

By the end of August war was evidently close. Three groups of Hitler's armies had massed on the Polish frontier as news of trouble in the German army and the General Staff flooded into Broadway, reports that reflected, as was the case in England, a marked lack of enthusiasm for war. Perhaps to check these reports, on August 27 Sinclair asked Cadogan whether the aircraft taking Sir Neville Henderson back to his post as ambassador in Berlin might also take "a spy." Cadogan and Henderson agreed, and the man deputed for the mission was Menzies's close friend, David Boyle, a shadowy character whose curriculum vitae read like that of an aristocratic odd-job man, but a proficient one.*

---

*Since 1920, when we last saw Boyle attempting to kidnap the future president of Eire, Eamon de Valera, in New York, Boyle was aide-de-camp to the Prince of Wales on his state visit to Canada. He escaped the November murders in Dublin by a whisker and at one time

Traveling in a Secret Intelligence Service aircraft and posing as a king's messenger, Boyle arrived in Berlin that same day. According to Robert Cecil, the reason for his mission at the eleventh hour was "the vain hope of enticing Goering to London" to avoid war. On his arrival in Berlin, Boyle almost certainly made contact with Kurt Jahnke, chief of the Jahnkeburo, Ribbentrop's private intelligence service, and originally a U.S. border patrolman and then a coffin maker, in which latter trade he made a great fortune out of the estates of dead Chinese in the United States who wished to be shipped home and buried with their ancestors.

A spy in World War I, Jahnke was a person of influence in Hitler's Germany, while at the same time he may have been one of Dansey's most important informants. As Brigadeführer SS Walter Schellenberg, head of the foreign counterespionage section of the Sicherheitsdienst, recounted under SIS interrogation after the war, Jahnke claimed to have "used every conceivable means to bring an English intelligence man to Hitler through Hess and Himmler." [33] Jahnke claimed also that he failed because Ribbentrop, leader of the prowar faction in the Nazi party, objected. And as Schellenberg also recorded

---

or another was a political and social agent for Cunard; a correspondent for the *Morning Post* in Shanghai and Danzig; director of the Anchor Shipping Line; officer of the Imperial Chinese Customs Service; tea planter in Ceylon, clerk to shipping agents at Ceylon; employee of the Bombay Burmah Timber Corporation and then with the Burmah Oil Company. He became, too, political officer to the Anglo-Persian Oil Company; assistant district commissioner on the Gold Coast; and he also earned his living by commissions obtained through the renting of grouse shooting in Scotland to Americans like Bernard Baruch, establishing associations that were useful to Menzies later on. He was also a king's messenger, one of the fraternity that carried the royal and secret mail between capitals.

All this was consistent with the record of a secret service "member," except in one respect. While in Burma he was offered, and accepted, the post of gold staff officer to the earl marshal of England and officiated at the coronation of George V. So efficient was he in this work that later he officiated at the coronations of George VI and Elizabeth II, while at the same time, when in London, he was chief of Section "N" of SIS, a supersecret organization that intercepted foreign diplomatic mail. Once intercepted, the mail was opened in a fashion calculated to escape detection by a team of thirty seamstresses employed for that purpose by SIS on behalf of the Foreign Office. These seamstresses occupied a house in Palmer Street, Victoria, close to Broadway, and when the mail had been opened, read, and copied it was returned to the envelope, the envelope was returned to the diplomatic bag, and the diplomatic bag was returned to its courier, all in a fashion calculated not to alarm the recipient. When the courier awoke from a passionate embrace, or alcoholic or drugged slumber, or a combination of all three, he found his bag at his side, apparently intact. This was a work requiring skill, and Boyle had that skill, it seems, in ample degree, for throughout their careers Boyle was never too far from Stewart Menzies.

under interrogation, Jahnke was suspected of being a British spy by the chief of the Gestapo, Mueller, who wanted to indict Jahnke for high treason, an indictment that was frustrated by Canaris.

Thus there were three different opinions about the reason for Boyle's journey. If any of them were correct, none prospered. But if Boyle failed to see Hitler, he did meet Otto Kiep, an informant who was until recently counselor at the German embassy in London. Boyle received an opinion on the political situation at the highest levels in Berlin; and when the Gestapo learned about the meeting, as they did much later, they hanged Kiep. By August 29 Boyle was back at Broadway, reporting what Cadogan called in his diary that day "interesting—and not unhopeful—items of news:" that the chief of the German General Staff, General Halder, intended to depose Hitler if he ordered the army groups on the Polish frontier to march.

Once again, however, that satanical, mystical genius, Hitler, outwitted and faced down his military advisers. The invasion of Poland began at 5:30 A.M. on September 1, 1939. The Franco-British governments gave Hitler an ultimatum: remove his troops from Poland, or war would follow. For two days Chamberlain wavered in the hope that through secret mediation Britain would achieve a German withdrawal and thus gain more time. But at length, and in Parliament, Leopold S. Amery, a Tory politician, faced Chamberlain and called upon him to "speak for England." Chamberlain then sent an ultimatum to Hitler: Get out of Poland, or war would ensue immediately. Hitler, confident that Chamberlain would not honor the ultimatum, ignored it.

At ten minutes past eleven o'clock on Sunday, September 3, 1939, Chamberlain resorted to what he called "the awful arbitrament of war." In a radio broadcast, he announced that a state of war now existed between the British Empire and the German Reich. Immediately Sinclair sent out the two-word war telegram: "Total Germany." World War II had begun. Winston Churchill was brought into the Cabinet as first lord of the Admiralty, and on that same day Chamberlain, without advising the Cabinet, agreed that Menzies's operation against Hitler should become "detailed." [34]

Some notion of what Chamberlain really intended—he did not intend to fight the Germans, but to overthrow Hitler and make peace with the German General Staff—was outlined by Sir Arthur Rucker, Chamberlain's principal private secretary, six weeks after the outbreak of war in a conversation with another of Chamberlain's private secretaries, John Colville. As Colville recorded in his diary:

Arthur Rucker says he thinks Communism is now the great danger, greater even than Nazi Germany. All the independent states of Europe are anti-Russian, but Communism is a plague that does not stop at national boundaries, and with the advance of the Soviet into Poland the states of Eastern Europe will find their powers of resistance to Communism very much weakened. It is thus vital that we should play our hand very carefully with Russia, and not destroy the possibility of uniting, if necessary, with a new German Government against the common danger. What is needed is a moderate conservative reaction in Germany: the overthrow of the present regime by the army chiefs.[35]

Obedient to their orders, Stevens, the passport control officer, and Best, of Dansey's "Z" organization, made their presence known to each other at The Hague. Then they proceeded under Menzies's direction to make contact through intermediaries with persons whom, they believed, had contact with the Beck-Goerdeler-Canaris group. As Menzies believed, accurately, that group intended to use units of the German army loyal to the conspiracy to overthrow Hitler, should the Führer order an offensive in the West, one code-named Case Yellow.

The original contact with "the German opposition" was made by Stevens through a certain Dr. Fischer, a politician in the Weimar government who had once been recruited by Dansey as a spy and then gone into exile in Paris when Hitler came to power. What Menzies did not know was that just before the outbreak of war, in an effort to reinsure his future against the possibility of a Nazi victory, Fischer had offered his services as a double agent working in the German interest to the Sicherheitsdienst, the Nazi party's intelligence service.

With Best's emergence as a British secret agent, Stevens insisted upon his seniority and controlled all communications with Menzies, with the result that Best's views about the reliability of Fischer were not relayed to Broadway. Personal relations between the two men were poor when at the end of September or the beginning of October Fischer reported to Stevens that he had made contact with "the German opposition," and that the German conspirators would send representatives to a village on the Dutch border. In fact, Fischer had informed the Sicherheitsdienst of the existence of Chamberlain's separate policy, and the men that Stevens and Best were to meet in the village were officers of the Nazi party secret service. Their objective was not a truce, but the identities of the German plotters, the names of whom had *not* been given by Menzies to either Best or Stevens or anyone else.

According to Best, Stevens discussed the contact with Menzies by coded telegram and telephone, and Menzies stated that "London was extremely keen about this business and had instructed that the matter should be prosecuted with the utmost vigour." In Menzies's mind, as he was to state after the war, there was enough evidence of the existence of a conspiracy against Hitler to warrant a meeting between the Germans and Best and Stevens. Arrangements were made by Menzies on or about October 11, at the request of Stevens, in which the preamble to the BBC's newscast to Germany—*"Hier Ist London"*—would be broadcast *twice* on a certain date. That was the signal that the British government would send agents to a village on the Dutch-German frontier on October 17.

At the agreed-upon hour and place, a single German appeared and announced that General von Wietersheim was prepared to meet the British representatives on October 20, at which time it was hoped that the British would be in a position to suggest terms for an armistice between the Allies and "a new Germany." That information was relayed to Menzies by Stevens, and a check with the London indexes confirmed the existence of a German general called Gustav von Wietersheim. Although not known as a dissident, Wietersheim was known to command the Fourteenth Panzer Corps in Poland. Menzies, the SIS expert on the German army and its politics, accepted Wietersheim's name as credible for the same reason he accepted the credibility of the other names: They were all *offiziers* of the old army of 1914–1918 who had remained with the Reichswehr after the Versailles Treaty and who despised Hitler and the Nazi party. As a result, according to Best, Stevens received a telegram from Menzies "regarding terms which would be considered acceptable."

Armed with these demands, Best, Stevens, a Dutch intelligence agent named Dirk Klop, and Fischer drove to Dinxperloo on October 20, where they met two intermediaries who gave their names as "Colonel Seydlitz and Colonel Grosch." Fischer warranted that both "Seydlitz" and "Grosch" were known to him as bona fide resistance members, when of course both were Sicherheitsdienst reconnaissance agents. Best and Stevens agreed to talk to the Germans, although Best was reluctant and suspicious. The German representatives had come, it was explained, to "spy out the land" for General von Wietersheim. Best then took the entire party to Arnhem, where a meeting was held at the house of a cousin, a certain Bigleveld. There, one of the German officers asked what terms Britain would demand in return for an armistice. Best replied in four words: "*Status quo* prior Munich." In other words, Chamberlain was prepared to end World War II between Germany and England only forty-one days after it had started. Then, according to the internal Sicherheitsdienst account of events, the British agents stated that the Chamberlain government intended to develop "a European League of States under the leadership of England and with a front against the progressive bolshevism."*

For their part, the German representatives announced the German army would make Hitler a prisoner and then establish a new democratic government formed with Hitler as titular head. They explained that Hitler's presence would be necessary because without him the new government would receive no popular support. But the true power of the German Reich would be in the hands of the German General Staff, of which von Wietersheim was an important member. With the staff firmly in the saddle, Hitler, too, would be liquidated.

Wietersheim required an assurance that neither the British nor the French would attack Germany while she dealt with her internal problems. Could Best give that assurance? Best replied in his excellent German that he had had no instructions from his principals, but he would consult and return at a later date. It was arranged that Wietersheim would personally attend the next meeting, which should be held at The Hague with Best undertaking to arrange safe passage across the frontier and transport to and from The Hague. Both Germans gave the Roman salute and then departed.

Afterward, Best claimed, he advised Menzies of his renewed unease, presumably because the men he had met were not officers and gentlemen but thugs, and that he had come to the "conclusion that they were Nazis and probably officers in the SS." There is some evidence that Best's suspicions were circulated by Menzies. Cadogan, who bore day-to-day political responsibility for the operation, noted in his diary on October 23: "[Sinclair] has got report on interview with his German General friends. I think they are Hitler agents." Menzies seems to have shared these suspicions, for he is said to have warned Stevens not to go too close to the frontier at the next meeting with the Germans.

---

*That statement would seem improbable were it not for Cadogan's diaries. These show that on November 13, 1939, Cadogan received such a proposal from the foreign secretary, Halifax, and Sir Orme Sargent, a colleague at the Foreign Office. What Halifax and Sargent proposed was "taking over the anti-Comintern Pact" formed earlier by Germany against Russia and "thereby roping in Italy, Japan, and Spain" against Hitler. Cadogan found the idea "attractive" and passed it to Sir Percy Lorraine, British ambassador in Rome, for development.

As for the question of the terms, as Cadogan recorded, in his diary the next day, October 24: "'C's' Germans have put 2 questions, and I discussed with H[alifax] answer to give them, and subsequently drafted it." He then "showed H my draft reply to Germans, which he approved," and they both "went over to No. 10 with it at 6.30. [Chamberlain] approved generally, with verbal alterations." The instructions were then relayed by Menzies to Best and Stephens at The Hague for presentation at the next meeting with the "German opposition" on October 30 at The Hague.

Best appears to have observed Menzies's warnings, for on that day he did not go to the frontier himself. Nor did Stevens. They sent a Dutch intelligence agent, Dirk Klop, the representative of the Dutch intelligence master Oorschot. On that day, three Germans arrived at the frontier and were driven by Klop to Best's business offices at Amsterdam. For the third time General von Wietersheim was not present. One of the Germans, a certain "Schaemmel," was really Walter Schellenberg, then chief of the foreign counterespionage branch of the Sicherheitsdienst. Schaemmel's colleague, "Martini," was Professor Max de Crinis, a Berlin psychologist and friend of Schellenberg. The third man was "Grosch," who had been at the Arnhem meeting. The Germans explained that Wietersheim was unable to attend because he had been called to a conference at Hitler's headquarters, and he had deputed Schaemmel to act as his representative. Best told later how "Schaemmel spoke with a certain authority and gave a clear picture of the plans which had been formed to take over the power from the Nazi Party." Best also recounted:

A protocol was drawn up of the proposals which the Germans put forward as forming a basis for peace negotiations. This included the evacuation of Czecho Slovakia [sic] and Poland, the holding of plebiscites in Austria, the Sudeten, and Danzig, and a request for reconsideration of the German colonial question. Jews to be placed in equal position with other Germans and disbandment of Nazi quasi military formations. It was stated that at a General Staff Meeting Hitler would be put under arrest whilst at the same time all government offices would be occupied by the army and all Nazi leaders arrested.

The Germans then wanted to know whether "after the revolution had been effected, representatives of the British and French governments would be prepared to come to Holland to arrange terms for an armistice and peace and, in that case, who in Germany would be considered an acceptable person to conduct these negotiations; whether Goering or some member of the ex-royal families."

This was a clear intention by "Schaemmel" to obtain the names of those Germans who were acceptable to the British government, and, scenting that more lay behind the question than was apparent, neither Stevens nor Best appear to have given any information other than that the Foreign Office was at that moment deciding whom they would accept as German representative. With that evasion, Best gave the Germans "a good dinner at his house"—Schellenberg recounted in his memoirs that the oysters served were the best he could recall—and afterward the Germans slept at the house of a member of the British service. Next morning Stevens gave them a two-way wireless set and arranged a code and a radio plan, and Schellenberg and his companions then returned to Germany. Stevens sent a long cable giving details of the protocol that had been drawn up and also telephoned Menzies, recounting what had occurred in what Best called "far more enthusiastic terms than I felt the situation warranted." [36]

On October 31, Menzies saw Cadogan, bringing with him the protocol. Having read that document, Cadogan's attitude toward "the German opposition" became slightly more favorable. "There's *something* going on in Germany," he wrote in his diary that day. "That's about all one can say." The documents were then sent to Chamberlain at 10 Downing Street, and on November 1, for the first time, Chamberlain informed the War Cabinet of the negotiations. The news that British agents had been negotiating with the enemy in time of war astounded the Cabinet, particularly Churchill, whom Chamberlain had brought into his Cabinet as first lord of the Admiralty. As Cadogan wrote in his diary after the meeting: "Cabinet were told of our contact with Generals and didn't like it. Told H[alifax] that first impact was bound to be unfavourable and rouse suspicion." But as Cadogan added, Halifax "mustn't listen too much to Winston on the subject of 'beating Germany.'" What they must do—and what in fact they were doing—was to "try every means of helping G[ermany] to beat herself."

Against that background Sinclair died on November 4 and Menzies was appointed acting "C." The Cabinet then began to review Menzies's fitness for the post of "C." Menzies's principal protagonist within the Cabinet was Lord Hankey, himself an officer of naval intelligence before and during World War I, secretary of the Committee of Imperial Defence between the wars and now Chamberlain's minister-without-portfolio in charge of the secret and special services.

As Hankey pointed out, Menzies had been a secret service officer for almost a quarter of a century, he was not yet fifty, he had held the highest posts. His fitness reports were uniformly excellent. Hankey felt that when the prewar history was written it would show that Menzies was the officer largely responsible for having kept the Cabinet fully informed on European political and military matters. Menzies's private life was unexceptional. He was fit. He was the only man who knew all there was to know about the secret service and its ramifications. He possessed a very wide range of connections throughout British and foreign society and particularly good connections with the French and Belgian intelligence services. Sinclair himself had nominated Menzies to the succession.

Contrary to the suggestions that Menzies was anti-American, he had performed important services that had almost led to an alliance with the Americans at the end of World War I. He was liked and respected everywhere. Above all he was discreet and dependable. Yet Menzies's suitability remained challenged by Churchill, who wanted a naval officer, Admiral Godfrey, for the post. And it was as the debate and inquiry extended over a period of twenty-six days that there occurred one of those devastating events that pockmarked Menzies's career from time to time.

On November 8 Hitler arrived in Munich, where he had two engagements. The first was to visit the Honorable Unity Valkyrie Mitford, a daughter of Lord Redesdale, member of a court-Eton-Life Guards family. Reputed to have been Hitler's paramour, Miss Mitford was an ardent Nazi and one who was so distressed by the outbreak of war between England and Germany that, according to a U.S. diplomatic report, she had attempted suicide. She was now in the hospital recovering from her attempt, and Hitler called on her to cheer her up.

Hitler's second engagement was at the Burgerbraukeller in Munich, a beer hall where old Nazis met with Hitler each year to commemorate the Führer's attempt at revolution in Munich in 1923. Hitler arrived at the beer hall at about 8:00 P.M. and began his speech ten minutes later. The speech ended at 8:45 P.M., when, suddenly and unexpectedly, he left the cellar and the city in the company of Rudolf Hess. Twenty minutes later a violent explosion destroyed the cellar and killed and injured a large number of party faithfuls. The city, plunged into darkness, was placed under martial law. It was thought locally that an attempt at a putsch was taking place.

Hitler traveled through the night aboard his private train, reaching Berlin at 4:00 A.M. About the same time, the official German spokesman announced that there had been an attempt to kill Hitler and voiced the "profound gratitude of the German people to the Almighty for watching over the Führer's safety." The spokesman then declared, "The instigators, the financial backers, the people who are capable of so infamous, so execrable an idea, are the same ones who have always employed assassination in politics! They are the agents of the [British] Secret Service! And behind them stand the British war agitators and their criminal satellites, the Jews!" [37]

Later that same day the German spokesman again tried to fix responsibility for the attempt, this time in equal measure, on Broadway and world Jewry and called attention to the demand of an American Jew, Max Rosenberg, that the U.S. government should release fourteen gangsters from prison on the condition they murder Hitler. [45] It is generally conceded, however, that neither Menzies nor Dansey had anything to do with the bomb, and that it was set by the Sicherheitsdienst to give the German government the public excuse it felt it needed to justify large-scale action against the Jews, the Dutch, the Belgians, and the Danes, to say nothing of the SIS. The Sicherheitsdienst also wished to create a wave of public support for Hitler that, unlike the demonstrations at the outbreak of World War I for the kaiser, were absent when the news was received in Berlin that England had declared war on Germany. That same night, therefore, Schellenberg, at Frankfurt preparing for his next meeting with Best and Stevens, received a telephone call from Himmler.

Schellenberg was to kidnap the two Britons, who were responsible for the attempt on Hitler's life, and bring them to Berlin for interrogation and trial. As Best and Stevens, and the Dutch secret service officer, approached the Cafe Bacchus near the border crossing at Venlo on November 9, they were seized by an armed group of men. Klop managed to resist, but in the gunplay he was mortally wounded. Best and Stevens were bundled into a car, which then rushed them across the frontier to the headquarters of the Gestapo at Dusseldorf and then on to Berlin.

On November 22 Heinrich Himmler, chief of the German security and intelligence services, announced that a Dutchman resident in Munich, a carpenter and bomb expert named Georg Elser, had been arrested while trying to cross from Germany into Switzerland and had confessed to making and planting the bomb at the instructions of the British secret service in Switzerland—Dansey's base. Himmler then claimed publicly that SIS planning for Hitler's assassination had begun "in September or October 1938" and that "the employer and financial backer of this undertaking was the British Intelligence Service."

Meanwhile, Best and Stevens were manacled and under interrogation at the headquarters of the Gestapo and the Sicherheitsdienst on the Prinz Albrechtstrasse, Berlin. Despite a standing order within Broadway that captured agents were required to give only their names and addresses, and details of their cover businesses, both men collaborated with their captors. The extent to which they collaborated did not become known until early 1940, so that their revelations could have played no part in the Cabinet's deliberations regarding Menzies's appointment. Later, however, it became evident that Stevens must have collaborated when Himmler made a public statement naming the higher executives at Broadway, including Menzies, and the names and functions of all sections of SIS. Only Stevens, not Best, possessed that information.

Furthermore, it became evident that Stevens must have revealed the names of all SIS station chiefs in western and central Europe. Again only Stevens possessed that information. The extent to which Best revealed the structure and mission of "Z" is not clear, although German documents captured later did reveal an extensive German knowledge of the activities and functions of Section Z. That information, however, did not necessarily come from Best, who, in any case, claimed later to have tried to deflect German interest in his affiliations and associations by prolonged and revealing discussions about the sexual activities of certain members of the British service. However, both men certainly compromised the neutrality of Belgium and Holland, for a statement was prepared for Himmler with the purpose of providing a casus belli against those two countries, and that statement revealed the names of all secret service agents, Dutch, Belgian, French, and British, operating from Western Europe against Germany. The statement was used by Himmler as justification when, in May 1940, the German army invaded Belgium and Holland.

In general, therefore, the damage to Menzies's espionage networks was confined to those operated by Best and Stevens. There was no basis for statements that SIS lost *all* its secret agents through Venlo. As will be seen, Menzies's agents inside Germany still operated as late as April 1940. Otherwise, at the end of the war it was discovered that the Germans had managed to obtain a copy of the political directive sent by Broadway to all chiefs of staff outlining British clandestine policy. That was thought to have been given to the Sicherheitsdienst by Stevens, for Best was not made privy to the directive. However, a search of Stevens's archives showed that his copy of the directive was in his safe. In other words, it was not on his person when he went to Venlo. That discovery raised the specter at Broadway that another senior officer of SIS was a traitor.

On November 22 the German Ministry of Propaganda announced that Best and Stevens had organized a plot against the life of Hitler and were now under arrest in Germany and would be brought to public trial for many offenses under the Third Reich's code of laws. These charges included murder and espionage, both of which were capital offenses, and the press and radio then began to speak of the British secret service's "time-honored method of assassination," denounced British "brutality and lack of scruple," and alleged that among the many others who had been killed by the service for opposing British ambitions were "Tsar Nicholas II, Archduke Franz Ferdinand, Jean Jaures, T. E. Lawrence, King Alexander of Yugoslavia, and Louis Barthou." [47] In documents captured at the end of the war, there was evidence that the Dutch and Belgian intelligence services had collaborated with what Himmler called "the obscure, asocial, and even homosexual 'Intelligence Service.' " [38]

Under these unpromising circumstances, the Cabinet had been meeting at 10 Downing Street to decide who should be chief of that service. This question proved laborious, for such was the importance and desirability of the post that all manner of names were considered. With the liquidation of Section Z, Dansey appeared in London from Switzerland immediately after the Munich and Venlo incidents to contest Menzies's appointment as "C." But he was never seriously considered, for apart from all else he was beyond retirement age. Dansey was just into his sixty-third year, while Menzies was yet to reach his fiftieth birthday.

When he was rejected, Dansey then placed such influence as he possessed behind Menzies, in the hope that he might at least be appointed as chief of the espionage services. At length, the choice came down to two men: Menzies and Admiral Godfrey, Churchill's nominee and the director of naval intelligence. On November 19 there was what Cadogan called "a tiresome" letter from Churchill about the succession; and as Cadogan complained, Churchill "ought to have enough of his own to do without butting into other people's business."

Churchill tried to prevent Menzies's appointment on a number of grounds. Menzies was a soldier, whereas until now the post had been held by sailors. Churchill felt that sailors had a sense of British imperial strategy and larger horizons than soldiers. Also, Churchill argued, Menzies was too closely identified with the military establishment, which he dismissed scornfully as men "whose nerves were much stronger than their imagination." The arrest of General Franklin Bell was remembered, along with the suspicion that Menzies might be anti-American. Churchill believed that sooner or later the United States would enter the war, and that the post would then require someone who could work in harmony with them. There was also some question about Menzies's loyalties. He had been too closely associated with Chamberlain and his policies for Churchill's taste. Had Menzies not been party to a covert policy that, without the Cabinet's knowledge, had been in existence since March 1938? And had not Menzies's conduct of that operation proven to be disastrous?

Menzies was not without support, however. At least two other powerful members of the Cabinet, Sir Archibald Sinclair (air minister) and Captain Euan Wallace (transport minister) spoke of Menzies's devotion to duty, his long experience, his skill and intelligence. These proved important sources of support. Sinclair was about to lay down the framework for that mighty force, Bomber Command. Wallace had helped to land a British army in France without a man or a gun going astray. The War Office establishment of which Churchill stood in such dislike was also influential, and it supported Menzies. Another powerful lobby backed Menzies, his own, that of the old Etonians, who formed what one of them was to call "an inner fraternity" in the government. All but one of the leading figures on the foreign affairs side of the government were old Etonians, although Cadogan was not prepared to elevate Menzies to the high post of "C" simply because he had been at Eton.

As the debate proceeded, Cadogan stated in his diary, he was "*not* satisfied" that Menzies was the right man to succeed. Nor did Cadogan readily change his opinion over the coming eighteen months, largely because he was not sure that Menzies would be "strong enough" (and by that he meant tough enough) for the job. But when Menzies's appointment had still not been confirmed or rejected by November 28, Cadogan, upon receiving a "tiresome letter from Menzies," expressed his sympathy for him and declared and that he would "try to binge up H[alifax] to get decision." Cadogan acknowledged Menzies was "in a difficult position" and declared that it was "silly of everyone to go on funking Winston." Halifax acted immediately. As Cadogan recorded of the events of a Cabinet on November 28, Halifax "played his hand well and won the trick." Menzies was confirmed as "C."

His appointment was not announced in any newspaper, not even the *London Gazette*, the official newspaper of the state. *The Times* breathed not a word. Neither did any gossip columnists make any hint. Yet from the start his tenure was not quite secure. When Halifax called Stewart to the Foreign Office to announce his confirmation and to congratulate him, Halifax was not quite reassuring. As Halifax remarked to the new "C," perhaps with Venlo in mind, there remained a "possible need of reviewing [SIS] organization."

In keeping with tradition, "C" went to Buckingham Palace for an audience with King George VI. Menzies related later that he half expected to receive a key from the sovereign that had been given first to Mr. Secretary Walsingham, chief of the secret service in the days of Elizabeth I. The purpose of the key had been to enable Walsingham to enter the private apartments of the queen without having to pass through the gossipy, spy-ridden court gathered outside. But if such a key still existed, the king did not give it to the new "C," although Menzies did receive a small plaque called "the Ivory." Its distribution was confined to the king's principal ministers and servants, and it gave the bearer the right to enter and leave Buckingham Palace through the Horse Guards entrance to St. James's Park during times of siege, riot, and war.

According to "C," the king showed interest mainly in the health of the old kaiser, Wilhelm II of Germany, who was in exile in Holland. During the brief audience, the king congratulated "C" on his appointment, and after a few pleasantries "C" left the audience. He had now become what the Russians believed, as they said in 1933, was "the power behind the throne." That was an exaggeration, but nonetheless it contained elements of truth. [39]

As for the Chamberlain conspiracy, the Sicherheitsdienst themselves closed down the operation with a personal, derisive message for Menzies. On New Year's Eve of 1939, Menzies received a signal from OM4, the call sign of the wireless set given to "Schaemmel" by Stevens during the meeting with Schellenberg at Best's offices just before the Venlo incident. As the message announced:

Negotiations for any length of time with conceited and silly people are tedious. You will understand, therefore, that we are giving up. You are hereby given a hearty farewell by your affectionate German Opposition.

(s) The Gestapo [40]

Four

The Battle of Britain
1940

1 "A CURIOUS, ARTIFICIAL VIVARIUM"

Stewart Menzies was on the eve of his fiftieth birthday when he became "C" and took over the chief's suite on the fourth floor of 54 Broadway, offices rising eight tiers above the Westminster skyline out of a narrow and crooked street just off Parliament Square. From the window to the right of his desk, he could look upon the busty mermaids of Jacob Epstein's sculptures "Night" and "Day," on the facade of the headquarters of the London Passenger Transport Board on the other side of Broadway. The headquarters of the British secret service were probably located on or near the site of the house where John Milton (1608–1674), the poet and Latin secretary for foreign affairs in Oliver Cromwell's government, began *Paradise Lost*, the greatest epic poem in the English language.

"C's" offices were comfortably furnished in the style of Edwardian government mandarins. On one of the walls was a painting of King

Edward VII at Balmoral, with his gundogs sniffing in the heather. On another wall was a painting of his favorite black, Amber A1, which he had ridden at Ypres. On a third wall was a signed photograph of Admiral Sinclair, Menzies's predecessor and a man who was greatly loved inside Broadway. Indeed, there were portraits of Sinclair in almost every office, although there were none of Menzies, then or later—Sinclair was always more popular than Menzies ever became. The office was large; it had a coal fireplace with copper coal tongs and scuttle filled with little nuggets of coal so neat in appearance and free from dust that they looked as if they'd been selected by hand, which was quite likely. In front of the fireplace was a club fender with leather pads on which visitors could sit—they called them "bum-warmers" at White's.

Set in a wall near Menzies's office was a concealed door that led to a passage connecting Broadway with "C's" official residence at 21 Queen Anne's Gate, a handsome house of mellow brick built by a governor of the Bank of England. There was a row of such houses, and these were regarded as being one of the best—and the best preserved—of early-eighteenth-century domestic architecture in London. The passage ended at another semiconcealed door set in the drawing room of Queen Anne's Gate. With it "C"—as Menzies was always known within the secret service—had no need to go out into the street, to get wet, or to meet strangers or colleagues. He could come and go between his apartment and headquarters unobserved, which was important in "C's" trade. For his essential task—the main objective of his service—was to maintain a *secure* system by which the state secrets of foreign powers were obtained and then disseminated, again under *secure* conditions, to the administration. All other tasks entrusted to the secret service, while often more colorful, were secondary to these.

Difficult and dangerous as those tasks were, those encountered in the procuring and transmission of such intelligence increased in wartime, when the outcome of a battle, and sometimes even of the war itself, could be decided by intelligence. The need for secrecy became an even greater responsibility when the secrets of foreign but allied powers were being handled, for a single misadventure might wreck the alliance and would certainly destroy the reputation of the service. Above all other factors in "C's" trade, therefore, was the need to protect the source, whether British or foreign. In that trade, the man who succeeded had to be discreet, a word that by its definition required the man who held the post of "C" to be prudent, wise, circumspect, and of sound judgment. And it was that requirement that made "C" more than almost all others the most desirable target for attack from a hostile power. Since secret intelligence represented political power, it followed that the better the intelligence, the greater the power and esteem. It also followed that if "C" could be compromised or embarrassed, then under certain circumstances a national resource could become a national liability, even a danger to national security.

That "C" possessed the quality of discretion was abundantly plain. But of itself discretion was useless without vigilance and an awareness that the danger of penetration or compromise was always present, day and night, on duty or off. For this reason, "C" expended much resource on a counterespionage service. Such an awareness accounts also for his marked reluctance to improve the system he had inherited, a system proved by the centuries. Why should it be changed? It had worked well in the past; why should it not continue to do so in the future? As he argued, any weakness lay not in the system, but in the character of the men it employed. If it was true that bad men made good systems bad, then it was also true that good men made bad systems good. The potential weakness lay not in the system, therefore, but in the men coming to it.

"C" insisted upon the maintenance of the traditional recruitment system. The best men for the British secret service were drawn from families he knew personally or were ex-officers of independent incomes recommended to him by a government department. Under Menzies's system, all officers of the service were, as they were in Cumming's and Sinclair's time, bound by the code of personal allegiance to the chief and by oath to defend the safety of the state. Only in the realm of the technical methods of acquiring intelligence—in technique—did he allow change. Those changes were far-reaching in their significance.

Since "C" was the chief, therefore, his personality and character were of fundamental importance in the formation of the character of the service. A secret service more than any other was, so it was said in the trade, the mirror image of the head of the service. At fifty "C" was fit, but not brisk or "military." He was, they said, calm, sly, wry, and waspish. The inner man within "C," the political and social man that few saw, was shaped by war and the currents of politics and society between 1890 and 1940. Behind the Regency elegance and style was a ruthless man, devious and subtle. Sir James Easton, who became a prospective successor, thought that if Philby had been detected as a Soviet spy at an early date, he would not have been shot or sent to prison. "C" would have posted him out of Broadway as a tutor at the Imperial Defence College or some such other moribund institution, then arranged that he be placed on permanent sabbatical and left to rot.

He could, however, be kind, considerate, and even generous. He was much admired in Whitehall for his care with public money, and Churchill declared later that one of "C's" virtues was that he ran the service on pennies. Even so, when Robert Cecil arrived from the Foreign Office as a personal assistant and found he could not live on his salary and was running into debt, "C" called him into his office and explained that he could do nothing about the salary, which was paid by the Foreign Office. He could, however, do something about the debt and wrote out a check in his ceremonial green ink for £500—a lot of money at that time—on Drummond's, an exquisite bank near Admiralty Arch. He then signed the check with his ritual "C" and told Cecil to present it immediately for cash. He did, the signature was honored as if it were that of Rothschild himself, and the matter of repayment was never mentioned.

In the management of his empire, "C" was personally assisted by a private office. He had two personal assistants, David Boyle, "C's" shadow and chief of Section N, and Peter Koch de Gooreynd, a close friend who was Menzies's "fixer." A member of a Belgian banking family, Koch was an amiable, charming, and discreet clubman in his late thirties. An Etonian, he had before the war followed a curious trade. Although he knew not a note of music, he had a great talent for making up the lyrics of popular songs in his head. He established a music publishing company to exploit these talents and those of others and had had several large successes, including "'Twas on the Isle of Capri That I Found Her" and "Silver Hair and Golden Eyes," which was sung by Richard Tauber, the Austrian tenor. Koch occupied an office close to Menzies, and they were boon companions at White's, where an etiquette evolved that they were not to be bothered when they were at the bar because it was understood they were " 'running the secret service, or something.' "

Also in Menzies's private office were three maiden ladies. There was the legendary Miss Kathleen Pettigrew, who had been secretary in turn to Cumming and Sinclair since 1921 and was the model for Miss Moneypenny, secretary to "M," James Bond's noiseless and secretive chief. Cecil found Miss Pettigrew to be a "formidable gray-haired lady with a square jaw of the battleship type," and all persons wishing to see "the Chief" had of necessity, at least until September 1942, to go through her. All Menzies's communications—during World War II Menzies sent out about eight thousand letters, mainly to Churchill, excluding the secret intelligence he distributed—went through her. Consequently she enjoyed great power. Assisting Miss Pettigrew were two other secretaries, Evelyn Jones, an attractive (and, some thought, beautiful) brunette, and Elaine Miller, an expert and discreet typist. Together they guarded "C's" door, which was of double thickness, one of the layers being padded with quilted leather as soundproofing. The door had two lamps above it. When the red light was on, no one was allowed into "C's" office until it went out and the green light came on.

Under the private office came the two men who operated the espionage and counterespionage services. Colonel Valentine Patrick Terrel Vivian, deputy chief of the secret service (D/CSS), born 1886, educated at St. Paul's School (with General Sir Bernard Montgomery), son of Comley Vivian, the Victorian portrait painter. Often confused with another Valentine Vivian, of Eton, the Grenadiers, son-in-law of the earl of Portarlington, member of the king's corps of gentlemen-at-arms, "Vee Vee" Vivian was of less gilded stock. Married to a daughter of the canon of Lahore in British India, the father of two sons and one daughter, he had joined the Indian police in 1906 and the secret service in 1923, remaining until 1951.

Tall, willowy, languid, erudite, well tailored, "Vee Vee" Vivian wore a monocle. He believed himself to be "C's" deputy and successor, as his title suggested, a belief that produced endless complications. Under "C's" direction Vivian created a global and efficient counterespionage and security service, one that attracted a large component of Oxford and Cambridge men. Considering "C's" suspicion of the intelligentsia, Vivian's was a surprising recruitment policy, the more so since it was "C's" belief (given the totalitarian nature of the espionage services of England's two main enemies at that time, Germany and Russia) that counterespionage was a more likely way of obtaining intelligence than orthodox espionage.

The second appointment was that of Lieutenant Colonel Claude Dansey, "C's" colleague—and rival—in the National Preventive Intelligence Service in World War I. Dansey's title was assistant chief of the secret service (A/CSS), a title that, later, was changed to vice chief of the secret service (V/CSS). Gruff, bearlike, intricate, both Dansey and Vivian circled around "C" like cats around a hot stew as they sought the succession.

In turn, "C" disliked and distrusted Dansey, although acknowledging that he was probably the best espionage man in the world. Dansey distrusted university men and recruited few. Such evidence as there is suggests that Dansey was right and Vivian wrong, for at the inquest on the disaster that afflicted "C's" service, it was noted that the treason, when detected, was in the counterespionage services. In short order, Dansey succeeded in displacing Vivian in "C's" counsel and came to be regarded by eminences such as Cavendish-Bentinck, chairman of the Joint Intelligence Committee, as the most able spymaster in the Allied camp. With Menzies, Dansey was regarded by the French intelligence service as the most proficient and most dangerous intelligence officer in Europe. And if the Americans did not share that opinion, Dansey was nevertheless unsackable, even by "C," who, otherwise, was a law unto himself throughout Whitehall. And it was this rivalry between Vivian and Dansey that gave Broadway the peculiar flavor that Professor Trevor-Roper, a counterespionage man, had in mind when in an essay after the disaster he wrote:

Colonel Dansey and Colonel Vivian, *ACSS* (or was it *VCSS*?) and *DCSS*— what old frustrations they call to mind! All through the war these were the grandees of our Service, the Aaron and Hur who, from right and left (but with eyes steadily averted from each other), held up the labouring hands of our Moses, *CSS* or 'C,' Sir Stewart Menzies. How we used to sympathize with Menzies! [1]

And as Trevor-Roper added of that murderous situation on the fourth floor of Broadway, displaying the very iconoclasm that made "C" pause before employing university men:

When I looked coolly at the world in which I found myself, I sometimes thought that, if this was our intelligence system, we were doomed to defeat. Sometimes I encouraged myself by saying that such an organisation could not possibly survive, unchanged, the strain of war: it would have to be reformed. In fact I was wrong both times. We won the war; and S.I.S., at the end of it, remained totally unreformed.

If "C" was killed, or was compelled to resign, neither of which seemed improbable in early 1940, who would replace him? Would it be Dansey? Or Vivian? The truth was that neither would have moved behind "C's" desk. There was no deputy and no successor. "C" alone was chief, as were Cumming and Sinclair before him. "C" alone selected the candidates for the succession, and "C" alone knew their identities. He told nobody who they were, not even the candidates, and when the time came to advise Cadogan of the identity of his nominees, as it did in 1944, "C's" nominees were to come from *outside* the service. One was a Foreign Office man, the other an airman, and neither had been previously employed by the secret service or, indeed, knew very much about that organization. Both were bureaucrats, not operational figures. Yet if both men were led to believe that they might become "C," and if Menzies appeared to favor one against the other at various times, "C's" intention was clear: he played Vivian against Dansey lest they unite against him, as was always possible in a savage place like Broadway.

Although it was easy to underestimate "C," he was a hard, tough Scot, and behind the agreeable and sometimes even diffident exterior was a strong-willed man determined to avoid any palace revolutions at Broadway. It is significant that there were none at any time during his thirteen years as chief. And although there *was* a tendency to underestimate "C," it was almost always by men who had not looked closely into his lineage—and especially at the character, personality, and ruthlessness of "C's" grandfather, Graham Menzies, the man who cornered the Scotch whiskey industry and whom "C" so closely resembled.

As for "C's" function, in early 1940 he was responsible globally for espionage and counterespionage on foreign territory; sabotage and subversion operations against the enemy; code- and cipher-breaking operations against the secret communications of powers of interest to the British government; the security of British (and later Allied) communications and codes and ciphers; aerial photographic reconnaissance; the transmission of the government's most secret communications; double-agent operations on foreign territory; and advising the sovereign, the prime minister, the foreign secretary, and the chiefs of staff concerning enemy capabilities and intentions.

To carry out these operations, Menzies maintained "war stations" at Oslo, Copenhagen, Stockholm, Helsinki, Tallinn, Riga, The Hague, Brussels, Paris, Berne, Budapest, Belgrade, Sofia, Athens, Rome, Madrid, Lisbon, New York, Buenos Aires, Istanbul. Section Z organization was withdrawn into SIS, "Z" having been liquidated after the Venlo incident. In Arabia and the Balkans there was an organization called British Secret Agents Middle East. "C" had representatives at the Intelligence Department of the British Indian government, and in the arc of Asia between Singapore and Hong Kong and as far east as Manila and Honolulu there was an organization called British Secret Agents Far East.

Beyond British intelligence, there was the French service. This was as advanced as Broadway and shared "C's" conviction that the best intelligence would derive not from espionage, but from counterespionage. "C's" confidence in the French intelligence service was not misplaced. General Gauche, chief of the Second Bureau, was the best-informed man in Europe, including "C," on the strength and intentions of the German army. The morale and capability of both the collection and analytical branches of his service were superior to the intelligence services of all other powers. Gauche himself claimed later that "the Second Bureau was able, at any moment, to present to the Command the synthesis of German military strength." Gauche's ability had been tried and tested since before World War I. There was no reason to believe that his service was in any way infected by the defeatism that affected the French government of 1939.

His reports were transmitted across the Channel, and when tested against British intelligence, it was found to be sufficient for the requirements of the Allied supreme command. When Churchill lunched in Paris on August 29, 1939, with General Alphonse Georges, deputy supreme commander of the French army, Georges "produced all the figures of the French and German armies, and classified the divisions in quality. The result impressed me so much that for the first time I said: 'But you are the masters.' " Why, therefore, should "C" attempt to duplicate Gauche's work? [2]

Consequently, the key intelligence collection agency was GC&CS at Bletchley. It was to Bletchley that the main personnel and financial resources went. It was from Bletchley that the most was expected. At the outbreak of war GC&CS had ninety men and women. At the height of the war there were nine thousand, most of them university graduates. So many came from King's College, Cambridge, that Bletchley was dubbed "Little King's." Yet at the start Bletchley was "C's" greatest anxiety.

The chief there was Alastair G. Denniston, born in 1881, an exschoolmaster who had been to the Sorbonne and Bonn University. Denniston believed that, given Teuton efficiency, the Germans' two primary systems, Enigma and Geheimschreiber, could not be broken. He was defeated before he started, therefore, and remained defeated despite the belief of a principal assistant, Alan Mathison Turing, "father" of the modern computer, that a cipher written by machine could be deciphered by a machine. In turn, that defeatism produced cliques that were, broadly, divided between those who believed that the German ciphers could not be broken and those who believed, like Turing, that there was no such thing as the ultimate cipher.

Such, then, was "C's" world, one that Trevor-Roper found a "curious, artificial vivarium," on the eve of the great battle.

2   AN EXERCISE IN NIMBLE WITS

The wartime relationship between Churchill and "C" began auspiciously. The first lord of the Admiralty and "C" met at Admiralty House at 6:30 P.M. on December 11, 1939, to discuss sabotage operations against supplies of iron ore from the Swedish ore fields to the Ruhr steel mills. But instead of talking about ore, "C" found Churchill preoccupied with news that a German commerce raider, whose name was unknown but which was believed to be a battleship, was loose in the South Atlantic. It was to be "C's" first battle of wits after the Venlo debacle—and a chance at vindication. [3]

Between December 2 and 13, she had sunk the *Doric Star*, the *Tairoa*, and the *Streonshalh*, whose radio operator managed to get out a message that a German battleship's shells were striking *Streonshalh* before his vessel went down. Captain Henry H. Harwood, commanding a British cruiser squadron of four warships in the area of the attack, had radioed that in his estimation the German warship was making for a British shipping concentration off the river Plate. Harwood requested aerial reconnaissance of the concentration area from Buenos Aires and Montevideo and requested also that any intelligence of the possible arrival of a German warship off the Plate be sent directly to his flagship.

Since "C" had responsibility for aerial reconnaissance at that time, Churchill asked him to authorize his war station at Buenos Aires to arrange for reconnaissance and to request the agents there for any information about a German warship's movements. Churchill's instructions to "C" proved timely, as did the British warships he ordered into the South Atlantic to assist Harwood's squadron. One of the "hunting groups" from Cape Town raced for Pernambuco. This group consisted of the battleship *Renown*, the modern aircraft carrier *Ark Royal*, and an escort consisting of cruisers and destroyers. That force had reached Freetown and had begun to cross the Atlantic in the direction of Pernambuco when, on December 13, Harwood's squadron, which consisted of the cruisers *Exeter*, *Ajax*, and *Achilles*, found and engaged the German battleship *Admiral Graf von Spee* off the Plate estuary. In the ensuing sea battle, the German was hit more than fifty times. The battleship then made for Montevideo, to repair ship and transfer casualties to a hospital, arriving in the Uruguayan capital late that same night.

If the *Spee* was to be sunk with the *Renown* battle group still in distant waters, it became imperative that the *Spee*'s captain be refused all assistance at Montevideo and, at the same time, be led to believe the *Renown* was closer to the Plate than she really was. Spee's captain must *not* learn that *Exeter* was little more than a burning hulk, that *Ajax* could fight with only two of her four turrets, that only *Achilles* was undamaged, and that all the British warships' magazines were down to one-seventh of their normal outfit of munitions. Churchill proposed to trap the German captain, Hans Langsdorff, by suggesting that Harwood's force was still operational, that reinforcements were on their way from the Falkland Islands, and that a powerful battle group was closing the Plate. If Langsdorff knew the truth—that Harwood's force was almost *hors de combat*, that the reinforcements on their way from the Falklands consisted of only one cruiser, the *Cumberland*, and that the battle group was perhaps a week away from the Plate—then he would surely sink the British squadron or gain the high seas and make either for a home port or the Antarctic.

The key requirement for the deception—the first major tactical deception of the war—was the control and, if need be, the doctoring of information released by London to the world's press and radio, whose imagination had been captured by the engagement in the South Atlantic. With the outbreak of war, the Defence of the Realm Act, the Official Secrets Act, and the "D" Notice Committee, a joint government-press committee through which the press was controlled in what it could publish, had all combined to prevent any disclosure that a British army was crossing the Channel and taking up positions on the Franco-Belgian border. The result was that not a man, ship, or gun was lost. At the same time a German agent, Snow, had been arrested under article 18b of the Defence of the Realm Act, which annulled the validity of habeas corpus, and placed in a cell in Wandsworth Prison, London, with his wireless set.

Under the direction of SIS, that agent was put to work with his wireless. He contacted his controller near Hamburg and, behaving as if he had liberty of movement, began to transmit information that suggested only a major headquarters had gone to France while the main force was moving to various points on the east coast ready to repel an expected invasion by German forces launched from the German Baltic ports. With the BBC collaborating in the dissemination of news and talks that appeared to substantiate the fiction that the British army was still in England, Churchill, whose philosophy was that all war was a combination of plausible fiction and maximum force delivered against a narrow sector of the front, succeeded in his first great task of the war—the movement of the British army across the English Channel without the German enemy becoming aware. Churchill now directed that same tactic be employed to entrap Langsdorff and the *Graf Spee.*

Here Langsdorff was vulnerable. Having surveyed his ship, he believed that the *Spee* could not get back to a German port in her present state of seaworthiness, and that he had sufficient munitions left only for a brief engagement if he encountered British warships on his homeward passage. He decided against bolting for the Antarctic on the grounds that he had to seek repairs and treatment for his casualties at Montevideo. Langsdorff himself was predisposed to believe from the outset that, with a more numerous and still dangerous enemy squadron outside the Plate, he could not escape. That state of mind was enhanced with the weakened intelligence capability of his own information service, the Etappesdienst, which had been neutralized by the American FBI and the SIS and British naval intelligence in the Americas shortly before the outbreak of war.

Thus began one of the most interesting and most successful tactical deceptions of World War II, and one of the most humiliating for the Germans. And if "C" was an instrument of war diplomacy, it was also one of the most interesting examples of the exercise of that craft of the war. The Uruguayan government was ready to assist through the presence at Montevideo of a British minister, Sir Eugen Millington-Drake, who had developed a paternal relationship with the Uruguayan ruling generation.

An old Etonian friend of "C" (in 1907, both were members of "Pop" and of the Oppidan Wall Team, and between the wars their careers at the Foreign Office were heavily intertwined), Drake virtually ran the political and economic life of Uruguay and frustrated all German attempts to get a foothold in the country by reminding the Uruguayans of the side on which their bread was buttered—Uruguay was England's butcher. Equally, just before the outbreak of war the marquess of Willingdon, who had important assets in the country, visited Uruguay and was received as if he were a royal when he and the marchioness, who was a Brassey,* toured the cities and the hinterland to distribute gold, silver, and bronze medals to hundreds of the Uruguayan ruling generation who had rendered the Willingdons valuable services for half a century or more.

The first frigid breeze was felt the moment *Spee* stopped engines and Langsdorff went ashore at 2:00 A.M. on December 14 to call on the Uruguayan minister of marine (whom Willingdon had made a member of the Order of the British Empire during the state visit) to ask that he be permitted to remain for fifteen days on the grounds that his ship was not seaworthy. As Langsdorff made his representations, the eight British merchantmen in the port—*Spee's* intended victims—surrounded the *Spee* at the order of the British naval attaché, Henry McCall. All flew the Red Duster, and all had a gun in their stern. Their purpose was to watch *Spee* and report all activity in and around her. At the same time Fray Bentos pensioners made contact with every victualing, lighterage, ship-repair, and welding concern in the city, inviting them not to assist Langsdorff. None did.

The Foreign Office in London then sent instructions, at Churchill's request, to Millington-Drake that he should bring maximum pressure upon the Uruguayan government to refuse any requests by *Spee* for technical and shipyard assistance, to refuse *Spee* oil and victuals, and to prevent the Uruguayans from expelling *Spee* within forty-eight hours (as the law required), in order to enable the *Renown* and *Ark Royal* to join Harwood's squadron off the estuary.

Since neither the minister, Millington-Drake, nor the naval attaché, Henry McCall, could afford to be seen engaging in belligerent acts in a neutral port, the business of denying the port facilities was given to "C's" agent in Buenos Aires and Montevideo, Captain Rex Miller, of the Manchester Regiment. Miller's other tasks were to deny Langsdorff accurate intelligence about the strength of the British squadron off the mouth of the Plate and its fitness for battle, while at the same time, and in concert with a deception program arranged by "C" in London, to exaggerate British strength there, thus (it was

---

*The marchioness was a Brassey and therefore the sister of the countess De La Warr and the aunt of Lady Avice, "C's" first wife. The marquess was one of the grandest figures in court and public life, having been in turn junior lord of the Treasury, lord-in-waiting to George V, governor of Bombay, of Madras, governor-general of Canada, viceroy of India, lord warden of the Cinque ports, and chancellor of the Order of St. Michael and St. George. Rex Benson, one of "C's" "honourable correspondents," was a nephew of Willingdon.

hoped) pinning *Spee* to Montevideo, where (it was also hoped) she and her crew of 1,100 men would be interned by the Uruguayan government.

Miller persuaded private Uruguayan and Argentinian aircraft owners to refuse his request that they spot for him at the mouth of the Plate. Miller secured the services of all tugs, to prevent them from being used as vessels from which observers could estimate the British squadron's fitness for battle and its strength. At the same time, one of Miller's assistants, a certain Edge, and his agents began to spread rumors calculated to support stories being put about in London that the *Renown* and *Ark Royal* had oiled at Rio de Janeiro on December 13 and were making south at thirty knots. Similarly, Miller and Edge were energetic in denying to Langsdorff the use of the shipyards at Montevideo and to prevent the movement out to the vessel of all ship-repair workers and their equipment.

In this Miller succeeded. Senor Voulminot, the Franco-Uruguayan owner of the only shipyards in Montevideo, the Reguschi y Voulminot, advised the German naval representative that he could give no assistance whatsoever. As Commander F. W. Rasenack, chief gunnery technician in *Spee,* recorded in his diary as a testament to Miller's efficiency: "Not a single man nor a single screw is provided for us by the local shipyards." When Langsdorff persuaded a German company, Siemens Schuckert of Buenos Aires, to send two lift experts to repair *Spee*'s four ammunition hoists, damaged during the fight with Harwood's cruisers, they were unable to procure tugs to get them and their equipment out to the *Spee.* When they found a small boat owner in Buenos Aires who was willing to charter his boat, they were prevented from starting work by the Uruguayan government even as they were arriving aboard *Spee* from Buenos Aires. With only a few exceptions of little importance, Miller was able to deny Langsdorff the use of any of the ship-repair and victualing services of Montevideo, while another British secret agent, Captain Lloyd Hirst, who had been in the service in South America since just before World War I, was able to delay or deny altogether the facilities of Buenos Aires. Thus Langsdorff was compelled to rely upon the resources available to him within his own ship.

Spee was trapped, although not as yet doomed. The battleship could still fight with all her guns, and her engines could still propel her to the high seas, where, in Harwood's estimate, she would have a 70 percent chance of reaching Wilhelmshaven. During the night of December 13, however, Churchill, working through "C," acted to close that option to Langsdorff by psychological means. That night the BBC broadcast that Harwood's squadron not only was *not* badly damaged, and therefore still capable of destroying *Spee* if she left Montevideo, but that the carrier *Ark Royal* and the heavy battleship *Renown* were closing the Plate, and the *Cumberland* was on station to prevent *Spee* from sailing south into the Roaring Forties, where, probably, she would be impossible to find. That story was picked up by the neutral press, and the sheer power of repetition seems to have transmuted bluff into fact; to Langsdorff the story seemed logical and, consequently, probably true.

The truth was different: *Renown* and *Ark Royal* had yet to reach Pernambuco, 2,500 miles and five days' north of Montevideo. In consequence, it became Millington-Drake's personal task not to force the Uruguayans to expel *Spee*, but to persuade them to allow *Spee* to remain until reinforcements were in place. This he achieved through diplomatic artifice. He ordered one of the eight British merchantmen in Montevideo, the *Ashworth*, to sail for the high seas that evening, and then in a note he drew the Uruguayans' attention to section 13, article 16 of the Hague Convention of 1907. This specified that a belligerent warship could not leave a neutral port until twenty-four hours after the departure of a merchantship flying the flag of its adversary.

The Uruguayans accepted the truth of Millington-Drake's note, and *Spee* was advised that she would not to be allowed to sail before 6:15 P.M. on Saturday, December 16, even if she wished to do so. When that hour was reached, Millington-Drake gained further time by ordering another merchantman, the *Dunster Grange*, to sail. Again the Uruguayans directed *Spee* to remain in port, this time until 6:15 P.M. on Sunday evening, December 17. At that point the Uruguayans realized what Millington-Drake's strategy was and ordered him to stop further sailings.

Meantime, the BBC had continued its reports of the assembly of the mythical squadron off the Plate, although the reality was, as one of *Achilles*'s officers stated, that the force amounted to more than "one and a half cruisers with six-sevenths of their outfit fired." But at about 10:00 P.M. on December 14 the heavy cruiser *Cumberland*, the fourth warship in Harwood's squadron, arrived from the Falkland Islands. With clever use of of light and distance, Harwood succeeded in creating the illusion, in combination with rumor spread ashore by Miller, that the *Cumberland* was really the battleship *Renown*.

Thus on December 15 at about 2:00 P.M. Langsdorff's chief gunnery officer, Commander Paul Ascher, reported from the gunnery control room on the foremast that he could see *Renown*'s masts on the horizon. Denied the use of spotting aircraft to check the report, Langsdorff was dependent upon the German embassy at Buenos Aires, and the naval attaché there *confirmed* that the report was true because *Renown* and *Ark Royal* were known to have been at Rio on December 13. The report that *Renown* was off was of the Plate then confirmed by Commander Rasenack, *Spee*'s chief gunnery technician, who recorded on December 14:

From the look-out we can see the battleship which our Gunnery Officer states to be the RENOWN. With her 14-in. guns and speed of 32 knots she is our worst enemy. Also the AJAX and the ACHILLES appear to be waiting for us. What was to be expected has happened. GRAF SPEE is blockaded in the port of Montevideo.

At that point, Langsdorff was doomed. Placing great reliance as he did on the reports of Ascher and Rasenack, he accepted that the *Renown* was just over the horizon waiting for *Spee* to emerge.

On December 15 the BBC continued to bend the facts to suit Churchill's stratagem, describing in graphic reports—reports that by now had begun to fasten the attention of the world on the cat-and-mouse at Montevideo—how a British heavy squadron had closed the estuary to the *Spee*, whose destruction was imminent. And again the BBC report was confirmed by *Spee*'s gunnery control officer, Ascher, who identified the carrier *Ark Royal* off the mouth of the Plate. That report appears to have affected Langsdorff's judgment of the situation completely, perhaps because it was soon followed by the news that another British battleship, the *Barham*, and the French battleship *Dunkerque* were about to join *Renown* and *Ark Royal* off the Plate. Langsdorff's decision seems to have been affected also by the visit of "C's" man in Buenos Aires, Commander Hirst, the British assistant naval attaché, to the Argentinian Ministry of Marine.

As Hirst recalled in a letter to Millington-Drake later, he obtained an interview with Admiral Scasso, a Fascist and the Argentinian minister of marine, and inquired "confidentially" whether, if *Renown* and *Ark Royal* arrived at Mar del Plata, an Argentinian port on the Atlantic not far from the mouth of the Plate, "within a day or so," would the entrance be dredged deeply enough for them to enter. Were there tugs big enough to handle them? Where would they be berthed? Could oil be supplied? Scasso replied that "fortunately a senior officer from Mar del Plata was in the building, and he was brought in to answer my questions." As Hirst hoped, "the popular evening news-paper *Critica* that night stated that they had learned from well-in-formed sources that within forty-eight hours the *Renown* and *Ark Royal* were due at Mar del Plata."

That report was picked up and broadcast throughout the Americas and all legations, and since Langsdorff had no means of checking the report, he accepted that he was blockaded into the Plate. He acted accordingly, declaring in a situation report to the *Admiralstab* in Berlin late on December 15:

(1) RENOWN and ARK ROYAL, as well as cruisers and destroyers, off Montevideo. Close blockade at night. No prospect of breaking out into the open sea and getting through to Germany.

(2) Intend to proceed to the limit of neutral waters. If I can fight my way through to Buenos Aires with ammunition still remaining I shall en-deavour to do so.

(3) As a breakthrough might result in the destruction of SPEE without the possibility of causing damage to the enemy, request instructions whether to scuttle the ship . . . or submit to internment.

That signal went to Hitler, who ordered Langsdorff not to permit the Uruguayans to intern the ship, and if there was no hope of making a successful breakout, then *Spee* must be scuttled. The end of the *Spee* came at just after sunset on Sunday, December 17, in view of great crowds. Having transferred most of her crew to a German freighter, *Spee* broke the Nazi ensign, made way as if for the open sea, and then turned westward toward Buenos Aires. Near a point in the estuary known as Whistle Buoy, *Spee* suddenly exploded and sank. There were no German casualties save one—Langsdorff. He survived the explosion and with his crew reached Buenos Aires, where he learned from the German legation that the *Renown* and *Ark Royal* had entered Rio de Janeiro approximately 1,100 miles to the north at about 1:00 P.M. that same day and were being oiled.

Following that report, Langsdorff, broken at the loss of ship, con-scious that he had been outwitted, went to his room on December 19 and wrote his government:

I can now only prove by my death that the fighting services of the Third Reich are ready to die for the honor of the flag. I alone bear the responsibility for scuttling the pocket battleship *Admiral Graf von Spee*. I am happy to pay with my life for any possible reflection on the honor of the flag. I shall face my fate with firm faith in the cause and the future of the nation and of my Fuehrer.

Langsdorff then borrowed a pistol, wrapped himself in the ensign of the German fleet, and shot himself. Millington-Drake contended at the time and afterward in an anthology that "the individual who probably did most by personal activity during those four days to bring about the final result was the Intelligence Officer, who . . . wished to remain anonymous." The officer referred to was Rex Miller of SIS.

The war had started well for "C." Although he had yet to face severe defeats and still more charges of incompetence, the *Graf Spee* incident served to persuade Churchill that "C" and his service might not be as ineffective as he had been led to believe. There were other reasons, too, for Churchill's delight at the outcome of the battle. Churchill had lost a succession of warships, losses that began to reflect on his administration of the Admiralty. In a few weeks he had lost the aircraft carrier *Courageous* in British home waters, the battleship *Royal Oak*, again in British home waters, and the armed merchant cruiser *Rawalpindi*, all with great loss of life. Now the score was even in circumstances that showed the enemy had been baffled as well as destroyed.

The *Spee* had not only been defeated by an inferior force, and trapped by superior wits, but the German navy had been bluffed into the humiliation of scuttling an important warship before the eyes of the world. Furthermore, Churchill wished to convey to President Franklin D. Roosevelt, with whom he was just beginning a correspondence of high importance, that the spirit of Benbow, Collingwood, Byron, and Blake was not dead, that England was not decadent. Indeed, Roosevelt was so impressed that, although neutral in the gathering storm, he wrote a note to Churchill congratulating him on the "the extraordinarily well fought action of your three cruisers."

3 CASE YELLOW

If "C's" standing with Churchill had improved through his skillful handling of the intelligence aspects of the *Graf Spee*, Sir Alexander Cadogan, permanent head of the Foreign Office, displayed no such satisfaction with "C's" performance during the early months of the war. On the very day of "C's" appointment, and the morrow of the Venlo incident, "C" went to see Cadogan to warn him that there was evidence Germany was once again about to invade Holland and then deliver the knockout blow that the Chamberlain government had expected against London since 1938. That warning caused Cadogan to explode in his diary:

Menzies this morning said that he had from the v. *best* source, report that Germans had abandoned any idea of offensive [against France and the Low Countries, which "C" had predicted earlier]. Tonight, report that telephone communication between Holland and Germany cut off! I believe all the stuff we get is put out by the Germans and put out to puzzle us! After all, that's what *we* do!

Cadogan's expostulations about "C's" capability and fitness for the job had several origins. One was "C's" conviction that, despite Venlo, there were severe differences between Hitler and his generals, as indeed there were. The second was "C's" inability as 1939 closed to predict what Hitler's next step would be. When "C" reported on January 19, 1940, that, as the French secret service was reporting, an "overwhelming German attack" was expected in the west from January 25 onward, Cadogan tended to discount the information with the observation in his diary that "C" was "rather mercurial, and *rather* hasty and superficial." [4] In fact there *would* have been an attack but for the severe weather that forced Hitler to postpone his offensive until the spring; and again in fact for one reason or another, Hitler ordered and then canceled an offensive in the west on no less than twenty-eight occasions that winter.

Then there was the problem endemic to most secret services, the friction created when secret service operations abroad caused difficulties for the local ambassador, as they were doing at that moment in Sweden. There, the ambassador, fearful about any British compromise of Swedish neutrality, complained constantly against "C's" plan to blow up the Swedish iron ore facilities at Oxelsund and so deny the ore to the Ruhr steel mills. But beyond all that there was the nagging worry created by "C's" report on the Krivitsky case.

Troubled by Stalin's purge of the Soviet administration in the second half of the 1930s, Walter Krivitsky, a high officer of the Soviet intelligence service, had deserted his post at The Hague instead of returning to Moscow as he was instructed and sought political asylum in the United States. After several unsuccessful attempts on his life, Krivitsky arrived safely in New York, where he began to make long and revealing statements concerning the Soviet service. One of his statements, which forecast the Nazi-Soviet Pact, came to the attention of Lord Lothian, the British ambassador in Washington. Arrangements were made with Krivitsky to go to London, where he arrived in late December 1939 or early 1940.

In London Krivitsky offered a mass of information, the value of which to the British security authorities was uncertain until he began to discuss the case of Captain John King, a Foreign Office cipher clerk who, Krivitsky claimed, had provided the Soviet service with much important information that included, by implication, certain Foreign Office ciphers. Under interrogation, King admitted treachery and was sent to prison for ten years. As Cadogan wrote in his diary, having read the report, King's admissions regarding the information he had given to the Russians revealed an "awful state of affairs" within the Foreign Office communications branch, the security of which was a responsibility of "C" as director-general of GC&CS.

On December 23, Ivan Maisky, the Soviet ambassador, called on Cadogan to protest the arrest of a Soviet Trade Delegation official, A. A. Doschenko. As Cadogan explained to Maisky, Doschenko had "unfortunately been indulging in activities which do not commend themselves to H.M.G." When Maisky called six days later to complain that Doschenko was still in prison, Cadogan dismissed the complaint with the statement, "That's nothing: you've been in prison. All my friends have been in prison. [President] Benes [of Czechoslovakia] many times, and a certain Delegate of the I[rish] F[ree] S[tate], with whom I made friends, had been in no less than six English prisons, and was none the worse for it."

The King incident played greatly on Cadogan's mind. A warning from Krivitsky that there was one and possibly two more younger Soviet spies "of good birth" at the Foreign Office served only to intensify Cadogan's dissatisfaction with "C's" administration, although the Foreign Office's security was the Security Service's responsibility, not that of Broadway. Krivitsky's own fate—on his return to the United States, he appeared to have been murdered in circumstances made to look like suicide—seemed further to suggest that all was not well at Broadway. Cadogan's diaries at this time—November 1939–April 1940—displayed a marked tendency to blame all England's misfortunes on poverty of intelligence.

As investigations were begun to identify the Foreign Office men mentioned by Krivitsky, a sudden surge of dangerous events overwhelmed the inquiry. On Saturday, April 6, "C" to no effect warned the prime minister's office that the Germans would invade Norway on Monday morning. Sure enough, Hitler attacked in the west with devastating consequences to Britain and to "C." General Sir Hastings Ismay, secretary to the Committee of Imperial Defence, described how he was awakened out of a deep sleep in the first hours of April 9, 1940, by the telephone bell to be told that the Germans were seizing Copenhagen and Oslo. [5]

Ismay hurried into his clothes for an emergency meeting, and as he did so, "I realised, for the first time in my life, the devastating and demoralizing effect of surprise." He had "always thought that Hitler's next move would be either an invasion of the Low Countries and France, or alternatively an air attack on the British Isles." The idea of "an operation of this scope against Scandinavia had never entered my head," and only recently the chiefs of staff "had recorded the opinion that any sea-borne operations against the western seaboard of Norway would be impracticable, in view of our great naval superiority." [6]

The rest of the government was as dismayed as Ismay, except for Cadogan, who thought it was a prelude to, and a distraction from, an attack in the west. Cadogan was right, but it was convenient for the government, and especially for Churchill, Godfrey, and the Admiralty, to blame the failure on "C," despite the warnings they had ignored.

As the government pursued their scapegoat, it ignored further warnings of still greater gravity: Gauche reported from Paris that there were now 190 German divisions, including ten or twelve panzer divisions, facing the western front, and that the panzers were almost all concentrated against the Belgian Ardennes, the traditional route of attack for armies marching against Channel ports. The Norwegian and Danish attack had made hardly any difference to the German dispositions in the west, and, Gauche continued, the main attack would come on or about May 10. On April 20 "C's'" war station at Brussels reported that German intelligence personnel in Belgium were being withdrawn to Germany, a sure sign that Belgium would be attacked.

Realizing that the warnings would be ignored again unless he acted forcefully and restored confidence in SIS's reports, Menzies broke with the tradition of silence maintained by the secret service in all events. He sent to Lord Hankey, the minister responsible for secret service affairs, a paper that, "C" believed, provided evidence that SIS had warned the government in ample time and on many occasions of Hitler's intention to invade Norway. Maintaining that his service was no more or less unprepared for war than the government or the

armed services, the paper laid responsibility for the Norwegian disaster at the desks of Churchill and Godfrey. Godfrey in particular
appeared to have been delinquent in not passing SIS reports upward
on the grounds that he did not trust them.

As "C" stated in the paper, since December 1939 all information
obtained and circulated by SIS "pointed quite clearly to the fact that
a German Expeditionary Force, continually exercised and trained in
embarkation and disembarkation," had been in the north German
ports "from about that time," and that information was "accepted by
the Service Departments and by the Foreign Office." As evidence
he enclosed a summary of the forty or so reports Dansey had sent
out in that time. Individually none of the reports provided *conclusive*
evidence of an imminent, major invasion of two countries vital to the
security of England. But in the form submitted by "C," they constituted *overwhelming* evidence that such a campaign was about to
begin. But, of course, they had not been collated but had been read
separately as they had come in, and consequently they had suffered
the fate of most of "C's" reporting at that time—the dead file.

Having read the report, Lord Hankey wrote to Sir Horace Wilson,
Chamberlain's closest adviser, and noted with satisfaction that Menzies's paper "exonerates S.S." of the charges that it had been negli-
gent. As Hankey also pointed out, most of "C's" information had been
sent to Godfrey, "as it was Naval business," but the Cabinet had not
got "any warnings so far as I can recollect from the Admiralty except
the general warnings that came from many sources besides S.S. that
ships were being prepared for embarkation purposes and that troops
were being practised in embarkation and disembarkation." As Hankey
continued, it was "not the business of S.S. to comment on the facts.
They merely furnish them to the Directors of Intelligence of the
Service Departments, whose business it is to send them to the appropriate authorities" and Hankey was "not satisfied that the Services
have done their job very effectively." Hankey then remarked on "C's"
summary:

A single report pointing in a certain direction does not mean much to any
of us. But a succession of reports set out in juxta-position as summarised
here by Colonel Menzies produce a cumulative impression of a very different
kind.

I am wondering whether we ought not to arrange that the Joint Intelligence Committee should make it their business to watch reports of this
kind and put them in series so as to give us better warning than we received
about the Norwegian affair.

After three hundred years of experience in intelligence work, it might have seemed elementary to a government that all information on a threatening situation might usefully be collated at a single point in a single file, in order to illuminate the nature and direction of the threat. But that was not done by any British authority, despite Menzies's support for expansion in the powers of the Joint Intelligence Committee after Beaumont-Nesbitt's correspondence on the need for a "Central Intelligence Bureau" at Christmas 1938.

General Ismay responded on May 5, 1940, as the Chamberlain government tottered at the point of collapse:

(a) The Joint Intelligence Committee should be instructed to prepare a special note on any particular development in the international situation whenever this appeared to any of the Directors of Intelligence (who are, of course, in close and continuous contact with "C") to be necessary.

(b) That copies of this note should be circulated at once (on paper of a special colour which is not used for any other purpose). . . .

(c) That I myself . . . should be charged with the responsibility of bringing the matter to the notice of the [responsible authority] at any hour of the day or night, and of taking his instructions as to action.

In what was almost one of his last acts as prime minister, Chamberlain approved Ismay's proposals on May 7, 1940. Menzies himself again stated that, although in the past SIS had, on the grounds of security, declined membership of any Whitehall committee, he himself would become a member of the JIC if invited to do so. "C's" membership was approved, but the re-formation of the Joint Intelligence Committee came too late to have any influence on a cataract of violent surprises in which, as Churchill remembered, "we were about to learn what total war means."

Striking with stupendous force and violence on a narrow sector out of the misty forests of the Ardennes on May 10, 1940, despite the sure knowledge in the hands of "C" and Gauche, the Germans took the Anglo-French supreme command by strategic surprise. For the third time since the war telegram was issued on August 1, 1939, the combined Anglo-French intelligence services, indeed those of the world other than Russia and Germany, were taken by surprise, this despite numerous warnings that Case Yellow—the German code name for a major offensive in the west, intended to drive England out of Europe and France out of the war—was at hand. The Nazi-Soviet Pact, the invasions of Norway and Denmark, and now the invasions of Holland, Belgium, and France—all were massive intelligence defeats for "C." The entire *raison d'être* for "C's" existence, and that of his service, had been to prevent these momentous occurrences, and he had not succeeded.

All the evidence had been in his hands. In November a high officer of enemy intelligence at Dresden, Paul Thummel, known to "C" as A54 and as an officer whose intelligence was so good that, as "C" declared, "when A54 reports, armies march," had sent a warning that Hitler would attack in the west in the second half of that month. The same warning was sent through the Vatican and by Canaris's deputy, Colonel Oster, through the Dutch military attaché at Berlin. "C" had verified that the main weight of the German panzer divisions were concentrated on the Dutch-Belgian frontier, and the Allied armies were brought to a state of immediate readiness for battle. But then nothing happened. Hitler did bring his armies to readiness on November 9 but then, through the weather, canceled the order on November 11.

At the end of November A54 reported that Hitler had reset the clock for mid-December. Again nothing happened. A U.S. diplomat in Berlin heard news that the offensive was timed for January 13. Nothing happened. From the wreck of a German aircraft in Belgium in January, the Allies captured the German air force air-support plan for an offensive by the German armies across Belgium to the North Sea. "Very odd," commented Cadogan when he received word of the existence of the plan. "But one can't ignore these things and all precautions taken." All Allied forces were again alerted. But again nothing happened, and Cadogan wrote in his diary on January 16:

I conclude that all this scare is *quite probably* a German fake. *But*, as I told H[alifax] before the Cabinet this morning—in case they felt they had been fooled—they must act *exactly* the same next time. If it was a fake, it was done . . . with the idea of "crying wolf" in the hope that we shall ignore the real information when it comes along. If therefore they are too sceptical in future, they will be playing the German game.

Then came the invasion of Norway and Denmark in April, in which Hitler obtained both tactical *and* strategic surprise, leaving Whitehall almost paralyzed with ignorance for two weeks or more. Between February and April, largely from the French secret service, "C" was able to provide intelligence that enabled his clients to establish with reasonable accuracy the German order of battle and also, again with reasonable accuracy, to fix the point of main attack—the Ardennes. He also was able to fix the approximate date of the impending offensive. What "C" could not do was inform himself as to the exact time and place of the attack, largely through Hitler's skill in concealing that information. But all that "C" did achieve, given the lack of signals intelligence during that period, was rendered worthless by the skepticism of Whitehall about the value of Broadway's information when it was not backed by technical or documentary evidence.

Although the Foreign Office had appointed Victor Cavendish-Bentinck of the Foreign Office as chairman, neither "C" nor any of the other principal suppliers of raw intelligence were brought on to the JIC, and still there existed neither the direction nor the vigor to produce authoritative strategic assessments of enemy intentions. Thus Cadogan's skepticism and Bentinck's languor left the Chamberlain administration as ignorant of enemy intentions after Norway as they were beforehand. Moreover, "C's" credibility was being undermined by the leakage of raw information, usually in the form of gossip, to Chamberlain's private office.

The only Broadway officer authorized to have contact with Chamberlain's private office was "C" himself, and unless there was someone else, "C" himself must have been the source of these leaks, seeking perhaps to reestablish the waning reputation for omniscience that Broadway had enjoyed in the time of Admiral Sinclair. If that was so, then the reaction to these tidbits was not productive. As John Colville, one of the prime minister's junior secretaries, claimed in his diary on May 10, an official of SIS had stated the day before that "there was no chance of an invasion of the Netherlands." The German activity against that country was, the official declared, "a feint" to disguise the actuality of Hitler's intentions, which was "an imminent" attack on Hungary. And, commented Colville, "so much for our renowned foreign agents."

Yet it seems unlikely that "C" was indeed the source of these leaks, for on May 9 "C" sent a "personal and most secret" report to Chamberlain and Churchill, recounting the findings of the Anglo-French secret intelligence committee meeting on the May 5. Also, on May 7 he circulated estimates of enemy intentions by General Gauche, chief of the French secret service, and Colonel Rivet, head of the German section. According to Gauche, his service forecast that the Ardennes would be the place of the attack, the date of the attack would be May 9–10, and the method employed in the attack would be blitzkrieg, powerful combined armor and aircraft columns aimed not at the seizure of political targets, but at the destruction of Allied military power. Gauche recorded "a grim meeting," one conducted in "a dismal and heavy atmosphere," "anxious faces" betraying the "disquiet aroused by the imminence of the decisive test which this time, everyone felt, could no longer be evaded or deferred."

Gauche also declared that the Germans possessed the initiative, and that France and England, indeed the world, "must expect a very hard time." A spy reported to Rivet, and Rivet reported to the conference, that he had gone through the entire German front in the west and had found that the "dynamism of the young men" of the German army was "prodigious," and that they believed "a mere flick of the fingers will make the French front collapse." *Date:* May 10. *Method:* Blitzkrieg.

Yet if that report was immediately available in London, Chamberlain was still in the same frame of mind on May 10 as he had been on April 13 when he wrote to his sister of an "accumulation of evidence that an attack [in the west] is imminent and formidable. [Yet] I cannot convince myself that it is coming." Although some of "C's" reports had pointed to the Ardennes over a considerable period, the French, but not the British, had continued to reject the view that the Ardennes was passable in wintertime, this despite the availability of important signals intelligence that again pointed directly at that area.

In the spring of 1940, the British Security Service succeeded in intercepting and decrypting traffic of the German intelligence service's radio link between Wiesbaden and their agents in France, Belgium, and Luxembourg; and MI5 noted that traffic "began to carry enquiries about defences, road blocks, troop dispositions, and other military topics" on the western side of the Ardennes. A54, moreover, warned London and Paris as early as April 25 that the *main* German attack would be launched through the Ardennes. In the attack the panzers would cross the Meuse north of Sedan and drive on the Channel ports.

As to the question of tactical surprise, the Allied armies could have been alerted to the imminence of the impending offensive had the great marshals and generals of France paid more attention to a single SIS bulletin that was verifiable: on May Day the Germans suddenly changed all their Enigma machine cipher settings; and that was, as "C" knew well from his experience in World War I, an incontrovertible indicator that a major attack was in the wind.

The survival of the state was at issue. For Chamberlain, the consequences were ignominious and fatal. They were almost as ignominious and fatal for "C" personally. All Europe began to fall to the German eagles. Yet even as Cadogan was recording in his diary that "everything's as black as black," he still made time to find a reason for the disaster in the west—"C." As he recorded on May 25: "[Lord Lloyd, the colonial secretary] at 3.30 with H[alifax]. He agreed to try and overhaul S.I.S., which wants it *badly!*" The situation for "C" personally proximated the meaning of the proverb "When the bull stumbles, the butchers begin to run."

From behind the government benches, Leo Amery hurled at Chamberlain the imperious words of Oliver Cromwell to the Long Parliament: "You have sat too long here for any good you have been doing. Depart, I say, and let us have done with you. In the name of God, go!" [7] And Chamberlain resigned.

It was widely supposed that the foreign secretary, Lord Halifax, would succeed because, remembering the abdication and his support for Edward VIII, King George VI "did not wish to send for Winston." [8] But in the event Halifax declined the succession, and almost by default it was offered instead to Churchill. At six o'clock during the evening of May 10, Churchill, now sixty-six, became prime minister and received the seals of office from King George VI. As he was leaving the palace, Churchill's detective, Thompson, noted that his master had tears in his eyes, and in the car Churchill remarked that he was "very much afraid his appointment had come too late." [9] It had. This time the Teuton legions could not be repulsed.

Only "C" knew at that time that the situation was not as "black as black," as Cadogan had said. For at Bletchley in the Buckingham-shire hills, a mathematical miracle had taken place in the very group of Oxford and Cambridge men who, before the war, had declared that they would not fight for king and country.

Enigma had been conquered.

4   THE CONQUEST OF ENIGMA

On May 22, 1940, as France began to fall and twelve days after Churchill became prime minister, the modern version of a miracle occurred. The code breakers at Bletchley Park began to decrypt regularly the German air force version of Enigma, the German machine cipher system that was by now in use by all main departments of the German government except the Foreign Office. Of that supreme moment in the intelligence history of modern times—and in the history of Menzies's own career—Sir Stewart Milner-Barry, an international chess champion who had been at Bletchley since February of 1940, was to remember:

What a moment it was! It was pure black magic. Turing, Welchman and Hugh Alexander had mastered a mathematical problem that had seemed beyond comprehension. Neither Denniston, the chief, nor Dillwyn Knox, the senior cryptanalyst, had thought it possible. This belief had been strengthened when, on May 1, 1940, the Germans made a change in the procedure used to improve the security of Enigma. This change wiped out the mastery we had gained over Enigma, and we had to start again from square one. But Welchman had never doubted the principle that all problems made by men can be solved by men, whatever their magnitude. And Welchman was proven correct. Only 21 days after the procedural change we had broken back into the German Air Force Enigma. Yet it was not so much a triumph for British intellect as it was a disaster for German carelessness. If they had followed their instructions on how to use the machine we would never have got back into the cipher. It was therefore a miracle based upon a German error; and because it was a German error they could have prevented us from reading their traffic at any time they wished, provided they obeyed the rules. Thus we began to live on the edge of a nightmare day and night for the next five years, for at any time, had they not continued to make mistakes in the procedure governing the use of Enigma, we could have lost the ability to read their secret traffic. Every night we went to bed wondering whether Ultra would be there in the morning. And if this was bad for us, it was a thousand times worse for "C."

During the rest of the campaign in France, which lasted no more than forty days, the breach of the cipher produced a flood of operational intelligence for which the staff at GC&CS was ready. Within a very short period—a day, perhaps, not more than two—GC&CS was decrypting, translating, interpreting, and circulating the very high grade intercepts at the rate of in excess of one thousands signals every twenty-four hours, thus starting an ever-widening breach of the German's high command communications system that lasted, with few interruptions, until the end of the war.

The value of the decrypts were immediately apparent, for if their existence could have no effect upon the irresistible German advance, they did enable London to follow the course of the German campaign with far greater clarity than was available in Paris. The earliest of these signals also influenced, and perhaps decided, what course British must follow. Evidence in the decrypts revealed that there was just time to evacuate the British army from Dunkirk; others indicated that the strength of the Royal Air Force should be conserved, not committed, as the French prime minister pleaded, to the battlefield, where, in the British view, the issue had already been decided by German power; and it cast light on that most important matter of all—whether after the defeat of France the Germans would attempt to invade England from the French and Belgian ports.

Immediately the new source began to produce. "C" employed the "venerable procedures" of Broadway to meet the imperative of the hour and of the days, weeks, months, and years ahead. That imperative was that the Germans should *never* become aware that they were making mistakes in the procedures governing their use of Enigma, and that they should *never* become aware that the British were reading their most secret command traffic. On June 6 Menzies held a meeting to discuss distribution and cover for the intelligence. That day was the morrow of the feast day of St. Boniface, the English missionary monk and martyr of A.D. 675–754, who was known in the church as the "Apostle of Germany."

"C" decided to attribute the intelligence "to Boniface," whom he described as being an "important agent on the German General Staff." That joke soon wore thin, and the cover did not work at all in places such as the Admiralty, where SIS's intelligence was distrusted, and it was replaced first by the word "Hydro" and then "Ultra." Churchill, however, called the intelligence "Boniface" for the rest of the war, and even President Roosevelt used the term at times.*

In what was one of his earliest precautions, with the avid support of Churchill, "C" confined circulation of Ultra to a small group of thirty persons. The staff at Bletchley was muzzled effectively by that severe instrument of law, the Official Secrets Act, which promised fourteen years' hard labor for those who offended against its more serious sections and death for the most serious infringements. Nobody was allowed to know of the existence of the source, and at first, at least, nobody but "C" saw all the intercepts, not even the production

---

*Although Churchill used the term "Boniface" to describe all intercept material throughout the war, for the convenience of the reader the term "Ultra," by which sigint (*sig*nal *int*elligence) became widely known, will be used from this point forward.

staff. "C" hand-carried the most important undisguised intercepts to Churchill personally. Nobody else in the entire administration, at first, saw anything other than the camouflaged version. When Churchill permitted "C" to expand slightly the number of those allowed to read the intercepts in their raw or processed states, that group became known to Churchill as "the secret circle," and in time that circle became an inner advisory group around Churchill.

For the rest of government there was the daily "Secret Situation Report," which had very limited circulation and in which the source was never revealed. For those important persons beyond the government, there was the *Dominions Wire*, a daily intelligence bulletin prepared by the Joint Intelligence Committee on the basis of intercepts and all other sources available. This was sent out routinely by telegraph to all dominions prime ministers and to President Roosevelt. But again Boniface was not revealed as the source. A special and less informative version of the *Dominions Wire* was prepared for the U.S. embassy in London. Such were the security precautions taken by "C" at this time, therefore, that there was only one leakage. Lord Kemsley, the press baron, learned of the existence of Ultra in a way that was never detected; but he was effectively silenced at a meeting with Churchill.

Since a major source of secret intelligence was, as it remains, political power, there can be no doubt that while those outside "the secret circle" continued to snipe at "C," as far as Churchill was concerned "C's" position was not again in doubt, at least not during the lifetime of the Churchill government. There were, from time to time, sharp words between the two men. Later in 1940 and again early in 1941, it seemed on occasions that the old antagonism might be revived. But these were short-lived, for Churchill recognized that "C" controlled the instrument that would enable him to steer the country through the tempest. Squadron Leader F. W. Winterbotham, who had responsibility for the distribution of the intercepts when "C" was absent, declared that at the time of the Battle of Britain, Churchill and "C" would have gone to *all and any* lengths to protect the security of the source.

As the battle unfolded, Ultra could contribute no intelligence that could prevent the fall of France. The panzer divisions proved invincible, accomplishing in forty days what the German army had failed to do in the four years of World War I. On May 15 the Germans broke across the Meuse between Mezieres and Namur as the Dutch army surrendered that same day. By May 27 the British, French, and Belgian armies were surrounded, and Belgium capitulated. The next day the British began evacuating their army at Dunkirk. On May 29 the Germans took Ypres in a flash and appeared on the English Channel. On June 5 the Battle of France began when the Germans forced the Somme. On June 9 the Norwegians surrendered. On June 10 Italy declared war on Britain and France. On June 14 the Germans entered Paris.

Three days later Marshal Pétain, the new president of France, announced that France had asked for armistice terms. The mood of the ruling generation was best expressed by Cadogan, who, as always, voiced himself in terms that reflected upon the competence of "C": "These days are dreadful, and my knees are beginning to go! Gather French haven't fought at all—simply shattered by air-tank attack. Our staffs living in the days of the Zulu war. . . . Never did I think one could endure such a nightmare." [10]

During that period, "C" succeeded in exfiltrating King Haakon of Norway: his person was considered essential to British causes because he controlled the Norwegian gold reserve and the Norwegian mercantile marine of three million tons. Out came Queen Wilhelmina and her government and their gold reserve. Leopold elected to remain in his country, despite a telephone call from "C" to the king of the Belgians, Leopold III, in which "C" reminded Leopold that he was an Etonian and that he had still an important duty to render the alliance. Charles de Gaulle, who proclaimed himself leader of the Free French Forces, his wife, their children, and a small staff arrived from Bordeaux to establish the Free French Forces.

The British Enigma team at French headquarters was evacuated, leaving not a shred of evidence that Enigma had been conquered, and bringing with them £13 million in French francs "found in a French courtyard." This would be, "C" decided, used to finance Broadway's operations in France. Section D officers seized industrial diamonds worth £7 million in a raid on the Amsterdam diamond mart. The French government refused "C's" transport to French North Africa, to continue the war from there. They elected to remain in France but did authorize one final gesture: they sent over a canister containing a new substance called "heavy water" to prevent it from falling into the hands of the Germans. They refused to send the fleet, however.

Then, on June 14, came the indignity of the hour. "C" was compelled to withdraw from Paris.

Charles Grey, an American boulevardier in Paris who had vol-

unteered for service in SIS at the outbreak of war, and who had flown
the Beechcraft biplane that SIS Paris had used to fly agents about
Europe, related afterward how the last man out was Commander
Dunderdale, chief of the Paris station. On June 13 Dunderdale and
Grey had been at the SIS offices in the Avenue Charles Floquet,
almost under the Eiffel Tower, when news was received that the
Germans were advancing on both sides of Paris. Dunderdale was
ordered by Dansey in London to abandon the station, and this he
did at about 11:00 A.M. The nine members of Dunderdale's staff had
left for London earlier. Since flying was too dangerous, and it might
be impossible to get out to Le Touquet where the biplane was han-
gared, Grey, who had a brand-new Talbot tourer, offered to drive
Dunderdale to Bordeaux. There Dunderdale could enter Spain or
obtain passage in a ship to England. Dunderdale accepted, mined
the safe, and then left Paris with Grey at the wheel of the Talbot.

On June 23 Dunderdale and Grey reached Bordeaux. There they
learned that a ship, a coaler, was calling that day to pick up British
citizens waiting at Arcachon, a pleasure port south of Bordeaux. But
at some stage Dunderdale received a message from "C" that an RAF
Anson communications aircraft was on its way to Bordeaux to exfiltrate
him. Grey then turned about and drove to Bordeaux airport, where
the Anson duly landed. "I'll be seeing ya, Charlie," Dunderdale called
back cheerfully to Grey as he boarded the old stringbag. The aircraft
then took off for England. At that moment for all useful purposes SIS
in Europe ceased to exist or had at least lost its ability to report to
London, for all lines of communication had come overland through
France, and these lines were now under German control. None of
"C's" agents between Brest and Yokohama were now able to report
direct to "C."

Yet for all the size of the disaster that had occurred, "C" would
allow none of the elegances of his service to be sacrificed to emergency. Somewhat later, Grey received a strange parcel at his hotel
room. In it was a beautiful solid-silver cigarette box with the British
coat of arms on its lid. Made by Spinks, the court silversmith, the
lid was engraved inside with Dunderdale's signature, the signatures
of the nine other members of SIS Paris, and the inscription "To The
First Volunteer, *L'Ange Bleu*,"—"the Blue Angel," which had been
Grey's code name. Grey was greatly moved by this gesture and recalled later how he thought, Well, the British certainly do things in
style, even when they're going under.

But as Dunderdale was to remember of that moment when the

red light changed to green and he strode into "C's" office, he found "C" "as cool as ever and quite unfussed" by the disaster in France. With him Dunderdale brought a message from Gauche. The new minister of defense, General Maxime Weygand, had ordered the French secret service to go underground. That was being done. If the French government had just signed Hitler's terms and had promised not only to cease secret operations against the conquerors, but also to liquidate the secret services, Colonel Rivet, the chief, had issued a counterorder: "The fight goes on, whatever happens." Rivet had also promised that he would *never* revoke the order.

"C" was down but not out. In these circumstances of triumph and disaster, "C" turned to a task in great secrecy. Since it was expected that the Germans would attempt to invade and conquer England, and it was also likely that they might succeed, some thought had to be given to the safety of the royal family, the government, and certain assets of importance—the gold reserve, the pictures in the National Gallery, and documentation relating to the atomic bomb, the jet engine, and radar. He, too, had to give thought to what plans he should lay for himself. To conceal his range of connections, he burned his private papers at Luckington and hid his jewelry and silver, as was done in Napoleon's time, in a hole in the Silk Wood at the Westonbirt arboretum. His mother was persuaded to burn her papers, too, although she proved less efficient than her son.

He then turned to his own services. Motor coaches were stationed permanently at Bletchley, to evacuate key personnel—the administration, cryptographers, and officials with any knowledge of the means by which Enigma was penetrated—to Milford Haven in Wales, where a warship would be made available to take them to "somewhere in the Americas." Much of the Secret Intelligence Service was already evacuated from London and scattered about the home counties in no less than eighteen large country houses. But the headquarters staff had remained in London, and "C" had to consider that with Best and Stevens in their hands the Germans knew exactly who he was (as indeed they did).

On the basis of information provided by Best and Stevens, the Gestapo and the Sicherheitsdienst had prepared a document entitled "Der Britische Nachrichtendienst" for use when they arrived in London. It named the headquarters "London Broadway Buildings near St. James's Park Station" and stated that "according to Stevens," Sinclair's deputy was "Colonel Stuart Menzies, a Scotsman, who succeeded his boss on the latter's death on 4th November 1939." Menzies's "ADCs were Captain Howard, Royal Navy, Captain Russell and Hatton Hall." The document also named all senior officers at Broadway and gave such detail as the floors on which they worked and the addresses of subheadquarters in London.

"C" was plainly a marked man. What, therefore, did he intend? Such evidence as there is shows that he would have accompanied the king's party or that of the prime minister to Canada with the fleet and resumed operations from there, returning to England at the liberation. "C" did get as far as giving an order that only Bletchley —at that time an organization of perhaps four hundred men and women—was to prepare for exile. But in the end the prime minister settled "C's" dilemma for him. There was a most secret proposal that the royal family and the government should be evacuated to Canada if the Germans invaded, and it seemed likely that they would capture London.

On May 27 the British ambassador in Washington, the marquess of Lothian, revealed that Roosevelt had told him that if Britain was really "in extremis," the United States "will come in." The president suggested that England—with the resources of the Allied empires and provided the navy remained intact—could carry on the war from Canada. But Roosevelt had also said that "the seat of government should be Bermuda and not Ottawa," as "the American republics would dislike the idea of a monarchy functioning on the American Continent." [11] That gave pause to all thought about the safety of the royal family and their evacuation from England.

While the pause lasted, Churchill's Cabinet debated whether England should surrender "in a certain eventuality"—if France surrendered. Meeting as a Cabinet for the first time in the underground war room at 2 Great George Street, between May 26 and 29, Cadogan produced a statement from Shakespeare's *King John* that, although slightly misquoted, had resounding effect: England should fight "come the three corners of the world, and we will shock them." [12] Churchill became greatly elated at these words, and they played their part in influencing the ministers, who sat like Bageholt's seers at the green beize table nodding and proposing. Eventually all voted for a policy not of surrender, but of war to the bitter end in the four corners of the world. That decision terminated all thought of evacuating anyone in an official position, for to have done so would have given the impression that the ship was sinking.

Churchill forbade all further discussion of evacuation, except that of children to Canada and America. When Kenneth Clark, director of the National Gallery, suggested that the paintings in the gallery should be sent to Canada, Churchill replied, "No, bury them in caves and cellars. None must go. We are going to beat them." And when the Foreign Office proposed evacuating the king to Ottawa whether the Americans liked English monarchs on the territory of American republics or not, Churchill again said no and forbade any discussion, declaring only that he was going to make the Germans regret the day they had attacked England, or words to that effect.

5 SEALION

With the decision to stand and fight, Churchill embarked upon his American policy. As his son, Randolph, recorded of his visit to his father on the morning of May 18, 1940:

I went up to my father's bedroom. He was standing in front of his basin and was shaving with his old fashioned Valet razor. He had a tough beard, and as usual he was hacking away.

"Sit down, dear boy, and read the papers while I finish shaving." I did as told. After two or three minutes of hacking away, he half-turned and said: "I think I see my way through." He resumed his shaving. I was astounded, and said: "Do you mean that we can avoid defeat? (which seemed credible) or beat the bastards" (which seemed incredible).

He flung his razor into the basin, swung around, and said:—"Of course I mean we can beat them."

Me: "Well, I'm all for it, but I don't see how you can do it."

By this time he had dried and sponged his face and turning round to me, said with great intensity:—"I shall drag the United States in." [13]

In those seven words, Churchill let slip one of the dogs of war: his war diplomacy, that most troubled—and troubling—aspect of war-making at the highest level. His basic principle was that of Machiavelli in *Discorsi III*:

Though fraud in other activities be detestable, in the management of war it is laudable and glorious, and he who overcomes an enemy by fraud is as much to be praised as he who does so by force.

And how did Churchill propose to entice a nation of 122 million people into a war that was then not popular, people who until lately, at least, were in general apathetic to British causes, disinterested in Europe's wars, and perennially suspicious of the British ruling class? Sharp wits would do the trick, Churchill thought.

John Colville, who remained one of Churchill's private secretaries at Chamberlain's departure, showed in his diary that the policy toward the United States was being implemented at an early date and what was entailed: "Indirect attempts are being made, through the Dominions' High Commissioners, etc., to bring the U.S. into the war *by painting to members of the Administration the most sombre portrait of what we expect from Germany*" (emphasis added). [14] Harold Macmillan, then a publisher and backbencher, spoke of a "policy of enticing" America into the war. And Churchill's earliest major act of statesmanship was to deliver a tremendous peroration to the world intended to force the American electorate to abandon its refusal, frequently stated and vigorously defended, not to become involved in "Europe's war." The speech was intended also to establish the basis of a war diplomacy: that England's cause was *just*.

The Battle of France was ending, the Battle of Britain was beginning, and then he reminded the United States of the immensity of the issues now being decided across the English Channel:

Upon this battle depends the survival of Christian civilisation. Upon it depends our own British life and the long continuity of our institutions and our Empire. The whole fury and might of the enemy must very soon be turned on us. Hitler knows that he will have to break us in this island or lose the war. If we can stand up to him, all Europe may be free, and the life of the world may move forward into broad, sunlit uplands; but if we fail, then the whole world, including the United States, and all that we have known and cared for, will sink into the abyss of a new dark age made more sinister, and perhaps more protracted, by the lights of a perverted science.

Let us therefore brace ourselves to our duty and so bear ourselves that if the British Empire and its Commonwealth lasts for a thousand years men will still say, "This was their finest hour." [15]

Churchill's words struck the American consciousness with appalling force, dislodging the isolationists from their position of primacy and awakening the American mind to the possibility that England's war might be, after all, not one of imperialist munitions makers and bankers, that it had a moral importance that transcended the large stock market rally the war itself produced in the spring and summer of 1940. The moral causes might after all be America's as well. The words acted like a bugle call in olden times in England and provided Roosevelt with the excuse, although not the legal basis, for entering a position of quasi-belligerence.

The new policy began to flower in late May. There was an exchange of most secret letters between Churchill and Roosevelt discussing the situation in France and Britain's need for a loan of fifty old American destroyers, the diversion to Britain of the largest-possible number of Curtiss P-40 fighters being manufactured for the U.S. Army Air Corps, a warning from Churchill to Roosevelt of what would happen if, through lack of American help, the Germans invaded England, if they succeeded in conquering the islands, and if Churchill's successors were compelled to parley "amidst the ruins." Churchill warned Roosevelt that he

must not be blind to the fact that the sole remaining bargaining counter with Germany would be the fleet [which Britain regarded as comparable to that of the U.S. Navy in power and size], and if this country was left by the United States to its fate, no one would have the right to blame those then responsible if they made the best terms they could for the surviving inhabitants. [16]

That statement played upon the one great fear of the U.S. strategists: the American fleet could not defend the American fortress, one protected by the Atlantic in the east and the Pacific in the west, if the German, Italian, and Japanese fleets acquired control of the British and French fleets. To reinforce those fears—and to place before the president clear evidence that the Americans were wrong if they believed, as they did, that England was a flaccid and corrupted democracy not worth assisting—Churchill sent Roosevelt the Admiralty's official report on the Battle of the River Plate. Roosevelt acknowledged receipt of the report in a brief but significant note on May 30:

My dear Churchill,

Ever so many thanks for that remarkably interesting story of the Battle of the River Plate—a grand job by your three cruisers.

You are much in my thoughts. I need not tell you that.

As ever yours,

FDR [17]

Those forty-one words were the principal sign so far that American history was changing. Until then it was a commonplace in Washington politics that, as Thomas Jefferson wrote to John Langdon in 1810, and repeated ad nauseam since, "the nature of the English government forbids, of itself, reliance on her engagements; and it is well known that she has been the least faithful to her alliances of any nation in Europe."

The function of all British agents in the United States was to destroy that myth once and for all. Roosevelt's personal attitude toward the Churchill government and the war was exceedingly equivocal. On the one hand Roosevelt recognized that if England failed, America would immediately be subject to extreme danger. He, too, was exceedingly suspicious of the Conservative party, deploring as he did all forms of British imperialism. His first impression of Churchill, stemming from Churchill's conduct at a legal dinner attended by Roosevelt in London in 1918 or 1919, was that he was what everybody had said he was—a coarse, aggressive, bibulous cad. Yet Churchill endorsed the New Deal in 1933 when he sent to Roosevelt the first volume of his *Marlborough: His Life and Times*. On the flyleaf Churchill had inscribed the words:

To Franklin D. Roosevelt from Winston S. Churchill
With earnest best wishes for the success of the greatest crusade of modern times. [18]

And it was Roosevelt who opened correspondence with Churchill when he became first lord of the Admiralty at the outbreak of war in September 1939:

PRIVATE
My Dear Churchill,
It is because you and I occupied similar positions in the [First] World War that I want you to know how glad I am that you are back again in the Admiralty. Your problems are, I realize, complicated by new factors, but the essential is not very different. What I want you and the Prime Minister [Chamberlain] to know is that I shall at all times welcome it if you will keep me in touch personally with anything you want me to know about. You can always send sealed letters through your pouch or my pouch.
I am glad you did the Marlboro volumes before this thing started—and I much enjoyed reading them.
With my sincere regards,
Faithfully Yours,
Franklin D. Roosevelt [19]

In a "fireside chat" over the radio on September 3, the day Britain declared war against Germany, FDR was again equivocal when, in declaring America's neutrality in the war, he nonetheless declared also that "this nation will remain a neutral nation, but I cannot ask that every American remain neutral in thought as well." Under the Neutrality Act of 1937, FDR prohibited the export of arms to the belligerent powers, but then, in a special session of Congress on September 8, 1939, he urged that the arms embargo be repealed. That was done on October 27 by the Senate (63–30) and on November 2 in the House (243–181).

Such was the relationship between the two men when in the spring of 1940 the New York *Herald Tribune*, which the State Department believed had been purchased or otherwise brought under the control of the British government, began to reflect the British viewpoint in exceedingly well informed terms. As Churchill continued speaking in eschatological terms of the peril of isolationism, the *Herald Tribune* began to express the view that "if *they* fail, *we* fail." The *Herald Tribune* emphasized English heroism, the malignancy and power of the Nazi anti-Christ, and the geopolitical calamity that would befall the planet if the anti-Christ succeeded, *without* directly telling America what her moral duty was—what the political warfare executive of the Foreign Office called, in a statement to the press of the Midwest, "the Nineteenth Crusade for civilization." This, so far as is known, was the first direct British political warfare attack on the "hearts and minds" of the American people.

Under Churchill, "C's" departmental policy had been changing under the pressures of war. Now responsible for the control of housing, communications, and, in some cases, the finances of the refugee intelligence services in London, he had embarked on a policy in which, through Dansey, those services would be employed for espionage in Europe. In the neutral capitals the Secret Intelligence Service would be responsible for carrying out those actions that the embassies could not afford to do for themselves if they were not to be seen to be committing nonneutral acts. With Ultra on stream, SIS increasingly became more concerned with clandestine politics than with espionage against the enemy (a role that intensified until, in the fifties, political operations of a secret nature had become almost the sole raison d'être for the existence of SIS). Hence "C's" insistence on the recruitment of field personnel drawn mainly from the same groups the Foreign Office used to draw its staff. The counterespionage service concentrated on operations calculated to destroy the enemy intelligence services and to mystify and mislead the enemy General Staffs, but it also engaged increasingly in espionage operations to draw in-

telligence from enemy agents. As for Churchill's war policy against
the United States, "C" was a man of principles, but one who acknowledged that war was also a stateman's game.

"C's" first action in Churchill's war policy toward the United States
soon came. With great reluctance he relieved Broadway's representative in the United States, Commander Sir John Paget, R.N., to
make way for William S. Stephenson, the Scots-Canadian businessman and member of Churchill's circle in prewar days. A member of
the old League of Gentlemen, Paget had been an effective agent,
discreet, well connected, not likely to get the country into trouble;
and he would have been an excellent man in the United States for
the covert side of Churchill's war diplomacy there. Paget was very
close to FDR's friend and intelligence master, Vincent Astor, and
privy to the advice of Sir William Wiseman, the World War I spymaster in America. Wiseman was a director of the Wall Street financial
house Kuhn, Loeb, so Paget was extraordinarily well informed on
the movements of that key ingredient in covert intelligence, money.
He knew everything, saw everybody, and said nothing except to "C."
But Churchill was insistent.

"C" was compelled to accept Stephenson, whom he had met in
1936 through Sir Ralph Glyn, one of his "honourable correspondents."
Menzies and Stephenson never liked each other, and Stephenson's
experience of Broadway during the Swedish iron ore operation only
heightened their differences. Stephenson did go to the United States
at "C's" request and under his orders, and as a CIA study of that
phase of Anglo-American defined Stephenson's task, he sought to
establish "relations on the highest possible level between the British
SIS and the U.S. Federal Bureau of Investigation." [20]

That mission, in April and May of 1940, came about through a
letter from "C" to FDR in which Roosevelt replied to the effect that
he would welcome such collaboration but that negotiations would
have to be conducted between a representative of "C" and the FBI
director, J. Edgar Hoover. Despite State Department opposition to
such collaboration, on the grounds that such a relationship might
embrangle America in England's causes (which was exactly what was
intended), Stephenson appears to have established relations with
Hoover. However, relations between Stephenson and Hoover personally did not become as close as "C" desired since, it appeared,
there was a misunderstanding or, worse, a calculated indiscretion.

According to a report placed before the U.S. Interdepartmental
Committee on Intelligence and Security, Stephenson told B. L. Cord,

the American industrialist, that Hoover had told him that the Axis powers were establishing an army of Fascist Spaniards in Mexico, one equipped with modern weapons that included artillery. Suspecting that Stephenson's remark was part of some British campaign to create trouble between the United States and the Axis, Cord reported that remark to the U.S. military intelligence service, and they reported it to Hoover. The matter arose at the next meeting of the Interdepartmental Committee on Intelligence and Security, at which Hoover denied that he had told Stephenson anything of the sort or that he had any knowledge of any foreign army gathering in Mexico.

Consequently, on Stephenson's return to England in May 1940, "C," having heard about the incident, expressed the view to Churchill, when discussing candidates for Paget's post, that Stephenson might not be suitable and, as an alternative, advanced the name of Rex Benson. Churchill pressed Stephenson's name upon "C," however, and "C" accepted Stephenson on the condition that, since "C" had executive responsibility for secret operations in the United States, he had control of Stephenson's activities. That did not suit Stephenson at all, for Stephenson had formed an adverse impression of "C" and "that gang at Broadway" [21], and, while quite prepared to go to New York, he would do so only if he had independent command with the right at all times of direct access to Churchill.

Only Churchill could resolve such an impasse, and that was settled when Stephenson, as he claimed, dined with Churchill on May 10, the day on which he was appointed prime minister. Stephenson discussed "C's" demands with Churchill privately after dinner, and as Stephenson also claimed, Churchill declared that it was Stephenson's duty to accept the post, but that, though he would have to accept "C's" directives, he would also have direct access to Churchill. Stephenson claimed further that Churchill assured him he would have a high degree of freedom in his operations, although in the interests of symmetry he would have to be subject to "C's" direction in fiscal, administrative, and communications matters. Churchill thereupon gave Stephenson his orders. He was to go to New York and help "assure sufficient aid for Britain, to counter the enemy's subversive plans throughout the Western Hemisphere . . . *and eventually to bring the United States into the war*" (emphasis added). [22]

With those objectives in mind, Stephenson prepared for his mission. Relations were not improved between "C" and Stephenson when the latter, who had had no previous training in either diplomacy or secret service, insisted upon taking with him a professional secret service officer, Colonel Charles H. Ellis. "C" opposed that request because Ellis was already employed on important diplomatic espionage work in London, and there was nobody to replace him. However, "C" relented largely because he had reasons for not wanting to keep Ellis inside Broadway—reasons that were not to emerge for several years—and Ellis was appointed as deputy to Stephenson.

Stephenson left England in mid-June, traveling by Cunarder with his American wife, Mary. Installing himself on the thirty-third and thirty-fourth floors of Rockefeller Center (which he obtained at a peppercorn rent from the owner, Nelson Rockefeller, a member of the old private intelligence organization, The Room, and of that exclusive diner, the Walrus Club), Stephenson created a large staff throughout the Americas with which to begin the contest of political wills with the German and Italian secret services and also to help the ambassador, the marquess of Lothian, in the task of guiding President Roosevelt in his step-by-step-toward-war policy.

Stephenson soon found himself in major contests with isolationist, Fascist, Communist, and pacifist groups—to say nothing of the FBI and the State Department—who were seeking to rally the U.S. electorate over to the side of nonintervention. The vigor with which Stephenson did his work again brought him to the attention of J. Edgar Hoover and Assistant Secretary of State Adolf Berle, chairman of the Interdepartmental Committee on Intelligence and Security at the State Department. And it was not long before "C" faced demands that Stephenson be recalled. But initially, in the late spring of 1940, Stephenson proved his value by making contact with a prominent Irish-American Catholic Republican lawyer, William J. Donovan, who was close to President Roosevelt.

At the suggestion of Vincent Astor, a mutual friend and the founder member of The Room and the Walrus Club, Roosevelt entertained Stephenson at his estate at Hyde Park, and at that meeting Stephenson told FDR of the concern in London over the defeatist nature of the reporting of the U.S. ambassador in London, Joseph Kennedy. Stephenson suggested that FDR send Donovan to London to make an independent estimate on the crucially important question of whether Britain would indeed, as Churchill had stated, fight the war to the bitter end. FDR thought highly of Donovan—they had studied law together at Columbia—and Donovan accepted the mission, leaving for London in a Pan-American Clipper flying boat on July 14.

Four days later Donovan was installed at Claridge's Hotel in London and met with Menzies. That this was an important encounter there is no doubt—and an unlikely one. On the one hand there was Stewart Menzies, Eton, Life Guards, GHQ, secret service, White's, Beaufort Hunt, praetorian spymaster, defender of the established order, Protestant, a descendant of the caste held responsible by the Irish for the production of the Celtic twilight. Now he was the secret instrument of a secret British policy intended to entice the United States into the war.

On the other there was "Wild Bill" Donovan, whose grandfather had been a Ribbonman, a member of a Catholic secret society devoted to the expulsion of the British from Ireland; his father had been a Fenian and a Catholic functionary at Buffalo; Donovan had commanded the Fighting Sixty-ninth, sons of the men come from Roaringwater and Courtmarcherry to build the Erie Canal. Born in the first ward of Buffalo, its poorest district, Donovan had married the richest Protestant girl in the city and had become a famous lawyer who was earning $500,000 a year at the height of the Depression; and they said in the twenties, when he was assistant attorney general in the Coolidge administration, that if he had not been Catholic, he would have become president of the United States. Silver-haired, silver-tongued, silver-suited, silver-mannered, one of the country's three authentic heroes of World War I, founding partner of one of the world's leading law firms, Donovan was a great example of the American meritocrat of the twenties and the thirties, the hired gun of the oil and movie companies.

From the outset "C" sought to use Donovan as an agent-of-influence to counter Ambassador Kennedy. That was vital if the United States was to provide the substantial aid that was necessary if, as Churchill was intimating in his private correspondence with the American president, Britain was to survive. Well aware of the American military belief that America's first line of defense was the east coast of England, "C" did everything he could to show that England would survive and even triumph *if* America changed the various laws governing her attitude toward the belligerents, *if* she sent the destroyers, aircraft, armaments, munitions, and foodstuffs, and *if* she abandoned her policy that the first business of the United States was business.

To prove these points, "C" went farther than he had gone with any foreigner at any time, while recognizing that Donovan was probably an antiimperialist in sheep's clothing. He opened every door except one—Bletchley's—to provide the evidence that Britain was not decadent, as was so widely believed in the United States, that she would fight as Churchill said she would. If the worst came and England was defeated, then she would not, as the French had done and as the Americans feared she would, surrender her fleet. Nor would she scuttle it as the Germans did when they were defeated in 1918. She would send the fleet and the government to the Americas to continue the war until Germany was defeated. The Donovan papers contain a rare letter by Menzies, which, while being a model of brevity and formality, demonstrated the importance of the doors being opened for the alien lawyer:

LONDON.

22nd July, 1940

Dear Colonel Donovan,

To confirm our talk, it has been arranged for you to visit Lord Gort [chief of the Imperial General Staff] at 10.30 A.M. on Wednesday next, the 24th inst.

Lord Gort is sending Captain Crayshaw to Claridge's at 10.25 A.M. to pick you up and take you to his office.

With best wishes,

Yours sincerely,

(s) S.G. Menzies [23]

For his part, it seems that Donovan's first encounter with Menzies, and the services that Menzies felt able to render him, met with Donovan's gratitude. As "C" remarked to Admiral Godfrey before Donovan left Washington, "He was told that he would find us 'difficult,' secretive, patronising. His actual experience, so he said, was exactly the opposite." [24]

The meeting with Gort was but a prelude to meetings with the entire group responsible for the direction of the war. Never were the doors of the great opened so rapidly as they were when Donovan arrived. People of power who in peacetime would not have dreamed of talking with an American lawyer gave him lunch, dinner, tea, breakfast, briefings, evenings at great country houses. The messages they left for him on Claridge's switchboard required the services of a full-time secretary. Donovan saw the prime minister, the king, the queen, the princesses, ministers, and secretaries of state, generals, admirals, marshalls of the Royal Air Force. The entire command, operations, intelligence, and administrative systems of the British war machine were opened to him.

As C.I.A. study shows, "Donovan scurried about London and its environs visiting every important government office and inspecting many of the military, naval, and air installations then girding for the defense of the islands." [25] Donovan's discussions "ranged encyclopedically over the full gamut of military, political, economic, and social factors relevant to the country's defense." These included the "expansion and training of the army, shipping problems, food production, conscription, the morale of the British population, and the very pressing need for destroyers, flying boats, bomb sights, and the training of pilots." He "discussed such subjects as intelligence, propaganda, the organization of the information ministry, subversion, and the Fifth Column."

One of Donovan's foremost contacts was Admiral Godfrey, who was to record in his journal that "the Kennedy influence had unfortunately spread to the Embassy staff, and infected the Naval Attaché (Kirk), who in June 1940 told me that Britain would be defeated before 4th August, unless America 'came in.' Donovan sensed this general air of defeatism at the Embassy, and felt it to be more marked among the Naval than among the Army representatives." Donovan on the other hand "quickly became aware of the spiritual qualities of the British race—the imponderables that make for victory but had evaded Ambassador Kennedy—and [decided] that there was still time for American aid, both material and economic, to exercise a decisive influence on the war."

Rarely before in the history of the two powers was an American so flattered with high confidences. Donovan spent his last night in England at Godfrey's home at Sevenoaks, Kent, and at this meeting Donovan promised to do what he could—and the secretary of the navy, Frank Knox, was a close personal friend—to obtain for Godfrey's naval intelligence department the U.S. consular reports from the French ports, which contained much important intelligence relating to the movement of U-boats and warships and the congregations of craft necessary to undertake an invasion of the British isles.

Then on August 3 Donovan left England for New York aboard the British flying boat *Clare*. With him he took a list of those materiels of war that the British needed most urgently. The list included "(a) Bomb sights (b) flying boats (c) 50 destroyers (d) squadrons of 'Flying Fortresses' [i.e. B-17s] with if possible pilots, mechanics and technical maintenance staffs (e) 25-pounder and 105 mm guns (f) motor boats (g) surplus Lee Enfield rifles (h) use of American airfields for the training of Canadian, Australian, and British pilots." In one way or another England got them all, although not quite so inexpensively as they had hoped.

On his arrival in New York, to the gratitude of the British government, Donovan, who had a wide following throughout the United States, announced boldly that, whatever happened, the Germans would not defeat Britain. He kept saying this, first to Secretary of the Navy Knox, then to the command of the U.S. Navy, then to the army command, which wanted to keep its weaponry within the United States, then to FDR and the White House, where Donovan presented the British list of required war materiels. And as Godfrey was to write: "Not only did Mr. Roosevelt accept Donovan's appreciation of our war effort, but he approved in principle the supply of material on a large scale. This developed into 'lend lease' and later full alliance." In the "sphere of technique and material, Donovan said he would be able to smooth out difficulties, as he had among his clients and his clients' relatives such a large number of industrialists of all sorts, many of whom were carrying out contracts for the British Government."

Donovan gave a national radio broadcast in which he spoke of England's resolution to fight and win. He met with members of both houses of Congress and most of the Cabinet; and he joined FDR for two days at Hyde Park on August 9. At their meetings he told FDR that Britain would withstand a German invasion, that British morale was excellent, and that the military needs of the country were both great and urgent. He said he was already considering whether the British would be able to take the offensive in the spring; and as for the need for old American destroyers, Stephenson was able to wire Menzies on August 21 that "Donovan believes you will have within a few days very favourable news."

Next day Stephenson wired Menzies again to state that "the figure of fifty destroyers had been agreed by the President and that forty-four were in commission for delivery." In short, as Godfrey was to recall, "it was obvious that we had a good friend in Donovan, and one who had the ear of the President and knew how to work with the British." [26] And if the destroyers deal was to prove the greatest sale of real estate in bankruptcy in history—for in return America received from Britain ninety-nine-year leases on naval and air bases in Newfoundland, Bermuda, the Bahamas, Jamaica, St. Lucia, Trinidad, Antigua, British Guiana, and all other English colonies, although none of the destroyers were battleworthy upon delivery, and few still were even seaworthy—that state of affairs was not Donovan's responsibility.

Yet for all the emerging intimacy between Menzies and Donovan, Menzies was not in any doubt that Donovan was, like himself, an instrument of power politics. Nor was he in very much doubt, like Churchill, that England would have to pay a stiff price for American support. Among the matters that Britain would have to undertake was a renunciation of imperialism and an abandonment of the empire. And that neither Churchill nor Menzies was prepared to countenance. Here, therefore, Menzies evidently decided, was an Irishman to watch. Most likely Donovan felt the same about "C." But for the moment it suited both men, as it suited both nations, to be cousins.

Writing on August 27, 1940, Donovan advised Menzies that "our conscription bill has been having hard going," but "at the request of the manager of the bill in the House and also of the manager in the Senate I have appeared before groups in both Houses and discussed your situation abroad." Donovan thought what he had to say had "helped a lot," and that he "knew" that "it was due to your thoughtfulness in opening so many doors that I was able to tell our people in authority the reasons for my conclusions," and this had given them "confidence in my report." All this had "inured to your benefit with our people." [27]

Aware that "C" might be disturbed by the appearance of Donovan's name over a series of articles in leading newspapers throughout the United States concerning German Fifth Column techniques, and aware, too, of "C's" reputation for being "a maniac" about secrecy, Donovan assured Menzies that this had been done "at the insistance of the President," who had, also, "let it be known in his own way to the various press services that my opinion was that your people were strong, determined, and would hold out." Donovan explained that he was "in touch with many of your representatives here," and "as I check with them—even though now you are taking a harder blasting—I find only confirmation of the opinion I stated to you while I was there." Donovan ended his letter: "I shall always remember your many kindnesses and I hope some time soon I will have the chance to reciprocate." [28]

In other directions, Churchill's American policy had been taking fresh forms to demonstrate to the Americans that Britain's was not only a moral cause of basic importance in the destiny of the world, but a practical one, one that the Americans must support, if only for their own good. Upon becoming prime minister, Churchill sought and was granted powers not hitherto awarded his office. His ministry became absolute, his method authoritarian. That caused great alarm, for as Colville recorded in his diary on May 23, 1940:

Yesterday the Government obtained permission from the House to take over fuller powers than any British Government has ever possessed. The purpose is largely that if we are invaded, or otherwise *in extremis*, the rights of individuals and institutions must not be allowed to stand in the way of the country's safety. Houses must be demolished to stop advancing tanks, labour must if necessary be coerced, industrial plant requisitioned. Now if ever *salus populi suprema lex*, and in a totalitarian war even a democracy must surrender its liberties. But what a precedent for the future peacetime Governments; and will state control, once instituted, ever be abandoned? [29]

Churchill was careless of the alarm. To demonstrate that his intention was not mere rodomontade, he ordered the arrest of everyone in high and low places he knew to harbor defeatist or treasonable thoughts. Fearing that a Fifth Column might develop through which the Nazi secret services could infiltrate to seize or influence the power of the state, Churchill authorized the detention of 436 persons, 150 of them described as "prominent," under Defence Regulation 18b. Under this order the government could detain members of any organization if "the persons in control of the organisation have or have had associations with persons concerned in the government of, or sympathies with the system of government of, any Power with which His Majesty is at war."

Two of the first three persons on the list were cousins by marriage of Clementine Churchill, the prime minister's wife. They were Sir Oswald Mosley (whose wife, Lady Cynthia Curzon, had been a bridesmaid at "C's" first wedding) and George Pitt-Rivers, who had been at Eton with "C" and with the Royal Dragoons in World War I, then served as private secretary and aide-de-camp to the governor-general of Australia. Of late, Pitt-Rivers had become convinced by Ribbentrop's argument that the Jews, Freemasons, and Bolsheviks had joined in a deliberate conspiracy to cause war between England and Germany. Another who believed this was H. St. John Philby, the Arabist and father of Kim Philby; he was detained and spent a year in Liverpool jail for arguing Fascist causes publicly. In all, the total of such persons arrested since the outbreak of war was 1,373. They were held in jail without indictment or conviction "at His Majesty's pleasure." Consideration was given to the arrest of George Frederick Steward, Chamberlain's press officer; MI5 telephone taps on 10 Downing Street just before the outbreak of war had shown that Steward was having possibly treasonable conversations with the Germans, perhaps on behalf of Chamberlain personally.

There was considerable unease about the activities and statements of the richest man in the empire, the duke of Westminster, whose income of £900,000 a year was double the Civil List for the king. A close friend of the duke and duchess of Windsor (Constance Edwina, duchess of Westminster, was also a close friend of Lady Holford, "C's" mother), Churchill warned Westminster against treasonable or defeatist utterances, then found he had to utter a second warning nine days after the outbreak of war when Westminster met secretly at Bourdon House with the duke of Buccleuch, Lord Arnold, and Lord Rushcliffe and read them a paper by a former member of Parliament, Henry Drummond-Wolff, an admirer of Herman Goering.

Lord Tavistock was found to be in secret communication with Ribbentrop through the German embassy in Dublin, and in January 1940 Tavistock actually received what were called "peace terms." These he sent to Lord Halifax, foreign secretary and Chamberlain's heir, and one whose enthusiasm for the war was not pronounced; and it was estimated that 34 percent of all English voters favored "peace at any price," almost all of them in the middle and upper classes who had suffered the most through World War I. A number of these people were in "C's" personal circle at one time or another. Euan Wallace, "C's" oldest friend, was not retained as transport minister, as he had been in the Chamberlain administration, because of his association with Mosley. Wallace was, however, appointed civil defense controller of London, a post he filled throughout the Battle of Britain with gallantry and efficiency.

Briefly, it seems, Churchill was again concerned with "C's" politics, for he associated with the titled group that Churchill had arrested. He was known to have argued in 1936 and 1937 that England should stand aside and propel Russia and Germany into mortal collision. Churchill had been gravely concerned to find in November 1939 that "C" was in charge of Chamberlain's attempt—the attempt that led to the humiliation of Venlo—to make an alliance with a German military regime from which Hitler and the Nazis had been extruded, one directed against Russia. Churchill was concerned, as he said, that Hitler had succeeded in taking England by surprise. How had this come about? Churchill remained convinced that British intelligence was still "the finest in the world," and happily for "C" he could not believe that Chamberlain's failure to foresee so many of Hitler's actions was really "the fault of the British Secret Service."

But Churchill's actions reflected the belief that Hitler's secret agents were ubiquitous, that their Fifth Column was at every hand, corrupting ministers, generals, high officials, and society at large. Churchill wondered whether "there is not some hand" in British officialdom that "intervenes and filters down or withholds intelligence from Ministers." As a consequence of these suspicions, he demanded of all his intelligence masters that he be shown "authentic documents in their original form." [30]

To insulate himself against German deception, Churchill appointed as his personal intelligence master Major Desmond Morton, of Eton, GHQ France (where he was aide-de-camp to Haig), and SIS. He was regarded with wonder in Whitehall because he had been shot through the heart and survived. Morton's instructions were to keep an eye on "C" and the intelligence services in general and to examine all intelligence destined for the prime minister. That, effectively, placed a barrier between Churchill and "C," who had the right of direct access to the prime minister.

"C" did not, however, concern himself too much about Morton, whom "C" regarded as a buffoon who would trip himself sooner rather than later. "C" was right. Although Morton remained in that office until the end of the war, he gradually lost authority. He was indiscreet, gossipy, a gin swigger, and one whose voice, as Colville declared, "would penetrate the ramparts of a medieval castle." [31] Morton let it be known in many quarters that he was Churchill's right-hand man, and so he seemed to be for a time. In the end, as Colville recorded, "because he had been over-ambitious, he died a sad and embittered man." "C," on the other hand, was cleverer: constantly he gave the impression that he was surprised to find himself where he was and was grateful to God—and Winston—for his elevation.

With the arrest of the lords of creation who found themselves on the wrong side, Churchill proceeded to his last and most important task in that regard, to clip the tongue and hobble the feet of Churchill's former king, now the duke of Windsor. This was very much "C's" business, for the duke was on foreign soil with the duchess, and both were making statements that could only bring aid and comfort to an enemy. Appointed a major general on the staff of the British military mission in Paris, Windsor's task included intelligence about French civilian and political attitudes at the highest levels. "C" sent his cousin, Rex Benson, a friend of Windsor, to Paris to keep his eyes and ears open. (Later, it emerged that the duke had corresponded with the old kaiser, Wilhelm II, who was in exile at Doorn, Holland, and that the kaiser was relating to the German minister at The Hague what Edward was saying.) When the Germans threatened Paris, the duke abandoned his post without permission, a court-martial offense, and fled to the south of France to rejoin the duchess at their villa on the Riviera. All British consular posts were warned of Windsor's disappearance, but the duke and duchess remained unsighted until they arrived in Madrid, the capital of a pro-German neutral. There the duke made several pro-German statements and, for a time, entertained the Spanish government's offer, one prompted by the Germans, of asylum in Spain, being offered a grand and sumptuously appointed castle as his residence. But the Windsors soon departed, this time for Lisbon.

They took up residence in the villa of a known Nazi informant at Cascais, Ricardo Espirito Santo Silva, the Portugese banker. There the duke was soon reported to have stated that England "faced a catastrophic military defeat, which could only be avoided through a peace settlement with Germany." [32] The U.S. ambassador at Madrid, Alexander Weddell, reported to Washington (and as Washington warned London) the duke's views reflected those of "an element in England, possibly a growing one, who find in Windsor and his circle a group who are realists in world politics and who hope to come into their own in the event of peace." Certainly these opinions came to the notice of the German foreign minister, Joachim von Ribbentrop, and early in July Ribbentrop proposed to Hitler a fantastic plot: kidnap the duke and duchess and, against a promise to restore the duke to the throne after a successful invasion of England, use the duke as the pretender. Windsor would remove Churchill and King George VI and then assume the political leadership of England.

To that end, later in July Ribbentrop sent for Brigadeführer SS Walter Schellenberg and ordered him to Lisbon to kidnap the duke and duchess of Windsor. Probably through "C," Churchill anticipated this plot, and since the duke of Windsor was a major general in the British army and therefore liable to military law, an order was sent to Windsor to return to England. Two Sunderland flying boats were sent to the flying boat dock on the Tagus at Lisbon to provide him with the necessary transportation, and at the same time "C" asked the Portugese security service, who were friendly toward SIS, to "provide the duke with protection." But the duke rejected his orders, pleading that he had no home or job in England, that his wife was not acceptable at court, and that he could not accept residency in England unless King George VI and Queen Elizabeth recognized the duchess as "Her Royal Highness," which hitherto they had refused to do.

With that refusal, the duke's and duchess's passports were retained by the British embassy in Lisbon. The chief of the Portuguese security service placed the duke and duchess under house arrest while Churchill sent the duke a personal telegram that implied a serious warning:

Your Royal Highness has taken active military rank, and refusal to obey direct orders of competent military authority would create a serious situation. I hope it will not be necessary for such orders to be sent. I must strongly urge immediate compliance with wishes of the Government.

The couple was placed under the personal surveillance of David Eccles, an acquaintance of the duke who was also a member of a British secret organization in Spain. During this period, the duchess was found to be in correspondence with Ribbentrop, causing further anxiety about the intentions of the duke. Eric Seal, Churchill's principal private secretary, minuted to Sir Alexander Hardinge, private secretary to the king, on July 9: "As I told you once before, this is not the first time that this lady has come under suspicion for her anti-British activities, and as long as we never forget the power she can exert over him in her efforts to avenge herself on this country we shall be all right."

Largely perhaps at the advice of Eccles, the duke agreed to return to England immediately aboard the Sunderlands that were still waiting for him in the Tagus. But at the last minute Churchill decided against having either the duke or the duchess in England at all, probably because he realized that both were friends of the duke of Westminster and that Westminster had offered Windsor his greatest estate, Eaton Hall, as a royal residence. At a time of emergency and siege, Churchill wanted no "trade unions of dukes" ganging up against his "war to the bitter end" policy and decided instead upon the banishment of Windsor to the minor post of governor of the Bahamas.

After much further difficulty over whether the duke and duchess might travel to the Bahamas by way of New York (FDR was not anxious to have them in the United States at such a dangerous time politically, for he feared they would become the darlings of the America Firsters), the duke agreed to leave Lisbon aboard the SS *Excalibur*, which was due to sail for Bermuda on August 1. With the duke's agreement,

Churchill then sent out Sir Walter Monkton, Windsor's legal adviser, to give the duke a warning in writing about his attitudes.

While elegantly framed and courteously expressed, the letter was nevertheless a warning:

Sir, may I venture upon a word of serious counsel. It will be necessary for the Governor of the Bahamas to express views about the war and the general situation which are not out of harmony with those of His Majesty's Government. The freedom of conversation which is natural to anyone in an unofficial position, or indeed to a major-general, is not possible in any direct representative of the Crown. Many sharp and unfriendly ears will be pricked up to catch any suggestion that your Royal Highness takes a view about the war, or about the Germans, or about Hitlerism, which is different from that adopted by the British nation and Parliament. Many malicious tongues will carry tales in every direction. Even while you have been staying at Lisbon, conversations have been reported by telegraph through various channels which might have been used to your Royal Highness's disadvantage. In particular, there is danger of use being made of anything you say in the United States to do injury, and to suggest divergences between you and the British Government. I am so anxious that mischief should not be made which might mar the success which I feel sure will attend your mission. We are all passing through times of immense stress and dire peril, and every step has to be watched with care.

I thought your Royal Highness would not mind these words of caution from

> Your faithful and devoted servant
> Winston S. Churchill [33]

By this time—toward the end of July 1940, when the Battle of Britain had begun the substratosphere over southern England—Brigadeführer SS Schellenberg arrived in Lisbon to kidnap the duke and duchess. Hoping to avoid violence, Schellenberg asked for a personal meeting with the duke at which he might explain his business. But on the eve of the sailing of the duke and duchess (and as rumor spread in Lisbon that if the duke did not sail in *Excalibur*, he was to be assassinated by the British secret service, a rumor spread probably by Schellenberg in order to frighten the duke into accepting Ribbentrop's offer of asylum in Spain and an honorarium large enough to permit a prince to live in the style worthy of a German guest), Windsor sent word that a meeting was impossible.

Soon after that message, Schellenberg fell ill and was later found to be suffering from a severe case of liver or gall bladder poisoning, an episode from which he never recovered and from which he died young. He always insisted that he had been poisoned by the British secret service. There was no interference from the Sicherheitsdienst, consequently, when the duke and duchess of Windsor left Lisbon for the Bahamas on August 1, in the U.S. liner *Excalibur.*

In the Bahamas they came under the "protection" of Stephenson's service in New York. They also became friendly with a Swedish millionaire who was a known Nazi agent-of-influence, Axel Wenner-Gren, who had an oceangoing yacht and who, it was feared in London, might be there to help the noble couple flee to Germany. Warnings from Churchill did no good, and at least until America's entry into the war in December 1941, Windsor made little secret of his sympathies. As he told a prominent American visitor, it was "too late for America to save Democracy in Europe," and that she had better "save it in America for herself." The duke was said to have written highly compromising letters to Hitler personally, ones that escaped the British censorship but were known to have been delivered. The duchess, too, was being watched by the FBI, for as Assistant Secretary Adolf Berle recorded in his diary on September 20, 1940, the eve of the day scheduled for the invasion of England:

Tamm, of the FBI, came down. They have uncovered some correspondence which looks as though the Duchess of Windsor was in constant communication with Ribbentrop. . . . It looks as though there has been some intriguing. . . . Maybe the Duchess would like at long last to be Queen. [34]

6 SOURCES

In the trade there is an axiom that no intelligence service is better than its sources. If that is true, then Stewart Menzies was better placed than was known in Whitehall, at the time or afterward. As Colville remarked:

Desmond Morton tells me that "C," the head of the Secret Service, has now received news of imminent invasion from over 260 *sources.* The main attack will be against the South [of England], with diversions against Hull, Scotland, and Ireland, which will be exploited if successful. Parachutists will be used only in the South. It is clear that all preparations have been made; whether they will be used depends upon Hitler's caprice. [35]

Colville added a sentence that was of high significance in "C's" tactics and strategy over the coming eight weeks of danger: "It is significant that German troops are concentrating in the East, and it is on the cards that Hitler has immediate designs against the Ukraine." That suggests "C" had special knowledge of Hitler's intentions, for in their private statements throughout the Battle of Britain, Churchill, the Foreign Office, and "C" all expressed the view that Hitler might invade if he could win control of the skies, but if he did not defeat Fighter Command, then he would turn on Russia. On what basis was that estimate forming—one that, incidentally, proved accurate?

Part of the official London view that Sealion, the German code name for the invasion of Britain, was little more than a ploy, sprang from "C's" knowledge of the Germans. Had he not begun to study them when he met the Garde du Corps in their pure white-and-gold uniforms at the funeral of George I in Athens in 1913? The rest was the intelligence he obtained from his sources. "C's" view almost consistently was that Hitler would not gain control of the skies and that he would turn east. "C's" chief, Cadogan, the man to whom "C" reported most days, if not by calling personally then by telephone, held somewhat similar views. Cadogan recorded in his diary: "Will Hitler invade? I, personally, doubt it, *but would never say so*" (emphasis added). Cadogan's statement is of high importance, for while his view was widely held within the secret circle, it was not communicated to the American embassy, even informally, on the grounds that silence might yet prove golden.

To prevent the diplomatic corps, including that of the United States, from learning any more than Churchill thought desirable about the true British capabilities, intentions, and knowledge, Churchill forbade all but necessary contact between his administration and foreign representatives. At the same time he directed that information to General Raymond E. Lee, the U.S. military attaché in London, should be greatly reduced. Lee was such an Anglophile that he had his uniforms cut in Saville Row and his hair and whiskers trimmed at Trumper's, the royal barber. When he learned of these instructions they made him angry, and suspecting that Churchill was tailoring the facts to his American policy, Lee warned the chiefs of staff in ominous fashion:

I do not believe that we can be too emphatic in pointing out that the U.S. Government must be kept promptly and fully informed of everything which has a bearing on the progress of the war.

The United States entered the last war in 1917 practically blindfolded because a great range of vital facts had been withheld from our representatives both here and in Paris. This has never been forgotten in Washington. It must not happen this time.

If the full support of the United States is desired, the President and his advisers are entitled to the complete and detailed picture, whether it is favorable or not, so that they can made their decisions with their eyes open.

The whole affair is now at a point at which Congress must decide whether the United States is to finance the rest of the war. If any impression gets about in Washington that any facts are being withheld on this side, so that our reports are partial, or biased, or misinformed, it is going to be too bad. [36]

As a result of that communication, Lee was recalled to Washington for a conference and did not return to London, being replaced by officials with less questing minds. Churchill did not propose to allow a niggling official of a foreign embassy to disturb the imagery being created of tiny, heroic England facing imminent and apocalyptic extinction at the hands of the German anti-Christ. With Donovan lobbying furiously for England in Washington, and U.S. intelligence in a worse state than it was before 1914, on what grounds could Churchill be censured if he chose to purvey England's version of the truth? This was total war, and total war required the calculated circulation of facts, which were a weapon always more deadly than bullets and bombs.

"C" played little part in direct political warfare. It was his responsibility to procure the facts. What other departments did with them was their business. But procure the facts he must, for the more he obtained about the enemy the better Churchill could pursue his American—and Russian—policies. "C's" sources were consequently as vital to the prosecution of strategy as they were to the business of defeating the enemy. The two went hand in hand, while the methods used to obtain the facts was the most secret business of the state.

First there was Ultra, but at that time Ultra was providing little or no strategic information about German intentions, only tactical intelligence that enabled the RAF, broadly speaking, to be at the right place, the right altitude, at the right time in order to intercept the German air force squadrons. There was little or no intelligence coming from Norwegian, French, and Belgian sources on the continent, for these had not as yet recovered from the disaster of May and June 1940. There was a little intelligence, albeit of a generally unreliable nature, coming from American diplomatic outposts in Europe, but nothing that would illuminate German intentions to the extent conveyed in Colville's diary entry and other statements like it made by members of the secret circle at that same time.

Of almost equal importance was the nature of "C's" sources in Berlin, if he had any at all. In discussions with American intelligence officers, "C" was asked if he had spies in Berlin, and he always replied that he had no spies "east of the Rhine." When Brigadeführer SS Schellenberg was captured after the war and interrogated, however, he claimed knowledge of ten suspected companies or individuals at work in the British interest in Berlin, other than the members of the Black Orchestra, the anti-Nazi movement around Admiral Canaris. These were:

Rosenkranz:
> A former director of the Reich Bureau for Mineral Oils, who had contact with two German directors of of the Shell oil company in Germany. These directors were also considered suspect. "Other of his business acquaintances were not entirely clear of suspicion either, for which reasons Rosenkranz was kept under observation. No definite proof of implication in espionage could be established against him.

Woolworth's:
> Suspect because it was an American firm and also because the activities of one American director in Berlin had come to the notice of the Sicherheitsdienst through "prima-facie suspicious actions." Watch was maintained on "5 or 6 American directors at Woolworth's head office, on other American personnel throughout Germany, and on various German directors." Schellenberg believes that after America's entry into the war this matter was reviewed more thoroughly but does not know the results.

The Schimmelpfeng Information Bureau:
> A German national and international commercial and private intelligence service that appeared in SIS's suspect lists during World War I as an enemy secret service, this organization operated from Berlin throughout Europe and Scandinavia and was regarded as being an excellent organization particularly in economic matters. So useful was Schimmelpfeng that after the invasion of Russia Schellenberg himself retained its services.

Opel, Limited:
> An automobile manufacturer, this company had close connections with General Motors whose European representative, a certain Hartmann, was Menzies's neighbor at Luckington Manor, the house which Treeck leased until his disappearance at the outbreak of World War II. Schellenberg was particularly suspicious of one of the Opel directors, a certain Winter, who was arrested on suspicion of espionage but released for lack of evidence. Another representative of General Motors in Germany, an

American called Mooney, alias *Stallforth*, was found to have had secret connections with dissidents within the German General Staff and with von Hassell, the German ambassador at Rome who was later executed for high treason.

Jauch & Huebner:

A Hamburg insurance firm with extensive connections, these enabled "Huebner to acquire information on such matters as the raw material situation, etc., and other matters incidentally important in economic espionage." The firm had a branch in Sweden, and it was believed that Huebner prepared reports on such matters and sent them there, though whether with guilty intent or for bona-fide business purposes was not established in Schellenberg's time with Department IV. He assumed that Huebner's guilt must have been established later as he was arrested in 1943 or 1944.

Hanau, gas-mask manufacturers, Berlin:

In the spring of 1941 Schellenberg's department investigated an allegation made by anonymous letter that the owner of this firm had sold particulars of its manufacturing patent to England via Sweden. By the time Schellenberg left the department the case was being investigated, but nothing had yet been established against the individual in question.

Kirchholtess:

A German diplomat who had been in overseas posts but had been dismissed by Ribbentrop, Kirchholtess was "a shrewd man with a large circle of social acquaintances who had come to the notice of some of Schellenberg's 'society espionage' informants." He was suspected of sending information to Sweden for Allied purposes by means of the foreign representatives [in Berlin] with whom he had contact. Nothing was proven against him.

Rhoderich Dietze:

Dietze, a member of the Ministry of Propaganda, had British nationality as late as 1938, and "difficulties" arose when, upon becoming a naturalized German subject in 1939, he claimed that he lost his British passport. A close contact and protegé of Josef Goebbels, the propaganda minister, "it was therefore considered too dangerous to arrest him."

Baron von Steengracht:

Steengracht "was a member of the German Foreign Office and suspicions against him implicated his wife. After the German invasion of the Low Countries, a slip was found on some Belgian official which showed that at some time prior to the invasion a telephone call had been received from the Belgian military attaché in Berlin, giving warning of the impending attack. There was no actual record of the text of the call, but [Schellenberg's department] set about tracing the circumstances of it, and found that at the time it had been made, the Belgian military attaché had been in the company of Frau Steengracht. There was, however, also the possibility that some member of the Papal Nunciatur in Berlin might have been responsible for the betrayal of the information, as having also been in telephone contact with the Belgian military attaché at about this time [sic]. Thus, the case remained open and nothing definite was undertaken against Steengracht or his wife."

Dr. Chaul:

This "Egyptian was a specialist in internal complaints, and suspicion concerning him rested partly on some remarks he had made in conversation and partly on the fact that he, a foreigner, had attended Hitler once during the war. Furthermore his mode of life was generally suspicious. Chaul's mail and telephone were put under check, but Schellenberg knows nothing further of the outcome of the case." [37]

At first there appears little startling about these sources, if they *were* sources. Certainly they did not compare to the Red Orchestra's ubiquity when that organization was uncovered. On careful reading, however, they may have been wider-ranging than it appears, especially the involvement of companies such as Woolworth's, which had stores in all main cities. Steengracht, too, may have been an important source, for he became deputy undersecretary of state in the German Foreign Ministry, a post he held until 1945. But if "C's" resources in Berlin were not substantial, then if a report by a French service is accurate, he *did* have access to the intelligence being obtained by the ubiquitous Soviet service of Lavrenti Beria.

Although a relationship between "C" and Beria seems unlikely on the surface, for not only were they ideological enemies, but Bolshevik Russia was an ally of Nazi Germany, on closer examination the *histoire* is not as unlikely as it sounds. Russia had everything to lose if Britain were compelled to surrender, for Hitler had made little secret of his intention to eliminate bolshevism once he had settled accounts with England and France. He had said what he intended to do in *Mein Kampf* and in several major speeches since the publication of that work. He had formed the Anti-Comintern Pact with Italy and Japan, with Spain hanging about on the fringes. Perhaps the very obscurity of Hitler's intentions would have forced "C" and Beria to collaborate, for it became known after the war that Hitler planned Sealion, the operation for the invasion of England, and Barbarossa simultaneously in order to confuse his adversaries about his intentions.

Plainly Stalin had reason to keep England in the war if only to gain the time necessary to complete his own rearmament program.

The more time he gained by giving England information calculated to stimulate her resistance and frustrate German operations, the more T34 tanks he would have when the time came for the invasion of Russia. Moreover, there had been intelligence cooperation of a sort before the war. Harold Nicolson, the parliamentarian, politician, diarist, and husband of Vita Sackville-West, a member of "C's" cousinhood in a roundabout way, had close contact with the Soviet ambassador, Ivan Maisky. Maisky was said to have told Aneuran Bevan, a left-winger, that he liked Nicolson because he was the only aristocrat he felt he could trust. Nicolson certainly had a soft spot for Maisky, for despite his Kalmuckian appearance, they saw much of each other. At one stage Maisky told Nicolson that British proposals for an Anglo-Soviet pact might be received by Stalin less frigidly than Chamberlain supposed. At another Maisky warned Nicolson of the possibility of a Nazi-Soviet pact. That information was passed to Broadway through Nicolson and Menzies's friend, Sir Ralph Glyn, one of Menzies's "honourable correspondents." Certainly there was an official exchange of Soviet and British secret service officers between Whitehall and the Kremlin after 1941, when Hitler invaded Russia.

The existence of a Beria connection was not, therefore, an unlikely proposition, and, indeed, when in 1952 the Soviet Politburo decided to execute Beria for high treason, they used as the primary reason Beria's connection with "C," which, it was said, went back to World War I and the British invasion of the Baku area. If it was so, the Beria connection probably only provided minimal intelligence in a manner calculated not to provoke Hitler or compromise Soviet neutrality. In turn, "C" did not hesitate to use the connection to plant reports on the Russians that were intended to split the Nazi-Soviet Pact.

Churchill in London and British Ambassador Sir Stafford Cripps in Moscow warned Russia of what might be in store for them at the hands of their allies. Churchill personally sent two warnings to Stalin that contained intelligence not circulated in Whitehall. Cripps referred to "our information" when as early as June 1940, immediately after the fall of France, he warned Moscow that Hitler contemplated an invasion of Russia. That was quite true: Hitler had ordered planning to start for an invasion of Russia, but, as the British official history admitted, at the time Cripps spoke, "no such information had been received in Whitehall." By August 1940 the Soviet government had become so nervous and suspicious that it added fuel to the fire by denouncing "the attempts of Great Britain to drive a wedge between

Russia and Germany." [38] Molotov reaffirmed Russia's friendship with Germany, a declaration that served only to provide the Foreign Office with yet more opportunities to scratch the wound by commenting:

M. Molotov's speech need not be taken altogether at its face value. The Soviet Government have no friends in the world and no spiritual affinities with other Governments. They merely enter into temporary diplomatic associations with countries for purely opportunist purposes. They distrust and are distrusted by those with whom they associate, but take care not to let their distrust by exploited by others. (i.e. by us). Hence the anxiety they display to re-emphasise on every suitable occasion the friendly character of their relations with Germany.

With a longer experience of war than any other world power in history, except possibly the Poles, Britain conducted its campaign with great skill, with "C" nourishing the rumor mills of the Political Warfare Executive (a dependency of the Foreign Office whose papers were still closed in 1986 with instructions that they were to remain so until 2015, at which time they "may be reviewed") with the gossip of half the chancelleries of Europe. They were also nourished with fact, for "C" was as well informed about what was happening in western Eurasia as any man.

As well as the chancelleries, there were other secret services working in the British interest with great energy and to great effect. Eleven Czech secret service officers escaped to London at the time of the Munich crisis, bringing with them an imprest of £30,000 and one agent of consequence. A54 was Paul Thummel, head of the Abwehr war station at Prague, and he corresponded with the Czech service in London by wireless. Trained in secret service on French principles, "C" had a high opinion of them and especially of their chief, Moravec.

Yet while A54 was certainly the source of some of the 260 reports mentioned by Colville, he was not responsible for all of them. The main source was the Polish intelligence service, which had remained intact despite the collapse of Poland in September 1939 and reached France under the command of a certain Gano. There Gano had begun to rebuild his service inside Poland, paying special attention to German military movements along the east–west railways that ran across Poland. At the French collapse Gano reestablished himself with the help of "C" in a large house at Prince's Gate, London, which remained highly operational as an espionage and communications center even as late as the 1950s, when, mysteriously, it was destroyed by fire.*

Gano's organization was skillful; again, it was trained in French principles, which were supposed to be more professional than those of Britain. It possessed efficient communications with the Polish secret army inside Poland, and German internal counterespionage services regarded Gano's organization with such professional admiration that at the end of the war they decided to establish their underground service on Polish principles. Thus Gano may well have been the source of the reports that persuaded Churchill as early as June 27 that, as he told Smuts, prime minister of South Africa, "If Hitler fails to beat us here, he will probably recoil eastwards. Indeed, he may do this without attempting invasion." The Polish reports may, too, have been the source of "C's" (and therefore the Foreign Office's) almost consistent belief that Russia, not England, would be Hitler's next target.

Nowhere was the queer world of "C's" existence more evident than in his Polish operations. At the beginning of 1940 the Gestapo inserted a spy into the Warsaw center of the Polish resistance movement. This spy reported that two ex-Polish officers were about to take courier—secret—mail by rail from Warsaw to Berlin. The spy provided descriptions, and Schellenberg's agents were able to follow one of the couriers. That man proved to be Kunzcewinzc ("K"), a Pole employed as an official of the Manchurian embassy in Berlin.†

The day after "K's" arrival in Berlin, he met a Polish woman in the Tiergarten in Berlin, and after he had given her a small package, the couple were arrested by German agents. The woman was a cook at the Manchurian embassy, and since neither possessed valid Manchurian passports, they were held in custody while the contents of the package were examined. In the package was a clothes brush and a tube of toothpaste that, Walter Schellenberg later revealed, "concealed microfilms which, on enlargement, produced three volumes of documentary matter on the position, movements, and origin of the

---

*The author, then a newspaperman, visited these headquarters in the early 1950s and saw perhaps ten wireless sets being worked in the basement by Polish emigrés. Presumably they were working to outstations inside Communist Poland. Menzies was still "C" at that time.

†The Chinese province of Manchuria was occupied by the Japanese army in 1932 and was thereafter run by Tokyo as, nominally, an independent state of importance to Germany as a source of metals, coal, fossil fuels, chemicals, and raw materials. Hence the "embassy" in Berlin. This was, however, no more than a Japanese control. Japan was, of course, allied to Germany through its membership in the Anti-Comintern Pact.

German forces in occupied Poland—valuable material at that period, namely the beginning of 1941." [39]

The arrest caused "profound alarm in Japanese official circles in Berlin." As Schellenberg related, the Japanese secret service was "tremendously active throughout Germany," but no counterespionage measures of any kind were undertaken against them because Japan was an allied power. The Japanese service controlled part, at least, of the Poles' Warsaw center and used it as an intelligence agency against both the Germans and the Russians. "K" gave the Japanese "access to the information in the possession of the Polish resistance, in return for which the Japanese issued him with a valid Manchurian passport (probably Diplomatic), thus enabling 'K' to travel unmolested between Warsaw and Berlin, and providing the Polish resistance with a diplomatically protected courier."

In addition, the Japanese assisted in the transmission of the Poles' courier, even though it was destined for Britain, sending it out of Berlin under Manchurian diplomatic protection to Stockholm and Rome. In Stockholm the courier was given by the Japanese military attaché, a certain Onodera, to a Polish intelligence officer, a certain Piotr, who sent the material to the Polish intelligence center in Stockholm. As Schellenberg confessed, despite the investigation, "the Germans never succeeded in finding out any details about this center or about the subsequent uses to which the material was put."

Plainly, however, it was communicated by wireless in Stockholm to the Polish intelligence center in Princes Gate, London. In Rome the material was passed by the Manchurian legation to the Jesuit general, Ledochowski, whom Schellenberg believed ran the Vatican intelligence service, Pro Deo ("For God"). And as Schellenberg also recorded:

"K" had made the Warsaw–Berlin trip as courier on several occasions, calling habitually at the same cover address in Warsaw where he received the material. The chief of an important section of the Polish resistance movement was a certain Polish professor, and it was in his excellently equipped technical laboratory that the micro-films were produced. This professor had also made the trip to Berlin two or three times without being caught by the train control check. Search for him in Warsaw by the agents of [Canaris's counterespionage service] was without result, and it was believed that the Japanese had warned him of his impending arrest.

Bewildering as "C's" world may have been to ordinary mortals, it was normal to him. He delighted in these convoluted schemes by which the stuff of state reached London, thus belying the contention of so many of his peers that he was really no more than a conventional member of the gentry. Yet if the Polish maze was bewildering, it was as straight as a freeway compared with that of the French.

"C's" relations with the French dated from July 1, 1940, when he met General Charles de Gaulle, leader of the Free French Forces in exile, and de Gaulle's intelligence officer, Colonel André Dewavrin, until lately a tutor at the French military college at St. Cyr and a staff officer with the Allied Expeditionary Force to Norway. By that time de Gaulle had been cashiered from the French army and sentenced to death in absentia for high treason. For a number of reasons, however, "C's" personal relations with de Gaulle were not congenial.

Following the fall of France, on June 24, 1940, the Royal Navy had begun a series of attacks on the French fleet to prevent it from falling into the hands of the Germans or the Italians, which seemed likely.* These attacks had produced a violent wave of French Anglophobia with everyone, including de Gaulle. Churchill was forced to realize that he might find himself at war not only with Germany and Italy, but also with Russia, Japan, *and* France. As he told the Cabinet on June 24: "Our relations [with the French government] might well approach very closely to those of two nations at war with each other."

At the meeting with de Gaulle on July 1, consequently, "C" could hardly have expected a favorable reception when he proposed the establishment of a Gaullist intelligence service in France subsidized by "C" and acting in the British interest under British control. Although de Gaulle did not know it, the subsidy was to be paid out of the £13 million in French francs that British secret agents had "found

---

*Thirteen days after the French surrender, Churchill acted to prevent the French fleet from falling into Axis hands. At Oran, Algeria, a heavy British squadron demanded that the French battleship squadron there choose (a) to join England and continue the war against the Axis powers, (b) accept internment in a British port, or (c) scuttle. On French refusal, the British squadron opened fire. Three French battleships were sunk, a fourth escaped, and five destroyers fled to Toulon. A French squadron at Alexandria, Egypt, which consisted of one battleship, four cruisers, and three destroyers, disarmed itself at British orders. Other such actions effectively neutralized the French fleet as an instrument of war, to the great relief in particular of FDR. The action embittered many Frenchmen; the Vichy government broke diplomatic relations with Britain, and for a time it seemed that war might break out between England and France. One of the reasons why Churchill undertook this action was to impress upon the Washington administration that Britain really intended to fight Germany and Italy to the bitter end, and it served mightily to persuade FDR to give Britain all assistance within his power.

in a French courtyard" as they were being evacuated from France. But both de Gaulle and Dewavrin were well aware that their existence, and perhaps their survival, depended upon their relations with "C." Nor was "C's" pressure any more easily resisted than that of the entire Foreign Office machine. As de Gaulle wrote later, to resist was a severe test, in which

without having experienced it oneself, it is impossible to imagine what a concentration of effort, what a variety of procedures, what insistence, by turns gracious, pressing, and threatening, the English were capable of deploying in order to obtain satisfaction.

De Gaulle had been given only £125 out of secret funds by the French prime minister, Reynaud, when he left France. That was hardly enough to pay the hotel bill, let alone raise the standard of France-in-exile. Both de Gaulle and Dewavrin agreed, therefore, to raise, train, and despatch secret agents to France under "C's" control. Within six weeks the first French secret agent, Major Gilbert Renault-Roulier, landed on the Breton coast and made contact with the French railroads executive to obtain intelligence about the movements of German invasion forces to the Channel ports. His means of communication: carrier pigeons.

During the withdrawal from Poland and Norway, "C" had established stay-behind espionage systems, and these had taken up his entire stock of portable wireless transceivers until a newer, lighter model was available. But at the time "C" had almost more faith in pigeons than he had in the wireless, and until quite late in the war there was a pigeon loft on the roof of Broadway. There was also one at "C's" home at Bridges Court, to be used by "C" to communicate with Broadway if England was invaded and London was cut off while he was spending a weekend in the country, as he did from time to time.

For control purposes—what Menzies called "liaison"—"C" did not place the Gaullist organization under the command of Dunderdale, the SIS station chief in Paris until the fall (and therefore the likeliest man for such an intricate Gallic task). Rather, he chose Commander Kenneth Cohen, a career officer who spoke French and was Dansey's staff officer in the Section Z.

Thus, reasonably good operational relations were established by "C" with the Gaullists at an early stage; and these relations proved of great value especially during the invasion watch that began late in

July 1940. At that time, "C's" first and sternest requirement was to provide the prime minister and the chiefs of staff with seventy-two hours' foreknowledge of a German intention to invade or undertake a large-scale raid. The extent to which Dewavrin was able to assist "C" in that high task during August, when the invasion was expected, if it was to come at all, was problematical: Renault-Roulier had only just entered the field by that time.

Shortly, however, "C" received the first feeler from Vichy, the old spa in the Auvergne that was the provisional capital of France while the Germans held Paris. Britain had no relations with Vichy, and throughout this period, communication between London and Vichy was as hostile as it was possible to get without an actual declaration of war. Moreover, it was the Vichy government that had sentenced de Gaulle to death, so it would have been unwise to reveal that "C" was dickering with both sides, the more so since the Gaullists and the Vichyites had begun to murder each other.

The feeler was from "C's" old friend, Colonel Gustav Bertrand, now in the employ of the Vichy "enemy." At the French surrender, the Germans occupied two-thirds of France, including the entire western coastline. The Vichy government was left with the remaining third, including the Mediterranean coast. The French armed forces and intelligence services were disbanded, and Vichy was allowed to retain only one hundred thousand men (as Germany was permitted under the Versailles Treaty) in uniform and under arms. From that point forward France became a control of the German police president in France.

On August 25, 1940, however, the chief of staff of the French army, General Revers, who appeared to be a Fascist and loyal to the German "new order," established an organization called the Bureaux des Menees Anti-nationalese (BMA). Officially the purpose of BMA was to protect the Army of the Armistice from British and Communist subversion and espionage, and for that reason the Germans allowed its formation. In truth, BMA was a bureaucratic cover for the French secret services underground. Colonel Rivet, a great friend of "C" despite the Royal Navy's savagery against the French fleet, was chief of the new secret service.

BMA's headquarters were at Royat, another spa in the Auvergne, and the executive head was a certain Colonel d'Ales. It had offices in every military district of the free zone of France. There was an active post in Paris under Commandant d'Autrevaux and in all the

French ports. A clandestine air intelligence section was established under Colonel Ronin, the prewar chief of French air intelligence and another of "C's" French friends.

Also, BMA established a commercial company called the Enterprise Generale de Travaux Ruraux (TR), the Country Projects Company. TR's head offices were at the Villa Eole on the Promenade de la Plage at Marseilles, and its code name within BMA was Cambronne, the name of the French colonel who, when called upon by the British to order his regiment's surrender at Waterloo, replied with one epic, startling word: *Merde*. The commerce engaged in by TR was trade in fruit, vegetables, wine, and the produce of various cottage industries. Its chairman was Commandant Paillole, lately chief of the German section of counterespionage, and its real task was "to neutralize the (Italo-German) Special Services on French Territory of the Axis Powers." It had branches throughout France, but, it appears, its principal post was that of Bertrand, a man of importance and delight in "C's" life.

At the fall of France, Bertrand, the man who brought the Polish Enigma to London with Dunderdale on the eve of the war, had been chief of P.C. Bruno, the French General Staff's cryptanalytical bureau. After the surrender, Bertrand liquidated P.C. Bruno without leaving a trace, and went underground and reestablished himself in the code-breaking business at a château at Uzes, between Avignon and Nimes. Bertrand called his new organization P.C. Cadix. With him was his team of fifteen Polish and seven Spanish cryptanalysts; he was funded by BMA, and his *post de commandement* was, for the next two years, one of "C's" main points of wireless contact in France. This wireless station first made contact with "C" early in September 1940, at about the time of the onset of the critical invasion period, and began to supply "C" with important intelligence about the German order of battle, the movements, locations, strengths, and equipment of their air, ground, and naval forces, on matters concerning intelligence, counterespionage, and policies until November 1942.

The intelligence derived from two main sources. The first was with an organization known to "C" only as "Source K." From the autumn of 1940 "Source K" began working on problems associated with the tapping of the main telephone and teleprinter cables that led from Paris to Berlin, cables used by the German high command for its land-line traffic. The intercept was established at the little French market town of Noisy-le-Grand, near Paris, and was sent via the French air postal service to another shadowy organization in Vichy known as ORA, of which Bertrand was a member.

Under Revers's indirect command, the Ordre de la Resistance de l'Armee (ORA) was an intelligence organization to which belonged regular officers of the French army who were on "armistice leave." By the autumn of 1940 ORA had begun to emerge as a complete though secret military intelligence and counterespionage substructure with agents throughout France and her empire. The first objective of ORA was to become capable of almost immediate reactivation as an army in the event of an uprising by the French nation or a British landing in France.

The politics of this organization were rightist, and its members accepted Marshal Pétain as the head of state, and, with reservations, they also accepted his notion of the corporative state. As the French intelligence service noted, ORA members were "obliged" to see Pétain as a "benign sovereign surrounded by pernicious advisors, and playing a long-range game with the Germans." ORA departed from Pétainism in one important respect: while it cooperated with the German occupation, ORA conspired to eject them. ORA members considered themselves to be "purely and traditionally French." They were "stubbornly" anti-German and also anti-British and anti-Communist. ORA existed primarily to "preserve the continuity of the Army and the moral position within the Army." Although the ORA had no popular support, drawing its strength entirely from the French officer corps, it did have the technical knowledge necessary not only to frustrate the Germans in their attempts to make France a German control, but also to ensure that the left did not seize the power of the state when the Germans departed. For ORA did intend that the Germans would depart France, and toward that end it created a plan for the seizure of state power.

Before the end of 1940 ORA had established two branches of the underground French secret service. The first was Ajax, a counterespionage service that, unlike TR, centered upon the French police force. Ajax existed largely to protect the second service, an intelligence arm of ORA, which was code-named Micromegas. The top echelon of ORA was a General Staff secreted in the offices of the Bureau of Foods in Paris, and the staff had dependent staffs at regional and departmental levels. It had representatives in each regiment and each branch of the army, men capable of receiving orders verbally and delivering them verbally throughout France.

In the second objective, news of the enemy, the Germans and Italians, Bertrand acted as the point of contact between "C" and Louis Rivet, chief of the old French secret service. Another part of ORA provided Revers and his colleagues with communications with SIS from December 1940 onward. At that time ORA made contact "with the War Office"—"C"—and "C" was disposed to listen. A Francophile, he knew and trusted the discretion and technical ability of the French General Staff more than he trusted any civilian clandestine group. Through military discipline, lore, and organization, the French General Staff possessed a capacity for intriguing without getting caught. They were men whose nerves were, like "C's," stronger than their imaginations.

The link between ORA and "C" was through Bertrand in France and Dunderdale in London. Adroit as always in his local politics, "C" judged that with Cohen at Broadway in charge of Gaullist affairs it would be wisest to find Dunderdale other headquarters. There were bound to be collisions between the Vichyites and the Gaullists, these were bound to infect the heads of the two desks, and there would be collisions in corridors, so "C" decided to send Dunderdale to the Admiralty. That not only kept the two factions geographically apart, but, felt Dunderdale, it provided admirable cover. Who would think to look for Bertrand's controller at the Admiralty, the place that had organized the arrest and devastation of the French fleet in June? And if word spread that England maintained secret relations with Vichy, the capital of a hostile power, "C" could claim, if pressed, that no such relations were being conducted at Broadway.

With the opening of communications with Bertrand in September 1940, Dunderdale found himself "down among the dolphins," working in the same room as Commander Ian Fleming, begetter of James Bond, the British secret service agent.

7 TROUBLE WITH WINSTON

On August 3, 1940, despite the existence of Ultra, Churchill produced one of those devastating one-page notes that sometimes meant the downfall of men such as "C":

I am not satisfied with the volume or quality of information received from both the occupied and the unoccupied areas of France. We seem as much cut off from these territories as from Germany. I do not wish such reports as are received to be sifted and digested by the various Intelligence authorities. For the present Major Morton will inspect them for me and submit what he considers of major interest. He is to see everything and submit authentic documents for me in their original form.

Further I await proposals from Colonel Menzies for improving and extending our information about France and for keeping a continual flow of agents moving to and fro. For this purpose Naval facilities can if necessary be invoked. So far as the Vichy Government is concerned it is not creditable that we have so little information. To what extent are Americans, Swiss, and Spanish agents being used? Colonel Menzies should submit a report on what he has done and is proposing to do. [40]

Churchill's action was unsatisfactory to "C" for a number of reasons. Despite Morton's deficiencies, Churchill had appointed him as a new intelligence master, thereby usurping the traditional position of "C." That left Menzies little choice but to resign; and but for the emergency created by the possibility of invasion, he would doubtless have done so. Second, Churchill had admitted Morton to the secret circle of Ultra recipients, thereby creating what might well result (given Morton's predilection for gossip with juniors) in the compromise of Ultra. Third, it hurt "C's" efforts to surmount a national disaster brought on, largely, by government parsimony over the secret vote over many years. Fourth, "C" could not possibly "submit a report on what he has done and is proposing to do," for in his view Churchill's private office was not secure—the leakage of the existence of Ultra to Lord Kemsley was sufficient evidence of that.

Given the gravity of the emergency confronting him, and the surprises that had so badly shaken his predecessor, it was understandable that Churchill should act to ensure that he received untainted intelligence. Nor was there good reason why he should not see documents in their original form, for such was the prime minister's depth of training and experience that he possessed what amounted almost to second sight and could see or sense indications of enemy capabilities and intentions in a document where, often, professional intelligence estimators could not. Yet even so, many of Churchill's memoranda at that time were conceived in late-night sessions with cronies— Cadogan referred to them as "Winston's midnight follies"—and reflected consistently a lack of understanding about what was happening inside Broadway. They also reflected Churchill's suspicions that, as in World War I, intelligence officers spent too much of their time intriguing.

In all this, Churchill underestimated "C's" loyalty, his sense of duty, and his ability. In part that underestimation was a consequence of "C's" own secrecy about his activities. At this stage, given his own dismay over the government's handling of the Russian decrypts during the Arcos affair of 1927, when "C" lost a major source through the uncomprehending actions of polititicians, he was not prepared to discuss his sources, extant or developing, with anyone outside Broadway. There is evidence that he concealed the existence of the Vichy source from Churchill until May 1941, in this case with the agreement of the chiefs of staff.

What "C" did about the situation created by Churchill will not become clear until 1995, when the rest of the file in London is opened. It is probable that the issues were settled by compromise. But it is also evident that Morton did not prevail. In September 1940 Churchill instructed "C" to send him "daily all Enigma messages." Thus began "the buff boxes." These were government despatch boxes, buff in color and the size of a large briefcase. They had first been used in Queen Victoria's time, for they were stamped with the initials "VRI"—"Victoria Regina Imperatrice." The sheer volume of the intercepts dictated that Churchill's order could not be fulfilled to the letter, but each day, and sometimes twice a day, one of the boxes arrived from Broadway, sometimes hand-carried by "C," containing the most important decrypts. The selection was usually made by "C." Only Churchill and "C" had keys to the box, and no member of Churchill's staff was allowed to open it.

When the prime minister was in the country, the decrypts were conveyed to him by pouch carried by an armed officer. When Churchill was abroad they were sent to him either in an air pouch specially constructed so that it would sink if the aircraft crashed into the sea, or wirelessed by a one-time pad cipher held only by Menzies and Churchill.

It is not known what the box contained before September 1940, but by that date the contents usually consisted of about twenty German air force decrypts, a summary of revelations obtained from work against other German ciphers, principally those of the German navy, against which the Bletchley attack was progressing only slowly. There were occasional decrypts of the Abwehr's traffic and decrypts of Gestapo and SS hand ciphers used in Poland. These revealed the extent and detail of the work of the SS squads busy executing Jews and Bolsheviks.

The purpose of these boxes provoked the greatest curiosity among Churchill's staff. Aware of this, Churchill warned Colville (who was then only twenty-five and learning the secrets of high places) as he unlocked one of them: "You will have to forget a great many things." Churchill then appended the advice: "Be wise rather than well informed. Give your opinion but not the reasons for it. Then you will have a valuable contribution to make." [41]

Yet if the improvement in relations between Churchill and Menzies promised a more agreeable future, it also provided a unique form of cavalry. Churchill was merciless with his midnight and early-morning calls to "C" from this time onward, as he was merciless with all his other principal advisers. After a long day running a major government department at wartime and even while air raids were on, Churchill would ring Menzies at Queen Anne's Gate and ask him to come to Downing Street or the central war room (CWR) in Great George Street, where Churchill had sleeping quarters, usually to discuss business, but just as often simply because the prime minister wanted to talk.

"C" would then stumble out into the black, cold, and often bomb-blasted night and stride out down Cockpit Steps and up Birdcage Walk to wherever Churchill was to be found. Often shrapnel from the antiaircraft barrage rained down, and occasionally a soldier or constable would step from the shadows and either demand his pass or order him to an air raid shelter. At the prime minister's quarters he would have to sit patiently and talk until the prime minister dismissed him, and then Menzies would have to trudge back to Queen Anne's Gate and be back at his desk at seven or eight in the morning.

These sessions, which often lasted until 2:00 A.M., were not a transitory feature of life with Churchill; they were a permanent part of his routine, and the more tempestuous the war situation, the more frequent "the Midnight Follies." As Robert Bruce Lockhart, director of the Political Warfare Executive, wrote of Churchill's demands: "Winston, I fear, is no organiser and, by sleeping half the afternoon himself and then flogging tired men to work half through the night, is killing more of his own countrymen than Germans." [42]

In all, Churchill's sharp memo proved little more than "Dessie" —as "C" called Morton, who was a bachelor—stirring the pot plus, probably, brandy in the belly after midnight. But even as Dessie stirred his pot, Churchill sanctioned a proposal by the chiefs of staff that "C" could not accept and for which he never forgave Churchill. Sound though the proposal may have been in theory, for "C" it proved calamitous in practice.

Churchill believed that if England was to survive and defeat Germany, the occupied countries of Europe would have to play their part at the moment when England "reentered" the continent and rebel against the conqueror. To organize, arm, and control the European underground movements on a large-enough scale, Churchill believed that he must take a leaf out of Lenin's book and establish a new secret service in London, one wholly given over to the establishment of a "democratic international" that at the right moment would rise against the Germans and make them see the sun, moon, and stars, thus reducing the number of armies Britain would have to raise for the task—and the casualties they would suffer.

That proposal emerged first on July 1, 1940, at a ministerial meeting held by Cadogan and attended by "C," who, as head of Section D, had a vested interest in the proposal. "C" did not object to the proposal. On the contrary, he acknowledged that "the multiplicity of bodies dealing with sabotage and subversive activities" should be replaced by "a Controller armed with almost dictatorial powers." Where "C" came to differ with Churchill was in regard to the command of the new service, which was to be called the Special Operations Executive (SOE). As the man responsible for secret service at that time, "C" visualized nobody but himself in charge of the new organization.

"C's" reasons were sound. SIS could operate safely and effectively only if silence and tranquillity existed in the target area. If SOE was created, its sole reason for existence would be to blow things up, slit throats, and stir the enemy up. When that happened, SIS agents were bound to become caught up in the inevitable German "rat hunts" (the technical term of the times for manhunts), and sooner or later SIS would find itself unable to operate at all. If that situation was to be avoided, SIS and SOE could operate on the same territory and across the same lines only if their operations were placed under the command of the same man—"C."

As "C" argued at these and other such meetings, there were other reasons for placing the new organization under his command. Rivalry would result if the two services operated independently. Then a situation akin to that of World War I would arise in which there would be competition for agents, with both organizations upbidding the price for a man's services. In World War I, there had been savagery in the field when several organizations had begun to work against each other, had murdered each other, and had sold their rivals to the enemy. The purity of intelligence would be seriously affected, for the Germans would soon learn, as they had in World War I, how to use rival services for the purpose of deception, planting information on one service and then "confirming" it through another. Above all, perhaps, the main danger of the new "international" operating independently of "C" was that ultimately there would be such confusion and competition between the two services that more time would be spent in "coordinating" the activities of the two services than in fighting the Germans.

All this proved to be a correct estimate of the dangers of Churchill's proposals. But "C's" warnings went unheeded. Politics intruded into the question, and another powerful man, Hugh Dalton, Socialist, Etonian, son of the vicar at Windsor Castle, minister for economic warfare, wanted the job for himself. Dalton began such an active lobby that shortly Cadogan began to complain that Dalton "was ringing up hourly to try and get a large finger in the Sabotage pie." He claimed, too, that if he was given the job by the end of the year, "the slave lands which Germany had overrun" would revolt, and that nazism would "dissolve like the snow in spring." "Regular soldiers," Dalton declared, "are not men to stir up revolution, to create social chaos, or to use all those ungentlemanly means of winning the war which come so easily to the Nazis." [43]

The prevailing attitude became hostile to "C's" continuing control. Menzies, so the arguments went, had his hands full restoring his service in Europe. The deputy prime minister, Clement Attlee, himself a Socialist, lobbied personally with Churchill, using the powerful argument that the left wing should be seen to be directing major operations against the right-wing Germans. But when the discussion seemed likely to go on forever, Churchill gave an order that Section D was to be taken over by Dalton in order to establish SOE as the instrument whereby Britain would "set Europe ablaze." Since Churchill had armed himself with dictatorial powers, nobody could contest the decision—and nobody did, except "C," who requested and obtained a formal meeting with the prime minister on July 16.

"C" made his case in detail but failed to impress the prime minister. When Stewart Menzies awoke the next morning, he found that during the night hours, without consulting him, Dalton had taken control of Section D. Protest was useless. The hour was too dark,

Churchill too busy to listen. Menzies accepted what was virtually a coup d'etat, and, to his credit, when the SIS men in Section D resigned that day rather than serve a new, civilian organization, Menzies told them to stay where they were and come back to him at the end of the war. But Menzies never accepted the graceless way in which Section D was snatched away.

Dalton did much to try and ensure that SOE worked with SIS, appointing a second Etonian, Sir Charles Hambro, a prominent merchant banker, as his second-in-command. In turn, Hambro brought in his Etonian crony, Gladwyn Jebb, as chief executive officer. As Jebb recorded, he was brought in precisely because he was an Etonian and because almost all the administrators on the foreign side of the government were Etonians. It was hoped, in particular, that Jebb might "smooth things over with 'C.' "

But in that aspiration Jebb failed, as did all his successors. Neither "C" nor Dansey accepted the separate existence of SOE and fought it tooth and nail until, at last, they succeeded in liquidating the new secret service. The operational difficulties between SIS and SOE proved basic—the former avoided trouble, the latter made it—and this in turn produced severe policy divisions that became political. And of all the troubles that Menzies had during World War II, none, except those involving his American counterparts, proved more troublesome than SOE. "C" tried constantly to tame "Dalton's Dragoons," even seeking Churchill's support for a unified service under SIS control. In this "C" failed, perhaps to his own greater good, for by 1944 SOE had swollen to some thirteen thousand persons.

Given his other responsibilities, as "C" remarked to Cadogan, he could never have found "all the time necessary to make sure that SOE blew up the right bridge." Moreover, as "C" predicted, the SIS-SOE relationship ended calamitously when their agents did indeed start to murder each other. It proved calamitous for "C" personally, also, for one of SOE's earliest recruits was Harold Adrian Russell "Kim" Philby.

At the outbreak of World War II, *The Times* had sent Philby as its correspondent to the headquarters of the British army in France. By June 1940, after the evacuation of the army from France at Dunkirk, Philby found himself back in London at loose ends. He embarked on his supreme task in the interest of the world revolution of the proletariat: he sought employment in the British secret service. A "mutual friend" arranged for him to see Frank Birch, a leading light at the Government Code and Cypher School at Bletchley. But Birch was also a leading light at Cambridge, a fellow of King's College, who understood the needs of secrecy and security. Birch checked Philby's credentials and then rejected him, although he was desperately in need of men with Philby's ability. The reason Birch gave for not employing Philby was that "he could not offer me enough money to make it worth my while." [44]

Philby then encountered his Cambridge friend and fellow Soviet spy, Guy Burgess, who had just been taken on by Section D. Burgess suggested that Philby, too, might find the work "interesting." Shortly Philby was at an interview with Miss Marjorie Maxse, "an intensely likeable elderly lady" who "spoke with authority" and was evidently "in a position at least to recommend me for 'interesting' employment" involving "political work against the Germans in Europe." A check was made with the Security Service (MI5), which reported "NRA" —"nothing recorded against"—on Philby. That was not surprising: the MI5 security indexes were in chaos; a fire had swept through the records only three weeks before Philby's application. The microfilm copy of the indexes proved illegible, and, moreover, MI5 was flooded with requests for security checks, not only for itself but with all other government agencies expanding to meet the emergency. Birch had not relayed his findings to the Security Service; and neither had anyone else who was at Cambridge, where Philby's politics were known.

Philby's employment was assured when the voice of Colonel Vivian was heard. Vivian, deputy chief of SIS in charge of counterespionage and security, had been a close friend of Philby's father, St. John Philby, since Rawalpindi days. While Vivian knew of Philby's left-wing associations at Cambridge, he noted on Philby's employment file that he had abandoned these on leaving Cambridge. Also, St. John Philby's own fate seemed to constitute additional evidence that the son had abandoned Marxism, for Philby, senior, was now in jail under Section 18b of the Defence of the Realm Act for having made pro-Fascist, anti-British statements. As for young Philby's marriage to a known Communist, Litzi Friedman, Kim told Vivian that he knew his wife was a Marxist, but he had weaned her away from such outrageous beliefs, and, in any case, they had separated and Philby had instituted divorce proceedings against her. Later events were to show that Vivian could not have checked to ensure that Philby actually obtained a decree; and that point proved important later.

The consequence was that Philby was appointed to Section D of SIS in no high position on July 17, thirteen days *before* Section D was transferred from SIS to the Ministry of Economic Warfare, which assumed control of Section D from July 30. Through bureaucratic accident, therefore, Philby just failed to obtain employment with SIS, his target. In SOE, his wage was £600 tax free a year, paid each Thursday in £5 notes. He was in Burgess's section, and since Burgess's symbol was DU, Philby, as a subordinate, became DU-D. With the arrival of Gladwyn Jebb, Burgess did not last long, however, for as Jebb was to state, Burgess was "quite exceptionally dissolute and indiscreet and certainly unfitted for any kind of confidential work." [45] Burgess was then fired, and Philby was promoted from DU-D to DU. Remote from London, and bereft of the companionship of Burgess, Philby began the dull task of teaching sabotage to trainee agents.

"C's" nemesis had entered the secret service.

8 "C's" FINEST HOUR

On Wednesday, August 8, 1940, the Joint Intelligence Committee, under the chairmanship of Victor Cavendish-Bentinck, met for its weekly meeting at 5 Richmond Terrace, opposite Downing Street. While serving in Warsaw in 1920, Bentinck was required to report extensively upon what was called "the Eighteenth Decisive Battle of the World," the defeat of the Red Army by the Polish army at the gates of Warsaw in August 1920. Now, twenty years later, Bentinck was required to report to the king and prime minister on what was considered to be the nineteenth decisive battle, the Battle of Britain.

"C" was present, for he had become a member of the committee in May 1940 after the Norwegian calamity. The finding of the committee, which had at its disposal all the intelligence resources of the state, was that "the result of Germany's delay in attacking this country is that a small cloud of doubt as to Germany's invincibility has arisen on the European horizon." And although Churchill deplored what he called "collective wisdom" in any form (and particularly that of the JIC), in this case the JIC was right. That cloud of doubt did not go away because, despite the air battle that raged in the skies of southern England throughout August, the German air force had failed to destroy the Royal Air Force.

Two weeks later "C" lunched with his old friend Euan Wallace, chief of civil defense for London, a large and vital position, and Menzies spoke more freely than had been his custom. Wallace recorded in his war diary:

I had lunch with Stewart Menzies at the Turf, and he gave me a lot of extraordinarily interesting information from the point of view of [SIS]. His people have always always been of the opinion that there was no possibility of the invasion taking place *before* the beginning of September; but it was only recently that this view has penetrated to the highest headquarters. On the other hand he had the best reasons for knowing that every preparation was complete and believed that in the next ten days at the outside they must either start it or chuck it. The Party as opposed to the German Army were desperately anxious that it should be tried.

Yet it is clear that "C's" estimates of German intentions were still not shared by the rest of the secret circle (except Churchill), for September brought with it an atmosphere of emergency and uncertainty, perhaps for the benefit of the Americans in London. In all this, the key factor was the weather in the Channel. While September was most often a month of good weather, from the onset of autumn on September 21 the Channel turned quickly into one of the stormiest and most unpredictable waterways in the world. If Hitler intended to land *and* supply armies across the Channel, then surely he had left it too late in the year.

The army, navy, and air force were all armed and ready. Despite what Lothian was telling Roosevelt, there were no serious shortages of any military materials. On August 9 both Churchill and Eden remarked in Colville's hearing that "the only real worry" was "the acute shortage of small-arms ammunition," a remark with which the chief of the Imperial General Staff did not agree. That same day Churchill declared that England would have *ten* armored divisions by September 1941.

Indeed, although as yet England had received no appreciable quantities of American military assistance, Churchill felt so confident that Hitler would *not* invade that he had directed that strong forces, including tank regiments, should be detached from home defense and sent out (a) to reinforce the army of the Nile, which was expecting an Italian offensive against Egypt, and (b) to seize the French West African port of Dakar. If the army had recovered from Dunkirk, if the population of England was resolute and hostile, if the air force remained in control of the sky, if one of the world's most powerful navies was intact and deployed, how were Hitler's hordes to get across the Channel in a ragtag fleet of merchantmen, trawlers, and barges and land on a strongly defended coastline? The truth was that he did not intend to do so at all, that he had other plans. Hitler intended to invade Russia, and Sealion was no more than cover for Barbarossa.

At the same time, from September onward it became evident that Churchill intensified his operations to "drag America in." England could survive, but she could not win the war and reestablish the prewar balance of power without active American military participation. From September 1 onward, therefore, all Churchill's actions were directed at securing American participation without being seen to do so. In all this, Roosevelt was well aware of what was happening in Europe, and he acquiesced to Churchill's strategy on the grounds of national self-interest: sooner or later America would have to fight whether the electorate wanted to or not. What Roosevelt hoped to obtain was time to establish what he called "the Victory Program" to fight with Britain if she did not collapse and to defend the United States and restore the status quo if she did.

The great game of nations reached its crux on September 1, when "C's" cryptanalysts "unbuttoned" a series of intercepts that indicated the German invasion of Britain might, after all, be imminent. These showed that accommodation and supplies were being prepared at fifteen airfields between Dunkirk and the mouth of the Somme for German dive-bomber and fighter units, and that all these airfields were to be occupied from September 4. Five other airfields along the coast were to be prepared as advanced airfields, and supplies of five-hundred-kilogram bombs, often the weapon used in ground attacks in support of the army, were to be distributed among them. Since the dive-bombers were the spearhead of the German army, the RAF analyst noted: "This congregation of Dive-Bomber Units in a small area opposite the Straits of Dover . . . may indicate their re-employment on a large scale in preparation for an invasion of the South and South-East coasts." The operative word in the estimate was "may," the underlying purpose bluff.

Two days later, the first anniversary of the war, Menzies took ominous news to Cadogan. The Luftwaffe was under orders to make its first major attack on London. Fur flew, for the information contained in the decrypt was inconclusive, at least as to the date of the attack. Cadogan, unable to understand the special technical language involved, seems to have failed to see the point in the signal. " 'C' came round with what looks like indication of Germans being ready for mass attack on 5th," Cadogan wrote in his diary. "But his information doesn't seem so watertight as it looks." Cadogan, who was inclined to testiness if it took more than thirty seconds to explain a complex subject, added: "He is rather a nervous babbler." [46]

Nervous babbler or not, "C's" decrypt was as accurate as was necessary. To bring about a decision in the Battle of Britain, Goering launched a series of attacks on British fighter airfields, radar stations, and aircraft and component factories around London between August 31 and September 5. It was intended that day's operations should culminate in a tremendous aerial attack on London, its purpose to force Fighter Command to give battle against odds so great that they were bound to lose. For reasons that are not evident, but which probably had to do with the problems involved in assembling and despatching nearly one thousand aircraft, the attack was postponed until September 7, although the target remained the same, as did the purpose of the attack.

Sure enough, the attack came at four o'clock on the afternoon of September 7. At that hour radar detected an assembly of three hundred bombers and six hundred fighters over Calais. Twenty-three squadrons of British fighters gave battle, but the air fleets got through to London and, in what was the first daylight raid on the capital, dropped several scores of thousands of firebombs on London docks. That night 247 bombers came back to stoke the fires, and by dawn on September 8, 306 civilians were dead and 1,337 seriously injured. Then, unbelievably, Goering switched his attacks from daylight to nighttime bombing, although Fighter Command was on the ropes. For seven nights the Luftwaffe pounded various docks, mainly on the Mersey. That week gave Fighter Command just long enough to rest and refit for the renewal of battle.

It came on September 15. Method: massed daylight attack. Target: London. Again "C" was able to show Cadogan the decrypts, and this time there was no outburst. From this time forward, so far as Cadogan was concerned, "C" had won his spurs. By the end of the day it was evident that Fighter Command had won a major victory over the Luftwaffe and that the German air force had failed to establish the preconditions necessary to enable Hitler to land his panzers in England. Now came "C's" finest hour.

On September 17 the decrypts spoke with clarity. A signal was intercepted from the headquarters of the German supreme command to the officer commanding the troop-carrying squadrons in Holland. He was authorized to dismantle the air-loading equipment on the Dutch airfields. It followed that if the troop carriers were being withdrawn, then Sealion had been canceled. "C" sent the signal to Churchill, and it was discussed by the chiefs of staff that night. At that meeting, the chief of the air staff, Air Marshal Sir Cyril Newall, "gave it as his considered opinion that this marked the end of Sealion, at least for this year." According to Squadron Leader Winterbotham, who claimed to have been present at the meeting, "there was a very broad smile on Churchill's face now as he lit up his massive cigar and suggested that we should all take a little fresh air."

Although London was badly damaged, England was not forced even to consider an application for terms, and in the long term Hitler's attacks so played into Churchill's hands that the U.S. electorate became profoundly alarmed and Roosevelt's reelection was assured along with his "Victory Program." On September 3 American and British representatives signed the bases-for-destroyers agreement; Churchill deemed the acquisition of the fifty destroyers essential in his campaign "to drag America in." On September 7, the U.S. Congress passed an appropriation bill for $5.5 billion, which included contracts for 210 warships. The first U.S. destroyers were taken over by the Royal Navy on September 9. On September 16 FDR signed the Conscription Bill, which provided for the registration of all males between twenty-one and thirty-five—16.4 million men—and for the training of 2 million troops and reservists. The presidential campaign had begun.

Thus the Battle of Britain came to an end as a triumph for the Royal Air Force, "C," and Churchill's war diplomacy. Nevertheless, for "C" this was a long period of tribulation and danger in which, as for all others in England, ordinary existence came to an end. Stewart Menzies's experience was typical of that of most men working in the government quarter of Westminister. Soon after 9:45 A.M. on September 11 a German aircraft appeared out of the low, dark rainclouds and unloaded a string of time bombs in St. James's Park close to Buckingham Palace, blocking the approaches to the palace by Constitution Hill, The Mall, and Birdcage Walk. On September 13 the palace was again attacked as two high-explosive bombs fell into the courtyard.

During the night, scores more of the two-pound firebombs fell in and around Queen Anne's Gate; and at 5:50 A.M. on September 14, a high-explosive bomb fell outside the front entrance of SIS headquarters but did not explode. The narrow street was partly blocked by the crater, and when the bomb was inspected by an army bomb disposal unit, they discovered one confirmed unexploded bomb in the crater and two suspected time bombs about twenty yards west of Queen Anne's Gate. [47]

That drizzle of bombs in and around the Broadway area continued throughout the winter. In all there were 1,462 "incidents" in Westminster, most between September 1940 and May 1941. And while a move was contemplated, SIS headquarters was not evacuated to the country, although Churchill recognized that the government quarter of London was the principal target and casualties were becoming heavy: By the first half of September, they numbered two thousand killed and eight thousand injured, four-fifths in London.

Churchill ordered that government servants remain at their posts and all government services be maintained, despite the destruction of the railways, utilities, blocked streets, and the dislocation of telephone, telegraph, and mail services and despite, in particular, the breaking of hundreds of thousands of panes of glass in government offices through blast. The loss of the glass meant that until the panes were replaced, windows could only be sealed by plywood and plasterboard, which made the use of electric light essential. But for most of the time all power was cut. Yet Churchill's order to stand fast was obeyed, although it was becoming progressively more difficult to maintain government. Menzies and his colleagues were, therefore, once more in the front line, a front line that was this time not at Ypres but at Menzies's own cherished St. James's.

For weeks on end Menzies and his staff slept at headquarters, using the former restaurant at 54 Broadway as a canteen. Menzies did not return to Luckington even for a few days throughout the period of the attack, which began at the start of July and did not end until the following May. Moreover, the incessant night raiding meant sleepless nights. But by October whatever doubts "C" had left about Hitler's intentions were removed when, from October 12 onward, "C" began to receive decrypts and gunroom gossip that reflected the contents of this signal from Field Marshal Keitel to the German commands participating in Sealion:

> Führer's Headquarters,
> 12 October 1940

1. The Führer has decided that from now on until the spring, preparations for landing in England will be maintained purely as a military and political threat.

Should the intention of a landing in England in spring or early summer 1941 be renewed, the necessary state of preparedness will be ordered in sufficient time beforehand. Until then the military groundwork for a latter landing will be further improved.

2. All measures concerning the relaxing of the state of readiness for attack must be regulated from the following viewpoints:

    A The English must retain the impression that from now on we are preparing to land on a large scale.

    B At the same time, however, German domestic economy will be relieved of a burden. . . .

(s) Keitel,

C.-in-C. Armed Forces [48]

That intelligence was supported by information from the Polish railway watching service in Poland, which revealed that Hitler was quietly transferring the best fighting divisions from the west to the east, replacing those divisions equally quietly with second-line divisions.

Hitler in fact had intended to invade Russia in the *late summer* of 1940. But Shark replaced Sealion. And as the sealed orders reaching the German supreme command in the west defined the code name Shark, the German command was now to undertake operations that would suggest southern England would be invaded in March of 1941, weather permitting. In fact Russia was to be invaded, not England. If Ultra conveyed little of those secret instructions, German eastward movements indicated something of the plan, and although Churchill himself did not believe that an invasion was now possible, he continued to declare otherwise in his telegram to FDR thirteen days after the transformation of Sealion into Shark.

As Churchill said in that telegram, which was originated after the St. Luke's summer period had come and gone, and winter had closed in upon his beleaguered islands, "I do not think the invasion danger is yet at an end," but he admitted that "we are now augmenting our eastern transferences"—the reinforcement of the Army of the Nile—and added hopefully, with an eye on Congress and the Lend-Lease Bill, that "the strain is very great in both theatres, and all contributions will be thankfully received." [49]

The strain was indeed great. Churchill was not altogether playing with the facts. The aerial bombardment of London and other great cities did not diminish. On the contrary, Hitler kept his air fleets at full strength in the west and maintained and even intensified the air attacks in order to give the substance of violence to the shadow-boxing of Shark. For sixty-seven nights—longer by far than any single bombardment that Menzies endured at Ypres in World War I—the Germans bombed London without a break. Westminister was badly devastated.

And then there was the Coventry disaster. Later, Squadron Leader Winterbotham, head of Ultra security, was to claim that "C" had two to three days' foreknowledge of the German intention to attack the Midlands industrial and cathedral city of Coventry, but that, to conceal the fact that the Luftwaffe's traffic was being read by the British, no attempt was made to reinforce the antiaircraft defenses of the city or to provide any form of warning to the fire, medical, rescue, and other services. That assertion was vigorously denied by the British government, but if Winterbotham was correct, then the price of Ultra was heavy. Five hundred and fifty-four people were killed and 836 seriously wounded, the center of the city was destroyed, and a total of almost 51,000 houses were destroyed or badly damaged. Yet as Sir William Stephenson was to state, "it was better to lose a battle than to lose a source of intelligence." [50]

And Coventry was a battle, not the war.

9   "C" AND CANARIS

Winter closed in, making the blackout over London as thick and black as the Styx. Stewart Menzies spent yuletide at the home of his mother at Dassett, near Woking in Surrey. Whether Pamela Menzies was present is not clear, for she was very ill. "C's" brother, Major Ian Graham Menzies of the Scots Guards, his beautiful wife, the former Lisel Gaertner, an Austrian, and her sister, Friedle, who was in cabaret in London, were also at Dassett. But there is evidence that whatever else, New Year's Eve at Dassett was Byzantine, for "C" was the sort of man who always took work home with him. Friedle Gaertner, who was as gorgeous as her sister, had been employed by the Security Service to infiltrate Nazi front organizations in London and had identified several of the persons now in jail for supporting Nazi causes. That New Year's Eve, however, Friedle Gaertner was present at Dassett for purposes other than penetration. She was there to meet an agent code-named Tricycle, a German spy under "C's" control.

"C" had been involved in double-agent operations against the Germans for much of his career, but in the special contact of Tricycle and other such spies, the practice was formalized as an activity of statehood with the establishment in September of the "W" Board. "C" became a member of the W Board with the three service directors of intelligence and a representative of MI5. The purpose of the board was to control and expand the nature of the intelligence being allowed to pass to the enemy through enemy spies under British control at home and abroad. This was highly dangerous work, for if the enemy was given information that was too good, then he might bomb a city or sink a ship. But if the information passed by the spy to the enemy was not good enough, he would quickly lose his credit in the enemy camp and would then become a burden rather than an asset to British strategists and tacticians. What was required, it was decided, was a committee with the seniority and authority to make the necessary calculations between profit and loss.

However, the W Board had time only to decide policy; it could not direct the operations of double agents. Therefore it was decided that a second organization had to be established to control the double agents on a day-to-day basis. That organization came to be called the "XX-Committee" and was placed for administrative purposes under the direction of MI5, with SIS collaborating with its double agents on foreign territory. The man appointed as head of the XX-Committee—the double X's represented not the roman numerals for twenty, but the sign of the double cross—was Professor J. C. Masterman of Oxford University. Born in 1891, Masterman had been a student, lecturer, and censor of Christ Church and was a cricketer, hockey player, and writer of intricate and subtle novels.

By November 1940 Menzies suspected that Hitler's eastward plans had begun to revive the dissension within the German General Staff that had marked the periods immediately before the Czech crisis and again before Case Yellow, the German attack in the west. The dissension, then as now, concerned those officers who supported Hitler's policy of expansion and those who believed that such a policy would produce calamity. For "C," therefore, the time had come to restore his contact with Canaris, which had been more or less dead since the fall of France. "C's" purpose was to establish the state of mind of the Abwehr, which in his estimation had been on the side of the defeatists and, consequently, ripe for penetration. An opportunity arose in December when a Yugoslav of good family, position, and education arrived in London from Lisbon. The Yugoslav's real name was Dusko Popov, his code name Tricycle. [51]

In his twenties, Popov worked as Lisbon representative for a consortium of Yugoslav banks while acting also as a German secret agent working against the British service. But Popov had never intended to be a German spy; he intended that he should use his position in the British interest against the Germans without their knowledge—in other words, that he should act as what the French called an *agent-doubles*. SIS Lisbon accepted that offer, and Popov, alias Tricycle, became the first British secret agent in direct contact with the Abwehr, supplying SIS with important information concerning the Abwehr's order of battle, its politics, and its personalities.

With the establishment of the XX-Committee, control of Popov passed from "C" to Masterman. Masterman invited Popov to London so that the new organization could acquaint itself with SIS's crack agent. It was suggested to him that he find a plausible reason for coming to London, one that would be acceptable to his German controller. That Popov did, with the explanation that he had to go to London to arrange the financing of bulk turpentine to be exported to England from Yugoslavia. Also, Popov suggested that he would make himself doubly useful by establishing an espionage ring in the British Isles for his German controller. The Germans authorized (and paid for) Popov's mission.

Popov arrived in London in December and was invited to White's to meet "C." At White's, "C" realized immediately that if Popov were given assistance in establishing an espionage ring in England—but one under the control of the XX-Committee—it would enhance Popov's personal standing within the Abwehr. This improvement in Popov's stature would lead to what Menzies really wanted—information on Canaris. "C" then invited Popov to spend the weekend of New Year's Eve 1940 with him at Dassett. Popov accepted and found himself at "a Victorian mansion set in a large park, the lawn perfectly manicured."

Lady Holford conducted "me into the drawing room, where several of the other guests were already assembled, and introduced me right off to the most glamorous creature I had set eyes on since arriving in England." This woman was Friedle Gaertner, who was there for a single purpose, to entertain Popov. In that she succeeded, and Popov and Fräulein Gaertner became close friends. As Gelatine she also joined Popov's XX-Committee network, Freak. This organization, which was financed by the Germans and controlled by the XX-Committee, reported to Germany by wireless telegraphy and included such agents as Artist, Popov's university friend and an Abwehr officer at Lisbon who maintained the contact between Popov and Abwehr headquarters in Berlin; the Worm, Balloon and Dreadnought. Freak was, however, no more than the witty hors d'oeuvres to the main dish, which was a special task that "C" had in mind for Popov.

During the weekend, "C" and Popov withdrew to the privacy of a study to discuss the main reason for Popov's visit to Dassett—Canaris. As Popov was to write of his conversation with "C":

Menzies took me into a small study. Deep armchairs, a fireplace where the flames were miraculously steady, book-lined walls—it was the traditional and perfect setting. What followed was not commonplace. Even now, many years later, I feel uncomfortable at the way he was able to assess me so clearly after knowing me only a few hours and probably by reading a dossier about me. At times, I felt he was disrobing my character and making me look at it for the first time in my life. And all this was done patiently and dispassionately. I could see why he was the head of the Secret Service, which was in the way of being 'master after God.' . . .

"We may regret that you don't belong to MI6 anymore." Menzies began what was to be a long monologue. "But you are a double agent and, as such, more vulnerable than an ordinary one. Your activity calls for the use of deception and the penetration of the Abwehr. You and your usefulness may live and last only if thoroughly protected and managed by a specialized body. I'm sure that the XX-Committee will accomplish that with the utmost efficiency, and they will exploit you to full advantage for their own game. It is an important game, but we mustn't let it reduce the possible crop to a limited field. My department wants to profit by your talents and your circumstantial position as well."

"I don't know about my talents," I said, not out of modesty. I was impelled to honesty by this man. I really did have doubts about my capacity when face to face with an intellect like Menzies.

"Dusko," he said, looking into the fire like a seer, "one man out of a thousand has the talent to play the fiddle. One out of a hundred thousand has the capacity to be a virtuoso, and one out of a million actually becomes one. My capacity is to assess values and measure them. If I do that properly I have fulfilled half my duty."

"C" went on:

"You have too many devices on your banner for my taste," he said, "but for your job that's ideal." I pondered this later, trying to decide exactly what he meant. Everything else he had said was to the point, whether I recognized myself by this description or not. This remark left room for speculation. It is true, I had been accused politically and socially of standing everywhere from conservative to radical. As far as I was concerned, my banner was that of liberty, but I suppose that can come in many forms, therefore the many devices.

"You have the makings of a very good spy," Menzies continued more specifically, "except that you don't like to obey orders. You had better learn or you will be a very dead spy."

On that solemn note, "C" proceeded to the main business. "We already have a fair amount of information about many officers of the Abwehr, including Canaris, but I want to know much more about everybody who is intimately connected with Canaris and also with Dohnanyi* and Oster.† I think you could get that information through Jebsen."‡

Tricycle agreed that Jebsen would know a great deal about the associations within the Abwehr, and as he recorded of the rest of the meeting, Menzies continued by stating:

It may be helpful if I explain the reasons behind this request. We know that Canaris, Dohnanyi, and Oster are not dyed-in-the-wool Nazis. They are what might be termed loyal officers, or patriotic Germans. In 1938 Churchill had a conversation with Canaris.§ Unofficially—he wasn't in office then. Churchill came to the opinion that Canaris is a sort of catalyst for the anti-Hitler elements in Germany. That's why I want to know more about the people he attracts. Eventually I may want to resume the conversation that Churchill initiated. In that event, I must be in a position to evaluate the strength of those around Canaris.

Popov continued:

I nodded my understanding. Menzies was contemplating a dialogue with Canaris or those close to him with a view to ousting Hitler.

"I am handling this matter myself," Menzies stressed. "All information you pick up is to come directly to me with no intermediary. Ordinarily," he added, "any information I request from you may be given either directly to me or to any of the MI6 officers with whom you are in contact."

*Hans Dohnanyi was a member of the Abwehr and a principal conspirator in the Abwehr ring operating against Hitler.

†Colonel (later General) Hans Oster was deputy chief of the Abwehr and a co-conspirator.

‡Johannes Jebsen was the XX-Committee's Artist and, for the Abwehr, a representative at Lisbon. Popov and Jebsen were close friends since their days together at Freibourg University. Dohnanyi and Oster were executed by the Sicherheitsdienst at the end of the war. Jebsen was murdered by the Sicherheitsdienst. Tricycle then executed Jebsen's executions.

§Although it is not impossible that such a meeting took place between Churchill and Canaris, there is no evidence of such discussions. There was a meeting, however, between an emissary of Canaris, Fabian von Schlabrendorff, and Churchill. This meeting took place at Churchill's country house, Chartwell, in Sussex, in 1938. Under the guise of visiting England to write a book about Queen Victoria's German relations, Schlabrendorff asked for a statement from Churchill that would encourage the German movement to action against Hitler. Churchill provided such a statement, but it was rendered in cautious form and its value was further negated by Prime Minister Chamberlain's concessions to Hitler at Munich.

The meeting came to an end, leaving a single surprise: that it had occurred at all. Menzies was a cautious man about whom he saw and to whom he spoke, and it was thought later that a double agent would be the last person to whom he would reveal himself. For as he was to state, in dealing with a double agent you could never really tell whether you were getting the lean or the fat. But perhaps Menzies felt more confident about talking to Popov in this fashion because of developments of the highest importance at Bletchley.

There had been a second miracle at Bletchley. After eight months' work, Alastair Denniston was able to read the main cipher of Canaris's intelligence service, the Abwehr. The service responsible at least partly for that triumph of cryptanalytical endeavor was Intelligence Service Oliver Strachey (ISOS). ISOS now became the staff of life of Menzies's Section V, the counterespionage branch, which was located near Bletchley in the cathedral town of St. Albans, twenty miles or so to the north of London. The man in charge of the war station there, Felix Henry Cowgill, was to recall of those first decrypts:

At first they were little more than fragments of German intelligence signals, in German, and either meaningless or almost so. But in a surprisingly short time, certainly less than a year, we were reading Canaris's traffic and that of the Sicherheitsdienst, too. From that basis we could, therefore, work towards first the control of the German intelligence service wherever and whenever it appeared, and then the liquidation of that service. [52]

Since that was "C's" intention in seeing Popov—to begin the process of destroying Admiral Canaris's service—by the end of 1940 "C" could look back on a year in which he and his service had made important progress in the twin tasks of informing the government and protecting the realm.

There were the usual Highland reels with all the men wearing the rose-red evening tartan of Hallyburton; and then back to business at Broadway. There was good news there and bad. At the beginning of July "C" had begun an action calculated to neutralize the specter in London of the situation that would arise if Spain declared war against England and attempted to seize Gibraltar. Captain Alan Hillgarth, a naval officer in charge of all British secret operations in Iberia, was instructed to "create a hostile attitude in Spanish Army circles towards Spain's entry into the war."

By the end of 1940, according to a statement by Hillgarth to an American secret agent, a fund of $2 million was established in New York to purchase the allegiances of some thirty senior officers of the

Spanish General Staff. The generals were paid the interest in pesetas in the form of half-yearly payments, and the principle was to be paid at the end of the war, provided the generals had kept Spain neutral. The main beneficiaries included General Aranda, the famous defender of Oviedo during the civil war and now the influential commandant of the Spanish War College, and General Orgaz, commander in chief in Spanish Morocco and high commissioner of the Canary Islands. Later the fund was increased to $13 million.

That doubtless was a satisfactory development. On the other hand, there was grave news deriving from telephone taps placed on the Japanese embassy in London. As Cadogan recorded in his diaries at year's end, "the beastly little monkeys"—the Japanese—had "decided to attack us." That was a grim-enough prospect. Worse still was the news that "the baby Dictator," Churchill, was *demanding* the hanging for treachery of Muselier, a French admiral on de Gaulle's staff. *That*, "C" may well have thought, would certainly wreck his arrangements with Bertrand and, perhaps, bring on a war between Vichy France and England.

Five

America and Russia

1941

1 PAMELA'S ILLNESS

As all Eurasia exploded in a cataract of murderous activity without precedent in warfare, the New Year of 1941 began disastrously for "C." At a time when he was still bedeviled by the major question of 1940—would Hitler invade Russia or England or both?—his burdens were made greater by news from home. The doctors had at last arrived at a diagnosis about the condition of "C's" wife, Pamela. Now thirty-eight, she was suffering from anorexia nervosa and its associated neurosis, bulimova, two of the most humiliating illnesses to afflict a woman of beauty. To make the degree of her illness worse, Pamela had suffered from the complaints since childhood, and they had been worsened by the uncertainties brought about by the war. At no time had the illnesses been treated, so that they were now imbedded in her personality. The prognosis, moreover, was poor. "C" had to face the possibility that Pamela might well either starve herself to death or, as was not uncommon, commit suicide.

Through inexact diagnosis during the illnesses' early stages, Pamela's condition had reached the point in which all ordinary domestic life became impossible. She hovered constantly between states of depression or elation, and she could rarely appear in public either in the country or in London. Such were the burdens of "C's" duties that he could not resign his post to attend to her, and he could not visit Bridges Court more often than he did—one day each fortnight—for an almost ludicrous reason: the government would not provide him with a telephone scrambler because such instruments were in such short supply and were given only to the prime minister, the minister of information, Lord Beaverbrook, and the American ambassador in London.

"C" wrote to the secretary of the Cabinet noting that more scramblers were now being distributed and asking whether he might be added to "this select circle," for "without being able to talk freely to my office from my home, I am virtually prevented from taking more than twenty-four hours' leave." [1] But it was not before September that the scrambler was installed at Bridges Court (in a boot-and-shoe cupboard), and for the rest of the war "C's" chauffeur, Cyril Lovelace, would leave Queen Anne's Gate at noon on Saturday and drive "C" the eighty miles to Bridges Court. Since Lovelace, too, was thus immured at Broadway for weeks at a time, "C" allowed him to bring his wife and daughter, and they rode in the front of the large staff car while "C," sealed off from the Lovelace family in the front seats by a glass panel, rode in the back, reading papers. At Bridge's Court, Lovelace and his family were accommodated in an apartment over "C's" stables. Then, after tea on Sunday, the party would return to Broadway.

There is little doubt that Menzies's regular presence at Luckington did help his wife, although a friend, Guy Vansittart, who lived next door at Luckington Court, recalled:

His wife's illness was very distressing to him, both because she was ill and, on occasions, she seemed like a wraith. We thought he might have been wiser to place her in custodial care, for his burdens in London were very great, much greater than almost any other man's, and he badly needed contentment when he came home. But that he did not find and he used to come regularly to our house seeking, we thought, respite. But even so Stewart would not hear of committing her, and he remained terribly loyal to her.

Nor was Pamela's illness the only bad news to reach "C" as he began the New Year. In the early part of 1941 he suffered three losses that brought the past flooding back. Menzies's old friend, Euan Wallace, civil defense controller for London, died of cancer on February 9. "C," Rex Benson, and many members of the government and armed services disregarded the order that mourners were not to congregate in one place because of the danger of a bomb. They attended his memorial service at St. Martin's-in-the-Field, where Wallace had been best man at "C's" wedding to Lady Avice twenty-three years before. As Benson recorded of Wallace's passing: "He has lingered for 2 ½ months with cancer of the stomach. It is a merciful relief. No man was fitter, stronger, or a better friend than Euan." "C" read the lesson, taking as his theme the marvelous lines by the Edwardian poet Rosetti:

> "Does the road wind uphill all the way?"
> "Yes, to the very end."
> "Will the day's journey take the whole long
>   day?"
> "From morn to night, my friend."

Wallace's death was followed by that of the countess of Airlie, Lady Bridget Coke until her marriage to the earl of Airlie in 1917. She was probably "C's" first love. Then another of Menzies's closest friends, the colonial minister Lord Lloyd, died, again of cancer, his investigation of SIS unfinished. Yet there was precious little time for mourning. "C's" entire life was being consumed by the problems of his office.

Flames of political menace from the war in Europe were flickering in Greece, Albania, and Yugoslavia, all of which were soon destroyed by Hitler's operations to secure his flanks for his campaign against Russia. The drift eastward toward Russia of the best formations of the German army continued throughout the winter. German agents were at work in Syria and Iraq to create bridgeheads from which to grab England's oil in Persia and Russia's in the Caucasus. The Germans had entered the Italian North African provinces of Cyreneica and Libya, to stiffen the Italians' march on Cairo and Alexandria and so cut England's main link with the empire east of Suez. The Japanese threatened the arc of Asia from the Aleutians to Delhi. The sheer immensity of the problems caused Churchill to remark to "C" at one of their late-night sessions before the New Year was a few hours' old that "in 1941 we will have a very big and very ugly war."

The German aerial bombardment of London and the other great cities continued, rising in tempo and ferocity. London burned and shuddered as the Luftwaffe drenched the capital night after night with firebombs and high explosives, destroying much of the center of the city and again rendering all ordinary life impossible. Buildings famous for a thousand years lay in ruins. Yet in failing to divine the strategic purpose behind the air raids—to bring England to political compromise while providing cover for the preparations for the Russian campaign—Whitehall could not and did not believe that Hitler would commit the ultimate act of strategic madness: invade Russia while England remained unconquered in the west. Nor was there doubt in Whitehall that Hitler would invade England before he attacked Russia. That belief bore heavily on "C," for his espionage services remained too weak to enable him to *guarantee* the prime minister and the chiefs of staff that he could provide three days' warning of any German intention to land, or raid, the home islands. The problems confronting "C" appeared to be infinite and insoluble, therefore, although he could not know that they had only just begun.

Yet during that savage interlude between the Battle of Britain and the battles for Russia and Egypt, "C" and his services came under such extreme pressure that it is surprising the system did not break down under the weight of work. That it did not was a tribute to the inherent strength of the system. The pressure came not only from the enemy; it came, too, from within the entire administration. "C" faced severe and determined attacks by colleagues who wished to grab control of Bletchley. Both the military and naval directors of intelligence believed they could do "C's" job better than he.

There were unending boardroom battles over what seemed to be "C's" failure to reestablish SIS in Europe. "C's" seniority was challenged constantly by Dalton, the chief executive of the Special Operations Executive, whose intention was to absorb SIS—as it was SIS's intention to absorb SOE. The bidding for aircraft and ships became ever more intricate; no transportation, no spies were in place. Serious trouble afflicted the heads of the two main branches of SIS, Dansey and Vivian, who, convinced "C" would not last or would not stay the pace, maneuvered for the position of successor. Constant arbitration was necessary to prevent "the professionals" and "the amateurs" from making war on each other. The dons at Bletchley sought control of cryptanalysis in a spirit not unlike the campus warfare in *Who's Afraid of Virginia Woolf*, with much shrill backbiting that threatened a breakdown of discipline. The troubles between SIS and

MI5 were endless and dangerous, as events were to prove. Only "C's" skills as a bureaucrat kept the machine from wrecking itself.

A serious case of influenza in the first three weeks of February 1941 limited Menzies's ability to impose as much control as the situation demanded. And although a main cause of his tribulations and fatigue was "the baby dictator" Churchill, "C's" relationship with the prime minister, once so unpromising, was a source of the authority that enabled "C" to keep the peace.

Early in 1941 Menzies began meeting with the prime minister in his bedroom at 9:00 A.M. each day when Churchill was in London. This was usually Churchill's first business meeting of the day and lasted from twenty to thirty minutes. Since the prime minister kept eccentric hours, he was generally in bed or in his bath and resembled a "nice pink pig" wrapped in mandarin robes. Among the wags, "C" came to be known lewdly as one of the "Companions of the Bath," a play on the name of the oldest of all British orders, the Most Honourable Order of the Bath, one that had been revived in modern times for "services in action." As "C" himself was to remember in 1967 of his relationship with Churchill in 1941, "Sometimes I had to talk to the P.M. when he was undressed and once when in the bath he mentioned he had nothing to hide from me." [2] Occasionally these meetings would provoke some bizarre incident, as "C" was to relate one of them:

On one of my morning visits to the P.M., I found him in bed. He told me not to speak and only produce my documents for his signature. He then remarked that I probably did not realise his motive and then pointed out his Persian cat who was looking out of the window over St. James's Park and said that I should have spotted what was happening. He then told me that [his cat Nelson] was in touch with the Pelicans on the lake and that they (the Pelicans!) were communicating our information via the cat to the German secret service! [3]

Menzies briefed the prime minister on the world situation as it had developed during the night and as it might emerge during the day, and the meeting included military, diplomatic, political, and intelligence matters, spiced with tidbits of high-level gossip, for Churchill greatly enjoyed higher clubland and parliamentary chitchat. These meetings led to greater intimacy and trust between the two men. Both Churchill and "C" liked indecent jokes, and "C's" fund of them, as an habitué of White's, was fresh and large—he possessed, as his son-in-law confessed years later, "a very dirty mind." That enabled

"C" to leave Churchill on a note of good humor, for whenever it seemed suitable as often as not he had a jingle or joke that left "the prime" chuckling. One, from Rex Benson in Washington, serves to illustrate the quality of the rest:

> The devil to prove all religion a farce,
> Invented a trick most sinister.
> He baited his hook with a cowboy's ass
> And landed a Protestant minister.

At first "C" always addressed Churchill as "Prime Minister." Only later did he become "Winston," and then only when they were alone together, as was usually the case. "C" was always "C" except when they met late at night or when they were discussing personal matters, or when Churchill was particularly pleased with his spymaster. Then "C" became "Stewart." When Churchill was grumpy about something, "C" became "General Menzies." To keep the peace, "C" was required to have a stomach made of lead, for at all hours of the day and night he was required to drink champagne, whiskey, brandy, beer, lager, gin, kümmel, soda water, lime juice cordial, tea, Benedictine, coffee, cocoa, Ovaltine, ginger beer, red wine, pink wine, white wine. Since at that time "C" still smoked—hand-rolled cigarettes with "gold spats" made by an exquisite Greek tobacconist on Jermyn Street—even at 2:00 A.M. it was prudent to accept one of Churchill's cigars and be seen to smoke it. Not surprisingly "C" thought that Churchill was "an unreasonable genius."

Yet "C" never forgot that Churchill was the prime minister and never forgot that, for all the charm, wit, and elegance of discourse, Churchill possessed a very nasty streak in his personality. He could be insulting, wounding, contemptuous, arrogant, vicious, rude, ill-mannered, vindictive, irritable, loquacious, and stubborn. It behooved "C" to watch what he said and did in Churchill's presence, and it speaks legions for "C's" conduct at these meetings that, unlike almost all others, he remained an intimate of Churchill from almost the beginning of the war until long after its end. Furthermore, Churchill was not the sort who expected his henchmen to be circumscribed by the terms of reference of their office. He was not above asking "C" to spy on people with whom Churchill had contact or in whom, for one reason or another, he was interested.

While appearing benevolent and considerate, Churchill was nonetheless a hard, ruthless, and, on occasions, unprincipled politician who showed much interest in other men's finances, politics, associations, characters, and domestic situations. All this required very careful handling, for Churchill did not take kindly to men who refused him. Domestic espionage was outside "C's" mandate, and how he handled Churchill's requests for personal information we do not know. But it is probable that he declined courteously for the obvious reason that any misuse of his services would, if discovered, redound unfavorably on Churchill and, in the worst situation, deprive the prime minister of the services of a man whose opinion and information had become important in the conduct of affairs. In other words, "C" might have to resign.

Yet there were rewards, for through these meetings "C" was able to persuade Churchill that the work of his department was not, as Churchill sometimes tended to believe, of little value, but of importance to the safety of the state. Therefore the service survived and triumphed when otherwise Churchill might well have liquidated SIS and transferred its most important assets to SOE, an organization in which he took great interest. At the same time, in a world such as Whitehall, where meetings with the prime minister often became the high point in a man's career, such meetings often provoked envy, jealousy, criticism, and resentment, especially when "C" displaced Desmond Morton as Churchill's sole intelligence adviser.

For a man with social and professional ambitions, which included a knighthood and perhaps a peerage, and a clutch of directorships to make his antiquity the more agreeable, Morton observed the extension of Stewart Menzies's influence with concern. That resentment became severe when Churchill, having received a snippet of intelligence from Menzies, would spring that intelligence on Morton and his other advisers. As often as not that snippet had not reached Morton and he could do no more than confess ignorance of what it was the prime minister was talking about. These were confessions that no wise man made too often. There was acrimony between Morton and "C," and, as "C" told a high officer of U.S. intelligence, he thought it "unwise" and not conducive to good order that there should have been such intimacy between himself and Churchill.

Within Broadway, meanwhile, the contest between Dansey and Vivian, the deputy directors, began to reach epic proportions of bureaucratic disorder. In January 1941, on the first anniversary of his appointment, Vivian felt compelled to write an enormous letter to "C" complaining that through a "want of definition" of his duties, he now found himself in an "unsatisfactory" position. [4] Since his appointment as deputy chief of the service, all Vivian found he had done for "C" was to sign a few checks, attend a few meetings, and deal with disciplinary problems. He had been able to learn "absolutely *nothing* of the policy, plans, methods or results" of Dansey's work, and Vivian had a "strong feeling" that "any interest I might show in" that respect would be "construed as curiosity or interference, and, until I know just where I stand, I would not care to risk a snub."

Vivian felt he was "rapidly losing my touch with SIS policy and performance generally except insofar as" he was "kept in the picture by my talks with [Menzies] himself." These talks were "all too rare" for either Vivian's "pleasure or profit." In consequence, Vivian announced, he was "squarely at the parting of the ways and, while I am blaming no one but myself for the situation, I have to recognize that it *has* come about and that I badly need your advice and guidance to decide which direction I am to take. But go I must."

If "C" wished to keep Vivian then, he suggested, Dansey should be evicted from his office on the (fourth or executive) floor of Broadway and that he, Vivian, should move in "so that you can get hold of me at a moment's notice." As Vivian reminded Menzies, the office presently occupied by Dansey was the room Menzies himself had occupied when he was deputy to Sinclair. But more than that, it was "fantastic" that the deputy chief of the secret service should be "distant from you at the furthest end on a different floor."

Vivian then recommended that Major Felix Cowgill, chief of the war station at St. Albans, should be given complete charge of Section V so that Vivian, who was presently overseeing Cowgill's work, would have more time to concentrate on his duties as deputy chief. He found he was spending too much time out of town when he should be at Broadway attending to his duties as deputy chief. If he was to be any use to "C," Vivian went on, he should be allowed to see all the sections' progress reports and all papers relating to policy, plans, methods, and results. He intimated that it would be desirable for him, if he was to be an effective deputy, to assist in the financial, financial planning, and expenditure sides of the secret service. To that end, if Vivian stayed, "C" should issue instructions that would "*ensure* my insight and control of all the key-points of organisation and constructive progress." And, as Vivian concluded his letter, he hoped "that you will wish me to go *forward* rather than *back*. Given the unmistakeable backing of your authority and the goodwill of the staff (the latter is almost entirely dependent upon the former) I am quite confident that there is much that I could do as DCSS to ease your position and to improve the cohesion, smooth working, and performance of the organisation as a whole."

"C" did not respond to this cri de coeur entirely negatively. He saw virtue in making Cowgill chief of Section V, for Cowgill was a first-class officer of the type that Menzies admired so much—neither brainy nor stupid, not so ambitious as to intrigue against the regime, loyal, and with a sense of discipline that all irreverent university men out at St. Albans required if there was not to be trouble. So "C" appointed Cowgill chief of Section V, freeing Vivian for more duties within headquarters.

"C" remained determined not to extend Vivian's duties to the point where the latter would become deputy chief in fact as well as title, and he certainly did not wish to have Vivian on the same floor. However, "C" did want order out at St. Albans. With Churchill's intervention, Menzies secured control of the Radio Security Service (RSS), a section of MI5 responsible for watching the air waves for clandestine enemy wireless traffic. With the RSS had come a new clutch of Oxford and Cambridge dons who needed the sort of firm hand that Cowgill possessed.*

In particular, the Iberian subsection of Section V, a particularly important operation, needed discipline. And in what proved a fatal step, "C" instructed Vivian to find somebody who could "get some order in Iberia" and in general help Cowgill to integrate "the amateurs," men such as Trevor-Roper, with "the professionals," the cadre of officers of the secret upon which the wartime service was built. In his anxiety to impress "C" with his skill and tact in touchy matters such as these, Vivian announced that he had found "just the man for the job." Vivian intended that this man should not only produce order to the Iberian subsection, but also act as conciliator between the two factions in Section V. The man was Kim Philby.

Vivian arranged Philby's transfer from SOE, and young Philby was brought in to St. Albans as Felix Cowgill's right-hand man at Section V, which was housed in two large villas on Lord Verulam's estate off King Harry's Lane. In bringing him into the service, there was, however, a vague sense at Broadway that Philby had once been

*Among them was Professor Trevor-Roper, whom "C" regarded as "an awkward and independent bugger" and who was chiefly noteworthy at that time for his book on Archbishop Laud of Canterbury, who, in the early 1600s, had resisted Puritanism and, for his troubles, was sentenced to death by the Commons. At that time Trevor-Roper was twenty-seven and had joined RSS at the outbreak of war. Before transfer with RSS to Broadway, Trevor-Roper had done some excellent work in the early attack on the Abwehr hand ciphers.

a Communist but that, as with so many others of his age, he had put that behind him with his other youthful illusions. But Professor Trevor-Roper recorded of Philby's appointment:

I admit that Philby's appointment astonished me at the time, for my old Oxford friend had told me, years before, that his travelling companion was a communist. By now, of course, I assumed that he was an ex-communist; but even so I was surprised, for no one was more fanatically anti-communist, at that time, than the regular members of the two security services, MI6 and MI5. It was quite inconceivable, in ordinary circumstances, that MI6 would want to employ anyone who had ever been a communist, or that the department of MI5 which supplied the "trace" . . . would clear him for such employment. . . . That these men should have suspended their deepest convictions in favour of the ex-communist Philby was indeed remarkable. Since it never occurred to me that they could be ignorant of the facts (which were widely known), I assumed that Philby had particular virtues which made him, in their eyes, indispensable. [5]

Perhaps Trevor-Roper was correct. Perhaps Philby did have particular virtues that made him, in "C's" eyes, indispensable. The war was widening, and Menzies was still under a directive from Churchill to do what he could to split the Nazi-Soviet alliance. And such was the theological nature of communism that, as in Jacobin times, when Catholics would talk only to Catholics, now Communists would talk politics only with a Communist. It was "C's" business to maintain dangerous associations, and these sometimes required the employment of dangerous persons. In any case, it was not long before "C" and Philby began to run into each other, and as Philby was to recall of an early encounter with "C":

Broadway was a dingy building, a warren of wooden partitions and frosted glass windows. It had eight floors served by an ancient lift. On one of my early visits, I got into the lift with a colleague whom the liftman treated with obtrusive deference. The stranger gave me a swift glance and looked away. He was well-built and well-dressed, but what struck me most was his pallor: pale face, pale eyes, silvery blond hair thinning on top—the whole an impression of pepper-and-salt. When he got out at the fourth floor, I asked the liftman who he was. "Why, sir, that's the Chief," he answered in some surprise.

At that stage, I knew precious little of the Chief. . . . As will be seen, I came to know him much better, and I hasten to say that I look back on him with affection and respect, though not necessarily with respect for those qualities on which he would have prided himself. [6]

Philby now began to play an extremely dangerous game, and if he ever wondered how dangerous it was, he had to look no further than Section V and the Armstrong case, a case about which "C" advised Cadogan on January 23, 1941, and which reached the public hangman in July even as Philby was joining the SIS executive.

In October 1940, George Armstrong, thirty-nine, a merchant seaman from Newcastle and a member of the Communist party of Great Britain, was observed by Stephenson's agents in New York to make contact with German consular and Abwehr representatives. Inquiries showed that Armstrong had deserted his ship at Boston, it seemed in response to a speech by Vyacheslav Molotov, the Soviet foreign minister to the Supreme Soviet in Moscow. The war was an imperialist plot, and, Molotov urged, to frustrate it munitions workers should strike, dock workers should refuse to load war materials, and Allied merchant seamen should jump ship in a neutral port.

Under the alias of George William Hope, Armstrong offered to supply the Germans with information concerning the sailing dates of British convoys from the United States, with as much information about their routes, speeds, and destinations as he could obtain. The Germans did accept his offer, but how much of that information Armstrong provided, and to what extent it contributed to the sinking of British ships by U-boats, was not revealed. Stephenson's organization was able to make a case against Armstrong, and he then advised the U.S. Immigration and Naturalization Service of Armstrong's illegal status in the United States and of his nonneutral intelligence work in the interest of Germany. Arrested in Boston on October 16, 1940, the United States deported Armstrong aboard a U.S. tanker, the *La Brea*, which arrived in Cardiff on February 21. Armstrong was then arrested on charges of high treason and taken to London. On May 8 Armstrong was tried at the Old Bailey, found guilty, and sentenced to death. His appeal was heard on June 23, the day after Germany invaded Russia. At that moment, as all Communists were advised by their party headquarters, the "immoral war" became a "just cause." But neither that proclamation nor the emergence of Russia as a fighting ally in the war against Germany served to change the sentence. Armstrong's plea was rejected, and he was hanged at Wandsworth Prison, London, on July 10.

Since "C" probably made the World War I case for hanging such men—the case of *"pour encourager les autres"*—when he met with Cadogan, it followed that Philby would be prudent to tred with great care. And that he did, so nimbly that even forty years later Mrs. Felix Cowgill spoke wonderingly of Philby's ability "to serve two hostile governments at the same time and with equal devotion."

Philby became the model secret service officer, one of the best to enter "C's" department.

2   THE APPOINTMENT OF A SECRET AGENT

Wild Bill Donovan had reappeared in London, meanwhile, as the envoy of FDR, this time en route to spend a hundred days in the Middle East. Churchill gave him lunch at 10 Downing Street and had placed him in "C's" charge. Menzies saw to it that Donovan received a great send-off at Paddington Station when he left by train for the flying-boat dock at Plymouth. There were no less than two field marshals, Gort and Dill, on the platform to wish the American colonel a safe journey, and all of "C's" stations throughout Arabia and the Balkans had been warned that Donovan was an important envoy who was to see everything he wished to see and was to be allowed to go everywhere he wished to go—everywhere, that is, except "C's" code-breaking establishments near Cairo and at Ramat David in Palestine.

During their talk at Claridge's beforehand, "C" mentioned to Donovan that, having established formal relations with the FBI and the U.S. military intelligence department in Washington, he would like to send Rex Benson to Washington as liaison officer at the War Department. Donovan had met Benson in 1936 when the latter approached him on the boat train platform at Waterloo Station. Donovan was in the company of a mutual friend, Sir Ralph Glyn, and Benson asked Donovan if he would take a parcel containing his wife's jodhpurs to her in New York. Donovan had agreed, and they had seen much of each other after that. As Donovan told "C," he thought Benson's would be a excellent appointment, for in Donovan's estimate Benson knew and liked Americans—had he not married Condé Nast's ex-wife?—and would be an asset in Washington. "C" kept Donovan's opinion for use when he next saw the prime minister.

In quaint circumstances such as this, the intelligence relationship between England and America was revived, twenty-three years after the Americans had abandoned it. When two FBI men arrived in London as "legal attachés," "C" asked the prime minister whether he might send Benson to Washington, and the prime minister agreed, suggesting that Benson could go as assistant military attaché with Lord Halifax when the new ambassador to Washington left England on January 16, 1941, in the British battleship *King George V* to take up his post.*

Accompanying Halifax would be Menzies's friend at Impey's, the director of military intelligence, Major General F. G. "Paddy" Beaumont-Nesbitt, who was to become military attaché. Thus if Benson accompanied Halifax, Eton would be well represented in Washington, for the earl of Halifax was himself an old Etonian, as were most of the members of his staff. "C" gave Benson his instructions at a meeting at Broadway early in January and left it to Benson to get himself aboard the *King George V* for what would be Halifax's entry into the United States—FDR was to come out and board the battleship off the U.S. naval base at Norfolk, Virginia, and then enter the port with full honors. That was a mistake, for if "C" had the support of Churchill, Halifax, and Beaumont-Nesbitt for Bensons's appointment, that did not mean Benson had the approval of the chief of the Imperial General Staff, Field Marshal Sir John Dill.

Dill objected first to Beaumont-Nesbitt's appointment "because he had not been under fire at Dunkirk" but then saw the point and approved it when Benson explained that Beaumont-Nesbitt had served under fire throughout the Battle of Britain, a victory, and that was "better than Dunkirk—a defeat—in the eyes of the Yanks." Then Dill objected to Benson's own appointment in what was, evidently, a reflection of the poor estate into which Broadway had fallen. Although there was space in the battleship, and "C" told the Army Council that Benson's presence in the United States was important, Dill declined to endorse the appointment because Dill's aide-de-camp, Captain Reginald "Narcissus" Macdonald-Buchanan (who had been at Impey's with "C" and Benson and whose grandfather was one of the co-founders with Graham Menzies of the Distillers Company Limited), thought that all Benson wanted to do was "loll about at Palm Beach." [7]

*The marquess of Lothian, Halifax's predecessor at Washington, was a Christian Scientist. He would not allow doctors to treat him when he fell ill late in 1940, and he died of uremic poisoning on December 11, 1940. He was a great loss to Britain and the United States and was considered to have been one of the best British ambassadors to have held the post. His ashes were deposited in Arlington National Cemetery and were then returned to Scotland in a U.S. cruiser in December 1945.

Benson's appointment was canceled, then approved, then canceled again. Finally it was approved, but too late to enable Benson to sail on the *King George V*. "C" saw Cadogan no less than three times in five days between January 9 and 14 to get backing for Benson's appointment. As usual, Cadogan was irritated with "C," exclaiming in his diary, "Menzies came in at 3:30—as garrulous as usual." But if Cadogan tried to do anything at the War Office, he failed. Benson then asked Oswald Birley, the society portrait painter, to talk to his friend Lord Halifax. That did not work, either, and Benson remained in London when the *King George V* left Scapa Flow for Chesapeake Bay in vice-regal splendor with the new ambassador and the new military attaché aboard.

Spending that day interrogating the Vichy French military attaché to Dublin on the off chance that he was a German spy, Benson exclaimed in his diary of the War Office: "I hope I never have the misfortune to work in the W.O. again. Inefficiency-delay-intrigue and a lack of confidence, which slows up the whole machine." Benson was still in London on February 21, although "C" had told him his mission was of the first importance. For by that time a new suspicion had entered the minds of Dill and "Narcisscus" Macdonald: Benson wanted the appointment because he had business interests in the United States. When he learned that, Benson was greatly annoyed and wished to resign, for as he recorded in his diary: "Is that what is in his mind over this? I can't think it. Why not send for me?"

Then "Narcissus" advised Benson that he was to go and told him to mark time by getting a detailed briefing from all government departments. It was during these briefings that, at the War Office, Benson discovered much secret intelligence was being withheld from the Americans despite the protest and warning from General Lee, the U.S. military attaché in London. As Benson wrote in his diary on February 6:

Short time in American section of [DMI]. Find important secret information about Japan withheld from U.S.A. Why? Surely they should be told everything. Picture as presented by MI about Japan quite alarming. They envisage a landing north of Singapore & short notice of entry of Japan into war against us [?United States].*

It was also during that briefing that a new task was added to Benson's mission. After spending a day at the Ministry of Information

---

*Rex Benson diaries, February 6, 1941. N.B. On that same date Cadogan recorded in his diary: "Instructed Halifax to pass on to U.S. Govt. our information about the machinations of these beastly little monkeys."

getting briefed on British policy toward the United States, Benson was told by the minister, Brendan Bracken: "PM wants America in the war, but go easy until the [Lend-Lease] Bill becomes law, probably February 28." [8] Nobody told Benson how he was to influence 131 million people into a declaration of war, however, and if his was regarded as an important task, it still did not produce fast transport. There would be no space aboard the BOAC or Pan-American Clipper for Benson, for as the air movements officer declared, although "C" had given Benson the highest priority for his journey, Benson had no priority.

Finally, on February 23, Benson was alerted to move. He hastened down to Norton Hall in the Cotswolds to bury the family treasure (including some George III and Queen Anne masterpieces, just as Holford's father had done when Napoleon threatened to invade England) in a concrete coffin in a corner of Beaufortshire. He assembled his half a ton of luggage, which included briefs on Ultra and a small cellar of choice wines. After an another muddle at the War Office over the name of the ship he was to sail in, Benson departed the Clyde on February 26 aboard the SS *Beaver Hill*, a six-thousand-ton tramp steamer that "burned Scotch coal which made a filthy smoke which could be seen seven miles away." [9]

Benson carried in his diplomatic baggage all data acquired from Bletchley relating to GC&CS's operations against the Japanese ciphers, which, so it was intended, should form the basis of the first Anglo-American intelligence alliance since the collapse of the relationship in 1919. The data included numbers of raw intercepts obtained from the monitoring of Japanese naval, military, and diplomatic traffic, and also numerous CX—secret service—reports on Japanese signals networks and procedures. All of this intelligence was most secret and of the highest importance to the United States. All was urgently required by the U.S. intercept service to improve the range of their own code- and cipher-breaking operations against Japan.

If the blossom was out, so were the knives. On Benson's arrival in Washington, the newspapers were full of Charles Lindbergh's statement in response to lend-lease that "the U.S.A. cannot help Britain because she is already beaten," while the advertising spots on the radio proclaimed the American Firsters' warning: "First our arms, then our money, then our boys." The lend-lease debate had brought to the surface all the old suspicions about England: "Imperialism was as bad as fascism; European power politics were un-American; trickery was to be expected of the corrupt British bankers and munitions-

makers; Britain had been the enemy since 1776." [10] Representative
Martin Sweeney, a professional Irishman from Cleveland, Ohio, proposed a new battle hymn sung to the tune of "God Bless America":

> God save America from British rule:
> Stand beside her and guide her
> From the schemers who would make of her a fool.
> From Lexington to Yorktown,
> From bloodstained Valley Forge,
> God save America
> From a king named George.*

Benson's orders read that "The King has been graciously pleased
to approve your appointment as Military Attache to His Majesty's
Embassy at Washington and His Majesty's Missions at Guatemala,
San Salvador, Tegucigalpa, Managua, San Jose, Panama, Port-au-
Prince, Havana and Ciudad Trujillo, with headquarters in Washington." Notwithstanding Benson's special connection to "C" personally
(which was not acknowledged in his orders), his orders enjoined him
specifically not to engage in espionage or other illegal acts of intelligence. As the orders stated in this respect:

You should take the greatest care to avoid any action liable to create the
suspicion that you are attempting to procure secret information by illicit
means. You must have no relations or communications with persons acting,
or professing willingness to act, as spies or secret agents, and you should
make a special point of conforming fully with all regulations or bye-laws in
force at places you may visit in the course of your duties. [11]

Likewise Benson was also ordered to avoid any display of political
activities, the formation and utterance of political opinions, and the
compilation and circulation of political reports. Any special information of importance that reached him on "purely political or commercial subjects" should "at once be brought to the notice of His
Majesty's Representative." Benson was to confine himself at all times
to the collection of intelligence about the armed forces of the countries
which he visited but only in conformance with his directive from the
War Office.

But those directives were meaningless. From the moment he
arrived in Washington, Benson became engaged in political intelligence on a very large scale and if he did not himself employ secret

---

*The new hymn was entered into the Congressional Record on June 19, 1941. See: CR,
77th Congress, 1st session, LXXXXVII, pt 12.

agents then Stephenson did and Benson had access to such persons and their reports.

The first joint Anglo-American conference regarding intelligence deriving from most secret sources was held on April 1, attended by General Beaumont-Nesbitt and Benson for the British and representatives of the U.S. Army and Navy intelligence services. From that conference sprang the document that guided the Anglo-American intelligence relationship for the rest of the war:

Existing military Intelligence organizations of the two Powers will operate as independent Intelligence agencies, but will maintain close liaison with each other to ensure the full and prompt exchange of pertinent information concerning war operations. Intelligence liaison will be established not only through the Military Missions [of the United States in London and the United Kingdom in Washington] but also between all echelons of Command in the field with respect to matters which affect their operations. [12]

On that basis, and with Benson's technical data on Ultra and Enigma transferred to the U.S. Army's cryptographic establishment, Arlington Hall in Virginia, the U.S. Army began to pass its technical data to GC&CS through the U.S. embassy in London. At the same time Benson began to receive Magic, the American decrypts of Japanese diplomatic and military traffic. As Benson's diaries show, from the start the intelligence content of Magic was remarkable. The Japanese diplomatic decrypts that flowed throughout the second half of April showed that there could be no room for doubt about Japan's allegiance to the Berlin-Tokyo Pact, that Hitler and Ribbentrop were keeping Baron Oshima, the Japanese ambassador in Berlin, fully informed about their intention to make war on Russia. Here, then, was "C's" window on the highest councils of the Axis in Berlin. Since Oshima reported *everything* he was told, "C" would not have been better served had he had a stenographer present at the discussions.

The first major intercept reached Benson almost immediately after Benson's arrival, on April 30. It was also almost the last piece of such intelligence. As Rex Benson's diary shows, on that day General Sherman Miles, the G2 of the U.S. Army, gave Benson the most important—and longest—decrypt so far received. In four parts each of about 240 words, the telegram was dated April 16, from Oshima to the Foreign Office in Tokyo. It showed that whatever else Hitler intended, he did *not* intend to—indeed could *not*—invade England. Based upon a briefing of Oshima by Ribbentrop, it showed that Germany intended to attack Russia, and that Japan would remain neutral in that war. It showed, too, that Japan's entire military strength would be available for an attack on the British and Dutch empires in Asia, except for that portion of her army which she agreed to keep in Manchuria to pin the Red Army in Siberia during the German attack on European Russia. Oshima had been urged to recommend that Singapore be attacked as soon as possible, presumably to prevent the British army in England from invading France while the German army was engaged in Russia. Oshima declared the Germans to be confident they could win a war on two fronts.

As for the United States, Oshima reported that the Germans believed she would not declare war but would continue her policy of assisting Britain with all steps short of belligerency. Both Germany and Italy believed that American aid to Britain would prolong the war but would not enable Britain to win it. In a conversation between Oshima and Grand Admiral Erich Raeder, the German naval commander in chief, Raeder conceded that the German fleet lacked the means to carry out an invasion of Britain, so Hitler had decided to marshal all his resources for his Russian campaign and be ready to attack Russia "when the harvest was ready." This attack would not commence before June, and, Oshima commented, all of this "pointed to a very grave crisis." [13]

Such was the importance of Magic that after it had been sent to "C," Beaumont-Nesbitt telephoned "C" to ensure that he had seen the decrypt, which may have been a mistake. Although Benson did not record the text of the conversation, it may be assumed that both Menzies and Beaumont-Nesbitt were cautious in what they said over the telephone, for at about this time "C," in a conversation with a colleague, described the transatlantic telephone as an open wire that every major power was tapping. The flow of Magic to Benson continued for fourteen days, until there was trouble.

On May 13 Benson attended a "long seance" with General Miles at which Miles announced there was evidence that the Japanese were aware that their diplomatic cipher was being read by the Americans. Miles complained that there had been a grave compromise of the Magic secret in Washington, and the U.S. Army Signals Corps was investigating how that leakage had occurred. Perhaps as a result of Beaumont-Nesbitt's telephone call to Menzies on April 30, Benson thought, Miles was "inclined" to blame Beaumont-Nesbitt as the source of the leak. Whether that accusation was justified was to take some time to establish, but in the interim the flow of Magic ceased.

[14] The first of what was to prove to be periodic bouts of mistrust concerning the security of cryptographic intelligence had occurred.

After much debate and examination of evidence, the most widely accepted theory was that the leak was the responsibility of the undersecretary of state, Sumner Welles, who, anxious to lure the Russians away from the Nazi-Soviet Pact, was said to have shown the intercept to Constantin Oumansky, the Soviet ambassador in Washington. It was believed that Oumansky then confronted Hans Thomsen, the German chargé d'affaires in Washington, with the warning. In his turn Thomsen warned the German Foreign Ministry in Berlin, which then warned Oshima.

On the other hand, the British embassy could not be excluded as a suspect, for as Benson acknowledged, it had no "method" for handling the most secret material: British embassy security methods were "still those of the peacetime 1900 period," and "their idea of security is wretched." [15] In the end, General Sherman accepted that the compromise was "probably" the fault of the State Department, and the crisis passed. In subsequent telegrams the Japanese revealed the nature of the precautions they were taking to mend the security of their ciphers, and that information enabled the Americans to remain a jump or two ahead of the Japanese security measures. Magic was preserved. The exchange of Magic for Ultra was resumed and in good time to enable Churchill to be informed fully of the events that led down to the German invasion of Russia and thence to Pearl Harbor.

3   THE RUSSIAN RIDDLE

In March 1941, as the new campaign season approached, "C" received what amounted to a rebuke from the chiefs of staff who, bedeviled by the continuing obscurity of German intentions—did they intend to invade Russia, England, the Balkans, or Arabia?—were concerned that "C" was still unable to give them seventy-two hours' guaranteed advance warning of an invasion of England. "C" was "required and requested" to "take every possible step to remedy this extremely unsatisfactory state of affairs." [16]

Whatever the basis of their discontent, it was not shared by Churchill. Nor could it be said that "C" himself had not already taken every step to remedy that state of affairs, with some success. In the second half of 1940, contact was reestablished with the permanent intelligence services of France, Belgium, and Norway. Dansey had established an important new Polish service across the German east-west lines of communication in Poland, and Broadway's intelligence structure had remained intact in the Balkans during the collapse in 1940. "C's" ninety-agent program for France was in effect and limited only by the availability of suitable aircraft, short-take-off-and-landing Lysanders for cross-Channel operations, and twin-engined Whitley bombers for deeper penetrations.

Other, bolder operations might have been possible but for SOE's constant intriguing for the very limited number of aircraft available. Irritated beyond measure by these intrigues, "C" warned Gladwyn Jebb, SOE's director of operations and policy, in a letter on March 10 that revealed steel claws. He could not, "C" declared, accept the view that SOE should have first call on any aircraft, because the director of military intelligence had just written to him "that he wishes me to insist on absolute priority on any intelligence operation affecting invasion." [17] But what could Menzies tell the director of military intelligence in the light of SOE's demands?

An amicable compromise might be reached between SOE and SIS, but "when I am being pressed the whole time for more and more information I am bound to say that I am thoroughly dissatisfied at the facilities at my disposal (this applies to boats as well as to aircraft)." And while he was about it, "C" raised the question of competition between SIS and SOE for agents among the French, Belgian, and Dutch troops in England. Since very few men had the qualities necessary to make a reliable secret agent, he was irritated to discover that SOE had "inspected between twenty and thirty of the French personnel, and that among these, there are a number of individuals whom I would have normally recruited" for the invasion watch. [18]

For the moment, this was little more than a minor squall, given the fact that Menzies was by now reasonably sure that the Germans would not invade in strength, although they might well make large-scale raids by commando-type troops on the ports. To Menzies the SIS-SOE relationship was an irritant, one made the worse by the tensions and aggravations of trying to wage war against a powerful enemy with only very limited means and against constant competition for these means from a rival and junior service. But as the year and the war ground on, these irritations were to turn into full-scale and dangerous brawls the like of which Whitehall bureaucracy had rarely, if ever, seen before.

As this quarrel came to a head, "C" undertook fresh measures to extend his intelligence coverage of the great Western European ports. Between January 27 and March 29, conversations were held in Washington between representatives of the American and British staffs. They were now producing a joint strategy should America enter the war, a plan called ABC-1, in which it was agreed that if and when America became a belligerent in a war with Germany and Japan, both the American and British forces would concentrate first upon the destruction of Germany and then Japan.

During these conversations, "C," acting with the authority of Churchill and Roosevelt, wrote to J. Edgar Hoover, director of the FBI, suggesting that the two services exchange liaison officers. As a result, two FBI officers came to London to open a relationship with Section V, "C's" counterespionage service. The U.S. military intelligence service also contracted an agreement with "C," with the knowledge and permission of Churchill and Roosevelt, that Ultra intelligence should be exchanged for its U.S. counterpart, Magic, and that the United States should concentrate its cryptanalytical effort against the Japanese while the United Kingdom continued to develop its penetration of German and Italian ciphers. Also, the U.S. naval attaché in Vichy, Captain A.C.J. Sabalot, had extensive contacts with French naval officers located in the Channel ports. Sabalot was obtaining important German naval information from these officers, and this, it was agreed under the Washington staff conversations, should be sent to London.

None of these arrangements could, however, provide the service directors of intelligence with the information they needed about German intentions against England. The result was that in March 1941 the service directors filed a formal complaint with Cadogan against Menzies. The basis of this complaint was the usual one. The directors of intelligence demanded more intelligence than they were getting and threatened that if "C" did not provide what they wanted to enable them to make their estimates of enemy intentions, they would establish their own collection agencies. It would be back to the same chaos caused by the various rival services in World War I—in fact, early in 1941 Churchill discovered that the RAF had begun what amounted to an espionage service, one reporting on bombing damage against targets in Italy. That discovery prompted a rare explosion of

anger from the prime minister, who was well aware of the danger—
and expense—involved when several espionage services attacked the
same targets.

Cadogan met with Menzies and the service directors at the Foreign Office on March 31. Menzies made a poor showing, and nobody
made a good one, for as Cadogan, reflecting his own continuing animosity for "C," recorded of the meeting:

A tiresome day. 11.30 meeting with Directors of Intelligence & "C." Object
was to drag former into [?the open] and make them formulate their complaints. But they didn't do much of this, and remain with their grouse. "C,"
as usual, a bad advocate in his own behalf. He babbles and wanders, and
gives the impression he is putting up a smoke screen of words & trying to
put his questioners off the track. [19]

From a man such as Cadogan, this was again severe criticism
bearing not only upon Menzies's competence but also upon his personal fitness for the work. Yet it does seem that "C" was indeed
"putting up a smoke screen of words & trying to put his questioners
off the track," for at this very period there had been major developments within the espionage and cryptanalytical services.

Through the work of Dansey's agents and those of Captain A.C.J.
Sabalot and his ring of French naval spies, comprehensive espionage
coverage was established in all the main ports between the end of
March and June 1941. With the appearance of the German battleships
Scharnhorst and *Gneisenau* in Brest, their point of departure for
commerce raiding in the North Atlantic, "C" was able to give Whitehall almost daily reports on the positions and seaworthiness of the
battleships as the RAF attacked them by night and day. These reports
were "especially useful because it was difficult to judge from photographic reconnaissance the effect of the bombing raids on the ships."
On June 20 "C" sent a collated report on both ships to the chiefs of
staff with the warning that, although the *Gneisenau* was out of action,
the *Scharnhorst* could sail at any moment.

From early 1941 the Polish intelligence service in France, while
itself subject to severe casualties through German counterespionage
attacks, was able to report to London the departure of U-boats from
Bordeaux. By June that service was extended to Brest and Le Havre.
A main tactic was the port laundries: when a U-boat crew collected
its washing, a sailing followed within a few hours. But if the Poles
could report the number and type of the U-boat, most often they
could report nothing about its operational area. Intelligence of that

description could be obtained only through Enigma, a copy of which was carried by each U-boat. At sea, U-boats maintained wireless silence except when sighting a convoy, when they reported the position, course, and speed of the convoy, or if they had made a successful attack, for the information of other U-boats in the same area. Otherwise the Admiralty had no information as to their whereabouts or movements apart from occasional sighting reports from the convoys themselves.

As a consequence, between June 1940 and March 1941 sinkings of merchantmen increased alarmingly, averaging 260,000 tons a month, double the previous rate. In all, two million tons were sunk by U-boats during that period while German surface ships and aircraft sank a further 1,119,000 tons. These sinkings were far beyond the replacement capacity of the British shipyards. Having declared unrestricted submarine warfare and a total blockade of the United Kingdom, all now depended upon GC&CS's ability to break into the German naval ciphers as the Germans introduced new tactics—wolf packs—with every expectation of cutting the North Atlantic supply routes and so bringing England to the point where she could no longer feed her population or bring in the fuel, raw materials, munitions, and equipment for her armed forces and factories. It was, therefore, a desperate period. But the future was not without hope, although the Enigma being used by the German fleet was infinitely more complex than that employed by either the German army or the air force.

In December 1939 "C" had pressed the Admiralty to undertake more operations against German shipping to produce the technical data required by Bletchley if the naval Enigma was to be penetrated as thoroughly as the air force Enigma. In February 1940 three Enigma rotor wheels, one of the key elements in a cryptanalytical attack, were captured from a member of the U-33. But otherwise the crew of the U-33 succeeded in destroying all paper data. The capture of the three wheels therefore did little to advance the attack. But in April 1940 the Admiralty by chance obtained some paper data from a German patrol boat intercepted off Norway, the VP-2623. That information enabled Bletchley to read during May the ship's naval Enigma traffic for six days in April. The important data—that the German navy relied entirely on Enigma for its communications—was secured. Just as important, evidence uncovered established that the German fleet used only two Enigma keys, one for home waters, the other for foreign, and that U-boats and surface warships shared the same key, transferring to the foreign key only for operations in distant waters.

Then, in March 1941—just before "C's" crucial meeting with the directors of intelligence—the Admiralty captured the armed trawler *Krebs* in a raid on a port in northern Norway. That raid enabled Bletchley to read much of the April traffic of the German fleet with a delay of between three and seven days. *Krebs's* information also enabled the Royal Navy to capture two weather ships, the *Munchen* and the *Lauenburg*. The intelligence contained in the wireless cabins of these ships permitted still futher advances. But it was the chance capture of the U-110 on May 9 that at last facilitated the major breakthrough into the home waters cipher, in which 95 percent of all German naval traffic was sent.

With the capture of the U-110, "C" authorized a larger naval staff to go to Bletchley, a staff that soon reached over a thousand men and women. At least one of the six *bombes* resident at Bletchley at the end of June 1941 was always available for work against naval ciphers. And after the first week of August 1941 "C" was able to report that the naval home waters Enigma had been mastered. That mastery persisted to the end of the war. Most of the traffic was read within thirty-six hours, although in December 1941 the delay increased temporarily to eighty hours.

Such, then, was the evolving situation when "C" met his critics in Cadogan's office in March 1941. In two directions—espionage and code breaking—he had reason to babble and wander, for he made it his golden rule never to reveal to anyone, including the prime minister, what his sources were. In still another direction, that of the security of British ciphers and Bletchley's capacity to read the German army's Enigma on a current basis, the directors' complaints were not unjustified.

In 1941 the Germans were breaking into so many British (and American) ciphers, and the intelligence being obtained was of such importance, the casualties inflicted so great, that the German propaganda minister, Josef Goebbels, wrote in his diary: "I can only hope that this is not the case with our own secret communications as well; for if the British knew in detail about us everything that we know about them it would have very grave consequences." [20] The casualties at sea were rising through German cryptanalytical success against British ciphers; all Britain's operations in the North African desert were being betrayed to Rommel as a result of the insecurity of the personal cipher being used by Colonel Bonner Fellers, the U.S. military attaché at Cairo, who had been given the freedom of the British front; and, Godfrey maintained, such German naval ciphers as were being broken by "C" were inadequate.

The boardroom battle remained, therefore, with "C" going about his business with all the energy and ability he could summon. For their part, the service directors remained merciless, for while it had become evident that both the Balkans and Arabia were German targets for operations that spring, in their mind they still could not accept that Hitler would invade Russia when England remained at war in the west. For his part, "C" believed that Hitler with 250 divisions (against the 30 in England and the 10 in the United States) was capable of invading England (provided they had air and sea superiority, which they had not secured), Arabia, the Balkans, *and* Russia at the same time.

In that estimate, "C" had the support of Churchill. As had so often been the case during Sealion, Churchill continued to maintain that an attack on Russia was as likely as one against England. So strongly did he believe this that he sent large numbers of trained forces from Britain to the Near East and elsewhere at precisely the time the War Office was predicting invasion in the spring. On January 31 "C," on the basis of SIS reports, declared that preparations for the invasion of Russia were "almost open." Troops were arriving in Poland from France. Men fluent in Russian were being recruited into the army and the Abwehr, while Russian emigrés were being drafted into German military intelligence units. A "continuous chain" of airfields had been, or were being, built along the railway line between Poznan and Lodz.

On February 5 "C" circulated Polish intelligence, which was highly regarded, showing that large numbers of German units, most of them armored, were reaching east Prussia, and there was congestion on the railways between Berlin and Warsaw. On February 21 the State Department actually obtained the Barbarossa directive from Sam E. Woods, its consul general in Geneva, but when it arrived in London it had been so garbled during transmission that, as Major Morton minuted in Churchill's private office, "the Book of Revelations read backwards would be more revealing." On February 24 Churchill commented that "Russia was now in an unenviable position and that her attitude was one of making concessions to Germany in order to gain time." [21]

Whether "C" had special knowledge—a special form of Ultra, perhaps—that he was communicating only to his immediate masters, the prime minister and Cadogan, we do not know. Such a postulation is not improbable, and such evidence rarely penetrated the intelligence files to leave a spoor for historians to follow. But special intelligence was certainly suggested when, on February 28, Sir Stafford Cripps, the British ambassador at Moscow, declared positively enough at a press conference that Germany intended to attack Russia, and that she would do so "not later than the end of June"—a report that was accurate. [22] If that statement was a provocation calculated to produce trouble in the Nazi-Soviet Pact, then it was significantly close to the truth. It suggests that Cripps was receiving—and, more important, believing—"C's" intelligence through the Foreign Office, for political provation was part of SIS's mission, and it also reflected the policy of the Foreign Office, Churchill, and Menzies.

Against that background of a looming and epochal clash between nazism and bolshevism, and of the new possibility that the war was exploding globally, "C" demonstrated afresh his determination to defend the secret of the existence of Ultra—that it was better to lose a battle than the key source of intelligence.

With the end of the battle between the British and German armies for Greece—a battle that was part of Hitler's grand strategy for Barbarossa inasmuch as it was part of a campaign to secure his Balkans flank against the large British army in the Suez Canal zone—"C" was confronted with a security problem resembling that which may have arisen over Coventry in November of 1940. During the Greek campaign, "C" discerned in Ultra a German intention to stage a large-scale airborne invasion of the important central Mediterranean island of Crete.

Whereas Menzies had agreed that Ultra could go to the British commanding general in Greece over a special GCHQ wireless link from Bletchley via Cairo, he balked at the prospect of allowing it to go to Crete, where, in the nature of airborne operations, army headquarters were liable to be captured at an early stage. Moreover, he had made it a cardinal rule, one on which he was prepared to resign if it was contested by Churchill, that Ultra was not to be sent to any headquarters under that of an army. His grounds were that brigade, division, and corps headquarters were liable to be overrun by the enemy, but army headquarters were located so far to the rear of the front that the men handling Ultra, an SIS organization called Special Liaison Units (SLUs), could be evacuated with their precious and revealing records if there was any sign that army headquarters might be captured.

Stewart Menzies's immediate family photographed at Tranby Croft, taken after the social ruin of Menzies's maternal grandfather, Arthur Wilson, in the Royal Baccarat Scandal of 1890. Wilson stands third from the left and his wife is seated directly below him. Stewart's father, Jack, is standing on the far right. Stewart, then about four, is seated on the left, his brother Keith on the extreme right. *(Menzies Family Archives)*

Stewart Menzies at Eton College in front of Edward Impey's house. Impey, Stewart's housemaster, was a major influence in Menzies's life. Eton was one of the prime forces that made Menzies the spymaster he later became in the service of Churchill—remote, elitist, ruthless, silent, and capable of great cunning. *(Eton College Library)*

Stewart Menzies lies prostrate in the middle of his teammates after attempting to score a "shy" in the Eton Wall-game, a form of football played only at Eton. Ruthless, tough, aggressive, and exhausting, it was through this game that England won its wars in the eighteenth and nineteenth centuries, or so the Duke of Wellington claimed. *(Eton College Library)*

Eton was founded in the fifteenth century by Henry VI as Catholic school for the poor, but over the centuries it became the leading college for the sons of England's ruling class. Its purpose was to train future Crown servants in the exercise of power. At the pinnacle of that quaint schoolboy republic was the Eton College Society, known as "Pop." In this photograph members wear the traditional habit of their office. Stewart Menzies, who became the society's president in 1909, is in the front row seated, second from the left; to the right, his lifelong friend and colleague in secret service, Rex Benson. A powerful group, it was said at Eton that "he who knows a member of 'Pop' knows enough." *(Eton College Library)*.

Susannah West Wilson *(left)*, later wife of Jack Menzies, mother of Stewart, Keith, and Ian. Lady Avice Sackville *(below)*, daughter of the eighth Earl De La Warr, whom Stewart married at the end of World War 1 in what was the first society marriage of the peace. *(Menzies Family Archives; Lady Avice Spicer Archives)*

After Eton the eldest sons either returned home to prepare for their inheritance or went on to university. Second and third sons entered either the military or the church; Stewart entered the military. After a year with the Foot Guards he joined the Second Life Guards, one of the regiments of the Household brigade responsible for protecting the royal family and their property. Lieutenant Menzies is photographed here in the full ceremonial of the Royal Horse Guards in 1911. *(Wombell Family Archives)*

Captain Euan Wallace, Menzies's lifelong friend, who succeeded Menzies as adjutant of the Second Life Guards. He became a member of the Cabinet of Prime Minister Neville Chamberlain at the outbreak of World War II, then was placed in charge of the civil defense of London during the Battle of Britain. *(Life Guards Museum)*

Colonel Sir George Holford, Stewart Menzies's stepfather, an aide to King Edward VIII and to Queen Mary. Holford married Stewart's mother after the death of Jack Menzies. He owned two great palaces and one of the finest private collection of Old Masters. *(Life Guards Museum)*

Keith Menzies *(left)* and Stewart at the beginning of World War I. This picture was taken in England just before they left for the great battlefield of Ypres in Belgium, a conflagration in which Stewart lost most of his Eton friends. *(Menzies Family Archives)*

At general headquarters. Captain Stewart Menzies began his career in the British secret service as chief of counterespionage in the intelligence section of the British commander in chief, General Sir Douglas Haig. Menzies is standing second from left. Seated in the middle is Brigadier General John Charteris, chief of the section who manipulated intelligence estimates, resulting in the deaths of a generation of young Britons. Seated second from the left is Walter Kirke, who wrote of Menzies: "Charming fellow...he'll do well." *(Life Guards Museum)*

The estate of Sir George Holford at Westonbirt. Holford's second palace was Dorchester House, which stood on the site of what is now the Dorchester Hotel in Park Lane. *(Menzies Family Archives)*

Stewart Menzies's first sport was his work—manhunting. His second was foxhunting, "the sport of kings." Throughout his career in secret service, except during World War II, he was a leading member of the grandest of all British hunts, the Beaufort. Here the hunt leaves the Duke of Beaufort's palace at Badminton. *(Menzies Family Archives)*

Stewart Menzies leads his only
child, Fiona, through the crowds at
the opening hunt of the season at
Badminton in 1937.
(Menzies Family Archives)

"C's" second wife, Pamela, who
suffered from anorexia nervosa
through much of their marriage.
(Menzies Family Archives)

Despite its enormous losses during World War I, the splendor of the British Empire was still in evidence in 1926 when the Life Guards presented their new colors to King George V at a ceremony on the Horse Guards Parade at Whitehall. Menzies was using the Life Guards as cover for his real activities, chief of the military section of the Secret Intelligence Service. *(Life Guards Museum)*

While the British intended to meet the German thrust at the island, therefore, "C" developed severe doubts about the wisdom of supplying the force commander, General Bernard Freyberg, with raw Ultra he needed to defeat the enemy. Yet the size of the impending operation, and of the imperial commitment to the defense of Crete, made it imperative that Freyberg be kept as fully informed about the enemy as Churchill and the chiefs of staff. The question was, therefore, how this could be done without risking the secret of the source. The solution proposed by Churchill was that an SIS officer should fly in to Freyberg's headquarters and brief him on what Ultra was, give him the raw texts, and especially those relating to the German intention to seize the airfields in the first stroke, and then destroy Ultra by fire after Freyberg had read them. The officer taking them out to Freyberg "would be answerable for their destruction in the event of engine failure en route. No-one should be informed but the General, who would give his orders to his subordinates without explaining his full reasons." [23]

When Menzies was asked to comment on this plan, he judged it too dangerous. The solution "C" proposed, and the one that was adopted, was that Ultra should be disguised as intelligence obtained by an SIS agent operating inside the German headquarters for the operation at Athens. The intelligence should then be sent to Freyberg in Crete over a special link, using one-time-pad ciphers. This was done, and as the New Zealand official history of the battle—many of the imperial troops involved were New Zealanders—was to acknowledge, "the nature and strength of the invasion was not only appreciated with remarkable accuracy, but by the time the battle was to begin there was little chance that even the obscurest fatigue man could be ignorant of what he was about to face."

"They're dead on time," remarked Freyberg as the Germans began parachuting in just as he was finishing his breakfast. Yet good intelligence rarely alone wins battles; only power does that. This battle was a disaster for both sides. The Germans came within an inch of losing, and the British came within an inch of winning. The narrow margin was lost to the Germans because Freyberg had not correctly understood that he was reading the German messages themselves in their disguised form. In attributing the origin of the intelligence to an agile spy (later Freyberg asked a senior intelligence officer, getting even the cover story wrong, "What's happened to that Foreign Office chap we had working in Berlin?"), Freyberg understood the importance of the intelligence he was receiving but did not allow it to influence him in the making of his dispositions as much as he should.

Instead of concentrating at the air-landing grounds that the Junkers 52 had to use to make the first penetrations, he allowed himself to cover points that were not absolutely vital. The result: the Germans just managed to make a lodgement, and Freyberg just failed to dislodge them. The paradox was that while the battle was lost, the fiction of Ultra was preserved; the Germans did not learn from the papers they captured at Freyberg's headquarters that Enigma was not as safe as they believed. On the contrary, like Freyberg himself, they believed that the British had a very efficient agent in the Germans' headquarters in Athens.

In all, thirteen thousand British troops were killed, wounded, or taken prisoner, with a further two thousand casualties in the large naval battles that accompanied the invasion. Sixteen thousand five hundred men were evacuated; and the Germans lost about seventeen thousand men. It was a pyrrhic victory for the Germans, for their parachute army, which Hitler reckoned to include his finest troops, was so badly damaged, its losses in transport aircraft so great, that Hitler did not again employ the survivors as a parachute force. They were not available for the one operation where they might have succeeded in obtaining a decisive victory—Sealion. Yet in defeat there was another paradox: such was the excellence of "C's" performance over the Crete invasion that it marked the point at which he became fully accepted as "C" by Churchill, for when Professor F. A. Lindemann, Churchill's friend and scientific adviser, was made Baron Cherwell and began signing his papers with the letter "C," Churchill minuted to him: "You had better sign yourself 'Cherwell,' as there is a 'C' already in my circle." [24]

The Greek and Crete campaigns had cast light on German strategic intentions, but the service directors of intelligence and their masters, the chiefs of staff, continued to believe that Hitler still intended to invade England. Nor did the directors' attitude change when Hitler invaded Yugoslavia on April 6, in reaction to a coup d'état by the Yugoslav air force commander in chief to replace the pro-German government of Prince Paul with the pro-British government of King Peter II. And the conviction of the Whitehall intelligence community was only partly shaken when, through the German invasion and the coup, "C" was able to provide Cadogan (who passed it to Churchill) incontrovertible evidence that Hitler intended to invade Russia, not

England, and that he would do so shortly. That information was another milestone in Menzies's career as "C."

On March 25, the day Yugoslavia joined the Tripartite Pact, decrypts showed that an important element of the German army in the Balkans, including the major elements of three panzer divisions, the SS Division Adolf Hitler, the headquarters of Panzerarmee Kleist, and a corps headquarters were all moving by rail from the Balkans to Krakow, Poland. Within a day of the Belgrade revolution "C" received more decrypts showing that the trains had been stopped and put into sidings. There they remained until April 26, when, with Yugoslavia's surrender, they resumed their movement to Krakow. These movements, as Churchill himself was to write, "illuminated the whole Eastern scene in a lightning flash." [25]

So confident was Churchill that the Ultras meant that Hitler intended war with Russia, he directed that a warning be sent through the British ambassador in Moscow to Stalin. That was done, and the prime minister's message read:

I have sure information from a trusted agent that when the Germans thought they had got Yugoslavia in the net, that is to say, after 20th March, they began to move 3 out of the 5 Panzer Divisions from Roumania to Southern Poland. The moment they heard of the Serbian revolution this movement was countermanded. Your Excellency will readily appreciate the significance of these facts. [26]

But if this warning reached Stalin, it produced no reaction. Nor was it acknowledged, for Stalin felt probably that here was yet another British provocation intended to produce war between Russia and Germany. Nor was the JIC any more impressed. Although it had before them the Ultra of March 25 (but not its sequel of April 26), in their paper circulated on April 10 the intelligence masters concluded that Germany's main objective remained the defeat of England during 1941, "by blockade and air attack if possible, by invasion if necessary." Germany would "continue her military preparations in the east with the double purpose of keeping Russia amenable and of enabling herself to take immediate action when necessary." A Russo-German clash was inevitable, the JIC opined, but only if Russia failed to meet the commitments she had made to Germany for the large-scale provision of raw materials, but in that respect, "Russia would do all she could to avoid the clash and—what was more to the point—so would Germany." [27]

4 RUDOLF HESS

On the night of May 10–11, 1941, the German air force undertook its most violent attack of the war on London and began a sequence of events of Proustian complexity. Churchill remembered that night:

The worst attack was the last. On May 10 the enemy returned to London with incendiary bombs. He lit more than two thousand fires, and, by the smashing of nearly a hundred and fifty water mains, coupled with the low tide in the Thames, he stopped us putting them out. At six o'clock next morning hundreds were reported as out of control, and four were still glowing on the night of the 13th. It was the most destructive attack of the whole night Blitz. Five docks and seventy-one key points, half of which were factories, had been hit. All but one of the main railway stations were blocked for weeks, and the through routes were not fully opened until June. Over three thousand people were killed or injured. In other respects also it was historic. It destroyed the House of Commons. One single bomb created ruin for years. [28]

John Colville, one of Churchill's secretaries, awoke that morning "thinking unaccountably" of Peter Fleming's novel *Flying Visit*, which Colville thought "an amusing fantasy, published in the early months of the war, about the embarrassment caused by Hitler's unheralded arrival in England by parachute." He was also, he wrote in his diary, "day-dreaming of what would happen if we captured Goering during one of his alleged flights over London." As Colville continued:

I walked out into Downing Street at 8.00 A.M. on my way to the early service at Westminster Abbey. It was really a sunny day with blue skies, but the smoke from many fires lay thick over London and obscured the sun. Burnt paper, from some demolished paper mill, was falling like leaves on a windy autumn day.

Whitehall was thronged with people, mostly sightseers but some of them Civil Defence workers with blackened faces and haggard looks. One of them, a boy of eighteen or nineteen, pointed towards the Houses of Parliament and said, "Is that the sun?" But the great orange glow at which we were looking was the light of many fires south of the river. At Westminster Abbey there were fire-engines and the policeman at the door said to me: "There will not be any services in the Abbey today, Sir," exactly as if it were closed for spring-cleaning. I turned towards Westminster Hall, on the roof of which I could see flames still leaping. Smoke rose from some invisible point in the pile of Parliament buildings beyond. I talked to a fireman. He showed me Big Ben, the face of which was pocked and scarred, and told me a bomb had gone right through the Tower. The one thing that had given him great pleasure during the night was that Big Ben had struck two o'clock a few minutes after being hit. It was still giving the proper time.

I stood on Westminster Bridge. . . . St. Thomas's Hospital was ablaze, the livid colour of the sky extended from Lambeth to St. Paul's, flames were visible all along the Embankment, there was smoke rising thickly as far as the eye could see. After no previous raid has London looked so wounded next day.

Neither Churchill nor "C" attached any political importance to the raid, except that it might be "a parting shot" before the Luftwaffe left France to begin the bombardment of Moscow and Leningrad. But even as the bomber streams made their way toward the burning capital, to their north flew a single Messerschmidt 110 fighter flown by the deputy führer of the German Reich, Rudolf Hess. The single aircraft was detected on British radar, night fighters were sent up to intercept it and shoot it down, but they failed to make the intercept. The radar noted that at a certain point over Scotland—near Dungavel, Stratheven, Lanarkshire, seat of the fourteenth duke of Hamilton, premier peer of Scotland—the aircraft began to spiral and then disappeared. It was thought at the time that it had been intercepted by a nightfighter, a Defiant, and shot down.

That was not the case: Hess had abandoned the aircraft by parachute, hoping to land in the grounds of Dungavel where he might have a conversation of a highly secret nature with the duke, a man Hess admired. But Wing Commander the Duke of Hamilton was on duty that night at an RAF base in Scotland and was not at Dungavel. In parachuting, Hess also failed to land on the grounds of Dungavel estate—the only mistake he made in what was otherwise a technically remarkable and flawless flight, especially in regard to navigation. Hess had flown from an airfield near Munich to a pinpoint near Glasgow, a distance of some seven hundred air miles in which he traversed two heavily defended air spaces and steered his way through major bomber streams proceeding both east–west and west–east.

Landing in a field, Hess was captured by a farmworker. He was still wearing the blue uniform of captain of the Luftwaffe. Hess was handed over to the assistant area controller of the Royal Observer Corps, Major Graham Donald, who identified "Captain Alfred Horn" as Rudolf Hess. At the outset, Hess told Donald that "he had a secret and vital message for the Duke of Hamilton, and that he must see the Duke at once." Donald then asked the German where he expected to find the duke, and Hess replied, "At Dungavel House," producing a map with a red ring drawn around the estate. After the brief interrogation, Donald reported to his duty controller and asked him to contact Wing Commander the Duke of Hamilton. "After this," Donald concluded his account, "I came to the conclusion that the safety of the realm was now securely in other hands and no longer the sole responsibility of our Group. So I went to bed." [29]

Next morning, a Sunday, Hamilton went to Maryhill Barracks, where Hess was being held, and noticed in Hess's effects the visiting card of General Professor Karl Haushofer and his son, Dr. Albrecht Haushofer. The former was Hitler's geopolitical adviser and the latter, well known to Hamilton up until the outbreak of the war, had been a secret agent in the special intelligence bureau run for Hess by Jahnke, that curious figure who had tried to get David Boyle into Hitler's presence in a last-minute attempt to avert war between England and Germany.

After the outbreak of the war, Hamilton recalled as he looked at the visiting cards, in September 1940 he had received a letter from young Haushofer, inviting him to a meeting in Lisbon. That letter had been intercepted by the SIS censorship service, where it found its way to the XX-Committee, Masterman's double agency. Hamilton had then been ordered to report to an office of the Air Ministry in London, where he was interviewed by two officials, one of whom was Colonel T. A. Robertson, an officer of MI5 primarily concerned with the handling of double agents. It was proposed that Hamilton go to Lisbon, establish contact with Haushofer, and that contact would be taken over by a secret service as a channel of intelligence that reached through many offices into the one that counted in Germany—Hitler's. That stratagem was still under consideration when Hess arrived near Dungavel. [30]

His memory refreshed, Hamilton went in to see Hess, and according to Hamilton's report to Prime Minister Churchill:

The German opened by saying that he had seen me in Berlin at the Olympic Games in 1936, and that I had lunched at his house. He said, "I do not know if you recognize me, but I am Rudolf Hess." He went on to say that he was on a mission of humanity and that the Fuehrer did not want to defeat England and wished to stop fighting. His friend Albrecht Haushofer told him that I was an Englishman who he thought would understand his [Hess's] point of view. He had consequently tried to arrange a meeting with me in Lisbon. (See Haushofer's letter to me dated September 23rd, 1940). Hess went on to say that he had tried to fly to Dungavel and this was the fourth time he had set out, the first time being in December [1940]. On the three previous occasions he had turned back owing to bad weather. . . .

The fact that Reich Minister Hess had come to this country in person would, he stated, show his sincerity and Germany's willingness for peace. He then went on to say that the Fuehrer was convinced that Germany would win the war, possibly soon but certainly in one, two or three years. He wanted to stop the unnecessary slaughter that would otherwise inevitably take place. He asked me if I could get together leading members of my party to talk over things with a view to making peace proposals. I replied that there was now only one party in this country. He then said he could tell me what Hitler's peace terms would be. First he would insist on an arrangement whereby our two countries would never go to war again. I questioned him as to how that arrangement could be brought about, and he replied that one of the conditions, of course, was that Britain would give up her traditional policy of always opposing the strongest power in Europe. I then told him that if we made peace now, we would be at war again certainly within two years. He asked why, to which I told him that if a peace agreement was possible, the arrangement could have been made before the war started, but since Germany chose war in preference to peace at a time when we were most anxious to preserve peace, I could put forward no hope of a peace agreement now.

He requested me to ask the King to give him "parole," as he had come unarmed and of his own free will.

He further asked me if I could inform his family that he was safe by sending a telegram to Rothacker, Hertzog Str. 17, Zurich, stating that Alfred Horn was in good health. He also asked that his identity should not be disclosed to the Press. [31]

Following the interview, Hamilton returned to his base and then telephoned the office of Sir Alexander Cadogan, head of the Foreign Office, but the "official at the other end of the phone acted with all the superciliousness of which the British Civil Service is Master." [32] It so happened that Churchill's private secretary, John Colville, was in the room in London and took over the call when Hamilton "demanded to see the Prime Minister without delay, as there might be something very important to report." The conversation was curious for a question which Colville put to Hamilton—"Has somebody arrived?"—which suggested that Colville was expecting somebody important to arrive. This was not the case, Colville asserted later. As Colville recorded in the editorial notes to his diary, when he entered the office of the duty officer at the Foreign Office for a gossip, he overheard part of a conversation that recalled his "early waking thoughts on Peter Fleming's book, and I felt sure that either Hitler or Goering had arrived. In the event I was only one wrong in the Nazi hierarchy." [33]

Having spoken to Hamilton, Colville then telephoned the prime minister, who was at his retreat at Ditchley Park near Oxford, the estate of Sir Ronald Tree and a place to which, for safety reasons, Churchill went on moonlit nights. According to Harry Hopkins—who was in England on FDR's business at the time—Churchill was watching a Marx Brothers movie at that moment, and he told the information minister, Brendan Bracken, to see what the trouble was. Bracken went to the telephone, listened to what was said, and then returned to the prime minister and announced that the call concerned the arrival of Hess in Scotland and that the duke of Hamilton wished to see the prime minister with important information.

Churchill is supposed to have replied to Bracken: "Will you kindly instruct the Duke of Hamilton to tell that to the Marx Brothers?" [34] The matter was impressed upon Churchill, who then instructed Hamilton to fly south to Oxford in his fighter. When the duke reported to Churchill, Colville recorded in his diary, "There has never been such a fantastic occurrence." [35] The affair was, however, to get still odder before it was concluded. When Hamilton had finished his report, Churchill asked him very slowly: "Do you mean to tell me that the Deputy Fuehrer of Germany is in our hands?" [36] That question seemed to indicate that Churchill at least did not know that Hess was coming, if indeed anybody, including "C," knew that Hess was flying to England that night, although later it would be suggested that "C" had trapped Hess into coming for the intelligence he might extract from such an eminent personality in the U. C. "G.", Greater German Reich.

When Churchill heard Hamilton's reply, he declared: "Well, Hess or no Hess, I am going to see the Marx Brothers." Churchill then ambled off to his host's private movie theater until about midnight, when he reappeared and began a three-hour grilling of Hamilton. He showed Churchill the copy of the letter from Albrecht Haushofer, which he had received from Robertson of the XX-Committee, and contended, as Douglas-Hamilton was to write, that "it was clear that Hess's flight involved a peace offer, and that Hess was stating terms which would be acceptable to Hitler, although the flight was made without Hitler's knowledge."

Having been sworn to secrecy, Hamilton was dismissed, and Churchill began to make arrangements for the formal interrogation of Hess. The man selected was Ivone Kirkpatrick of the Foreign Office, a close friend of "C." Kirkpatrick had been counselor at the British embassy in Berlin during the period leading up to the outbreak of war. He had asked to be recalled from his post on the grounds that his antipathy for the Nazis had become physical, and he was no longer able to report or advise objectively. As Kirkpatrick remarked to the duke of Hamilton as they flew to Scotland, "Behind all the bombast, histrionics, and hysteria Hitler remained the most treacherous, calculating, and cold-blooded devil in the world."

On their arrival at Maryhill Barracks, Hess delivered a long speech in German, which consisted of a eulogy of Hitler and a review of Anglo-German relations since Edward VII. He then declared his understanding of Hitler's terms. These resembled closely those that had been offered by various Germans from Treeck through "General von Wietersheim" before Venlo to the present: "England should give Germany a free hand in Europe, and Germany [would give] England a completely free hand in the Empire, with the sole reservation that we should return Germany's ex-colonies which she required as a source of raw materials."

At that point, Kirkpatrick tried to draw out Hess on Hitler's plans toward Russia, for by now all the intelligence reaching London indicated that Barbarossa was probably inevitable and imminent. In other words, had Hess come to secure an understanding with the British that would render England acquiescent while Germany attacked Russia? Kirkpatrick recorded in his report to Churchill, "C," and the Foreign Office that Hess

reacted quickly by remarking that Germany had certain demands to make of Russia which would have to be satisfied, either by negotiation or as the result of war. He added however there was no foundation for the rumours now being spread that Hitler was contemplating an early attack on Russia.

They had reached the crux of the Hess affair. Kirkpatrick, who was skeptical, irritable, and impatient throughout the interrogation, felt that "Hess was so much out of things that he really did not know" about Hitler's plans for Russia. Hamilton, a highly intelligent man, did not agree, declaring that he thought "Hess looked as if he had over-reached himself when he mentioned the possibility of war against Russia, and that he tried to recover his balance by denying that Hitler was thinking of an early attack."

At the end of the session Hess made a statement that seemed to give political reasons for the violent attack on London during Hess's

flight. As Kirkpatrick and Hamilton were leaving the room Hess delivered a parting shot. He had, he said, forgotten to emphasize that
Germany could not negotiate with Churchill and that "if we rejected
this chance it would be clear proof that we desired no understanding
with Germany and Hitler would be entitled, in fact it would be his
duty to destroy us utterly, and keep us after the war in a state of
permanent subjection."

Throughout these and the many subsequent interviews of Hess,
"C" was kept closely informed, for although Hess was nominally a
charge against the prisoner-of-war department of the War Office, he
was in fact "C's" special prisoner with "guardians" provided by "C."
Both officers Thomas Kendrick (formerly chief of the Vienna station)
and Francis Foley (formerly chief of the Berlin station) were members
of Section V. In addition to the interrogations carried out first by
Kirkpatrick and then by Lords Simon and Beaverbrook, they undertook a long series of "conversations" with Hess. Foley had known
Hess in Berlin between the wars; he was detached from all other
duties and spent a year in Hess's company. Yet his reports have never
been made public. Nor was the fact that "C" was involved ever admitted publicly by the British government, although well-weeded
official files relating to Hess's flight to England showed "C's" involvement beyond doubt. [37]

Through the information reaching him from *all* sources, "C" reached
certain conclusions that were not made public. These were (a) that
Hitler *did* intend to attack Russia shortly; (b) that Hess was sent to
England with Hitler's permission to arrange a truce that would (c)
enable Hitler to overcome the strong opposition to Barbarossa within
the German General Staff (which historically feared the consequence
of a war on two fronts against two major enemies); (d) that Hitler was
prepared to take any gamble to end the war with England, which he
believed would support a campaign against Bolshevik Russia because
(e) he continued to believe that a powerful group of Englishmen, of
which the duke of Hamilton was a member, believed that Russia, not
Germany, was the ultimate enemy; (f) that once Hitler had liquidated
Russia he would then turn his full, undivided power against England,
unworried by the prospect of finding himself facing America as well,
for he did not regard that country as being morally powerful.

Meanwhile, there had been the repercussions, which were not
without elements of black comedy. In London, Churchill declared
that Hess's flight was "the worm in the apple." In Rome, Count Ciano,
Italy's foreign secretary, noted in his diary: "In my opinion, it is a

very serious matter; the first real victory for the English." In Berlin, disastrously, Ribbentrop advised the world that Hess suffered from gallstones and through the pain he had become an "astrological fadd- ist" and was mad. Ulrich von Hassell, political adviser to the Beck- Goerdeler underground group, noted this meant that for months and even for years the man whom Hitler had presented to the people as his heir apparent had been partly and perhaps completely insane.

As the British began to play cat-and-mouse with their prisoner, early on Monday morning, May 19, eight days after Hess's landing, two parachutists landed near Luton Hoo, an estate in Bedfordshire. The parachutists were promptly captured and proved to be members of the SS in plain clothes. In their possession was a map with circles drawn around certain places, one of which was the duke of Hamilton's home in Lanarkshire. The nature of their mission was never revealed, and there was no statement that it had even taken place. But Lord James Douglas-Hamilton stated that "the British Secret Service picked them up, and drove them to a secret establishment, where they were identified, interrogated and executed." [38] And as Douglas-Hamilton also recorded, Hess's "secret mission astonished the British, bewil- dered the Americans, horrified the Germans, and struck fear into the Russians." Puzzled at the time by Churchill's silence, FDR remarked to an aide: "I wonder what is *really* behind this story," and continued to believe that there remained in Britain a small but potentially pow- erful minority who wanted peace conversations and were in fact hav- ing them. [39]

But beyond all else was the speculation that "C" had lured Hess to England for the intelligence he might extract from his victim and to exact satisfaction for the humiliation "C" had suffered through the Venlo incident. Although nowhere was there explanation as to *how* "C" could have lured Hess to England, that he did trap Hess was as good an explanation as any other for what was the most important mystery of World War II, except, perhaps, for Pearl Harbor. There is no doubt that "C" was aware that Haushofer had tried to get in touch with Hamilton in September 1940, for the letter was in British hands. Nor was there much doubt that Haushofer was acting for Hess. Where the doubt has always been was whether Hitler himself sanc- tioned Hess's flight to Scotland in a last, desperate attempt to enlist England as an ally in his war against Russia.

The fact that Hess was placed in "C's" custody supports the notion that there was a grand stratagem involved, but does not, of course, prove the case. Certainly the sequence of known events suggest "C's" knowledge that Hess was anxious to talk, if not "C's" connivance in his journey. But as impressive as the circumstantial evidence remains, it is circumstantial. "C's" service was as capable of provocation as any other, particularly when the prize was an eminence such as the deputy führer of the German Reich. Moreover, the case for the theory that "C" set a trap for Hess is strengthened somewhat by the fact that the principal interrogation of Hess, conducted by Lord Simon, was conducted under the supervision of "C," and that the reports were sent to Churchill not by Cadogan or Simon, but by "C" personally. It is therefore the more significant that one of the three parts of Simon's interrogation was either withheld at the request of Churchill or destroyed.

Conversely, there was clear evidence that Churchill was irritated and embarrassed by the presence of Hess in England, and Cadogan appears to have been quite ignorant of his coming, indifferent when he was notified that Hess was in the country, and outraged at the amount of work Hess caused him. "In all the years I have kept this beastly diary I have never been so hard pressed," he exclaimed indignantly on May 12. "Mainly due to Hess, who has taken up *all* my time and I am 48 hours in arrear with work." It was not before June 11, 1941, that Cadogan simmered down and began debating (in terms that reflected the fact that Hess was not a welcome guest, nor one in whom Cadogan had much interest) how he could "best exploit Hess—mendaciously." [40]

Since "C" would never have undertaken such an operation without the permission of the prime minister and the knowledge of Cadogan, this was a strong factor for the case against there having been a trap. It is true that the first thing Cadogan did before he sent Kirkpatrick Scotland to interrogate Hess was to ensure that "C" did not object —a measure that appears by implication to support the notion of a trap—and it is undeniable that the XX-Committee was involved. The case must therefore remain open, for as Stalin suggested to Churchill much later, Hess had been "invited over by our Secret Service," and he remarked that "there are a lot of things that happen even here in Russia, which our Secret Service do not necessarily tell me about." [41] Perhaps not, but this bizarre affair now moved to its inevitable, vast climax.

At 3:00 A.M. on June 22 (after Hitler had requested divine assistance in his order of the day: "May the Lord God help us all in this struggle!") 17 panzer, 13 mechanized, and 110 infantry divisions crossed into Russia under the covering fire of 7,100 guns, 2,770 aircraft, and

3,300 tanks. Within a week the three German army groups of Ritter von Leeb, Fedor von Bock, and Gerd von Rundstedt had shattered the Red Armies in European Russia.

Churchill spoke to Russia and the world over the BBC and declared that Britain would render all assistance in its power to the Soviet Union. "No one has been a more consistent opponent of communism than I have for the last twenty-five years," the prime minister declared, continuing, "I will unsay no word that I have spoken about it." But the past "with its crimes, its follies, and its tragedies, flashes away." The "Russian danger" was "our danger, and the danger of the United States, just as the cause of any Russian fighting for his hearth and home is the cause of free men and free peoples in every quarter of the globe." [42]

For all Churchill's magnanimity, "C," the archetype of the Bolshevik-Russophobe, seemed at first to be uncertain about the extent to which he should collaborate with the Soviet Union. He indicated that he was not prepared to place Ultra at the service of the Soviet state. Two days after the German attack, Menzies, displaying considerable knowledge of Soviet codes, advised Churchill and the chiefs of staff against sending the Red Army General Staff raw Ultra "in view of the insecurity of their ciphers." [43] In reality this insecurity seems not to have been very pronounced. By the middle of July Enigma decrypts were revealing that the Germans were reading some Red Air Force ciphers, understood the signaling system used by Russian aircraft in the Leningrad area, and that they were decrypting some Russian naval traffic.

On July 12, however, his duty became evident. The Soviet government announced that the war, hitherto an "imperialist conflict," had become a "liberating and anti-Fascist one." They renamed the conflict "the Great Patriotic War," and with that the subterranean war between the Secret Intelligence Service and Russia was suspended. [44] The Soviet service's mission arrived in London and found offices in Bush House next door to the office of Lammins' Enterprises, a Broadway cover company administered by David Boyle. And for the politicians, but not for the secret services, yesterday's foe became today's friend. The murdered tsar's nephew, King George VI, the embodiment of the enemy of the world revolution of the proletariat, signed an agreement (which was transmuted in May 1942 into a twenty-year alliance) with the Russians for "joint action in the war against Germany." That document required the high contracting parties to "mutually undertake to afford one another military and other assistance and support of all kinds in the war against Germany and those States which are associated with her in acts of aggression in Europe." [45]

With those solemn words before him, "C's" duty was now to support Russia, a task he approached with no great enthusiasm: it must have crossed his mind that the Ultra intelligence he could provide the Russians would result in the Red and German armies clawing the life out of each other, which meant that at the end neither would be in much shape to claw the life out of the British army. It must also have crossed his mind that the longer the Red Army survived, the longer delayed would be the evil day when Germany would be able to concentrate her full might against England.

Twelve days after the signing of the Anglo-Russian agreement, "C" and the chiefs of staff bowed to Churchill's insistence that the Russians be sent "the more important" Ultra in disguised form, "provided no risks are run." [46] The intelligence sent by "C" through the military missions in Moscow to the Red General Staff was always from "a highly-placed agent in Berlin" or suchlike. From time to time "C" objected, for example when the prime minister required him to send intelligence that could have come only from Enigma.

"I am always embarrassed at sending the Russians information obtainable from this source," he minuted to Churchill on that occasion, adding again that many of the Russian ciphers were legible to the Germans. Nor was "C" unjustified in his "embarrassment." [47] Through Barbarossa and the vast increase in German wireless traffic produced by the campaign (most of which could be intercepted by British stations in England and Palestine), in the first six months of the campaign GC&CS developed five major new sources that enabled Churchill and Menzies to follow the campaign almost as closely as if they were present at Hitler's map table.

By October these fresh sources were telling "C" as much about the German army as the Russian command itself knew. Under pressure from Churchill, "C" relented, but only to the extent of providing Ultra to the Russians in heavily disguised form and even then only those Ultras that might prove decisive in the defense of Russia. Yet as the German and Soviet armies tore the heart out of each other on the great plains of White Russia, Churchill was evidently not satisfied that "C" was doing his best for the Russians. For some time "C" had been able to read the Communist International's secret wireless traffic with its supporters in Britain and elsewhere. On September 5, two months after the outbreak of the Russo-German war, there was evidence of the Soviet desire to negotiate a peace with the Germans, and on September 9 Colville noted in his diary:

[Churchill's personal assistant for intelligence] Desmond Morton tells me that we know from secret sources that the (Comintern) has given orders to its followers in this country to keep alive discontent with the alleged inadequacy of support for Russia in order to use this to overthrow the Churchill Government when the time is ripe. Further he says that Stalin is lukewarm in his determination to go on fighting and Molotov is definitely opposed to so doing; but there are others, representing Russian youth organizations, who are resolute.

If Morton was correct (and we may assume that the intelligence came to him from "C" or MI5 because Morton had no intelligence sources of his own), then it would seem to have been irresponsible of "C" to continue to send disguised Ultra to Russia; for if there were successful negotiations, the first thing the Russians would reveal to the Germans was the fact that the British were reading their ciphers. Nonetheless, Churchill insisted, perhaps because Morton's report, as was so often the case, was little better than gossip.

On September 9, even as Morton's intelligence made the rounds, "C" provided Churchill with Ultra evidence of Hitler's "great plan" to destroy the three Red armies guarding the approaches to Moscow. In consequence, "C" sent a number of warnings to Moscow between September 20–24. On September 22 Ultra provided intelligence that the Germans were about to resume their attack against Moscow. Constituting as it did the greatest offensive operation undertaken by the Germans—fourteen of her twenty-one panzer divisions were involved along with eight of the sixteen motorized divisions—"C" kept Churchill and the Whitehall intelligence community "fully and promptly informed" about every phase of an offensive that culminated in the evacuation of Moscow to Kuibyshev in the Urals foothills.

Then, as the Germans destroyed the main Russian armies in Europe, "C" was able to report that Stalin was now bringing up his Asian armies from the Japanese front. When the weather and Soviet resistance finally forced Hitler to halt his offensive on November 13, that fact, too, was faithfully reported to Moscow by "C." Even so, Churchill felt compelled to order "C" at the beginning of the offensive to "show me the last five messages you have sent out to our missions [in Russia] on the subject."

"C" obliged, sending not five but the nine messages he had sent in the five days between September 20 and 24. Yet Churchill still pressed "C" in terms such as "has any of this has been passed to Joe"—"Joe" being the British code name for Stalin. "C," however, had little confidence that the Russians would hold the Germans in their drive on Moscow.

At their meeting on October 10, the Joint Intelligence Committee estimated that it would take the German army about one hundred days to remount Sealion after they had captured Moscow and Russia had surrendered. Once more "C" came under pressure from the chiefs of staff to be in a position to give three days' warning of any attempt at an invasion of England during the autumn and winter months. As if to remind "C" personally that the Germans were not far off, on October 16 a land mine—a weapon eight by three feet laden with 1,750 pounds of high explosive of a type that, some nights earlier, had rendered 300 houses uninhabitable in Battersea and over 1,500 people homeless—fell on Queen Anne's Mansions. It did not go off, but had it done so, it would have blown the dainty row of houses where "C" lived to kingdom come.

Elsewhere, "C" had been increasing his investment in Colonel Donovan.

5 "C" AND "Q"

On December 17, 1940, as Donovan was arriving in London on his second secret mission for FDR, Sir Alexander Cadogan sent a note up to the foreign secretary, Anthony Eden:

["C"] tells me that Mr. Stephenson, who travelled over with Colonel Donovan, has impressed upon him that the latter really exercises a vast degree of influence in the administration. He has Colonel Knox [secretary of the navy] in his pocket and, as Mr. Stephenson puts it, has more influence with the President than Colonel House had with Mr. Wilson. Mr. Stephenson believes that if the Prime Minister were to be completely frank with Colonel Donovan, the latter would contribute very largely to our obtaining all that we want of the United States. [49]

The British ambassador in Washington, the earl of Halifax, agreed. Donovan was, Halifax signaled to Cadogan, "one of our best and most influential friends here with a great deal of influence both with the Service Departments and the Administration."

To persuade Donovan that England meant business in regard to Germany, the night before Churchill and Donovan were to lunch at 10 Downing Street, Royal Air Force Bomber Command bombed the major German inland port and industrial center of Mannheim, which gave credence to Churchill's announcement that, when the matter came up at luncheon, Britain was placing requests for lend-lease weapons and munitions to a total value of $750 million.

Although Donovan left no account of his long talk with Churchill—it lasted from 1:00 P.M. until about 5.00 P.M.—Donovan told his law partner and close friend, Otto C. Doering, Jr., the Sears, Roebuck heir, that "the prime" discussed at length his strategy for the defeat of Germany. Churchill believed that Britain would surely founder as a world power if it suffered again casualties on the scale of those of World War I, and that to avoid such casualties, he had begun his ministry by looking at the map in other ways. Churchill showed Donovan on a globe that Germany was more vulnerable to an attack from the Baltic or the Mediterranean than from the west across the Channel. What he proposed, therefore, was a strategy of the circumference against the center as his illustrious forebear, John, duke of Marlborough, had used in the war of the Spanish succession to defeat Louis XIV, the sun king of France.

At some stage during their conversation, Churchill mentioned the importance of secret service in his strategy. He called it not "the Fifth Column" but "the Fifth Arm," one used to raise the populations of conquered territories against the German invader and to weaken their will and energy to fight before the British "armoured legions" landed on the far shore to begin their march on Berlin. Donovan showed great interest in, and some knowledge of, secret service matters, particularly in areas of sabotage and subversion, although he seemed to know little about intelligence and displayed less interest in that aspect of clandestine affairs. That did not go unnoticed by "the prime."

Largely at Churchill's suggestion, Donovan accepted an invitation to visit Arabia and the Balkans, where the British army was waging a major campaign against the Italo-German armies and secret services. Donovan left London on Christmas Eve in a train from Paddington Station. Everywhere thereafter Donovan was treated as royalty. Between January 1 and March 18 he visited Gibraltar, Malta, Cairo, Athens, Belgrade, Sofia, Istanbul, Nicosia, Jerusalem, Lisbon, Madrid, and Dublin. At all times "C's" men were in attendance, and at all times Donovan's bills were met from the secret vote. He saw everything he wanted to see (but not "C's" cryptanalytical establishment near Cairo) and was provided with a thorough tutorial of secret service in action everywhere he went.

There is no doubt that Wild Bill Donovan made a great name for himself during his one-hundred-day tour through the Arabian-Balkans theater. Speaking as he did in the name of the president, his presence with the British ambassadors, counselors, admirals, generals, and secret agents demonstrated to the world that an Anglo-American alliance was in the making. Moreover, Donovan was sincere when he stated in his report for FDR and the U.S. Cabinet that "England has done a superb job in the area from a strategic, tactical, and administrative standpoint," the quality of which could be "truly appreciated only by actually seeing that so much has been done with so little." [50]

The telegram, which constituted an urging to give England everything that the United States could afford, arrived in Washington as the lend-lease debate was making what seemed to the British to be an interminable, legalistic passage through Congress, and served to strengthen the arguments of those who supported the bill, particularly those of the secretary of the treasury, Henry J. Morgenthau. And as Churchill wired FDR on March 10, 1941, "I must thank you for the magnificent work done by Donovan on his prolonged tour of the Balkans and Middle East. He has carried with him throughout an animating, heart-warming flame." [51]

There was a purpose behind such magnanimities, purposes other than Churchill's policy of "dragging America in." "C" wanted the United States to form its own secret intelligence and special operations executive, with Donovan at its head and working with, not against, the British services and British interests. British technical assistance would be provided the new service by SIS and SOE (although in "C's" view SOE was in no position to be of much assistance to anyone) and by the Political Warfare Executive. The plan appears to have been hammered out at a series of meetings in London with "C" and also at a weekend meeting at Chequers, "the prime's" official country residence. Donovan had visited Chequers before, while traveling through Europe as the agent of J. P. Morgan. In 1921 he was the guest there of Lord Lee of Fareham, the owner of the estate before he gave it to the country as a gift in perpetuity for the use of prime ministers. What "C" also desired was that, in scrupulous fashion, he should control the new service by indirection through Donovan.

Whether Donovan agreed to propose the creation of the new service to FDR on his return is far from clear, for Donovan knew his political Washington well enough to recognize that any such proposition would cause tumult in the existing intelligence agencies, which were exceedingly jealous of their turf. That silence proved to be prudent, for news of his talks with Churchill and "C" preceded Donovan's return to Washington and caused great alarm.

Spasms of anxiety and opposition of ever-increasing severity besieged the FBI, IRS, State Department, INS, Treasury, and other, lesser bodies concerned with intelligence. It affected in particular J. Edgar Hoover and Adolf A. Berle, the assistant secretary at the State Department in charge of intelligence and security affairs. Berle had been in the Russian section of U.S. military intelligence at Versailles during the peace conference after World War I and had formed a deep and abiding suspicion of the British secret service and the use to which the British delegation had put secret intelligence to achieve political objectives. He had insisted that the British so rigged their intelligence estimates that the United States was trapped into supporting Britain's anti-Bolshevik policy. Worse, by such means they had succeeded in grabbing almost all Arabia from the Turks, except for that small part they gave to the French.

Berle viewed William Stephenson's presence in the United States and his close association with Donovan, therefore, with suspicion and came to believe that if Donovan succeeded in his purpose, the United States would find its foreign policy dominated by the British. Berle also began to suspect, as did Hoover, that Stephenson was forging or falsifying intelligence sent to the administration, in order to intensify American unease at Axis activities in the American hemisphere.

These suspicions foreshadowed what was to become one of the most violent and prolonged interdepartmental battles in modern Washington history, as all the established intelligence departments in Washington closed rank and opposed both man and concept. With all the senior representatives of the British secret services in the United States advising Donovan, his wife, Ruth, was recording in her diary of the scene at their mansion in Georgetown: "Bill has British Empire for breakfast." All were present: Stephenson, Benson, David

Bowes-Lyon (brother of Queen Elizabeth and chief of the Political Warfare Executive), Colonel Ellis, and Professor J. W. Wheeler-Bennett of the New York office of PWE. It was a war council the purpose of which was to establish a U.S. secret service with Donovan as its chief. [52]

By April 26 Donovan had completed a long paper on the subject, the theme of which was "the instrumentality through which the British Government gathers its information in foreign countries." On May 5 Stephenson sent a signal to London that he had been "attempting to persuade Donovan into the job of coordinating all U.S. intelligence." Among those whom he lobbied in order to develop a constituency for Donovan were Robert E. Sherwood, the playwright and FDR's speech writer, and the U.S. ambassador in London, John Winant. And at about this same period Stephenson discovered that he was under FBI wiretap and physical surveillance.

On June 4 General Sherman Miles of Army G2 warned that there was "a considerable amount of talk going on in Washington of forming (somewhat after the British pattern) a Central Secret Bureau of Information." Such, indeed, was the alarm in Washington that Donovan was a British control that for a time FDR decided against Donovan's appointment as chief of the new secret service. Although FDR indicated that Donovan was one of those he was considering for the job of heading the "bureau for constructive counterespionage work," a month later FDR recommended Donovan first as head of a "sort of ballyhoo committee" under Mayor Fiorello LaGuardia of New York and then, on June 2, offered Donovan a "bond drive job" in New York State. [53]

During all this, the *Bismarck* and the *Prinz Eugen*, the powerful new German battleship and its attendant heavy cruiser, entered the North Atlantic at a time when twenty lend-lease supply convoys were on the high seas. The Washington polity was gripped by acute anxiety, and on May 27 Roosevelt took another large step toward war and proclaimed a state of "unlimited national emergency." That state of national emergency remained in force even though Benson was able to write shortly in his diary: "Hurrah! We have destroyed Bismarck. She must have died a wild boar's death with many dogs around."

Although *Bismarck* succeeded in sinking the greatest British battle cruiser, *Hood*, with a single shell (in going to action stations, it is thought, someone left an armored door open and the lucky shell penetrated into an armory, where it exploded, blowing up the entire ship), the Stephenson organization succeeded in capturing the imagination of the American public to such a degree that the battle was transmuted into a grand British victory, which it was. His hands greatly strengthened by the new emergency powers, and the alarmed mood of the country to support him, Roosevelt ordered the U.S. occupation of Iceland, and as the thirty-second of the emergency measures he pushed through at this time, Roosevelt also directed that a U.S. secret intelligence and special operations service be established. He gave instructions that a department of the government be formed called the Office of Coordinator of Information (COI), with Donovan as director.* He received no salary, only expenses, and he was *not* appointed to the rank of major general, for the U.S. General Staff had objected to the man, the office, and the mission.

The British were elated, for as Stephenson telegraphed London on June 18: "Donovan saw President to-day and after long discussion wherein all points were agreed, he accepted appointment. He will be coordinator [of] all forms of intelligence including offensive operations equivalent SOE. He will hold rank of Major General and will be responsible only to the President. Donovan accuses me of having 'intrigued and driven' him into appointment. You can imagine how relieved I am after three months of battle and jockeying for position in Washington that our man is in a position of such importance to our efforts."

At about the same time Desmond Morton, ever indiscreet, wrote to Colonel E. I. Jacobs, a member of Churchill's private office:

Another most secret fact of which the Prime Minister is aware but not the other persons concerned, is that to all intents and purposes U.S. Security is being run for them at the President's request by the British. A British officer sits in Washington with Mr. Edgar Hoover and General [sic] Bill Donovan for this purpose and reports regularly to the President. It is of course essential that this fact should not become known in view of the furious uproar it would cause if known to the Isolationists. [54]

Although it was twenty-one years almost to the day since President Woodrow Wilson liquidated the Office of Special Counsellor, the first U.S. secret intelligence service, and broke up the original Anglo-American intelligence alliance, "C" sent no word to Donovan personally, leaving it to Dansey. "Congratulations," Dansey wrote from Boodles, "Believe me, I read of [your appointment] with great

---

*Although Donovan's service was known as COI until June 1942, at which time it was reorganized, placed under the jurisdiction of the U.S. Joint Chiefs of Staff, and renamed the Office of Strategic Services, to avoid confusion in the mind of the reader Donovan's organization will henceforth be called the Office of Strategic Services or, for short, OSS.

pleasure—and by no means unselfish pleasure, for I think we shall have every reason to be thankful to your President's selection, which cannot fail to bring fruitful cooperation. Good luck to you." [55]

These agreeable sentiments were not initially misplaced. But almost immediately the politics of Ultra supervened as something resembling full-scale bureaucratic warfare broke out between Donovan and the established intelligence agencies. As Benson (who by this time was in the process of succeeding Beaumont-Nesbitt as military attaché) advised "C," there was much trouble in Washington over the president's order establishing the Donovan organization. By October 21 the War and Navy departments' hostility for Donovan came into the open when Benson received a warning from the office of Field Marshal Sir John Dill, who was now head of the British Military Mission to Washington. That warning was, according to Benson's diary, that "we should not deal with [Donovan] until U.S. Services say OK. Otherwise we shall get in wrong with [Navy and War departments]" concerning the Magic exchange.

Under various agreements relating to the Ultra-Magic exchange, the intelligence could be handled only by the FBI and the army and naval intelligence services. "C" realized that the Ultra-Magic exchange might be endangered if the established agencies saw that SIS was working too closely with the Donovan organization; he decided, therefore, to put a measure of distance between himself and Donovan, leaving the management of the Donovan organization to Stephenson. The desirability of such a step was emphasized on November 12, 1941, when Benson warned Stephenson to be "careful about the purely naval or military information which he asks Donovan to get for him." That warning was a reflection of Berle's preoccupation with the possibility that Donovan was supplying Stephenson with U.S. secret information, a thought that was increased when it was alleged that somebody gave Benson a copy of a secret U.S. bulletin, *The Defense Record*, which dealt with supply and production problems in U.S. industry. As a result, Donovan's name was removed from the distribution list but restored when Donovan protested to FDR. Nevertheless, the damage was done, and it was now believed widely by his numerous antagonists that "Q"—as Donovan came to be known in London—was no more than one of Stephenson's controls.

Here everyone was in error, including "C," for Donovan had misled the intelligence world in supposing that he was little more than one of "C's" "honourable correspondents." "Q" was his own man, and what was more, he was devoted to the proposition that the world would be a good deal safer if the ideology of imperialism was liquidated. Even so, he was loyal to Stephenson, as Stephenson was to Donovan. But where "C" was concerned, Donovan's real attitude was a very different matter. For in the meantime, Donovan's first chief of station had arrived in London.

Aware of Menzies's sensibilities, and his preference for educated men of good background, good manners, and independent finances, Donovan's first choice for the post of chief of OSS London was a shrewd one, although not as shrewd in the end as Donovan expected. William Dwight Whitney was well known to "C." Lately personal assistant to W. Averell Harriman, President Roosevelt's special representative in London in 1940–41, Whitney had been the intermediary between the president of General Motors Overseas Corporation, James D. Mooney, who was known to "C" as Stallforth, one of the men whom Brigadeführer SS Schellenberg claimed later was a spy for England in 1940. There seems little doubt that Stallforth was a spy, for Whitney saw Stallforth in Washington with Donovan just before he left Washington to take up his appointment.

As a director of Opel, Stallforth had important connections with General Oster, Canaris's deputy, and with other German dissidents, including Ulrich von Hassell, the conspirators' chief political adviser. In September 1941 Stallforth arrived in Washington from Berlin and on the thirtieth met Donovan and Whitney at 1647 30th Street, N.W., Washington, D.C. Stallforth stated he had been in Berlin from May 1, 1941, onward and during that time had had contact with dissident officers in the German General Staff. He claimed there were two grounds for the renewal of the dissidence. First there was "disgust" at orders from Hitler that the German army was to engage in a very large program of executions—the so-called commissars decree. Second, Hitler had issued a new directive concerning the Russian front on August 21, which the General Staff considered would lead only to disaster. Hitler laid down that the most important objectives before the onset of winter were the seizure of the Crimea and the industrial region of the Donets, the cutting of the Russian oil route from the Caucasus, and the besieging of Leningrad. Only when these objectives had been achieved would the offensive be renewed against Moscow.

That directive had spurred a renewal of hope and heart in the anti-Hitler opposition movement. Stallforth had received an invitation to a private luncheon given by General Ernst Udet, one of Goering's principal deputies in the Luftwaffe and a man Stallforth had known for several years. Present at the luncheon were "officers (not the top officers, but the second men) in each of each of the military establishments,—General Staff, Army, Navy, and Luftwaffe." The course of the conversation, according to Whitney's account of it for FDR and "C," ran as follows:

THEY: We are still confident that we will conquer Russia, but we are anxious at all costs to avoid war with the United States of America and wish to know what the USA wants.

I: We will make no peace with the present German government, and neither would Great Britain.

THEY: What if Hitler and Goering were to disappear or to resign?

I: That would not be enough. No party member would be accepted by the USA today, but I personally believe that the USA and Great Britain would likely make peace with a new constitutional government in which every private citizen would be recognized and have full normal rights.

THEY: How about a monarchy?

I: That would do, I think; if it were a constitutional monarchy on the English model.

A few days later, Stallforth continued, he received a visit from a single German officer, and this conversation followed:

HE: Suppose—always suppose—that the army replaces the present regime and offers peace.

I: I think that it is possible that the USA and Great Britain would treat with the army under those circumstances.

HE: The army's condition would then be: (1) No double crossing of Germany, as happened after Germany's acceptance of Wilson's Fourteen Points; (2) The army to remain in control to avoid cooperation and thus of course disarmament could not be immediate [sic].

I: I think something could be arranged.

HE: Whom would you suggest to meet with you?

I: I suggest Donovan, [Wendell] Willkie [the Republican nominee for the presidency], and General [Robert E.] Wood [chairman of the American Firsters]. (I thought of these three men to show that America was united, and to negative [sic] the idea that Willkie or Wood would not cooperate with the President.)

As Stallforth went on to report, the German emissary "further explained to me that they did not even ask who would be the emissary from England as they would have full confidence in England, but indicated that they would prefer energetic men like [Lord] Beaverbrook [chairman of the *Daily Express*, London]." Stallforth added that the German army "hate us more than the British because we are spoiling their success; whereas they rather like the British." He indicated "they would likely send [General Alexander von] Falkenhausen [the German military governor in Belgium], [General] Halder [chief of the German General Staff], and [General Karl Heinrich von] Stulpnagel [the German military governor of Paris and the occupied zone of France]." The civilian member would be Ulrich von Hassell, a former German ambassador at Rome. And as Stallforth continued in his interview with Donovan and Whitney:

It was further explained to me that:

(1) Everything against Hitler and the regime must originate from Germany. The German people must not get the idea that the disposition of Hitler had been organized from outside, as then they would line up to protect him.

(2) If we consider their plan at all, we must do so very promptly, before hatred of the USA gets worse in Germany.

(3) But as soon as it becomes plain to the German people that the change means peace, they will let Hitler go, as they put peace first in their affections and Hitler second.

(4) The German army fears that the President or Churchill would kill any such plan, as they have been convinced by their own propaganda to the effect that the President and Churchill as individuals have a special and violent animosity against Germany while all the rest of the USA and Great Britain understand them. I of course explained that this was absurd and that the USA and the UK were definitely behind their two chiefs, but mere explanations do not surmount months of skillful propaganda. This does not of course mean that they would not be glad to deal with Churchill and the President, but they think that the President and Churchill would, for reasons of blind hatred, refuse even to consider reasonable solutions. [56]

That proved to be vital information to "C," for he supported the opinion that the German army's failure in Russia would re-create the circumstances that had existed before England's declaration of war and before Case Yellow: The German General Staff would, if given suitable guarantees by the United Kingdom and the United States, overthrow Hitler and his regime. Thus Whitney could bring vital connections to strengthen Dansey's operations. But more to the point, in "C's" view of Whitney, he was an ardent Anglophile who could be depended upon to present to Donovan the British point of view in the undercurrent of antipathetic politics that beclouded the political relationship between Churchill and FDR. In fact, it seems, "C" regarded Whitney as a British control.

In his secret work, Whitney was to work with "C" in London and would have an office next door to that of General Ismay, who was by now Churchill's chief of staff, a man who was called "the perfect oil-can." Whitney would send no intelligence to Washington without first showing it to Ismay. As Ismay further defined Whitney's job in London, he would work with Ismay to supply "correctives to what we may consider misinterpretation or unjust criticism [in the United States] of British activities." Ismay hoped, too, that Whitney "might particularly reflect and emphasize the British view-point," for Whitney had "connections so pre-disposing him in favour of the British cause and viewpoint . . . that it might reasonably be hoped that he would be at pains to represent it." [57]

General Ismay's confidence in Whitney's Anglophilia was not misplaced, although he took no chances that Whitney might not have a change of heart. As Ismay wrote to Churchill on Whitney's arrival, there were "obvious dangers" in having Whitney at the heart of British affairs, and he should therefore "have a watch-dog, not only on the military, but also on the civil side of his work." He suggested that he, Ismay, should keep an eye on Whitney on the military side while Desmond Morton should guard the civil side of Whitney's interests. "Yes," replied Churchill to Ismay's memo, reflecting his own caution about permitting a foreign secret service in the British capital at a time of war, "but watch [Whitney] vigilantly." [58]

Ismay then directed Major Denis Capell-Dunn, one of his assistants, to be the channel through which Whitney received his military intelligence. Ismay stressed that while Whitney "should be shown as much as you think reasonable," he should be shown "NOTHING (repeat NOTHING) which relates to future operations or which is derived from 'Most Secret Sources' "—such as Ultra. Whitney was excluded from Ultra, and while Capell-Dunn was to do his "best to help him in his work," he was also to "consult me if you are in any doubt about any particular item of information."

Donovan was kept informed about these strictures on Whitney's access and function and did not object, at least at first. But the strictures did demonstrate Churchill's and "C's" suspicions of the Donovan organization in the British capital. They demonstrated, too, that they were prepared to send Ultra to the United States only through the established agencies. Moreover these strictures, imposed largely for security reasons but also because Churchill and "C" were aware that the Donovan organization might contain Anglophobes who might not be as cooperative or as trustworthy as Whitney, limited the usefulness of the Donovan organization and made his telegrams suspect in Washington.

That suspicion became particularly strong when Whitney fell ill in January 1942 and returned to the United States for treatment. One of Whitney's assistants, Percy Winner, by trade a New York newspaperman and radio broadcaster of distinction, was then appointed locum tenens. Although Morton knew Winner well and considered him to be "as safe and sound as Major Whitney," Ismay wanted nobody as bright as Winner with access to the inner offices of British power and replied to Morton that he did not propose to give Winner anything like the same facilities he had given to Major Whitney and, Ismay declared to Morton, "I hope you will be able to ride him off." Winner was ridden off.

In these unpromising circumstances, the foundations of the "C"-"Q" relationship were laid. Gradually Whitney and his colleagues found themselves isolated and dependent upon Broadway not only for intelligence, but also for permission to operate from England into Europe. Nor was this isolation and control confined to London. It occurred everywhere within the empire and particularly in Delhi and Cairo, the main imperial bastions outside Whitehall. There, as Lieutenant Colonel Paul West, chief of OSS special operations at Cairo, was to report of the situation by early 1943:

There are three general difficulties in setting up an operation in any theater or location, namely (1) The British (2) The native difficulties, and (3) The United States State Department. . . . The British are really only interested in protecting the Empire, and in that they will stop at nothing. [59]

6 PEARL HARBOR

Donovan's first headquarters were in the Executive Office Building, a muddle of turrets, mansard roofs, Victorian, Greek revival, Italian, and French architecture next door to the White House. His first employee was a receptionist, Mrs. Cushman, an extraordinary and exotic creature who had startled New York a few years before by getting married in red, thereby becoming the inspiration for the movie *The Bride Wore Red*. Donovan soon displayed the basic element in his official personality, what was called "a marked tendency to desire to undertake anything he thought was a good idea." And frequently Donovan had to be told "No." He also proved to be a man who was "principally gifted for inspiring rather than organizing."

The earliest manifestation of Donovan's personality at work in the secret service was an attempt, one approved by the Bureau of the Budget, to bribe the German chargé d'affaires, Dr. Hans Thomsen, into defecting. A prominent Quaker and an American friend of Thomsen was authorized to pay $1 million to Thomsen if he would refuse to return to Germany and allow himself to be used to overthrow Hitler. Then he would become head of a new German government, formed by the German General Staff. This plan was, evidently, an outgrowth of Stallforth's contact with the German generals in August. Thomsen at first showed interest in the proposition. But for his fears about Washington's discretion, this operation might have worked. Thomsen also declared that he would discuss these matters only with two men: the president and Donovan.

In the end, Thomsen withdrew from the proposals, but not before the eve of Pearl Harbor. The talks then terminated in cordial fashion, and Thomsen was deported to Germany. But the entire incident did display in Donovan's personality an imaginative and conspiratorial touch possessed by few law-abiding Americans at that time. He thought on the grand scale. But otherwise he knew nothing of the first essential of secret service—the establishment of a sound, secret, and secure bureaucracy.

To establish such a bureaucracy, Stephenson's deputy, Colonel Charles Howard Ellis, was accepted by Donovan as his adviser, the first of several SIS men who were attached to all departments and sections of OSS. Thus "C" could expect to be well informed about what was happening inside Donovan's offices. Throughout the Pearl Harbor period and until the beginning of 1943, except for a brief mission to Cairo in the spring of 1942, Ellis was at the center of Donovan's affairs. He had an office close to "Q's," and he consulted and assisted in all phases of the development of Donovan's organizations—its financing both overt and covert; its selection of secret agents and their training; the establishment of Donovan's worldwide communications systems; the briefing of agents going out on secret missions; the establishment of Donovan's special operations and counterespionage services. He was responsible for such matters as the provision of a cover and documentation department; the development of secret inks and special weapons; and providing advice and assistance in the formation of Donovan's overseas bases. Also, he was consulted on the nature of Donovan's contacts with the enemy services.

In all aspects of his operations, Donovan cooperated loyally and closely with Stephenson, too closely for the comfort of J. Edgar Hoover and Adolf Berle. For shortly Stephenson was confronted with what was the first serious charge against him, that he had fabricated intelligence being sent by Donovan to FDR. On September 5 Berle wrote to the secretary of state to discuss Stephenson's information that a German raider had appeared off the Dutch Guiana coast, an access point to important fields of gold, diamonds, bauxite, manganese, and possibly oil. Stephenson was anxious that the area be occupied by either British or American troops, but what Berle wished to know was how the notion got abroad that there was a German raider busying itself in Guianian waters. For as he advised Hull:

A personal letter from our man in Paramaribo to one of the men in the State Department gives some reason to wonder what is really going on. The news of a possible German raider came via a British Intelligence agent and was promptly relayed by a British Commander Furse,* "British Naval Attache to the Americas." He stirred up the Governor of Dutch Guiana; and later in a conversation suggested that it might be all a hoax and remarked, "Well, anyhow we bullied the old man (the Governor of Dutch Guiana) into asking for help." The story of the raider has not been confirmed so far as I know.

In this connection it ought to be noted that the British Intelligence, under date of August 2, approached our Embassy at Bogota, suggesting that they collaborate in "planting some forged documents" placing responsibility for a minor riot in Bogota on the German Legation. . . . The British Intelligence has been very active in making things appear dangerous in this area. I believe that there is considerable basis for concern in view of the poor defences and some of the secret work, notably, the secret airfields which have been built in Colombia. But I think we have to be a little on our guard against false scares. [60]

The Furse incident, resembling so closely as it did that of Stephenson's suggestion to Cord in May 1940 that a Hispano-Fascist army was gathering in Mexico complete with artillery, was followed rather too closely by another such incident. In October the State

*Almost certainly this officer was John Paul Wellington Furse, born October 1904. Furse was a submariner who became, as his *Who's Who* entry discloses, "Assistant Naval Attaché, Europe and the Americas, 1940–43." That title was used as cover by "C's" officers. Furse later became rear admiral in charge of naval aircraft development, having served after the war as commander of various submarine flotillas. If Berle's statement has substance, then deception and provocation was one of Furse's intelligence functions.

Department reported what it called a "secret Nazi map showing their ultimate plans for the political reorganization of South America." [61] How this document found its way into the White House is far from clear, but at that stage it was not difficult or impossible to plant such deceptions for, as Lord Halifax remarked, the administration was "so ill-coordinated" that it resembled "a disorderly day's rabbit shooting."

President Roosevelt either believed the document or it suited his purposes, for he discussed it at length in a "fireside chat" on October 27 as evidence of Axis conspiracies in South America, an area in which the United States had traditionally exhibited sensitivity. But when the White House pressed the War Department for the original, it could not be found in any of the relevant departments, and upon learning that the original source was Stephenson, Berle concluded that it was a British plant, for as he stated in a paper for Cordell Hull and Sumner Welles:

You are familiar with the fact that we recently took up with the British Government the fact that British Intelligence had given us documents which they had forged; and on one occasion had approached our people to collaborate with them in certain other forgeries. The FBI, therefore, has regarded all British Intelligence information of this kind as subject to check.

Without going into a long mess of detail, I believe that the British Intelligence probably has been giving attention to creating as many "incidents" as possible to affect public opinion here. When they work up such an incident they apparently use the *New York Tribune* as the means of publication, much the same as they used to use the *Providence Journal* in the World War. Consequently before we shoot off I think we should have some check. [62]

Stephenson rejected Berle's allegation in an interview in 1986, declaring that the map was not a British forgery but a genuine document, although he did agree that it might have been no more than the brainchild of some low- or medium-level official of the Nazi party and might not therefore have represented the geopolitical intentions of the German government.

But whatever the truth behind Berle's assertions, the fact remained that the British intelligence service in the United States was engaging in a wide range of actions that were against American law and might compromise U.S. neutrality in the war. Moreover, J. Edgar Hoover feared, the British service might actually be engaged in espionage operations against the United States and was, as Berle wrongly believed, using FBI communications to get the material to London.

Berle was not aware of the existence of Ultra, nor of the arrangements made to transmit summaries to the White House and the U.S. chiefs of intelligence of the U.S. Army and Navy. Nor was he aware that this channel was being used by Churchill and Roosevelt for their personal messages to each other. The challenge to British communications privileges in the United States—and also to those of the FBI in London—was therefore deflected.

For his part, Donovan had no doubts about Stephenson or his activities. He sent President Roosevelt a paper that dwelt further on the extent of Nazi activities in South America:

Please read the attached. [It is] based on long, detailed, and comprehensive investigations by the British. The views and conclusions stated are those of Mr. Stevenson [sic], in charge of British Security Coordination. I know him well and have the greatest confidence in his judgment. [63]

Against that background of distrust between the higher reaches of the American and British intelligence establishments in Washington, events continued to march inevitably on toward Pearl Harbor and the Japanese invasion of Hong Kong and British Malaya.

On July 24 the Japanese occupied French Indochina, a measure that provoked FDR and Churchill into freezing all Japanese credits in the United States, thus bringing Anglo-Japanese-American trade to a virtual standstill. Roosevelt nationalized the armed forces of the Philippines and placed them under the command of General Douglas MacArthur, who was named commander in chief of U.S. forces in the Far East. Churchill then promised that the British Empire would go to the assistance of the United States in order to avoid war should negotiations break down between American and Japanese representatives. In view of the darkening world situation, Roosevelt proposed a secret meeting with Churchill, and arrangements were made for the two statesmen to meet in Argentia Bay, Newfoundland, aboard the British battleship *Prince of Wales* and the American cruiser *Augusta* on August 9. Roosevelt then vanished from Washington "on a fishing holiday in the Caribbean."

That meeting, the first of nine between the two leaders during the war, was noteworthy for two reasons, although "C" played little direct part in it. If there was cordiality between Churchill and Roosevelt personally, there was evidence that the traditional American attitude toward the British government—a combination of admiration and suspicion—persisted. The main issues were the old ones: the Americans' detestation for, and ignorance of, the British Empire and

British economic imperialism; and the British suspicion that the Americans intended to fight World War II as they had fought World War I—with European blood and American money. There was evidence, too, in the British view, that American moralizing on British imperialism and colonialism merely concealed an American intention to "pick up the pieces of the British Empire"—a phrase Churchill used from time to time—after the war and establish a U.S. world economic hegemony. Certainly "C" himself believed this, as did all high Tories.

Furthermore, FDR revealed that behind the amiable facade he was the new Machiavelli—of whom he was a student—and that he was the fount of U.S. antiimperial policy. Churchill was forced to be amiable, too. Confronted as he was by an electorate disinterested in fighting another war, FDR nevertheless had moved since 1939 from a position of total neutrality to near belligerency by skillfully conducting step-by-step executive action assisted by equally skillful British propaganda and diplomacy. As Churchill defined FDR's policy in a discussion with his War Cabinet on his return to London, FDR "had said that he would wage war, but not declare it, and that he would become more and more provocative" in the Atlantic. [64]

On his return to Washington, FDR implemented immediately the second part of the agreement. On September 4 he ordered the U.S. Navy to "shoot on sight" if German or Italian warships were encountered in U.S. "defensive" waters, which included half the Atlantic Ocean by that time. And as an example of FDR's utilization of British propaganda to assist him with his policy, in a speech just after the German torpedoing of the U.S. destroyer *Kearny* off Iceland in which eleven American sailors were killed, FDR claimed that "history has recorded who fired the first shot." He then claimed, too, to possess documents proving Hitler's intention to conquer Latin America and to eliminate religion. FDR then called upon Congress to amend the Neutrality Act to permit U.S. merchantmen to be armed and carry munitions into the British war zones. Shortly, Congress amended the act to the great benefit of Great Britain.

As to the Pacific, U.S. ambassador Joseph C. Grew warned FDR on November 17 that the Japanese might make a sudden attack, a warning he had made before. Churchill, suspecting that the Japanese might attempt to do to the Americans what they had done to the Russian fleet at Port Arthur in 1904—sink the American fleet in a surprise attack without a declaration of war—authorized the first of several major attempts to ensure that whatever else happened, the

United States was *not* taken by surprise if war broke out in the Pacific. The W Board,* of which "C" was a member, authorized a special operation involving Tricycle.

Dusko Popov, Tricycle, had been accepted by the Germans as what J. C. Masterman would call "a leading and highly placed agent in England." [65] Such was the Germans' trust in him, indeed, that when the head of the German service in New York, Major von der Osten, was knocked down and killed by a taxi while crossing Times Square, Popov's German employers decided to send him to the United States as von der Osten's successor. Since Popov was greatly valued by the British, the case went up to W Board, which decided that, since the XX-Committee controlled other important German agent organizers in the United Kingdom, Popov's presence in the United States at this tense and critical time might have great advantages. The W Board agreed to let Popov go to New York, his control being transferred from Masterman to Stephenson.

The wisdom of the W Board's action was soon proved, for while in Lisbon between June 26 and August 10, Popov's German controller gave him a questionnaire to which Popov was to supply answers while in the United States. Part of this questionnaire was prepared by the Japanese intelligence service, for whom the Germans acted in areas where their allies found it difficult to operate. Such an area was Pearl Harbor. The questionnaire was concealed under several microdots on documents carried on Popov's person. As important as the document itself were the reasons underlying the Japanese request that the Germans make a reconnaissance of the great U.S. naval base in the Pacific.

On November 11, 1940, British carrier aircraft had made a surprise attack on the Italian fleet at Taranto, using specially designed torpedoes to pass under the Italian antitorpedo nets and detonate beneath the keels of the target ships. Only a small force of Swordfish torpedo carriers were available, but in the attack three of the five Italian battleships were sunk. As a consequence the Royal Navy held supremacy in the Mediterranean. The attack marked the point at which the aircraft carrier and its strike planes became the dominant weapon of naval warfare. For that reason the Japanese displayed great

---

*Recall that the "W" Board consisted of "C," Guy Liddell, chief of counterespionage in the Security Service, and the three service directors of intelligence. Its purpose was to authorize information of a sensitive nature to be passed to the enemy through the double agents of the XX-Committee.

interest in the operation. Accordingly they asked German intelligence to obtain a full report from the Italian navy on the operation. Their interest indicated that the Japanese were contemplating similar action at Pearl Harbor. The questionnaire read:

Hawaii—Ammunition dumps and mine depots
　　1 Details about naval ammunition and mine depot on the Isle of Kushua (Pearl Harbor). If possible sketch.
　　2 Naval ammunition depot Lualuelei. Exact position? Is there a railway line (junction)?
　　3 The total ammunition reserve of the army is supposed to be in the rock of the Crater Aliamanu. Position?
　　4 Is the Crater Punchbowl (Honolulu) being used as ammunition dump? If not, are there other military works?
Aerodromes
　　1 *Aerodrome Lukefield.*—Details (sketch if possible) regarding the situation of the hangars (number?), workshops, bomb depots, and petrol depots. Are there underground petrol installations?—Exact position of the seaplane station? Occupation?
　　2 *Naval air arm strong point Kaneche.*—Exact report regarding position, number of hangars, depots, and workshops (sketch). Occupation?
　　3 *Army aerodromes Wicham Field and Wheeler Field.*—Exact position? Reports regarding number of hangars, depots and workshops. Underground installations? (Sketch.)
　　4 *Rodger's Airport.* In case of war, will this place be taken over by the army or the navy? What preparations have been made? Number of hangars? Are there landing possibilities for seaplanes?
　　5 *Airport of the Panamerican Airways.*—Exact position? (If possible sketch.) Is this airport possibly identical with Rodger's Airport or a part thereof? (A wireless station of the Panamerican Airways is on the Peninsula Mohapuu.)
Naval Strong Point Pearl Harbor
　　1 Exact details and sketch about the situation of the state wharf, of the pier installations, workshops, petrol installations, situations of dry dock No. 1 and of the new dry dock which is being built.
　　2 Details about the submarine station (plan of situation). What land installations are in existence?
　　3 Where is the station for mine search formations [Minensuchverbaende]? How far has the dredger work progressed at the entrance and in the east and southeast lock? Depths of water?
　　4 Number of anchorages [Liegeplaetze]?
　　5 Is there a floating dock in Pearl Harbour or is the transfer of such a dock to this place intended?

As Masterman, chairman of the XX-Committee, concluded from this document:

It is noticeable that, whereas all the other questions (in the entire document) are more or less general or statistical (e.g., "Reports regarding U.S.A. strong points of all descriptions, especially in Florida"; "How much is the monthly production of bombers, fighting planes, training places, civilian aeroplanes?"), those connected with Hawaii are specialised and detailed (e.g., details of named aerodromes, if possible with sketches, and the situations of hangars, workshops, bomb depots, and petrol depots are demanded). [66]

Masterman added: "It is therefore surely a fair deduction that the questionnaire indicated very clearly that in the event of the United States being at war, Pearl Harbor would be the first point to be attacked, and that plans for this attack had reached an advanced state by August 1941." However, "Obviously it was for the Americans to make their appreciation and to draw their deductions from the questionnaire rather than for us to do so." [67]

When Stephenson read the questionnaire he found the German interest in Pearl Harbor "striking and significant," and, having seen Magic, which showed plainly that the German and Japanese intelligence services were working hand in glove, Stephenson was to state, "I had no doubt that Pearl Harbor was *a* target and perhaps *the* target."

Popov left for the United States by Pan-American Clipper on August 10 and was met in Bermuda by John Pepper, one of Stephenson's assistants. Pepper then took Popov on to New York to meet the director of the FBI, J. Edgar Hoover. But if Masterman thought the questionnaire "startling," the suspicious Hoover displayed little interest, and the document was *not* circulated to the Interdepartmental Committee on Intelligence and Security even for information purposes.

To the contrary, Hoover became increasingly hostile to Popov when FBI agents watching Popov uncovered evidence that he was committing offenses under the Mann Act, which provided punishment for those who transported women across a state line for purposes defined by the act as being immoral. Popov left the United States with much of his mission a failure and with much explaining to do to his German controller in Lisbon. Indeed, it was not clear whether Popov was "blown" with the Germans.

Meanwhile, "C" had personally taken a further curious step. In

June Major Gerald W. Wilkinson emerged from his cover at Manila, where he was the manager of an important Pacific trading post. He presented himself to the U.S. intelligence authorities at both Manila and Pearl Harbor as a "British Secret Agent, Far East." Wilkinson was investigated by the FBI, whose report showed that Wilkinson was "thoroughly reliable and trustworthy," and that he was the "properly accredited branch manager in Manila for Theo. H. Davies & Co., Ltd., one of the five largest corporations in the Territory of Hawaii. His wife, Lorna, was the granddaughter of Theo. H. Davies. The report noted that Wilkinson's representative in Hawaii was one Harry Dawson, manager of the steamship department of Theo H. Davies & Co., and that Dawson was a British subject and also British vice-consul for Hawaii.

What the FBI/ONI report did not state was that Wilkinson knew Churchill well enough to lunch with him, perhaps because Lorna Davies's uncle, Sir George, was a Conservative member of Parliament and government Whip, a lord commissioner of the Treasury, and vice-chamberlain and then comptroller of the king's purse between 1935–37. Wilkinson was, therefore, well connected.

During his discussions with the authorities at Manila, Wilkinson successfully established friendly relations with the U.S. Army and Navy intelligence chiefs, but when the U.S. Army chief was succeeded by General Charles A. Willoughby, the relationship collapsed. Willoughby, an Anglophobe, formed a deep suspicion of Wilkinson and the intelligence he had to offer. Indeed, it was peculiar that "C" should have authorized such a roundabout way of getting British intelligence to U.S. authorities at Pearl Harbor and Manila when, presumably, it could as easily have been sent over the established London–Washington intelligence link. The most probable answer was that "C" wanted to establish a *direct* channel to U.S. intelligence authorities to ensure that the U.S. fleet in the Pacific was not "Tarantoed." If he learned anything regarding Japanese intentions during this dangerous period in the Pacific—and "C" did have important intelligence sources about the Pacific that the U.S. did not have— he could communicate that intelligence directly to the U.S. commanders in chief by fast and reliable means. A second goodwill attempt again foundered upon official U.S. suspicion of British intelligence.

But if Wilkinson failed at Manila, he succeeded at Pearl Harbor. There, working through Harry Dawson, he regularly shipped SIS reports aboard the Pan-Am Clipper from Manila to Shivers, the FBI man at Pearl Harbor; the Army G2, Colonel Bicknell, and Captain Mayfield, the ONI chief. Despite some initial reserve, Wilkinson appears to have been accepted as "reliable and trustworthy," although the information he supplied between June and October 1941 was considered by Admiral A. G. Kirk, director of naval intelligence in Washington, to be "not of importance or of particular interest to the Division of Naval Intelligence, because it was too detailed in its nature, too local in its application, and too late in its reception." [68]

By the third week of November, when it was evident that diplomatic conversations between the U.S. and Japanese governments in Washington had reached the final crisis stage, Wilkinson had established fair relations with the authorities at Hawaii. Against that background on November 20, the Japanese ambassador communicated to the U.S. government proposals for a modus vivendi in the Pacific. On November 24 Secretary of State Cordell Hull told the British ambassador, Lord Halifax, that the United States wished to examine these proposals "primarily because the heads of our Army and Navy often emphasize to me that time is the all-important question for them, and it is necessary to be more fully prepared to deal effectively with the situation in the Pacific area in case of an outbreak by Japan." [69]

When FDR advised Churchill (and Chiang Kai-shek of China) of the proposals on November 24, Churchill expressed "disquiet" about the proposal, while Chiang Kai-shek's reaction was described as "hysterical." [70] It seemed to Churchill that, in the light of intelligence reports reaching him from "C," the Japanese, too, were playing for time to get their forces in and around French Indochina into position for an invasion of British Malaya. The congressional inquiry into Pearl Harbor subsequently found it of interest that on November 26 Wilkinson received and circulated this message from Broadway, a message that seems to have been sent also to Washington:

Secret source (usually reliable) reports that, A. Japanese will attack Krakow Isthmus from sea on Dec. 1, repeat Dec. 1, without any ultimatum or declaration of break, with a view to getting between Bangkok and Singapore. B. Attacking forces will proceed direct from Hainan and Formosa. Main landing point to be in Songkhala area. Valuation for above in No. 3, repeat 3 (i.e. only about 55 to 60 per cent probable accuracy).
American Military and Naval Intelligence informed. [71]

Having read that message, Secretary of War Henry L. Stimson, as he related in his diary, telephoned the president and asked him whether he had heard that the Japanese had "started a new expedition from Shanghai down toward Indo-china." The Japanese had warned several times not to land further troops in French Indochina and to evacuate those that were there already. Since FDR had promised Churchill that America would declare war, whether she herself was attacked or not, if the Japanese attacked British possessions in Asia, the president was, Stimson recorded, "shocked and at once took it as further evidence of bad faith of the Japanese." It was now clear that the Japanese were indeed using the modus vivendi proposals as cover to gain time in order to get a major expedition into place for an attack on British Malaya. The Japanese proposals for modus vivendi were rejected, and, as Hull advised Halifax:

the diplomatic part of our relations with Japan was virtually over. . . . It would be a serious mistake for our country and other countries interested in the Pacific situation to make plans of resistance without including the possibility that Japan may move suddenly and with every possible element of surprise and spread out over considerable areas and captured certain positions and posts before the peaceful countries interested in the Pacific would have time to confer. . .

Stephenson received Colonel James Roosevelt, the president's son, at his headquarters in the International Building in New York to deliver a telegram from Roosevelt to Churchill that declared, according to Stephenson's recollection, "Negotiations broken off. Services expect action within two weeks." Also on November 26, and presumably at FDR's instructions, all commands of the U.S. Armed Forces were sent this signal by the U.S. Naval Department in Washington:

This dispatch is to be considered a war warning. Negotiations with Japan looking toward stabilization of conditions in the Pacific have ceased and an aggressive move by Japan is expected within the next few days. The number and equipment of Japanese troops and the organization of naval task forces indicate an amphibious expedition against either the Philippines Thai or Kra Isthmus or possibly Borneo. Execute an appropriate defensive deployment preparatory to carrying out tasks assigned in WPL 46. Inform District and Army authorities. A similar warning is being sent by War Department. [Special Naval Observer London] inform British. Continental districts Guam, Samoa directed to take appropriate measures against sabotage. [72]

Although "C's" message to Wilkinson of November 26 was by no means the only indication the U.S. government received that the Japanese might be about to invade Malaya, it was an important one.

The origins of the intelligence were debated by the Pearl Harbor inquiry, if only because a modus vivendi that did not include Britain would be, from the British point of view, undesirable and perhaps even dangerous. The British had, in consequence, every reason not to support the modus vivendi proposals and, indeed, to support their rejection. The Joint Congressional Committee on the Investigation of the Pearl Harbor Attack, exploring whether FDR and Churchill had been in league to bring the United States into the war against its will, paid much attention, therefore, to "C's" message of November 26. But for reasons that are not clear, the Pearl Harbor inquiry did not dwell upon this subject and did not establish the factual basis for the message. There was, however, more success when the inquiry tackled two subsequent messages. [73]

On November 25 "C" sent further intelligence to Wilkinson and Washington. This message was plainly an Ultra intercept of a communication from the Japanese foreign minister in Tokyo to the Japanese chargé d'affair in London, and it was the famous "winds" message:

No. 098127.
Date 25 November 1941

From: The Foreign Minister, Tokyo.
To: The Japanese Charge, London.
Date: 19th November 1941
   To be treated as Chef de Mission Cypher.
   The international situation is tense and we cannot tell when the worst may happen. In such an event, communications between the Empire and the enemy countries will immediately cease. Therefore when our diplomatic relations are on the point of being severed, we shall broadcast, as the weather report, the following phrases in the middle and at the end of the news in Japanese in our overseas broadcast service:
   (1) If Japanese-American relations are in question: "Higashi no kaze ame" (East wind, rain).
   (2) If Japan and the Soviet are concerned: "Kita no kaze kumori" (North wind, cloudy).
   (3) In the case of Japan and Britain (including the invasion of Thailand or an attack on Malaya): "Nishi no kaze hare" (West wind, fine).
   The appropriate phrase will each time be broadcast twice in a resolute voice and you should accordingly [group corrupt: ? Destroy by fire] codes documents, etc.
   The above is to be treated strictly confidential.

There can be no doubt about the authenticity of that message. Separately and independently the same message, or a variant of it, was intercepted by various U.S. agencies, although due to a heavy backlog it was not translated and circulated until after the British message. Thus on the basis of "C's" decrypt, a listening watch was instituted for what came to be called the "winds execute" message. At the congressional inquiry, Captain Laurence F. Safford, chief of the U.S. Navy cryptanalytical service, insisted that a "winds execute" message was intercepted by a U.S. station on the East Coast "during the evening of December 3, 1941 (Washington time), which was December 4 by Greenwich time and Tokyo time." This message indicated that England *and* America were both to be attacked. But no evidence existed that such an intercept was ever produced because the message itself, and the papers relating to it, vanished. And it was for that reason the inquiry paid so much attention to the third of Wilkinson's reports, which was dated December 3, the same day Safford claimed he had seen the "winds execute" message.

Evidence of the involvement of "C's" service was provided the inquiry by Colonel Henry C. Clausen, an army lawyer establishing whether there was a basis for court-martial proceedings against certain senior army officers at Pearl Harbor. Clausen maintained before the inquiry that he formed an impression during his investigation that there was a "winds execute" decrypt in the messages received from the British. Senator Homer Ferguson, Republican of Michigan, and a member of the congressional board, pounced on this statement and asked Clausen: "Did you find in the British file any suspicious message?" Clausen replied that the last of the messages circulated by Wilkinson did contain a statement that could have been made only by someone who had seen a "winds execute" message. Dated December 3, this message was produced from Clausen's file for the congressional inquiry, and it was the message upon which most attention was focused. It stated (the italics are supplied to give additional emphasis to that part of the message derived from "C's" Ultra):

Urgent cable received from Manila night of December 3, 1941. We have received considerable intelligence confirming following developments in Indochina.

A-1. Accelerated Japanese preparation of air fields and railways.

1. Arrival since November 10 of additional 100,000 repeat 100,000 troops and considerable quantities fighters medium bombers tanks and guns (75 millimeter).

B. Estimate of specific quantities have already been telegraphed Washington November 21 by American military intelligence here.

C. *Our considered opinion concludes that Japan envisages early hostil-*

*ities with Britain and the United States. Japan does not repeat not intend
to attack Russia at present but will act in South.* [74]

That suggested British knowledge that war was imminent on December 3, a fact that supported Safford's evidence that he had seen
a "winds execute" message that showed America as well as England
were to be attacked. As Clausen explained to the congressional inquiry, he went to London to seek evidence about the source of Paragraph "C" of the December 3 message, and he "talked with the
British party in charge of all this magic stuff," but he found *no* evidence that that message had been based upon a "winds execute"
message. On his return to the United States he went to see Wilkinson,
then working in Stephenson's organization in New York. Clausen
showed Wilkinson the message and asked him what the source was,
and Wilkinson replied that he did not know. Clausen then asked
Wilkinson to find out for him, and as a result "this came from the
British to the Americans in Washington." [75]

Clausen submitted this telegram from "C" to a man called Jones,
displaying marked anxiety not to become involved in the Pearl Harbor
inquiry on the grounds that the security of Ultra might be placed at
hazard:

TOP SECRET ULTRA

From London, 31st August 1945
ULTRA   IMPORTANT
GOR 682 from GCCS 11279.
    Following from C.S.S. for Jones.
    A. Colonel Wilkinson who was stationed at Manila and is now with 48000
[48 = U.S.A. 000 = Stephenson] and is temporarily in U.K., was recently
approached by Lieutenant Colonel H. C. Clausen, of Judge Advocate General's Department U.S. Army, in connection with investigation of General
Short and Admiral Kimmel for Pearl Harbour disaster. He carried credentials
from Secretary of War. [76]

Menzies continued: "Colonel C. anxious to know basic source of
para. C of telegram of December 2nd [sic], and in particular, whether
this was in 'special' category." In point of fact, Menzies went on, "para
C was based on B[lack]J[acket] [the code term for diplomatic Ultra].
Wilkinson was unaware of source and passed information to Honolulu
as he appreciated that I possessed no direct communications." Menzies then told Jones: "You should consult with G2 [of the U.S. Army],
as security Ultra at stake if this evidence made public." [77]

Continuing his testimony, Clausen introduced evidence that showed if the U.S. Armed Forces failed to place the correct interpretation on the intelligence they were receiving from London—that they were about to be attacked in the Philippines—then the commercial house to whom Wilkinson showed the message did not fail to do so. On the contrary, the president of Theo. H. Davies & Co., Ltd., John E. Russell, was so impressed by the text that he decided war was imminent and canceled important shipments of goods to Manila. Also, he ordered all his ships on the high seas into safe harbor.

On that note, the congressional investigation proceeded to other business, without making a conclusion concerning Clausen's evidence. It remains, therefore, one of the great mysteries of the Pearl Harbor inquiry and its literature that the role of the British, who had the most to gain through America's entry into the war, was not investigated as fully as were all the other aspects of the disaster. That, doubtless, was because the U.S. government had no jurisdiction over "C's" affairs and because of the need in 1945 to preserve the secret of Ultra on the grounds that British cryptanalytical capabilities developed in the war might have utility against the Russians.

The British position, only formally stated in public for the first time in 1981 (in the official histories of the war), was that nothing was known in London about Japanese intentions that was not known in Washington, and that in the British archives there was "no intelligence of any importance that was not available to the Americans, who, indeed, had much that was not available in Whitehall. . . ." While making no reference to what may or may not have been known to Churchill or "C," the official historians did record that the Joint Intelligence Committee did issue a paper that proved to be the last on the subject. On November 28, nine days before the Japanese attack on Pearl Harbor, the committee "implicitly excluded the prospect of a direct Japanese attack on U.S. possessions" and concluded that if Japan attacked, she would "move against" Thailand in preparation "for an attack on Malaya in the favourable spring weather." Since the file containing that appreciation remained closed to the public as late as 1985, the official opinion can be neither probed nor contested.

Inevitably, therefore, there was speculation in Washington that the United States might have been the victim of British duplicity. Churchill himself fueled such suspicions when, in a broadcast on February 15, 1942, the prime minister declared that he had "dreamt of, aimed at, and worked for" America's entry into the war. The use of the words "worked for" were troublesome because, as Lord Halifax wrote to Anthony Eden, the foreign secretary, the phrase gave the idea that "simple innocent people" had been "caught asleep by others cleverer than themselves." Eden then wrote to Churchill to advise him of the suspicions and that the phrase was "being kept in cold storage for sharper use later on." Churchill responded: "I don't think there is much in this. *Qui s'excuse, s'accuse. Qui s'expliquer, compliqué.*" There the suspicions petered out under the welter of war, leaving not so much suspicions as belief that there were grounds for suspicion.

So there were in regard to modus vivendi, although not in regard to the disaster itself. Britain had nothing to gain by having the U.S. fleet sunk. The disaster was a U.S. intelligence failure, one very similar in its causes to those that had occurred in Whitehall in 1938–40 before full powers were vested in the Joint Intelligence Committee. The bulletins based upon Ultra sent to Washington, and perhaps also to Honolulu, certainly showed the strongest evidence of imminent hostilities. If read with the U.S. ambassador's warning from Tokyo in January 1941 that the war would commence with a surprise Japanese attack on Pearl Harbor, with the subsequent warning from the U.S. ambassador that a surprise attack might be imminent, with the Popov questionnaire, with the large body of intelligence generated by the Americans themselves, and with the knowledge of the disappearance of the Japanese main carrier force, then it would have been obvious that Pearl Harbor was threatened. Had that conclusion been reached, the fleet would not have been double-parked at its buoys that Sunday morning. It would have been at sea, and all guns at Pearl Harbor would have been manned when the Japanese attack aircraft appeared out of the dawn twilight. Furthermore, even if the United States had possessed no intelligence service of any description at that time, the decrypts sent by Menzies *after* the "winds code" message of November 25 should have been sufficient to warn the U.S. commanders in chief in Hawaii that they were in danger of being "Tarantoed" at any moment.

In all other directions, "C" did what seems to have been his best by his American associates. In all, according to the evidence given to the Pearl Harbor inquiry, he sent forty-one Ultras to Washington relevant to Japanese intentions.* Yet if the evidence suggests that "C" was entirely loyal to the spirit of Anglo-American relations, there was at least one curious incident that displayed that he might *just* have known more about Japanese intentions than was recorded by the official historian. Rex Benson suddenly left Washington for Cairo on December 6. That in itself would not have been noteworthy, except that he did precisely the same thing on the eve of the German invasion of Russia.

Nor would Benson's movements have been really noteworthy but for another curious circumstance. Although the period December 5–7 was a weekend, it was a time when ordinarily most key people would be away from their offices. But this was not an ordinary period at all, it was a time of extreme emergency, one so intense that the imminence of fateful events was palpable in Washington. It might have been expected therefore that everyone would have been available, yet this was not the case. As it was at Pearl Harbor, so it was in Washington: almost everyone in the highest positions appear to have been everywhere and anywhere *except* at their place of duty, and as at Pearl Harbor most remained remote or unavailable for much of the crucial first few hours. As it was in Washington, so it was in London. There, both the U.S. ambassador, John Winant, and the second most important American in London, Averell Harriman, were with Churchill at his official country residence, Chequers, on December 7. At their dinner that evening, Harriman later recalled, "the Prime Minister seemed tired and depressed. He didn't have much to say throughout dinner and was immersed in his thoughts, with his head in his hands part of the time."

As for Rex Benson, the circumstances of his departure "for Cairo" were as follows: On November 25 FDR advised Churchill that because of the high importance of the campaign in Arabia and Italian North Africa being fought by the British and German armies, he intended to send a special representative, William C. Bullitt, to Cairo "to report to me and to be of what assistance he can to you[r] supply and similar problems." Bullitt would leave Washington on December 1. That decision could not have pleased Churchill, for Bullitt had been U.S. ambassador in Paris at the fall of France.

A passionate Francophile, Bullitt had then felt that the British had betrayed France because of Churchill's refusal to send its Home Defence fighter squadrons to France. Bullitt had been also "bleakly defeatist" in his estimates of Britain's will and ability to win the Battle of Britain, and, it must have been feared, he might be equally defeatist in his reporting from Cairo. Since recently the U.S. Neutrality Act

*See appendix for crucial evidence.

had been revised to allow U.S. merchantmen to carry arms into the war zone, including the Middle East, and there were at that moment no less than forty U.S. merchantmen at sea carrying arms, equipment, and munitions to the British in the Middle East, it was thought to be essential that Bullitt be handled "correctly."

The man to handle Bullitt "correctly" was the one who knew him best, Rex Benson. As Benson recorded in his diary on December 6, he left Washington for Cairo with Bullitt in a B24 Liberator carrying 7¾ tons of thirty-seven-millimeter ammunition, among other war stores. Benson sat in the radio room of the aircraft most of the way. On landing at Miami to refuel the aircraft for its transatlantic flight to Bathurst in Africa, Benson suddenly left the aircraft, leaving Bullitt to continue the flight alone. He did not confide to his diary *why* he so suddenly abandoned such a vital mission. But the thought arises that at some stage during the flight or on landing he learned something that exceeded the Bullitt mission in importance. What could this have been if it was not information that war between America and Japan was indeed imminent? Moreover why was Bullitt, the special assistant to the secretary of the navy, flying to Cairo when the U.S. fleet was about to be attacked at Pearl Harbor? We do not know.

It was true that Benson suffered from diverticulosis and had been suffering from stomach pain so severe that he had been absent from the embassy throughout the previous week. It was true also that Benson had need of an enema. But treatment for his complaint must have been available at the Miami airfield, a major entrepôt, and if he needed to take an enema with him, one could easily have been supplied. But that he did not do. As his diary shows, what he did was stay with friends, Peggy and Percy Frazer, at Hibiscus Harbor in Miami. There, during the evening, he recorded of the situation: "Japan news looks like certain war."

Since it was axiomatic in the service that there was often good reason for eccentric behavior, there may have been such a reason in this case. For apart from all else, Benson was able to play several rounds of golf while at Hibiscus Harbor that weekend. The news that Pearl Harbor had been attacked reached Benson, the man who had been instructed before leaving London to do everything he could to help bring America into the war, while in a Miami drugstore. And as he recorded of the attack:

The blow has fallen. . . . It is clear that the Japs have gone all out to get the first blow in and it looks like being a pretty shrewd one. I guess many planes destroyed on the ground and quite a few ships. Rumours that "Oklahoma" and aircraft carrier are amongst them. If this is true it will "unify" this country in a brace of shakes & they will realise early that their teething troubles are going to be plenty.

Then he went off to play more golf.

At 7:55 A.M. Hawaiian time on Sunday morning, December 7, 1941, Japanese torpedo-carrying aircraft and bombers from a Japanese carrier task force, the *Kido Butai*, which was 275 miles to the north, attacked the U.S. fleet, just as Popov's questionnaire had foreshadowed. Within thirty minutes American naval power in the Pacific was virtually destroyed, except for the fleet's aircraft carriers *Enterprise*, *Lexington*, and *Saratoga*, which were at sea. Of the 8 battleships, 3 were sunk, 1 had capsized, and 4 were seriously damaged. Of the 231 army aircraft, 166 remained intact or reparable; of the navy and marine aircraft, 54 of some 250 were flyable. More than 3,000 navy and marine officers and men were killed and 876 wounded, while among the army losses were 226 killed and 396 wounded.

The U.S. garrisons on Wake Island and Guam were overwhelmed; the British crown colony of Hong Kong was invaded and surrendered on Christmas Day. Thailand and northern Malaya was invaded as expected, but not on December 1; the invasions took place on December 7–8. On December 10 the last Anglo-American capital ships, the *Prince of Wales* and the *Repulse*, were caught and sunk in the South China Sea by Japanese aircraft based in southern Indochina. Japan was now master of the Pacific and Indian oceans. "We are," FDR told Churchill on the transatlantic telephone the day of Pearl Harbor, "all in the same boat now." [78] At Chequers there was what Winant termed "incredulity," although whether it was incredulity at the attack or the casualties was not debated.

Churchill, who until now had held his head in his hands at the dinner table, rejoiced at the prospect of a Grand Alliance of the English-speaking peoples and Russia against the Nazi foe, declaring later in his memoir of that moment:

No American will think it wrong of me if I proclaim that to have the United States at our side was to be the greatest joy. . . . We had won the war. England would live; Britain would live; the Commonwealth of Nations and the Empire would live. How long the war would last or in what fashion it would end no man could tell, nor did I at this moment care. Once again in our long island history we would emerge, however mauled or mutilated, safe and victorious. We should not be wiped out. Our history would not come to an end. We might not even have to die as individuals. Hitler's fate was sealed. Mussolini's fate was sealed. As for the Japanese they would be ground to powder. All the rest was merely the proper application of over-whelming power. . . . Being saturated and satiated with emotion and sensation, I went to bed and slept the sleep of the saved and thankful. [79]

In the United States, the reactions were confused and uncertain. Few men could free their minds of the suspicion that there had not been a Rooseveltian conspiracy, connivance, or plot. That belief intensified with time, and Admiral Husband E. Kummel, the officer whose fleet was sunk, reflected a national suspicion when he was allowed at last to read the intelligence available to FDR *before* Pearl Harbor. He was "appalled" at what he discovered and wrote the statement that "Nothing in my experience of nearly forty-two years service in the Navy had prepared me for the actions of the highest officials in our government which denied this vital information to the Pearl Harbor commanders."

The sense was widespread that America had been led by a new Machiavelli. Yet nothing was proved even when, in 1980, Donovan's own papers were discovered, unedited and untouched since 1946 when they were consigned to a room under the ice-skating rink at Rockefeller Center in New York City. The file on Dr. Hans Thomsen, the German chargé d'affaires in Washington, the man to whom Donovan offered $1 million if he would desert his post and attempt the overthrow of Hitler, did show that Thomsen had warned that the Japanese intended to attack the United States at Pearl Harbor, and that he had passed that intelligence to Donovan. Yet if that was true, there was nothing in Donovan's papers to show that that warning was sent to FDR.

As for FDR's bearing immediately after Pearl Harbor, when Donovan visited the president at the Oval Office with Ed Murrow, the American broadcaster, he did not find the president surprised that the United States had been attacked and was at war. What FDR's statements indicated was a state of shock at the fact that the war warning uttered to Pearl Harbor and all other key military and naval centers on November 28 had been ignored. As FDR exclaimed to Donovan and Murrow when they came into the room: "They caught our ships like lame ducks! Lame ducks, Bill!" He then went on: "We told them at Pearl Harbor, and everywhere else, to have the lookouts manned. But they still took us by surprise." The president added: "They caught our planes on the ground—on the ground!"

As for the British representatives in Washington, their reaction was much the same—not surprise at the attack, but surprise at the casualties. As Rex Benson recorded in his diary on his return to the embassy from his inexplicable journey:

Found everybody composed & facing up to the new situation. The Fleet came back to Hawaii from exercises on Saturday night and simply tied their ships up and went for a Sunday leave. Not even steam up!! This in spite of plenty of warnings and a knowledge that the Far Eastern situation was critical! No air patrols up on Sunday. Everything caught completely unprepared. Most of the aeroplanes destroyed included all [B17] Fortresses. 3 battleships sunk in the harbor. It is unbelievable. . . . Fear they will make all mistakes we made & worse.

Six

Year of Decision

1942

1 THE COUSINS

While Churchill was in Washington establishing the Grand Alliance that yuletide of 1942, and the British Empire in Asia was being swept away by the Japanese along with "C's" service, Menzies emerged briefly from his clandestine twilight at Broadway on the evening of January 5, 1942, to dine at 5 Belgrave Square, the home of that rich and charming old gossip and intriguer, Sir Henry "Chips" Channon.

In his late forties, Channon was an Anglo-American born in Chicago and grown rich. He lived in splendor in London and at Kelvedon, a great house in Essex. He had married a Guinness, had a son at Eton, and a safe seat in Parliament, but he described himself a writer. Just before the war he published a marvelous biography of King Ludwig of Bavaria. Why "C" was there is not known, although it may have been that Channon was one of "C's" "honourable correspondents."

Channon was supposed to have been the lover at Oxford of Prince Paul, regent of Yugoslavia, and "C" sent Channon to Belgrade or at least provided the technical means of getting him there and back safely, with a personal letter from King George VI advising Paul against joining the Axis Pact. But the letter had no effect. Paul signed his country into the Axis alliance at Belvedere Palace in Vienna on March 25, 1941. That act caused a counterrevolution assisted by British secret agents in which Paul lost the regency and Peter II was placed on the throne. Hitler then bombed Belgrade, invaded and occupied Yugoslavia, restored Yugoslavia to the Axis, and Peter and Paul fled to Cairo aboard aircraft provided by SOE. The entire affair wrecked the Karageorgevic dynasty that had ruled the triune kingdom of Serbs, Croats, and Slovenes—Yugoslavia—since the liquidation of the Austro-Hungarian empire. It also inspired two oppositions: a royalist guerrilla force whose leader was called Mihailovoic and a Communist force under a leader called Tito. Hence the connection between "C" and Channon.

The dinner was a grand affair. "C" appeared in black tie wearing for the first time the "Red Riband," the much-prized badge of the Order of the Bath suspended by a crimson ribbon around his neck. "C" had been admitted to the order in the New Years' honors list, which meant that "C's" services had been recognized and that, provided he watched his P's and Q's, he might expect to be advanced in the order to the rank of knight. And as Channon burbled breathlessly in his diary entry for that night: "I gave one of the most *reussi* dinner parties I have *ever* given, the *clou* being Stewart Menzies who is 'C,' that is, head of the *entire* Secret Service." [1]*

Although Channon's windows were boarded and sandbagged against bomb blast and shrapnel, inside the colonnaded mansion burned Channon's thousand lighted candles. The guests had their cocktails in the orange-and-silver anteroom. When called to dinner, they went in to the Blue Room, an imitation of the dining room at the Amalienbourg Palace, created by Channon in 1936 so that he could entertain his neighbors, the duke and duchess of York, in a style still greater than that to which they were accustomed. The room was a shimmering cascade of blue and more silver, with twenty-two-karat gold plate and hundreds more flickering candles. Present, too, was

*Reussi = (f) successful. Clou = (f) literally nail, but in this context the principal guest.

the acting prime minister (while Churchill was away), Clement Attlee, a Socialist. For "C" doubtless it was an agreeable and informative evening. But these flashes of the toff in "C's" personality were becoming rare as the war widened and became ever more overpowering in its complexity.

As it did so, "C's" operating policy changed again, this time into a form that was to last at least for the next decade. The espionage branch of the secret service, which was known as Intelligence Service British Agents (ISBA), and which was administered by Dansey, became responsible for the direction of the refugee intelligence services in London. These became primarily responsible for espionage within occupied Europe, leaving British-born secret agents with the main task of very high level political reporting on the basis of clandestine sources recruited within the capitals where they were stationed. Dansey's service became, therefore, an adjunct to the diplomatic services. Only rarely were they interested in operations, and their targets were not only the enemy, but also the Allied diplomatic and intelligence services. Beyond that, "C's" main interest overseas was counterespionage.

At "C's" direction, Section V under Vivian and Cowgill expanded widely, its purpose to defend British interests against the activities of the Germans, Italians, Vichy French, Spaniards, Japanese, Russians, and, now, the Americans. In 1651 the English philosopher Thomas Hobbes wrote a celebrated book called the *Leviathan*, in which he developed the political philosophy that man was by nature a selfish, individualistic animal at constant war with all other men. In 1942 that stage had been reached. With respect to the Americans, "C" now believed that the United States had been propelled into the war not through political and moral decision, but as the consequence of hostile action. The Grand Alliance was not, as it was being represented, a natural alliance between powers bound by the ties of common blood, language, and shared danger, but by self-interest.

With the development of the Donovan organization, "C" held that his services would have to deal with a complex situation in which Donovan was not only a colleague in a common fight for existence against a powerful group of enemies, but also an instrument for the execution of FDR's policy of anticolonialism. Even as the Anglo-Saxon world collapsed under the Axis hammer blows, FDR, using lend-lease as a threat that became increasingly explicit, pressed Churchill at Washington and constantly thereafter to concede home rule for India. So acute did the pressure become that at one stage during the first half of 1942 Churchill contemplated resignation rather than submit to the pressure.

FDR warned Churchill that U.S. public opinion "could not understand why, if the British Government is willing to permit the component parts of India to secede after the war, it is not willing to permit them to enjoy what is tantamount to self-government during the war." Churchill, a man never very impressed by the rights of public opinion in wartime, received FDR's proposals with what Harry Hopkins described as a "string of cuss words [that] lasted for two hours in the middle of the night." And as Churchill wrote to FDR (in a letter he did not send), "I should personally make no objection at all to retiring into private life" if FDR continued to press him. He could not feel that the "common cause would benefit by emphasizing the serious differences which would emerge between our two countries if it were known that against our own convictions we were conforming to United States public opinion in a matter which concerns the British Empire and is vital to our successful conduct of the war in the East." [2]

As an instrument not of the Grand Alliance but of Churchill and the Foreign Office, it became the task of Broadway to frustrate not only enemy but Allied political activity inimical to British interests. In the context of imperial policy, the empire was not to be propelled through foreign interference into a revolutionary postcolonial era, but through an orderly process in which Britain's hegemony would be maintained in the form of commonwealth. Since the Americans could not be expected to acquiesce in such a policy, they would have to be resisted and frustrated in what they did want, which was economic hegemony. At the same time, however, "C" was authorized by the War Cabinet to maintain a strong, active service in the United States, where the object of all British activity was to maintain lend-lease policies untrammeled by political obligations, impose British control on strategic policy, and ensure that Britain obtained a powerful voice at the peace conference.

By his actions before Pearl Harbor, "C's" man in New York, William Stephenson, had caused anxiety at the FBI and the State Department. Now that the United States was in the war, a movement started, one led primarily by Berle and J. Edgar Hoover, to stop British intelligence and propaganda activities in the United States. On January 2 a bill was introduced into Congress that would make it an offense to conduct propaganda on U.S. territory without the consent of the U.S. government. Then followed a measure to outlaw all foreign espionage activities on U.S. territory, the McKellar Act. This bill struck directly at "C's" and Stephenson's activities in the United States and produced what Berle called in his diary "a terrific undercover row."

As Berle described the causes of that row in his diary on February 2, 1942:

Briefly, the British Intelligence who maintain a lively and not too creditable spy system (masked under the name Security Coordination Police) don't want any such act because they don't want their spy system interrupted. They intervened with the Embassy but the Embassy said they could do nothing about it. Thereupon they intervened with Bill Donovan, who promptly put in a memorandum to the President asking him to veto the bill which was on his desk. I am impressed by Donovan's courage though I don't think much of it in terms of national wisdom. Why should anybody have a spy system in the United States? And what will anyone look like a little later when someone finds out about it?

With the quiet intervention of FDR, it seemed that the administration's concerns might abate and that the act might be adjusted to allow agents of a foreign power allied to the United States to operate on U.S. territory, provided the permission of the FBI and State Department was obtained. But then somebody on the British side blundered. On February 13 Edward Tamm, an official of the FBI, warned Berle that a British secret agent, a certain Paine, was attempting to "get the dirt" on Berle's private life. The object of the operation had been to obtain information that, when leaked to the press, would discredit Berle. The FBI ordered Paine to leave the country immediately or be deported. [3]

Bristling with indignation, Berle called Derek Hoyer-Millar, a senior official at the British embassy, to his office and protested at "the attempt of the British so-called Security Coordination to spy upon and thereafter to arrange for a press campaign against a high official of the Government of the United States." Berle "requested" that the ambassador, Lord Halifax, send Berle informally "his personal word" that there would be no repetition of the incident. Hoyer-Millar undertook to convey Berle's views to the ambassador.

The disturbance simmered on until March 5, when Lord Halifax and Sir Ronald Campbell, counselor at the embassy, met Berle, Attorney General Francis Biddle, and Hoover. As Berle recorded, he "indicated that the President and the Cabinet were unhappy about Stephenson's activities and presence in the country." Berle said they had concluded that "the activities of the British Intelligence here ought to be liaison rather than operations, and, second, that they probably needed a different type of man to head it."

Lord Halifax replied that "he understood from Stephenson that "everything he did was submitted to, and passed upon by, and approved by Mr. J. Edgar Hoover," but, Berle continued, Hoover "promptly said that the statement made by Stephenson did not correspond to his impression at all." Stephenson "reported only after the fact what he had been doing, and on occasions not even then." Hoover also declared that "he had no quarrel with Mr. Stephenson, and had pleasant relations with him" but Hoover did not feel that "they were on terms of such confidence" as to "make close working relationships possible." The FBI "were never sure whether they were getting the whole story; and they knew that in many cases they were not." Hoover then discussed incidents in which "British Intelligence had tapped wires and shanghaied sailors."

When Halifax heard Berle's and Hoover's statements, he felt his "mental structure was altered on learning that there was not a close working relationship between Mr. Hoover and Mr. Stephenson." Halifax promised to investigate and remarked that "intelligence was headed up under Menzies in London, who was not a publicly known figure." At that time Attorney General Biddle asked for "first, a list of all Stephenson's men working here; and second, a careful, detailed statement of activities." Stephenson should, moreover, "cease all activities other than those of a liaison officer between the British and American intelligence services."

With that declaration the meeting adjourned, to be resumed on March 10 at the British embassy. By that time Halifax had consulted "C" and perhaps even Churchill. Halifax came down firmly on Stephenson's side. Stephenson had done nothing "except with the direct authority and cooperation of the American officials." That *must* be understood, Halifax insisted. But he did agree that Stephenson's position should be "liaison, pure and simple," and that operations should not be carried out except with the agreement of Hoover. Halifax added, too, that there were "only" 137 officials in the British intelligence service in the United States. Halifax then dismissed the American charges against Stephenson and declined to discuss the matter further.

On that uncertain note the dispute closed, but only for the moment. Stephenson was accepted as chief of the British secret service in the United States, acting purely as a liaison, and while he was permitted to operate from New York into non-American territory in the Western Hemisphere, he could do so only with the knowledge and authority of the U.S. government. The effect of that stricture was to make Stephenson more secretive in the measures he and his service took to elude Hoover's surveillance. As a result, an odd mixture of cordiality, suspicion, and irritation developed in Anglo-American intelligence relations within the United States, one that remained for the rest of the war and even into the peace.

That queer association was not confined to the United States; it was to be encountered wherever the American and the British services met, particularly in the capitals of the empire. That situation also characterized the personal relationship between "C" and "Q." It is doubtful whether "C" and Donovan ever liked each other as men, and there is some evidence that "C" actually distrusted Donovan as a political opportunist and an unregenerate Fenian. For his part Donovan regarded "C" with respect but never with affection, and it seems that "Q" never doubted that behind his calm and mild manner was a man the Irish had fought for centuries.

The full force of their antipathies had not as yet developed, although Donovan was said to have exclaimed after the first morning's business with "C" that he now knew what it must have been like when Horatio Gates tried to argue terms with General Burgoyne at the Saratoga Convention. "Perhaps," "C" replied, adding: "And I do hope that 'Q' will not suffer Gates's fate." [4]*

The differences between the two men and their services were the differences in the relationship between America and England—they were fundamental. The British believed that the Americans had been taught to dislike the English in their history books, and that American republicans intended to demolish the empire. The Americans felt, as Robert Bruce Lockhart, director-general of the Political Warfare Executive, reported in 1942: "The British had pushed the world round for the last hundred years, and now the Americans were going to do it." [5] Donovan wanted power, and "C," for operational reasons, did

---

*Horatio Gates was a British soldier, born at Maldon, Essex, in 1727. Before the American Revolution he left the British army in America and settled in West Virginia. During the revolution he joined the colonial army, became a general, and defeated General Burgoyne at Saratoga in 1777. The Continental Congress appointed Gates president of the Board of War, and he became a serious rival of George Washington. It is believed that the so-called Conway Cabal tried to make Gates president but failed, and Gates was then sent to command in the Carolinas. There he was defeated through incompetence, and he resigned in disgrace. Although regarded as an intriguer, he was reemployed by the U.S. Army. But his reputation had not recovered from his involvement with the cabal, and he died in 1806, not quite a traitor but not quite a hero, either.

not intend that he should obtain it at the expense of British national security. "C" did not propose to relinquish his primacy to an amateur such as Donovan.

As for "Q," he had become the chief of a new, rich, ambitious, aggressive, dynamic, largely untrained service that had no New Dealers and was allied closely to big business, especially big oil. He waved the flag of the four freedoms and intended to become, as Stephenson was to state, "No. 1 in the entire world."

There were agreeable moments between the two men. General Edwin L. Sibert, chief of intelligence to the commander of the U.S. forces in London, remembered that on June 4, 1943, the birthday of the patron at Eton, George III, "C," and "Q" and a mixed group of OSS and SIS men were at White's for lunch. They spent about twenty minutes at the bar drinking the traditional blackstrap and then drifted upstairs to the luncheon room, "C" and "Q" leading the way. When the two men got about halfway up they stopped and sang the chorus from the one undying song of World War I:

> Oh, mademoiselle from Armentieres, parlez-vous?
> Oh, mademoiselle from Armentieres, parlez-vous?
> Oh, mademoiselle from Armentieres,
> She hasn't been kissed in forty years.
> Hinky dinky, parlez-vous?

For the rest, their relationship ranged from zero to freezing, and, so Donovan claimed, whenever he had a meeting with Menzies at Broadway he noticed that "C's" favorite portrait, that of Edward VII with his gundogs in the heather, had been taken down and an oil portrait of George III had been put up. That, according to "C's" assistant, Patrick Reilly, was not true. But what was true was that at the top, as in all politics, the rivalry between Menzies and Donovan assumed a gentlemanly aspect—lunches at "Q's" favorite hotel, Claridge's, followed by dinners at "C's" favorite club, White's.

Earnest efforts were made to resolve their differences, especially those concerning where the secret intelligence branch of OSS London could or could not operate, and each engagement usually seemed to end in a measure of agreement. But that proved not to have been the case next day. Then "C" would find that "Q" was offering financial subsidies and liaison offices in Washington to those refugee intelligence chiefs whom Donovan felt might be useful, especially the French chief, Dewavrin, and Menzies would send a gentlemanly note to the refugee chief reminding him of the obligations he had undertaken in

1940. Their relationship was relatively good-humored, and "C" displayed great patience with Donovan, but when that patience withered, their association seemed never too far from rupture.

And the first of the serious ruptures came that June of 1942. So far as "C" was concerned, his objectives were two: to protect the secret of Ultra and to prevent Donovan from learning about the nature of his connection with Vichy, for the existence of that connection would have detonated a major political explosion in the liberal Allied press. That meant it was imperative for "C" to deny to Donovan contact with the refugee secret services in London. In obedience to that imperative, "C" conducted himself without regard to obligations that he might have to "Q." In turn that produced from Donovan ever greater pressure upon Whitney to act more independently of the British and to penetrate the refugee intelligence services. The result was that Whitney resigned on April 16.

Echoing "C's" attitude, Whitney declared in his letter of resignation that since the American and British armed forces now worked in harmony, there was no need for U.S. secret intelligence services in London. Most of the work now could be done through U.S. naval and military attachés. As for making contact with the emigré intelligence services, Whitney explained that he felt his "British connection" was "too intimate to permit me adequately to handle those relationships." Where they were "handled *through* the British, I am not needed. Where they are to be handled independently of the British, I would not be the right man." In other words Whitney was not prepared to work in Donovan's interest *against* those of "C." Whitney ended his letter in a fashion that suggested he was going to work for "C":

As to the British secret services, I will always be available for an odd errand or consultation, but it is plain in practice that you deal best directly through the British. If you want to call me in personally to help, you can get the message to me through them. [6]

Donovan was furious at what he considered "the greatest betrayal of American interests since Benedict Arnold." [7] That was a profound exaggeration of the facts concerning Whitney's association with the British, but Donovan was given to such exclamations. "C" never used Whitney as a spy against Donovan, any more than Whitney would have allowed himself to be so used. But in any case, there followed a long period in which Donovan was allowed to maintain but not operate a war station in London. Several replacements were sent to

London. All proved to be untrained zealots operating solely in the U.S. national interests. None survived until the arrival of David K. E. Bruce, an acceptable Virginian country gentleman, lawyer, and legislator of ample means who, having married into the Mellon family, epitomized all that was elegant in American society.

2 REVOLT AT BLETCHLEY

Bletchley first became fully operational by the spring of 1941, employing about 1,800 men and women (a population that rose to 9,000). The influence of Cambridge was so great that Station "X" was sometimes called "Little King's." Cambridge in the thirties resembled fifteenth-century Venice, with its little palaces (colleges), its little princes (tutors), its general citizenry (undergraduates), and the Council of Ten (the proctors). Similarly Bletchley grew up as a collection of huts, heads of sections, the workforce, and the SIS officers that administered the station. Each group was split by the need for secrecy and security into "the cliques," which lived separate existences within the structure of that strange principality of brainpower in the Chiltern Hills.

Many of the population of the war station were markedly eccentric or precious, or both, and spent much of their time quarreling and intriguing among themselves. The place seethed with passions, ambitions, tempers, fits, explosions, tantrums, loves, hates, plots, rivalries, and many conjugations thereof, just as they had done at Cambridge. "C" reigned over this world as the chancellor reigned over Cambridge or as Cesare Borgia reigned over Venice. "C," they said, was "about as remote and as God-like and just about as mysterious and powerful as The Doge." [8]

They neither understood nor cared for that special type of bureaucracy, the iron-fisted discipline that caused so much trouble between "the professionals" and "the amateurs" at Broadway and St. Albans. They were immured outside a dreary redbrick railroad town; they lived mostly in lodgings with indifferent landladies; they subsisted on such alien foods as whale steak, Woolton pie, and cod and chips; they worked a system of night-and-day shifts; the wives of the war station frequently complained; the males could not tell their wives what they were doing; they were very poorly paid; and above all they lived the existence of the provincial civil servant. Bletchley bore no resemblance to the exquisite worlds of Oxford and Cambridge, with its high tables, candlelight, and medieval ceremonies and elegances. Many indeed did not know the reason for their work.

The chief of station was still Denniston, and, concerned as he was primarily with operational problems, he ran Bletchley through Commander Edward Travis, "C's" representative at Station X. Travis was a tough customer, an ex-naval officer with a face that looked like "a study for a carving in Spam" and a "great table-thumper" in manner. Through the different prewar collegiate associations, and of the different, very secret, and highly specialized tasks that had been thrust upon Station X, a series of cliques had grown up, again not unlike the governing system that developed in medieval Venice. These cliques, too, constantly quarreled among themselves. The mathematician Isaac Jack Good had not been at Bletchley for more than ninety days when he realized that he was sitting on top of the intellectual equivalent of a time bomb.

Bletchley had come into existence in haste at the outbreak of war as a small code-breaking bureau dealing mainly with diplomatic ciphers. But within a short time, and largely through the large-scale and unexpected breach of Enigma in May 1940, Station X in the second half of 1941 had evolved into the headquarters of a signals intelligence service operations throughout the world. More than that, it was the main signals intelligence production center attacking enemy military codes and ciphers; and at the same time it had become a major, advanced research center. As Station X's responsibilities increased, so did its staff, until by the end of the summer of 1942 the population had increased to 3,293 employees. Yet in its administration and organization, Bletchley remained as it had been when it was opened at the outbreak of war—a group of cliques.

As "C" was well aware, there would be trouble at Bletchley for which he would be held responsible. In reviewing the organization, he suggested structural reforms to bring the camp under Denniston's central control. But perhaps in the flurry of developing Ultra sources still further, little was done. This was the period when the station was breaking into more and more German air force, army, naval, SS, and Abwehr codes on a scale never contemplated at the establishment.

Discontent bubbled at Station X throughout the spring and summer of 1941, mostly due to "C's" regime and staff and equipment shortages. But some of the unrest was a result of the fact that so many brilliant dons had been crammed into a small estate, forming a critical mass of talent that might prove disorderly at any moment. Aware of the discontent, Churchill visited Station X to encourage the staff, accompanied by "C," who kept well in the background. Churchill toured the entire project and appeared to be greatly impressed by what he saw and the high spirits he encountered; he described all and sundry as "the geese who lay the golden eggs and never cackled." At the end of the visit he gave a short address to a large number of Bletchleyites, using the bole of a demolished tree as a platform. He is supposed to have referred admiringly to the "conditions of creative anarchy" that he had encountered and remarked to "C" that "I know I told you to leave no stone unturned to find the necessary staff, but I didn't mean you to take me so literally." [9]

There is no doubt that those present were greatly heartened to receive two visits from illustrious personages—Cadogan and Churchill—and a movement took hold among the "creative anarchists" that a Bletchley council could run Station X better than Commander Travis. By October 1941 that view had become so pronounced that the four cryptanalysts who headed the attack on the Enigma keys—Alan Turing, Gordon Welchman, Hugh O'Dowd Alexander, and Stewart Milner-Barry—met at the Shoulder of Mutton, an inn at Old Bletchley. They decided that the crisis in manpower was so serious, and the administration so slow in dealing with it, that they would ask the prime minister personally for assistance in overcoming the problems.

As Sir Stewart Milner-Barry was to recall, the proposal came initially from Gordon Welchman, a diffident man who had been a professor of mathematics at Sidney Sussex College, Cambridge, but who also who had "fire in his belly—an ability to get things done." Together, the four cryptanalysts wrote a letter of warning and protest to Winston Churchill:

Prime Minister:
    Secret and Confidential
    Prime Minister Only

                                    21 October 1941

Dear Prime Minister,
    Some weeks ago you paid us the honour of a visit, and we believe that you regard our work as important. You will have seen that, thanks largely to the energy and foresight of Commander Travis [who was responsible for

all questions relating to cryptanalytical machinery], we have been well supplied with the "bombes" for the breaking of the German Enigma codes. We think, however, that you ought to know that all this work is being held up, and in some cases is not being done at all, principally because we cannot get sufficient staff to deal with it. Our reason for writing to you direct is that for months we have done everything we possibly can through the normal channels, and that we despair of any early improvement without your intervention. No doubt in the long run these particular requirements will be met, but meanwhile still more precious months will have been wasted, and as our needs are continually expanding we see little hope of ever being adequately staffed. [10]

The letter was long and dwelt mainly upon what was a failure of the Women's Royal Naval Service ("the Wrens") to provide a sufficient number of assistants to the cryptanalysts. It pointed out that without such assistance on a large-enough scale, the entire system of production of Ultra would collapse. Welchman then had to decide what to do with the letter to ensure that it did not pass through the routine chain of command, which lay through Travis, Denniston, and Menzies to Churchill, for they feared that Denniston in particular might not transmit it. At that point Welchman decided to go over the heads of their superior officers, including "C," and deliver the letter personally to Churchill.

Welchman dated the letter October 21, 1941, Trafalgar Day, the 136th anniversary of the Battle of Trafalgar between the British and French fleets, perhaps the greatest day in the modern history of the Royal Navy, in the belief that, being the man he was, and in light of the historical significance of the anniversary, Churchill might be better disposed to take action on the group's complaints without also instituting disciplinary action against them.

Milner-Barry was deputed to take the letter that same day to Churchill at 10 Downing Street, and he set out from Bletchley by train to London, getting as far as the hall of 10 Downing Street without difficulty. But there he was intercepted by Brigadier George S. Harvie-Watt, Churchill's parliamentary private secretary. Milner-Barry explained to Harvie-Watt that he had come from a secret establishment and was charged with the delivery of an important secret letter to the prime minister personally. Since Harvie-Watt knew nothing of Ultra, nor of the existence of Bletchley, and Milner-Barry could not tell him, Harvie-Watt was perplexed. Such was Milner-Barry's security awareness that he said nothing more about the establishment for which he worked, and Harvie-Watt declared that it was quite impossible for the prime minister to see anyone without an appointment.

Milner-Barry did not, however, lack courage or determination; he stood his ground and insisted that the matters concerned were of the highest importance to the security of the state, and that he was not empowered to discuss them with anyone who was not authorized to know about them. He had no Foreign Office pass to prove his identity, and he had nothing that would prove he was on secret business. But he was able to show that he was present when the prime minister visited Bletchley. Harvie-Watt knew of that visit, and while he continued to insist that Milner-Barry could not see the prime minister without an appointment, he did promise to place the letter unopened before Churchill personally, without going through his private office.

Satisfied, Milner-Barry gave Harvie-Watt the letter, and he then left 10 Downing Street to return to Bletchley. There the quartet "awaited the wrath of God," fully conscious that, having taken the unprecedented step of going over the heads of the entire chain of command, "C" was not going to like this.

Harvie-Watt was as good as his word. He did place the letter before Churchill, and Churchill reacted as the Bletchley quartet had hoped he would, with speed and purpose. Churchill wrote to "C" through his chief of staff, Ismay, on October 22:

ACTION THIS DAY
Make sure they have all they want on extreme priority and report to me that this had been done. [11]

And, as Milner-Barry recalled, Menzies appeared at Bletchley and "was very cross." He had a "private session" with Welchman, to whom "C" delivered "a vigorous sort of rocket" for having gone over the heads of his superior officers in writing directly to the prime minister. Menzies then went to see Denniston, the director of GC&CS, and, as Milner-Barry recalled, "from that moment things began to happen." [12]

Staff requirements at Bletchley Park were given "extreme priority," and on November 18, 1941, Menzies reported to Churchill that "every possible measure was being taken." Though the new arrangements were not then entirely completed, Bletchley's needs were being "very rapidly met." [13] So they were; but by the end of the year anarchy again threatened the establishment. And the official historian noted that "the spate of argument and recrimination was damaging efficiency and threatening a breakdown of discipline." [14] "C" therefore appointed an independent investigator, General K. J. Martin, a former deputy director of military intelligence, and by February 1942 Menzies had the investigator's report before him and acted ruthlessly.

In what was one of "C's" unhappier decisions, he replaced his old friend Alastair Denniston as director. "C's" reason: As long as Denniston was director, Bletchley would remain a series of cliques and would never become the highly integrated, mechanistic center for the production of decodes that "C" needed to deal with the volume of the intercepts and, at the same time, produce the high morale needed for such work. Denniston's place was taken by Commander Travis. "C" gave himself the new title of director-general of Government Communications Headquarters, the new name for GC&CS, and Denniston was appointed deputy director in charge of diplomatic and commercial code breaking. Denniston was then moved out of Bletchley and back to London, together with the diplomatic section.

As part of what was a judgment of Solomon, "C" also placed the military and air sections in charge of Air Ministry and War Office representatives at Bletchley. Still under "C's" control, Denniston and the diplomatic section were housed in a seven-floor building in Mayfair behind the facade of Madame Riche, couturiere des dames. For months after that supersecret group took possession—they were responsible for attacking the German, Japanese, Arabian, and clandestine Hebrew, Portuguese, Spanish, "and other" political ciphers for "C"*—distinguished ladies called to see their favorite clothes de-

---

*Until Pearl Harbor, the Diplomatic Section was reading the State Department's cipher. On February 25, 1942, in a personal letter to FDR, Churchill wrote:

My dear Mr. President,

One night when we talked late, you spoke of the importance of our cipher people getting into close touch with yours. I shall be very ready to put any expert you care to nominate in touch with my technicians. Ciphers for our two Navies have been and are continually a matter for frank discussion between our two Services. But diplomatic and military ciphers are of equal importance, and we appear to know nothing officially of your versions of these. Some time ago, however, our experts claimed to have discovered the system and constructed some tables used by your Diplomatic Corps. From the moment when we became allies, I gave instructions that this work should cease. However, danger of our enemies having achieved a measure of success cannot, I am advised, be dismissed.

I shall be grateful if you will handle this matter entirely yourself, and if possible burn this letter when you have read it. The whole subject is secret in a degree which affects the safety of both our countries. The fewest possible people should know.

I take advantage of the Ambassador's homeward journey to send you this by his hand, to be delivered into yours personally. . . . [15]

signer, and on occasions several penetrated into the inner sanctum, to be puzzled by the silence and the all-male, official-looking staff members who intercepted them and escorted them back to the street.

Denniston was bitter at his removal, for at that moment his prospects of a knighthood vanished. Something of a vendetta grew up in the Denniston family against "C" in the mistaken belief that Menzies had ploughed Denniston under to strengthen his control of that turbulent dominion. "C" moved Denniston because if he was kept at Bletchley, all attempts at reform would be blocked. Since "C" himself disliked reform, the poacher had turned gamekeeper; but his reason was pure—what had begun as a cottage industry was now a major undertaking and required special management.

And although Travis exercised his new powers so authoritatively that he came to enjoy the nickname "der Fuehrer," the passions at Bletchley began to subside, and from that moment forward GC&CS embarked upon "what was to become an all but unbroken chain of success against the enemy's high- and medium-grade Service and police cyphers." [16] In that unbroken chain of success "C" owed much to a source called "K."

3 SOURCE "K"

By the summer of 1942 "C" was able to report that GC&CS had conquered twenty-six German army and air force keys, representing about half of the fifty-odd different keys then in use throughout the two German services. These sources were providing "C" with thirty-nine thousand signals a month (twenty-five thousand army and German air force, fourteen thousand navy). Thus Ultra had become the principal source of intelligence in the Atlantic theater, as Magic had become the main source of intelligence in the war in the Pacific. But of all the sources of intelligence that enabled the cryptanalysts to "unbutton" the German keys, few were more important than Colonel Gustav Bertrand of the Deuxieme Bureau, the officer whose contact with the German traitor Hans Thilo-Schmitt enabled the Poles, French, and British to penetrate Enigma in the first place.[17]

Just before the fall of France in 1940, the French equivalent of

Bletchley, P.C. Bruno, was quietly demobilized and its personnel scattered to the four winds. Although German technical experts conducted a large investigation into French cryptographic work going back to the turn of the century, *no* evidence was found that Enigma was compromised. On the contrary, everything they found confirmed them in the belief that Enigma was beyond penetration. Bertrand had succeeded in evacuating his Spanish and Polish cryptographic teams to Algiers, where they went underground in the care of the French secret service. They were, therefore, never available to the Germans for interrogation. Bertrand himself was not identified with P.C. Bruno, nor did the Germans discover its existence.

In due course Bertrand presented himself for demobilization at Vichy, the new French capital. On July 8, 1940, he proposed to "his chief"—he was never identified—that he be allowed to restart "my factory" under another name in the unoccupied zone of France. That proposal was "not welcomed with enthusiasm" because it implied reviving the liaison that had existed between P.C. Bruno and Bletchley. "The chief" wanted nothing to do with "C" after the British attacked the French fleet at Mers-el-Kebir. But "the chief" did agree to the establishment of a new signals intelligence organization, one code-named P.C. Cadix, under Bertrand's sole command.

Bertrand recovered the archives of P.C. Bruno, which contained the technical data obtained through the Anglo-French-Polish attack on Enigma in the 1930s. With due regard for French property laws, and financed, it appears, from the appropriation of the Bureau M[enees] A[ntinationale], an organization established to guard the purity of the Vichy French ideology against foreign influences, a château was purchased in a remote corner of the free zone of France. This was the Château des Fouzes, not far from Uzes on the road toward Bagnols-sur-Ceze, in the Gard, a beautiful mountainous region with rural fertile valleys. Authority for these purchases came from General Maxim Weygand, who was creating an infrastructure for reintroduction of France into the war against Germany, a task in which he failed and for which he was sent to a concentration camp.

The château appeared to belong to "a M. et Mme. Barsac"—Bertrand—who held them in trust for the outlawed French secret service. Its existence as an outpost of the French secret service was unknown except to "the chief" in Vichy, but it did receive the protection of the ORA organization, Ajax, which warned *resistants* if they became the subject of German or hostile Vichy French interest. To dissuade chatelaines of the area from calling, rumors were spread that the château was "in the hands of Communists," a story that helped mightily to keep away the curious and the dangerous.

By October 1, 1940, both the old "D" team of P.C. Bruno, mainly Spaniards, and the "Z" team of Polish cryptanalysts had been brought back from Algiers and reassembled at P.C. Cadix. In all, there were thirty-two persons at the château, all paid monthly and surreptitiously by B.A. Vichy. Three motor vehicles were always ready to evacuate them in the event of a German or Vichy raid, which was an expectation at all times. Given the chaos and terror of the times in France, all this was remarkable, and "C" always held that it was the most extraordinary piece of secret service work carried out under hostile circumstances of the war.

But the most remarkable phase had yet to begin. The task of P.C. Cadix was to keep "the chief" advised of German *and* British activity within France. To keep "the chief" informed, therefore, required certain equipment that, Bertrand knew, could be obtained only at one factory in Paris. This equipment consisted of components of Enigma still being manufactured for Bertrand, as they were before the fall. To get to Paris he had to board the mainline express at Vichy, which required a special pass, and undergo a special check at Moulins en route; to get out of the station at Paris he had to undergo a further check.

All this Bertrand succeeded in accomplishing by obtaining a special, high-ranking orange *ausweis* that was given to him as the manager of a factory at Grasse, the center of the French perfume industry, which represented him as delivering perfume essences to Paris for production into perfume for sale to the German armed forces. In all, Bertrand made twenty-six journeys to Paris and suffered no embarrassment or indignity at any time from any of the German army railway police who traveled on each train—his work was, it seems, too important.

At some stage during 1942—the precise date is not known— Bertrand went to Maxim's, that most famous of all restaurants, for dinner. While there he met an official of the German embassy, whom he identified only as "Max." Although Bertrand was not fluent in German and "Max" was not fluent in French, they became firm friends, although sometimes they had to resort to a dictionary to make themselves understood. Bertrand, who was infinitely more subtle and clever with other men, never declared whether he turned "Max" into a traitor. He did claim that "Max" was not "another Asche"—a reference to the German who had sold him the original Enigma secrets in the mid-thirties. But from time to time Bertrand did hint that "Max" was far from being the devout Nazi that his position in Paris might have indicated, and that he was a very high ranking man.

Bertrand visited "Max" at the German embassy, and as Bertrand was to record, "After a while the concierge saluted me when I arrived and once even the guard presented arms. In return, I saluted the portrait of Hitler at the head of the staircase with the necessary 'Heil Hitler!' " Bertrand also stated that "Max" enabled him to travel between Vichy and Paris so frequently without hazard from the German control authorities, who were very vigilant. "Max" made Bertrand the escort for the German diplomatic mail sent between the embassy in Paris and the German Armistice Control Commission at Vichy. "Max" provided him with the special metal pass of a German diplomatic courier, and Bertrand was able to transport the equipment necessary for P.C. Cadix as German diplomatic mail. It also, it appears, enabled Bertrand to render "le colonel Ming-eez" the greatest service since Bertrand handed over the data he had received through his subornation of "Asche," alias Schmitt.

The facts are vague, but Denniston was to record in a 1944 paper on the work of GC&CS between 1919 and 1944 that he noted in 1919, when he and "C" worked together against foreign ciphers at the Paris peace conference, the German diplomatic delegation at that conference introduced two new new ciphers to ensure the security of their communications with the German government. One of the systems was the one-time pad; the other one had no technical name and was, therefore, called "floradora." [18]

Although GC&CS worked on the cipher on and off throughout the interwar years, and although they discovered what the system was, they "diagnosed it as unbreakable" until 1942, when there occurred what Denniston called in one place in his paper "an amazing scrap of physical compromise." In another place, referring again to floradora, he described what he called "three chances. 1. The basic book fell into our hands. 2. Close co-operation with USA. 3. S[ecret]S[ervice] work by an able ally who obtained first hand information and one page of figures from a German cypher officer." Almost certainly this officer was Bertrand and "Max" was either head of chancellery at the German embassy, the official who controlled the cipher room operations, or the head of the German cipher office. Denniston is, however, unclear about the extent to which the "three chances" enabled GC&CS to "unbutton" the German diplomatic cipher, although he does state that floradora was "broken in 1942" thanks to those "three chances." Later events suggest that Allen Dulles of OSS Berne and Philby of Section V provided technical evidence in 1943 that led to the large-scale decryption of floradora from late 1943 onward.

For the moment, however, it seems Bertrand had provided the vital connecting technical evidence between the basic discoveries of 1919 and the interwar years and the ability to read the German diplomatic cipher in 1942. If so, this was an astounding conquest, one made the greater by Bertrand's skill, devotion, and daring. But, he claimed, he never knew who "Max" was, and their association came to an end in January 1944 under very dangerous circumstances.

For the moment in the history of P.C. Cadix, it is necessary to state only, as does Bertrand, that "one element was missing." That element was a radio transmitter with which to restart liaison with Broadway and Bletchley. Arrangements were soon made with "C" and Dunderdale, despite an order from Bertrand's chief that he was to give the British nothing that was of "operational value." By that "the chief" meant presumably that he was to give "C" nothing that was of cryptographic operational value. If he did, then Bertrand disobeyed that order, at great cost to himself.

After much secret communication, Bertrand and Commander Dunderdale met in the hothouse of the Botanical Gardens in Lisbon in March 1941. There, Dunderdale turned over the transceiver. Bertrand then transferred the transceiver to the French secret service representative in Lisbon, who consigned it to Vichy in the diplomatic pouch. It was collected in good operational order by Bertrand on his return to Vichy and then taken by him for installation at P.C. Cadix.

It was now necessary for Bertrand to obtain German wireless intercepts, the raw material of cryptanalysis, for Bertrand himself possessed no intercept stations. These intercepts were obtained, again in remarkable circumstances, from one of the great heroes of the French subterranean world, Gabriel Louis Charles Romon, a communications expert with the French posts and telegraphs organization, P.T.T.

In his mid-thirties, and the head of technical services at P.C. Bruno before the armistice, Romon was attached to the Groupement des Controles Radioelectriques de l'Interieur, the mission of which was to locate the clandestine transmissions of resistance and other illegal organizations. This organization was established with the agreement of the Germans under the provisions of the armistice. But

Romon was a determined French patriot who really worked for ORA, the resistance organization within the French army of which General Revers was chief of staff. One of Romon's main functions was to provide Bertrand with the radio intercepts obtained by his six intercept stations in France, and his headquarters at Hauterive, near Vichy.

Although under constant German surveillance, with the exercise of skill and cunning Romon managed to seem to be obeying the terms of the armistice and the requirements of the German Control Commission and the Vichy government while in reality working as an ORA communications center. At first Bertrand collected the results of GCR's intercept operations and took them to P.C. Cadix each week. Then, from February 1942, because the delays between interception and decryption were too long, Romon succeeded in passing the intercepts to P.C. Cadix quickly by means of the air postal service aircraft, which continued to operate in France under Luftwaffe control at both departure and arrival points. Despite that control, neither Bertrand, who collected the bag after each flight at Nîmes, not far from the château, nor Romon was caught. These intercepts were of great value to Broadway and Bletchley, to which Bertrand communicated the most important over Dunderdale's wireless each day.

As Bertrand shows, this was heavy traffic and, therefore, dangerous to handle, for the Funkabwehr, the German wireless intelligence service, was cunning and competent in detecting prolonged transmissions such as were emitted by P.C. Cadix each day. Much of the intercept material provided by Romon derived from Source "K," the taps placed by Romon on the long lines that connected Paris with Berlin through Metz and Strassbourg, and especially the tap that existed for many months on the long line that passed through the small country town of Noisy-le-Grand outside Paris.

In sum, Romon's intercepts consisted of Gestapo, German army, Luftwaffe, kriminalpolizei, German Control Commission, embassy, Sicherheitsdienst, Abwehr, and other German traffic that passed over the land lines and was not, therefore, available to Bletchley. The traffic included, according to Bertrand's account of it, military, political, economic, diplomatic, aviation, and intelligence administrative, operational, and secret service activities concerning Austria, Belgium, Bulgaria, Crete, Denmark, France, Holland, Hungary, Libya, Poland, Rhodes, Syria, Czechoslovakia, the USSR, and Yugoslavia.

On receipt, the traffic was decrypted by the Poles and Spaniards at P.C. Cadix and was then transmitted by Bertrand and his French colleagues to the SIS wireless station at Hanslope Park in Buckinghamshire in SIS ciphers. Bertrand had a special cipher reserved to himself for communications between himself and Dunderdale, and as Bertrand recorded of the volume of traffic between P.C. Cadix and Hanslope Park between March 1, 1941, and November 5, 1942, the number of messages sent totaled 2,748 (or 228,771 groups of cipher). The number of messages received from "Y"—the code letter for Broadway—was 2,296 (152,879 groups). This link functioned for 610 days; the volume sent and received was therefore about eight telegrams a day, or 625 groups of cipher and an average of three hours of transmission time each day. And as Bertrand himself was to exclaim at the volume of traffic, which was to bring about his downfall, "What a pasture for the Funkabwehr!"

Indeed it was to prove to be a pasture for the Funkabwehr, the radio-locating service of the Germans in France. Soon, all too soon for "C" and Bertrand, the first German radio location vans were seen circling Uzes with their crews dressed in the dark blue overalls of repairmen of the posts and telegraphs service.

Against that background "C" received his directives concerning the first Allied counteroffensive of the war, Torch. The Combined Chiefs of Staff elected to invade French Algeria, Morocco, and Tunisia to establish a southern front from which to strike at the southern ramparts of Fortress Europe. Of all the operations of World War II, Torch was at once the most difficult and dangerous, the one least likely to succeed. The operation entailed the sailing of one great task force across four thousand miles of the North Atlantic from the Maine and Virginia ports at a time when the ocean was not fully under Allied control, with two more sailing across eighteen hundred miles of embattled ocean from Scottish ports.

In reviewing the operational proposals, "C" decided that Torch could succeed only if the enemy were taken by surprise. Surprise could only be achieved through good security. Security might be achieved if the enemy intelligence services were not only mystified and misled about Allied intentions, but were also thrown into basic confusion during the pre-Torch period. Here, then, was one of the reasons, and perhaps the main reason, why "C" agreed to an action to kill a German intelligence and counterespionage officer whom Hitler called "the man with the iron heart."

4 THE KILLING OF REINHARDT HEYDRICH

Although OSS was forever dreaming up schemes to kill or kidnap Hitler, "C" believed that since no such operation could work, British interests were best served by keeping Hitler in his present position: as long as he was "Führer," no really efficient strategist could emerge to take command of the war—as had occurred in World War I when the Hindenburg-Ludendorff coalition had emerged to replace Kaiser Wilhelm II as supreme commander—and create more trouble for the Grand Alliance than it had already. But there were men in Hitler's administration who *were* dangerous, and one of them was Reinhardt Tristan Eugen Heydrich.

Heydrich's father was an opera singer, and his mother was an actress. He was named, therefore, after one of the characters in Wagner's opera *Tristan und Isolde*. Born in 1904 at Halle in the Teutoburg forest, Heydrich was the apotheosis of the Nazi doctrine of Nordic racial supremacy. Everything he did he did well. An excellent naval officer, he passed his examinations for entry into naval intelligence with honors. He could speak English, French, and Russian beautifully. He became an excellent aviator. As a violinist, he made women weep with his beautiful fingerwork and his mellow, delicate tone. In appearance he was tall, slim, blond, with a thin Van Dyck face and an excellent figure in the midnight black and silver of an obergruppenführer in the Schutzstaffel. He flew and fenced like a master. His wife, a Miss von Osten, was also the apotheosis of the Hitler *madchen*, with golden ringlets, long white dress, white stockings, and black shoes: the virgin at the SS ball.

Anxious to further her betrothed's career, in 1931 Miss von Osten had introduced Heydrich to Heinrich Himmler, who then had a chicken farm at Waltrudering near Munich. Himmler, a pedant by trade and, it was suspected, a pederast by inclination, was immediately impressed by young Heydrich's high intelligence and good looks. Then in charge of the Nazi party's security section, Himmler gave Heydrich exactly twenty minutes to write a plan for the formation of the Party's secret intelligence and security service. Heydrich wrote the plan on time and was given the job of establishing the Sicherheitsdienst.

Heydrich rose quickly in the Nazi councils of power. His chief talent, a young Walter Schellenberg recorded, was his "incredibly acute perception of the moral, human, professional, and political weaknesses of others." [19] In 1941 Schellenberg was appointed by Heydrich from the counterespionage section of the Sicherheitsdienst to the post of chief of the foreign secret intelligence branch, largely through the efforts of Miss von Osten, who was taking as much interest in Schellenberg's career in 1941 as she had in her husband's a decade before. As Schellenberg was to define his relationship with the wife of a man as powerful and merciless as Heydrich, they became firm friends. Although there was much gossip about the relationship at headquarters in the Prinz Albrechtstrasse in Berlin, "there was never any foundation for the suggestion that this friendship was other than innocent." [20]

As "C" knew, if Heydrich was assassinated, then the Sicherheitsdienst, the most formidable of the German services, would be greatly weakened, for if Schellenberg was cunning enough to take it over, he could not do so for long because of ill health. He had suffered a heart attack through the excitement of the Venlo undertaking and now had severe liver and gall bladder trouble through the case of suspected poisoning at Lisbon while there to arrange the kidnapping of the duke of Windsor. Furthermore, he was a defeatist who wanted to strike a deal with "C" against the Russians. So, with the treason, disaffection, and defeatism in the General Staff's secret service, the Abwehr of Canaris, the German intelligence community would be greatly disadvantaged by Heydrich's death, while "C" would be greatly convenienced.

"C" found Heydrich's superefficient counterespionage service made it difficult for Dansey to get his men into Fortress Europe, or at least it was Heydrich who made their survival problematical. Heydrich had already liquidated A54, the Abwehr officer turned Czech spy whom "C" considered to be such an important and reliable source that armies marched on the strength of his word. Moreover, "C" had evidence that Heydrich was soon to be sent to France to put an end to the burgeoning underground movement. That included ORA, and Bertrand and all the Allied agent chains were, therefore, at risk.

In 1941 Heydrich became reichsprotektor of Bohemia and Moravia; on February 22, 1942, the interrogation of A54 had begun; and to make matters worse, on May 21, 1942, Heydrich and Canaris met at Heydrich's headquarters in Hradcany Castle, the great Gothic residence of the kings of Bohemia on the peak of a hill overlooking Prague and the river Moldau. Here Heydrich accused Canaris of "political unreliability"—a crime akin to treason in the Third Reich

—and charged also that "at certain levels" there was "unfortunate inefficiency." [21] Heydrich then "commended" to Canaris the acceptance of what came to be known as "Heydrich's decalogue," a system for the efficient operation of the German counterespionage services in which the Sicherheitsdienst obtained primacy over the Abwehr.

Unless "C" was careful and acted forcibly, he would find himself confronted by an efficient German intelligence coalition. And where would "C's" agents be then? They were finding it hard enough to survive and operate with a divided service. How much more formidable would the German counterespionage service become if "Heydrich's decalogue" was put into effect? Informally at the Joint Intelligence Committee—matters such as assassination were never put on paper—"C" indicated to Brigadier Colin Gubbins, chief of the London Group at the headquarters of the Special Operations Executive, that he would not object if Gubbins proposed the assassination of Heydrich. However, "C" did acknowledge that in the *ratissage*— French counterespionage terms dominated Broadway, and this one meant, literally, "rat-hunt" or, technically, the manhunt that always followed an SOE coup de main—the Czech secret service might suffer badly. Colonel Franciscek Moravec, head of the Czech service in London, did not object, however, and he provided Gubbins with two assassination agents known as the Anthropoids. Their names were Jan Kubis and Josef Gabcik, both of whom possessed British army paybooks. They were parachuted into the Bohemian hills near a village called Lidice by the light of the December half-moon of 1941. With them went a wireless operator, a Lieutenant Bartos, and three cipher clerks. All landed safely and submerged into the extensive Czech underground.

On May 23, 1942, through a stroke of good fortune, an antique clock in Heydrich's office at Hradcany Castle gave trouble, and Josef Novotny, a repairman, was called to make it work. As he examined the clock Novotny noticed a piece of paper with Heydrich's itinerary on it for May 27. He screwed the itinerary into a ball and threw it into the wastepaper basket, from which it was retrieved later by one of the charladies, Maria Rasnerova. Shortly the itinerary was in the hands of Kubis and Gabcik, who now planned the killing for just outside the Prague suburb of Holesovice at the point where the Prague–Dresden road makes a hairpin bend down to Troja Bridge. At that point Heydrich's chauffeur would be compelled to slow down in order to negotiate the bend.

At 9:30 A.M. on May 27, Kubis and Gabcik were in position, with Gabcik's lover, Rena Fafek, some distance away to signal the approach of Heydrich's big green Mercedes. Right on time Heydrich's car, unescorted, came into view. The Anthropoids opened fire and rolled grenades under the car. They then vanished on cycles, leaving Heydrich for dead. But Heydrich was not dead, although he was badly wounded. He tried to give chase, firing at his attackers as they pedaled away. Then he collapsed and was taken to a hospital.

At first his wounds were thought to be slight; an X ray revealed a broken rib and some fragments of metal and cloth in his stomach. The doctors decided to operate to extract the debris, which was found to be small pieces of burned leather, upholstery, and uniform cloth near the spleen, with shreds in the pleura. The operation was successful, the debris was extracted, and it was felt that Heydrich would survive. And he would have done so, had there been antibiotics. But there were none, and he contracted blood poisoning and gangrene and died on June 4.

Heydrich's successor, Karl Hermann Frank, was appointed immediately and decided to administer "a special repressive action to give the Czechs a lesson in propriety." All the inhabitants of Lidice, the village that had sheltered the Anthropoids, were killed and the village leveled. All the Anthropoids were trapped and executed, and Heydrich was given a state funeral.

Guarded by the Leibstandarten SS Adolf Hitler, Hitler's personal bodyguard, Heydrich's coffin was lashed onto the breech of a rubber-tired cannon and taken to the Reichschancellery on the Wilhelmstrasse for the state obsequies. Hitler wore a black band on his dove-gray tunic and, laying a wreath of orchids beside the coffin, declared that Heydrich was "one of the greatest defenders of our greater German ideal." He was "the man with the iron heart." [22]

At the cemetery, Himmler spoke to the assembled officers, who included Brigadeführer SS Schellenberg, of "your murdered chief," and abjured them all to give of their best in that "special sector" where their work "still did not compare with the work of the British secret service"—that mystique again. The swastika-draped bier was then unloaded, Heydrich's death mask was placed on the flag, and Schellenberg was to write how he was struck by what he called the "deceptive features of uncanny spirituality and entirely perverted beauty, like a Renaissance Cardinal." [23]

Among the other mourners, Schellenberg noticed, was Canaris, whose vivid blue eyes brimmed with tears and whose voice choked with emotion. "He was a great man," Canaris said to Schellenberg. "I have lost a friend in him." But the reality for Canaris was that Heydrich's murder had come not a moment too soon, for, it was to emerge, at the time of his death he was under Hitler's orders to set down his post as reichsprotektor of Bohemia and Moravia and proceed to Paris as the *höher SS und polizeiführer*, the man responsible for the ideological purity, loyalty, and security of France. And if Heydrich had taken up that post, the clandestine war inevitably would have been much more ferocious than it became.

Heydrich, "C's" cleverest enemy, was dead. If we do not know how he reacted to that news, we may assume at least that he had an extra glass of kummel that night at White's. What "C" may not have known at that time was that at the obsequies in Berlin Himmler also addressed all the senior officers of the Reichsicherheitshauptamt (RHSA), which Heydrich had also commanded and which was the highest headquarters for all SS and party intelligence, security, and ideological control throughout the greater German Reich. In adding the RHSA to his own swelling empire during that speech, Himmler mentioned Schellenberg alone by name and described him as being "the Benjamin of our Leadership Corps." After the funeral Himmler spoke to Schellenberg privately and declared that, according to Schellenberg in his final interrogation report by "C's" organization, "although Schellenberg was young, he considered him as diligent, trustworthy, and incorruptible in money matters."

From that moment forward Schellenberg began to enjoy some of Heydrich's powers and much of Himmler's private confidence. As Schellenberg's final interrogation report also showed, his conduct remained consistent with a man who intended to overthrow Hitler, appoint Himmler as an interim führer while Schellenberg went to London as ambassador to negotiate a peace with the British, destroy Russia, liquidate Himmler, and then appoint himself as chancellor of the greater German Reich—an ambition that bespoke the surreal quality of life within the reich's intelligence services. [24]

Against that background, the armed forces of the Grand Alliance prepared their greatest military undertaking, Torch, with the German intelligence services in disarray and corroded by treasonable thoughts.

5 THE TORCH PERIOD

Torch was to be the first major test of how well "C's" and Donovan's organizations could cooperate. To help him meet that test, "C" accepted Cadogan's proposal to bring in a personal assistant from the Foreign Office to advise him on the political aspects of secret operations and the needs of the Foreign Office in the collection of secret intelligence and to bring Broadway into closer, more direct contact than was possible through the occasional meetings between "C" and Cadogan. The man who came to Broadway was Patrick Reilly, son of Sir D'Arcy Reilly of the Indian civil service.

Reilly arrived in September 1942 and took an office across the passage from "C's" office. What Reilly discovered was not an orderly process of state business, but a sort of "organized chaos" in which "C's" health was being undermined through the morass of work that, unnecessarily, engulfed him each day. As Reilly later defined what he believed was Broadway's chief weakness:

At Broadway there were an extraordinary collection of characters, but among the more senior people there was jolly few who had been to university. This struck me so much when I got there, for, I believed then as I do now, that the main benefit of a university education is and was that it taught you to look at issues on their merits, and to try and eliminate emotion and prejudice in making judgements. I found that recommendations from the staff to "C" tended to be full of slant, bias and prejudice. . . .I found that "C" was not being given an honest account of the facts. Dansey was a prime example, and Vivian and Cowgill were pretty guilty of it, too. Winterbotham was amongst the worst. As a result there was about Broadway an atmosphere of prejudice, bias, that people were not looking at things dispassionately and honestly. [25]

The second most important weakness, Reilly felt, was the absence of an orderly decision-making process. Having burrowed into the inner structure of the secret service, Reilly secured "C's" permission to undertake administrative reforms. Surprisingly, given her power, he also won the cooperation of the formidable Miss Pettigrew. The system of "ugly rushes" whenever "C's" green light came on was abandoned. All who wished to see "C" had first to submit their proposal in writing along with the papers to Miss Pettigrew, and she then sent the documents forward to Reilly. If he thought the proposal of sufficient importance, it was sent to "C." All files sent to "C" were reduced to the minimum necessary to make a case, and the system whereby an entire file went to him was abandoned.

In effect, Reilly, who was then only thirty-three, became "C's" deputy. "C" was delighted that somebody had come in with enough authority, tact, diligence, and time to take some of the weight off him. A close bond developed between the two men, one in which the element of compassion proved strong. So far as is known, Reilly was the only man in Whitehall to whom Menzies confided that his wife was anorexic. Reilly, too, had tragedy in his life—one of his daughters, a brilliant child, had caught whooping cough at school. She had become a permanent invalid and was about to be committed to a home where she was to spend the rest of her life.

"C" was much moved by this tragedy and was especially impressed by the realization that a man carrying such a burden could devote himself to his work so completely as Reilly. But order was not achieved without cost—Reilly lasted a year before he found himself "worked out." As Reilly wrote to his father in India upon his appointment, without revealing what his work was: "I have been extraordinarily lucky to get this job, which is a remarkable experience for a chap in our service. And my master couldn't be a nicer chap to serve. He has a terrific job, and much of it he does superbly well." [26]

With Reilly's appointment, "C" entered what may be called the Torch period of his career. The British Eighth Army in Egypt under General Sir Bernard Montgomery would first strike westward toward Tripoli. Then an American army was to land from ports in Scotland, Maine, and Virginia and seize a number of ports between Casablanca and Algiers. When the Americans had captured Algiers, the British First Army was to land to the east of Algiers and seize Tunis, the capital of French Tunisia, and Bizerta, the main port, *before* the Italo-German armies could launch a counterriposte and land in Tunisia themselves.

All these operations were to be concentrated within a span of no more than a month, and, as always in major amphibious operations, success lay in surprise. The enemy was to be kept guessing until the last moment about where the Allied task forces would invade, and that implied a combination of vigilance and security of the first order. An additional major factor had to be considered. If bloodshed was to be minimized during the landings on French territory, then the co-operation of the French army in North Africa had to be obtained before the landings. Since relations between the United States and

Vichy France were thought to be better than those enjoyed by England, Donovan's organization became responsible for all clandestine operations on French territory intended to procure French cooperation in Torch.

Outside French North Africa, and especially in Spain, which, it was feared, would enter the war on the side of Germany if Allied armies landed in North Africa, clandestine operations were the responsibility of "C's" services and of SOE. "C" was also aware that the Donovan organization might be liquidated. As late as April of 1942 Donovan's future, and that of his organization, appeared to be so much in doubt that Field Marshal Sir John Dill, the chief British representative on the Combined Chiefs of Staff in Washington, sent Whitehall the following warning: "Donovan's stock is in my opinion falling," that his "whole status is under discussion on a high U.S. level," and that the British should do nothing concerning their relationship with him that would put the country "in wrong with" the U.S. service departments. [27]

Benson also warned Menzies in similar terms, and in May FDR was reported by the British embassy—accurately—to have remarked to Berle that "he had been trying to get a brigadier-generalship for the Colonel; after which he was thinking of putting him on some nice, quiet, isolated island, where he could have a scrap with some Japs every morning before breakfast. Then he thought the Colonel would be out of trouble and be entirely happy." [28]

As a consequence "C" began to build an espionage organization with clandestine communications with Gibraltar *in parallel* to Donovan's work, but not known to him. This organization was to lay silent in French North Africa and start actual operations only if the Donovan organization collapsed, and then only at the personal command of "C." Thus there were two Allied clandestine organizations forming in French North Africa. In June, while Donovan was in London, Roosevelt suddenly and unexpectedly abolished the Office of Coordinator of Information (COI), carved off its largest branch, that responsible for political warfare, and made it into a separate department. He then authorized the establishment of a new organization, the Office of Strategic Services (OSS), and transferred control to the U.S. chiefs of staff.

The "fly-by-night civilian organization headed up by a wild colonel trying to horn in on the war"—as Donovan's rivals called his organization—now became a military organization subject to military law and discipline. Donovan was almost sent out to some Pacific island but succeeded in hanging on. But there were serious doubts that OSS would be able to handle its responsibilities, and "C's" actions to establish network and communications organizations parallel to OSS were formally authorized, although their existence remained unknown to Donovan.

"C" had a number of responsibilities under Torch. First, he was required to keep the Allied commanders in chief advised about the whereabouts of the powerful U-boat forces in the North Atlantic, so that the naval task forces could be routed around them. Second, he was to keep the Allied commander in chief, General Eisenhower, informed of what the enemy thought the Allies intended, so that if the hostile intelligence services caught wind of true Allied intentions, "C" then could provide Eisenhower with due warning, and alternative plans could be adopted. Third, "C" was to inform the chief of the deception organization of the degree to which the enemy was accepting the Allied cover plans.

These cover plans indicated that the targets were Dakar in French West Africa, combined with a landing in Norway and, to explain the large concentrations of Allied shipping in and about Gibraltar, a major resupply operation to the key British naval and air base of Malta. All these operations placed large responsibilities upon Broadway, Bletchley, and St. Albans, the headquarters town outside London of Section V.

Beyond this, "C" acted to maintain control of all intelligence operations in the Atlantic and Mediterranean theaters. In the first place, he acted to prevent the careless use of Ultra that might betray its existence to the enemy. This required great tact, for the commander of Torch was to be an American officer, General Eisenhower, a man with little prior experience of inter-Allied operations and none at all of actual warfare—he had not yet commanded even a battalion in action when he was placed in command of an army group in what was the most complicated politico-military operation of World War II. "C" had no reason to suppose that Eisenhower was experienced in the ways of Ultra. To ensure that Eisenhower understood the importance of Ultra, Churchill personally inducted the new commander in chief into the secret at a meeting at 10 Downing Street soon after Eisenhower's arrival in London, one that, Churchill intended, should be followed by a formal briefing on what Eisenhower could and could not do with "the golden eggs."

At the same time, Eisenhower was given a copy of the Anglo-American security agreements governing the use of Ultra. That document explained that "Special Intelligence"—SIS called it "MSS" or "Most Secret Source" intelligence—was "the designated term for highly secret information obtained by intercepting and reading enemy messages which have been enciphered in cryptographic systems of a high security classification." [29] As the regulations continued:

The extreme importance of Special Intelligence as a source of reliable information concerning enemy activities and intentions has been repeatedly proved. Preservation of this source requires that the enemy be given no reason to suspect that his communications are being read. If from any document which might fall into his hands, from any message he might intercept, from any word revealed by a prisoner of war, or from any ill-considered action taken upon the basis of such intelligence, the enemy were given cause to believe that his communications are not adequately safeguarded against the interception which he knows to be employed against him, he would effect changes which would deprive us of knowledge of his operations on all fronts. Extreme secrecy is therefore required and these regulations are to be strictly observed.

To avoid a situation arising similar to that at Crete the year before, all messages or other documents with special intelligence contained the code word "Ultra" buried within the body to indicate the source. No less than sixteen pages of regulations governed who could read Ultra, how it was to be handled, and how and when it could be used as the basis for action against the enemy. These were complex, technical, and legalistic but phrased with clarity so that, as Winterbotham was to remark, "even a general might understand them."

The document, once signed, placed *absolute* responsibility upon Eisenhower to ensure the safety of Ultra and guarantee that he would obey the rules governing its circulation and the operational use to which it might be put. In particular, Ultra could *not* be used simply to save the lives or liberty of officers and men under Eisenhower's command, which was one of the temptations of Ultra.

All Ultra was to be destroyed by fire after reading; it could be retained "only for the minimum period necessary for reading and discussing it, and Eisenhower was to see to it that the special security staffs seconded by "C" to his headquarters were "never required to go where they would be subjected to the risk of capture." Nor should the meaning of the code word "Ultra" be disclosed to any person not authorized to receive Ultra.

In all, the regulations placed severe constraints on Eisenhower and all other commanders, British as well as Americans, who were authorized to receive the intelligence. And it is not at all clear that either Eisenhower or the U.S. War Department accepted all the conditions, particularly those clauses relating to the use of Ultra to save lives and units. But it is assumed that Eisenhower raised no serious objections, for Ultra was released to him, but only under British control. To ensure that that control was effective, Eisenhower accepted a British chief of intelligence on his personal staff. The chief of the Special Liaison Unit at Eisenhower's headquarters was a Bletchley officer whose staff was entirely British.

After Eisenhower's indoctrination by Churchill, Eisenhower and his deputy, General Mark Clark, underwent a detailed explanation from "C" of Ultra and what intelligence Eisenhower and Clark could expect to derive from it. Eisenhower learned that he would receive not only the German high command communications between Hitler and Keitel at German supreme headquarters and the German supreme commander in the Mediterranean, Field Marshal Albert Kesselring, but also communications between Kesselring and the German air force and army commanders, including those of the commander of Panzerarmee Afrika, the famous General Erwin Rommel, who was facing Montgomery on the Egyptian frontier.

Eisenhower could also expect to receive most of Rommel's communications with his higher headquarters, including the German supreme command in Berlin and the commando supremo, the Italian supreme headquarters at Rome that controlled all military, air, and naval supply operations to Rommel's armies in Libya. He might also receive extensive intelligence about the military capabilities and intentions of the Spanish armed forces, which might intervene. Beyond this "C" had a substantial ability to read French army, navy, and air force communications, and, he stated, he had an extensive system of agents in place in both the free zone of metropolitan France and within French North Africa, the zone of operations.

If Eisenhower appeared to be impressed by the intelligence that would be available to him, General Clark was not. Squadron Leader Winterbotham, who was present and watched the reactions of the Americans closely in order to establish how seriously and responsibly they regarded this unprecedented access to the most secret channels of information available to the British, found Clark

restless from the start. I explained not only what the source was, but in an endeavour to catch Mark Clark's interest gave some pertinent examples of what it could do. I had intended to follow this with an explanation of how the information would reach him, and the security regulations which accompanied its use. But Mark Clark didn't appear to believe the first part, and after a quarter of an hour he excused himself and his officers on the grounds that he had something else to do. [30]

Winterbotham said he felt "it was a bad start and Menzies was considerably upset." He felt sure, however, that Eisenhower would ensure Ultra was used properly. There is evidence that Clark did not believe Ultra could assist him in his operations in any way until June of 1944. And there is also evidence that, despite the restrictions he had agreed to, Eisenhower did not honor them. Shortly after his appointment as commander of Torch, as his diaries show, without consulting his Ultra adviser, Eisenhower informed his aide-de-camp, Commander Harry C. Butcher, about Ultra. What Eisenhower may not have known or suspected was that Butcher was keeping a detailed diary every day of Eisenhower's every movement, and that he confided the Ultra secret to the diary. However, as Winterbotham recalled, "Eisenhower was surprised at the meeting at the extent of our penetration of Enigma, and thoughtful afterwards at lunch. He had every reason to be, for not even the most inexperienced general should lose a battle if he has on his breakfast table the enemy's own reports as to his capabilities and intentions that day."

Yet for all the breadth of intelligence available to Eisenhower, there was one worrying gap in "C's" knowledge of German operations. Torch was to be mainly, in its opening phase, at any rate, a major maritime operation. But "C" had lost the ability to read the U-boat ciphers at a time when the largest and the most important Allied convoys would be on the high seas carrying the forward elements, totaling over one hundred thousand men with all equipment. Grand Admiral Karl Doenitz had become suspicious that the Enigmas used in his U-boats were no longer secure, so Doenitz introduced a modification calculated to improve the security of Enigma. That development had been foreshadowed in various decrypts, and much was known about the nature of the modification. Nonetheless, when the modification was introduced into service throughout the U-boat command and fleet in February 1942, it became evident at Bletchley that a new, faster *bombe** would have to be designed if the U-boat Enigma was to be repenetrated.

Since German naval ciphers were now the responsibility not of "C" but of Admiral Godfrey, director of naval intelligence, Godfrey was severely criticized for not having been more energetic than he

---

*The spelling *bomba* denotes the original Polish version of this machine. Later British-designed models were referred to as *bombe*.

should have been in pressing the need for the new *bombe* upon the Admiralty. (Godfrey was replaced as director of naval intelligence in mid-1942 and sent out to command the Royal Indian Navy—a navy that mutinied not long after he took it over.)

But if the removal of Godfrey permitted a fresh and more congenial figure to take command of naval intelligence, nothing could be done to speed the design and production of the new *bombe*. The Americans were not able to assist as yet because the U.S. Navy had not been introduced to British *bombe* technology and was concentrating on the Japanese ciphers. (Not until the summer of 1942 were the Americans sufficiently inducted into the naval Ultra program to begin the design and manufacture of a high-speed *bombe*.)

It was true that the existing *bombes* at Bletchley could penetrate the new cipher, but only if very large numbers of them were employed at the same time. But Bletchley had thirty of the standard *bombes*, and these were all fully committed to air and military targets. Too few of the *bombes* could be diverted to the new U-boat cipher—it took six of the old *bombes* seventeen days to break a setting for a day, and one existing *bombe* had to work twenty-six times longer against the new cipher than it had taken against the old.

The solution lay in the very rapid design and manufacture of "old" and "new" *bombes* on both sides of the Atlantic simultaneously. The outcome of the Battle of the Atlantic lay not in naval power, but intelligence—the knowledge of where a U-boat could be found and thus destroyed. At no time between February 1942 and March 1943 was there any certainty that the new *bombe* would prove successful or that during the period when the new *bombe* was being designed and made, the Germans would not introduce some fresh modification that would invalidate all the work on the new *bombe*.

It seemed that after his brilliant start against Enigma, Menzies was at a disadvantage and might remain so throughout Torch which saw "the most valuable convoys ever to leave these shores." [34] Certainly the casualties at sea seemed to indicate that a disaster might result if Torch were undertaken. In August, September, October, and November of 1942, U-boats sank fifty, twenty-nine, twenty-nine, and thirty-nine ships in convoy, and fifty-one, fifty-eight, fifty-four, and seventy sailing independently. These losses were far beyond the replacement capacity of the combined U.S. and empire shipyards, and by March of 1943 the Germans came as close as they ever would to disrupting commerce between the New World and the Old.

The convoy system was all but destroyed as an effective defense against U-boats. The Admiralty asked "C," as director-general of GC&CS, to focus "a little more attention" on the U-boat cipher problem, which by this time had been code-named Shark. The U-boat war was "the one campaign which Bletchley Park are not influencing to any marked extent—and it is the only one in which the war can be lost unless BP *do* help." [31]

Yet for all the extraordinary exertions at Bletchley, the new U-boat ciphers remained inviolable throughout the Torch invasion period. This greatly increased the dangers to the four task forces destined for French North Africa, or "the Far Shore," as the invasion coasts were known for security reasons. These forces were huge—twelve aircraft carriers, six battleships and battle cruisers, fifteen cruisers, eighty-one destroyers, nine submarines, eleven corvettes, five sloops, twenty-six minesweepers, fifty-six ships carrying the 65,000 U.S. and British assault infantry, fifty-five ships carrying their tanks, trucks and other equipment, twenty antisubmarine and minesweepers, seven tankers, eighteen motor launches, one seaplane tender, two cutters, five antiaircraft ships, one monitor, and one hundred and seventy merchantmen bringing the followup forces and supplies. Casualties were expected to be correspondingly large.

Much, however, could still be told about the whereabouts of U-boats from "Y" signals intelligence; more could be deduced from the Ultra sources, for the new security provisions were confined to the U-boat fleet. Through Y intelligence, the whereabouts and movements of U-boat packs could be plotted and estimated at the Operational Intelligence Centre at the Admiralty, the squadrons and advancing ships could be routed around the waiting wolf packs, and wolf packs waiting in areas of the sea where maneuvering was not possible could be lured from the path of the approaching task force by decoy convoys.

"C" was able to advise Eisenhower, if he chose to do so, that he had broken into a number of important enemy intelligence ciphers that would keep Eisenhower advised about what the enemy knew about Torch. These ciphers were as follows:

Orange 1, which was broken from December 10, 1940, and remained broken until the end of the war. This was the SS general-purpose key.

Railway, which was broken in February 1941 and was the Enigma key used by the German railway system to secure railway military movements.

ISK, being the Abwehr Enigma, which was broken in December 1941 and remained broken to the end of 1944.

GGG, from Eisenhower's point of view the most important, for it was the Abwehr Enigma key between Berlin and the Abwehr's stations in the Gibraltar area. This was broken in February 1942. There is no record of when, or if, the ability to read GGG was ended.

Quince, being the main SS general key, broken on August 14, 1942, remaining so until the end of the war.

The breaking of these keys was one of the epics of the war and not only produced important intelligence, but also cast long shadows. In the first place, it was because of the GGG decrypts that "C" and Philby maintained close and frequent contact, the result of which was that "C" personally formed the highest regard for Philby's ability. In June 1942 Philby discovered in the GGG decrypts the code word Bodden in the context of the Pillars of Hercules. As was often the case with German code words, the meaning contained a significance from which the intent of the code word could be deduced. Such a word was Bodden: Philby's research showed that the word had to do with the bottom of the sea.

Further decrypts revealed that the Abwehr was building, with Spanish naval assistance, a chain of sixteen infrared and sonic ship-reporting stations in the Straits of Gibraltar across the very routes where the Torch convoys must pass to land their forces in Algeria and Tunisia. The sonic-reporting system was being laid on the sea bottom; and the effect of both systems would be to prevent British convoys from slipping from the Atlantic into the Mediterranean after dark without being detected. The reporting stations also had communications with U-boats inside and outside the Mediterranean; the submarines could be radioed and directed on to the ships.

Plainly such a system could not be tolerated, for the existence of the stations posed a threat to the success of Torch and the operation would be rendered too costly to undertake unless the stations were neutralized. With the discovery of the Bodden line, the Joint Intelligence Committee met to decide what should be done about the stations. Philby was required to attend the meeting and make a report, but he made a mistake. In Whitehall it was an unwritten rule that persons attending business meetings wore either uniform or mufti. Anybody who did not was considered improperly dressed, and that always caused comment.

But Philby did not know this—no one had told him—so he appeared in his Glenalmond clothes, which consisted of his father's World War I tunic and a pair of old corduroys. On this occasion, as the chairman, Cavendish-Bentinck, remembered, Philby's shirt was orange. Startled by the ensemble, Cavendish-Bentinck nudged "C" as Philby entered the room and made his way around the committee table to some visitors' chairs set against the wall and asked in a pewlike whisper: "Who's that scruffy bugger?"

Menzies replied: "Young Philby. St. John Philby's son. He's with me. Good lad."

Cavendish-Bentinck retorted: "Looks like a damned Bolshevik to me."

Cavendish-Bentinck regretted later that he did not ask somebody to give him a report on Philby, for he claimed knowledge that Philby had been a member of the Cambridge University Socialist Society, and that he knew, too, that that club was heavily infected with the Marxist line. But he did nothing, and the meeting continued. The Admiralty representative recommended that the stations should be destroyed by commandos landing from submarines—a proposal that was abandoned in favor of a diplomatic demand made personally on General Franco, the Spanish dictator. That demand was successful, and when the stations were dismantled the way was opened for Torch to take place.

Through Bodden, "C" saw Philby frequently during the summer of 1942, and although Menzies never allowed younger members of the service to get too close to him, Menzies did begin to send for Philby when Felix Cowgill, Philby's chief, was absent. For all this slight extra attention, Philby, who was himself really an "amateur" and displayed much of the disdain of that group, was grateful to "C" for this recognition, for as Philby himself was to write, he found himself "on the up-and-up." He was later to record—from his sanc- tuary in Moscow—the impressions he made of "C" during their meet- ings on the question of the Bodden line:

I think that I have already made it clear that I look back on the Chief with enduring affection. He was not, in any sense of the words, a great intelligence officer. His intellectual equipment was unimpressive, and his knowledge of the world, and views about it, were just what one would expect from a fairly cloistered son of the upper level of the British Establishment. In my own field, counter-espionage, his attitudes were schoolboyish—bars, beards, and blondes. But it was this persistent boyish streak shining through the horrible responsibilities that world war placed upon his shoulders, and through the ever-present threat of a summons from Churchill in one of his whimsical mid-night moods, that was his charm. His real strength lay in a sensitive perception of the currents of Whitehall politics, in an ability to feel his way through the mazy corridors of power. Capable officers who knew him much better than myself spoke of his almost feminine intuition—by which I do not mean that he was anything but a whole man. [32]

6 KINGPIN

Of all the political tasks confronting "C" during the pre-Torch period, none was more important than the selection of a Frenchman with the stature necessary to detach the French army from its personal oath of allegiance to Marshal Pétain, president of the New Order state of France, and then lead the French army in North Africa, a potentially powerful force, over to the Allied standard. "C" had no doubt that a revolt was a realistic possibility, for he had been involved in various secret staff talks with French officers and intermediaries ever since Christmas of 1940. In December 1940 a French staff officer operating under the code name Lancelot appeared at Tangier with a suggestion that the French army might change sides if given the signal to do so by the commander in chief, General Maxime Weygand.

Nothing came of those talks, for, largely through gossip obtained from Major Morton, an American newspaperwoman in London, Helen Kirkpatrick, revealed the existence of secret contacts between London and Vichy. But in 1941 a trade agreement was established between Washington and Vichy through which the French in French North Africa received limited American aid, consisting primarily of food, domestic heating oils, and medical supplies. In return Vichy agreed that, ostensibly to ensure that the American supplies did not reach the enemy, the United States might establish twelve consuls in the capitals and main ports of French North Africa from Tunis to Casablanca. These consuls were used to obtain intelligence about the allegiances of the French armed forces in French North Africa, and especially those of Weygand, and to establish a cadre upon which a larger espionage and special operations organization could be built when the need arose.

"C's" plot took a further important step forward in the spring of 1941 when a high officer of the French secret service, Colonel Georges

Groussard, who doubled, clandestinely, as chief of Ajax, the security service of the French army's underground service, had a meeting with General Charles Huntziger, the Vichy war minister. At that meeting Huntziger appointed Groussard chief of all ORA's espionage and counterespionage services and received agreement on one major point: that he should work in direct liaison with "C" in London and with Dewavrin, de Gaulle's spymaster. Huntziger also approved a proposal that Groussard should go to London.

As Groussard himself was to define his purpose in making such a dangerous journey across the lines of war:

It was necessary for the British policy-makers to understand that, at Vichy, the sound element of the Ministry [of war] wanted to aid the anti-German struggle as efficaciously as possible, and intended to reach a positive understanding with the Allies. In the event of my succeeding in my mission, the British would no longer be tempted to treat the Vichy State as a kind of secondary enemy; they would regard it as a trump-card and, in the realization of certain of their plans, would act in concordance and harmony with it without any the less giving their support to General de Gaulle's Committee, with which Committee I would make every effort to make contact. [33]

In approving Groussard's mission, an approval that may well have led to Huntziger's death by murder, Huntziger declared:

Sooner or later the English and ourselves must come to an understanding, and that is why it will never be superfluous to repeat to Churchill that we people desire the German defeat in Vichy, too. I spoke to you about the present state of the secret struggle, because I consider it of capital importance—perhaps more important than anything else, that you make them understand the danger there would be in trying too soon to light a fire that the Germans would too easily put out with a sea of blood.

Arrangements were first made for Groussard's journey to London via Lisbon through Bertrand's radio link with "C," P.C. Cadix. Then in June 1941 Groussard left for Lisbon. There "Georges Guerin" became "George Gilbert," a French-Canadian survivor of a ship that had been torpedoed, and "C's" war station in Lisbon issued him with papers in that name. On his arrival in London Groussard was met by Dewavrin, de Gaulle's intelligence master, and taken to the De Vere Hotel in London. He was met that same evening by Commander Dunderdale, chief of "C's" Vichy desk, who took him to Downing Street to meet with Churchill and "C."

The meeting lasted two hours, during which time Groussard was "amazed. Churchill might have come straight from Occupied Paris, so well-informed and so well-considered was his knowledge of it. His impartiality was stupefying. Here was the man who really understood the tragic situation of France." During that time Groussard laid out the arrangements by which "C" could expand his intelligence service in France with the assistance of ORA. Groussard laid out, too, how the French army might assist the Allies if and when they landed on French territory. At the conclusion of the meeting, Groussard recorded that as he rose to leave, "the Prime Minister, speaking still of his desire to see France glorious again, accompanied him to the door. He clasped Groussard's hands and bade him farewell with tears in his eyes."

"C" appears to have been concerned only with policy. The technical details he left to Dansey, whom Groussard knew as "the Old Colonel." Of his dinner with Dansey, Groussard wrote that he felt Dansey was the real chief of the secret service, a belief Dansey fostered with foreigners with "C's" knowledge and approval, his purpose to deflect attention from "C." As Groussard wrote of that dinner:

Like many Secret Services, British Intelligence has a double organization. The Old Colonel was in charge of all that was ultra-secret; he made the most important decisions; he was probably the most feared man in the world—however that may be, he was certainly the most feared among the fighters of the secret armies. . . . The Old Colonel was about sixty, of medium height, powerfully built, bald; his movements were measured, his expression tranquil. He spoke perfect French. His exact and ample data on France impressed Groussard. . . . I had the impression that he knew more about my own country than I did.

The Old Colonel told Groussard that he considered his plans realizable. Circumstances had never been more favorable for an understanding between the sound elements of Vichy and the British. "If you come to grief over it, I think those who come after will do no better. Huntziger will go, Weygand will have his hands tied more and more, and, as for Petain, the more time passes, the more he is in danger of weakening and letting himself be abused by the maneouvres of the Nazis and their lackeys."

The Old Colonel's glance darkened with a shade of regret.

"What a pity," he said, "that you were not able to come to London immediately you had reached an understanding with Huntziger. I am not saying it is too late now, but the atmosphere of Vichy has become so charged . . . that not only will a lot of caution and cunning be needed, but also, in fine, a lot of luck." The Old Colonel was silent for a moment. Then he added, "You have a fifty per cent chance. That's not too bad."

Neither "C" nor Dansey left any record of their impressions, though subsequent developments showed that "C" at least trusted Groussard. But even so, Churchill was always disposed to be suspicious of Vichy emissaries, and as Colville recorded in his diary, Desmond Morton in particular took a highly adverse view of Groussard:

Desmond says there are signs that Vichy is playing a double game and that the emissary from Petain and Huntziger, who came the other day, was not all that he appeared to be. The aim may be to cause a breach between ourselves and de Gaulle.

Subsequent emissaries from Vichy were not taken to see Churchill, therefore, their meetings being confined to "C" and the chiefs of staff.

Nor did Dansey's estimate of the conspirators' chances of success appeared to be exaggerated. In November 1941 "C's" plans for bringing the French army back into the war suffered a severe setback when General Huntziger vanished in an aircraft "accident" over the Mediterranean. Two days later Weygand was suddenly retired and then sent to a German concentration camp—the Germans apparently were reading the State Department cipher.

By December 1941, therefore, Menzies's operations seemed moribund. But in that month an officer of the French General Staff appeared in London and was interviewed "by a representative of the British General Staff." During that interview, the intermediary made a proposal that constituted fresh evidence that the French General Staff in Vichy contemplated a resumption of the war against Germany and Italy.

According to a paper by Field Marshal Brooke, chief of the Imperial General Staff, the emissary, who was again sponsored by "C," requested that when Allied forces invaded, a relief convoy with instructors, arms, equipment, and supplies should be despatched from the United Kingdom to the ports of Bordeaux and La Rochelle for the support of the French Armistice Army, and that the French forces for their part would secure these ports and hold a corridor connecting them with unoccupied France.

The conversation at this interview was of a purely exploratory nature, but it was agreed that "C" should arrange for "a secure means of communication" and that the French General Staff should forward their detailed requirements. [34] Later these were sent to "C" through Bertrand's wireless post at Uzes: they wanted equipment for ten divisions together with French plans for an uprising of the ORA's

Corps Francs de Pommies; an underground army of sixteen thousand demobilized French soldiers would create a major diversion at Bordeaux if the British landed in Europe later that year.

For the moment the Anglo-French talks did not proceed, largely because, following the death of Huntziger and the arrest of Weygand, there seemed to be no figure in France powerful enough to contest Pétain. General Charles de Gaulle, head of the Free French Forces, was considered to be a renegade by the French officer corps and therefore rejected. De Gaulle was not popular in French North Africa because of his support for the British destruction of the French fleet and the Anglo-Gaullist invasion of French Syria in the spring of 1941. As "C" wrote to the head of SOE on January 10, 1942, "De Gaulle had not a great following but only a symbolic value." [35]

"C" felt that General Henri H. Giraud, who had commanded with distinction the French Seventh Army during the Battle for France in 1940, was "a much better bet from our point of view." There was, however, a problem with Giraud: he had been taken prisoner in 1940. When the Germans overran his army headquarters facing the Ardennes, he was taken prisoner by the Germans and held in that most formidable of all German jails, Koenigstein Castle on the Elbe in Saxony deep inside Germany. General Revers, chief of staff of the French Armistice Army and head of the ORA, did have contact with Giraud and with "C," again through Bertrand in France.

"C" conceived a plan for Giraud's escape. As "C," he controlled an important escape organization known as MI9, and it is likely that he discussed this operation with Cadogan on March 25, 1942, for Cadogan recorded in his diary: "Interesting talk with 'C' about Lucas & future plans." Lucas was, it appears, Broadway's code name for Giraud. In April 1942 Giraud escaped, shinnying down the high walls of the fortress on a special rope concealed in jars of preserves that reached him in his prisoner-of-war food parcels.

Giraud could not easily be concealed, as he was sixty-three and six feet three inches tall. With a price of 100,000 gold marks on his head, there was a good deal of traffic in the Sicherheitspolizei ciphers that "C" could read, so he was able to follow Giraud's progress across Germany toward Switzerland with some accuracy. Also, there seems no doubt that Canaris facilitated Giraud's escape.

On April 21 Giraud entered Switzerland. He was held for four days while the Swiss checked his identity and determined whether he should be returned to the Germans. They did not do so because

Giraud was a *retired* officer of the French army, and such was Swiss law that they did not feel obliged to send him back. On April 25 Giraud was released, and on the same day the Germans acknowledged that their most important prisoner had escaped.

While in Switzerland Giraud made contact with "C's" organization there and, presumably with their help, made his way to his home at Lyon with the assistance of Ajax, the ORA organization in the Vichy French police. At Vichy Giraud was called to Pétain's office and there made a promise that he had no intention of keeping: in return for his liberty, he would eschew all political activity.

Shortly, Giraud was in communication with Revers and the British chiefs of staff through Bertrand and "C." At that stage Giraud was re-code-named Kingpin, an indication that in the mind of "C," at least, Giraud was the man to lead France back into the war. Plans were laid by "C" to bring Giraud from France to Gibraltar. On May 16 "C" advised the chiefs of staff that an emissary had arrived from Giraud. They agreed that "knowledge of these plans should be greatly restricted," and that "it was unnecessary to inform the Prime Minister or Foreign Office until discussions were about to start." [36] Moreover, nothing was said to Donovan, whose future was still in doubt.

To further complicate matters, some controversy developed over Giraud's suitability as Kingpin in an operation into French North Africa. "C" felt that Giraud was the embodiment of the old France that he admired so much: tall, slim, fit, impressive in physique, dignified, politically honest, the apotheosis of St. Cyr. Harold Macmillan, the publisher and parliamentarian of Eton, who was Eisenhower's British political adviser, thought otherwise. He pointed out that Giraud's experience included too much imprisonment and defeat—he had been captured by the Germans in *both* World War I and World War II.

Giraud was of the age of the post–Franco-Prussian War, a French humiliation. He had served in the French army that was almost defeated by the Germans in World War I. He was a general whose army had been smashed by a German general in World War II. He had been sent to Koenigstein. Macmillan believed Giraud's attitudes "bore the same relationship to modern strategy and ideas as did the ideas of the German and Austrian generals to the genius of Napoleon." He was, Macmillan insisted, largely obsolete and therefore dangerous. As to the Americans, so it was said, Giraud did not admire their army but did admire their "energy and enthusiasm." [37] On this occasion Macmillan was to be proven right and "C" wrong—very wrong.

In June Donovan came to London for staff conversations, and it appears that Menzies and Donovan worked out an agreement that "C" should handle Giraud and all external intelligence matters bearing upon Torch, while Donovan should retain control within the zone of operations. The quid pro quo was that selected OSS men would be allowed to train in counterespionage. On June 5, the first OSS officer—Colonel David K. E. Bruce, future chief of OSS London—visited Section V headquarters off King Harry's Lane, St. Albans. But even as that agreement was being struck by "C," the lines to Giraud became dangerously crossed.

A French secret agent code-named Aumeron claimed to represent a "high French general" and endeavored to make contact with "C's" representative in Lisbon. Aumeron failed, so he saw Donovan's representative, Colonel Robert D. Solborg. Having interviewed Aumeron, Solborg wired Donovan that he had been invited by a pro-Allied group in the French staff to meet their representative at a pinpoint off the Algerian coast. Properly, Solborg requested instructions but received none because at that time Donovan was on his way to London for meetings with "C." Had Solborg waited, he would certainly have received an order from Donovan to break contact with Aumeron. But Solborg did not wait.

Assuming that he would receive permission to develop the contact, he did what he had been forbidden to do in his *ordre de missions:* he entered French or Spanish North Africa without authority and established contact with a Vichy official. Ignoring his directive—by their very presence in a country, agents could betray a military intention—Solborg left his post in Lisbon despite a warning from Washington that he had been identified by the Germans as an American secret agent.

Solborg went first to Tangier to meet the representative of the "high French officer." If the Germans had Solborg under surveillance—which was likely—then they would conclude in short order that there was a conspiracy in violation of the armistice agreements between the French General Staff and the OSS. The consequences of such an assumption would be manifold. Certain officers, at least, would find themselves in a concentration camp. Some might even find themselves in front of a firing squad. They might also assume that the Americans were about to invade French North Africa, which would allow the Germans to deploy U-boats and aircraft to make such an expedition a costly one. At worst the Germans might invade Tunisia to forestall such operations.

On learning that Solborg had gone not only to Tangier, which was under Spanish control, but also to Casablanca, which was French, Donovan ordered him back to London. But as Donovan's cable file shows, Solborg did not obey that order. He wired Donovan, "I hope you will excuse my not keeping London appointment because of importance of my present mission here." Deeply embarrassed by the position in which Solborg's action had placed him with "C" and with the War Department, Donovan shot back one of his cold and angry telegrams:

I have informed you previously and you had already given your word that you would not carry on activities of any kind in North Africa. You are directed to return to Lisbon at once, no matter what you are doing, and await further word from me. State Department is being advised. [38]

To that telegram Solborg replied that he was "surprised greatly" by Donovan's order to leave French North Africa. He claimed to have "established contact and assurance of leadership on highest plane" and added that "I now question utility of my further contributing to [OSS] as your peremptory cable has produced most depressing effect on me." Acting on his own authority entirely, Solborg then left Casablanca not for Lisbon but for Algiers and conducted secret conversations with representatives of the French General Staff.

Solborg's adventure caused anxiety and consternation in Washington and London, particularly at "C's" office, for Algiers had become the center for the political negotiations concerning Torch. "C" felt that Solborg had been so widely trailed across French North Africa, which was riddled with hostile agents of all kinds, that the enemy would be on the alert, an assumption that was confirmed shortly by Philby, who was now in control not only of Iberia, but also North West Africa. (Also, Solborg undertook his action at a time when the U.S. chiefs of staff were considering the liquidation of OSS on the grounds that their function would be more effectively carried out by the military intelligence service.)

Donovan ordered Solborg to report to his deputy, Edward Buxton, at OSS headquarters in Washington. Solborg obeyed that order and flew there immediately by Pan-American Clipper from Lisbon. In Washington it was made clear to Solborg that by his foolhardiness he might have betrayed a major military undertaking to the embarrassment of the United States and its secret intelligence service. There was also anxiety that Solborg might have made promises of financial or military assistance to the persons with whom he had contact. And who was the high military personage that Aumeron claimed to be representing?

General Giraud, Solborg stated. At Algiers, Solborg claimed, he had had a talk with Giraud's representatives, one of whom commanded the Algiers division, the other the Casablanca division. At that admission, Solborg was told to write a full statement on what he had done, whom he had seen, and what, if anything, he had promised. In that paper, Solborg admitted that he had assured the representatives—and he could not guarantee that they were not agents provocateur of Vichy—that "our intervention could only take place at an express invitation from them." This was an indiscretion that, if honored by FDR, would preclude the United States from invading French territory without an invitation from the French General Staff.

On July 9 Edward Buxton, having read Solborg's papers, wrote an appreciation of them for Donovan, who was still in London and up against "C" and the British chiefs of staff over the affair. Buxton declared, "I do not see anything in all of this except insubordination, direct disobedience of orders, which [Solborg] appears to assume are of no importance because of certain arrangements which he regards as of extreme importance to the United Nations." [39]

Solborg was fired. Through the chaos and uncertainty caused within the Allied secret circle by the Solborg affair, the final decision to undertake Torch was delayed while "C" undertook an inquiry through all his sources (but mainly Ultra, ISOS, and Bertrand). This in turn made the planning and preparations for Torch uncertain until almost the eleventh hour, and that in turn increased the risks of what was already a very risky operation. Those uncertainties were increased when "C" discovered that U.S. Treasury representatives had been purchasing huge amounts of French North African francs, which again indicated that French North Africa was to be the area of major military operations.

OSS once again was found at fault when it was discovered that, without Washington's authority, the Vichy French harbor master at Casablanca, a man knowledgeable about harbor conditions, currents, tides, and the surf along the Atlantic coast around Casablanca, had been brought out of Casablanca and taken to a U.S. naval headquarters to give one of the U.S. task force commanders advice on the sea conditions that were likely to prevail at the time of the disembarkation of the troops. That exfiltration pointed plainly to an Allied intention to attack at Casablanca. There was, moreover, evidence from Vichy that both General Giraud and Admiral Darlan, the French naval commander in chief at Vichy and a foe of England, suspected that the Allies intended to land at all points between Algiers and Casablanca. It had to be assumed, therefore, that Berlin, Rome, and Vichy knew far too much. "C" was not able to give Torch a clean bill of health, but he did feel able to provide a guarantee that *if* the enemy did become aware of the objectives and timing, then he would be able to warn Eisenhower in time.

With that part guarantee, the combined chiefs decided on August 25 to proceed. "C" took charge of two preparatory operations from his desk at Broadway. The first was to land General Mark Clark and his all-American party on a beach at Cherchel, about forty miles west of Algiers, to discuss questions of U.S. military assistance with a representative of Giraud. The second operation was to take place when Clark reported that he had reached agreement at Cherchel. This involved the evacuation, with the assistance of British and French agents in southern France, of Giraud from a point on the French Mediterranean coast to Eisenhower's headquarters in the rock at Gibraltar.

As General Sir Bernard Montgomery prepared to launch Lightfoot, a massive counteroffensive against the Panzerarmee Afrika of General Erwin Rommel at El Alamein, Clark and his party flew from England to Gibraltar on October 19. At Gibraltar a British submarine, *Seraph*, was waiting to take the Americans to the pinpoint, a beachhouse near Cherchel.

Clark had been "admitted to the Ultra club," one of the main rules of which was that no one who knew of the existence of Ultra was to be placed in a position where he might be captured by the enemy. Why "C" relaxed this regulation for Clark is not known, but it may have had to do with Clark's demonstration of disbelief in the existence of the decrypts during his indoctrination by "C." In any case, there was nobody but Clark (except for Eisenhower) with the authority required for the mission, and "C" had judged that it would be useless to send a Briton since the Vichy French, and particularly Giraud, had stated that they would not deal with the British, only with an American officer.

Landfall was made just before daybreak on October 21, and *Seraph* lay submerged until after dark that day and then moved in to a point five hundred yards from the beach. Clark and his party paddled ashore in canoes with an escort of three Royal Marine commandos, the only Britons in the party. At the beachhouse where the conference was to take place, Clark met the French representative, General Charles Mast, commander of the French army's garrison at Algiers and the "spokesman for General Giraud." As Clark declared on meeting Mast, "the Allies had decided to send to North Africa large American force, supported in the air and on the sea by British units." Clark then asked if Mast would indicate whether the French army would resist to such a landing.

Mast replied that Algiers might not resist but that Casablanca and Oran were in the hands of pro-Vichy administrators. Resistance would certainly occur at these two cities. The only man who could bring *all* French forces over to the side of the Allies was Giraud. Clark stated that aircraft and warships were ready to bring Giraud out of France, but Mast answered that Giraud was insistent that he would come only if he was given command of all Allied forces operating on French territory, reflecting Giraud's conviction regarding his own superiority as a general.

Clark's response to that condition was vague; he replied only that Giraud would be appointed commander in chief of all French forces in French North Africa and that all other command matters would have to await a letter from Eisenhower as Allied commander in chief. There was more than a hint of finessing on this point, but Mast seemed to accept the situation and then turned to French military aid requirements. These were huge: rearmament for eight infantry and two tank divisions, plus separate tank, artillery, and service units, all ready within one month—in all, 1,400 aircraft, 5,000 tanks, 3,000 cannon, 30,000 machine guns, and 160,000 rifles with 62 million rounds of ammunition. Clark promised "all aid" to the French.

At that point the discussion broke off as the police raided the beachhouse. Clark, Mast, and their parties hid in a dusty wine cellar. Then, when the police had gone, apparently satisfied that the only occupants were the owners, Mast returned to Algiers, and Clark returned to *Seraph*. During that night, better equipped with intelligence than any general in modern times, Montgomery launched the Eighth Army against Panzerarmee Afrika at El Alamein; and that same day some of the Torch convoys in the ports of Maine and Virginia came under sailing orders.

At the same time, "C" was coming under extraordinary day-and-night pressure from Churchill, whose nerves were becoming as unsteady as his imagination. As Cadogan recorded in his diary, "Smuts [confided?] to me that a weekend at Chequers was 'like a tornado'!" On November 3: "P.M. v. over-excited. Night before last he sent for 'C' at 11 P.M. About 11.15 he said, 'You look v. tired; you'd better go to bed.' 'C' admitted he was, and would. At 2.15 A.M. P.M. rang him up to ask a quite unnecessary question—and then apologised!"

It was now that "C" undertook the second half of his special political operation—the evacuation of Giraud to Algiers, where, as the Allies came ashore on D-Day, he was to make a radio broadcast to all French forces to obey his orders and then take command in North Africa. Since there was no U.S. submarine within three thousand miles, Seraph was used again. But since Giraud might not board a British warship, this time she sailed as the USS Seraph. Aboard was an American naval officer, Captain Jerauld Wright, who had only nominal command until the submarine reached the pinpoint, at which time the British commander, Lieutenant N.L.A. Jewell, was to hand over full control to the American. This was the first time in history that a British warship had sailed under the American flag.

On October 27 Seraph sailed for the pinpoint in the Gulf of Lyons, a beach at La Fossette, a village near Le Lavendou on the French Riviera. It was thought there was ample time to take Giraud off the beaches at La Fossette and then land him with the U.S. assault forces at Algiers. Such was the importance of the operation to Eisenhower that a second submarine, the Sybil, sailed almost immediately after Seraph, her task to take over if Seraph was unable to carry out the mission.

But by November 5 it was evident to "C" that something had gone wrong at La Fossette, although it was known that Giraud had left Lyons and hidden at Marseilles for several days. The muddle had been created because the Algiers wireless operators' signals had been illegible on receipt at Gibraltar, which required their retransmission. That could not be arranged quickly, as the Algiers station had closed down for six hours. But whatever had happened, wherever Giraud had disappeared to, he was in the hands of the Ordre de la Resistance de l'Armee in France. The agent involved may well have been Bertrand, for he had a safe house in a nearby village and knew the Riviera coastline well.

By the evening of November 5, Seraph was so close inshore at Le Lavendou that when she surfaced into a rough sea, the men in her conning tower could see the headlights of cars on the roads around the village. At 11:30 P.M. *Seraph* received advice from Gibraltar that Kingpin might be an hour late, his fishing boat would come eight hundred yards to seaward before making a recognition signal, and when he did so *Seraph* was to signal the letter "S" by dimmed blue light. This was confirmed by a further signal within a few minutes, which came in with news that the weather situation was deteriorating rapidly and might make it impossible for Giraud to transfer from the fishing boat to *Seraph*.

Ashore, Giraud and his party had narrowly escaped the police and gone back to the house, where it was intended that they would meet the captain of a fishing smack. From that point forward all proceeded normally. A light in the house flashed the signal "O-N-E-H-O-U-R," which was seen by the signalsman in the conning tower. A German E-boat appeared briefly and then sheered off, raising fears that *Seraph*, too, might be ambushed. But then as expected a white-painted fishing boat appeared and, as one of the American officers in the conning tower of Seraph recorded in a diary:

In the stern sat General Giraud—6-feet odd, dressed in civilian clothes and wearing a grey fedora. His gloved hands were folded over a walking stick and a raincoat was thrown over his shoulders like a cloak. It was the first time I had ever seen him and he looked rather like an old-time monarch visiting his fleet. [40]

As Giraud came aboard only the Americans in the crew spoke to him, but when the British commanding officer, Jewell, made a mistake and welcomed him on board in a noticeably British accent, "he wondered what Giraud would do if he unmasked the deception—he could only jump overboard and swim back to France if his anti-British complex was powerful." [41]

When Captain Wright read out the text of the proclamation Giraud was expected to make, calling upon all French forces to join the Allies when they landed in French North Africa on D-Day, which was two days away, Giraud declined on the grounds that, as he stated in the crowded wardroom, he was a soldier, not a politician. It was an ominous sign of what was to follow.

With that, *Seraph* submerged and made for a patrol line some seventy miles from the French coast, where, since it was impossible to get Giraud to Algiers before H-Hour, they were to meet a Catalina flying boat that would take the French general to Gibraltar and Eisenhower.

Since *Seraph* was under orders to remain submerged all day—
Allied aircraft had been instructed to attack any submarine on the
surface during the hours of daylight—she now proceeded toward
Gibraltar underwater until just after dusk, when she surfaced to send
a signal that Giraud had refused to read the proclamation. Soon after
the signal had been handed in, however, it was discovered that the
transmitter had broken down, and there was no reserve. The signalsman worked throughout the night but could not repair the equipment. As one consequence, *Seraph* failed to make her nightly report.
A second was that unless Catalinas were on constant patrol down the
rendezvous line, there was no way of getting Giraud to Gibraltar
before D-Day. When *Seraph* failed to report, aircraft were sent from
Gibraltar down the line of the course she was known to have been
taking when she went silent. Aboard the submarine, Wright and
Jewell agreed that they should remain on the surface, despite the
danger of bombing; and their luck held.

Just before nine o'clock on November 7, a Catalina was sighted;
Seraph fired flares, and the flying boat landed close by. Giraud was
successfully transferred. At that point the Stars and Stripes was lowered and the White Ensign was hoisted. For *Seraph*, the operation
was over. For Eisenhower, it began when Giraud, bedraggled and
irritable, arrived in the commander in chief's office at about 7:00 P.M.
on November 7, the eve of H-Hour. There, the atmosphere was thick
with tension as the task forces approached their appointed positions
off the northwest African coasts. For now was the most dangerous
time for the convoys. There was little room for maneuvering and less
still for escape if an undetected wolf pack lay in the area.

As church bells rang in England in salute to Montgomery's smashing victory over Rommel at El Alamein, all Torch convoys had been
able to avoid the U-boat wolf packs despite Bletchley's inability to
read the U-boat cipher. No ships had been lost in the transit from
The Clyde, Maine, and Virginia. During the approach to the Far
Shore, as the Y intelligence showed, one task force was in peril from
a pack of eight U-boats lying just to the west of the Canary Islands.
This was convoy UGF1, part of General George S. Patton's western
assault force. UGF1 consisted of thirty-eight troop and supply ships
and fifty-six escorts. Miraculously (and by design rather than by accident), a British convoy of empty merchantmen, SL 125, England-
bound from Sierra Leone, was running east and north across the bows
of the advancing convoy. The U-boats spotted SL 125 first and gave

chase in what was a running battle fought all the way from the Canaries to the western approaches. In all, the British convoy lost twelve ships, but the American task force was able to slip in behind the U-boat patrol line and was not spotted.

At Gibraltar, meantime, Eisenhower received Giraud. With Torch still at risk, Eisenhower was astounded when, immediately following the usual exchange of courtesies, Giraud announced abruptly that he had come to take command of Torch. When Eisenhower reminded him that that appointment had been made by the Combined Chiefs of Staff in Washington, and that he (Eisenhower) had been made commander in chief of all Allied military operations in the theater, Giraud replied that "the honour of himself and his country was involved and that he could not accept any position in the venture lower than that of complete command." [42]

Eisenhower sought to explain why this demand would be impossible to meet. The selection of the commander had been an involved process, requiring the agreements of all governments concerned, and that therefore no subordinate officer in the expedition could legally have accepted an order from General Giraud. Apart from all else, Eisenhower reminded Giraud: "at that moment there was not a single Frenchman in the Allied Command. On the contrary, the enemy, if any, was French." Giraud then announced that he would be "a spectator in this affair." When Eisenhower spoke of the "constant fear at the back of our minds of becoming engaged in prolonged and serious battle against Frenchmen, not only to our sorrow and loss, but to the detriment of our campaign against the Germans," Giraud went to bed.

That night Eisenhower wrote to his chief of staff, General Bedell Smith, who was still in London: "It isn't this operation that's wearing me down—it's the petty intrigue and the necessity of dealing with little, selfish, conceited worms who call themselves men. All these Frogs have a single thought—ME."

"C's" operations to bring the Vichy French forces over to the side of the Allies had been technically superb and blessed with a fair measure of good fortune. The secrets of the operation had been kept, the enemy was mystified about the intentions of the Allied convoys, agreement had been struck between the Algiers commander of the French army and the U.S. Army, and Giraud had been successfully brought to Gibraltar to become commander in chief of the French forces in French North Africa. But now these plans had foundered.

Giraud was not quite the great and gallant French soldier that every-one had thought. At that crucial hour he proved to be no more than just another French general concerned only with his own reputation, career, and pension. No proclamation therefore went out to the French army in North Africa; and the French armed forces, which were numerically superior to the Allied forces but poorly equipped, pre-pared to resist whatever was to follow. "We've backed the wrong horse," declared "C" at Broadway in the presence of Reilly. And so he had.

The armies of Torch began landing in the dawn twilight of No-vember 8, 1942, losing only one troop ship damaged by torpedoes. Even that vessel, the British liner *Scythia*, managed to stay afloat. That was a miracle of seamanship, tactics, strategy, intelligence, coun-terespionage, security, and deception. The new machine had worked beautifully. Yet Eisenhower found little encouraging in the first battle reports. At all points Donovan's clandestine plan failed; nowhere did the Vichy French army welcome the Americans as liberators. Fighting erupted, and for a time it seemed that the Grand Alliance and France would find themselves at war by the end of the day.

At Casablanca Patton threatened to level the city by naval gunfire if the French did not surrender. But the Vichy French generals had remained in command, despite an attempt to jail them, and they had ordered all the French armed forces in Morocco to resist. Patton's task force encountered the fire of two French battleships and a num-ber of cruisers and the torpedoes of destroyers and French subma-rines. The French shore batteries fired on the U.S. covering warships, and as Eisenhower learned, the actual landings would have been a terrible failure if there had been German forces ashore: the surf had been especially heavy and had disorganized the incoming flotillas.

The most dangerous situation existed at Algiers, the political cap-ital of French North Africa. There, as had been arranged with General Mark Clark, the pro-Allied French staff had seized Algiers at H-Hour under the control of the U.S. political officer, Robert Murphy, and all other key points were seized in what was the first phase of operations to establish Giraud's political and military control over the French empire in northwest Africa. But then the revolutionary leaders had encountered an unexpected factor: the Vichy French vice-president, Admiral Jean F. Darlan, who commanded all Vichy French armed forces in France and in the empire, was in Algiers, visiting his son, Alain, an officer in the French navy, who was said to be dying of an incurable illness.

Darlan was the most hated Frenchman in Washington and London, a diehard of the German New Order. A foe of England, he was determined upon revenge for the destruction of the French navy battle squadron at Mers-el-Kebir in June 1940. "C" had secured evidence that it was Darlan who, far from destroying the document, gave the French copy of a main British naval cipher to the Germans. He had assisted Rashid Ali's rebellion against the British in Iraq in 1941. Again, it was Darlan who had arranged for French merchantmen to carry supplies to Rommel's army. And had he not supplied the transportation in French North Africa to get those supplies, and those run into French ports by Italo-German ships, to the German front in Libya in 1941 and again in 1942?

In October 1942, however, "C" had received a message from Darlan, probably through Bertrand, requesting the supreme command of the rumored American expedition to French North Africa and claiming that he could rally the French army there to the Allied side if he was appointed. No reply was sent to Darlan, it seems. But that a month later Darlan should be in Algiers was, as the official American historian noted, "a coincidence fraught with such impressive consequences that it has been attributed to premeditation and prearrangement." It seemed certain that the intentions of the Allies had reached Vichy in some way, although it seemed equally certain that Vichy had kept this information to themselves and had not passed it to Berlin or Rome.

(That certainty increased when it was discovered that a week or two before the landings, apparently, there had been a flood of French francs from the banks in France into those of French North Africa, the purpose to take advantage of the stabilization in the value of the franc that, it seems to have been known in Vichy, would follow the American occupation of French North Africa. The result was that the French metropolitan banks were estimated by the U.S. Treasury to have profited by at least $500 million on the rate of exchange.)

In seeking an explanation for Darlan's presence, Cadogan and "C" at least concluded, on the basis of what subsequently occurred at Algiers, that Robert Murphy, the U.S. consul-general at Algiers, had been in league with Darlan all along. It was noted that Murphy's mistress, the princess de Ligne, and the pretender to the French throne, the comte de Paris, both of whom were in Algiers, were strong supporters of Darlan.

Plainly there was evidence of leakage and conspiracy to further the political interests of Darlan, for, although he appeared surprised and irritated when he learned of the Allied landings, he knew enough to secure control of the city. In taking control of the apparatus of state, he arrested Murphy, Mast, and all others who had taken part in the Cherchel conspiracy to place Giraud in command and executed some of those French guides who led the American assault forces toward Algiers during the assault phase. Darlan then ordered all French forces to resist the invaders.

There was one compensation: Hitler at least had been taken by surprise. As the Allied convoys entered the Mediterranean and began landing on the Atlantic coast of French North Africa, Hitler was aboard his private train, rumbling through the hills of Franconia on his way to Munich, where he was to attend the nineteenth anniversary of the 1923 beer hall putsch. From dawn onward, teleprinted reports had reached the train that a mighty Allied armada of transports and warships—some said four million tons—was approaching the coast of French North Africa from Casablanca in Morocco to Bougie in Tunisia. But no one knew the destination of the convoys. Hitler's chief planner, Jodl, announced that "on the basis of somewhat vague reports, there are indications that the Anglo-Saxons intend multiple landings in West Africa."

All the available evidence pointed to the great French West African port of Dakar. Here, it should be said, an OSS secret agent, Donald Q. Coster, a "vice-consul" at the U.S. legation in Dakar, had been extraordinarily successful in his manipulation of two Austrian double agents, Lederer and Valikis, who were homosexuals spying for the German consul-general, Hans Auer, who was also chief of the German Armistice Control Commission in Dakar and chief of the Abwehr. Coster reported Auer was "a well-known pervert" who had taken an interest in Valikis and Lederer. Under Coster's direction, from June 1942 onward the young Austrians had supplied him with information "stolen from the American secret service" that the main Allied landings would be at Dakar, which was what the Germans were inclined to believe themselves. All Axis authorities from Hitler downward accepted the probability that an attack on Dakar was likely.

On the evening of November 7, Hitler had retired in his train parked beneath the Beerberg. At 2:00 A.M. an aide woke him and advised that the Allies were landing at all key points in French northwest Africa. Such was the surprise that the Allies could assemble such power that even eighteen months later Hitler recalled how startled he was and how he had exclaimed, "And we didn't even dream of it!" As it had been when the Germans took Whitehall by surprise in

April 1940 when they landed in Norway, so it was with Hitler. Hitler's "confidence in Canaris was completely destroyed" for "having failed to foresee and to inform the Reich authorities of the impending attack." [43] But if Hitler and Canaris were discomfited, the Allies had not as yet won the battle of Torch.

With Darlan in command in Algiers and Giraud still refusing to cooperate at Gibraltar, Eisenhower still had no French figure with the authority to replace Darlan. A broadcast had gone out to all Frenchmen in Giraud's name, but without his knowledge, calling upon them to render all assistance to "the valiant American Army wherever and whenever it appears," but that order of the day was largely ignored. Following much argument and threat, Giraud did relent and agreed to go to Algiers immediately, provided he did not have to fly in a British aircraft. Eisenhower accepted that condition and ordered a plane to be made ready to fly Giraud to Algiers, only to discover that there was no suitable American aircraft available at Gibraltar. An RAF Hudson was commandeered, its colors were replaced by those of the United States, and Giraud was then flown, still in civilian clothes, to Algiers to try and persuade the French army to cease fire.

That attempt failed, as Harold Macmillan was to remember, because Giraud had lost his uniform, that of a five-star general. The uniform had been sent from Gibraltar, but the package had been mislaid, and Giraud declined to act in civilian clothes. Macmillan exclaimed in his diary: "How to make a coup d'etat in a bowler hat? What a problem!" [44]

A new uniform was procured, but a precious day was lost, and when Giraud, properly dressed, confronted Admiral Darlan, he lost his nerve and placed himself under Darlan's orders. Later, it emerged, Giraud approved the award of Croix de Guerre with palms to certain French soldiers. But what for? Macmillan wished to know:

For resisting the landings. And how—by fighting English and American soldiers? Not even that—which (from one point of view) is a brave and meritorious act on the part of the individual soldier. No. For shooting two de Gaullist or pro-Ally irregulars who were helping to guide our troops. [45]

In these circumstances of black comedy, the French army resisted for a week, thereby delaying the disembarkation of the British First Army, which had the task of taking Tunis and the French port and naval base of Bizerte. By the time the army was ready to march, the timetable for the stab through the mountains to Tunis was wrecked, and the autumn rains had set in. And too late Eisenhower agreed to Darlan's insistence that he be recognized as the high commissioner of French North Africa and commander in chief of the French armed forces. The Germans and the Italians had succeeded in landing in Tunis before the British army could get there from Algiers. In consequence Eisenhower now faced a major military campaign.

When the guns under Darlan's command went silent, Allied casualties totaled 530 killed, 887 wounded, and 52 missing. All but 4 dead, 50 wounded, and 11 missing were American. When the guns in Tunisia went silent six months later, Allied casualties consisted of *Americans*, 2,715 dead, 8,978 wounded, 6,528 missing; *British*, 6,415 dead, 21,630 wounded, 7,835 missing; *French*, 1,100 dead, 8,080 wounded, 7,000 missing. The total, therefore, was 70,281 casualties, of whom 10,230 were dead.

If these developments took the Allied command by surprise, "C" at least was ready for them. As part of his operation to install parallel espionage and communications networks to those of OSS, four networks of secret agents began transmitting from Tunisia at the moment of H-Hour. As if by the wave of a wand, sixty-seven full-time subagents were activated to supplement Ultra. Three of the four groups of Tunisian agents had been in place since the spring of 1941.

They were led by a member of ORA code-named Tom Brown. Tom Brown had been in Tunis long enough before Torch to have developed all those assets necessary to survival and operations— trustworthy subagents, safe dwellings, sources of finance, wireless telegraphy with "C's" base at Malta, contacts with the beylical, municipal, police, and French colonial authorities, communications with the other SIS organizations in the country, and contacts established at all airfields, ports, and rail and road centers. It was the twenty-fourth such service formed by "C's" war station on Malta, these being purely espionage organizations scattered about Italy, Sardinia, Corsica, and North Africa.

Tom Brown's organization consisted of his own network and three subgroups code-named Lulu-Dupont, Y.Y.Y., and the Hirondelle Group. All four were in operation during the battle period, which lasted from November 8, 1942, until May 7, 1943, and their personnel were Britons, French, Maltese, and Tunisian natives. At first all four reported by wireless to "Station Alpha"—Malta—but as the battle developed, communications were opened to Eisenhower's headquarters at Algiers and to the British First Army advancing on Tunis. Casualties were heavy. Of the sixty-seven spies in or associated with the Tom Brown group, about 20 were known by February 5, 1943, to have been captured and taken to Germany as prisoners.

But as the battle report claimed, the operation was successful. In all, Tom Brown transmitted by radio a total of 585 messages during the four months of operations until his capture on February 24. That figure was remarkable, for during that entire period, according to the battle report, "the principal members of this group appear to have led a veritable 'Robin Hood' existence, never remaining in one place for more than a week or two and frequently escaping across the roofs of the native town, while the Gestapo was hammering on the door of their hastily vacated quarters."

These messages constituted a principal source of human intelligence from November 10, 1942, when the Germans and Italians began landing and it became evident that despite the Clark-Mast deal at Cherchel and the Darlan-Eisenhower deal at Algiers, the Tunis division of the French army would not resist the Italo-German landing in Tunisia and the commander of the Tunis division would collaborate with the arriving Axis command. That information was vital order-of-battle intelligence. Still more valuable was Tom Brown's warning to the First Army on November 14, 1942: the Germans had landed the new Tiger tanks. Mounting an eighty-eight-millimeter gun, they were heavier and better armored than any of the American or British tanks in Tunisia. He warned, too, that the Germans were using "Siebel ferries," seagoing craft with a drafts so shallow that at normal settings torpedoes from Allied submarines would pass *under* them. These craft were being used in large numbers to bring German armored fighting vehicles, transport, and munitions to Tunisia.

Taken together, Bletchley decrypts of German army and air force, Italian naval traffic, and SIS Tunisia provided what was to be described as "a virtually complete record of the shipping making for and arriving in Tunis and Bizerta from Italy and Sicily." It does appear that Tom Brown and his agents were of especial value in reporting on shipping arriving and departing the smaller Tunisian ports. But at all times Tom Brown was not more than a valuable adjunct to Ultra. Ultra remained the main—and the most trusted—source of intelligence throughout the campaign.

Yet if the renaissance of Broadway had begun, it did not occur without disaster. On September 3, 1942, Bertrand advised Dunderdale that on a recent visit to Paris he had seen "Max" of the German embassy. [46] "Max" had warned him that Hitler would, if the Allies invaded French North Africa, occupy all France. Of the forty-nine divisions in northwest Europe, eleven would be used to occupy the unoccupied zone, and two panzer divisions were already massing at Dijon ready to strike south to Marseilles down the Rhône valley. A similar movement was to take place from the Bordeaux area of southwestern France. At the same time, the Italians would march from their positions in southeastern France. That movement, Bertrand warned, would place P.C. Cadix in great danger. If the Germans marched, Bertrand thought that he would be compelled to evacuate P.C. Cadix. He was, he said, particularly anxious to get the Poles to London, for they knew far more about the Enigma attack than was good for their health.

With that warning, Dunderdale arranged the evacuation of the Spaniards by sea, leaving Bertrand, his wife, Mary, and the fifteen Poles at P.C. Cadix. Arrangements were made for their escape by sea, again to Algiers, while the Bertrands were to be brought in the first instance to London by air. The code name for the movement, to be broadcast on the French service of the BBC, was "The harvest is good." A British warship was sent to the area of La Napoule on the Riviera coast, but for reasons that are not clear the Poles were not embarked. Nor is it clear why the Bertrands were not immediately evacuated to London.

The last message from Bertrand to Dunderdale was dated November 5, 1942, when Bertrand indicated that the French intelligence service at Vichy and the Vichy government had not the slightest idea that the Allies intended to invade French North Africa, and, indeed, the feeling at Vichy was that they would *not* do so. After that message—which was confirmed by all others from all points—there was only silence.

The Funkabwehr had at last located P.C. Cadix. A number of radio-location vehicles were seen in the village near the château on November 3. Bertrand escaped immediately. By dawn on November 6 the Germans visited two farms near the château but did not try to enter the château because, so they were told, "Communists lived there." They did, however, keep the château under observation, so during the night Bertrand hid all secret materials. On November 8 they learned from the BBC that the Allies had landed in French North Africa.

Having secreted all equipment and archives during the dark hours, Bertrand and his party left the château at 1:00 P.M. on November 6, taking with him his secret archives as he passed through the German lines. Six days later the Germans raided the château. At Cannes

Bertrand rented four different apartments under four different identities. Arrangements were then made by radio to evacuate the Z team by British submarine, but that proved impossible when Bertrand discovered that the shoreline was occupied entirely by Italian troops. When that attempt failed, Bertrand then contemplated exfiltrating his wife, himself, and the Poles in French military aircraft leaving Istres, the airfield near Marseilles, but these planes left without Bertrand on November 11 with parties of French intelligence officers.

Bertrand then considered sending the Poles out into Switzerland, but again that proved impossible, partly because some of the Poles were drinking liquor so heavily that they might attract attention and partly because all roads were blocked by the invading German and Italian forces. Bertrand then returned to Cannes, where the party remained at great peril until January 14, when the first party of Poles left Cannes for the Franco-Spanish frontier at Perpignan. They were followed by the second party on February 4. On or about February 5, however, the Poles were sold out to the French or German border guards by their Spanish guide. Two of them, Fonk and Lenoire, were captured by the Germans. Both died in German hands, Fonk of an illness and Lenoire during an Allied bombing attack. Both died without revealing their secret to the Germans. The rest—and these included the people who knew the most—were captured by the Spaniards but rescued by "C," who exfiltrated them to England.

Meanwhile, Bertrand and his wife had returned to their home at Theoule, where Bertrand placed himself at the disposal of an SIS intelligence network Kleber, resuming contact with Dunderdale over Kleber's wireless. Bertrand remained with Kleber for a year until January 1944. And then he, too, was captured by the Germans.

7 THE MURDER OF ADMIRAL DARLAN

By mid-November the outcry within the Grand Alliance against Eisenhower's recognition of Darlan as the political and military leader became a crisis. Churchill warned Roosevelt:

I ought to let you know that very deep currents of feeling are stirred by the arrangements with Darlan. The more I reflect upon it the more convinced

I become that it can only be a temporary expedient justifiable solely by the stress of battle. We must not overlook the serious political injury which may be done to our cause, not only in France but throughout Europe. . . . Darlan has an odious record. . . . It is but yesterday that French sailors were sent to their death against your line of battle off Casablanca and now, for the sake of power and office, Darlan plays the turncoat. [47]

To restore harmony and allay the concerns, Roosevelt made a public statement that Darlan's appointments were indeed no more than a temporary expedient, and that no permanent arrangement had been made with him. But this did little to restore confidence at the Foreign Office. Cadogan felt increasingly sure that U.S. political authorities had been, as he recorded in his diary on November 17, "playing with Darlan all the time." He added: "I wouldn't put it past them. But if it could be proved, I would have a God Almighty showdown with them." The Americans were "becoming impossible at all points, and are lecturing us now on Persia, about which they know nothing. I urge that we should put our foot down *now*—it will only be more difficult and more dangerous later."

With the German occupation of the Vichy zone of France, and the subsequent breakdown in such organizations as the Ordre de la Resistance de l'Armee, all "C's" intelligence assets were swept away or disorganized. Those assets that remained in place in northern France were badly demoralized by the Darlan deal. The militant Socialists in Europe were declaring in their telegrams that there was no point in fighting the Germans if the Allies made pacts with the very forces they were fighting—fascism, nazism, and extreme right-wing nationalism. As "C" warned Cadogan, as long as Darlan remained in place, Churchill's policy of "setting Europe ablaze" through the underground movements had little chance of prospering. The Communists in France in particular would not fight if they believed that the real Allied policy was to place men such as Darlan as the leaders of the liberated territories.

The anger and dismay was, if anything, intensified when on November 22 Darlan announced at Allied headquarters in Algiers to all French diplomats abroad that he had "taken military and *administrative* control of the French *Empire*!!" Cadogan added, with more menace than admiration, "He *is* a card!" The British Parliament went into secret session to discuss the crisis (the Donovan agency being secretly provided with the minutes for transmission to FDR, to ensure the president was aware of the depth of the pools stirred by the deal). Underlying the crisis was a sense that the Americans had neither the training nor the international experience to handle charlatans such as Darlan, who, as Cadogan observed in his diary, was running rings around the U.S. command in Algiers. Such were the dangers that at one stage Eisenhower's chief of staff, General Walter Bedell Smith, proposed to Churchill that Cadogan should fly to Algiers to act as Eisenhower's political adviser, and all arrangements were made for Cadogan's departure.

By November 25 the crisis had further deepened when one of the main reasons why Darlan was appointed—his claim that he could bring the French fleet over to the side of the Grand Alliance—proved illusory. The French commander in chief in France ignored Darlan's orders, and as the Germans were arriving in the port of Toulon to seize control of the fleet, French officers scuttled seventy-three ships there. At that point Cadogan began to contemplate action to remove Darlan from the scene. That had been the work of "C's" Section D until Churchill created the Special Operations Executive in 1940 to "set Europe ablaze." Cadogan, however, regarded SOE as an amateurish organization capable of working only at a low political level. The liquidation of Darlan required "C's" political skills and discretion.

Those signs became clearer when Cadogan confided to his diary on November 14, 1942, the ominous words "The Americans and naval officers in Algiers are letting us in for a *pot* of trouble. We shall do no good until we've killed Darlan." Cadogan showed afresh what was in his mind again, this time at a dinner at the Savoy Hotel on December 8, 1942, in the presence of Foreign Secretary Anthony Eden, General de Gaulle, General Catroux, and an assistant undersecretary of state, William Strang. As Cadogan's diary entry shows, whenever he raised the Darlan issue, "De G.'s one remedy is 'Get rid of Darlan.' My answer is 'Yes; but how?' No answer."

In what was one of the most mysterious of the several crises affecting "C" personally, Fernand Bonnier de la Chapelle, in his early twenties, a Royalist zealot undergoing training as a secret agent of SOE, entered the Palace of State in Algiers on Christmas Eve and hid. As Darlan returned from luncheon Bonnier shot him to death. Darlan's last words were said to have been "The British have finally done for me."

When Bonnier was arrested and interrogated, he admitted that he was a lieutenant in the Corps Franc d'Afrique, a paramilitary organization formed by Giraud. This organization wore the British uniform and was being trained in special means at a joint OSS/SOE base at Ain Taya, just outside Algiers, to be parachuted into France by OSS or SOE to lead the Maquis, a French underground movement that had sprung up immediately after Torch. So far as was known, Bonnier had no connection with "C's" organization, which was concerned solely with espionage and deception.

Immediately after the murder, however, strong rumors spread from the French high command that not only was "C's" service behind the assassination, but it also intended to murder others in order to enable Churchill to annex French North Africa to the British Empire. The other victims, the rumors held, included Eisenhower, Giraud, and Robert Murphy. Within a week these rumors had become so strong and damaging that Admiral Sir Andrew Cunningham, commander in chief of Torch naval forces and the deputy supreme commander of Torch, telegraphed the first sea lord in London on December 29, advising that Giraud, who by now was in French North Africa in command of the French army, had told Murphy that "the French" had discovered

an assassination ring in Algiers and that they have been led to believe that the British Secret Service is behind it. Eisenhower told me of this and he is reporting [the discovery to General Marshall]. . . . The first three names on the list are reported to be Giraud, Bergeret, and Murphy. The French are taking it very seriously and the above mentioned are being very heavily guarded. [48]

Expressing anxiety at the effect the rumors might have on his French relationships, "C" placed the question before the Defense Committee, the organization through which Churchill directed the British war, on December 30. The committee thereupon took an unprecedented step: it made a public comment on matters pertaining to "C's" service. As Cadogan recorded in his diary for December 30, 1942:

5:30 went to see [Admiral Sir Dudley] Pound [First Sea Lord] to arrange telegram, to Cunningham authorising him to deny charges that Secret Service was in any way connected with Darlan murder.

Accordingly, Admiral Pound replied to Cunningham that same day:

Whatever French may have discovered, it cannot incriminate any branch of British secret service, who do not indulge in such activities, and you may of course give General Eisenhower formal assurance to this effect. Defence Committee have no doubt that you took early and energetic action to stop spread of these absurd stories. [49]

However, the British and American secret services may have been more deeply involved in Darlan's murder than that signal acknowledged. The murder weapon, a Colt Woodsman, a powerful hunting pistol, had belonged to Bonnier's commanding officer, Major Carleton Coon, former professor of anthropology at Yale. Coon claimed the weapon was stolen from his locker at Ain Taya a day or two before the murder.

Coon also admitted that he was in the vicinity of the Palais d'Ete at the time of the murder, having come into Algiers, he explained, to obtain treatment for a head injury received in accident at Ain Taya while showing the Corps Franc d'Afrique how to use plastique explosives. Coon stated that he was also in the city to attend a Christmas Day celebration with a Colonel Eddy, but that Eddy ordered him to leave the city immediately and join a combined OSS/SOE unit on operations at the front in Tunisia. He did so dressed as a British army officer and carrying papers showing him to be a "Captain Ritinitis," a man who had been killed while on operations. As Coon explained, Eddy had ordered him out of town—at a time when the French security authorities were placing all British and American secret service and special operations personnel and property under surveillance—"it seemed to be a good idea" for Coon "to drop out of sight" for the "sake of others as well as himself." [50]

To increase the murkiness surrounding Darlan's murder, it emerged that Coon had written a memorandum (a copy of which has survived) advocating assassination as an instrument of politics in cases where it was necessary to nip "the causes of potential disturbance in the bud" in political relations. He recommended for that purpose a specially trained force of Anglo-Americans whose job it would be to "throw out the rotten apples" in political affairs "as soon as the first spots of decay appear." [51]

Whatever the influences that lay behind Bonnier, therefore, the affair was further obscured by the activities of a drumhead court-martial, established by Giraud, which sat in judgment upon Bonnier during the middle of the night of December 25–26, 1942. Bonnier was found guilty of the murder of Admiral Darlan and was executed by a French firing squad immediately afterward. These proceedings took place in secrecy without the presence of any Allied officer.

The French Imperial Council, which was responsible for the administration of French North Africa, then met on December 27, and, at last, Giraud was appointed high commissioner of French North Africa and, as "C" had intended, commander in chief of the sizable

French forces in the territory. The council then acted again in proceedings intended to annul Bonnier's sentence and to restore his civil rights posthumously on the grounds that documents had been found that "showed conclusively that Admiral Darlan had been acting against the interest of France and that Bonnier's act had been accomplished in the interests of the liberation of France." [52]

The outburst of French nervousness so often stimulated by anything to do with *l'intelligence service* then subsided; and it might have died away altogether but for the fact that "C," the man who never went anywhere beyond St. James's unless in the imperial interest, was in Algiers secretly at the time of the murder. Indeed, he may well have left London for Algiers within a day or two of Cadogan's discussion with de Gaulle. The date and circumstances of his sudden journey are known, for as "C's" personal assistant, Patrick Reilly, was to recall:

This was perhaps the strangest episode of my term as "C's" personal assistant. At the beginning of December 1942 "C" asked me whether I would like to take a short leave. I was surprised at this suggestion, for it was the only time he made such a suggestion. I was rather tired and I accepted gratefully, and when I went on leave "C" was at his desk. When I got back "C" was still at his desk. I did not know he had been away on a foreign journey and did not know until forty years later that he had been away, and then only when Winterbotham wrote to me and asked me if I knew why "C" had gone to Algiers. I then saw that the coincidence was remarkable, although I still cannot say that "C's" journey had anything to do with Darlan's murder, except that "C" was in Algiers when it took place. I am now inclined to the view that he gave me leave at that time because he wanted me out of the way while he was abroad. Had I not been on leave, I would have been at my desk at Broadway and I would certainly have known that he had gone to Algiers. [53]

As for the reason put about for Menzies's journey, Winterbotham, who visited Eisenhower's headquarters in Algiers on Ultra business at that same time, was to record in a memoir:

When I got back to Algiers [from the Tunisian front] I was overjoyed to find that my old friend Georges Ronin [of the air section of the French secret service] in Paris had managed to get out of France, when the Germans [invaded the unoccupied zone of France], in a small civil aeroplane and had flown, along with his late chief, across to Algiers. When Stewart Menzies had heard the news in London he flew out so that he could meet [Colonel Louis Rivet, chief of the old French secret service] and between us perhaps start up a new French Intelligence service based in Algiers.

On Christmas Eve, the day of Darlan's murder, Winterbotham continued:

Colonel Rivet and Georges Ronin gave Stewart Menzies and me a splendid lunch on the sun-drenched roof of a little house in Algiers. With the coffee came the news that Darlan had been shot in his house a few hundred yards away. [54]

But according to Winterbotham, the murder occasioned no surprise and no great discussion, and it appeared that "they could not have cared less."

In all, therefore, it is possible to suggest that "C" was in Algiers to ensure that the "immobilization" of Darlan—to use the French term for assassination—was not botched. Cadogan had referred twice to the need to kill Darlan, although Cadogan argued later it was never meant literally.

Whatever the truth was, however, we shall not know it. Nobody was better than "C" at keeping a secret. That he was back in London in time for New Year's Eve there is no doubt. As for what "C" was doing in Algiers, there was, naturally, not a word in Cadogan's most secret and personal diary. All that Cadogan recorded in his diary for New Year's Eve was: " 'C' at 3:30. Very little work & not much news." As for the situation in Algiers, all he wrote was that he had had "a more cheering telegram from Eisenhower" but that "we must see what happens."

With that vague comment the foreign affairs of England entered 1943.

Seven

Triumphs and Troubles

1943

1 "SAFEGUARD OUR PRECIOUS SECRET"

In the New Year's Honours List of 1943, the *London Gazette* announced that Stewart Graham Menzies was created a Knight Commander of the Most Distinguished Order of St. Michael and St. George, a Foreign Office order of chivalry established by George III in 1818. "C" was invested with the order at a private ceremony at Buckingham Palace on February 1. Menzies bowed, advanced to the kneeling stool, knelt by his right knee, and was tapped lightly on both shoulders by the king with a short sword, a custom that originated in the knighting of faithful servants on the battlefield.

This was a proud moment experienced by few men. When Menzies rose he was no longer a commoner but a knight of the realm, one styled Brigadier Sir Stewart Menzies, K.C.M.G., C.B., D.S.O., M.C. "C's" wife became Lady Menzies. He was fifty-three and the first member of his immediate family to receive a knighthood. The king congratulated his latest knight and then Menzies left the royal presence, bowing as he went, into the daylight and a world at war.

A shoal of congratulatory letters descended upon him.

General Ismay's letter was generous. "Dear Old Stew," it began. "I wish it had been a 'G,' " using the Whitehall slang for the senior degree of the order, that of the Knight Grand Cross, adding:

It would have been if I had had any say in the matter. Anyway, it is nice to have. I am glad the powers that be have at long last realised to some extent what a hell of a job you've done these last 12 years. No answer.

Yours Ever,
Pug

There were many other such letters from all the members of Churchill's inner circle, but from Churchill, who was at Casablanca with Roosevelt, charting the future course of the war, the only message "C" received was an irritable signal on January 18, 1942, concerning Ultra: "Why have you not kept me properly supplied with news? Volume should be increased at least five-fold and important messages sent textually." [1]

The ceremonial over, "C" returned to the reality of the war. Charged by the Casablanca conference to do all in his power to defeat the new U-boat cipher, there was nothing in his past that equipped him for this decisive task of intelligence in World War II, a task that Churchill defined obliquely only much later:

This was the secret war, whose battles were lost or won unknown to the public, and only with difficulty comprehended, even now, by those outside the small high scientific circles concerned. No such warfare had ever been waged by mortal men. The terms in which it could be recorded or talked about were unintelligible to ordinary folk. Yet if we had not mastered its profound meaning and used its mysteries even while we only saw them in the glimpse, all the efforts, all the prowess of the fighting airmen, all the bravery and sacrifices of the people, would have been in vain. [2]

"C" understood neither the high sciences nor the people involved. He did, however, understand the need to protect "the source," how to baffle the enemy about its existence, and how to direct him away from the truth when he began, as he did, to inquire into the causes of his defeats and discomfitures. Here, then, developed the ultimate campaign of the war, a campaign in which nuance, subtlety, hunch, intuition became all. In defense of Ultra, "C" and his colleagues developed a form of intuition, almost of second sight, as they scrutinized each Ultra that bore upon the security of what Churchill called "our precious secret."

With the output of Ultra rising to 84,000 items *a month*—two every minute of a calendar month—"C" knew exactly how the source could be secured. Although a basic law of life held that a secret known to three people was not a secret, and that if a secret had to be kept from an enemy, it should not be imparted to a friend, this was nevertheless what "C" attempted, but only according to Broadway's procedures, the system that "the amateurs" regarded with such scorn. "C" had demonstrated the lengths to which he was prepared to go in defense of Ultra over the Crete affair. The defense of Ultra became "C's" most important task of the war, and in the end he became a prisoner of the secret, for he could not reveal it even in his own defense. Such a secret did it become, indeed, that at the bar of history Churchill felt compelled to dissemble about it even twenty years on. Yet there were several close calls. The German invasion of Crete, for instance, and two years earlier when the Americans had cut off Magic.

Yet even as the Americans resumed the supply of Magic to the British, a third threat to Ultra had evolved. Between May 7 and July 11, 1941, naval Ultra disclosed the whereabouts of eight of fifteen German supply ships sent to support the German battleship *Bismarck* when she sailed into the Atlantic to raid British convoys. In the initial engagement, HMS *Hood*, a British battle cruiser, was sunk with the loss of almost all aboard, about fourteen hundred men. *Bismarck* did not herself escape damage in the engagement, and she made off with British warships in pursuit.

During the night, however, the shadowing British cruiser *Suffolk* lost the battleship, causing great anxiety within the Admiralty. Since *Bismarck* maintained complete wireless silence, the Admiralty had no means of locating the battleship's whereabouts and bringing her to battle with the very powerful naval force sent to the area. Had *Bismarck* turned back to Germany? Was she making for Brest on the French Atlantic coast? Or would she escape by heading deeper into the Atlantic? *Bismarck*'s captain, Admiral Lutjens, settled the problem for the Admiralty.

In the erroneous belief that he was still being shadowed at daybreak on May 25, and that his position was known to the British, Lutjens sent two long signals to a shore station. Those signals were intercepted by Y stations in England, they were identified as messages from a large warship, and the position of the transmitting ship was plotted. The *Bismarck* was intercepted and sunk in what was one of the epic naval engagements of the war.

Since *Bismarck* was located by wireless intelligence, not through Ultra, "C" was not concerned with the intelligence methods used to locate the battleship until the navy began to sink or capture all but one of the fifteen support ships. Although the loss of eight of these vessels owed nothing to Enigma, and although the Admiralty had ordered that some ships be allowed to escape to prevent suspicion falling upon "the source," the Admiralty was nevertheless embarrassed by its victory. However skillfully the Admiralty had conducted the operations in order not to bring down German attention upon Enigma, "C" feared that the Germans would undertake such a searching inquiry into the loss of so many ships in so short a time that they would learn Enigma was penetrated. Then they would attribute *all* their losses to that cause and withdraw Enigma from service throughout the German armed forces. However, Enigma continued in the German service.

"C" did become alarmed at four incidents between July and November 1941 in which Ultra might have been compromised:

1 = The commander in chief South Atlantic repeated to one of his destroyers the three U-boat positions that had been sent him in an Ultra. Had that signal been intercepted and read by the Germans, they would inevitably have concluded that the naval Enigma was compromised.

2 = The officer commanding submarines at Malta sent to one of his submarines almost the exact text of an Ultra giving full details of the arrangements made for sailing an Italian convoy to North Africa. The danger to Ultra was obvious: if the submarine was captured or entered after it was sunk, as could always happen, then the copy of the signal would have been found and compared to the Italian original. Then it would have been discovered that the Italian machine cipher was penetrated.

3 = The commander in chief Mediterranean transmitted to the naval attaché at Ankara, a man who was not an authorized Ultra recipient and one who was based in a neutral country, the contents of a decrypt that revealed that the enemy knew of an Allied plan to pass Russian tankers in the Black Sea.

4 = The flag officer commanding the North Atlantic at Gibraltar repeated to ships and other authorities, none of whom knew that Ultra was a state secret, three U-boat positions sent to him in an Ultra. [3]

In each case, these incidents occurred through carelessness or an imperfect understanding of the Ultra regulations governing the circumstances under which Ultra could be used to intercept enemy warships. And if these regulations were irksome, sensible men did not doubt their necessity. These actions brought "sharp rebukes" from the Admiralty. They also brought equally sharp reminders of the need for care, attention, and skill in ensuring that whenever Ultra was used to make an intercept the Germans were *always* provided with plausible evidence that showed some source *other* than Enigma for the otherwise inexplicable appearance of a British warship.

These rebukes and reminders were effective since there were no more such scares for almost a year. "C," however, did have trouble with Churchill, who in April 1941 began to display irritation at Menzies's insistence that all decodes be paraphrased before they were sent to the Middle East commands. Here his complaint focused on the conviction that paraphrases "were not reflecting the full flavour of the original decrypts," and he pressed "C" and others for a greater exploitation of Ultra. But "C" did not relent on this issue. Not until November did Churchill again fully recognize the need for care. At the same time, "C" recognized Churchill's point about the need to convey the full flavor of authenticity. He agreed to send Ultra in its "raw" state, but only to commanders in chief who knew the importance of the source to the country.

In that fresh spirit, Churchill sent this message to General Sir Claude Auchinleck, commander in chief in the Middle East, in November:

C is sending you daily our special stuff. Feel sure you will not let any of this go into battle zone except as statements on your own authority with no trace of origin and not too close a coincidence. There seems great danger of documents being captured in view of battle confusion.

Churchill's caution ended: "Excuse my anxiety." [4]

Yet if Auchinleck was well informed about his German adversary, General Erwin Rommel, commanding general of the Italo-German Armeegruppe Afrika, Rommel was better informed. His cryptanalysts were able to read the cipher of the U.S. military attaché in Cairo, Colonel Frank Bonner Feller, who was kept fully informed of British strength, morale, capabilities, and intentions, either by Auchinleck personally or by his deputy. Intercepted by the German B-Dienst, the equivalent of Bletchley, Feller's cipher was then relayed to Rommel by secure means. Add to this Rommel's superior generalship, the skill and resolution of his men, and the superiority of some of his equipment, and it becomes possible to explain the series of defeats that marked the desert war in 1941 and the first half of 1942.

Even so, by the second half of 1942 the weakness of Feller's cipher had been detected by the Y service, Feller was removed, the Ultra service had expanded, and the official historian was able to write that

the British forces in North Africa were supplied with more information about more aspects of the enemy's operations than any forces enjoyed during any important campaign in the Second World War—and, probably, of any earlier war. In time, the intelligence helped them to turn the tide in the North African campaign.

General Auchinleck believed that, but for Ultra, "Rommel would certainly have got through to Cairo" in June 1942. With the arrival of General Sir Harold Alexander as commander in the Middle East and General Sir Bernard Montgomery as commander in chief of the Eighth Army, combined with the exhaustion of the Italo-German armies, the front was stabilized at El Alamein, a halt on the Cairo–Tripoli railroad on the Mediterranean near the Libyan-Egyptian frontier. The British then prepared for a major counteroffensive to drive Rommel out of North Africa, coincidentally with the Allied Torch landings.

The transmission of "raw" Ultra to Auchinleck appears to have been carried out without alerting the enemy. But then in June 1942 the first American security failure proved to be the gravest breach of Ultra security so far. And it occurred just as the first Americans—Paul K. Whitaker, Selmer Norland, and Arthur Levenson—arrived for work at Bletchley. That failure concerned the Battle of Midway, fought between the American and Japanese fleets off Midway Island in the Pacific in June 1942, one of the most critical battles of the war fought at the war's most critical juncture. That the U.S. Navy was able to defeat the Japanese task force with inferior forces was a victory derived from Magic.

Armed with complete intelligence about the capabilities and intentions of the Japanese task force commander, the American commander was able to deploy his forces effectively and smash the Japanese fleet. Despite the security agreements, the British representatives to the Combined Chiefs of Staff were stunned when, while lunching at the U.S. Navy headquarters canteen on Sunday, June 7, 1942, they overheard a conversation at the next table in which a man in civilian clothes told a party of eight that "the United States authorities could read the Japanese naval ciphers, and as a consequence they knew the movements of the Japanese vessels before-hand." [5]

After the lunch a British official took the man aside and questioned him. He was an official of the Australian Purchasing Commission, a certain Van Valzah, who declared that the information he had imparted was "public knowledge." It certainly was. It had been published earlier that day by the *Chicago Tribune* under the headlines:

JAP FLEET SMASHED BY U.S

2 CARRIERS SUNK AT MIDWAY

NAVY HAD WORD OF JAP PLAN TO STRIKE AT SEA

KNEW DUTCH HARBOR WAS A FEINT

That same story had appeared simultaneously in the *New York Daily News*, the *Washington Times-Herald*, and four midwestern newspapers associated with the *Chicago Tribune*. Rear Admiral Layton, the U.S. Pacific fleet's intelligence officer, who investigated the leakage, was to recall:

My personal horror of the situation was greater, because it appeared that the information on which the story was based had been taken directly from our Cincpac bulletin, which had been sent out to all task force commanders on 31 May. [6]

Layton's horror was no less than that of "C" when he heard about the breach, for he had been pressing the Americans to do something to limit the American press's freedom to publish stories involving signals intelligence. Had a law been in force, the press discussion that flowed from the *Tribune*'s disclosures would have been limited. But there was no such law, and the press discussion became national. A national columnist made the statement in the public print that "when the history of these times is written, it will be revealed that *twice* the fate of the civilized world was changed by intercepted messages," explaining further that he could not enlarge on what he had said because "it is military information." [7]

The result was inevitable. The Japanese withdrew the cipher involved, JN-25, from service at the very time it seemed possible that they would invade India, Australia, and Ceylon. Consequently, relations between "C" and the U.S. military and naval intelligence departments became "very bad" from the *Tribune* affair until April 1943, the period of the negotiations intended to establish full state agreements relating to the exchange of Ultra and Magic.

Donovan made his own contribution to those bad relations when, in an operation he had authorized, OSS agents burgled the Japanese consulate at Lisbon to obtain the cipher used by the Japanese military attaché. The operation was successful except for the fact that the Japanese discovered the cipher was missing and warned Tokyo that it was probably compromised. Tokyo withdrew the cipher from use. It turned out that both the Americans and the British had been reading the stolen cipher on a current basis for over a year. The source was therefore lost, an incident that did nothing to improve OSS's poor standing.

Miraculously, it seems, the Germans took little if any interest in the *Tribune* or Lisbon affairs and did not connect them with their own misfortunes in the Atlantic and Mediterranean theaters. But that failure provided "C" with little comfort, for all too soon afterward there occurred yet another serious breach. This one was made even more serious because the man responsible was no less a person than Britain's leading fighting general, Montgomery, an officer who should have known better.

On August 24, 1942, Bletchley decrypted a message from Rommel to the German supreme command in which Rommel announced that he was seriously ill and asked to be relieved by General Heinz Guderian, the armored warfare specialist. He suffered from liver trouble, severe desert sores, and a general debility so often suffered by high commanders fighting in inclement climates. That signal made a great impact at Montgomery's headquarters, for an intense rivalry had developed between Montgomery and Rommel. Moreover, that Rommel was hors de combat was important news to the fighting men. Such was Rommel's legend for omnipotence and martial skill that even Churchill felt compelled to pay tribute to Rommel in a parliamentary speech. "We have a very daring and skillful opponent against us," declared Churchill, "and, may I say across the havoc of war, a great general."

As the import of that Ultra circulated, "C" began sending General Sir Harold Alexander, the new commander in the Middle East, decrypts that gave Montgomery, commander of the Eighth Army in the field, a complete picture of Rommel's plans and intentions for his next attack. To be made in the direction of Alam Halfa, about fifteen miles to the east of El Alamein, the attack involved a very powerful right hook of tanks, self-propeled guns, and lorried infantry intended to cut Eighth Army's lines of retreat back into Egypt. Churchill was at the front at that moment and witnessed what occurred.

Taken to a key point southeast of the Ruweisat Ridge, there "amid the hard, rolling curves and creases of the desert," Montgomery had hidden "the mass of our armor, camouflaged, concealed, and dispersed, yet tactically concentrated." Every crevice of the desert was "packed with camouflaged concealed batteries." In all, some four hundred guns were so sited that, without Rommel's knowledge, they could play on his main point of attack. At the same time, Montgomery, already aware from Ultra that Rommel's main problem was motor and aviation fuel, also became aware from Ultra that the Italians were about to send no less than twenty tankers and supply ships to Rommel's ports.

With that supply train disrupted by the Royal Air Force, Rommel's attack began on the night of August 30. He drove into Montgomery's trap ambush, the artillery decimated his columns, and then the armor moved onto the battlefield to complete Rommel's defeat. Rommel had suffered a blow from which he did not recover.

After that battle, news about Rommel's bad health began to circulate in Cairo, London, and Washington. The consequences were inevitable. The news leaked into the world's press in the first week of September 1942, as Eisenhower prepared for Torch and Montgomery did likewise at El Alamein. By that time there had already been indications in German military decrypts that the Germans, alarmed by Axis shipping losses in the Mediterranean, had set up an inquiry about the security of their ciphers. The press stories about Rommel's illness produced much alarm at Broadway and Bletchley, therefore, the more so since Axis diplomatic intercepts indicated that the source of the leak was in London. Ultra security now became a Cabinet matter.

On September 9 Churchill asked the Cabinet secretary, Sir Edward Bridges, to investigate, and as he was doing so a further decrypt, one dated September 11, showed that the Germans were now "highly suspicious" that Montgomery had had foreknowledge about Rommel's plans at Alam Halfa, as indeed he had. It was true that the Ultra indicated the source of Montgomery's foreknowledge was Italian prisoners-of-war. Nevertheless, the "Prime Minister suspected that General Montgomery had been too free with the Engima intelligence, using Italian POW statements as cover, and that this cover was far from adequate." Montgomery was "rebuked" and told to be "more careful." [8]

Following the Alam Halfa incident, when "C" and Churchill met they decided that Ultra carrying with it a high risk of provoking gossip should be withheld from general circulation and confined to "C" and the prime minister. They would then decide whether the decrypt should be withheld completely or sent to the appropriate commander with a special warning. In all, about 540 such signals were withheld, mainly involving Hitler's and Goering's signals to the fronts, allegations concerning war crimes by American troops, matters concerning Allied prisoners-of-war, and German orders of the day, along with entire series concerning German intelligence activities and all diplomatic decodes. Yet even those security measures could not stem the leakages and gossip.

"C" found no fault with Montgomery's handling of the decrypts during the El Alamein battle and the pursuit of the German and Italian armies along the North African coast to the Tunisian frontier, but he did find severe fault with the statement of one of Montgomery's tank commanders, a man who under the regulations should have had no knowledge of, or access to, Ultra.

In what was the eleventh known security mishap since November 1941, any one of which could have alerted the enemy to their peril, General Alexander H. Gatehouse, commander of the Tenth Armoured Division, which had done well at Al-Alamein, was sent to Washington after the battle to describe for the benefit of the U.S. press how the great battle was won. Gatehouse opened his American tour with a lunch and address at the National Press Club in Washington on August 16, 1943. He announced that the British "had broken the German code after El Alamein." [9] That declaration caused consternation in the Joint Staff Mission, where the Ultra secret was an even more closely held secret than that concerning the atomic bomb.

An inquiry into Gatehouse's statement showed that the remark went unnoticed by the large numbers of American newspapermen there, but not by the Reuters representative, an Englishman. He understood the significance of the remark, if not its secrecy, and had sent the statement to London for dissemination. The Reuters man was "put on the mat," but what action was taken to suppress dissemination in London (for dissemination was suppressed) is not known. However, the chairman of the board of Reuters, Sir John Chancellor, *was* a close friend of "C."

As for Gatehouse's career, he did not get a knighthood, which was almost automatic for divisional commanders. He was not reemployed in a fighting capacity for the rest of the war. Later he became British army representative in Moscow and then aide-de-camp to the king before being retired at the age of fifty-two in 1947. He was not court-martialed, however, for that would have drawn attention to the original indiscretion. Gatehouse was quietly ruined in a fashion that would become apparent to the rest of the General Staff.

"C" acted in a similarly indirect fashion to make OSS conform to the security program for Torch. Already totally excluded from Ultra and from all cryptanalytical activity by presidential order, "C" was authorized to establish an organization with the code name Lonmay at Gibraltar. This was under the command of Wing Commander Hugh "Bombshell" Mallory, and its purpose was to watch all OSS wireless traffic to ensure that the ciphers were secure and gave nothing away to the enemy. That operation was skillfully conducted, OSS cipher discipline was enhanced, and despite the weakness of State Department ciphers—they were so primitive that it was claimed they could be "unbuttoned" over tea—the enemy learned nothing from OSS that he was not intended to learn.

Even so, Lonmay did little to resolve the antagonisms between OSS and Broadway. The OSS men in Tangier learned of the existence of Lonmay and, misunderstanding its purpose, believed that here was an example of Broadway spying on OSS. And if Mallory did enforce secure communications, it did him little good personally. The OSS investigated his activities and background, and the investigator, Carleton Coon, accused Mallory in a report of being a German spy.

As Coon advised OSS headquarters in Washington, Mallory took "an undue interest in the technical aspects of the OSS cipher." That interest caused Coon to become suspicious of Mallory, and Coon alleged that there was "strong evidence to support the thesis that Mallory was a traitor." That allegation caused great anxiety at British headquarters at Gibraltar, but in the end it was found that Mallory's greatest crime was to have failed to realize the elementary principle of Anglo-American clandestine relationships: the Americans did not mind learning from the English, but they did resent being instructed by them.

As that drama unfolded, and Torch was lit, Churchill again became concerned about the expansion in the number of persons who had been cleared to read Ultra, and on November 21 he wrote to "C": "Pray consider whether, at this period in the operation, it would not be wise to have a general campaign to reduce to one-third the circulation of Boniface [in London], in the Middle East, and at the Torch headquarters." What he had in mind was that "there would be 2 classes of Boniface, starred and unstarred. The starred would only go to the new restricted circle. The unstarred would continue as at present, but would gradually die away, it being suggested that the hens are laying much less, or even not at all."

Soon, however, there was another serious breach of the Ultra regulations. This time the culprit was the naval commander in chief of Torch and deputy supreme commander, Admiral Sir Andrew Cunningham. What had occurred was explained by the official historian in terms that reflected the extreme intricacy of the wireless game being played on both sides:

On 11 December 1942 the Naval Officer in Charge [of] Bone delayed a convoy movement in a signal which was made in a cypher that Whitehall suspected of being insecure, and which gave as his reason the fact that he expected an E-boat attack. This expectation was based on a decrypt of which the gist had been sent to Algiers by GC&CS. To make matters worse, NOIC was not an authorized Ultra recipient. To make matters worse still, it was now confirmed that the cypher used by the NOIC was being read by the enemy: the enemy cancelled the E-boat attack and it was an Enigma decrypt ordering the cancellation and reproducing the NOIC's signal which brought the incident to Whitehall's notice. [10]

That incident, combined with other evidence, led "Whitehall"— "C"—to the startling realization that for many months the Germans had themselves been reading British Naval Cypher No. 3, one of the ciphers used by the American, British, and Canadian navies to communicate with each other. Since it had been suspected for some time that this cipher might have been penetrated, no references to Ultra were ever sent over that link, such references being confined to the U.S. Electrical Cypher Machine, which was considered secure by the Admiralty. The Germans, therefore, learned nothing through their reading of messages sent in the compromised British cipher.

But the slips continued. By now Rommel's suspicions about the security of his communication were again aroused. "All wireless is treason," warned General Erich Fellgiebel, the German chief signals officer. Henceforward Rommel reduced his communications to the barest minimum, and all that he did he enveloped in serpentine cover stories. He took such skillful security precautions regarding his communications during the preparatory phase of the battle—precautions caused by his earlier suspicions regarding Ultra—that he took the Americans completely by surprise at Kasserine Pass in Tunisia, a battle that opened on February 14, 1943. American casualties were severe, and Brigadier Mockler-Ferryman, Eisenhower's chief of intelligence, was sacked for what was called "over-dependence upon a single source of information." [11]

That battle was not a breach of Ultra security regulations, but Rommel's success demonstrated to him that he could succeed when he was careful what he said on Enigma. Aware of Rommel's continuing suspicions, both "C" and Rommel began to play an increasingly complex game, the former to conceal his intentions, the latter to deflect Rommel's suspicions from Enigma to other sources of possible leakage.

"C" played upon a German predisposition to believe that their defeats were due not to any insecurity in their communications, but to the treachery and incompetence of their Italian allies. He leaked information to the Germans that seemed to show there was a group of Italian spies at Naples and elsewhere on the Italian mainland, and that they were reporting the departures, course, and speeds of supply ships sailing for North Africa. To account for the press leakages and what seemed to be the leakage of Rommel's personal signals to the enemy, "C" suggested that the British intelligence service had spies in the Italian *commando supremo* at Rome. Rommel was quite prepared to believe anything of the Italian supreme command, which he regarded with contempt.

Such was the state of Italo-German relations, and such was the skill with which the intelligence was imparted to the Germans by "A" Force, the British deception agency in the Mediterranean, that concerns about Enigma were neutralized with all but Rommel. He continued to believe that through some extraordinary intelligence means, the British were reading his communications; and that belief seemed again to be confirmed at the great battle with Montgomery at Medenine near the Libyan-Tunisian frontier, a battle that opened on March 6, 1943—the fourteenth time in twenty months that the glare of suspicion had fallen upon Enigma. And again fault was found with Montgomery's handling of Ultra.

This was to be Rommel's last battle in North Africa, for decrypts had shown that his health continued to deteriorate.

Rommel himself signaled to the supreme command of the German army: "I report: The state of my health has suffered greatly in the last six months. After reaching the Mareth position, I shall probably no longer be in a position to command the German-Italian Panzer Army for any length of time." "C" confined the circulation of both signals to Churchill and himself, and there was no leakage to the press. Nor was there gossip.

During the preparatory period for the Battle of Medenine, Churchill sent an imprecation to Montgomery to "safeguard our precious secret so far as possible in your dispositions." [12] But again Montgomery ambushed Rommel in much the same way as at Alam Halfa and using much the same foreknowledge. When Rommel attacked with 160 tanks and 200 guns, he found himself opposed by 400 tanks, 350 field guns, and 470 antitank guns. The RAF had doubled its forward strength so that the German air force was badly outnumbered. In consequence, Rommel's casualties were so severe that he terminated the battle and then left Africa convinced that his defeat was due to yet another breakdown in the security of his communications. Those assertions were disregarded by the German supreme command for much the same reason that they had disregarded most of Rommel's earlier complaints: he was a defeated general looking for reasons for his defeat.

But if Montgomery had won the decisive battle in the march on Tunis and the destruction of all enemy forces in Africa, he received only a rebuke from London, one engineered doubtless by "C." Ultra on March 9 revealed that, from British prisoner-of-war statements and captured documents, the Germans had concluded that Montgomery was aware in advance not only of Rommel's intention to attack, but also of its strength, place, and time. But there was no evidence in the decrypts that the Germans assumed Enigma was the source of Montgomery's intelligence. In fact, Ultra was not the source of Montgomery's foreknowledge. But as the British official historian was to remark:

[T]he revelation naturally caused alarm in Whitehall; and as the [Chief of the Imperial General Staff, Field Marshal Sir Alan Brooke] pointed out, while the references to prisoners' statements and captured documents did not "necessarily mean that matters of the highest secrecy have been compromised," they did point to "an alarming lack of security" which "might well produce German cypher security counter-measures which would deny us all the use of Ultra." [13]

Montgomery was not, it seems, reprimanded on this occasion. How was it possible to reprimand a national hero, one who had defeated Rommel and was in the process of ejecting the Italo-German armies from Tunisia? But the anxiety produced in Whitehall did not die down.

If "C" was making himself few friends over his powerful and unrelenting defense of Ultra—one of the reasons why he never became a beloved or popular figure in World War II history or mythology—the secret Ultra nevertheless remained secure when, at last, the campaign came to an end in North Africa in May 1943. In the last week of March decrypts had shown that again the enemy was suspicious about signs of Allied foreknowledge, this time in connection with the land fighting at Maknassy and Al-Guettar. As the official historian recorded:

The decrypts made it clear that the suspicion was based on a "sure source"—that is, on interception of Allied wireless communications. They offered a variety of possible explanations for the Allied foreknowledge—the interrogation of POW and the cutting of landlines by the Allies, Allied air and ground reconnaissance, and Allied Sigint derived from the use of plain language or of careless signalling by Axis troops. But they contained nothing to suggest that the enemy connected it with the security of Enigma. Perhaps for this reason Whitehall took no action. [14]

On that uncertain note, a flurry of apocalyptic decrypts marked the end of the North African campaign. The German quartermaster instructed the *commando supremo* in Rome not to send any more ammunition because there was no petrol for the trucks to move it. The last decode out of Tunisia came on May 12 when the enemy commander, Colonel-General Jurgen von Arnim, wirelessed to German army supreme headquarters: "We have fired our last cartridge. We are closing down forever."

Then there was silence. General Sir Harold Alexander, the Allied land forces commander, signaled Churchill on May 13: "Sir, it is my duty to report that . . . all enemy resistance has ceased. We are masters of the North African shore."

The Axis had lost 620,000 men (one-third German), 2.4 million tons of shipping, 8,000 aircraft, 6,200 guns, 2,500 tanks, 70,000 trucks—casualties and losses far greater than those inflicted by the Russians on the Germans at Stalingrad. British casualties were 220,000, French about 20,000 men, Americans about 18,500. The main cause of the Axis defeat had not been the prowess of the Allied armies, although Montgomery's march from Egypt was one of the great campaigns, but the failure, nourished by Ultra, of the Italo-German supply convoys to get through the ring of Allied warships around the Axis bridgehead. Arnim found himself, as had Rommel, without the supplies of fuel, ammunition, replacements, and food he needed to march on Cairo. Then both generals found themselves without the means to resist being overwhelmed by superior force.

In the end, therefore, Hitler's grand strategy was confounded, Churchill's enhanced. The Allies now threatened the entire southern coast of Fortress Europe from the Franco-Spanish border to the Graeco-Turkish frontier. Compelled to garrison Italy and the Balkans, forty-nine divisions were eventually pinned down in southern Europe. There they waited, idly, anxiously, uselessly, and expectantly, when they might otherwise have been available for service on the western or the eastern fronts. Thus that desirable state of affairs was attained in which, as Wellington was said to have declared to Blucher before meeting Napoleon's army at Waterloo, "Sire, my strategy is one against ten, my tactics ten against one."

The end of the campaign did not, however, bring with it relief for "C" in the defense of Ultra. On April 18, 1943, U.S. fighters, working from Magic, intercepted and shot down the aircraft carrying Admiral Yamamoto, the Pearl Harbor naval colonel in command, as he was flying from Rabaul to Bougainville. Since no cover story was disseminated to explain how it was that the American airmen had been able to intercept a single aircraft in all the vastness of the Pacific, the Japanese concluded that their ciphers had been compromised.

But "C's" belief that the Yamamoto affair was a compromise of the Anglo-American agreements went beyond the compromise of yet another source. In "C's" view it demonstrated a predisposition in the command of the southwest Pacific theater to use Magic for purely tactical or prestige purposes. It was not being used for great occasions only, as Churchill said it should be. As "C" argued at the Anglo-American meetings, what use was Yamamoto's death to the Allies? By killing him, the Americans had removed from the scene a man whose strategies and tactics were well known to them, and the likelihood was that he would be replaced by one whose conduct of battles was unknown. That could cause serious trouble.

But more to the point of Magic security, the action accepted the risk that Magic might be compromised at the very moment when, on a grander scale, it was being used to transform Japan from a first-rate marine power to a third-rate naval power whose operating radius was rapidly being confined to home waters. Was that desirable state of affairs to be risked for what was no more than an act of vengeance worked for propaganda purposes?

"C" thought the killing of Yamamoto was an act of self-indulgence, not a military operation, and pointed out that on numerous occasions the British could have killed Rommel in much the same way as the Americans had killed Yamamoto but had not done so because if they had, it would have cast suspicion again on Enigma. There was, in consequence, a long pause in the negotiations to produce the Anglo-American agreements for a full exchange of Ultra and Magic. But when that pause was over, the alliance was established.

The first rewards of that alliance were apparent immediately. At the Casablanca conference between Churchill and FDR on January 19, 1943, the Allied supreme command made its recommendations for the conduct of the war in that year. The first of the military conclusions was that "the defeat of the U-boat must remain a first charge on the resources of the United Nations." That directive concerned "C" directly, for since the loss of Shark, the U-boat cipher, the war at sea was being lost. In February 1942 the average number of U-boats at sea in the Atlantic was thirty, but by October 1942, with Shark still illegible, there were one hundred, and for the first time monthly sinkings in the Atlantic exceeded 500,000 tons.

But then another cryptanalytical miracle occurred in what was one of "C's" bleakest hours. On October 23, 1942, the U-559 was sunk in shallow water during naval action off Port Said. Divers working for Bletchley succeeded in entering her signals room, where they found Enigma and related data.

By mid-December 1942 that documentation enabled Bletchley to break into Shark again. But as Churchill had stated, the Battle of the Atlantic was nothing if not "hard, wide-spread, and bitter, a war of groping and drowning, a war of ambuscade and stratagem, a war of science and seamanship." The flow of Shark intelligence proved to be sporadic, for the Germans had in the meantime introduced yet more security procedures to protect their communications. It was not for another eighty days that Shark was penetrated by a combination of brainpower and the new high-speed *bombes*.

Largely through Ultra intelligence, on July 14, 1943, Churchill was able to advise Roosevelt that seven "canaries"—U-boats—had been sunk in thirty-six hours. On July 16 Churchill cabled FDR again: "My cat likes canaries and her appetite grows with eating. . . . We have altogether 18 canaries this month." On July 25 Churchill reported afresh: "Up to date in July, we have caught 26 canaries, which is good for 25 days. There should be quite a good meal for our cats when the time comes." On July 31: "35 U-boats had been sunk for a total of 85 in 91 days."

By August the U-boat commander in chief, Grand Admiral Doenitz, acknowledged defeat and withdrew from the Atlantic battle. As Doenitz recorded in his 1956 memoirs by way of explanaton:

We found ourselves bound to admit that . . . we had not succeeded in finding . . . the convoys for which we had been searching. As a result of these failures we naturally went once more very closely into the question of what knowledge the enemy could have of our U-boat dispositions. . . . We repeatedly checked our security instructions in order to ensure as far as possible that our intentions were not being betrayed. That a widespread spy network was at work in our bases in occupied France was something we obviously had to assume. An efficient intelligence service must in any case have been able to ascertain the distribution of U-boats among the various bases, the dates of their sailing and return to port, and possibly also the sea areas allotted to boats proceeding on operations. Our ciphers were checked and rechecked, to make sure they were unbreakable; and on each occasion the head of the Naval Intelligence Service at Naval High Command adhered to his opinion that it would be impossible for the enemy to decipher them. And to this day, as far as I know, we are not certain whether or not the enemy did succeed in breaking our ciphers during the war. [15]

Doenitz was defeated, and worse, he was baffled. In later years, "C's" detractors were to contend that Menzies's job was saved by the code breakers. There is limited truth in that assertion, but it may also be said that by the skillful employment of his procedures, by nagging Churchill constantly about the foolishness of generals and admirals, by compelling the Allied war machine to recognize that neither Ultra nor Magic were secrets to be expended in the pursuit of short-term advantages, publicity, or propaganda—by doing all these things, "C" not only directed Bletchley to the most rewarding targets, but also saved the code breakers themselves from the oblivion that is, in government, the reward of those whose usefulness has departed.

In short, "C" was Ultra. Nobody else could make that claim.

2 "I HAVE COMMUNISTS IN MY ORGANIZATION"

Through his control of Ultra and of transport into northwestern and southern France, "C" had become the most powerful figure in the western intelligence alliance. Through his connecton with Churchill he had become not only the eyes and ears of the Anglo-American alliance, but also an influential principal in the secret aspects of its grand strategy in Europe. Churchill conceived, "C" advised and executed.

The alliance with America and Russia had become so unnatural that its contradictions had become evident to Hitler, largely from the U.S. press, which found itself incapable of discretion even in the midst of the largest war in human history. Hitler did not need an intelligence service at Washington; he could make a fairly shrewd estimate of the strength and unity of purpose of the Allies by subscribing to the airmail editions of *The New York Times*, *The Washington Post*, and the *Washington Times-Herald*. So revealing was the press that, indeed, later on Hitler was able to define the geopolitical position confronting him more realistically than anyone in the Allied camp was prepared to admit.

But Churchill realized that if England was to emerge from the war as a great power, there could be no headlong confrontation with Germany in Europe until the Third Reich was so bloodlet as to be incapable of prolonged, determined resistance. Therefore, Churchill knew it was imperative that Russia be kept in the war, if necessary strengthened, so that the Wehrmacht and the Red Army would claw each other into exsanguination, leaving the Western powers' strength intact to impose the will of England and America at the peace conference. For that reason, Churchill *ordered* "C" to send disguised Ultra to Russia, "C's" protests notwithstanding.

During 1943, "C" detected through Ultra that the Germans were assembling very powerful forces to annihilate the Red Army at Kursk in the Russian central sector. With priceless inside intelligence about German capabilities and intentions flooding into Whitehall, one decode was of special importance. On April 25, 1943, Bletchley decrypted a long message signed by Generalfeldmarschall Maximilian Baron von Weichs, commander in chief of Army Group South on the Russian front. It was Weichs's appreciation of the capabilities and intentions of the Red Army in light of Operation Zitadelle, which was to be the greatest tank operation in the history of warfare until that time. The purpose of the operation was the elimination of the Kursk salient and all Russian forces inside it, a sort of second Ypres operation.

Other such signals were intercepted and decrypted in due course. All were relayed at "C's" direction but disguised as communications from an SIS spy at German headquarters, to General F. F. Kuznetsov, who was thought to be chief of the Red Army's foreign secret military intelligence service in Moscow. Although in the operational orders Hitler had *demanded* maximum concentration of force on a narrow front and *surprise*, this was denied the Germans when the vast offensive was opened on July 4. The Red Army was waiting in readiness for a battle that was to engage two million men. When the battle ended a year later on August 23, German military power on the eastern front was broken. The moment had arrived for the Red Army to start their march into central and Eastern Europe from the Baltic almost to the Adriatic. The irony was that "C"—"the terrific anti-Bolshevik"—whose service had tried so hard to strangle the Bolshevik infant at birth, was now providing it with the intelligence that would assist Russia in becoming a political colossus.

Plainly it was imperative that if Churchill's Russian policy was to succeed, both the source of Churchill's intelligence and the policy itself must remain a state secret held by only a few Britons and *no* Americans, for FDR believed it would be possible to form a brotherhood with the Russians after the war. It followed, therefore, that the organization of the keeper of the secrets, "C," had to remain secure. But how secure was Broadway? Had it been penetrated by alien forces? And in particular, did "C" know that Philby had been a Communist, and if he did know, why did "C" continue to employ him?

In the first place, it is possible to state with certainty that in July 1943 "C" knew that Communists had infiltrated the secret service. In July 1943 two Communists were arrested on charges of spying for a foreign power. Douglas Frank Springhall, forty-two, described in court as an organizer of the Communist party in Britain, stood accused of obtaining information relating to the design and production of the first British jet engines, a technology in which Britain was at that time a leader. Springhall was followed by Captain Ormond Leyton Uren, who was alleged to have provided the Russians with information relating to the internal structure of the Special Operations Executive (SOE), of which he was a member. Both men were sent to prison for seven years for "obtaining information in respect of munitions of war, and, for a purpose prejudicial to the interests and safety of the State, information calculated to be useful to the enemy." [16]

These convictions convinced "C" that despite the clause in the fifty-year Anglo-Soviet Treaty of 1942 in which both powers undertook to refrain from interfering in the internal affairs of the other, the Soviet government was actively engaged in espionage against the United Kingdom. "C" himself had had few doubts that the Soviet service had remained active in Britain, but until those convictions there had been little evidence. Consequently, "C" felt that it was time his chief of security, Colonel Valentine Vivian, the man who had introduced Philby into the secret service in 1941, examined the service to see whether any other Communists had crept in through the expansion from peacetime to wartime establishment.

At the same time, through the Security Service, "C" asked the FBI whether the U.S. government was having a similar experience. Immediately after the convictions, the FBI representative in London reported to Washington that he had been advised by "our friends" —the Security Service—that "they were aware that the Soviet Government was actively engaged at the present time in obtaining espionage information concerning the British Government." They had stated that "the Soviet espionage organizations seemed to operate through two channels: one directly through the Communist Party of England, utilizing the Party organization and the English Communists who are in the armed services and the Government to collect espionage data." The second Soviet espionage group "is apparently completely separated from the Communist Party of England and operates on what our friends described as a diplomatic level." That activity involved the Russian embassy in London as well as their consular offices throughout the country, and the various Russian trade commissions that were accredited to the British government and enjoyed quasi-diplomatic immunity.

By mid-August Vivian was in a position to report his findings. There *were* Communists in Broadway and elsewhere in the secret service. One of these, Vivian felt, was almost certainly David Footman, head of the political section at Broadway and the man who had introduced Guy Burgess to SIS. Footman's job was to assess the value of political intelligence reaching Broadway before it was sent on to the Foreign Office. "C" never said why he suspected Footman, but he did tell a colleague later that he felt Footman was suppressing intelligence that, if circulated, would be against the Soviet interest. As Sir James Easton was to state: " 'C' had a bee in his bonnet about Footman and even almost a decade later whenever we were discussing possible security risks 'C' would state: 'And don't forget to to see to it that Footman's name is on the list.' "

In consequence of Vivian's report, "C" called on Cadogan at the Foreign Office, and as Cadogan recorded in his diary concerning the subject they discussed: " 'C' about Communists in his organisation." That statement was a major development in the history of the Philby affair, one that showed plainly and beyond any doubt that "C" was alert to the dangers of clandestine communism in Broadway and its outstations. It is evident, too, that either "C" or Cadogan, or both, advised Churchill, for the prime minister wrote to Anthony Eden, the foreign secretary, and Duff Cooper, Churchill's representative to de Gaulle in Algiers, stating:

I suppose you realise that we are weeding remorselessly every single known Communist from all the secret organizations. We did this after having to sentence two quite high-grade people to long terms of penal servitude for their betrayal, in accordance with Communist faith, of important military secrets. [17]

It is now, at that point between August of 1943 and February of 1944, that we encounter the first sign of the mystery in the association between "C" and Kim Philby. As the second half of 1943 progressed, "C" received reports that Philby's work at St. Albans was outstanding. So outstanding was it indeed that, with the surrender of Italy in September 1943 and the absorption into Broadway's structure of the Italian secret service, one of the best in Europe, Philby's area of operations was expanded from Iberia and North Africa to include Italy.

Philby's power, already considerable in the Broadway firmament, was further extended to the American services when the first members of OSS X2, Donovan's counterespionage organization, began to arrive in London late in 1943. "C" badly needed manpower for the looming invasion of Europe, Overlord, and these were the best men that Donovan could find. At this time, Section V was withdrawn from St. Albans to central London, to offices located at 7 Ryder Street, an apartment block close to St. James's and White's. Built at the turn of the century, the front entrance carried the sign "Charity House," while the passes by which officials gained entrance to the building reported that the bearer was a member of the Greenwood Country Club.

The Americans had been hand-picked for their ability to work with Britons and included Hubert Will (a future federal judge in Chicago), Robert Blum (professor of European history), Dr. Dana Durand (Rhodes scholar), Frank Holcomb (son of a commandant of the U.S. Marine Corps), John Oakes (member of the Ochs family and later an editor of *The New York Times*), Ben Welles (son of Undersecretary of State Sumner Welles), Hayes Hayes-Kroner (former assistant military attaché in London and chief of the U.S. military intelligence service), Akeley P. Quirk (graduate of Stanford law school and head of the foreign lands department of Standard Oil of California), and James Jesus Angleton (who had attended an English public school and became chief of counterespionage in Italy, part of Philby's territory, and later on the chief of the CIA's counterespionage branch).

Most if not all the American arrivals had attended a counterespionage school in the United States and were given an orientation course, usually by Philby. Philby's tutorial involved mainly the security arrangements governing the use of "Ice" (later "Pair"), the X2 code name for the German intelligence decrypts. And it was a condition of this first and only admission of OSS into the secret circle that X2 accepted that all traffic mentioning or concerning "Ice" was sent and received only by British signalmen using British ciphers. A party of such signalmen were to be attached to each U.S. Army group before, during, and after the invasion.

In these circumstances, Philby came to know the X2 men intimately. His advice was sought constantly. He was popular with and trusted by them, and his judgment as a counterespionage officer was admired to such an extent that he was brought into the Anglo-American Commission established in both London and Washington to investigate a source of intelligence that the Americans code-named "the Boston Series."

In August 1943 an official of the German foreign office, whose code name became George Wood, presented himself to Allen Dulles, then chief OSS representative in Bern. Wood offered to supply Dulles with a selection of the most important foreign cables coming across his desk from the German diplomatic outposts in all parts of the world. Dulles checked the man's background. Convinced that he was not an agent provocateur, he accepted George Wood's offer. Wood then produced 186 copies and synopses of messages prepared by him.

By Dulles's standards (for he knew nothing of Ultra) these were extraordinarily revealing. But prudence dictated that they be surveyed against other sources of intelligence, and for that purpose he sent them to Washington for analysis. That analysis lasted from the time of receipt of the first consignment in Washington, probably in September, until January 1945. Between September 1943 and March 1944 Wood's telegrams were tested against all known Allied sources of intelligence in both Washington and London, where Philby's opinion of the telegrams was sought. If Philby's account of events has merit, both Dansey and Cowgill felt that the Woods traffic was a German plant intended to influence Allied strategy and tactics during the coming invasion period. Late in 1943 Cowgill went to Washington for discussions with Donovan about joint counterespionage operations for Overlord. At that time Cowgill gave the task of testing the documentation to Philby to complete. Philby was to write:

About this time, a project was forming in my mind which needed a cautious approach. I was very anxious to get a certain job [i.e. chief of the anti-Soviet section of SIS, which was under preliminary discussion at Broadway at this time] that would soon become available, and I could not afford to antagonise any of the people who might help me towards it. Cowgill, Vivian, Dansey, MI5, the Foreign Office, the Chief—they were all pieces of the jig-saw, and it was exceedingly difficult, from my comparatively lowly position, to see how they would fit when the moment came for action on my part. I had, however, long since reached the conclusion that, although political man-oeuvre can produce quick results, those results are lasting only if they are based on solid and conscientious work. I therefore decided to study the Dulles material on its merits. If it was unequivocally genuine or spurious, I would say so. If the outcome of my study was inconclusive, I would then reconsider the political aspects of the affair before deciding on which side to throw my weight. [18]

At length Philby, although aware of Dansey's belief that the Woods traffic was an enemy plant, concluded to the contrary that here was high-grade intelligence of great value to the British government. Hav-ing collected notes to that effect from the various departments to which Philby had sent the traffic for evaluation, especially Denniston, chief of the diplomatic code-breaking branch, Philby then went to see Dansey about the material. He was to write of that meeting, which was an important one in Philby's career both as a British secret service officer and a Soviet spy:

The visit lasted a very uncomfortable half-hour. As was to be expected, Dansey was furious. But he was sobered by the fact that I had studied the material and he had not. Denniston's minute deflated him a little. He did not understand the argument, but the conclusion was plainly stated. Anger mounted in him again as he read the eulogistic comments of the departments. He composed himself with some difficulty to read me a lecture. Even if the documents were genuine, what of it? I was encouraging OSS [which Dansey detested while envying them for their money] to run riot all over Switzerland, fouling up the whole intelligence field. Heaven knew what damage they wouldn't do. Such matters had to be handled only by officers with experience of the pitfalls that beset the unwary. For all he knew, OSS, if egged on in this way, could blow the whole of his network [in Switzerland] in a matter of days.

Philby was, however, nothing if not a consummate tactician and continued in his account of the meeting:

When Dansey had exhausted his reckless improvisation, I asked him with puzzled deference how OSS came into the business at all. I had not circulated the material as OSS material. Not even [SIS] circulating sections, let alone the departments, knew that OSS were involved. They regarded it as *our* stuff, they were asking *us* for more. It seemed that the credit would be ours. When I faltered to an end, Dansey gave me a long, long stare. "Carry on," he said at last. "You're not such a fool as I thought." When Cowgill returned, I took him the file and explained what I had done. To his immediate anxious enquiry about Dansey's attitude, I explained that I had consulted him and that he had approved my action. With relief, Cowgill handed me back the file and asked me to handle any sequel. To my surprise, the case was by no means closed. Our German friend proved to be an intrepid operator, and paid several more visits to Berne with his useful suit-case. [19]

More than any other factor, it was that intrepid operator with his useful suitcase, and the X2 group at Charity House, that brought Philby into close contact with the future U.S. intelligence establishment. That did not go unnoticed by Vivian, Philby's principal patron. Broadway was a place where there were few intelligence officers who had either the time or the inclination to make friends with the American intelligence services, and, so Vivian concluded, young Philby was not only a first-class intelligence officer but one who was liked by his American colleagues.

At a time when relations with Donovan's service were in a sorry state, Vivian reached an important conclusion. Although "C" already had an American desk, it was responsible only for the assessment and distribution of intelligence relating to the Americas; it had nothing to do with relationships. Indeed, such was the secrecy in which the section operated that it was not supposed to have relations with American services at all.

Aware of the serious problems affecting relationships, and having no time to deal with those problems personally, in mid-1943 "C" gave thought to the appointment of Philby as his personal assistant in charge of American affairs. He abandoned that idea when Cowgill objected because Philby was as close to being indispensable as a man can be with the approach of major military operations—Overlord, the invasion of Europe.

With Philby unavailable, "C" then decided to appoint Benson, whose tour of duty as military attaché in Washington was coming to an end. When the matter was discussed, however, he discovered that Benson's attitude toward the United States had changed sharply with the intensification at medium levels of the administration of pressure upon Britain to declare that, in return for a continuation of lend-lease, she would adopt a policy of decolonization and, in particular, declare that she would grant India the powers of self-determination at the end of the war. By mid-1943, that advocacy was no longer concealed in Washington. It had became explicit. And Benson had wearied of his high task.

3 SPECIAL RELATIONSHIPS

If Benson's diaries are an accurate reflection of his duties, then his job in Washington was to act as a confidential adviser to the ambassador, Halifax, and to "C," while at the same time acting as an agent-of-influence within the Washington administration in favor of British policies and interests. By 1943 that was a difficult task, for the administration was itself seeking to wrest strategic control of the war from Churchill while the geopolitical interest in the liquidation of the British Empire had become explicit.

Benson was a member of Halifax's "Little Cabinet," and he operated at the highest levels, mainly at the War Department. He was also involved in matters concerning the security of Ultra and also in attempting to counter the work of the antiimperialists in American politics. He met frequently with Secretary of War Henry L. Stimson, Stimson's personal assistant, Harvey H. Bundy, and Robert Lovett, a former partner in Brown Brothers Harriman, the New York private bankers, and now a special assistant to Stimson.

Benson maintained a wide range of connections beyond the War Department. These included Harry Hopkins, the Lend-Lease Act administrator and presidential adviser, Bernard Baruch, the American multimillionaire and presidential adviser on war and postwar plans, Walter Lippmann and Arthur Krock, the leading American political commentators, and General Donovan. Through these persons he sought to counter the antiempire attitudes of Americans such as Henry and Clare Booth Luce, with whom Benson had a running feud over their articles on British India.

As Benson wrote of the Luces in his diary on February 8, 1943: "Personally I have no use for her & am tonguetied in consequence. She is a clever hard-boiled ambitious young lady backed by a wrong-thinking husband for whom success as a big newspaper man & money has & probably is still the main object of living. The less these two try to practise the art of statesmanship the better." And he added in his diary following a particularly stinging attack on the British administration in India in *Life*:

> On things in no way us concerning,
> Each loves his wits to exercise.

How clearly each can analyse!
Yet look! Beneath your very eyes
Your house has nearly finished burning.

As Benson remarked in his diary about the Luces on a further
occasion after lunching with Lord Halifax and Bernard Baruch: "B.
B. in excellent form. . . . Wants us to be nice to Clare Booth Luce
& husband. Told him that husband could help clear himself by writing
factually accurate article about India in 'Life.' " He was equally sharp
with Donovan. "Lunched with Bill Donovan, Paddy [Beaumont-
Nesbitt] & some of Bill's myrmidons," he wrote in his diary just after
Torch. "Much discussion over North Africa. Told Bill I thought the
fact could not be denied that the [OSS] show was an amateur one."
Reflecting his belief that U.S. concerns about India were not moral
but commercial, when a U.S. colonel of intelligence stationed in New
York requested of Benson "much commercial and industrial information about India," Benson demanded to know: "What for?"

The incident that most influenced Benson was his discovery that
at a school at Charlottesville, Virginia, for U.S. officers about to go
overseas on occupation duties in Germany, Austria, Japan, Italy, and
elsewhere, the curriculum was almost entirely on anticolonialism and
contained nothing about enemy ideologies. He was particularly in-
censed when he also discovered that many of the lecturers "openly
talk anti-British" and when one of the lecturers began by stating
(unaware that there were two British colonels present), "Of course,
I take it that most of you here are anti-British."

When in New York for a meeting with William Stephenson, he
read Stephenson's paper for Churchill and "C" on Anglo-American
relations, a task that took him ninety minutes. As he commented on
"geopolitical groups in the USA," Benson wrote in his diary: "Am not
frightened of the big business side of the Republican Party after the
war. British can cope with them." What worried him was the party's
"obsession" with "U.S. strategic policy."

By mid-1943, Benson was irritated and concerned not with American devotion toward the prosecution of the war, but the realization
that there were groups of powerful Americans who supported the war
for postwar financial and political gain and power. His diaries also
reflected his concerns, which were reported to London, about the
fighting capabilities of the U.S. Army. "U.S. troops & leadership still
terrible," he wrote on April 17, 1943, just after the Battle of the
Kasserine Pass. "They are quite unfit to go to battle with any success

against the Germans." Nor did his friend Harry Hopkins, one of the most powerful Americans, escape his ire when, after dinner and bridge with the Hopkinses at Benson's house in Georgetown on July 17, 1943, he wrote: "H. H. disagrees with W[inston's] politics—no wonder. He is an advanced New Dealer with all the tripe etc. about India. He thinks W will get into a big fight with U.S.A. State Department after the war."

Plainly, by the second half of 1943, Benson had tired of Washington and was ready for fresh work, when there occurred what may be called "the Wallace Affair," which wrecked whatever use Benson might have had to "C" as liaison officer to the American intelligence services.

In 1942 Wing Commander Roald Dahl, a young fighter pilot with a gallant record who had been shot down while on operations over Greece in 1941 and was badly burned, reported for duty as assistant air attaché at the British embassy. After the war Dahl became a well-known novelist and contributor to *New Yorker*. Benson came to know Dahl well, and perhaps at Benson's suggestion, Dahl transferred to Stephenson's organization, British Security Coordination, while remaining on the staff of the embassy.

Dahl possessed a number of contacts that were useful to Stephenson. The First Lady, Eleanor Roosevelt, as Dahl stated later, "took a liking to the young RAF fighter pilot who had been shot down and rather badly burned and I was invited more than once to dinner at the White House and to week-ends at Hyde Park." He "got to know Cabinet ministers Henry Morgenthau,* Will Clayton,† and Jesse Jones,§ and these people were inclined to speak more freely about affairs to an innocent-looking young serviceman than, let us say, Halifax." [20]

Dahl also became friendly with Vice-President Henry Wallace. Wallace was an Iowan agronomist who had done important work in developing new strains of corn and strawberries. As Wallace's diaries show, he and Dahl regularly walked to work together, played tennis, and Dahl told Wallace that he was in the British secret service. Stephenson was greatly interested in Wallace's politics, which to say the least were of the left, and Stephenson was concerned about what

---

*Henry Morgenthau, Jr., secretary of the treasury.

†William L. Clayton, secretary of commerce, 1942–45, asst. secretary of state, 1945.

§Jesse H. Jones, chairman Export-Import Bank (1936–43), a member Board of Economic Warfare, War Production Board (1942–45), Economic Stabilization Board (1942–45), and others.

would occur should FDR die and be succeeded as president by Wallace. Wallace was strongly pro-Russian and was much influenced by the wife of the new Soviet ambassador, Andrei Gromyko. It was felt also that he was strongly anti-British.

From the summer of 1943, Dahl's main work in Washington was to keep "pretty careful tabs on his [Wallace's] Communistic leanings and his friends in those quarters" and report to Stephenson. As Dahl was to state of Wallace, "He was a lovely man, but too innocent and idealistic for this world." Their relationship became so close that Wallace used to send Dahl a bag of special plant fertilizer as a Christmas present. Elsewhere, however, Wallace was not regarded with the same affection. "C" regarded Wallace as "that menace," one who was rather too closely associated with Nicholas Konstantin Roerich, a Russian mystic. [21]

Roerich was by trade an artist and scene designer who had been connected with the Moscow Art Theater and the Diaghilev ballet. His sets for Stravinsky's *Sacre du printemps* were astoundingly beautiful, and he had an important following in the New York avant garde, who built a museum in his name. In the mid-1920s Roerich spent much time painting and exploring in Tibet and the other Himalayan kingdoms, and the five hundred or so pictures he produced were purchased by all the main European and American art collections. However, Roerich's expeditions also attracted the attention of the British secret service in India, and particularly that of Major Felix Cowgill, then a specalist in Marxist subversion in India. Cowgill had written an official volume on clandestine communism in the arc of Asia from Istanbul to Hong Kong, a work entitled *Communism in India*. It was published confidentially by the government of India at Delhi in 1932, and in that volume Cowgill asserted that Roerich was a clandestine agent of the Communist International. Roerich had been, Cowgill asserted, in the Kulu Valley of Tibet, a country in the British sphere of influence in central Asia, attempting to raise the Tibetans against their treaties and agreements with the British Indian empire by spreading the belief that the second incarnation of Buddha, which was expected in 2083, would be a Bolshevik.

In short, the vice-president was already known to the ruling incumbency at Broadway when, in the early summer of 1943, Dahl discovered that Wallace, with the help of John Carter Vincent and Owen Lattimore, both of the State Department and both gentlemen of the extreme left, had written the draft of a pamphlet entitled *Our Job in the Pacific*. That document was published in the spring of 1944 by the Institute of Pacific Relations in New York, a distinguished organization that, however, was being taken over by U.S. antiimperialist Sinophiles, some of whom were also of the far left. In 1945 the IPR became embroiled in a serious spying case known as "the Amerasia affair."

While visiting the house in Washington of Charles E. Marsh, a Texan newspaper owner and a power in the Democratic party, Dahl encountered another of Marsh's associates, Wallace. They were both reading Wallace's draft, and after Wallace had left, Marsh gave it to Dahl to read and asked the young airman for his opinion. What Dahl read "made my hair stand on end." Wallace's draft proposed American postwar economic assistance for the industrial development of Asia, a trade policy for the Asian countries, the emancipation of colonial areas in Asia, the demilitarization of Japan, and what John Morton Blum, editor of Wallace's papers, was to call "international control of air power in the Pacific." The paper also advocated the "emancipation of colonial subjects" in the British Empire countries of India, Burma, and Malaya, the French empire of Indochina, and the Dutch empire in the East Indies. As Dahl recounted:

I saw immediately its importance from the British point of view and excused myself saying that I was going downstairs to read it. I quickly phoned the only contact I knew in [British Security Coordination] and told him to meet me on the road outside Marsh's house fast. I handed the draft through his car window and told him he must be back with it in fifteen minutes. The man buzzed off to the BSC Washington offices, and duly returned the manuscript to me on the dot. I returned it to Marsh without comment. A copy of the pamphlet went to Stephenson and thence to "C" and then to Churchill and I was told later that Churchill could hardly believe what he was reading. [22]

Among much else the document contained what Dahl called "a lot to do with postwar civil aviation and how the American government, people like Adolf Berle, were conspiring with Pan Am (Trippe) to take over the commercial aviation of the entire world after the war was over," a proposal that, together with its decolonization plans, "stirred Winston to cataclysms of wrath." If that was so, Churchill's reaction was not surprising, for as he had declared at the time of Torch, he had not become the king's first minister in order to preside over the liquidation of the British Empire. Nor was Benson's change of heart about America surprising, for here was a declaration of the policy of the Democratic party, co-written and signed by the vice-president of the United States.

The offending manuscript caused major resentment within the British official community in Washington. Wallace himself recorded in his diary how he was approached by Dahl, who told him that "the entire British Secret Service was shaking with indignation as well as the British Foreign Office." Dahl had also remarked to Marsh, "This is very serious. You know Churchill is likely to ask the President to get a new Vice President." Marsh was said to have retorted: "Don't be a child. Grow up. Don't you know that the most certain way to be sure that Wallace will continue to be Vice-President is for the word to get around that Churchill is against him?" [23]

At Churchill's request, Lord Halifax drew the attention of Cordell Hull, the secretary of state, to the "regrettable" statements made by the vice-president concerning the internal affairs of an ally as major military operations were developing—Overlord was just about to be launched—while other Britons, including Stephenson, remarked on British concerns at the security implications of some of Wallace's statements. As a result, as Stephenson was to state, "I came to regard Wallace as a menace and I took action to ensure that the White House was aware that the British government would view with concern Wallace's appearance on the ticket at the 1944 presidential elections." This he did through an intermediary, Ernest Cuneo, a lawyer and friend who had married a member of the staff of Stephenson's organization and acted as liaison between the White House and the British secret services.

And as Dahl was to recall of the history of the Wallace affair, Stephenson played a part in his fall from power, although the extent to which British objections to Wallace really influenced the administration is vague, perhaps because they played no part at all. Stephenson "could be very devious," Dahl recalled, and acted indirectly through Lord Beaverbrook, the British press lord, and Lester Pearson, the Canadian external affairs minister. But as Dahl was also to remember: "Menzies was always avid for everything he could get out of the White House and the Cabinet in regard to U.S. intentions, and especially anything that had to do with U.S. intentions towards the Empire." [24]

As for the Institute for Pacific Relations and its plans for subjects of the Crown in Asia, "C" was in an excellent position to keep the prime minister informed. In September 1943 he had sent to New York a familiar figure—Colonel Gerald Wilkinson, "C's" man at Manila at the time of Pearl Harbor and afterward "C's" representative on the staff of General Douglas MacArthur. Wilkinson's task in New

York was to establish an espionage ring in New York that would keep "C" informed about the activities of the Japanese government in China and those of the Chinese war lords.*

On his arrival in Washington, Wilkinson saw Donovan and succeeded in obtaining his support for a joint Anglo-American-Canadian operation code-named Oyster, the purpose of which was to recruit a number of leading Chinese in the United States and use their connections in China to obtain the intelligence required in Wilkinson's orders. Hitherto Donovan had declined to take part in any joint Anglo-American intelligence operations, but he agreed to this one and placed $25,000 at Wilkinson's disposal and left Wilkinson in charge. Wilkinson recruited a number of agents in New York, whose contacts included the closest personal friend of the mistress of Tai-Li, Generalissimo Chiang Kai-shek's spymaster at Chungking. In due course a number of subagents were recruited, including a certain Willie Lim, Chinese representative at the Institute of Pacific Relations in New York. Lim approached Wilkinson's chief agent, Dr.

---

*"C's" orders to Wilkinson have survived, remarkably, for it was not often in the history of SIS that a British secret agent's orders have come into the public domain. These orders read: [25]

Far Eastern Section, 48-Land

Cancelling all previous communications and other arrangements, it is understood that your Far East Section (section 6) in charge of 48982 will be maintained and developed under the following directive:

1. To procure from North and South American sources and from the American areas of command in the Pacific and Far East all secret intelligence of Imperial interest relating to Far Eastern matters that is not available to H.M.G. through official channels, or other existing S.I.S. representatives.

2. To achieve this, 48982 to develop liaison (within the terms of the Registration Act) with any organization or individuals in 48-Land areas described in my immediately preceding Paragraph, at your discretion, provided that care is taken to avoid (a) overlapping with British Army Staff, YP, or other British official organizations; (b) conflict with McKellar Act.

3. Section 6 to supply London and appropriate S.I.S. representatives in other areas (particularly as defined in paragraph 4) with all secret intelligence of interest to them, and in turn to be kept fully supplied with Far East secret intelligence (whether this be for transmission to 48-Landers or only for the information of your station.) Duplication and consequent overvaluation of intelligence so exchanged to be avoided by each transmitter stating the local distribution that has taken place in the area of despatch.

4. Section 6 to supply all secret intelligence concerning Military, Naval and Air matters of interest to S.E. Asia command to London and 69000 only, apart from 48-Land distribution.

XYZ

Translated, the codes in these orders read: 48-Land = SIS code designation for U.S.A. 48982 = Wilkinson's designation. He was the 982nd SIS official in 48-Land. YP = SIS bigraph for the British embassy. McKellar Act = The 1942 law restricting the activities of foreign intelligence agencies on U.S. territory. 48-Landers = Americans. 69000 = SIS chief of station at South East Asia Command. XYZ = Menzies's telegraphic signature.

Konrad Hsu, a socially prominent Chinese in New York and a wireless manufacturer by trade, "for some way of earning money on the side to supplement his meager IPR pay." Lim wanted $200 a month paid in gold in Chungking.

Yet if "C" was informed about IPR and the manuscript, nothing could be done to prevent its publication. On the other hand, FDR himself acted to remove Wallace from the ticket for the 1944 presidential elections, replacing him with Senator Harry S. Truman. Wallace did, however, remain in the Cabinet as secretary of commerce until after FDR's death and Truman's accession. Then, concerned at Wallace's neo-Marxist attitudes, Wallace was removed from Truman's Cabinet and found himself in the political wilderness, a man guilty of no great crime except his political innocence.

Meanwhile, Benson had been working out his last weeks in Washington. His relations with the U.S. military intelligence service of General George V. Strong were little better than they were with the Luces, and the fact that they survived at all was a result of Benson's tact, diplomacy, charm, and his ability as a marathon pianist, all of which had stood him in such good stead since Eton. To the range of British popular airs he added America's, and such was the nature of Washington political society that he was forgiven British policy in India when he played the piano nonstop for two or three hours on end at parties. He was perhaps one of the most popular foreign diplomats in Washington. In the end his relationship with Strong, a very difficult man whom Benson regarded as "a narrow patriot of little education and less experience of the world," foundered altogether on a relatively petty issue.

Benson was already weary of Strong's assertions that Britain was fighting the war to the last Russian, that it was also fighting to the last American, and of Strong's frequent proclamations about what the U.S. Army was doing to win the war. But Strong also took exception to an invitation by Benson to three prominent members of the Maryland State Guard to visit England, which had been extended without consulting Strong. As Benson wrote in his diary after meeting with Strong about the "discourtesy," he found he had "a nasty taste in my mouth about Strong who acted like a child & a rude one at that" and felt that the U.S. Joint Chiefs of Staff "ought to find someone better & younger and less ignorant as head of G2."

Not long afterward Benson received instructions from the War Office to prepare to return home in December as his tour of duty had expired. This was almost certainly to enable Benson to take up his appointment as "C's" personal assistant for American affairs. Benson sent his wife, Leslie, to London to open one of their houses, while he cleared up his affairs and introduced his successor. Meanwhile, he continued his ordinary duties when, on September 25, he learned, probably from Ultra, about the German missile threat to London that had been developing since February.

With that grim warning, Benson prepared to leave Washington. Stimson, Bundy, and Robert Lovett gave him a special luncheon, at which there was talk about the war and Anglo-American relations. As Benson wrote in his diary on that day, he said to Bundy "frankly that, as I was leaving, I thought he should know that we were very far from being together with the War Department." Strong and General Leslie J. McNair, chief of the Army Ground Forces and a power in Washington, were, Benson thought, "the big stumbling blocks." Bundy replied that he "realised this" but said they were "having difficulty in replacing Strong." Benson had not been wise in being so candid, for somebody repeated to Strong what he had said.

Benson was waiting for an aircraft at Miami when he received a note from his successor warning him that General Strong had made the grave charge against him that in a letter to his wife, Benson, on the basis of Ultras regarding the impending rocket attacks, had warned her to leave London. This, Strong alleged, had been a "gross breach of security." [26] Upon receiving the warning, Benson wrote two letters, one to General Sir G. N. MacReady, chief of the British army staff in Washington and a representative on the Combined Chiefs of Staff, a man who was a close friend, and the other to Bundy. In both letters Benson denied the charges, but ineffectively, it seems, for Strong also made that charge against Benson with the director of military intelligence at the War Office.

On his arrival in London everything went wrong for Benson. His mother had just died. His brother, Guy, never well through his experiences in World War I, was almost in a state of nervous collapse at the bombing and the general war situation. Benson's bank required reorganization if it was to survive, and Benson himself was in serious financial trouble, having spent far more of his own money in the service of the Crown in Washington than he should have done, and was compelled to sell jewelry at Cartier's to pay his surtax.

The "little Blitz" on London began the moment he landed, and the great guns and rocket launchers barked every night all night. His lovely house in Sussex was almost a ruin: "Everything very dirty. [Air raid shelter] leaking. Dry rot." [27] The concrete coffin in which he had buried the family treasure on a hillside in Beaufortshire before setting out for Washington in 1941 was found to have leaked lead-impregnated water, badly damaging the Queen Anne silver and ruining his miniatures of Napoleon. Then he found that his insurance did not cover him for the loss of the treasure. "It is difficult to adjust," Benson wrote gloomily in his diary on January 18, 1944. "No car, no secretary & must do most things in the house." His doctor told him his nerves were bad and prescribed some special pills to calm him.

Benson ran into Stewart Menzies, Donovan, and David Bruce, the new chief of OSS London, at Claridge's, and "Bill came to our table for a minute & hinted that they were going to ask me to do a job for them!" [28] Perhaps Donovan was trying to even the score with "C" for the time he gave Whitney a job back in 1942. But even worse, it was clear to him that the War Office had been poisoned against him by Strong's charge. On February 10, after thirty-six years in the army and its reserve of officers, Benson received the coldly formal letter from the War Office terminating his services:

With references to the provisions of Articles 522 and 717, Pay Warrant, 1940, I am directed to inform you that as you have exceeded the age limit of liability to recall, you will cease to belong to the Regular Army Reserve of Officers with effect from 21 March 1944, after which date you will no longer be liable to be recalled to army service. The requisite notifications will appear in the London Gazette (Supplement) on or about 21 March 1944, when you will be granted the honorary rank of Lieutenant-Colonel under the terms of Army Order 209 of 1942, but you will not be permitted to wear uniform. I am to conclude by expressing regret that the time has now come for you to leave the Regular Army Reserve of Officers.

If Benson's career was over as a soldier, it was not as a spy. What his role became is not evident, except that "C" did not reemploy Benson, as he intended, as his personal assistant in charge of American relationships. If this had to do with the allegation against Benson that he leaked Ultra regarding missiles to his wife, there is no evidence. But Benson was, it seems clear, retained by "C" in his old role, that of an "honourable correspondent." For despite the charges made against him, by Christmas Benson was back in New York visiting Stephenson, almost certainly on "C's" business, which had to do with Stephenson's tenure in New York.

Throughout this period "C" had been plagued by the old complaints about Stephenson from the State Department and the FBI. At length, however, "C" felt the Anglo-American relationship might be better served if Stephenson were replaced. In appointing Gerald

Wilkinson to Stephenson's organization as chief of the China section, Menzies intimated that Stephenson's days might be numbered. As Wilkinson recorded in his diary: "In reply to a question from me C admits that Little Bill may be leaving us for another job in the United States, but he states that this would not diminish and might increase the prospect of my usefulness there." Moreover, "C" felt that Stephenson's organization, which was an amalgamation of the functions of all three British secret services, was giving British intelligence a bad name in the United States.

It is evident that Menzies spoke to Churchill about his concerns, as was prudent, for Churchill and Stephenson remained close friends. After Churchill's arrival in Washington for the Trident conference, Ernest Cuneo, one of Stephenson's intimates and also OSS's liaison officer with the White House, was approached by the attorney general, Francis Biddle, who told Cuneo that Churchill had asked Roosevelt for an opinion of Stephenson. Roosevelt agreed and asked Biddle to furnish the report, taking care not to provoke speculation. Biddle then called Cuneo to his office for an opinion, and Cuneo expressed the view that Stephenson was an important and reliable officer of the alliance. That view was not shared by everyone, but it was supported by Donovan and others within OSS, although the anti-Stephenson element within the FBI, the State Department, and military intelligence all opined that it was time for a change.

But as Cuneo also recalled, when Biddle asked the White House how the report was to be sent to Churchill, he was instructed to send it to the representative of Lloyd's of London in Chicago. That instruction surprised Cuneo, for he had always believed that Stephenson was Churchill's personal intelligence officer in the United States, as well as being head of BSC. But, Cuneo added, "It didn't surprise me that that second channel was centred in Lloyd's of London for it was well known that Lloyd's had a superb intelligence service." Although Cuneo "understood" that the report on Stephenson was "generally favorable," he never saw it. Nor did he hear any more about it. But the report does not appear to have been sufficiently favorable to persuade "C" to stop his measures to replace Stephenson.

Throughout the period between the summer of 1943 and the spring of 1944, Stephenson received a string of visitors from London, all of whom he thought were " 'C's' spies." First there was Colonel Vivian, who by now had been shunted aside by Dansey and was Menzies's "chief security advisor." Vivian was then followed by Major Cowgill, and after Cowgill came the chairman of the Joint Intelligence

Committee, Cavendish-Bentinck. After Cavendish-Bentinck came one of "C's" deputy directors, Air Commodore Lionel G. S. Payne, whose nickname in the service was "Lousy."

Stephenson suspected that Payne, at least, and probably his other visitors, had been sent over by "C" to gather evidence against him, and Payne might be Stephenson's replacement. Since Payne seemed to be interested in Stephenson's financial relations with Donovan, and the efficiency with which the secret accounts were kept, Stephenson was to claim later that he decided the time had come to act. He told "one of my ruffians" to burgle Payne's room at the Hotel Carlyle in New York, examine Payne's papers, and bring to Stephenson any that suggested Payne was in New York to spy on him. And as Stephenson was to claim: "When *all* Payne's papers suggested that he was in New York to spy on me, and perhaps to replace me, I called Payne to my office and told him to get out of the country before I threw him out."

Toward the end of 1943, Cuneo had moved to New York and lived at the Hotel Dorset, where Stephenson had the penthouse. He saw a great deal of Stephenson and "sensed" that Stephenson was in "great trouble" with Broadway. "Nothing was said, but," Cuneo remembered, "Stephenson was depressed, inactive, and never went near his office." Then, suddenly, Stephenson was back at work with all his old vigor, and Cuneo assumed that "the heat was off." It seemed to Cuneo that Churchill had intervened in favor of Stephenson and he was back in business. The record certainly suggests this, for thereafter there were no signs that Stephenson was in trouble or that Menzies was still trying to replace him. [29]

On the contrary, a reluctant friendship developed between the two men that survived at least until 1969. For this, Stephenson and Menzies probably had Rex Benson to thank, since, although their relationship was formal at the start, Benson and Stephenson formed a strong bond. At the end of 1943, when Benson was due to return to London, he recorded on several occasions his admiration for Stephenson. "Stayed the evening with Bill Stephenson," Benson wrote in his diary on December 5, 1943. "I am sorry to leave him. He is in his way a very able little man and has built up a remarkable organization." Benson was, indeed, so impressed with Stephenson that at a meeting in New York toward the end of the war he offered Stephenson a directorship in his merchant bank, Robert Benson and Company.

What Benson did not record in his diary was the nature of his other mission to the United States, which was some rather ticklish business. Beatrice Eden, wife of the British foreign secretary Anthony Eden and "C's" cousin by marriage,* had become the mistress of C. D. Jackson, a Princeton man and the senior vice-president of Time Inc. before becoming Eisenhower's American deputy for political warfare in England.

This was considered a security matter (to say nothing of the possibilities for a major scandal), for Beatrice knew a great deal about the personalities and politics of state. Benson was known to and liked by both parties involved, but it does not appear that this mission met with much success, for the relationship continued until 1947, when the affair came to an end and Eden divorced Beatrice and later married Clarissa Churchill, one of the prime minister's nieces. But Benson may have persuaded Jackson and Beatrice Eden to discretion, for no word of the affair leaked into the press, although it did leak out into OSS and thus into the diaries of David Bruce, OSS chief in London.

Yet "C's" life was nothing if not beset by tumult. And of all the tumults with which he had to deal at this time, none was more intricate and noisy than his relationship with Donovan.

4 "WE ARE NOT A REFUGEE GOVERNMENT"

By July 1943 "C's" official relations with Donovan and the OSS had gone from bad to worse. With the establishment of Algiers as the main Allied base for operations against the southern ramparts of Fortress Europe between Gibraltar and the Dardanelles, "C" formed a new Secret Intelligence Service just outside the city. Called the Inter-Services Liaison Department (ISLD), it was also known as "Little Broadway."

It was a large base, and the station chief was Captain Cuthbert Bowlby, son of Harold Macmillan's tutor at Eton. Throughout, ISLD remained separate and remote from all other secret services. It had several missions, not the least of which was to report on the capability and performance of Eisenhower and his staff, on the attitudes and

---

*Stewart Menzies was married to Pamela Beckett, daughter of Rupert Beckett. Beatrice Eden was a daughter of Sir Gervase Beckett, Rupert's brother.

morale of the U.S. Army, on French politics in French North Africa and metropolitan France, and on the activities of the American and French intelligence services. It also fought the enemy.

Its separateness and the reasons for it were studied by the chief of OSS SI in Algiers, Henry B. Hyde, a young New York lawyer:

Since they were professionals in a game where rules of security breed an inevitable reluctance to reveal anything, we never managed to get an inside view of SIS operating methods. This was because the British Intelligence Service were always mindful of the fact that wars, in which countries may pool their total efforts, are succeeded by periods of peace, when it may be advantageous not to have given away too much. Thus, they were instinctively loath to open up the secret of their operating methods, carefully built up by trial and error over a great number of years. [30]

Hyde was sensible in his judgment, but there were others less well disposed toward "C's" service, among them Kenneth W. Downes, a former schoolmaster who had worked as an agent for SIS before joining OSS as a founding member. Downes was in charge of an important operation called Banana to land OSS spies on the Spanish coast at Malaga. Since OSS had no transport of its own, SIS loaned OSS a sardine fishing trawler, HMS *Prodigal*, to put the agents ashore. But when OSS asked for the use of the trawler for a second mission, one needed to land a substitute radio set to replace the Banana party's original set, which would not work, SIS refused on the grounds that an order had been received from the Foreign Office in London to refrain from the insertion of secret agents into Spain while sensitive matters were being discussed with Franco—there were signs that the Bodden infrared ship-reporting line was being reestablished on Spanish territory by the Germans in the Strait of Gibraltar.

That action left Downes, a man with considerable influence at Donovan's court, greatly distressed, for as Downes complained in a telegram to Donovan about the Banana affair: "This left our reception committee, with whom we could not communicate, on the Malaga beach to wait, at great danger to themselves and the whole Malaga show, for three nights for a relief that was not coming." Downes's concern was the greater because, as he went on, "this episode was, unfortunately, far from unique." [31]

The sum of the OSS Historical Unit's reports does make it appear that by the autumn of 1943 there was a concerted policy on the part of both SIS and SOE to limit, control, or prevent OSS in the nature of the work it could undertake within the empire and from British or

British-controlled capitals. Whatever the truth of Downes's assertion, even David Bruce, the new chief of OSS London, perhaps the most blue-blooded Anglophile of the American power brokers of the period, felt he had cause to complain.

A rich man who had married a Mellon and was a prominent politician and lawyer, Bruce was liked and trusted by Menzies and accepted him promptly. But if Donovan hoped by Bruce's appointment to succeed where Whitney had failed, in obtaining "C's" license to operate in Western Europe, Donovan was disappointed. "C" proved no more prepared to grant freedom of action to Bruce than he had been to his predecessors. Although Menzies and Bruce became close friends, and remained so, Bruce was not able to operate at will from England into Europe, and he was not permitted to develop relationships with the refugee intelligence services. As Bruce was to record of his relations with "C":

Throughout the early history of [OSS secret intelligence] the attitude of SIS towards us was, on the whole, consistently friendly and cooperative. They gave us generously their intelligence during a period when we had little to offer in exchange. As we expanded and became more expert and more productive they may have viewed our growth with some jealous forebodings, but there was never any rift between us. I am sure that they feared the emergence of an American system that might compete globally with their own, but they bowed to what may have seemed to them the inevitable. [32]

Whatever Menzies's personal attitudes were toward Americans and America, "C" recognized that the United States was England's main ally and a main source of supplies, and that "109"—Donovan had long since abandoned the cipher "Q" given to him by him Stephenson—must have a place in the war. But could he be allowed to operate in northwest Europe at this time? That was the area in which "109" wished to operate, for obvious reasons.

Having deliberated at length, "C" had to advise Donovan that at the present time he could *not* be allowed to operate in northwestern Europe at will. "C," "109," Dansey, and Marshall-Cornwall ("C's" old friend from the days at GHQ in France in World War I, who had recently joined SIS as Dansey's heir apparent) met at Broadway. "C" explained the nature of the new threat. Since February it seemed likely that the Germans were preparing to bombard London with a revolutionary form of weapon, the flying bomb or cruise missile and the stratospheric rocket tipped with a one-ton warhead. That threat required that "C" impose complete control over all operations into northwestern Europe, Allied as well as British, if the lines now being laid by Dansey were not to be impossibly tangled.

In view of the emergency within the British government created by the discovery of these weapons, "C" asked Donovan not to undertake intelligence operations from North Africa north of the line of the Loire River, and not to undertake any missions from any point into Holland, Belgium, and northern France. Always courteous and mild-mannered, "109" (Menzies felt) seemed to accept his points, especially in regard to operations into northern France, Belgium, and Holland at that time.

Menzies's hopes were entirely misplaced. In entering into this agreement, Donovan intended not to honor but to build a case against "C" to prove to the Joint Chiefs of Staff in Washington that when "C" used the word "coordinate" he meant "control" of OSS activities in Europe. Colonel Arthur Roseborough, chief of Donovan's secret service, commented on the proposals that "C" was being "aided and abetted" by the G2 of the U.S. Army commander in London, General J. C. Crockett, the U.S. ambassador to the European governments-in-exile in London, A. J. Drexel Biddle, and his military attaché, Colonel O. N. Solbert.

Roseborough alleged that they had "ganged up" with "C" because, as they had jointly complained to Washington, "OSS is an unnecessary and disturbing element in the general secret intelligence picture and its activities in France in particular, if not closely coordinated by and with the British would add to the 'chaotic' conditions resulting from the activities of the other Allied services. Furthermore, it was alleged by the group that OSS had been 'slick' in its dealings with the British and its efforts to avoid "British control of our operations."

Persuaded that "C" was acting not out of his immediate concerns regarding the emplacement of missiles, but out of a long-range intention to so control the refugee intelligence organizatons that, when they provided the nucleii of the postwar governments in Europe, they would endorse Britain's proposals at the peace conference. Donovan began his contest of will with "C." He first tested "C's" ruling with a request to the U.S. Joint Chiefs of Staff, his masters, for authority to begin both secret intelligence and special operations in the Low Countries, northern and southern France, Norway, Spain, Portugal, Poland, Czechoslovakia, and Germany.

Without comment, the U.S. chiefs sent the paper to the Combined Chiefs of Staff, who in turn sent it to the British chiefs of staff. Having met with "C" and the new head of S.O.E., Brigadier Colin Gubbins, the British replied that OSS could work as a full partner in the secret war so long as their operations were "coordinated" with those of Broadway. In other words, "C" had conceded not a point. The British chiefs of staff stated also that they could not provide transport for OSS and that therefore the U.S. chiefs of staff must provide it.

That reply produced almost a rupture in relations between Donovan and Menzies. Donovan cleared all British personnel from OSS headquarters, including Colonel Ellis, who had worked inside almost daily for eight to ten hours a day since January 1, 1942. At the same time, Donovan sent a directive to all headquarters that all OSS personnel were to prepare to terminate relations with SIS personnel, and he also examined proposals for the imposition of security procedures at OSS headquarters in London intended to prevent SIS men from visiting OSS installations and offices without invitation and also to guard against the possibility that "C" might seek to place agents inside OSS.

Careless of the main reason for the rejection of the Donovan plan—if accepted it would introduce a new element to confuse the already confused intelligence scene in Western Europe—Donovan called for comment on the British chiefs of staff note.

David Bruce, chief of OSS London, replied to Donovan that if the paper were accepted by the U.S. chiefs of staff, OSS would be reduced to the "same completely subordinated and subservient status that the Greek, Jugoslav, and other refugee foreign services are permitted by sufferance to enjoy." Bruce went on, "We are not a refugee service," and submitted that OSS "should not be reduced to such a satellite position. The strongest nation in the world which is in addition doing the bulk of the financing for the United Nations is certainly entitled to the right to maintain a secret intelligence system free of control by any Allied or associated nation, so long as its operations do not threaten the security of such a nation." Bruce added that he felt SIS should be informed that "as an agency representing a free and sovereign co-belligerent country," OSS was "entitled to the same measure of independence as the British Government grants to SIS."

Armed with these and other such opinions, Donovan sent his views to the U.S. Joint Chiefs of Staff. He began: "I should say this at once—without the assistance of British SIS, we would have had a most difficult time in setting up our organization." For that, OSS had been grateful, but at the same time "we have . . . made it entirely clear that it is our obligation and our purpose to establish a strategic intelligence service . . . independent of that of any other nation."

He recognized "in Allied operations the propriety and importance of a definite line of demarcation between military and paramilitary operations and strategic intelligence." Also, he recognized the need for "unity of command" and agreed that it was necessary to insure security and avoid conflicts." But, he declared, the British paper "involves a question of principle which, if ignored, may seriously affect our national sovereignty." If the paper was accepted, then a "large and important part of the European Continent would be denied American intelligence operations except on British terms." OSS SI would be reduced to a "subordinate and subservient status."

Donovan said he believed it would "ultimately not only do harm to the good relations between the two countries but will hamper the united war effort by destroying any effective American intelligence service in that theater." He warned the Joint Chiefs of Staff that if the paper was accepted, then OSS would become no more than part of SIS, and the intelligence the American military command would receive would be no more than materials "processed and evaluated through British machinery." Virtually "complete control will continue to be exercised by the British, since the supreme Allied commander and the American [Army] Group commander will have only that intelligence which has met the British test." This was not in the common interest, for it would "shut out entirely one complete set of brains."

Donovan's paper worked its magic with the U.S. chiefs of staff, who were well aware of the British administration's campaign to maintain strategic control of the war. On December 28, 1943, they notified their British counterparts that they did not accept the British paper. They were, they said, of the opinion that "the interests of both nations will be better served by the continuation of independent operations by OSS under the control of the Commanding General, U.S. Forces in the European Theater, whose responsibility it is to effect the necessary coordination with the corresponding British agencies."

The U.S. chiefs of staff added also, "The British SIS and SOE, in discharging their responsibility to the British Chiefs of Staff under appropriate British direction, likewise are afforded independence of operations," and it was "our view that complete reliance must be placed in these agencies to effect coordination among themselves in good faith and on a common sense basis."

In the event, that is not what occurred. In making their recommendations, the U.S. chiefs of staff had not reckoned with "C's" skill in and knowledge of the corridors of power in London. OSS London was placed under the control of the U.S. Army, which was well disposed toward "C"—from July 1943 onward Broadway and U.S. military intelligence shared Ultra, and U.S. military and naval personnel were being introduced on a large scale into the Ultra production process both at Bletchley and at all other points—and Menzies's officers were being attached to all American armies, as they were attached already to all British armies, to control the dissemination of Ultra in the field.

General Jacob L. Devers, U.S. commanding general in London, had no wish to disturb the Ultra relationship by granting OSS freedom to operate wherever it wanted. He was well aware of the great dangers that might arise at any time from the missile bombardment, dangers that could make it impossible to use England as a base for the cross-Channel attack now planned for the spring of 1944, and he backed "C's" case. Whenever OSS asked Devers for permission to undertake espionage operations in northwestern Europe, he sent the proposal to Broadway. If Broadway approved (which it very rarely did), then the operation was undertaken. Consequently, Donovan found himself pinned to England until after the invasion, a setback from which neither he nor his agency recovered. He was unable to gain the laurels required to obtain the support he needed in Washington for the formation of the Central Intelligence Agency. Rejected as well was Donovan's hope that OSS might become the permanent secret intelligence service of the United States.

"C" gained few supporters in Washington and New York by pinning Donovan to England before the invasion. Furthermore, at this same time "C" found himself involved in an even more noisy scuffle, this time again with the Special Operations Executive, which Churchill had created by taking a rib out of Broadway's chest—Section D—in 1940 to "set Europe ablaze" coincidentally with the invasion.

Along with the Donovan decision, that scuffle established "C" as the most unpopular man inside the secret circle.

5 THE DEATH OF PROSPER

On August 3 Churchill wrote to Ismay, his chief of staff, on the eve of his departure for the Quebec conference with President Roosevelt and the Combined Chiefs of Staff:

It will be very necessary for me to be kept fully informed during these critical days. Particularly I must have good "C" stuff. At any moment a larger crisis may arise, and risks may have to be run. . . . Make sure that full pouches by air including "C" stuff await me at H[alifax, Nova Scotia]. There will be time for a long read up in the train. [33]

The news and opinion was indeed momentous. Germany had been mauled at El Alamein, Cap Bon, Kursk, Stalingrad, in the Atlantic, and during the Pointblank day-and-night heavy bomber campaign against German cities. Consequently the Joint Intelligence Committee circulated the opinion that Germany might collapse in 1943 as suddenly as she had done in 1918, even while Churchill was at Quebec. Mussolini had been swept away, and as Churchill told the Chinese foreign minister, T. V. Soong, "his paraphernalia had disappeared overnight—like snow at Easter." [34] Italy was near surrender, and "C" was able to advise Churchill on August 6 that a Signor Berio, an Italian diplomat (and a friend of Rex Benson), had appeared at Tangier with authorization from the new Italian government to negotiate on terms. At any moment, so it seemed, an Allied army might have to land in northwestern Europe to secure the Continent upon the German collapse.

At any moment the U.S. chiefs of staff might also have to scrap their plans for an invasion of France from England that year and instead invade Italy. Hence Churchill's anxiety to obtain as much " 'C' Stuff" as possible, for during the Atlantic crossing little could be sent or received because of the need to maintain wireless silence against the possibility that U-boats had come out to intercept the great liner. Churchill was out of England and could not adjudicate or intervene, therefore, in what was becoming the most dangerous conflict within the British administration, the quarrel between Broadway and Baker Street, headquarters of the Special Operations Executive.

There were many causes for the trouble between Stewart Menzies and Brigadier Colin Gubbins, chief of SOE. Ordinarily, they might have liked and admired each other, for both were professional army officers, both were about the same age, both were of Scots origins, both were courtly and amiable clubmen, both were conservative Loyalists, both served with distinction in the Great War, and both had had distinguished careers in the secret services of England.

Both were spirited men, although Gubbins was the more evidently so—he believed, as he wrote, that the tommy gun was the best weapon for close combat, and that the thing to do with an informant was to kill him quickly. "C" on the other hand disliked noise and violence in his work, preferring silence and stealth. When Menzies captured a spy, execution did not necessarily follow immediately: he preferred to keep the man alive on the grounds that a live spy had utility, a corpse had none. This was a difference of tradecraft, and it was a difference that caused much of the trouble between the two men and their services.

Menzies had never taken kindly to the memory of that day in 1940 when Gubbins had taken control of Section D, "C's" sabotage and special operations section, without informing him. With the authority of Hugh Dalton, minister of economic warfare, Gubbins had welded several organizations into a single department known as SOE. That Gubbins managed to put together an organization at all was one of the bureaucratic epics of the war. But most of Gubbins's recruits came from the city or the liberal arts, and there was, consequently, an independent, almost revolutionary spirit that was magnificent but "amateur."

Rapidly, Gubbins began to challenge Menzies everywhere. In New York he succeeded in winning the support of Stephenson. That was, perhaps, inevitable, for Gubbins and Stephenson had become firm friends in the 1930s when both were in Churchill's political circle. But Menzies could not be expected to like the situation, for Stephenson was "C's" man in New York.

For operational reasons—Broadway required quiescence if it was to operate successfully, SOE existed to create uproar within the German Fortress Europe—by the midsummer of 1943 relations between "C" and SOE had become so serious in all theaters where they operated together that, a high American officer testified later, "they used to cut each other's throats at the drop of a hat." [35]

At that time, the French section of SOE, which was commanded by Maurice J. Buckmaster, was intensifying its operations to seed France with British agents. The object: Create and lead the national insurrection that was expected to break out when the Allies landed in France. That such an insurrection would break out was evident from one of "C's" decrypts, for they received the intelligence from, so to speak, the horse's mouth.

A decrypt reached Broadway showing that on July 1, 1942, seventy Sicherheitsdienst officers stationed in France met in Paris to discuss the French internal political situation. The minutes of the conference were transmitted to Sicherheitsdienst outstations in various parts of Europe. These minutes were intercepted, decrypted, and translated by Bletchley. They showed, as Standartenführer SS Bickler warned the conference, "ninety-nine per cent of the French population are openly hostile to us. The French despise the Germans. They will not even forgive us for treating them so decently." Bickler continued: "A wind of insanity blows over the whole of France," and "Everywhere there is the possibility of an outbreak of collective hysteria, as in the times of Bartholomew's Eve and the great Revolution." [36]

By the summer of 1943, Buckmaster had created a system of skilled aircraft handlers at various points in France. Their task was to supervise the reception and departure of RAF aircraft bringing agents in and out of France. The RAF also carried secret mail that supplemented wireless as the most important method of communicating between London and occupied France. This was difficult and hazardous work requiring great technical skill and courage. A French aviator, Henri A. E. Dericourt, was regarded as the best of the aircraft handlers, and the most important, for he controlled all clandestine air traffic into and from the Paris region. [37]

In 1939–40 Dericourt served in the French air force as a test and transport pilot. In 1941 Dericourt and another French pilot, Leon Doulet, were brought by Dansey from Syria, where they had been captured in the Gaullist-British invasion, to London. Both were examined by the Security Service, and during this interrogation Dericourt admitted to having been a courier for the Sicherheitsdienst, carrying letters and packages for them between various cities while flying airliners for Air Bleu, a French aviation company at Marseilles. As the MI5 report stated, Dericourt did not seek the work, had not engaged in intelligence for the Germans against France or any power, and had acted only as a courier between two addresses. Dericourt's point of contact within the Sicherheitsdienst was Hans Boemelburg, head of Section IV of the Sicherheitsdienst in Paris, the section responsible for counterespionage in France. Boemelburg was an elderly and alcoholic homosexual who, as one of the "Big Four" at the Sicherheitsdienst's headquarters near the Arc de Triomphe, was one of the most hated—and the most feared—members of the German secret service in France.

Doulet faded from the story, but when Dansey met Dericourt it seems evident that he knew of the latter's connection with Boemelburg. Persuaded that Dericourt was entirely pro-Allied, Dansey decided to use Dericourt to penetrate the Sicherheitsdienst in Paris through Boemelburg. Dericourt was trained in the clandestine flying and handling of Lysanders, the heavy single-engined aircraft that, because of their ability to make very short landings and takeoffs, were employed extensively for the insertion of agents into northwestern France. He was also trained in the flying and handling of Lockheed Hudsons, small twin-engined aircraft that were used for agent penetration deeper into France. Dericourt conducted himself satisfactorily and was made a flight lieutenant in the Royal Air Force.

Dericourt then was offered to Buckmaster as air movements officer for the Paris sector of France. This was their first connection, and Buckmaster could not later remember who made the introductions, except that it was not Dansey. The official who made the introduction was almost certainly Air Commodore Archibald Boyle, director of intelligence at the Air Ministry, who was well known to Dansey. There is no reason to doubt that Dansey used Boyle to introduce Dericourt to Buckmaster in order to further his plan to penetrate the Sicherheitsdienst in Paris, nor is there any reason to doubt that Dericourt was cooperating with Dansey in that stratagem. In arranging the introduction by a third party Dansey could establish Dericourt's cover for the real purpose of Dericourt's return to Paris—to "get into" the Sicherheitsdienst.

Coming as he did with powerful recommendations, Buckmaster accepted Dericourt's services gladly, for he had great need of a man with Dericourt's qualifications. Buckmaster was not, however, told of Dericourt's association with the enemy counterespionage chief, Boemelburg. One man in Buckmaster's organization may have known, however. He was Dericourt's prewar friend, Nicholas Bodington, Reuters correspondent in Paris before the war and now a member of the senior staff of Buckmaster's office. Bodington may have been not only Dericourt's protector but, it was asserted later, as part of the allegations against "C" and Dansey, one of "C's" men placed in the Special Operations Executive to report on Gubbins's activities in particular and what SOE was thinking and planning.

Buckmaster arranged for Dericourt to enter France on the night of January 22–23, 1943. He was parachuted blind—that is to say, without a reception committee to meet him—near Orleans. Dericourt headed first for Marseilles, where he collected his wife, and then made his way to Paris. Dericourt and his wife spent the first three nights of their arrival in Paris at the home of Dericourt's former mistress. They then moved to the Hotel Bristol, a hotel requisitioned for the exclusive use of the Sicherheitsdienst for Germans and others visiting Paris on SD business. Since no French person was allowed to stay at the hotel without a pass from the Sicherheitsdienst, it must be assumed that Dericourt and his wife stayed there with the knowledge and permission of Boemelburg. If that was the case, then Dericourt was knowingly and wittingly in contact with the enemy from the time he first arrived back in Paris. There is acceptable evidence that Boemelburg did meet Dericourt on his return, and that Dericourt told Boemelburg that he was back in France as the air movements officer for Buckmaster of "F" Section. There is also acceptable evidence that Boemelburg gave Dericourt a case officer, Hermann Goetz, the Sicherheitsdienst's specialist in wireless.

From this point forward Dericourt met Goetz regularly in a flat in the Place des Ternes in Paris, and at an early meeting Dericourt gave Goetz the time and place of a Lysander bringing in agents from London. Goetz then contacted the headquarters of the German air force with a request that German aircraft stay away from the Lysander. Thereafter Dericourt kept Goetz informed of *all* air movements into and from France from his airfields, of which there were fourteen. [48] Dericourt himself admitted that he told the enemy about the whereabouts of the airfields, although he claimed that he told the Germans only about those airfields he had selected but which he knew the RAF had *not* accepted.

That Dericourt told the Germans of the fourteen airfields, and that the Germans believed him, is evident from the decrypt of the Sicherheitsdienst conference in Paris. This decrypt showed that Dericourt was probably the Sicherheitsdienst's principal informant about the British secret services in France. It also shows the highly significant fact that while Dericourt told them everything they wanted to know about Buckmaster's F Section in the Special Operations Executive, he told them little or nothing about SOE's first rival, Broadway.

In discussing what Hauptsturmführer SS Weezel called "the oldest and the most dangerous service"—SIS—Weezel declared that the Sicherheitsdienst did not "have an organizational plan" of SIS in France, and all that Weezel could tell the meeting about the SIS was the obvious, that "from the interrogations of those captured one can conclude that it contains three sections: (1) counterespionage, (2) section for operational espionage, and (3) economic espionage," and that "in the whole of France there are possibly only some agents of the SIS who, however, work with a considerable number of French collaborators." [38]

On the other hand, the same decrypt did reveal that the Sicherheitsdienst knew all it needed to know about F Section's operations in France. In short, F Section had been blown completely, at least primarily by Dericourt—the key evidence here is the reference to fourteen airfields. Also, in reviewing British sabotage operations in France, Obersturmführer SS Keller stated:

The English Ministry of War has . . . built up . . . its own resistance organization in France; this is called "French Section"; it is made up of French people but commanded by British officers. This "French Section" receives ammunition, explosives, and weapons by air for the execution of sabotage and for the installation of weapon depots for guerrilla fighting in the case of a landing. A further task of the organization consists of the location of suitable landings fields. The organization is divided into three sections: (1) Sabotage (2) Radio (3) Air landing. It takes care of nine sections in occupied territory. It maintains closest relations with the Communist Party, which it supplies with weapons, while it refuses to supply the bourgeois resistance groups with weapons and ammunition. Eleven planes kept up regular contact with England; *fourteen airfields* were made available for this purpose. All subleaders of the organization were brought to England by plane for a training of several weeks. The "French Section" in southern France has even larger supplies of weapons to be reckoned with. [39]

The decrypt revealed no evidence that Dericourt had given any information on those air movements in which SIS agents or mail alone were involved. Nor could any aircraft casualties be attributed to him.

By the end of the summer of 1943, therefore, Dericourt had performed superbly well in his duties. There had been no aircraft casualties, although it was known by Buckmaster that some of the agents he had handled had been captured by the Germans. But in that same month the Dericourt story became caught in the web of Starkey, a major strategic deception operation to make it appear to Hitler that the Allies would invade northwest Europe that year and that operations in Sicily and Italy were no more than a diversion from Starkey. This deception operation also sought to pin down German divisions in France that might otherwise be moved to either Russia or Italy and also to bring the Luftwaffe to battle, where it might be destroyed, which was one of the essential preconditions of the real invasion of Europe, Overlord.

It caught, too, Buckmaster's chief organizer in northern France, a man whose real name was Major Frances Suttill, an Anglo-Frenchman born at Lille in 1910 of an English father and a French mother. Suttill was educated at Lille and at Stoneyhurst and was a lawyer of Lincoln's Inn. He was barely thirty-two when he parachuted onto a French meadow near Vendôme, the old walled city about 110 miles south of Paris. His mission was to establish what was to be F Section's largest circuit, Prosper. Prosper made his way to Paris. By the early spring of 1943 Suttill had established Prosper, and he had helped to develop Physician, Donkeyman, Bricklayer, Chestnut, Butler, Satirist, Cinema, Orator, Surveyor, and Priest, all SOE networks. Some of them were large, with membership of up to two or three thousand persons—far too large for safety.

Dericourt came to know and like Prosper and handled most of Prosper's incoming and outgoing agents and his secret mail. Suttill's principal method of communication was wireless, with secret mail going in and coming out on Dericourt's Lysanders and Hudsons. During the first five months of 1943 Suttill received no less than 240 containers of arms and explosives, much of which Suttill distributed among the clandestines in the "Red Belt" of Paris. And by the spring of 1943, as one of Suttill's associates was to write: "Germans are killed daily in the streets of Paris," and "90 per cent of these attacks are made with arms provided by us . . . to the Communists." [40]

Neither murder nor sabotage was Suttill's main task. His principal mission was to prepare the French resistance for the invasion of Europe, which was then expected in the late spring or late summer of 1943. However, by the late spring Churchill had decided that a cross-Channel invasion through France was out of the question. Instead he had conceived a large-scale strategic deception scheme to suggest to the Germans that the Allies *would* land that year. The main element of this plan was called Starkey, which through feints and misinformation was intended to convey to the Germans that the Allies would land in September 1943. And with the acceptance of Starkey, events began to assume a sinister aspect.

On the night of April 22–23, 1943, "at London's orders," Dericourt flew to England in one of his own Lysanders from a field about ten miles west of Vendôme, presumably to be briefed about "the invasion." Dericourt was to suggest that his orders to return came not from SOE but from SIS, although Mr. D. Foot, the official historian of SOE in France, was to assert that "nothing in the files of any British service bears this out." The reason for that journey, Foot was to state, was that Dericourt was "to receive a reprimand" for having "endangered a Lysander through an ill-placed flarepath" sometime earlier.

We may regard this as a cover story for his actual purpose in coming to London. If it was the real reason, then it took an uncommonly long time to reprimand Dericourt and for him to recover. Dericourt remained in London for twelve days when twelve hours would have sufficed. He returned to France by parachute during the night of May 5–6, 1943, but as Foot was also to write in his official history, Dericourt had held "staff discussions" while in London.

Whom these staff discussions involved is nowhere revealed. But it may be assumed that Dansey was involved, for he received a daily report on all persons arriving in and departing from Great Britain. It is also clear that at least in part these staff discussions involved the question of Dericourt's contact with the head of German espionage in Paris, Boemelburg, for as Foot revealed, there was a note in Dericourt's personal file by Dericourt's friend in SOE, Nicholas Bodington, stating, "*We know he is in contact with the Germans and also how & why.*" [41] That notation was significant because, without it, Dericourt's contact with the Sicherheitsdienst could only have been construed as treacherous. With it, it was clear that the contact was being condoned. And the reason why Dericourt was allowed to maintain this highly dangerous contact concerned, as we shall see, the secret mail relating to the whereabouts of the missile launching sites.

With Dericourt's return to France, seven days later, Prosper himself was then called to London, arriving in England in one of Dericourt's Lysanders during the night of May 13–14. Foot did not advance any reason for Suttill's flight to London so soon after Dericourt's journey. Buckmaster, too, claimed at first not to know who issued the order for Prosper to come to London. As late as 1983 Buckmaster was still stating, "I was not aware of the *real* reason [for Suttill's return to London]. All I knew was that Suttill had to be brought back, right? Well, we made the arrangements and brought him back." [42]

However, in 1983 both both Foot and Buckmaster regained their memories and indicated that the order to Suttill to return *involved Churchill*, and that while he was in London Suttill went to see Churchill. Thus, for the first time with clarity, we encounter Churchill directly involved in the propagation of that most dangerous of all gambits in warfare—deception. Suttill was told personally by Churchill that there *would* be an invasion of Europe across the Channel later in 1943 and that Suttill was to prepare himself and his networks for that operation. Plainly Churchill was lending his authority to Starkey. In a 1983 interview with Larry Collins, the American reporter and novelist, Foot stated of the meeting between Churchill and Suttill:

This was Churchill doing a bit of deception on SOE. . . . Yes, I've heard this story from several sources. That certainly would have been SOE being used without its knowledge for deceptive purposes. A direct coup by the PM towards an SOE agent whom he'd insisted on seeing. With Gubbins' knowledge we must presume. He was supposed to have been present. But never let on. It's almost too impossible to believe. But in fact it is so perfect that I think that it does ring true—it's true because it's so impossible.

Suttill returned to France on or about June 12 with what Foot called an "alert" signal, "warning the whole circuit to stand by" for an invasion that summer. When interviewed in 1985–86, two survivors of Suttill's networks, Jacques Bureau and Pierre Culioli, both confirmed that Suttill told them the long-awaited invasion was only a few weeks away. That autumn, again according to Foot, the BBC broadcast "warning messages to every active SOE circuit in France, indicating that the invasion would come within a fortnight," although the "action messages that should have followed, on the night of the landing, were not sent." [43]

Foot contended that these warnings "formed a small part of the deception plan that covered the Italian surrender and the Salerno assault (8 and 9 September)." As Foot himself concluded: "No doubt word that these warnings had gone out was passed round, too far for the safety of the resistance circuits, so that the Germans heard of it; for this the indiscretions of local subagents were responsible." Foot then added by way of a reprimand that the French resistance movement could be used so callously: "The staff [in London] concerned with deception *relied on indiscretion*, and might have thought more about safety." [44]

By that time, however, Suttill had been captured. He was arrested at 10:00 A.M. on June 24, ten days or so after his return from London, by German police waiting for him when he returned to his hotel room in the rue de Mazagran, an address to which he had only recently moved. That the Germans had obtained his new address so soon, Foot acknowledged, was "suspicious." Here we come to the kernel of the allegation that Prosper was betrayed by Dansey. Foot stated that it was "said to be widely believed in France that Suttill's circuit was deliberately betrayed by the British to the Germans; even 'directly by wireless to the Avenue Foch.' " But as Foot was also to state in repudiation of that notion:

An assertion as absurd as this last one calls to mind the Duke of Wellington's reply to the man who called him Captain Jones: "Sir, if you can believe that, you can believe anything." The Avenue Foch could only be reached by wireless by someone who knew the frequencies it used; and it was the task of one of the British intelligence departments to hunt for these frequencies and, having found them, to watch the traffic on them. It is not seriously conceivable that any transmission could have been made to the Gestapo direct from any British-held set without giving rise to widespread and elaborate inquiries involving several different secret services: how on earth could they all be hushed up? Such a conspiracy to betray Prosper, whether *per impossibile* by wireless or by any other means, appears in any case quite pointless. What object useful to British strategy could have been served by it? [45]

The official historian was badly informed and obfuscating at this point, for the fact was that there *had* been a major deception in World War II involving Prosper, one that had badly disrupted Anglo-French relations in the sixties to the point where General de Gaulle, by then president of France, voted against allowing England into the European Common Market. Thus, still wriggling on the very sharp hook of an old deception operation, Foot answered his own question as best he could:

Only one conceivable object has ever been hinted at in print: that this circuit's downfall may have been part of some elaborate deception scheme to draw the German's attention away from the invasion of Sicily; but not in a form that carries conviction . . . to send a few SOE agents into France primed with rumors that France was going to be invaded in 1943, on the off chance that some of them would fall into German hands and pass the rumors on, would have been a project lacking alike in bite, finish, and viability. Besides, it is undoubtedly the case that no use was made of SOE's work in France for any purposes of deception, then or later: no one trusted the agents enough for such delicate tasks. [46]

In the light of Foot's subsequent discovery concerning Churchill's statement to Prosper, that explanation was no longer blessed with conviction. There could be no better instrument than Prosper, the chief of all British special operations networks in northern France, to convey to Hitler that an invasion was coming that year, for Hitler knew of Prosper, and his agents were watching that tragic figure for the signs that an invasion was impending. Also, Hitler, who spent at least fifteen minutes of his morning conferences discussing resistance operations in general and Prosper in particular, himself gave the order to demolish Prosper in the belief that, if they were destroyed, then the Allied high command would be so unhinged by their loss that they would abandon the invasion. In reality, therefore, *nobody* but Prosper could give Starkey the full flavor of authenticity that Starkey required if it was to succeed in its purpose.

But did the design succeed? Did Suttill tell his captors what Churchill had told him, that there was to be an invasion that year? The evidence indicates that Suttill said nothing to his interrogators, who did not hesitate to torture him. He may well have continued to say nothing until his execution by firing squad at Sachsenhausen concentration camp. All his deputies, too, appear to have maintained silence, except one.

Flight Lieutenant Gilbert Norman did break and actively collaborated with the Sicherheitsdienst in arresting all Prosper's helpers and arms dumps—until, when Norman was of no further use to his captors, they shot him, too. The total number of casualties caused by the collapse of Prosper's clandestine empire could never be calculated. The conservative estimate was that four hundred men and women were taken, the outside being fifteen hundred. This did not quite destroy Buckmaster's organization in northern France, for some individuals and even chains survived to fight another battle.

But did the loss of the Prosper networks indicate that "C" meant what he said when he remarked to Robert Bruce Lockhart at their meeting on January 29 that if Gubbins's organization in France "could be suppressed our Intelligence would benefit enormously"? Gubbins, by now chief of all special operations in Western Europe, thought so. Gubbins soon learned of the collapse of the Prosper network and formed the impression that Dansey was involved. As Stephenson claimed in January 1986, he was in London in September 1943—a claim borne out by Gerald Wilkinson's diaries—and

Gubbins advised me that Dansey had betrayed to the enemy a number of his key agents in France, and that the casualties were extremely heavy. He told me, too, that he had informed the prime minister. Because Gubbins was not a man who lied or exaggerated, I believed this, for I myself had formed the impression that Dansey was an evil man who would stop at nothing to get someone out of his way. That was why Stewart employed him. [47]

As Stephenson added, far from being knighted, as Dansey was in June of 1943, Dansey should "have gone to the Tower of London, and Menzies with him, for Menzies bore executive responsibility in all this." When asked if he had any documentation to substantiate his statement, Stephenson said that he had destroyed all his World War II records. However, the BBC magazine, *The Listener*, in May 1986 in an article concerning a television program on Prosper, printed what it represented as being the text of a letter from Gubbins to Stephenson. This contained the statement, "Since I told you about the Dansey menace in May and you talked with Stewart about it, Dansey has somehow accelerated his jabbing interference to the point that I am losing good men." [48]

Stephenson claimed that he saw "C" about Gubbins's allegation and, according to the author of the article, Robert Marshall, who was also the producer of the television program, "C" and Stephenson "held a series of meetings with other concerned [SIS] men and with Desmond Morton, Churchill's intelligence adviser." Then Stephenson went to see Menzies personally, and after "a heated discussion" Menzies "angrily assured" Stephenson that "the destructive, nonsensical interference [by Dansey] would cease from that moment, and whatever action was necessary to assure compliance" would be taken. [49]

Was the Prosper disaster directly attributable to Starkey? If Prosper did reveal under interrogation by the Germans what the prime minister had told him, then it was. If he did not, then what Prosper told his networks as a consequence of his meeting with the prime minister certainly had the effect of encouraging the *resistants* to put their heads up when they should have been keeping them down. Churchill's statement was, then, *one* of the causes of the Prosper disaster. London knew from the decrypts and Dericourt's reports that Prosper was a doomed man and, despite Foot's assertions to the contrary, he was primed with statements by no less an eminence than the prime minister that France was to be invaded that year in the knowledge, and perhaps the belief, that when tortured he would talk. Prosper was therefore to that extent a victim of the deception.

But there were two other causes of the disaster, and Churchill was not responsible for these. They were (a) the contents of the secret mail and (b) Prosper's insecurity and the insecurity of his assistants.

Suffering as they did from the clandestine's greatest weakness—
loneliness—they gathered together at their favorite restaurants and
bars when they should have had no contact with each other except
through cutouts. A special paper by the senior members of ORA in
France, General Guillane de Benouville, defined exactly Prosper's
predicament and the mistakes of certain of his helpers:

An agent . . . has more money than he otherwise would. He is keyed up
and treats himself too well. He eats when no one else has food. He drinks
at expensive bars every now and again. Stool pigeons at these bars get to
know him. He has women. They may not personally betray him, but they
make him conspicuous if he takes them about or they keep him from moving
alone and bring him back to his old address. He moves himself up in the
social scale so that his cover no longer fits him. He travels first-class when
he ought to be in third, either from vanity, or because he has made the last
four trips standing and is tired. He has a white collar but he spits on the
floor. His table manners do not suit the restaurant he selects. He believes
that he is important and he hates to be utterly obscure.

The agent by conviction is liable to need a sense of solidarity. There will
be determined lone figures, but there will also be determined beer hall
patriots who will be noisy, talkative and boastful. In short, they all get out
from under their cover at one time or another. They grow tired or lazy; they
linger one night too long in pleasant surroundings, and so are caught. Such
agents are on the periphery of an organization, but they can lead to its
center. Their arrest is of value, or they should be followed, or approached
by penetration agents. In theory, there are cut-outs between them and the
higher ups, but it is natural for a man to want to know his superiors and
commanders by sight. [50]

But if this explains why Prosper became a pawn—he was in the
position of the battalion commander who finds that he has been sacrificed to enable an army to gain its objectives—it does not explain
why Dericourt was used by Dansey. There are two explanations: (a)
"C" required a man such as Dericourt to keep him informed of the
activities of Buckmaster's agents in the field; and (b) Broadway's secret
mail had to be protected at all costs. As it was to emerge, SIS's mail
contained data regarding the missile sites; Buckmaster's mail was
largely valueless except to the Germans.

It is evident, therefore, in his relations with Boemelburg and
Goetz that Dericourt allowed them to see SOE's mail while concealing
SIS's courrier. Intelligence regarding the exact whereabouts and
structure of the missile sites, their lines of fuel and munitions supplies,
their missile dumps, and their headquarters and barracks became the

most urgent of all intelligence business before, during, and after the Prosper disaster. In order to ensure that SIS mail reached London safely, Dericourt, who controlled the air mail in northern France, surrendered SOE's mail to Boemelburg, who was delighted to get it because of Hitler's interest in the Prosper case.

Having read the files, Foot acknowledged that "much of" F Section's mail with London "was watched by the Gestapo, probably with Dericourt's agreement." And the casualties were caused because, as Foot also discovered, "one of the rash things the agents did was to send long reports home by Dericourt's aircraft, either inadequately coded or altogether *en clair*." The agents were "so blindingly trustful of their colleagues that most of them were in clear—names, place names, addresses, everything." [51]

As Foot also wrote, from Prosper's mail "a very fair picture of agents' modes of life could be built up. Worse, agents' addresses and the areas they were interested in exploiting could be deduced from these papers as well. The Germans thus secured a substantial body of intelligence about F's operations round Paris and in the Loire and Gironde valleys. They noted it down and bided their time." These statements were supported by the Germans.

A leading Abwehr counterespionage officer, Hugo Bleicher, was to claim that it was "through the mail" that the main Prosper arrests occurred, Bleicher also claiming that "the Germans saw nearly all the Prosper mail." A colleague of Boemelburg, Kieffer, deposed after the war that the "material which Boemelburg had had photographed by his agent [Dericourt] and which was kept in my safe" was "put to very good use during the interrogation of Prosper." [52]

But beyond all this remains the final question: Who betrayed Prosper's personal address, the address in the rue de Mazagran where he was caught by the German security service? Since he had moved to that address only the night before, and of all the members of his networks he was the one determined lone figure of which Benouville spoke, who knew that address? Presumably Dericourt was given it by Prosper; but there is no evidence. Certainly Dericourt was about the only man he would have given it to, for only Dericourt had a need to know it.

It was this point that always confounded those Frenchmen who, for reasons both personal and national, became curious about the underlying circumstances of the destruction of Prosper's networks. If it was Dericourt, then Dansey was an accomplice. According to Patrick Reilly, at about the time of Prosper's arrest

Dansey came into my room and asked me with delight all over his face: "Have you heard the news, Reilly?" I thought, "Gosh, we must have pulled off some gigantic coup against the Germans," I replied: "No. What has happened?" Dansey replied as if this was the most important moment of his career had come: "SOE's in the shit. They've bought it in France. The Germans are mopping them up all over the place." I felt quite sick inside and I then realised that Dansey was the most evil and the most wicked man I had met in public service, and nothing since then has made me change my mind.

Yet if that grisly conversation marked the end of Prosper, it did not mark the end of Dericourt. He remained in place until February 1944, at which time SOE brought him back to London at gunpoint for interrogation. Since that operation is narrated at its correct time and place, it is sufficient at the moment to state only that SOE did not succeed in its efforts to bring a treachery case against Dericourt: Dericourt found powerful protectors when he got to London. As for Starkey, it proceeded as planned. All Europe quivered with expectancy as the BBC London—for everyone was involved in the deception, including England's mistress of truth, the BBC—announced on August 17, 1943:

The liberation of the occupied countries has begun.

We are obviously not going to reveal where the blow will fall. The people of the occupied country that is to be the first to welcome the armies of liberation will be notified at the last minute.

Pending the hour when we shall be in a position to enlighten you on this crucial point, we are today addressing a preliminary appeal.

It is time for you to prepare all your actions, to perfect your preparations. All these elements that are to contribute in any way whatsoever to the success of operations on French metropolitan territory must be fully equipped to carry out their task.

You must prepare yourselves, day by day and week by week, for the role that you will have to play at a future date, which may be near, in the liberation of your country. [53]

The United Press told the world from London that "an unofficial source states that the Allies will move against Germany by the autumn, and the race for Berlin is on with Anglo-American forces poised to beat the Russians. Signs multiply that they may land in Italy and in France within the next month." The Associated Press and Reuters picked up the broadcast and made it world news. The French Committee of National Liberation warned all patriot forces to stand by for an Allied invasion that "may come any day now."

The United Press then announced that "French underground leaders were revealed today to be confidently expecting an early invasion of France, and coincidentally there was widespread speculation in Great Britain that zero hour for the assault on western Europe was approaching." From Quebec, in a broadcast to the Canadian people, Churchill announced that Europe would be invaded "before the leaves of autumn fall"—without saying *where* in Europe the Allies would land. "C's" agents everywhere dropped hints here and there throughout the world. *The New York Times* on August 19, 1943, carried the deep page-one headlines:

ARMIES READY TO GO SAYS EISENHOWER
ALLIES BID PEOPLES OF EUROPE PREPARE

Churchill signaled from the Quebec conference to the chief of deception, Colonel John Bevan, a friend of Menzies: "Good luck to Starkey!" The "invasion fleet" assembled on the east coast of England as the RAF and the USAAF launched 3,215 fighter and bomber sorties at "invasion targets." On September 9 the USSAF launched a further 1,208 aircraft against the French coast. The "fleet" sailed.

Sadly, Churchill's good wishes were not realized, for Starkey failed. The German supreme commander, Field Marshal Gerd von Rundstedt, recognized all the activity for what it was—a feint. Instead of keeping his armies alert and expectant in France, he actually removed a number of divisions from the French to the Italian and Russian fronts. Of the thirty-six German divisions in the west between April and December 1943, twenty-seven were sent to other fronts, mainly Russia, being replaced by burned-out divisions from the other fronts. Indeed, so certain was Hitler that the forces in Britain would not invade because they could not—they were not sufficient for a major sustained operation on the Continent—that of the four infantry and two panzer divisions in Brittany, one of Starkey's main targets, the equivalent of one panzer and two infantry divisions were withdrawn for other assignments, thus leaving Brittany practically denuded of German troops.

With the failure of Starkey, "C" did undertake measures to prevent a recurrence of the Prosper disaster. He appointed his old friend, General Sir James Marshall-Cornwall, senior general in the British army, as Dansey's deputy. The threat was clear to Dansey: he was reaching sixty-five and was already far beyond mandatory retirement age.

6 THE CROSSBOW MAZE

By the autumn of 1943, the optimism that had infected the Churchill administration just before the Quebec conference had subsided. The Germans did not collapse. On the contrary, the immensity of the missile threat and the performance of her armies on the battlefields showed that Germany still possessed the power to fight her enemies at least to a standstill. Between Churchill's return from Quebec and the tripartite conferences at Cairo and Teheran in late November and early December—the conferences at which it was decided that the United States and Great Britain would invade northwestern Europe on or about May 1—Churchill's thoughts were dominated by the missile menace.

In "C's" Europe-wide espionage inquiry into that menace, he owed much to the prescience of a young scientist who, back in 1941, had almost been sacked by Menzies for impertinence. In February 1941 Dr. R. V. Jones, Menzies's chief scientific adviser, invited Charles Frank, a thirty-year-old grammar schoolboy who had taken a doctorate of philosophy at Oxford and had since studied physics at the Kaiser Wilhelm Institute in Berlin, to join his staff at Broadway. Jones and Frank had known each other at Cambridge, and Jones had been impressed by Frank's ability to express himself in terms Jones could understand. Frank accepted the invitation knowing only that he was to join the "Scientific Civil Service"—which did not exist—and arrived in London without having arranged lodgings.

Since Jones's wife was having a baby and Jones himself could not put him up for a fortnight, arrangements were made for him to sleep in the basement of Broadway. Within a few days there was trouble. Concerned that he was about to lose the services of one of the most brilliant of the younger physicists, Jones set to work to piece the incident together, and "it seemed that Charles had sat down at the breakfast table where a middle-aged man had been chatting to the duty secretaries and something that the man had said was known by Charles to be incorrect. Charles, who had a rigorous feeling for truth, intervened in the conversation and told the man where he was wrong. The man turned out to be Stewart Menzies, who was understandably put out at being contradicted in front of the secretaries of an organization in which he was Chief." [54]

As Jones was to recall, it was a "desperate moment because I knew that Charles's help was going to be invaluable. And so

although I had not met Menzies before, I asked to see him as soon as possible. I told him that I understood that my chap Frank had upset him, but that I would very much like him to stay because he was one of the ablest men I knew. "That's alright then," said Menzies. "I'll stand anything if a man's efficient—he can stay!" This episode, which looked so disastrous, in fact put me into cordial contact with Menzies, to the benefit of my standing with the organization.

Jones was proved correct; Frank did do able work in the scientific intelligence branch of SIS. And two years later almost to the day there came an episode that was to prove the start of a long intelligence inquiry that not only reestablished the Secret Intelligence Service but acted as a vivid example of its reason for existence. It was, Jones recalled, a Saturday afternoon, March 27, 1943. Frank was sitting at his desk opposite Jones when he remarked: "It looks as though we'll have to take those rockets seriously!" Frank had been reading the transcripts of conversation between two captured German generals in a bugged room in the SIS interrogation center near London. Both had been commanding generals of the Afrika Korps. One was General Ludwig Cruwell, the other General Wilhelm Ritter von Thoma.

During their conversation Cruwell was heard to say: "But no progress whatsoever can have been made in this rocket business. I saw it once with Feldmarschall Brauchitsch, there is a special ground near Kunersdorf. . . . They've got these huge things which they've brought up here. . . . They've always said they would go 15 km into the atmosphere and then. . . . You only aim at an area. . . . If one was to . . . every few days . . . frightful. . . . The Major there was full of hope, he said, 'Wait until next year and then the fun will start. . . . There's no limit. . . .' " Von Thoma remarked by way of reply that "he knew their prison was somewhere near London, and since they had heard no large explosions, there must have been a hold-up in the rocket programme."

Frank's remark, and the transcript, defined what had been common knowledge since 1934, when the German army was known to have begun to take an interest in missiles as weapons of war, little more than a miasma of menace into reality that seemed imminent and omnipresent. Suddenly, that ancient institution SIS was confronted with an ultramodern technological threat involving new sciences such as rare, high-calorie fuels, the theoretical science of stratospheric trajectories and ballistics, very lightweight airframe construction, and remote-control missiles.

Jones went to see "C," and the danger was laid before Churchill on April 15 with a note that there had been five such reports of the existence of missiles since the end of 1942. The chiefs of staff considered that four aspects required immediate further study: How reliable was the evidence, and could more be obtained? Was a rocket really feasible as a weapon of war, and what was the most likely form of its mechanism and projection? Where was the weapon being deployed and what countermeasures could be employed against it?

To the irritation of "C" and Jones, the chiefs of staff established an investigatory body under the chairmanship of a man who had had some slight experience of British antiaircraft missile testing, although he knew nothing of heavy, long-range missiles. That man was Duncan Sandys, Churchill's son-in-law and joint parliamentary secretary to the Ministry of Supply. Code-named Bodyline,* what had begun as an SIS inquiry had in a flash become a crisis of state.

Menzies was "requested and required" by Sandys to begin a major intelligence attack. Menzies passed the matter to Dansey and briefed the controllers of the espionage organizations in northwestern Europe on the basis of primitive intelligence. Since few of the controllers or agents possessed any technical knowledge, none knew precisely what they had to look for. As a result, there was confusion as to the nature of the threat, and even whether several weapons or one were involved, even within the highest ranks of the government. Once again "C" and his services found their intelligence severely challenged and themselves facing a form of inquisition.

At the same time, two other forms of intelligence inquiry were begun. If these weapons were being test-fired, as had been suggested, at Peenemunde, a small town on the Baltic, the likelihood was that they were being tracked by radar in order that some estimate could be made about their trajectory and performance, and, as Jones knew well, since the German army had little radar and in any case radar experts would be required for the tracking, then it might be a good idea to keep an eye on the fourteenth and fifteenth companies of the German Air Signals Experimental Regiment. That task went to Professor Frederick "Bimbo" Norman, reader in Medieval German at

---

*Bodyline was the code name for the Sandys inquiry, Crossbow for the aerial campaign against the German missile program. Since the use of these two code names is liable to cause confusion in the reader's mind, the code word Crossbow is used to define both the inquiry and the campaign.

King's College, Cambridge, a leading student of German heroic poetry and the specialist translator at Bletchley who did outstanding
work in the unbuttoning of the Abwehr's Enigma. Norman was to
inform Jones if either of these two companies appeared at Peenemunde. Their wireless traffic was to be followed as closely as possible.

At the same time a specialist RAF photographic reconnaissance
unit was established to keep an eye on Peenemunde. On the first
sortie, on April 22, 1943, the pilot came back with photographs that
showed a large, busy establishment on the dunes beside the Baltic
and the issuance of a large cloud of what looked like steam. This was
thought to be exhaust from a rocket jet being tested. On June 18 the
unit acquired a photograph of "something that could be a whiteish
cylinder about 35 feet long and 5 or so in diameter, with a bluntish
nose and fins at the other end." At that moment Jones "experienced
the kind of pulse of elation that you get when after hours of casting
you realize that a salmon has taken your line."

Having verified the existence of the object with Charles Frank,
Jones was to write:

Now the only question was how we should play the advantage that the
discovery had given us in demonstrating to the Intelligence world and the
politicians that the "old firm"* had done it after all, despite all the effort
and fuss that had been created by the Sandys approach.

The fate of Jones's discovery belongs in the realm of Whitehall
politics; it is sufficient to say that when Jones conveyed the discovery
to Sandys, the prime minister's son-in-law did not acknowledge receipt of the intelligence, nor did he ask Jones in for any technical
conversation. Since his periodical bulletin was in circulation, Jones
merely published an appendix announcing the fact of the discovery
and by indirection suggested that the microscopic object on the photograph was the result of his processes. If Jones had been more experienced, he would have given the discovery to Menzies to handle;
Menzies had weight in Whitehall and would have known how to use
the photograph to the advantage of SIS. As it was, a further sortie
produced a further and unmistakable photograph of a rocket with the
same dimensions and appearance as that of June 18. The result was
a full meeting of the War Cabinet Defence Committee (Operations)
at 10:00 P.M. on June 29, 1943, at which Churchill presided and at
which there were present the chiefs of staff and a number of ministers.

*Within the service, from "C" downward, the secret service was known colloquially as
"the Firm," as if it were a factory or corporation.

With the information before Churchill that the start of the missile attack on London might be imminent, and that it had been estimated that a single missile would—not might—cause up to four thousand casualties, a number of major decisions were made. These were remarkable, given the fact that the missile was a novel weapon. Radar was to be established to detect the firing points of the missile in France; the "most searching and rigorous examination of the area in North France within a radius of 130 miles of London" was to be organized and maintained. [55] Peenemunde and its inhabitants and factories were to be destroyed by air attack at the earliest opportunity. Plans were to be prepared for air attack upon suspected rocket bases in northern France as soon as these were located.

What was not known in London at this time was that the Germans had either begun work, or were preparing to do so, on forty-five sites between the Pas de Calais and Cherbourg, with a main base at Watten, near St. Omer in the Pas de Calais. These were for missiles known to the Germans as the A4—the same missiles that Jones had detected on the photographs at Broadway. The German command had called for a production of 3,080 A4s by December 1943, with a monthly production of 950, and the bombardment was to start on November 1, 1943, from an underground bunker at Watten. By June 1943 Broadway knew something, but by no means everything, of these preparations. What was not known was that the Germans were preparing to introduce a second missile, the FZG 76, which was to become known as "the flying bomb" to one generation and the "cruise missile" to a later one.

With work starting in August 1943, there were to be sixty-four main sites, with another thirty-two in reserve, situated in a belt from Cherbourg to St. Omer, with eight armories each containing 250 weapons. These sites were to be completed by November 1, 1943. Of this second range of weapons and sites, little or nothing was known in London although men such as Lord Cherwell, Churchill's scientific adviser, believed that a "pilotless jet aircraft" did exist and that the reports concerning the A4 heavy rocket were cover for it. He insisted and kept insisting that the A4 could not exist: there was no propellant or guidance system that could give accurate flight to such a vehicle.

Cherwell was supported in that belief by SIS reports now flooding in, which, when studied by the Sandys committee, men without knowledge of the dynamics of missiles or even of science, resulted in an inability to sort fact from fiction. The system became clogged with intelligence calculated to mystify and mislead the British about the truth concerning the missiles.

It was evident that the Germans knew the British knew about their secret weapons. It was evident, too, that the Germans had begun to "blossom"—the German technical term for a deception operation—the British in an effort to mystify and mislead the Crossbow inquiry. In that, at first, the Germans were successful. By July 9, 1943, Sandys, the man responsible for analyzing the reports and making the conclusions upon which counter- and defensive measures could be undertaken, confessed that it was not possible to assess the reliability of the SIS and diplomatic reports. The Joint Intelligence Committee, of which Menzies was himself a member, concluded skeptically:

There are some signs that we are receiving too much information about a rocket or a long-range weapon and there are, therefore, grounds for hope that German experiments in this direction are proving unfruitful. On the other hand there are, for the most part, not unreasonable explanations why we should be receiving so much information; and therefore we would not be justified in relaxing any precautions and must still be prepared for the possibility that the Germans will use the long-range rocket.

Nevertheless, if there was confusion about the nature of the missiles, there was certainty that they existed and that they were being manufactured and tested at Peenumunde. The decision was made, therefore, to destroy the testing grounds. The attack on Peenemunde took place on the night of August 17–18, the earliest date at which the night was long enough to permit the entire flight from England to the target and back to take place in darkness. A force of 597 RAF heavy bombers hit the experimental establishment in what was intended to be a precision bombing operation. Forty bombers were lost, thirty-two more were damaged, and Peenemunde was severely damaged. Many people had been killed, key technicians among them, but the target marking by the master bomber had been imperfect, and a sufficient number of key personnel, most of the records, and many of the facilities had survived. The German missile program could, therefore, continue, although the manufacturing and deployment of the attack was probably delayed.

On August 12, 1943, however, the picture changed fundamentally with the receipt by SIS of what was described as "a detailed report about the state of development of German long range weapons" from

"a quite unusually well-placed and hitherto most reliable source."
The source was a German traitor of rank in the Army Weapons Department in Berlin (Waffenamt). This source advised that there was
not one missile but two. One was the PHI7 flying bomb, the other
a rocket projectile known as A4. The PHI7 was launched by a form
of catapult, but beyond that the Waffenamt official was unable to give
details, as PHI7 was an air force, not an army, project. As to the A4,
which was an army project, the information the English possessed
was correct as to length, but not to diameter. The source had stated
that one hundred A4s had been fired and one hundred were in hand,
and he declared that Hitler had set October 30, 1943, as the date for
the beginning of the attack. Hitler had ordered also that thirty thousand A4s be ready, although "this rate of production was beyond the
bounds of possibility."

At this point it became clear that there might be two weapons,
and there might be more of them ready for action than was supposed.
Menzies himself attended the ministerial meeting at 10 Downing
Street on August 31, 1943, at which Clement Attlee took the chair
in the absence of Churchill, who was at the Quebec conference. The
principal skeptic was, as usual, Lord Cherwell, who took the view
that there could be only one weapon—the pilotless aircraft—and that
the A4 rocket was a mare's nest intended to deflect the British intelligence attack.

By late September the entire Crossbow investigation had become
so obscured by German propaganda, the inexperience of SIS and its
agents in high-technology espionage, and Cherwell's preconceptions
that the War Cabinet Defence Committee instructed Sandys to obtain
a statement from "C" about the reliability of the intelligence he had
produced so far. In other words, Cherwell contended that "C" was
being hoaxed and, in turn, was misleading the committee. Menzies,
who was no scientist, sprang to the task of defending his intelligence
with the assistance of Dr. Jones, who by now had received two further
reports pointing to the existence not only of the A4, but of the PHI7
as well.

On August 22, 1943, a small pilotless plane bearing the number
"V83" had crashed on a turnip field on Bornholm Island in the Baltic
and had been photographed and sketched by the Danish naval officer
in charge on the island, who had sent the photographs and sketches
to Commodore Paul Morch, chief of the Danish naval intelligence
service. These were being sent by three separate clandestine channels
to Broadway, and one set, which consisted of some poor-quality pho-

tographs of a small aircraft in a field, arrived at Broadway on August 27, five days faster than the peacetime mail.

The second report was still more remarkable. Indeed, Jones thought that the report and the circumstance in which it was acquired placed it with the most remarkable espionage reports of World War II. Founded immediately after the French collapse in 1940 by Georges Loustaunau-Lacau, Alliance was a right-wing espionage organization operating in the British interest and controlled by Commandant Clam—Commander Kenneth Cohen at Broadway—through Lisbon. With the capture and execution of Loustaunau-Lacau, the network was taken over by his secretary, Marie-Madeleine Fourcade. Under her control the network expanded to some three thousand members, of whom some five hundred were executed during the lifetime of the organization. They knew each other by the names of birds and beasts. Hence the code name Noah's Ark, by which it became more popularly known.

The most notable achievement of Noah's Ark came from a twenty-three-year-old woman named Jeannie Rousseau (who later became the viscomtesse de Clarens), who used her sexual charms to extract the table of organization of one of the two German missile organizations that were now, late in 1943, being emplaced in northern France.* Her victim, or seducer, was one of the German officers involved. [56]

In 1943 Mlle. Rousseau, code-named Amniarix, encountered a German officer whom she had met for the first time in 1940 while working as an interpreter for the mayor of Dinard at the headquarters of General von Reichenau's army group assembling for the invasion of England. This officer, whose identity was never revealed, offered Amniarix a post with a new organization responsible for launching the V1 flying bomb missiles at London. Mlle. Rousseau accepted,

---

*In a lecture on SIS to the British air staff after the war, Dr. R. V. Jones, "C's" chief scientific officer, who received Noah's Ark reports, stated that these tactics were known at Broadway as "Dirty Work." Of that type of espionage he stated: "It is difficult . . . to trust 'Dirty' work, although it may sometimes produce very valuable results. Valuable early information about V1 and V2 came, for example, from a German officer on the staff of the General responsible for development in the German Army Weapon Office; this was pure treachery. In the 'Dirty' category also comes information obtained through women spies by seduction of foreign nationals. It is only fair to mention here that during the war there was one outstanding report obtained in this way, when a young French girl in August 1943 seduced a German officer attached to [the German missile research and development center on the Baltic called] Peenemunde, and obtained from him a remarkably detailed account of the embryonic Flying Bomb organization (although she much confused the issue by telling us that it was for the Rocket). Apart from this one report, no mistress turned up anything valuable as far as is known."

and by the late summer she had handed her controller, Georges Lamarque, this report for transmission to Broadway: "The missile-launching organization was known within the German Army as Flak Regiment 166W; it appeared to consist of 16 batteries of 220 men. Its headquarters would be near Amiens, with batteries spread between Amiens, Abbeville, and Dunkirk. These batteries were to have at their disposal a total of four hundred catapults; and the commanding officer's name was Wachtel."*

That report was the first to give in detail the order of battle of the German missile attack program and therefore of the highest importance to London. Furthermore, on September 7, 1943, even as Jones was preparing a draft review of the SIS evidence for Menzies, there came two crucial Ultra signals. Hitherto, despite the vigilance of Professor Norman at Bletchley, Ultra had played little part in the Crossbow inquiry. But on that date two German air force signals referred to Flakzielgerat (flak target apparatus) 76. In one of the intercepts, the headquarters of the Third German Air Fleet asked urgently for antiaircraft gun protection for the ground organization of Flakzielgerat 76 "following the capture of a British agent who had had the task of establishing at all costs the position of the new German rocket weapon, and in view of the fact that five 'reception stations' had already been attacked, some of them repeatedly, by the Allied air forces."

The second decrypt had made it evident that Flakzielgerat 76 was in Belgium and northern France. From these two decrypts Jones concluded that Flakzielgerat was a code name for a rocket-driven weapon intended, presumably, for the long-range bombardment of England; that the weapon was much more likely to be a pilotless aircraft than the long-range rocket. And if the conclusions drawn from Amniarix's report and the decodes were correct, then a ground organization existed for the operational use of the flying bomb that did not exist for the A4 rocket.

Against that background of facts known and unknown, Jones drafted the paper on SIS intelligence for presentation by "C" on September 25. It was a well-written document with an elegance of form and logic that was not often bettered during the war. It revealed how extensively and rapidly Broadway had developed since those calamitous days of 1938–40. And the issue was grave—whether SIS had been

---

*The viscomtesse de Clarens's report, which was considered to be a model of espionage reporting, is reprinted in appendix E.

effective in obtaining intelligence about weapons that were intended shortly to batter London and the ports and cities around it into ruins, and so prevent the region from being used as the base for the invasion of Europe, which all knew must come soon.

The first serious evidence about German rockets was contained in the Oslo Report* of November 4, 1939, which described several new German weapons developments. Nearly all the weapons described in the Oslo Report had by now been used. The latest to appear was the radio-controlled rocket-driven glider bomb, which was anticipated in the Oslo Report in some detail and was said in that report to have been developed at Peenemunde. As "C" noted: "The Germans in 1939 could hardly have been contemplating a hoax four years ahead, nor has there been any suspicion of a hoax in any part of the very competent Oslo Report, which has proved a valuable guide in many fields of Scientific Intelligence." "C" thought, therefore, that "in 1939 the Germans were developing a large rocket, but experiencing control problems."

Little further of consequence was heard of the German long-range rocket until December 18, 1942, when three reports were received that a Professor Fauner of the Berlin Technische Hochschule and Engineer Stefan Szenassy had witnessed trials near Swinemunde, twenty miles southeast of Peenemunde, of a rocket containing five tons of explosives with a range of two hundred kilometers and "a danger area of ten kilometers square." This weapon had "automatic steering." This source, "C" stated, had added little to the Rocket story but had since provided valuable information in other directions, most noticeably the transmission to Broadway of drawings and photographs of the Lichtenstein aerials on a German nightfighter, which "we know to be accurate and which, from a German point of view, would have provided us with information valuable to our bomber

*The "Oslo Report" was a document sent to the British naval attaché at Oslo by an unknown person shortly after the outbreak of war. While the document was first regarded as a hoax, combat experience of the weapons detailed within the document showed that it was genuine and contained breathtaking intelligence about an entire range of new German weapons. Since no one person could have known the technical detail about such a range, and since very few would have had the authority to know of their existence at all, it is assumed that it was compiled by a technical man acting under the direction of Admiral Canaris, chief of the Abwehr, the secret service of the German General Staff. At that time, General Franz Halder, chief of the German General Staff, and Canaris were plotting to overthrow Hitler, and it was assumed the Oslo Report was an attempt to alert the British to the dangers facing them, to persuade them of the good faith of the conspirators and to prevent their use at all because, if such weapons were employed, any hope of a political settlement in any way favorable to Germany would vanish.

offensive." Therefore, "although the first long range rocket warning came from an untried source, he has since shown himself to be efficient and reliable."

At least four other reports were received during the first quarter of 1943 that drew attention to trials of a long-range rocket at Peenemunde. Although at that time these reports could conceivably have been "plants," a "convincing pointer" came from the conversation of General von Thoma. The information revealed by von Thoma "agreed with our knowledge where this existed," and while it might now be regarded as slender evidence, it nevertheless represented a crucial point in the intelligence picture at that date, "for it appeared that he must have seen some experimental long range rocket development." Furthermore, it would have been "remarkable had this been the one 'plant' in all his conversations with Cruwell," so "his statements had more weight than the earlier but unchecked secret reports."

The existence of a very large experimental station at Peenemunde was then confirmed by photography. "C" continued, since plainly Peenemunde was an establishment of great importance in the German Reich, "It was very unlikely that the Germans would carry a hoax so far as to incite us to attack it." It followed that any secret reports mentioning Peenemunde were very probably made in good faith, and any development seen there was most likely genuine.

Information had also been received from "an officer at Peenemunde" who was in touch with French sources (such as Amniarix). This officer had stated that a "special Flak Regiment 155W under Colonel Wachtel was going to France in October-November to operate the weapon, which would be launched from 108 catapults. A further 400 might be operated by the army." There was "no external check" available on the reliability of this source, but the report "contained many circumstantial details" such as the passes necessary to enter Peenemunde, which added to its accuracy where checkable and suggested an inside and genuine contact with the German air force. Later it was to emerge from Ultra that Flak Regiment 155W was indeed the unit charged with the task of opening the missile bombardment of London, although this information was not on hand September 25.

These, then, were the "keystones in the evidence for the reality of the rocket." In analyzing the general run of the secret reports, "C" acknowledged that there had been "a few reports from sources who have suggested that the Germans have put the story out as a bluff, either completely fictitious or based upon a genuine but forlorn development." But against these there was "a vast body of reports supporting the keystones."

As for the question of a hoax, "C" observed:

While it would be unwise to underestimate the German capacity for hoaxing, no technical hoax of any magnitude has hitherto been played upon us. For the rocket story to be a hoax, it is necessary to suppose that information, much of it oblique, has been planted upon many of our secret sources and upon German prisoners of war, over a long time and in many places. In addition, the effort of building a fake establishment, complete even to the detail of possessing a fire-raising decoy, would have been enormous and beyond human thoroughness. Therefore, if the rocket story is a complete hoax, it is the most consummate ever conceived.

"C" continued: "It has been suggested that long range rockets are a cover story for radio-controlled pilotless aircraft," but, he believed, it was "unlikely that a successful rocket hoax would sufficiently direct our attention from the aircraft because while looking for the one we should almost certainly stumble across the other." It would therefore be "a poor hoax which succeeded in making us bomb Peenemunde, not only from the viewpoint of other G.A.F. research, but also from that of the very weapon which the hoax was designed to protect." It followed that the hoax must have been intended to cover "some weapon other than pilotless aircraft, but even supposing that there was such a weapon, Peenemunde is still a high price to pay." It would be surprising, "C" asserted, if "none of our sources had discovered the new weapon."

The last alternative to believing in the existence of the rocket was that "our sources had observed something genuine at Peenemunde, but that it is not a long range rocket." It was necessary, therefore, to examine those points that appear to conflict with physical expectations. The "torpedo" had a rounded nose, which appeared to be designed for subsonic speeds, while a long-range rocket would travel at much greater speeds over most of its trajectory. Having studied all the technical evidence to support this postulation, "C" concluded:

If the torpedo-shaped objects are not the long range rockets . . . it is hard to find an alternative. They are unlikely to be true torpedoes, for the naval torpedo establishments are elsewhere, and the only torpedoes likely to be found at Peenemunde would have to be airborne. It would require an impressive aircraft to carry one of the objects photographed.

"C" now turned to evidence relating to the date and scale of the attack. Declaring that it was "hard not to conclude that the Germans have been conducting an intensive research into long range rockets at Peenemunde," he felt nevertheless that it was possible the "German leaders have been persuaded to devote much effort to the long range rocket by scientists with more enthusiasm than judgement." The "ardour of the inventor may have prevailed."

In these circumstances, it was "difficult to determine when these rockets will, if ever, be available for operational use." Few sources had been in a position so far to give reliable information. It had been reported by the high officer in the German Army Weapons Department that Hitler had demanded they be brought into operational use as soon as possible. The starting date had been postponed from the beginning to the end of July 1943 and might yet be postponed still further.

In early August this source had stated that at a conference in the last week of July, Hitler had "regretfully" recognized that the "rocket aeroplane" was not yet ready but had ordered increased numbers to be ready for the spring of 1944. The Foreign Propaganda Department had been instructed to soften the reprisal threats. But a few days later this same source had advised that Hitler had now revised his earlier decision of waiting until the spring and had fixed October 20, 1943, as zero hour for the opening of the rocket bombardment. These shifting dates might "well represent the conflict between the anxiety of the Fuehrer and the difficulties of the rocket development," for even "the keenest intentions cannot always be kept in face of the hazards of war and the snags of experiment, and it is likely that the rockets are still some months from the operational stage." If this stage was attained, "our secret sources and photographic reconnaissance between them should have a good chance of discovering the emplacements."

"C" then turned to the bedeviling question of the flying bombs. He maintained that there was nothing in the rocket story that detracted from the suggestion that the Germans were developing such weapons to launch against the big cities of England. In fact, much of the critical evidence pointed to both weapons, and it was at least plausible that while the German army was developing the one, there was keen rivalry with the air force developing the other. Long-range guns were similarly not excluded. Since none of the technical difficulties of the rocket stood in the way of the flying bomb, "C" said he would not be surprised if flying bombs were used first, nor even that launch sites for this purpose were now being built in northern France.

Lastly, it was possible that "the German Air Force has been developing a pilotless aircraft for long range bombardment in competition with the rocket, and it is very possible that the aircraft will arrive first." This last observation was to prove correct. On October 25 the War Cabinet Defence Committee met with Churchill in the chair with Field Marshal J. C. Smuts, premier of South Africa, in attendance together with a total of twenty-three ministers, members of the chiefs of staff committee, and members of various advisory committees—a large number to be crammed into the small underground Cabinet war room at Storey's Gate. "C" was present to represent his services, Jones to defend the views of his scientific intelligence establishment at Broadway.

The subject was introduced by Churchill, just back from the summit meeting at Quebec. He declared there were many indications that the enemy was preparing some secret weapon for use against this country. The two "crucial points" to be considered were, first, "can such a weapon as the long range rocket be made, and second, for what purpose are the many unusual works in Northern France being constructed?"

The minutes of the meeting showed a growing acceptance among those centrally responsible for assessing and countering the attack that both the A4 and the PHI7 existed, and that the extensive construction work taking place in a broad belt behind the French coast from Cherbourg to the Pas de Calais were launch sites. When Churchill asked Menzies to express an opinion, according to the minutes, "C" stated:

As regards the German long range rocket, we had collected a vast amount of evidence. Our task had not been made easier by the fact that the Germans had been aware that we were making enquiries and had therefore put out a certain amount of false information. This did not, however, mean that they had not developed a large rocket. It was impossible to determine the stage reached in the development of this weapon, but the effort they had put into the large constructional works in the Pas de Calais area indicated that they expected to use it in the reasonably near future. There was a good deal of evidence to show that these works were connected with projectors of some type. We also knew that extensive measures had been taken to ensure their security, and that very large areas of the Baltic had been closed for experimental work.

Many key decisions flowed from this and the other opinions expressed at that meeting. Of these the most important was "the highest priority" should be given to the destruction of the suspected launch sites and of the factories believed to be engaged in the project; intensive reconnaissance by ground and air of northern France for other such sites; the chiefs of staff were instructed to consider the use of gas against the sites and the advisability of passing a warning to Germany that Britain would retaliate with gas attacks on her civilian population.

Churchill declared that a secret session of Parliament would be held in a week's time to discuss the threat. And as a further expression of the gathering anxiety, Churchill for the first time advised President Roosevelt of the threat. In a telegram transmitted after the meeting, Churchill summarized the evidence but did not state definitely that two weapons existed, or that any existed at all, but that there was a definite suspicion of the existence of such weapons.

Meanwhile, after nearly seven months of watchfulness, Jones's long shot had begun to provide indications to confirm the view that the principle weapon in the bombardment would be the flying bomb, not the rocket. At the end of June Jones was advised that the Fourteenth GAF Signals Experimental Company had detachments specializing in radar on Bornholm and at Stolpemunde. There were no further intercepts until GAF Ultra revealed that two groups of plotting stations were at work.

One—Group Wachtel—was carrying out firing experiments and tests of explosives with a battery located at Zempin. The other—the "Insect Group"—was experimenting with catapults and was tracking by radar objects being fired in a northeasterly direction across the Baltic. Bletchley had unbuttoned the plot reports, which were in a simple code, and these showed that a weapon was involved, not a manned aircraft. The decrypts of the traffic of the Fourteenth Company showed that the maximum range was about 120 miles, and that the missile could travel at between 216 and 420 mph. The expression used by the Fourteenth Company to describe the object they were tracking was "koerpe," which hitherto had been used in connection with the HS-293 glider bomb used against Allied warships and merchantmen in the Mediterranean and the Bay of Biscay from September of 1943 onward. The decrypts showed also that the "koerpe" was under either gyroscopic or radio control and could change its course.

On November 13, 1943, the RAF's Central Interpretation Unit at Medmenham, a place skilled in the examination of aerial reconnaissance photography, noted on a fresh set of photographs of Pee-

nemunde that there was an aircraft smaller than those hitherto photographed, and this was judged to be, from its size, an expendable
pilotless aircraft. This aircraft was in an area quite separate from the
rocket test site, but there was no proof that this was the "koerpe."

In all, therefore, the inquiry continued to support the existence
of a flying bomb while not permitting the rejection of the existence
of a rocket. On the other hand two different types of special-purpose
sites were being constructed in France. Dansey's networks in France,
and especially the Alliance service, had detected six major structures
each employing up to six thousand French workers: Martinvast and
Sottvast near Cherbourg just within a mean range of 140 miles of
Bristol; and Mimoyecques, Watten, Lottinghem, Siracourt, and Wiz-
ernes in the general area of Calais-Boulogne. Four lay within a range
of 120 miles of London Bridge. The one at Siracourt was at the heart
of a concentration of smaller sites scattered all across the Pas de Calais
from the Somme to Calais—when plotted on a map they formed a
coherent and identifiable corridor two hundred miles long by thirty
miles wide. All were set back from the coast up to twenty kilometers,
which ruled out commando raids. These smaller sites resembled a
ski on its side, and each had a strip of concrete and a line of posts
aligned on London. By the end of November seventy-five of the
smaller sites had been identified in the Pas de Calais and seven around
Cherbourg.

The spreading rash of such installations led to a further inquiry
into the entire phenomenon by the minister of aircraft production,
Sir Stafford Cripps. Stewart Menzies and the head of the military
section of SIS, Colonel Hatton-Hall, gave evidence again. Of their
evidence Cripps recorded that, realizing the British authorities were
now fully aware of the existence of what was probably a major missile
program, the Germans were trying to "build up a war of nerves based
upon this secret weapon and the new and devastating explosive it
contains."

A large number of suspicious installations had been identified; and
those near Cherbourg, at least, were clearly not an attempt to confuse
the administration, for they were all sited for the best concealment,
all were camouflaged, and although they had all been detected, none
of the cluster in that area had been reported by agents. This suggested
strongly that they all had a definite and similar purpose, and that this
purpose was not propaganda. If it were, the agents would have reported their existence. As it was, in such reports that existed all were

described as being for the purposes of "internal security." Cripps concluded, therefore, that there was a strong case to be made that the flying bomb would be used against London first.

But then, on December 10, Bletchley decrypted a further signal from the "Insect Group" connected with the Fourteenth Company on radar plotting in the Baltic. The group was informed by its higher headquarters that "you will be used now and again for measuring the A4 from Ost. You need merely attempt to pick up the ascent vertically and to hold it as long as possible. W/T as for 76." And as Menzies and his colleagues on the Joint Intelligence Committee noted in its report on December 18, this first Ultra reference to the A4 confirmed that it was a weapon undergoing trials in the Baltic and left little doubt that it was a high-altitude rocket. London was confronted not with one but with two major new weapons of attack.

As Churchill minuted to his administration, when there was talk of evacuating certain components of the government and industry from London: "On no account must anything be done which will give rise to panic or the suggestion of the wholesale movement [from the capital]," although he did sanction the making of plans "discreetly and privately" for the departure of "firms or plants which are of unique importance and the linch-pins of important processes."

Among those who would be evacuated at short notice were "those sections of 'C's' organisation which are responsible for obtaining Crossbow information, and also for training Agents for despatch to Western Europe" for operations concerning Overlord, the invasion of Europe. Beyond that Churchill stated he had given "no authorization for any general order."

7 THE DEATH OF LADY HOLFORD

Although Broadway had obtained thousands of fragments of intelligence as the year drew to a close, two threats had begun to emerge: (a) a missile or missiles existed for an attack on London, but (b) were they flying bombs, what would later come to be called cruise missiles, or rockets? Or did the Germans have both weapons? These questions bedeviled Broadway, as they bedeviled the entire London intelligence community for the good reason that the Germans were using the existence of the one as cover for the other. The decision was made to destroy the detected sites. On Christmas Eve the U.S. Eighth Air Force launched the first of what was to total 28,000 RAF and USAF missions against the missile sites that winter. In that first operation 1,300 medium bombers dropped 1,700 tons of bombs on the sites in the general area of Calais and Boulogne.

Shortly, Broadway received a new series of telegrams from Amniarix, the French girl inside German headquarters for the attack. As Jones recorded, the Christmas Eve raid led Wachtel, chief of the missile-launching organization in France, to conclude that "we knew too much about his organization, and [he] tried to throw us off the scent." As Jones first heard the story:

He aimed to suppress the name "Flak Regiment 155 (W)" and replace it by "FlakGruppeCreil," pulling back his headquarters 100 kilometres southwards from Doullens to a chateau near Creil, about 45 kilometres north of Paris. To change his personal identity he dyed his hair, grew a beard, and changed his name to "Max Wolf." The whole move was carried out in secret, even to the extent of his entire headquarters staff driving into the back streets of a town and re-emerging on the other side in different uniforms and with different transport. In this it was reported to have been so successful that its laundry never caught up with it. [57]

But through Amniarix, who traveled with the headquarters staff, Jones quickly caught up with Wachtel. But Georges Lamarque, Amniarix's chief in the field, surrendered to the Germans, having volunteered his person in return for a German promise that, if he surrendered, they would not harm the inhabitants or the village from which he had been transmitting the Amniarix reports to London. Lamarque was then executed. When news of Lamarque's execution reached Broadway, the decision was made that Amniarix should be evacuated, and she was instructed to go to the Breton town of Treguier. This she did, accompanied by two other members of the Druides.

Sadly, the German security service caught up with her, and she was sent first to Ravensbruck concentration camp. She was then transferred to Konigsberg punishment camp and thence to Torgau concentration camp in Saxony, where she was liberated at the end of the war. Although Ultra and signals intelligence dominated the Crossbow inquiry, Amniarix demonstrated that in the world of high-tech espionage the courageous spy could still carry out major coups beyond the reach of even the most advanced machines at Bletchley.

By mid-December of 1943, there was virtually an army of spies at work in France to locate the missile sites. Evidence unearthed the existence of a third secret weapon, the V3 cannon, five of which were being installed in a hillside at Mimoyecques. Each possessed a barrel 416 feet long, the whole of the length lying in inclined, concrete-lined shafts driven into the limestone. All the shafts were aligned on London Bridge. False haystacks concealed the six-inch muzzles of the gigantic guns, which were designed to fire a finned shell weighing about three hundred pounds, of which fifty-five pounds would be warhead. Hitler intended that the charge should be incendiary rather than high explosive, his purpose to set London afire. The designers intended that the V3 should be capable of sustained fire at the rate of six hundred rounds *an hour* from late summer of 1943 onward.

On December 18, an hour or so before he was due to attend a War Cabinet Defence Committee meeting to discuss intelligence that such a tremendous weapon might exist, Menzies received word that Lady Holford, his mother, was dying. Sending a message that Dr. Jones would attend in his place, Menzies managed to reach Dasset just in time. Shortly after his arrival, Lady Holford passed away, her three sons at her side. The funeral was held privately, and, it is thought, Lady Holford was then cremated and her ashes laid with those of Sir George.

Churchill had been at Teheran and Cairo conferring with President Roosevelt and Marshal Stalin and was at Marrakesh in Morocco recovering from pneumonia. He and Mrs. Churchill had known Lady Holford well, for he had once tried to marry her sister, Muriel, all those years before at Tranby Croft. Churchill signaled "C" on December 22:

Personal for "C":
I was so sorry to hear of the death of your mother. My wife and I send you our deep sympathy in your loss and hope that you will have been able to take a few days off from your vital work.

To this telegram Menzies replied on Christmas Eve 1943:

I am deeply touched as well as assisted by the very considerate message which you and Mrs. Churchill so kindly sent me. I earnestly hope that your health will be soon fully restored.
C.

It is not known where Menzies spent Christmas Day, but he was probably at his official residence in Queen Anne's Gate. For there had been grave intelligence that more of SOE's networks in Europe might have been penetrated, and he had been asked by the Joint

Intelligence Committee to examine the evidence. And it was while he was in the middle of this task that dramatic news arrived from Bletchley, where "C" was due for the Christmas pantomime.

For years the battle cruisers *Scharnhorst* and *Gneisenau* had hypnotized the British public, who knew the twin battle cruisers variously as "the S.& G.," "the Salmon and Gluckstein," and as the "Sodom and Gonorrhea." Although each weighed only 26,000 tons, they seemed to be mistresses of the seas whenever they appeared. They were fast, powerfully gunned, heavily armored, well manned, and reckoned to be emblematic of the prowess of the German fleet ever since their escape from Brest through British home waters to their home ports in 1942.

They were damaged in that escape, and *Scharnhorst* lay immobilized at Wilhelmshaven until early in 1943, when she appeared at Altenfjord in north Norway, to begin operations against the Anglo-American supply convoys to the north Russian ports. There had been several daring raids by *Scharnhorst* on these convoys when, on Christmas Day 1943, Bletchley circulated an electrifying Ultra from the German admiral northern waters to the German admiral polar coast indicating that the battle group of which Scharnhorst was part might have sailed to attack a large Allied supply convoy, JW 55B, which was near Bear Island, on its way to deliver war stores to the Russians at Murmansk.

During the late afternoon of December 26, "C" left London for Bletchley to attend, as he did each year, the pantomime. He took with him his new personal assistant, Robert Cecil (Patrick Reilly had left "C's" staff to join Harold Macmillan at Eisenhower's headquarters near Naples). Thus, it seems, "C" had just arrived at Bletchley when the epic news was received that *Scharnhorst* had been intercepted by the radar of a British warship at 8:40 that morning, before she could attack JW 55B. Fire was exchanged between *Scharnhorst* and the battleship *Duke of York* at 9:26, contact was lost, and it was feared for a time that *Scharnhorst* might have escaped in the savage winter storm that lashed the northern seas.

But contact was restored just after noon on December 26, and the *Duke of York*'s gunfire slowed her. Three hours later *Scharnhorst* was sunk by torpedoes delivered by destroyers of the home fleet. A total of 1,864 German sailors perished when *Scharnhorst* went down. Such was the satisfaction at *Scharnhorst*'s destruction in both London and Washington—her destruction meant that a large number of warships were relieved of the task of watching out for her and could now be deployed for Overlord—that FDR sent a rare signal of congratulation to the Royal Navy:

Personal and Secret from the President for the Former Naval Person:

The sinking of the *Scharnhorst* has been great news to all of us. Congratulations to the Home Fleet. Roosevelt.

At Bletchley, on the first night of the pantomime, the occasion was chiefly remarkable for the appalling pun used by the leading man to mark the end of *Scharnhorst*. "Scharnhorst," he declared, "is not nize-now* anymore." Four hundred men and women who were present in the Assembly Hall jeered. [69]

"C" was back in London on December 30, for the memorial service for his mother, which was held at St. Mark's in North Audley Street, Mayfair, just around the corner from the house where Stewart Menzies had been born a day short of fifty-three years before. Princess Helena Victoria and Princess Marie Louise, descendants of Queen Victoria, sent representatives. "C" and his brothers were all present with their wives, except Pamela Menzies, who remained too ill to attend. There was a large number of peers and peeresses at the service, and an equally large number of prominent persons were present from Beaufortshire. Also present were Dansey and Guy Westmacott, a founder member of the League of Gentlemen. While the Westmacotts were close friends, this was the first and only sign that Dansey was ever an intimate of "C's" family.

On that sad note "C" entered that epic year, 1944.

---

*A play on the name of *Scharnhorst*'s sister ship, *Gneisenau*.

CHAPTER

Eight

Neptune

1944

1 THE CAPTURE OF BERTRAND

Early in 1944 "C" was made a major general "while specially employed in the Offices of the War Cabinet," thereby becoming the first Life Guards officer to be made a general in the 285 years since the formation of the regiment by the cavalier, Lord Gerard of Brandon. Menzies's portrait was hung in the officers' house of the Life Guards at Windsor along with all the other great oils of commanding officers. Indeed, it was still there in 1987. At the same time "C" became a member of the Committee on Overlord Preparations, a ministerial committee. It met each Wednesday under the chairmanship of Churchill to assist the supreme allied commander, General Eisenhower, on matters concerning British sovereignty involved in Neptune, the assault phase of Overlord.

For all practical purposes, "C" enjoyed ministerial rank in everything but name (there was no precedent for "C" having been made a minister). He was issued a special identity card, number 500376, to permit him to enter and leave at will the heavily guarded area around Downing Street.

Yet if the promotion and privilege were agreeable, it came just when another crisis struck "C's" key source, Ultra. On January 5, 1944, the Abwehr captured Colonel Gustav Bertrand, the man who knew more about the Enigma attack than anyone except "C." The Germans had arrested Bertrand while he attended the services for the Twelfth Night, the eve of the Epiphany, at the Basilica of the Sacre-Coeur in Paris. Bertrand had gone there to receive a wireless set that had been sent to Bertrand by "C" to enable him to resume personal contact with Broadway. "C" assumed that Bertrand was in the Abwehr's security indexes and that they would soon learn who he was, if they did not know already, and would use all their means to extract from him the technical knowledge that was his. "C" recognized that every man could be made to talk, and the fact that Bertrand was a brave and expert clandestine made no difference. Therefore the Enigma secret—what the British chiefs of staff declared to be "our most important source of intelligence"—was considered at risk.

Bertrand's arrest had the gravest implication for the conduct of the Neptune plan—the landing phase, the most dangerous and difficult of the entire Overlord operation. "C" had certain specific duties of high importance. The first required the final elimination of the German intelligence services as an effective and coherent part of their defense system. The second required precise knowledge of the strength and whereabouts of the enemy forces, the extent of their command's knowledge about Allied intentions, and the whereabouts of the main enemy offensive divisions, in particular the tank divisions.

"C's" third major task was to provide Eisenhower with the necessary intelligence for him to predict whether the Allied armies could obtain tactical surprise. If the enemy knew the time and place of Neptune, and assembled sufficient forces to repel it, then the supreme commander would have to take the final decision about whether to proceed with the operation, with all the vast political and operational consequences, if Neptune had to be abandoned.

Never before in the history of warfare had so much been *demanded* of an intelligence master. The key remained Ultra. In January 1944 "C" began a large program of expansion and technological modernization at Bletchley for the purposes of Neptune and Overlord. But at the same time he encountered serious trouble in two different directions. From the autumn of 1943 onward the Germans had begun to introduce major security improvements to Enigma, which remained the mainstay of their communications. As Menzies advised Eisenhower and the chiefs of staff, these improvements were "more fundamental" than any made by the Germans since the Triton cipher system was introduced into the U-boats in 1942 with such calamitous consequences in the Battle of the Atlantic.

By January 1944 these improvements had created a situation as complex and dangerous as any hitherto experienced. On January 20, as the British chiefs of staff handed over responsibility for Neptune and Overlord to Eisenhower and his land forces commander, Montgomery, "C" felt compelled to advise that "the Allies could at no time exclude the possibility that they would lose access to a large part of the Enigma traffic on which they depended for their intimate knowledge of Germany's strengths, dispositions, movements, and other responses to developments in every theatre of the war." [1]

Meanwhile, only a minimal amount of Ultra could be obtained about the German forces *in France*, which had been the situation since September 1940 when the Germans began switching from wireless to teleprinter and telephone land lines. That meant no wireless traffic existed to intercept and hence no Ultra. It was true that the Allied air forces were attacking the telecommunications systems to force the Germans to use wireless, but that tactic had produced little change. In consequence, Ultra revealed little about the Germans' plans and intentions when Normandy was invaded, although "C" received the usual mass of Ultra intelligence concerning the Russian and Italian fronts and all other sectors of the German war machine. But in France, the most important of the sectors, there was virtual silence except for Damsey's espionage reports.

By now Ultra dominated or influenced every aspect of the war, including Overlord planning, security, and deception. It provided sure knowledge of the enemy economy and morale; aerial bombardment targeting, and especially the Crossbow campaign against the (by now) large-scale German missile concentrations; counterespionage against the enemy intelligence services; the war at sea over which the men and the munitions were streaming in convoy for the grand invasion; the size, effectiveness, and allegiances of the European resistance movements in Europe; the capability and intentions of the enemy land forces throughout western Eurasia.

In providing these services, the Government Code & Cypher School (GC&CS) had become a large industry, employing men and women of many trades and disciplines and requiring a large and complex management. Since the management of Bletchley had functioned well under Commander Travis, in the interests of efficiency in the trial to come, "C" turned the directorship of GC&CS over to Travis and appointed himself director-general, a term that implied the duties of a chairman of the board. The staff increased to 7,723 men and women. During Overlord it increased still further until, by January 1945, it was to reach its wartime peak of 8,995. As for the performance of Bletchley, in the autumn of 1943 the number of German army, air, and naval decrypts had reached over 84,000 *a month* (48,000 army and air and 36,000 naval signals). Denniston's diplomatic section produced 14,050 decrypts in 1943, the best of the year, and the number remained almost as high for the rest of the war.

In all, GC&CS's penetration of the German war machine represented an achievement without precedent. Despite ever-increasing German security innovations, GC&CS broke into fifty new Enigma keys* in the year June 1943–June 1944, compared with twenty-seven in the previous twelve months. Nor could any of these breaches be considered unimportant. Each represented the sort of penetration of the enemy's command system that could not have been achieved even if "C" had a spy, or spies, in every major headquarters of the German armed forces.

Any one of those penetrations would, in isolation, have been a triumph of intelligence. Taken together, they constituted a breathtaking vision of the inner workings of the German war machine. Moreover, they displayed a picture of a nation more powerful, more fully mobilized, more fanatical in its determination and its support for its leadership, more inventive, and better organized for total war than any of its adversaries.

Yet of all the triumphs, none was more significant than the conquest of the second of the two principal German machine cipher systems, the Geheimschreiber. The existence of this machine was first reported to GC&CS by Broadway as early as 1932. It had been watched ever since, it had first been broken into in 1942, and by 1944 it had been established that the system had two main exchanges,

*So vast was the cipher manufacturing capacity of Enigma that it could, and did, provide a different key for every major service, agency, headquarters, ship, and in many cases aircraft operating in the German war machine. These keys were changed, usually daily, providing the same type of security that a Yale lock provided every house in a conurbation. As no two Yale locks were identical, so no two Enigma keys were the same. This, so the German Reich signalmaster believed, provided each user with a high degree of security against external as well as internal enemies.

one for the western front at Straussbourg near Berlin and one for the eastern front at Konigsberg in East Prussia. The exchanges' twenty-six links served as the German army supreme command's connection with the highest operational headquarters on the eastern, western, and southern fronts. Code-named Fish at Bletchley, the Geheim-schreiber system commonly contained intelligence of the decisions and orders of the German supreme command, the Oberkommando der Wehrmacht (OKW).

The Germans were not unaware that formidable skills were being employed by the Allies to penetrate Enigma and Geheimschreiber systems and regularly introduced innovations intended to prevent the Allies from breaking in. In December 1942 Menzies agreed that Fish might become unreadable unless more advanced, high-performance machinery capable of locating the keys was designed. The prototype of that machinery, code-named Heath Robinson, became available in May 1943, and, although primitive, it proved satisfactory enough to order twenty-four copies to be made. But still more advanced machinery became necessary as the Germans introduced more modifications on both Enigma and Geheimschreiber to improve their impenetrability.

Although the scientific concepts behind these battles of mathematical theory were far beyond the understanding of either Churchill or "C," both understood the need to advance the machinery of attack in order to maintain superiority over the Germans' machinery for defense. Churchill himself wrote of the unending struggle for scientific supremacy:

This was the secret war, whose battles were lost or won unknown to the public; and only with difficulty comprehended, even now, by those outside the small high scientific circles concerned. No such warfare had ever been waged by mortal men. The terms in which it could be recorded or talked about were unintelligible to ordinary folk. Yet if we had not mastered its profound meaning, and used its mysteries even while we saw them in the glimpse, all efforts, all the prowess of the fighting airmen, all the bravery and sacrifices of the people, would have been in vain.

Throughout, the struggle was dominated by the minds of Oxford and Cambridge; and of all the minds employed on that high scientific task none was more important, none more tragic, than that of Alan Mathison Turing. The grandson on his maternal side of the man who did more than any other Englishman to preserve the British Empire in India—he invented Stoney's Patent Silent Punkah-Wheel, a system that stirred and cooled the air and thereby made the subcontinent habitable to the British middle classes—Turing was one of the few authentic modern English geniuses.

Turing attended King's College, Cambridge, where he appeared to be too eccentric even for the Apostles. He possessed very strong homosexual impulses, although he was not exclusively homosexual in his behavior—I. J. Good, one of the men who conquered Geheimschreiber, found him late one night in hut three, the most secret installation at Bletchley, attempting to copulate with a lady who later became his fiancée. Turing's genius was that his fanciful notions contained sufficient utility to influence and shape theory. The essence of that genius was reflected in his assertion that a machine could be built that would understand a sonnet written by another machine. His "abstract universal computing machine" could duplicate the behavior and performance of other, far more advanced machines. In short, he was talking about the computer.

Menzies had known that Turing was a practicing and aggressive homosexual; this had emerged soon after his employment at Bletchley. But since he caused no offense to his colleagues at Bletchley, and since he was perhaps the only man in Menzies's service who might have been called "indispensable," his services were retained with a quiet and gentle warning from Commander Travis, the director at Bletchley.

However, Turing soon found his sexual impulses stronger than his wisdom. Early in 1944 a suspicion arose that he might have been the man responsible for molesting schoolboys at the main public library in Luton, a large industrial town not far from Bletchley. While no proceedings arose, it was decided that the need for good order and discipline required his removal—but not before he had done his finest work.*

*Turing's talents were too great to be lost to the secret service altogether. He was transferred to the supersecret SIS wireless laboratory at Hanslope Park, a large eighteenth-century mansion in a remote corner of north Buckinghamshire. This unit was under the command of "C's" radio expert, Brigadier Richard Gambier-Parry, who had been in the Royal Flying Corps and was known universally as "Pop." Here Turing worked on a speech encipherment project of his own design code-named Delilah, which was intended for communication between aircraft and secret agents on the ground. He also worked on a mathematical study, "taking up" John von Neumann's "Mathematical Foundations of Quantum Mechanics" and in general engaging in extremely advanced secret work the product of which was intended not for this war, but for the next one. While at work in the Delilah hut, according to Turing's biographer, Andrew Hodges, "Alan suddenly dropped into the conversation, with apparent casualness, the fact that he was homosexual. His young Midlands assistant was both amazed and profoundly upset. He had heard mention of homosexuality only through jokes at school (which he was not the sort

Although "C" regarded homosexuals with as much suspicion as he regarded Marxists, the time had not yet been reached when it became evident that there was often a close relationship between Soviet spies and "nancys," as "C" generally called homosexuals. To "C," as perhaps with Philby, Turing had utility in the secret world: "nancys" confided in "nancys." Furthermore, Turing's mathematical theories found their embodiment in Heath Robinson. But with further German modifications to enhance the impenetrability of their cipher machines, "C" felt the need for still more machines. One of these, Colossus, was again an expression of Turing's theories.

Persuaded by the experts at Bletchley of the need to retain Turing's services against the possibility that he might develop still more valuable concepts, and persuaded also of the need for Colossus, in February 1943 Menzies went to see Churchill about the program. It was given the highest manufacturing priority. Shortly Heath Robinson gave way to the Colossus I, which was introduced into service at Bletchley in February 1944. With 1,500 valves, far exceeding the number in any previous electronic device, the pioneer programmable electronic digital computer had been created.

By then new security devices introduced by the Germans required new Colossi. Colossus II came into service on the very eve of D-Day. It had 2,400 valves, giving it far more power than its predecessor. Both Colossi were described as "fairly specialised" general computers with circuit elements that included "binary adders, binary and decade counters, AND, OR, NAND (ie mod 2 add) and NOR logic gates, and short registers." The sequence of operations was "determined mainly by setting of external switches and by plugboards, but in Mark II some conditional branching could be determined by data generated and stored in the machine."

The internal memory "was of very limited capacity, the main data—the long cipher texts—being read photo-electrically from a loop of perforated tape. The tape drive was purely frictional; whereas on Heath Robinson the tape drive worked on the sprocket holes, on Colossus these were only read to control the timing." The basic speed

---

of person to find amusing) and through the vague allusions to 'grave charges' employed by the popular Sunday newspapers reporting court cases. It was not only what Alan told him that he found repellent, but the unapologetic attitude." Even so, Turing was not released from the service even at the end of the war, being retained by "C" for other, highly secret communications intelligence work. Turing died in odd circumstances after the war, by which time he had become a serious security risk.

of circuit operation was five thousand tape positions per second, but "with parallel processing the bit-processing rate could be five times this." [2]

The introduction of Colossi II was a development of the first importance to the success of Overlord, the defeat of the German armies, and for the future. It represented one of the great technological achievements of the twentieth century. In terms of the battle, it permitted the penetration of Jellyfish, the Geheimschreiber cipher used between German supreme headquarters and the headquarters of the German commander in chief in the west, Field Marshal Gerd von Rundstedt. Colossi II was built largely for Neptune, and the penetration of Jellyfish was therefore Bletchley's most important conquest of 1944, one that was to be "of the greatest value" to the Allied supreme command.

By the spring of 1944, consequently, no great power's war machine had been as thoroughly penetrated as Germany's. Moreover, this astonishing achievement occurred on the very eve of and during the invasion of Europe, an operation that was of itself the emotional and strategical climax of the war. Yet there were dangers of overconfidence and overdependence upon "the source." Above all, the danger always existed that Ultra would come to be regarded as a commonplace source and that its users would reveal its existence to the enemy through carelessness. Nor could German ingenuity be ignored.

To prevent that loss through carelessness, Menzies acted to make Eisenhower *personally* responsible for the safeguarding of Ultra intelligence throughout the campaign in northwest Europe. At the request of Field Marshal Sir John Dill, chief British representative on the Combined Chiefs of Staff in Washington, General Marshall, the chief U.S. representative, wrote to Eisenhower in suitable terms on March 15, 1944. This letter established Menzies's primacy in intelligence in the Atlantic theater of operations, for Marshall advised Eisenhower of the "supreme importance" the War Department attached to Ultra and directed Eisenhower to give the matter "your personal attention, and take all necessary steps to insure that the security regulations governing the dissemination of 'Ultra' intelligence are meticulously observed." [3]

Menzies emphasized the importance the British command attached to Ultra and its security in May 1944 with another of those ruthless actions that characterized "C's" control of "the source." In August 1943 there had been indications that the ciphers being used by Tito, the Communist partisan leader in Yugoslavia, were insecure.

When Tito's attention was drawn to the evidence that the Germans were reading his ciphers, the British offered to supply replacements that would be secure. Tito did not accept their offer and continued to use his compromised system for his communications within Yugoslavia and with the Allied supreme command in Italy. Tito's rejection of the British system was, in all likelihood, a reflection of his fear that if he accepted the British ciphers, the British cryptographers would be able to read his communications, a risk that, as a highly trained Comintern man, he did not wish to run.

The consequences were inevitable. By May 25, 1944, "C" possessed clear evidence from his decrypts of the wireless traffic of a major German headquarters operating against Tito's partisans that they were about to drop an SS parachute battalion on Tito's headquarters in the caves at Drvar. Their intention: to kill or capture Tito and thereby wreck the partisan movement.

"C" recognized that if the partisan movement collapsed, the nineteen German divisions operating in Yugoslavia would be released for service in France, Italy, or Russia. The question arose, therefore, whether Tito should be sent "a general warning" of the danger in which he stood. But the warning was overtaken by events. It was not sent, despite the presence of the prime minister's son, Randolph Churchill, as a liaison officer at Tito's headquarters. In short, "C" was not prepared to make any use of Ultra in circumstances where the Germans might deduce that either Enigma or Geheimschreiber had been penetrated. "C" personally warned Churchill on March 9 that Ultra should not be sent to Tito on the grounds that if the intelligence was captured, it would inevitably arouse German suspicions about Enigma.

It does seem, however, that both Churchill's son, Randolph, and Churchill's representative at Tito's headquarters, Fitzroy Maclean, did receive some form of warning of what was to occur, for both left Tito's headquarters shortly before the Germans began a raid in strength on the headquarters at 6:30 A.M. on May 22. First, German bombers attacked the area while German troop transports and gliders landed about one thousand paratroopers and glider-borne soldiers. Lieutenant Colonel Vivian Street, acting chief of the British mission, had also moved mission headquarters to a new location about a mile away because, as he explained in his after-action report, his suspicions were alerted by the "very careful" German aerial reconnaissance of the area that preceded the attack, reconnaissance that Street felt was the harbinger of a bombing attack.

When the attack started, Tito and his staff were in a cave over-looking Drvar; as Street reported, "It was clear that the Germans knew the exact location of this cave, for soon after the attack started a party attempted to reach it but were driven back." The Germans then covered the path leading to the cave with machine-gun fire, which made it impossible for anyone to enter or leave the hideaway by the normal route. Tito and his staff were trapped for some hours until, by late afternoon, they succeeded in tunneling their way out of the back of the cave and escaping. The Germans pursued Tito and his party for eleven days and at times came close to capturing him.

By June 2 Street concluded that Tito's capture was certain unless he was evacuated by air to the Allied special forces base at Bari in the heel of Italy. Street succeeded in getting a signal to Bari, and that night an aircraft, a Russian DC3, arrived as arranged on the airstrip at Kuprus Polje. After a day or two at Bari, Tito then elected to reestablish his headquarters on the Yugoslav island of Vis, which was in the hands of British commandos. There he arrived in the British destroyer *Blackmore* on June 9, safer and wiser.

2 THE SUICIDEX PLAN

For all the strictures placed upon Ultra distribution and discussion, it was evident to "C" that even the most highly trained men might leak the Ultra secret. The Germans themselves possessed a large signals intelligence base at Urville-Hague near Cherbourg directed at the immense wireless traffic being generated each hour of the day in England. Until it was destroyed by aerial attack just before D-Day, that base remained a threat not only to Ultra, but also to the security of Neptune plans. But if the destruction of Urville-Hague removed a principal source of danger to the security of Ultra, there remained other such bases and dangers. "C" could not guarantee that an Ultra shut-down might not be imminent. [4]

That Ultra had survived so long was already miraculous, and in preparing for the worst Menzies began to undertake Sussex, the main joint venture of the war between Broadway and Donovan's secret intelligence service. Originally proposed by "C" to Colonel David Bruce, chief of OSS London, the British and American secret intelligence services, in collaboration with the Gaullist intelligence agency, began to plan for the provision of military intelligence to the Allied armies upon their invasion of France through a group of about ninety pairs of agents. Each pair consisted of an observer and a radio operator, trained in England at a joint SIS/OSS school, to be landed in France by parachute. The code names for the two main operations were Brissex, for the forty-five SIS teams to be dropped on the British sector of the invasion front, and Ossex, for the similar number of OSS-controlled agents to penetrate the American sector.

"C" expected that Sussex would absorb the interest and energies of Donovan's young lions in London and, while enabling him to assure Churchill that he was collaborating with Donovan, also provide Eisenhower and Montgomery with battlefield intelligence from the far shore, the assault area in Normandy. Donovan was, however, far less ready for operations than he thought he was, and his staff for Sussex did not arrive in London until September. The group was led by Lieutenant Colonel Francis P. Miller, a Rhodes scholar, a high official of the Council on Foreign Relations, one of the organizers of the destroyers-for-bases campaign in 1940, and a well-known Democrat. They took over a house in Grosvenor Square to plan and carry out the Ossex operations.

Although Miller had had no previous experience of clandestine warfare, he came imbued with Donovan's desire for "an equal, independent, and coordinate secret service" in London. Miller soon became as dissatisfied as Bruce over the status of OSS London. As Bruce observed, the inclination "on the part of some SIS representatives to treat SI [OSS] as a less than equal partner in intelligence operations naturally tended to slow to some extent the development of the Sussex plan." As late as September 1, Colonel Maddox reported to Washington that "in its slow and measured pace, Broadway has shown some indication of working with this Branch on Sussex, although it is evident that they regard us as a distinctly junior partner." Nor was this criticism of Plan Sussex confined to the Americans. It was shared by the French, who denounced "C's" strategy as the "the suicidex plan."

Unaware of the underlying reasons for "C's" recommendations regarding Sussex, Miller soon fell under the influence of Lieutenant Colonel George Renault-Roulier, de Gaulle's controller for Sussex. "C" believed that the less people in France knew of Sussex, the better it would be for Sussex agents. The German security services were very powerful in the area of Sussex operations, the area behind the

Neptune assault area, and it was well known at Broadway that to some degree or another the Germans had penetrated or even controlled British networks in the Pas de Calais and Normandy. For that reason, "C" proposed that agents be parachuted "blind" into their operating areas.

"C's" view was rejected, however, by Roulier, on the grounds that he doubted whether any agent could survive more than half a day in the invasion area unless he had contacts on the ground who could hide, advise, and feed him. Miller therefore wrote to "C," drawing his attention to the French description of the plan in terms that supported Roulier's apprehensions:

For some time I have had a doubt in my mind as to the wisdom of our plan to drop the Sussex agents blind. Perhaps the phrase dropping blind is not intended to exclude the agents from having the name of at least one reliable person in the locality whom they could eventually contact if necessary. My own opinion is that the amount of intelligence secured will in many instances be relatively negligible unless the officer in charge of each unit is given at least one contact in the locality where he is dropped. Without such a contact I should think the hazard of the undertaking would be considerably increased.

"C" replied four days later that he had been "considering the same matter" and had, in fact, "been instructing some of Broadway's existing organizations in northern France to prepare suitable hiding places so that agents would not be dropped completely blind." "C" also advised that the plan was to select some one hundred "nodal" points on the Germans' main lines of communication "so that we can select suitable hiding places as near as possible to these points." He anticipated that immediately prior to operations practically all road travel for civilians in France would be prohibited, and consequently "agents must have a good contact center quite close to the point where they will have to operate."

At length, Roulier's suggestion was adopted: to use "Pathfinders," agents who knew no one within the existing intelligence networks in northern France but were either from, or knew, the region. They would be dropped into France before the main body to locate safe houses and obtain food coupons. By the end of 1943 about three-quarters of OSS London's staff was devoting the better part of its time to preparations for Sussex. Supreme headquarters listed for both OSS and SIS the key points in northern France on which it required coverage. These included communications and railway centers, main motor transport and tank parks, enemy headquarters, airfields and repair centers, and bridges and fords over the rivers Seine and Loire. These targets were assigned equally to the Brissex and Ossex organizers, and Donovan obtained the funds, manpower, and authority to build a large, new OSS wireless station, Victor, on the grounds of Ladye Place, a small country house near the village of Hurley in Berkshire.

All agents were French. No Franco-Americans were recruited on the grounds that they would have become too Americanized to be able to submerge into the pastoral French scene where, mainly, they were to operate. A special school was opened for their training, which lasted from twelve to seventeen weeks, and each pair of agents were examined at the end of the course for their physical and mental fitness, for the degree of compatability between the men of each team, and for the impression they conveyed of their devotion to duty. Their cover stories and papers were prepared by the fake-papers section of Broadway.

But if through Sussex "C" had hoped to deflect Donovan's complaint that Menzies's iron control of Neptune intelligence ran counter to U.S. sovereign interests, he failed. Relations between the two planning organizations continued to be marked by irritability. Menzies resolutely forbade OSS SI to undertake any operations other than Sussex, and as Miller reported to Donovan on his relations with Broadway on February 4, 1944:

Our work is carried on under the friendly sufferance of Broadway, which means that we are liable at any time to have our status called in question and also liable in some instances to be kept in a position of subservience from which it is not within our power to escape. [5]

Also, in February 1944, Commander Kenneth Cohen, of Broadway, chairman of the Main Committee (which controlled all Sussex operations), made several final attempts to bring Donovan's secret intelligence service in London under "C's" control. At a meeting with Miller at Broadway, Cohen stated that "C" had begun to wonder whether Sussex should not be under one "central and unified control." Cohen thought that the commander of the assault forces, General Sir Bernard Montgomery, "would not be happy if he learned that he was receiving his intelligence from two separately controlled groups of agents in France." The practical implications were that "all intelligence from all Sussex agents would be transmitted through British communications, and," Miller warned Donovan, "the American SI

[OSS] would have little to do except to receive the intelligence which was handed to it."

Miller's rejoinder to these proposals had been that the new scheme would render Victor, the special wireless station built to handle Ossex traffic, an expensive white elephant, and that "it would involve placing the offices of our joint operations section" in OSS headquarters, because "C" had "observed in my presence that he would not allow American officers to work regularly in his building." Also, "the logic of the reference to General Montgomery's views, if pressed to its conclusion, would mean that General Eisenhower's views would also have to be ascertained." In the end, Miller advised Donovan, he succeeded in defeating "C's" proposal. [6]

With that defeat, "C's" attempts to gain absolute control over Donovan's secret intelligence service in the European theater changed direction. By now, "C" possessed what he believed was the world's finest clandestine communications system and laboratories in Section VIII. Located at Whaddon Manor not far from Bletchley, and headed by a fellow Etonian and friend, Richard Gambier-Parry, Section VIII handled all Churchill's correspondence, the transmissions of all British diplomatic and secret agents throughout the world, and also all Ultra communications at home and overseas. With a large scientific staff engaged on a range of very advanced clandestine communications devices, "C" decided to consolidate his takeover of Donovan's service in an area in which he knew his service was superior to OSS.

Again, at a February 1941 meeting of the Main Committee, Cohen announced that Broadway had developed a device called Ascension for telephone conversations between an agent on the ground and an aircraft flying overhead. Cohen announced that Broadway wished to use this device for collecting the Sussex agents' intelligence, that twenty copies of the system had been made, and that SIS proposed to fly two or three Mosquito light bombers over the Sussex agents each night to pick up the agents' reports on a recording device installed in the tail of each aircraft. Since Ascension would cut back on agents' wireless transmissions, and since Ascension was itself relatively immune to rapid goniometry—counterespionage radio-detection vans that the Germans had in large numbers—casualties would be reduced.

Having ensured that the introduction of this equipment was handled in such a manner that only the British had the planes and the equipment, as Miller wrote to Donovan, "It is extremely late for us to try and catch up with them in the sense of matching their equipment," and therefore OSS would lose control of communications with Ossex agents. The only answer if OSS was to regain control was helicopters.

In a letter to Donovan, Bruce pressed for an allocation of the new Sikorsky YR-5 helicopters, which were then in preproduction manufacture at New Haven, Connecticut. These had a range of 450 miles, and the first operational machines were expected by March 1944, thus opening up a vast new horizon in the difficult and dangerous work of inserting secret agents into hostile territory. But, sadly, the YR-5 proved "extremely unstable" in flight, flight itself was difficult, it could only be operated in clear weather, and the rotors were "highly vulnerable to small arms fire."

With the U.S. decision not to allocate helicopters to OSS, and with the control of all intelligence, sabotage and subversion, and political operations passing to supreme headquarters, except those of SIS, which remained under Foreign Office control as a sovereign instrument of state, Donovan's last prospect for gaining independence for OSS London before D-Day had vanished. This he neither forgot nor forgave, for as he remarked to his executive officer, Otto C. Doering, the passage of control of OSS London and Algiers from sovereign American control to that of the Allied supreme commands marked OSS as a wartime emergency organization that could be liquidated when the emergency was over, and that made it the more difficult to persuade Congress of the need to establish a central intelligence agency—the term was already in use by D-Day—to guard the peace.

Meanwhile, on February 8 a British aircraft dropped the first Pathfinder mission blind onto the meadows near Châteauroux. Familiar with the area, the Pathfinders possessed personal contacts to locate pinpoints for the main Sussex *parachutage*,* temporary and permanent safehouses, shelters for the wireless operators, and informants. The Pathfinders were under instructions to avoid all existing SOE and SIS networks, and they appear to have been given no information about either French or British secret agents in the area into which they were dropped.

The Sussex operation did not begin well. Most of the Pathfinders' supplies were parachuted wide of their pinpoint. When the Pathfinders tried to find their personal contacts, they discovered that most

*The French technical term for the insertion of secret agents by parachute into enemy territory.

had been moved, deported, or arrested. This led to slow progress, too slow for the chief Pathfinder, and he ignored his instructions and made contact with the local *maquis*. This did not prove fatal, and they succeeded in establishing shelter and informants over most of northern France from the Loire River to the Belgian frontier. By D-Day there were twelve Brissex and ten Ossex teams in France. The rest followed by degrees after the start of operations.

But then disaster struck the OSS operation in circumstances that could not wholly be written off against the hazards of the trade. As agent Raymonde, a woman and the leader of the OSS Pathfinder team, was to report, her teammate, agent Clauzel, had been caught by the German geheimefeldpolizei and, in Bruce's diary account, "tortured in the most horrible manner before he died." [7] Clauzel's death, however, unnerved three other Ossex teams operating in the general area, teams Filan, Calere, and Salaud. Deciding that they were overexposed in a rural area, the six members of the three teams, who included one woman, agent Chammonet, decided to make for Paris and continue their work there. They stole a German army truck and some uniforms of the Organization Todt, the German field construction battalions in France.

Having donned the uniforms, they began the drive to Paris. Just outside Vendôme, a small town on the Loire on the Tours-Paris road, they were stopped by geheimefeldpolizei, who began to search the truck. Almost immediately the German sergeant in charge found the teams' radios, and the party was arrested. As they were being taken to the German headquarters for interrogation, one of the agents, Laurent of team Filan, jumped out of the car and, although fired at, managed to escape. The rest, Ferriere, Girard, Dutal, Maurin, and Mlle. Chammonet, were interrogated and then executed. But they were not executed in the accepted fashion, by a firing squad and blindfolded. As Bruce was to recount, they were all, including the woman, "shot through the groin."

3 THE DEFEAT OF SOE

From the moment he took office, the most basic of all Churchill's concepts about how Germany would be defeated was that there should be created throughout German-occupied Europe "an army of the shadows." This shadow army would leap to arms at the moment of "the Return to Europe" and "set Europe ablaze," thus "confusing and confounding" the Germans as they sought to defend the immense empire Hitler had created. It was for this purpose that he formed the Special Operations Executive (SOE) in 1940. "C" had never taken kindly either to Churchill's action or to the new secret service, which Menzies came to regard, as he stated repeatedly, as "amateur, dangerous, and bogus." Yet SOE had survived and expanded into a large undertaking of perhaps six thousand men and women that, by the winter of 1943–44, could claim to have carried out many brave, important, and notable operations.

But during the summer of 1943, "C's" intelligence sources began to show that, in his view, the Special Operations Executive did not possess the degree of control necessary if the resistance movements were to succeed in setting Europe ablaze at the moment of the great invasion. To "C" the French resistance movement resembled gangs, guerrilla groups, or private armies each operating at the whim of the chief and beyond the control of General Gubbins. Hitler had created the most redoubtable apparatus of surveillance and repression Europe had ever known. That apparatus had penetrated the government of every state and impregnated the life of every European. Each and every attempt to establish national underground forces had been smashed; and if the "armies of the shadows" reappeared and became ever larger and better organized, as they did by the winter of 1943–44, then the forces of repression and penetration became ever more ruthless.

The first evidence that SOE's networks might have been seriously compromised to the point where they might be a danger to the security of Overlord reached "C" in the week of July 1943, almost certainly through the agency of Henri Dericourt, the air movements officer in the Paris region who figured in the Prosper disaster in the late summer of 1943.

During the night of July 20–21, 1943, Dericourt handled a Lysander landing near Tours. Since there was space in the aircraft, Dericourt seized the opportunity "for a flying visit to London" and was met at RAF Station Tangmere by a friend, Andre Simon, the French wine expert who, like Dericourt, appears to have inhabited a place in the no-man's-land between SIS and SOE in London. Simon took Dericourt the sixty miles to London and put him up at his own flat near Cavendish Square. There Dericourt made a report on the security and capabilities of the French resistance networks in the Paris area in the wake of the Prosper disaster.

Whether that report was for "C" is far from clear, but five days after Dericourt's arrival in London, "C" submitted a report to the British chiefs of staff and the Joint Intelligence Committee. The report, CX108, was entitled "SOE Activities in France." The substance could have come only from someone such as Dericourt, who was intimately connected with French resistance operations *in France*. [8]

The content of CX108 was contained in the JIC findings. For some time past "reports have been reaching 'C' indicating that the resistance groups in France" were "to a considerable extent compromised and that the enemy must be in possession of much detail regarding those resistance groups." The report continued, " 'C' had passed on all reports of this nature to S.O.E. as soon as received," and that SOE had informed the committee that these reports were "substantially true." "C" added that "at the present moment resistance groups are at their lowest ebb and cannot be counted on as a serious factor unless and until they are re-built on a smaller and sounder basis." That observation was rejected by General Gubbins, chief of SOE, as "misleading."

The report also stated that CX108's contention that some "45% to 50% of air operations for S.O.E. are abortive for one reason or another, of which some 30% to 35% are now due to failure due to reception arrangements." Of the effective operations, "some 20% eventually fail through activities of the enemy." As the JIC went on to note in what was a reprimand of SOE, all this had come to the attention of the committee through "C," not from SOE, which had failed to inform the committee of the grave state of its organization in France. The committee concluded, therefore, that the chiefs of staff "may well consider the desirability of recommending some re-organisation to bring [the SIS and the SOE] more closely together."

The Joint Intelligence Committee recommended accordingly that SIS retain the priority it had over SOE in France. The underlying purpose of the figures cited was that SOE had failed in so serious a fashion that SOE was not worth the air effort being expended upon it. If the French resistance was to have any value at all, then the present SOE command structure in London must be liquidated and SOE placed under the control either of the chiefs of staff or of "C." [9]

These assertions provoked the gravest dispute thus far between

"C" and Gubbins. "C's" allegations were investigated by the War Cabinet Defence Committee, with Churchill attending as chairman and Lord Selborne, the minister responsible for SOE, present. Despite the Prosper evidence, he claimed that the resistance movements against Hitler had been "booming" (which could hardly have been true, at least in the Paris area) during the last eight months, and that he was "convinced" of the "increasing value" of the contribution SOE would make. Selborne continued by declaring that when the time came for the invasion of Western Europe, the resistance movements "should be" capable of "vitally important work in the destruction of enemy communications." Churchill agreed and "emphasised the immense value to the war effort of stimulating resistance among the people of Europe." He recognized that "acts of rebellion against the Germans frequently resulted in bloody reprisals," but the "blood of the martyrs was the seed of the church," and the result of these incidents had been to make the Germans hated as no other race had ever been hated. [10]

Support for "C" came from Sir Charles Portal, commander in chief of the RAF, who was impressed by CX108. He opposed granting SOE the 117 aircraft it requested to enable it to expand its operations. He proposed instead that fifty-eight heavy bombers be set aside for SOE operations, and that proposal was accepted. Portal was equally impressed by "C's" argument that any increase in the allotment of aircraft to SOE would mean a decrease in the number of aircraft allotted to SIS for espionage purposes, which might prove fatal to the major operation that he now had in hand, establishing the whereabouts of the missile sites that were now known to be aimed and armed for operations against London.

The quarrel had become a fight between Menzies and Gubbins, with yet more charges by each that the other was betraying his agents to the Germans. Shortly after Churchill left England for the Teheran conference in November, the North Pole affair burst upon the secret circle. Its effect upon "C" and, indeed, the entire attempt to set Europe ablaze coincidentally with Neptune, proved staggering.

As part of the preparations for what was called at the time "the Return to Europe," both SIS and SOE, sometimes jointly and sometimes separately, began in 1940 and 1941 to insert secret agents into Holland. The agents involved were well trained and dedicated, and all of them were imbued with that special sense recalled, poignantly, by one of them, Hubert Lauwers. One of the few agents to survive the North Pole disaster, Lauwers described the relationship between the secret agents and the faceless services (in a few cases some of the agents did not know which service they were working for) on whose business they were prepared to run such hideous risks:

All of them had one thing in common—a deep love of their country and, in their duties, a blind trust in their superiors. The long-standing reputation of the British Secret Service throughout the world and the training which the agents received brought their trust in their service to the heights of an almost mystical belief. Without this confidence not one of them could have been brought to undertake the dangerous tasks which lay before them. [11]

Of his own training as a secret service officer, Lauwers felt that added to a sense *mystique* was an "unshakable confidence—a boundless faith in the Service to which we belonged." Indeed, they had been selected for an important undertaking, to be the vanguard of Overlord. But now that mystique and confidence would be put to the most savage of tests. By March 20, 1942, sixteen secret agents had been parachuted into Holland from England or landed on the beaches of the Dutch coast by motor torpedo or fishing boats. Of these sixteen, eight had been selected by the Dutch government-in-exile working with Broadway to transmit intelligence and to smuggle to England various people selected by Queen Wilhelmina and the Dutch prime minister, P. S. Gerbrandy. The other eight agents had been sent by SOE to establish sabotage groups. One of SOE's missions, however, had a purely political mission, to contact the Socialist leader Koos Vorrink.

Of these sixteen agents, three from SIS and two from SOE were captured. The Abwehr tried to use the captured agents for the purposes of what was called Englandspiel, wireless games with the London headquarters of the captured agents, the object of which was to set traps for further agents being sent in and widen the Englandspiel until all Allied secret agents in Holland were under German control. The German code name for that operation was North Pole. Through it, the German controllers fervently hoped that they would be able to obtain intelligence concerning Allied invasion plans. With this intelligence in their possession, the German armed forces could repel all attempts to invade Europe until Allied casualties and disasters became so numerous that the Allies would accept Germany's terms for a political settlement to the war.

The first attempt failed. But the second—the manipulation of Hubert Lauwers, the wireless operator who testified so eloquently about the pride he felt in having been selected for work by the British secret service—succeeded. Although Lauwers managed to insert the prearranged mistakes in the text of the signals he sent to London under German control, those mistakes and code words were not detected when the signals were received. As a result, and despite Lauwers's repeated attempts to warn London, the Germans over a period of fourteen months were able to arrest a total of fifty-five secret agents. Using their radios, the German controllers of North Pole succeeded in making contact with SOE London over seventeen different links.

Most of the captured agents were executed at Mauthausen or Gross Rosen concentration camps in Silesia. As evidence later obtained indicated, a number of important SOE networks in France were penetrated as a result of this "infection," some 150 Dutch coworkers lost their lives, and fifty crew members of the twelve RAF aircraft intercepted and shot down by the Luftwaffe as a result of information obtained by the Englandspielen also lost their lives.

Although from the spring of 1943 onward suspicions had developed in London about the Dutch networks, they were not confirmed until two of the captured Dutch agents escaped from German detention at Haaren to Berne, Switzerland. These men were Dourlein and Ubbink, and at Berne in November 1943 they warned a Dutch official that, as the official reported to London:

The Germans have been maintaining code links with England for a long time, acting as if they themselves were the dropped agents.

At that point "C" was warned, presumably by his war station at Berne. He directed that Dourlein and Ubbink be brought out over his escape chain to Gibraltar. Thence they continued to London for interrogation, where, as a result of what they told "C's" men, the vice-chiefs of staff (who were acting in the absence of their chiefs at the Teheran conference) were informed.

Coming as soon as it did after the Prosper affair and CX108, this information caused consternation in the secret circle, for, with other evidence, it began to seem that the entire SOE system in Europe was at least penetrated by and perhaps under the control of the enemy. An investigation began immediately, undertaken by "C" and his colleagues on the Joint Intelligence Committee, and their inquiries lasted throughout the Christmas and New Year holidays. At the same time, "C" himself had to ensure that SIS's networks had not been penetrated through the infection that had pervaded Holland. Since it was feared that the SOE networks laid in preparation for Overlord were compromised, all "C's" services were now given a second task, to establish the degree to which SOE in Europe *as a whole* had been penetrated.

Such, then, was the complex of events confronting "C" when, on January 3, 1944, the chairman of the Joint Intelligence Committee, Cavendish-Bentinck, presented his report on SOE security and management to the office of the minister of defence. This was done with some apprehension on the part of Cavendish-Bentinck, who was to declare later that "there was no doubt that SOE had been too happy-go-lucky. SOE would gladly have murdered me. I arranged with Victor Rothschild [a scientist employed by one of the secret services] that if I suddenly died he was to carry out an autopsy." [12]

Although the Joint Intelligence Committee's papers relating to the inquiry were closed by the government until 1994, the case of Lord Selborne, who had ministerial responsibility for the Special Operations Executive, was released, and his documents show the JIC paper contended that the SOE's secret *apparats* in Denmark, Norway, Belgium, Poland, France, and Holland all had to be considered penetrated for one reason or another, either through enemy action or through the domestic policies of the countries concerned. In Norway the JIC expressed concern that the Norwegian government's secret army might compromise SOE's operations to the Germans because it was the policy of the secret army to do nothing that would provoke the Germans into counteraction, and to lie low and be ready to restore the established order at the moment of liberation. The JIC drew attention to the "highly dangerous" independent status of the Polish government, particularly concerning the large credits given that government by both the British and American governments. These credits were being used "in a manner which if the Russians knew would have a disastrous effect on Anglo-Russian relations." [13]

As for France, in light of intelligence that became available later, it was evident that the Joint Intelligence Committee had underestimated the degree of German penetration of SOE and Gaullist networks, drawing attention only to the dangers inherent in de Gaulle's policy of unifying and centralizing its organizations in the French underground, a policy intended to facilitate de Gaulle's seizure of power when France was liberated. Otherwise, JIC felt, "those organizations in France directly controlled by SOE seem at present to be reasonably secure."

The JIC was severely critical of SOE's handling of the situation and especially its decision after it had become known in London that SOE's networks in Holland were probably compromised: two supply aircraft were sent on missions to Holland to "test" the extent of the penetration, and both were shot down by the Luftwaffe.

Replying in two papers to the JIC's findings, Lord Selborne asserted that, with the exception of Holland, "the SOE continental organization has not been penetrated, and that to the contrary SOE had been remarkably successful in its operations." [14] Up until the end of 1943, 1,467 agents had been sent in to fifteen countries and 322 were known to have been captured or killed. A total of 3,106 operations had been undertaken of which 1,920 were known to have been successful, a success rate of 61.8 percent. Forty-four aircraft had been lost. In the Lysander agent operations, there had been sixty-seven sorties, fifty-three of which had been successful, thirteen of which were unsuccessful, with one aircraft missing. And as Selborne opined:

When we consider the excessively dangerous nature of the work for these aircraft flying low and unescorted over enemy country on moonlit nights to predetermined spots known to numbers of the local inhabitants, I submit the percentage [of loss] is extraordinarily low.

During 1943 alone, SOE had despatched to enemy-occupied countries 1,075 agents and 6,545 tons of weapons and explosives. As the prime minister had said, "This is a very dangerous war." Selborne himself declared: "SOE work is among the most dangerous in the whole war, and these brave volunteers knew that they were taking their lives in their hands on each journey." He felt the JIC report revealed "certain grave misapprehensions on matters of fact." These misapprehensions had resulted in an impression in the paper that "the work of SOE has been neither very sound nor very effective." Selborne therefore rejected the report on the grounds that

the danger of penetration is inherent in the work of a secret organisation, as I think SIS will confirm; it is the enemy's counter-attack, and on the whole I consider SOE has successfully met it.

As for the proposals that the Special Operations Executive should be restored to "C's" control, Selborne felt that the functions of SIS and SOE were "quite distinct and, as SOE work inevitably comes more into the limelight (e.g. Greece and Yugoslavia), the desirability of keeping the organisations separate increases." He felt that—and here Selborne was wrong—that relations between SIS and SOE "has been greatly improved during the last eighteen months," was "now on the whole satisfactory," and it would, Selborne felt, continue to improve. As for SOE, its work and scope has enormously increased during the last eighteen months. It is now playing an important part in every theatre of war, is conducting unacknowledgeable operations of infinite variety, and the importance must increase as the war moves to its climax.

With all the papers on his desk, Anthony Eden, the foreign secretary, found himself unable to resolve the problems without prime ministerial authority and sent Churchill at Marrakesh a "personal & most secret" minute in which he declared that he found the JIC paper "most disquieting" and believed that there was "need for the matter to be fully gone into" by a ministerial inquiry. But, Eden added, he did not think "we can do this effectively in your absence." [15]

That is what happened: the entire affair was allowed to mark time until Churchill returned to London on January 18, 1944, having recovered from his pneumonia. In what was his first business, the prime minister sent for "C," having heard that "C" had threatened to resign when he learned that, despite the JIC paper, SOE was being given priority over SIS operations in order to restore its position in Holland and expand its operations in France. Presumably, Churchill persuaded "C" to abandon thoughts of resignation, for "C" did not resign—at least for the moment. Otherwise, little came of this discussion except that Menzies accepted yet another offer by Cadogan to attempt to arbitrate.

But then Gubbins presented "Ratweek," a big scheme for the assassination of Sicherheitsdienst officers in France, a scheme that "C" deplored on the grounds that such operations would provoke large-scale reprisals throughout France and as a result, inevitably, affect his intelligence operations. Churchill continued to back SOE on the grounds of his personal conviction that SOE still had too much to contribute to Neptune, despite the penetration of its networks. RAF missions on SOE business rose from 107 in the last quarter of 1943, through 759 in the first to 1,969 in the second quarter of 1944. Although there was a long-standing agreement between Churchill and "C" that SIS would have priority of claim on the services of such aircraft as were available, "C" feared that his priority had been superseded through SOE salesmanship. In this he may not have been wrong, for most of the 220 arms containers parachuted into the Haute Savoie in February fell into German, not French, hands.

Churchill had become conscious that "C" was disturbed by the degree of prime ministerial support being given to SOE despite Carendish-Bentinck's adverse report. He wrote to his chief of staff, Ismay:

"You should show 'C' exactly what has been decided about helping the Maquis in France." Churchill instructed Ismay also that the refreshed SOE airlift would involve just Stirlings, which "C" used only occasionally, not the Lysanders used for his agents and courier. "Someone," declared Churchill, "has been stirring him up and making mischief."

Churchill thought that "someone" was Bomber Command, which was always reluctant to provide airlift to SOE. Also, Churchill maintained, the documents that "C" had shown to Churchill that day "if anything convinced me of the wisdom of supporting the *maquisards.*" The airlift involved was "a tiny fraction of our Air," and it was worthwhile because the actions contemplated had "high political importance." The only comment Churchill made about the question of resolving the SIS-SOE dispute through an amalgamation under the chiefs of staff was an acknowledgment that "there is also the warfare between S.O.E. and S.I.S. which is a lamentable, but perhaps inevitable, feature of our affairs." [16]

In fine, the airlift to the *maquis* continued, although the troubles did produce a decision regarding the future of SOE. As each country was liberated, the SOE section concerned was to be liquidated and the management of clandestine affairs within that country transferred to "C." Gubbins's days were numbered.

4 THE VERMEHREN AFFAIR

On occasions in the secret world there occurs a single incident, involving people of little account in the great affairs of state, which nonetheless has large consequences. Such a case was the Vermehren incident of February 1944 at Istanbul. [17]

Erich Vermehren was a member of an old Lubeck family that had had strong trading ties with England; twice he had been awarded a Rhodes scholarship to Oxford, and on each occasion he had been prevented from accepting it by the Nazi authorities. He was related to Dr. Franz von Papen, the former German chancellor and now, in 1944, the German ambassador at Turkey. Vermehren's wife, the former Elizabeth Countess von Plettenberg, was an ardent Catholic from Westphalia. Both were anti-Nazi activists, and both had been recruited into the Abwehr by Canaris's deputy, General Oster, and sent to Turkey to report on the British political position in the Near East.

Both Vermehren and his wife were known to Section V, for early in 1943 they made an unsuccessful attempt to defect to the British at Lisbon. In November 1943 they offered to defect again but were instead recruited into the XX-Committee as double agents. Early in 1944, the representative of Section V at Istanbul, Nicholas Elliott, son of a former headmaster and provost of Eton, received yet another defection overture from Erich Vermehren. At the same time, other German secret agents at Istanbul intimated their willingness to defect to OSS at Istanbul.

By now "C's" decrypts of Abwehr and Sicherheitsdienst wireless traffic had begun to reflect the severe tensions that had existed between the Party and the General Staff over the control of secret intelligence in Germany. Popov's inquiry (commissioned by "C" at Christmas 1940), the XX-Committee's double agents, an agent of "C" who had succeeded in obtaining employment as an officer on the Abwehr staff in Berlin—all reported that Canaris's reputation had not recovered from his failure to predict the times and places of the invasions of North Africa, Sicily, and Italy. Seen against the menaces of the looming invasion—in Directive 51 to the armed forces Hitler himself claimed the mortal blow to Germany would come not from the east but the west—Canaris's defeatism, sabotage, and ineptitude could be tolerated no further. If the Atlantic wall was to prevent such defeat, then the armed forces must have foreknowledge of the enemy's capabilities and intentions.

The time had come, therefore, for "C" to throw a spanner in the German works. That he did in February 1944. In rapid succession the Abwehr suffered exposure in the Argentine and, induced by irresistible Anglo-American diplomatic pressure, expulsions of high personnel in Spain. Then came the Turkish desertions. Four German agents went over to the OSS chief at Istanbul, Lanning Macfarland, the Vermehrens to Elliott. The consequences in Berlin were almost seismic.

For years Reichsführer SS Heinrich Himmler had complained to Hitler "of the defeatism and lack of Nazi sympathies of so many Abwehr officers." Hitler's reaction to the run of misfortune in the Abwehr was to summon Canaris to his office. When Canaris pointed out that the defections were no more than an indication of what was a fact—that Germany was losing the war—Hitler flew at Canaris, knocking over the table that separated them. He dismissed Canaris as chief of the Abwehr and placed him under a form of arrest in a castle in Franconia. At the same time a flurry of angry signals flew between Himmler and Ribbentrop and the German ambassador in Turkey, Franz von Papen.

To intensify the Abwehr's embarrassment and the Führer's anger, a press "leakage" reached the Associated Press in Istanbul, which sent out this bulletin on all wires:

Istanbul, Feb. 9 (A.P.)—A German who deserted the Nazis and gave himself up to the British several days ago was officially identified by Allied spokesman today as Erich Vermehren, clerk to the military attaché in the German embassy here and son of Petra Vermehren, German authoress.

Vermehren's wife, the former Countess Elisabeth Vermehren, accompanied him. His mother is now in Lisbon.

The 24-year-old attaché and his wife declared that they have deserted the Germans because they were disgusted with Nazi brutality. He is said to possess detailed information of greatest value. At the German embassy he served directly under Dr. Paul Leverkuehn, assistant military attaché in Turkey.

Vermehren said that he and his wife reached Allied controlled territory despite every effort by Germans in Turkey to apprehend him. Ambassador Franz von Papen interrupted a vacation in the Bursa mountains to go to Istanbul to direct an investigation into his disappearance.

Allied propaganda used the Vermehren defection to suggest a German Reich administration crumbling under the overpowering aerial bombardment. Only four months before the invasion, Hitler signed a written order that the Abwehr, the intelligence service of the German General Staff, and the Sicherheitsdienst, the Nazi party's intelligence service, be amalgamated into a single service under Party control. The consequences of that order were, for Germany, calamitous. Over the next six months, the German intelligence community underwent a complex and fundamental upheaval at a time when the secret services should have been giving their entire attention to the task for which they had been created: watching out for the invasion and guarding the Third Reich against the internal and external enemies of national socialism.

A series of high-level administrative conferences began on February 20 and lasted until September 1, 1944, in other words for the duration of the invasion period, the most critical period of World War II. The object was to break up the Abwehr and divide its parts between Brigadeführer SS Schellenberg and his foreign espionage service and Heinrich Mueller, chief of the Gestapo, a process that succeeded only in splitting the German intelligence community into two antagonistic parts. These conferences were accompanied by the large-scale reshuffling of personnel, files, furniture, offices, telephones, communications, procedures, and the installation of new filing equipment. For example, all Abwehr and Sicherheitsdienst files were consolidated into a single system using the new American Hollerith machine filing system, which was complex and broke down frequently, often requiring the services of the Waffen SS for emergency repairs.

The most intensive part of the reorganization took place in May 1944, when the German services would otherwise have been entirely preoccupied with operations to divine the intention of the Allies. In the end little was achieved. The German intelligence community had exactly the same personnel doing exactly the same work but under different leadership. By the beginning of June, only a few days before the invasion, the authorities established a new military intelligence service, one called Amt Mil, and an entirely new combined Party–General Staff headquarters. In establishing this new service, Schellenberg drew his inspiration partly from the organization and discipline of the Society of Jesus, but more from the social composition and objectives of the British secret service. Professor Trevor-Roper, who later wrote a study of Schellenberg, recorded of that inspiration:

Like many Germans, he was an admirer, a despairing admirer, of the British Intelligence Service,—an organisation of which indeed he knew very little, but of which he had evidently read much in those amazing novelettes which filled the reference library of the Gestapo. From these he had learnt much about that all pervasive, incessant engine which, founded by Edward III and perfected by Oliver Cromwell, has secured the otherwise unaccountable success of British diplomacy and politics, and which, operating through the Y.M.C.A., the Boy Scout Movement, and other dependent organisations, has overthrown dynasties, altered governments, and assassinated inconvenient ministers throughout the world. To create such a universal, "totalitarian" intelligence service was the ambitious dream of Schellenberg.

Instead, Schellenberg succeeded only in creating inefficient muddle at a crucial time in the destiny of the nation that employed him. The new spymaster of the German Reich was the psychotic product of a psychotic regime. To intensify the disturbed state of his mind, three murderous rivals challenged him constantly: Ernst Kaltenbrunner, chief of the Sicherheitsdienst; the chief of the Gestapo,

Heinrich Mueller; and Standartenführer SS Otto Skorzeny, who had come to prominence through his success in snatching Mussolini from his mountaintop prison in the Gran Sasso in Italy in September 1943. Skorzeny was in charge of SS special operations.

Only thirty-four, the son of a Saarlander who made pianos for a living, a lawyer by trade, Schellenberg was soft, gentle, persuasive, effeminate, seductive. Indeed, it may be said that the chief instrument in Schellenberg's capture of almost supreme power was seduction of just about everyone he met who mattered from the time he was a student at Bonn university. With his arrival at the side of Reichsführer SS Himmler, it was not long before Schellenberg made a startling discovery about the man who in Germany was politically the second most powerful man after Hitler, and who held the actual reins of power. Himmler suffered from cancer of the rectum, although Schellenberg never revealed his evidence. But as his Broadway interrogator was to observe later: "A remarkable feature of his career is the strange friendship Himmler 'the school-master' adduced for him in 1939, at a time when Schellenberg was still a comparatively unknown and unimportant figure. His rapid rise to power thereafter is undoubtedly mainly due to this friendship."

Schellenberg's capture of Payne and Best at Venlo, and the poisoning he suffered at Lisbon in attempting to do the same to the duke and duchess of Windsor at Lisbon, left his mind in an unstable state. Far from being the instrument that dealt efficiently with the vital but boring minutiae of intelligence, Schellenberg's foreign political espionage service became what Cowgill's excellent survey of the enemy services called an "extremely secret information network" devoted to the task of keeping "a close watch on the endangered spheres of life of the people, to see that the state of the people is sound and that no harmful tendencies emerge." The enemy without was of little interest to Schellenberg as he became ever more involved in bizarre plots and intrigues to kill Hitler, using Himmler as his instrument, to establish a Fourth Reich with himself first as ambassador to London and then as chancellor with a "western orientated" policy.

In pursuing this ambition, Himmler had placed himself in Schellenberg's power, for Schellenberg had discovered that Himmler was greatly dependent upon a Finnish doctor of German birth, Felix Kersten, who was, Himmler maintained, the only man who could relieve him of the pain he was suffering through his cancer. In consulting Kersten in an attempt to alleviate his own liver and gall bladder troubles—troubles caused by, he insisted, his poisoning at Lisbon—

Schellenberg discovered that Kersten held political opinions very similar to his own, that Hitler must be liquidated, the war must be ended with the western powers, and the western powers must be brought into an alliance with the Fourth Reich against Russia. When Kersten was introduced to Himmler, Himmler made what Schellenberg called the "express wish that Kersten should not be used for intelligence purposes in case he should be brought into a compromising situation and Himmler should lose his services."

But it was too late: Kersten had already confessed to Schellenberg treasonable thoughts about Hitler and the Third Reich, and he had also committed treasonable actions. Through his association with a Chinese lady of great beauty whom Schellenberg named Mrs. Kou, Kersten revealed that he had connections with the British and Russian secret services at Stockholm. It is thought that "Mrs. Kou" was Mrs. Wellington Koo, wife of the Chinese ambassador in London.*

As Himmler must have realized, Schellenberg had only to advise Heinrich Mueller of his suspicions regarding Kersten, and Himmler would lose the services of the one man who could cure his pain. Moreover, there had been a similar treasonable association between Kersten and a certain Abram Hewitt, an OSS secret agent in Stockholm. That connection served to reinforce the hold that Schellenberg had over Kersten personally. In what was one of the more bizarre episodes of the war, in October 1943 Schellenberg acted to bring the reichsführer SS over to his political beliefs—that is to say that Himmler must kill Hitler.

For some years Himmler had been susceptible to astrology. This was known to Kersten, who, according to Schellenberg in his SIS interrogation, "evolved the idea of introducing Himmler to a Hamburg astrologer, a certain Wulff, with a view to influencing Himmler with his and [Schellenberg's] political beliefs." At his interrogation Schellenberg described Wulff as being "100 percent anti-Nazi" but because of the Hess affair "astrology was in very bad odour." Therefore, Schellenberg introduced Wulff to Himmler as "a professor of Sanskrit who could advise Himmler on Indian matters." While awaiting the interview Wulff worked out the horoscopes of Hitler and

*Vi Kuiyin Wellington Koo, Mandarin Ku Wei-chun, 1887. Chinese nationalist diplomat, b. Shanghai. Educated Columbia (BA 1908; MA 1909; Ph.D., 1912), specialist in international law. 1912, secretary to Yüan Shih-kai, president of China; 1936–41, ambassador to France; 1941–46, ambassador to Great Britain; 1946–1956, ambassador to the United States. At various times he was foreign minister and prime minister of nationalist China; he headed the Chinese delegation to the San Francisco conference that in 1945 founded the United Nations. From 1957–1967 he served on the International Court of Justice at The Hague.

Himmler, and these he passed to Schellenberg for perusal. As Schellenberg went on to relate at his SIS interrogation:

As regards Hitler, Wulff predicted endangerment to his life in the period around July 20th, 1944 as well as a subsequent illness in November 1944. He furthermore foretold Hitler's demise before May 7th, 1945 but stated that the cause of death would never be discovered, though it would be in point of fact due to alkalies (alkaloid).

For Himmler little was foretold, except that the year 1945 was going to be an important one for him. Schellenberg commented [to his interrogator] that no doubt Wulff was well aware of the real prognostication but deemed it wiser to suppress this for the time being.

Schellenberg's own horoscope had not at this time been prepared by Wulff but was given later as follows:

1 Danger for Schellenberg round about July 20th, 1944.
2 Important events in 1945.
3 His imprisonment in April or May 1945 with threat of extreme danger.
4 If nothing materialised then, position might improve in 1947 or 1948.

Having read Hitler's horoscope and his own, Schellenberg advised Wulff "to keep the following three points in mind in his relations with Himmler":

1 The strength of Schellenberg's position
2 His influence over Himmler.
3 That Himmler had to end the war and liquidate Hitler.

With those three points in mind, Wulff now met Himmler personally in March 1944 in Berlin, and, Schellenberg claimed, "Himmler showed the greatest interest in Wulff's forecasts." Wulff began to supply Himmler with regular horoscope readings. From that point forward, Schellenberg claimed he had little difficulty in offsetting the influence of his closest rival, Kaltenbrunner, head of all Sicherheitsdienst services, and throughout the closing days of the Third Reich, during which time Himmler became the most powerful man in Germany, "Himmler seldom took any steps without first consulting his horoscope reading beforehand."

With Schellenberg's control over Himmler's mind and body, he acted to acquaint Churchill with what was going on inside the German government, using one of the most enchanting women of the period, Gabrielle "Coco" Chanel, the Parisienne parfumeuse. Chanel had come to world prominence first as the mistress of the duke of Westminster, the richest man in the world, then as the most influential clothes designer of her time, and then as creator of the perfume

Chanel No. 5. Known to "C" and and still more so to Pamela Menzies and her mother, "Coco" Chanel was also well known to Churchill.

Madame Chanel was deeply interested in politics, and especially in fascism, exhibiting a violent detestation of bolshevism. Her views, and the passions unleashed when she held forth about her opinions, attracted her to Churchill, for when they met Churchill had just made his famous statement on Italian fascism:

If I had been an Italian, I am sure I should have been wholeheartedly with you [the Italian people] from the start to finish in your triumphant struggle against the bestial appetites and passions of Leninism. But in England we have not yet had to face this danger in the same deadly form. We have our own way of doing things. But that we shall succeed in grappling with Communism and choking the life out of it—of that I am absolutely sure. [18]

In April 1944, as the armies gathered for Neptune, a man named Schiebe mentioned to Schellenberg that "a certain Frau Chanel" should be used to get in touch with Churchill in London. Schiebe assured Schellenberg that Chanel was "a person who knew Churchill sufficiently to undertake political negotiations with him, as an enemy of Russia and as desirous of helping France and Germany whose destinies she believed to be closely linked together." [19]

Schellenberg then instructed that Chanel be brought to Berlin, where she arrived with a certain Dincklage, an "honourable correspondent" of the old Abwehr. At their meeting, Madame Chanel proposed to Schellenberg that "a certain Frau Lombardi, a former British subject of good family then married to an Italian, should be released from internment in Italy and sent to Madrid as an intermediary."

Mrs. Lombardi was an old friend of Madame Chanel, and her task would be to hand over a letter to the British embassy. Madame Chanel herself wrote the letter to Churchill. Schellenberg approved the scheme, and within a week Mrs. Lombardi had been released and was on her way to Madrid. But there the plan foundered, for as Schellenberg admitted later in his interrogation, on her arrival in Madrid, instead of carrying out the part that had been assigned to her, she denounced all and sundry, including Madame Chanel, as German agents to the British authorities.

Himmler himself may well have been involved in the Chanel episode, for as Schellenberg recorded, shortly after the operation collapsed Himmler called Schellenberg into his presence and raised the points recorded about him in Wulff's horoscope "and in particular

the question of concluding peace with the Allies and liquidating Hitler." Himmler was wavering, as he was to do frequently in the near
future, "and asked Schellenberg exactly how much importance could
be attached to Wulff's prophecies. Schellenberg took the opportunity
of pouring a little oil on the flames but Himmler found himself still
unable to come to a definite decision" regarding Schellenberg's demand that he kill Hitler.

Such, then, was the poor estate into which the German intelligence service had fallen as, through "C" and his colleagues, the Allied
supreme command spun its "silken curtain" to mystify and mislead
the Germans about the times and places of the various phases of the
invasion. Nothing that Schellenberg had done, except Venlo, entitled
him to the term so often accorded him by those whose job it was to
study the young German spymaster, that of being "a genius." As
Squadron Leader G. W. Harrison, the man who interrogated Schellenberg when he was captured, stated: "His demeanour at this camp
has not produced any evidence of outstanding genius as appears to
have been generally attributed to him. On the contrary, his incoherency and incapability of producing lucid verbal or written statements have rendered him a much more difficult subject to interrogate
than other subjects of inferior education and of humbler status."

As to the quality of Schellenberg's new intelligence service, as
Chester Wilmot, perhaps the leading war correspondent associated
with Neptune and afterward the author of one of that operation's most
important histories, was to record:

In trying to estimate Allied intentions, the German High Command was
working under a serious handicap, for its Foreign Intelligence Service, now
in Himmler's sinister control, was producing information of the most doubtful
character. Himmler's absorption of the Abwehr in March could not have
come at a less opportune time. Inefficient though Canaris's organisation was,
it did exist, and Himmler had no adequate substitute. For the most part
the Gestapo types whom he sent abroad were gauche thugs, ignorant and
inept. Their big ears picked up every canard which British agents spread
abroad in neutral capitals, and in the weeks immediately preceding the
invasion Himmler's men were deliberately swamped with "secret information" which they had neither the time nor the wit to sift and appraise. The
German Intelligence machine became clogged, and the material sent in by
the Abwehr who were still in the field was lost among the rubbish. After
the war in the records of the German Admiralty the Allies found a dossier
containing some 250 individual reports from agents dealing with the time
and place of invasion. Of these only one, from a French colonel in Algiers,

was correct, but this had been filed away unheeded with the dross. The majority opinion gave July as the month and the Pas de Calais as the place. [20]

That majority opinion reflected exactly the intelligence leaked to the Sicherheitsdienst under the main tactical deception plan, Fortitude.

Yet there were still dangers to the security of the secrets of Neptune, for if the Sicherheitsdienst showed itself to be more interested in the sciences of the next world than this one, their counterespionage service remained the most redoubtable, ruthless, and omnipresent of any power in modern history, including Russia.

5 TO THE EVE OF D-DAY

Standing amidst the ruins of the chamber of the House of Commons, Winston Churchill remarked to the assistant secretary of war, John J. McCloy, upon "the number of his early contemporaries who had been killed during what he called the hetacombs of World War I." [21] Reflecting exactly "C's" own attitude toward a headlong confrontation with the German army, Churchill reminded McCloy of a fact that had never been impressed upon the American nation—that an entire generation of potential British leaders had been cut off at Ypres, Passchendaele, and the Somme, and that England could not afford the loss of another generation. It was, he declared, vital to the future of the world that both England and America should possess "vigorous and competent leaders at hand to ensure the peace and democratic government."

All might succeed, Churchill declared somewhat later, but only if the Germans remained in ignorance of the time and place of the assault. If they learned those key secrets, they might still retain the power to assemble overwhelming power at the points of landing and destroy the invasion. And what then? Would it be possible to mount a second such invasion? Could England be destroyed by a deluge of missiles as the second invasion was being mounted? Above all, what was to become of Europe if the invasion failed? Would Hitler become master of Europe? Or would the Red Army succeed in advancing to the English Channel?

Churchill wrote to Anthony Eden on April 1, concerned about Soviet policy. "Once we get on to the Continent with a large commitment, they will have the means of blackmail, which they have not at present, by refusing to advance beyond a certain point, *or even tipping the wink to the Germans that they can move more troops into the West.*" [emphasis supplied] Although he had tried "in every way to put myself in sympathy with these Communist leaders," Churchill went on, "I cannot feel the slightest trust or confidence in them. Force and facts are their only realities." The issues carried a great burden and would require remarkable cunning if they were to be resolved.

The supreme Allied commander, Eisenhower, had visions of the English Channel running red with the blood of the troops under his command. He wrote to a friend that "we are not merely risking a tactical defeat; we are putting the whole works on one number." [22] Brooke, chief of the Imperial General Staff, felt "very uneasy" and wished "to God it were safely over," for at best Neptune would fall "very far short of the expectations of the bulk of the people, namely all those who know nothing about its difficulties"; at worst "it may well be the most ghastly disaster of the whole war." [23]

"C," the instrument of Churchill's cunning, remarked to Colonel Bevan, the chief of deception, that he could not get out of his mind the physical pain he had felt that night in his cottage at Verbrandenmolen after the First Battle of Ypres when he discovered that almost everyone in his regiment was dead, wounded, or missing. Was England now to lose another generation on the far shore?

The sense of fear was palpable throughout the armies and the islands. And there were several reports that the Angel of Mons had reappeared in the sky over southern England. Hitler himself recognized that here was the supreme moment of the war, for as he had declared at a staff conference on December 23: "If they attack in the West, that attack will decide the War. If that attack is repulsed the whole business is over. Then we can withdraw troops right away [for the Russian front]."

For the purposes of Neptune, "C," who hitherto had avoided direct contact with the Supreme command, now became ever closer to it. The management of the command consisted of General Eisenhower, supreme commander, who was little more than a figurehead at that time, although he became more prominent later; Air Chief Marshal Sir Arthur Tedder, deputy supreme commander; General W. Bedell Smith, chief of staff; Admiral Sir Bertram Ramsay, commander in chief of Allied naval forces; Air Chief Marshal Sir Trafford Leigh-Mallory, commander in chief Allied air forces; and General Sir Bernard Montgomery, commander of the Twenty-first Army Group, the headquarters that was to command Allied land forces in the invasion. These consisted of the U.S. First Army of General Omar Bradley and the British Second Army of General Sir Miles Dempsey. Under these arrangements, Eisenhower bore executive responsibility for Neptune while Montgomery had operational command until the time was reached on the far shore when a separate American army group was established. Then Eisenhower would assume direct command of all land forces.

The plan for the invasion, a vast document weighing thirty-six pounds with appendices, contained two elements of high importance to "C." One was Bodyguard, the intent of which was to mislead the German supreme command about where *in Europe* the Allies would invade. The second was Fortitude, intended to baffle the Germans about where the Allies would land *in northern France*. The object of the plan was to present the enemy with a number of different major threats through the medium of false intelligence, thereby compelling him to disperse his forces in Europe on the principle that in trying to be strong everywhere, he would be weak everywhere.

The plans were prepared by Churchill's deception officer, Colonel John Henry Bevan, a close friend of "C" and chairman of the London Controlling Section. Plan Fortitude was arranged by Bevan with Eisenhower's and Montgomery's headquarters through an organization called the Committee of Special Means. The main aspect of Fortitude was to provide evidence to the enemy that would convince him that he was correct in the assumption he held already, that the Allies would land in the place closest to England, the Calais area, when in fact the Allies would land in the area between Caen, the capital of Normandy, and Cherbourg.

To lend conviction to Fortitude, through "C's" and the XX-Committee's double agents Bevan had been building up the belief in the German mind that the Allies would possess three groups of armies for employment in the invasion, when the reality, the heavily concealed reality, was that they would possess no more than two. Under Fortitude, Montgomery's Twenty-first Army Group would lead the invasion with the purpose of diverting German forces from the point of main attack. The Twelfth United States Army Group would then land behind Montgomery to divert the German panzer divisions still further. But, as Fortitude misrepresented the Allied battle plan, there was a *third* army group in Britain, Army Group Patton, named after the American tank commander, General George S. Patton. Although Army Group Patton did not exist as anything more than a deceptive formation, under Fortitude it was to make the "main" attack in the Calais area two to three weeks after Montgomery's forces had landed. Therefore, the purpose of Army Group Patton was to compel the Germans to maintain and even reinforce their Fifteenth Army in the Calais region and thereby prevent Hitler from using that formation as reinforcements for the Seventh Army on the Normandy coast.

To maintain that fiction, an individual of importance and interest in both the short- and the long-term aspects of "C's" career was placed on the Bolero committee, which oversaw the arrival of American troops in England. John Alexander Drew was a British civil servant whose task it was to provide transportation and accommodations for the incoming American forces and in general to act as liaison officer between the civil power and the American command in England. But Drew was also a member of the XX-Committee, the double agent group. In that capacity it was his task to secure, with the agreement of the American command, documentation that, when played into German hands, would provide factual evidence that the United States was establishing not the one million men of one army group in England, but the two million men of two army groups. This was a repetition of the "Document 'X' " deception in World War I, in which GHQ succeeded in inflating American strength in France to such an extent that it became one of the factors in which the German commanders Hindenburg and Ludendorff received favorably Woodrow Wilson's Fourteen Points. Through clever and judicious cooking of the books, under Bolero Drew succeeded in approximately doubling the strength of the American army in Great Britain, a piece of dexterity that earned for him so much admiration within the American command that he was awarded the Medal for Merit by President Harry Truman.

Under these command and deception arrangements, "C" remained responsible only to the British government, but his intelligence was sent to the supreme command through Eisenhower's chief intelligence officer, who was always British. As was customary when "C" became involved in major military operations, he took direct control of certain key sources of intelligence throughout the Neptune period. These were: (a) all major Ultra decrypts relating to the strength and dispositions of the German army in France, (b) the diplomatic bag intercept service of David Boyle, because from such intelligence

"C" could gauge the effectiveness of the misinformation being spread within the large diplomatic corps in London and also of the security precautions that had sealed England from the rest of the world, and (c) all important intelligence deriving from the French section of Broadway relating particularly to the emplacement and employment of missiles and also the movements and whereabouts of the German panzer and mobile divisions. All other intelligence flowed through their normal channels unless any part of it was thought by "C" to have a direct bearing on the situation or the battle about to be fought on the far shore.

During the planning of the operation, it was decided that the limited number of ships and aircraft available for the operation imposed restrictions upon the size of the assault force. This, therefore, could consist of no more than three airborne and five infantry divisions, four tank brigades, five regiments of self-propelled artillery, with two infantry divisions in reserve in the immediate rear of the invasion fleet. That limitation on "lift" meant that in the first two days of the invasion 176,475 men and 20,111 vehicles, including 3,000 guns, 1,500 tanks, and 5,000 other armored vehicles, could be landed.

In turn, the limitations dictated that the assault could succeed only if the enemy had no more than twelve mobile divisions in reserve in Western Europe at the time of the invasion, and if there were no more than three of these divisions in the vicinity of Caen on D-Day, with no more than five by $D+2$ and no more than nine by $D+8$. Further, to give Neptune a "reasonable chance" of success, the Allied air forces must establish absolute air and sea superiority over the English Channel and the area of operations, which was to be in the Bay of the Seine between the capital city of Normandy, Caen, and the great Atlantic port of Cherbourg.

Through these preconditions, and the limitation on the air and sea lift, "C" was required to obtain intelligence that would answer four questions: How many German divisions would there be in the west on D-Day? How would these divisions be disposed? How many of them could be pinned down away from Normandy? How effectively could the battlefield be isolated and the movement of German reserves be frustrated or delayed by bombing and sabotage?

"C's" ability to provide answers to these questions were dictated in large degree by what happened on the Russian front. There, the gigantic Russian winter offensive drew off a number of Rundstedt's best divisions in February and March, which revealed that for all the power at his command, Hitler possessed no central reserve upon which he could call in an emergency. But in the second week of April 1944 the spring thaw began, and the Red Army's attack was halted in a sea of mud until June. At that point Hitler, who had the advantage of excellent east–west road and rail communications, began to switch divisions back to France. But while all that movement was taking place, "C" had no clear idea of where all the panzer divisions—the main threat confronting the assault forces—were located. Then, on April 20, 1944, like manna from heaven, Bletchley circulated an Ultra showing the itinerary of the inspector-general of panzer troops, General Heinz Guderian, who was due to begin a tour of inspection of *all* panzer forces in Western Europe that same day.

In a flash all other intelligence relating to the whereabouts of the panzer divisions was confirmed. When all the confirmations were plotted on a map, they reflected the enemy's essential ignorance about *where* and *when* the Allies would land, for the divisions were located either outside the Neptune area or in equal divisions in both the Neptune—Normandy—and the Fortitude—Calais—areas. That there was no concentration on Normandy reflected the obvious fact that the enemy did *not* believe the Neptune area to be any more endangered than anywhere else on the French coast.

But how powerful were these divisions? Ultra supplied the answer to that question fairly soon after the Guderian decrypt. The Second SS Panzer Division had 412 officers, 2,536 noncommissioned officers, and 14,077 men. It was only in the sixth week of its basic training for operations in France. Only one battle group of three was ready for offensive operations. There were deficiencies in NCOs, men, motor transport, and signals equipment, and motor fuel was short. The state of the Twelfth SS Panzer Division was somewhat similar. And more would have been known about Rundstedt's ability to counterattack if Bletchley had decrypted earlier two returns regarding his tank strength in the west. But those two intercepts were not decrypted until D-Day and D + 1 because they were sent in a new format whose paragraph headings were not as yet understood by Bletchley. But just before D-Day a further decrypt showed that the Seventeenth SS Panzer Grenadier Division was in its twenty-second week of training, short of officers, noncommissioned officers, and transport, but well provided with guns.

An examination of the intelligence available showed that the German Fifteenth Army in the Calais area continued to receive priority, on the grounds that Hitler was placing his missiles there for the bombardment of London, a bombardment that was intended to open at the moment of invasion. In February, March, and April the Fifteenth Army's infantry strength increased from ten divisions to fifteen. Other reinforcements went to the Mediterranean coast, and some went to Brittany. But none went to Normandy, where the invading armies were to land.

To the supreme command, "C's" intelligence seemed too good to last. By mid-April aerial reconnaissance photography detected that the Germans were building posts as obstacles to the landing of gliders in the area where the glider formations of the British Sixth Airborne Division were due to land in the area of Caen. The question, therefore, was whether the Germans had got word of the plan. More aerial reconnaissance in the Fifteenth Army area, however, showed that such obstacles were being constructed everywhere, and for the moment the alarm was allayed—but only for the moment.

In the first week of May "C" began to report exceptionally heavy rail traffic into the region between the Seine and the Loire, the area where the invasion was to take place. Agents' reports revealed that the Twenty-first Panzer Division was being moved toward Caen and Falaise, the same area in which the Sixth Airborne Division would be landed and hard by the beaches on which the British Second Army would come ashore. At the same time "C" advised that the formidable Panzerlehr Division, now in Hungary, was moving back to France, where it would be stationed near the nodal points into the Cherbourg and Breton peninsulas, only one day's march from Caen. That movement was regarded as the more ominous because the Panzerlehr had gone into an area where there had been no tank division previously. With the arrival of two more panzer divisions in or near the Neptune sector, the Allied armies would now face a total of four German divisions. It seemed certain at Broadway therefore that Hitler had either discovered, or deduced, that Normandy was *the* target.

Further intelligence received by "C" on May 25 heightened that alarm. The Ninety-first Air Landing Division, trained to destroy airborne landings, was suddenly rerouted while on its way to Brittany. Its new destination: the root of the Cherbourg peninsula. There it joined Sixth Parachute Regiment across the dropping zones for the U.S. 82nd and the 101st airborne divisions in the Cherbourg peninsula. Finally the Seventeenth SS Panzer Grenadier Division, hitherto positioned around Thouars and Poitier for the defense of the Biscay coast of France, was found to be under orders to move up to Normandy. The supreme command thus faced the fateful question: How much did Hitler know of the Neptune plan?

With only ten days until D-Day, it seemed he knew too much to give Neptune "the reasonable chance of success" on which the operation was based. Montgomery had reckoned that the U.S. airborne and seaborne divisions due to land in the area of Utah beach on D-Day would meet six German divisions. With these fresh German reinforcements, the American force at Utah might meet eight divisions on D-Day and another four by D + 2. In short, the ratio might prove to be five American to eight German divisions. Furthermore, the firepower of the average German was slightly superior to that of an American division, and a large number of the German troops had been battle-trained in Russia. Moreover, the Allied air commander, Leigh-Mallory, doubted whether more than 50 percent of the U.S. paratroops and 30 percent of the glider loads would, given the route, moonlight, and altitude at which the sky trains were to operate, even reach the dropping zones.

A mood of grave crisis enveloped everyone planning the airborne landings, including "C" personally, the begetter of this grim and unwelcome intelligence. The information proved so grave in its implications that "C" was reminded of some of the intelligence General Charteris had withheld from Field Marshal Haig before the First Battle of the Somme and the Third Battle of Ypres in World War I, on the grounds that Haig's nerve might collapse if he knew the worst. As Eisenhower said after the war, the fate of the airborne divisions became one of the two heaviest burdens he had to carry. A less skilled and practiced intelligence officer than "C" might well have decided, as Charteris had done, to spare his commander in chief the worst news.

But "C" did not do that. As we have seen, he had resolved during World War I to provide the commander in chief with *all* news, good or bad, at whatever the cost to his own career. It is possible that he took this decision anew on the eve of Neptune. He left his resignation as "C" with Cadogan in the event that his intelligence proved inaccurate, corrupted, or incomplete, so that his replacement might follow rapidly and without debate.

Eisenhower decided the airborne assault must be made, whatever the dangers, if the landings of the U.S. Fourth Infantry Division at Utah beach were to succeed. The Fourth's mission was to capture the great Atlantic port of Cherbourg, without which Allied operations in northwestern Europe could not succeed. Therefore, the airborne and seaborne operations were indivisible and had to be undertaken.

But by May 15 "C" had obtained still more evidence that Hitler might have perceived the truth through the fog of war. On the basis of all intelligence, the Joint Intelligence Committee was guardedly pessimistic, for as it appreciated on that date:

1. *Area of main assault.* Main assault is expected against Northern coast of France from Boulogne to include Cherbourg inclusive. Although German High Command will until our assault takes place reckon with possibility it will come across the Straits of Dover to Pas de Calais area, there is some evidence that Le Havre-Cherbourg areas [the Neptune area of the actual assault] . . . are regarded as likely and perhaps even the main point of attack. [24]

In the same bulletin, JIC indicated that the German supreme command seemed to know not only *where* the invasion would occur, but also the other key secret of Neptune—*when* it would take place. The JIC continued: "Enemy appreciates that Allied preparations are sufficiently advanced to permit operations any time now and that from the point of view of moonlight and tide *first week in June* is next likely period for assault."

Despite the omens, on May 20 the Joint Intelligence Committee decided that the two main preconditions for the invasion to proceed had been met: (a) German fighter strength in the west had been so reduced as to promise aerial superiority over the Channel and (b) the number of fully mobile, first-class German divisions would not exceed twelve in Western Europe at the time of the invasion. Technically, therefore, the Neptune undertaking could proceed to its final phase before the launching of the assault in the first week of June.

But despite the deception operations, still more evidence appeared that Hitler had discovered the truth. What "C" did not know was *how* he had found out. Was it a matter of deduction, or had there been treachery in London? The answer to this question was sought but never obtained. When JIC issued its next bulletin on the German situation in Europe with regard to Neptune on May 30, it found:

During the last week there has been little evidence to modify our former conclusion that the enemy appreciated that our main assault was likely to be made in the Channel area, from Boulogne to Cherbourg inclusive. The recent trend of movement of German land forces *towards the Cherbourg area* tends to support the view that the Le Havre-Cherbourg area is regarded as a likely, and perhaps even the main, point of assault. . . . The enemy still considers that Allied preparations are sufficiently advanced to permit of operations at any time now, and that from the point of view of moon and tide the first week in June is the *next likely period.* [25]

Even as that ominous appreciation was circulated, very significant movements took place across the Channel in the final period before D-Day. These movements were not fully detected by "C," only partially so. The 352nd Infantry, which was rated as "good," had inched silently *and without detection* by "C" into the bluffs overlooking Omaha beach, the assault area of the U.S. V Corps. And here was the mystery. "C's" agents had reported the 352nd in the area of St. Lo as early as March and around May 23 that the 352nd might be encountered during the assault. Then, on D-2, Brigadier Williams, Montgomery's intelligence officer, passed on the warning to both the First U.S. and Second British armies through the medium of the *Twenty-first Army Group Weekly Neptune Intelligence Review*. As Williams wrote: "It should not be surprising if we discovered that [the] 352nd Division has one regiment up and two to play."

Perhaps the British colloquialism mystified the U.S. First Army G2, Colonel Benjamin A. "Monk" Dickson. But whatever the cause, this intelligence failure proved to be the main intelligence failure of Neptune, one that resulted in very heavy casualties for the U.S. First Army. For it meant that the coastal defenses were one-third stronger than shown on Bradley's order-of-battle maps. In the intelligence appreciation of May 15, that division was reckoned to be twenty-eight miles away from the *Omaha* beaches and could not be in action until H + 17. In reality it was an entrenched, powerful force of 12,769 men, with firepower superior to a U.S. infantry division, possessing parity in infantry howitzers and with a heavy superiority in automatic weapons.

Moreover, it had two regiments "up to play"—not one, as Williams forecast.

6 D-DAY

With clouds lowering, winds increasing, and the sea rising, the first elements of the task forces began sailing on Saturday, June 3, 1944, from Belfast, The Clyde, and the Devon ports. By Sunday morning a storm blew up that was so fierce that Eisenhower postponed the start of Neptune by twenty-four hours, from June 5 as scheduled to Tuesday, June 6.

During the evening of June 4, as the invasion fleets were sailing and only two days before D-Day, "C" called on Cadogan at the Foreign Office and made it known that he was prepared to resign his appointment. Cadogan recorded in his diary: " 'C' this evening showed me quite a lot of good news [about the invasion]. Discussed his successor (if one has to be appointed in a hurry—he doesn't want to go)." Cadogan then recorded that Menzies had nominated two men for consideration as his successor. One was Ivone Kirkpatrick, of the Foreign Office, the other Air Vice-Marshal William Elliot, a brilliant young air staff officer who at that moment commanded the Allied air forces at Gibraltar. As Cadogan added, Menzies recommended that both names be "put on record," both were "good" candidates, and as Cadogan concluded his diary for that day ominously: "Starting to rain tonight: gale raging merrily. This *would* happen."

Whatever the reason for "C's" resignation at such a moment in modern history, forty years later no archive and no survivor could provide an answer for it. The reason for the resignation, which must have been grave, remained a state secret. Indeed, the resignation appears to have slid into the background with the onrush of great events. The first of those great events for "C" was the miraculous location and evacuation of Colonel Gustav Bertrand, "C's" old friend in the Deuxieme Bureau and the "father" of Ultra. [26]

After months in hiding Bertrand had managed to get a message to "C," who managed to get a reply to Bertrand at his hideout near Nîmes, and he was exfiltrated during the night of June 2–3, 1944, the eve of the day before "C" went to see Cadogan. During that period, "C" had seen Bertrand at Broadway and heard his odyssey. It was indeed an odyssey and a tribute to "C's" resources in France.

After his capture in January at the Basilique du Sacre-Coeur de Montmartre, Bertrand was taken to the headquarters of the Abwehr in Paris. There he found himself confronted by Rene Masuy, a well-known interrogator and executioner known to be corrupt. To establish his *moral* domination over Masuy, Bertrand announced who he was: Colonel Gustav Bertrand, *commandant technicien* of the Deuxieme Bureau of France. Overcome by the prominence of his captive—for Bertrand was one of the most famous names in the French secret service, and one of the most wanted—Masuy arranged for Bertrand's not in jail but at the five-star Hotel Continentale near the Place Vendôme. There he was offered a deal by "Rudolf," chief of the Abwehr in Paris. If Bertrand would help in a *tauschmaneuver*, a radio game with the British calculated to establish the time and place of the invasion, Bertrand would, as he told "C," receive "a heated house at Neuilly, the servants of my choice, a car, as much gasoline as I wanted, and a salary of 200,000 francs a month [against the 6,800 francs he was receiving at the time of his arrest], plus a percentage of the profits of intercepted parachutages." He would also receive a card showing that he was a member of the Abwehr, a document that would have made him "untouchable even to the Gestapo."

Bertrand accepted this deal, which was then sealed with a bottle of rare wine drunk from a *tastevin*, the ceremonial French cup; then, about a week after his capture, and after he had been reunited with his wife, Bertrand vanished. He and his wife were on the run with the help of the Ordre de la Resistance de l'Armee until April 27, when they received a message from an agent code-named "Fa-Fa" that "Y"—Broadway—was sending an aircraft to collect them in the vicinity of Orleans. But owing to the intensity of German *ratissages** going on at that time, they missed that plane and another that came by the May moon.

It was not until May 31 that they received instructions from London that led to their escape. On that evening they heard their *message personnel* from the BBC: "Les lilas blancs sont fleuris." (The white lilac is flowering.) The aircraft would land on a lilac field at a farm at Charmont fifteen kilometers northeast of Pithiviers. Bertrand recorded of their escape to England:

Drink, rest. We leave again for a barn where a Jesuit is waiting for us. The caravan then goes on foot at Lilas. Indian file. Night falling. 4 kilometers along a muddy lane. The moon is at its height. Dogs bark. Finally we got to Lilas where we were ordered to hide in an alfalfa field. 11 P.M. We have to wait in silence until 0100. In the distance an Allied bombardment lights up the sky and unfortunately the Lilas field. Noise of a motor at the correct time. We give the agreed light signals. On closer view it is a Messerschmitt. At 0330 in the morning the plane has not come. We return to the barn at Grange. Sleep until 4 P.M.

2 June 1944. The message is transmitted by the BBC. We remain shut up in the farm. Phillippe sent a code message the key of which was taken from the Ave Maria. I cleaned his black crocodile shoes scale by scale. At 11:30 P.M. left by truck to return to Lilas. The moonlight is magnificent, the morale is excellent. Everybody takes his place on the field Lilas. Again

*Literally the French for "rat hunt" but, in the context of espionage, used by secret services and the French underground as the term for manhunt.

in the distance an aerial bombardment. The Allies are raiding the German air force base at Chateaudun. Tracer balls stripe the sky. Eight bombers fall in flames. We counted eight when they exploded and hit the ground. At 1 A.M. another bombardment, much closer. Nearest German post is 10 kilometers. After another half an hour, the noise of a motor. We light up the ground signals flashlights which are in the shape of an arrow pointing to the direction of wind. The aircraft responds with its lights. It lands like a dragonfly. It does not turn off either its motor or its light. A passenger gets out. Three passengers got on with all the mail. In three minutes the change is complete.

The RAF pilot made me translate the rules on board. The rules are simple. If you see a Messerschmitt to the left push a green button, if it is to the right press the black button. The plane is a Lysander 3. The Polish courier is aboard. He is a Jesuit, a real one. Moonlight. Altitude about 1,000 meters. I see another set of signals for another pickup. The Jesuit gets air sick, throws up. I give him my bottle of rum, he drinks *a la Polonais*. Clear sky. No Messerschmitt. Over water for a long time. Pass over lighthouses, islands and the Channel sparkles and finally—land! England certainly. The Jesuit and I embrace so great is our joy. We fly over aerodromes lighted for the return of the bombers. I count eight fields. We land on the ninth, which is in darkness. The landing is very hard. I get out of the plane and make the sign of the cross. The flight has lasted four hours. I give the pilot the traditional bottle of Armagnac.

People run from the darkness. It is Philippson [an official of Broadway's air section, apparently] and some men from the RAF. They take us into a shed on the edge of the field. Day is breaking. Whiskey? Gin? For me a whiskey, and not a light one. For Mary [his wife] a gin. We are completely knocked out and deaf as the motor was not silent. We do not realise yet how generous Providence has been towards us. We are taken to the RAF house neighbouring the field where we are received by Mrs. Bart and [Wing Commander] Sophianu [of the SIS air section].

3rd of June. Rest until 10 A.M. Real breakfast. Then departure for London in a car 150 kilometers. The airfield is near Cambridge. Ouf! What a curious feeling to still be alive. Arrive in London towards 12:30. All the way military convoys marked with the white star which are going to the invasion. Alliance house on Caxton Street where Bill Dunderdale and "Uncle Tom" [Greene] are waiting for us. The two principals of this special operation. Hugs, congratulations. I give my report of my arrest and escape to Bill. Bill gives it to his photographer, Ptitchkin, who will copy it and give it back to me at 5:30 P.M., the time at which [the chief of French counterespionage] Paillole will come and see me at Bill's. Lunch at St. James's Court. Then we are installed at St. Ermin's Hotel in Caxton Street in a comfortable room, flowers everywhere, and a battery radio on a table to enable us to follow events. Later on I will go to see General Menzies, chief of the IS, who I have known for many years and who organized our escape. . . . This evening the third of June BBC during three broadcasts will tell our friends in the whole world *"Michel a rase sa moustache."* [Michael has shaved his moustache]. Which is true. This I did the moment I arrived and before they took my pictures for my identity card.

Bertrand's joy at his arrival was not shared by his French colleagues in London, who shunned him then and for years afterward for having provided "C," not de Gaulle, with his technical intelligence and for having been "a British secret agent." Such indeed was the feeling against Bertrand that not until 1967, twenty-three years later, did Bertrand receive any form of recognition from the French government. Even then, when he was awarded the Legion d'Honneur from President de Gaulle, it was for his postwar secret service work, not for anything he had done during World War II.

Meanwhile, at 3:30 A.M. on June 5, Eisenhower and the Allied commanders in chief met for the last time to hear the weather report and make a final decision whether Neptune was to be launched or postponed for two weeks, when the moon would again be in the right quarter for nighttime airborne operations. As they made their way to the meeting place, they encountered weather that was far from encouraging for an assault beginning just after midnight on the night of June 5–6. The rain and wind beat down even as the meteorologists presented their final forecast. They were able, they stated, to offer "some hope" that there might be a break in the foul weather in the Channel that night. That good weather *might* last thirty-six hours, but they could not predict what would occur at the end of that time. On the basis of that advice Eisenhower held to his decision to proceed if there was a chance of better weather on D-Day. The commanders in chief agreed with him, and with that agreement Eisenhower announced his decision to proceed with Neptune with the words— words that were both fateful and graphic—"Halcyon plus 5 finally and definitely confirmed."*

That evening "C," Dunderdale, Dunderdale's wife—the former June Morse, granddaughter of Samuel B. Morse, inventor of the Morse code—and the Bertrands dined together at the Dunderdales' home in Walton Street. And as Bertrand was to record of that event:

5th June. General Menzies invited to dinner at Bill and June's. . . . He congratulated me on my brilliant conduct during the course of my resistance, during the course of my arrest and escape. He told me that he was proposing

*Halcyon was the code word for June 1, 1944. "Plus 5" indicated June 6, 1944.

me for a British decoration as a reward for the services I had rendered. The DSO!*

As they dined, the Allied invasion fleets—five thousand ships of all sizes carrying the armies and their equipment, with an escort of six hundred warships—approached the far shore. The task forces plunged and heaved in the worsening gale, and none within the ships would forget that night of growing tensions, seasickness, and suspense. Nor would they quite forget one element that puzzled all who were there. As the official British historian recorded:

During the few dark hours of the early morning thousands of ships and craft of many sorts were streaming across the Channel, thousands of airborne soldiers were landing in France, and a thousand or more heavy bombers were plastering key points in the Atlantic Wall. Yet the enemy made no sign at all. His complete inactivity at sea and in the air was disconcerting, even sinister. Had he something unforeseen up his sleeve?†

*Bertrand's Distinguished Service Order, given for "distinguished services under fire, or under conditions equivalent to service in actual combat with the enemy," was gazetted at the end of the war. The citation read:

1-This officer has worked for more than five years in close liaison with the British Intelligence Service. Just before the war he succeeded in obtaining possession of secret German documents of the greatest importance and promised to keep them hidden at the risk of his life. Not only were these documents of very great value to the Allies but if the Germans had recovered them it would have been a serious drawback to our war effort.

2-At the time of the French surrender in 1940 he organised an underground intelligence service in occupied territory. He established radio communication with London and a quantity of information of very great value was transmitted. Thanks to his official contacts, he was able to furnish reports of prime interest confirmed by authentic documents in many cases. All branches of intelligence were covered, including secret weapons and chemical warfare. Reports on the order of battle of the German army and air force were received regularly. Without considering the personal risk involved in his delicate situation, he undertook several special missions for the Allies.

3-Arrested by the Germans at the beginning of 1944, he succeeded in escaping shortly afterwards. Obliged to hide, he was evacuated in dangerous circumstances in June of the same year.

4-During the whole period of German occupation of France this Officer has rendered invaluable services to the British Intelligence Service and also to the Allies.

†In all, 350,816 men were in the assault. These figures comprised 78,244 Britons and 20,380 Americans in the warships, with a further 4,988 in the ships of other navies, mainly French; 32,880 Britons and 30,009 Americans in the landing ships, craft, and barges; 25,000 (estimate) from the Allied merchant navies. A total of 75,215 British and Canadian and 57,500 American troops were landed by sea. Incomplete records show that 23,000 airborne troops (7,900 Britons and 15,500 Americans) were landed from the air. During the night of June 5–6 and D-Day there were 14,000 air sorties, involving perhaps an average of five men to each crew, the total number of airmen directly involved being in the region of 70,000 men. Therefore, probably 425,000 men came within sight of the Norman shore on D-Day. Behind these stood a roughly equivalent number of members of the Allied armed services and civilians involved in transportation and services of supply. In all, about one million men and women were directly or indirectly involved in the assault.

The Germans did have something up their sleeve, although it was not what the Allies thought, some secret weapon or gigantic ambush. As "C" knew well from contacts between German peace emissaries from Berlin during May, the German high command had become fatally flawed through defeatism, conspiracy, and treachery against Hitler. That defeatism existed especially within the command in the west, where important officers were prepared to allow the Allied armies to march ashore rather than fight their way—if only England and America would come to terms with the German General Staff regarding Russia.

7 DINNER AT THE CHÂTEAU

After Schellenberg took over the Abwehr, Admiral Canaris was confined briefly at a castle in Franconia. Then, curiously, he was released and given the post of chief of the German economic warfare service, evidently a sinecure since Germany was in no position to wage economic warfare against anyone. His new appointment did, however, enable him to travel. In May, Canaris appeared in Paris and met with a representative of "C" in Paris, Major Philippe Keun. [27]

Commander Dunderdale had known the Keun family for many years and was a close friend of Keun's father, Georges Keun, a Sephardic Jew with a Danish passport who was one of Europe's leading traders in pharmaceutical opium. Georges Keun lived in great splendor at Taneh Merah on Cap d'Antibes, where Dunderdale was a frequent house guest. Keun's son, Philippe, went to Downside, the Catholic college in England, and to the College Stanislaus, a leading French school for the sons of wealthy and influential Catholics. But young Keun had abandoned Catholicism for communism during the era of the Front Populaire and went to work as a laborer in Turkey, where, being a clever linguist, he began to translate Shakespeare into Turkish.

At the outbreak of World War II, Philippe Keun returned to France, was captured when the French army collapsed at Sedan in 1940, escaped, and made his way to Bordeaux. There, through Catholic connections, he met a Jesuit who was serving in the French secret service with the rank of colonel. This man was the formidable "Colonel

Claude Ollivier," whose real name was Arnould and who was working under cover of being a coal merchant. In 1943 Keun and Arnould formed an intelligence organization called Jade Amicol, the word "Jade" denoting networks operated by Claude Dansey, and the word "Amicol" being a composite of Keun's code name, Admiral, and Arnould's, "the Colonel."

They made their headquarters in the convent of the Sisters of St. Agonie, a branch of the Lazarites, a religious and military order founded in Jerusalem about the middle of the twelfth century. The convent was situated at 127 rue de la Sante, a building under the walls of the Sainte-Anne lunatic asylum. With the nine sisters and the Mother Superior, Madame Henriette Frede, acting as couriers, the convent became one of "C's" main radio posts in Paris and also the center for the collection of Broadway's secret mail for London. A transceiver was secreted in a small loft over the sacristy, and there were wireless outstations in various parts of Paris, including one in the loft of the Hotel Scribe.

By mid-1944 Jade Amicol had become one of the largest and most secure networks in Europe, with some fifteen hundred subagents, mainly former French officers and soldiers, railwaymen, and clerics. Their chief success had been to secure the plans of the Atlantic wall, that formidable and extensive line of fortifications along the coast of Europe from the north cape of Norway to the Spanish frontier. In the course of these operations Keun made connection with an Austrian baron, Posch-Pastor, who acted as private secretary and adviser to the German military governor of Paris and northern France, Colonel General Karl-Heinrich Baron von Stulpnagel, a close associate of Canaris, Beck, and Goerdeler.

Stulpnagel was at the head of the very extensive anti-Hitler conspiracy in the west, the existence of which was known to the German commander in chief, Field Marshal Gerd von Rundstedt, and to the German commander on the invasion front, Field Marshal Erwin Rommel. The conspirators included many of the most prominent members of the German General Staff in France and was in direct contact with the center of the conspiracy to overthrow Hitler in Berlin: the Black Orchestra (the Gestapo code name for the right-wing opposition to Hitler). The new leader was Colonel Klaus Philip Maria Count von Stauffenberg, a member of a prominent Wurttemburg family and related by marriage to Cadogan. After his recovery from wounds suffered in Africa, Stauffenberg became chief of staff to the commander in chief of the German replacement army in Berlin. Since it was the responsibility of that army to induct and train new troops, Stauffenberg had direct and frequent access to Hitler at the Führer's headquarters in the East Prussian woods at Rastenberg.

By May 1944 Stauffenberg was ready to undertake a plan, code-named Valkyrie, to kill Hitler and replace his regime with a government drawn from trusted fellow conspirators in the German General Staff and from the right, center, and left of the civilian sector. The new chancellor was to be General Ludwig Beck, who was still at large despite a long history of conspiracy against Hitler. But in May he decided to seek assurances that the Allies would not attack Germany during the civil war that, almost inevitably, would follow the assassination of Hitler. Stauffenberg intended to murder Hitler personally, using a special bomb found in SOE war stores.

To obtain those assurances, in May 1944 Stauffenberg instructed Stulpnagel to make contact with the British secret service in Paris. This was one of four such contacts established with American and British secret agents in Paris and the neutral capitals. With Stulpnagel's personal adviser, Baron Posch-Pastor, acting as the intermediary in Paris, according to Arnould, Canaris met Keun in Paris to advise Broadway of the plot and of German political requirements if it was to succeed.

Keun flew to England by Lysander on or about May 30, 1944, almost on the eve of D-Day. Dunderdale confirmed that Keun did come to England at that time, and that he met Keun off the Lysander at the clandestine air base at Manston in Kent and took Keun to London. (However, Dunderdale never knew why Keun had come to England, except perhaps to receive instructions about the part Jade Amicol was to play in the invasion.)

Keun was only briefly in London and saw "C" and perhaps Churchill. Arnould claimed that "C" gave Keun a letter to take back to Paris, one intended for Canaris, and that Keun was back at the convent "three or four days before the *debarquement*," the French term for the invasion. There, again according to Arnould, Keun told Arnould that he had brought a letter from London that must be given to Canaris without delay. Arnould then claimed that he telephoned a contact at Stulpnagel's headquarters whom he met later that same day at the confessional at the Cathedral de Notre Dame. Arnould asked the intermediary to tell Canaris, who was believed to be still in Paris, to be at the windmill beside the racetrack at Longchamps at eleven o'clock on the morning of June 3.

Canaris appeared at about a quarter past eleven, according to

Arnould. He was "a short man in a dark suit, easily identifiable because of his silver hair," and he climbed the steps to the windmill
and then began to walk around the path, as if he were looking over
the race course. Arnould recalled approaching Canaris from behind
and introducing himself as "Colonel Ollivier." Arnould told Canaris
that he had received a letter from London, but that it was too dangerous to bring by hand and too important to send by messenger or
to commit to the post. Arnould invited Canaris to come to the convent
at six o'clock and collect the letter, and if there was any reply, it could
be discussed over dinner.

At six o'clock that same evening the bell on the old door of the
chapel entrance to the convent rang. Sister Frede, the Mother Superior, had been told by Arnould that he was expecting a visitor, and
she answered the bell personally. Aware that it was to be a confidential
meeting of importance, she had confined the sisters at the convent
to their quarters so that none might observe the arrival or departure
of the visitor. When Sister Frede opened the door, she found a man
with silver hair in his late middle years whom she had seen previously
by chance with Keun shortly before he had gone to London. The two
men had been walking near the Lion of Belfort in the Place Denfert-
Rochereau, not far from the convent.

According to Sister Frede, the man seemed "nonplussed" and told
her that he had come to pray. Sister Frede asked the visitor to follow
her, which he did, and they walked down the narrow stone-flagged
passageway that led to the clinic and entered a medium-sized room
that the Mother Superior used as a combination of office, sitting room,
and dining room. There was a large table in the center. Arnould was
waiting there, having arrived by the clinic entrance. The two men
shook hands, and then Sister Frede left the room, to be ready to
serve what she called a "simple but wholesome dinner."

Arnould produced the letter, which was in an ordinary white
envelope. From where Arnould stood, the letter appeared to contain
two sheets of paper; it was typewritten and bore a signature, but the
paper was white, not the blue notepaper and green ink that Menzies
habitually used for his correspondence. Canaris sat down in one of
the room's easy chairs to read the letter, and when he had finished
he was quite white and gave a little gasp. *"Finis Germaniae!"* he
declared in Latin. Then, after a brief meal, he left the convent.

Arnould concluded from the desultory conversation that he had
with Canaris during their meal that the letter constituted a rejection
of certain political proposals, although Canaris did not permit him to

read the letter and would not discuss its contents in any detail. It is difficult to say, therefore, what the letter contained to cause Canaris's exclamation, but if it was a rejection, then it is possible to make an informed guess at its contents, for during that same period similar proposals had been received from the conspirators in Berlin by Allen Dulles, the chief American secret representative in Berne, and Rita Winsor, one of "C's" agents in Lisbon. The Donovan papers contained a medium-sized file of proposals from the conspirators to open the Atlantic wall to the Allied armies and also to facilitate the landing of Allied airborne divisions at key ports such as Hamburg and Kiel.

As Dulles reported, the conspirators included three former chiefs of the German General Staff, Beck, Halder, and Zeitzler; General Adolf Ernst Heusinger, one of the heads of the operations branch of the army high command; and General Friedrich Olbricht, deputy chief of the replacement army. A little later still, Dulles reported to Washington that the German commander in chief in the west, Field Marshal Gerd von Rundstedt, would under certain circumstances open the Channel front to the Allied armies.

Twenty days before D-Day, Dulles further advised that the group included Wilhelm Leuschner, a Socialist and the former interior minister of Hesse; General Hans Oster, Canaris's right-hand man until his arrest for alleged currency offenses in 1943; Karl Goerdeler, the former lord mayor of Leipzig, who had been plotting with Canaris against Hitler at least since 1938. Dulles thought it likely that the movement would be supported by General Alexander von Falkenhausen, military governor of Belgium, who would be, Dulles assured Washington, "ready to cease resistance and aid Allied landings, once the Nazis had been ousted." Also, Dulles reported, his contact thought "a similar arrangement might be worked out for the reception of Allied airborne forces at strategic points in Germany."

Since none of Dulles's reports evoked any statement either of collaboration or encouragement to the conspirators by FDR, as Dulles hoped, it can be assumed that the object of the contact between Keun, Arnould, Posch-Pastor, and Canaris was to obtain a similar form of understanding between the conspirators and "C." That being so, it is evident that "C," obedient to the dictate of unconditional surrender arrived at between America, Britain, and Russia as a result of the Casablanca conference, was compelled to reject the overture.

The plan for the rebellion had provided for the assassination of Hitler, Goering, and Himmler. At that point General Friedrich Olbricht, deputy commander in chief of the replacement army in Berlin, was to be informed, and all communications between Hitler's headquarters and the outside world would be blocked by the chief signals officer of the German army, General Erich Fellgiebel. The assassin, Stauffenberg, would use a bomb provided by Colonel Georg Hansen, chief of Amt Mil, the successor organization to the Abwehr, and then fly to Berlin and join Olbricht. Upon receiving a code word that the assassinations had been carried out, Olbricht would then send a signal to key people aware of the plan. These conspirators were located in each major command, military district, and occupied territory. Upon reading the code word Valkyrie, each was to open a sealed envelope declaring that the three German leaders had been murdered by the SS and that the army had been empowered to form a new government with General Ludwig Beck at its head and Field Marshal Erwin Witzleben as commander in chief of the armed forces.

The letters then placed the commanders of all war districts and occupied territories under Witzleben and required them to arrest all senior members of Hitler's administration from ministers down to Nazi district leaders. All Waffen SS units were to be incorporated into the army, and all resistance was to be ruthlessly suppressed. When the Fourth Reich was secured, a provisional government would be established under Beck, with Goerdeler as chancellor, Olbricht as war minister, Stauffenberg as secretary of state for war, and Witzleben as commander in chief of the armed forces. At that point, envoys would seek an armistice in the west. In all, plan Valkyrie appeared to be an impressive document. However, the plan could succeed only if the conspirators moved efficiently and quickly, and the German army accepted the leadership of Beck, which it was likely to do. Given modest good fortune, it could be expected to succeed. It had been, after all, created by the masters of military planning.

Among the officers in the field who were privy to the plot was General Hans Speidel, chief of staff of Field Marshal Rommel's Army Group "B," the force responsible for destroying the Neptune invasion at the water's edge. The headquarters of the army group were at the Château de la Roche Guyon, a great castle on a bend of the Seine near Vernon, to the west of Paris. Apart from his military duties, Speidel's main task was to influence Rommel to support the overthrow of Hitler. Speidel had very nearly succeeded by D-Day. And if Rommel had not decided just before D-Day to go to Germany to attempt to persuade Hitler to agree to a redisposition of the panzer divisions, and then go to his home near Stuttgart for his wife's birthday celebrations, he might have succeeded altogether. As it was, Rommel left the château only partly committed to the objectives of the con-spirators, leaving the army group in Speidel's hands.

By the eve of D-Day, therefore, the command of the German army in France was not merely riddled with defeatism—it was in-efficient to a point that strongly suggested treachery. On the nights of June 1 and 2, listeners heard the BBC send an unusually large number of *messages personnels* ordering the French resistance into a state of alert. The Sicherheitsdienst knew the meaning of twenty-eight of the messages, a sign that "C" had not been wrong in his apprehensions about the degree to which the French resistance had been penetrated by the German security services. Sicherheitsdienst headquarters in Berlin reported these intercepts on June 3 to Grand Admiral Doenitz and warned that "invasion could be considered pos-sible within the next fortnight." [28]

At the admiral's headquarters, these warnings were not taken very seriously, and it was thought that perhaps an exercise was in progress. But on the evening of June 5, the headquarters of Field Marshal von Rundstedt intercepted the "action" or "B" messages. At least one of the Germans' intercepts produced a reaction. That message was a couplet from the poem "The Violins of Autumn" by Paul Verlaine, the French poet. The meaning of the couplet was known to the Germans, but they had misinterpreted its importance, believing it to be the signal for a general call to action to the French railroad workers. In fact it was a call to arms to the Ventriloquist circuit, an SOE F section network operating in the Loir-et-Cher. The first line of the poem, "The long sobs of the violins of autumn," meant that Ventriloquist was to prepare for action. The second line, "Fills my heart with languorous sorrow," was the order to destroy the German land-line system so that the German commanders would be compelled to use wireless, when the signals could be intercepted and decoded by Bletchley.

Through rare good intelligence work the Sicherheitsdienst had learned the meaning of the Verlaine couplet, as they had learned the meaning of the twenty-seven other messages. In consequence, the German intelligence chief in Paris announced to all commands in Western Europe that the invasion was imminent. But the German commander in chief in the west, Rundstedt, did not believe that the British would be so foolish as to publicly broadcast that the invasion of Europe had begun. Therefore he took no action to bring his army, naval, and air forces to a state of maximum alert, largely because through feints the German defenses had been put on alert so often during the past month that the troops were exhausted. Furthermore, Rundstedt believed that the gale raging in the English Channel would make an invasion a technical impossibility.

But then, during the evening of June 5, the eve of Neptune, the BBC broadcast the action line of the couplet, "Fills my heart with languorous sorrow," fifteen times in all. The result was that the commander of the German Fifteenth Army in the Pas de Calais, the area in which the Germans *thought* the Allies would land, encouraged by the Fortitude deception plan, placed his army in a state of maximum readiness. But the German Seventh Army in Normandy, where the Neptune forces *would* land, was not alerted. General Bodo Zimmermann, Rundstedt's operations officer, claimed afterward that all commands in the west were placed on alert.

Thus—if Zimmermann's version was correct—the entire German group of armies, with the navy and the air force, should have been in a state of maximum alert by the time the first Allied soldiers started to land by parachute. But they had *not* been mobilized; afterward Hitler suspected that treachery had intervened.

He may not have been wrong, for Colonel Anton Staubwasser, Rommel's intelligence master at Army Group B, told quite a different story. At about 8:00 P.M. that night, he was informed by telephone by the intelligence officer of the Fifteenth Army that one of these code words had been intercepted and that the Fifteenth Army had alerted its troops. Staubwasser reported this immediately to Speidel, who directed him to obtain a decision from Rundstedt about whether to place the army group on alert, as, Speidel claimed, he did not know what the couplet meant because he had not been informed by the Sicherheitsdienst.

At that moment, Speidel was giving a small dinner party. Present were Dr. Horst, his brother-in-law, and Juenger, the philosopher, both of whom were also in the anti-Hitler German resistance. The purpose of the dinner party was to discuss the draft of a twenty-two-page document that Juenger intended to be used by Rommel as the basis for an armistice with America and England. When Staubwasser contacted Rundstedt's headquarters, he claimed: "In the course of the ensuing conversation, which I held personally, a special missions staff officer—after a short while—conveyed to me, by order of [the commander in chief west], the command to desist from alerting the troops in the area of Army Group B." [29]

The Seventh Army on the invasion front was *not* alerted. Yet that was not the end of the queer occurrences that evening: about a third of all senior officers were on leave, another third were attending war games at Rennes, and the rest were confident that the Allies would not invade that night because they could not, since the weather in the Channel was too bad. Thus "the sledgehammer of God," as the kaiser once called the staff of his army, was asleep that night of June 5–6 when, at 2:00 A.M., the lead sticks of an Allied paratroop army began landing in the water meadows at the root of the Cherbourg peninsula and in the area around Caen.

If there was truth to the story—for the relevant documentation was never found to prove it—one deception was of crucial importance. Since December 1942 the naval section at Bletchley had been reading a German hand cipher known as the "K" code at Bletchley. It was used for communications to and between German coastal artillery batteries and radar stations on the English Channel coast of France and in the Mediterranean. In the small hours of D-Day a single K-code signal was intercepted from a shore station in the battle area that said, "Cancel state of readiness." Who sent that signal, and why, is still a mystery forty years later. But if it *was* sent, then it would explain how and why it was that that night, at 0230 hours, the three Allied parachute divisions managed to land in Normandy from 1,300 aircraft without alerting the entire western front until after daybreak.

At 1:30 A.M., Rundstedt, the Third Air Fleet, and Admiral Krancke, the naval commander in the west, were all informed of the airborne landings, but at that hour all three took the view that "no major enemy landing is imminent." The weather, they believed, was too severe. [30] In fact, an entire airborne landing was in progress, and for the first time, and *on their own initiative*, the German Seventh Army in Normandy and the Fifteenth Army in the Pas de Calais placed themselves in a state of "the highest alert." Five and one-half hours had passed since the circulation of the second line of the Verlaine couplet.

At 2:15 A.M., the chief of staff of the Seventh Army, General Max Pemsel, telephoned both Rundstedt and Speidel and announced that his outposts had heard the sound of engines at sea and that the admiral commanding the Cherbourg sector had reported the presence of ships in "the sea area Cherbourg." In Pemsel's view this activity pointed to a major operation. Neither Speidel nor Rundstedt agreed and maintained their earlier opinion that Rundstedt did not "consider this to be a major operation." [31]

From that time forward, reports of ships and aircraft multiplied rapidly from many quarters. At 4:45 A.M. Seventh Army advised Army Group B, Speidel's headquarters, that a "large-scale enemy assault" was about to take place. With the start of the aerial and naval bombardment, these reports multiplied still further. Both the Seventh and the Fifteenth armies were now thoroughly alarmed and alerted. Then Fifteenth Army asked Speidel for permission to move the Twelfth SS "Hitler Youth" Panzer Division closer to the coast, but Speidel refused.

It was not until 5:00 A.M. that Rundstedt gave orders for the "Hitler Youth" division to begin moving up and to be ready for "immediate intervention." He also ordered the Panzerlehr Division, a formidable tank division, to prepare to march. But Hitler's headquarters countermanded the orders on the grounds that these divisions could not move without the Führer's approval, and he was asleep and could not be disturbed.

Nor was any attempt made to prepare another powerful tank division, the Twenty-first Panzer Division, which was only twenty-two miles from the British landings, for an immediate counterattack before daybreak. It was clear from the outset that the Allied invasion and hence the battle for Europe might well be decided *in the first hours*. Everything hung upon immediate and determined responses to the intelligence received. But those determined responses were not made, partly through German muddle, partly through the uncertainties created by Allied deceptive actions, and partly perhaps through treachery.

The Channel front had been opened, and Montgomery had achieved that most important of all conditions in warfare: tactical surprise. At 6:30 A.M. the assault divisions of the American First and the British Second armies began landing. As they did so, General Strong, Eisenhower's G2, circulated a strategic appreciation of the German army on the eve of battle. These figures demonstrated better than all the words written and spoken about political and military argument over Allied strategy since Pearl Harbor. The German army was spread-eagled at all points of the compass just as Churchill intended when he introduced his strategy of the circumference against the center:

Russian Front: 122 infantry divisions, 25 panzers plus one brigade, 17 miscellaneous divisions plus 1 brigade.

Norway & Finland: 21 infantry divisions.

Italian and Balkans Fronts: 37 infantry divisions plus one brigade; 9 panzer and 4 miscellaneous divisions.

Denmark: 2 infantry plus 1 panzer division and 2 tank brigades.

France and the Low Countries: 41 infantry, 11 panzer, 9 miscellaneous.

Units in Germany or en route between fronts: three infantry divisions plus 1 brigade, 1 panzer division plus 2 brigades, 4 miscellaneous divisions plus 2 brigades. [32]

When "C" retired for the night, both the strategy and the intelligence campaign that had preceded Neptune seemed triumphant. The precondition for victory first enunciated by Churchill's illustrious forebear, John, duke of Marlborough, on the eve of Waterloo, had been obtained. "Sire," the duke advised the sovereign, "my strategy is one against ten, my tactics ten against one." So it was now. At that moment, in an effort to be strong everywhere, the German army was weak everywhere, or at least too weak to defeat the forces that could be brought against it at any one point.

As General Warlimont, deputy chief of operations at Hitler's supreme headquarters, wrote later: "On 5 June 1944 the German supreme command had not the slightest idea that the decisive event of the war was upon them."

8 H-HOUR

After breakfast in Whitehall, "C" met with the Joint Intelligence Committee in the War Cabinet offices in Great George Street, a small thoroughfare linking Parliament Square with St. James's Park. A bulletin based upon all reports received during the night was prepared for the chiefs of staff meeting at 10:30 A.M. and for the teletype to Eisenhower. The discussion was brief and confined to an almost disbelieving expression of the fact that the Allied armies had obtained a degree of tactical and, perhaps, strategic surprise.

But as Cavendish-Bentinck, the chairman, recalled, "C" thought this was due more to bad weather in the Channel than either to skillful generalship or the success of the deception plan. Nobody said very much, as Cavendish-Bentinck recalled, and his committee confined itself to the obvious:

The Allied armies will have to overcome desperate resistance by the maximum forces which the Germans can bring against them without denuding the coasts of France and so enabling the Allies to effect an unopposed landing elsewhere. [33]

At German supreme headquarters, located at Berchtesgaden in the Bavarian Alps, the chronicle of events was different. When Hitler awoke he was advised of the landings, but instead of calling a supreme command conference to decide upon some masterstroke to drive the landings back into the sea, he did little all morning other than authorize the release of the Twelfth SS Panzer Division to Rundstedt's command while maintaining that the Panzerlehr was to stand fast. Neither divisions were to be committed to the battle without OKW —Hitler's—authority.

The matter of the battle rested for the next four and a half hours while Hitler lunched at Klessheim Castle, far distant from his staff, with the new Hungarian prime minister, General Dome Sztojay. Dutifully, the staff of the Oberkommando der Wehrmacht, the German supreme command, trooped after him, maps under their arms. They did not meet with Hitler until about 2:00 P.M. According to General Warlimont, OKW deputy chief of operations:

As we stood about in front of the maps and charts we awaited with excitement Hitler's arrival and the decisions he would take. Any great expectations were destined to be bitterly disappointed. As often happened, Hitler decided to put on an act. As he came up to the maps he chuckled in a carefree manner and behaved as if this was the opportunity he had been awaiting so long to settle accounts with the enemy. [34]

Hitler was in a sprightly mood, and his first words were, "So! We're off!" Not until 2:30 P.M.—over twenty-two hours after circulation of the first warning that the invasion was imminent—did Hitler release both the Twelfth SS and the Panzerlehr to Rundstedt's command. But by then the cloudy skies over Normandy had broken, and swarms of Allied fighters and bombers operating from England ranged over the battlefield to attack anything they saw moving. That activity made the panzer divisions' movements impossible until after dark. Consequently it was not until June 8 that the main elements of the divisions could join the battle.

"C"

Two of the greatest figures of the twentieth century meet—Stalin and Churchill. During World War II "C" had over fifteen hundred meetings with Churchill; Stalin, for his part, executed those people whom he suspected of being too close to "C." *(National Archives)*

Hitler. While the world strove for the defeat of Germany in World War II, much of "C's" work was connected with the Black Orchestra, the anti-Hitler movement inside Germany. They almost succeeded in assassinating Hitler on July 20, 1944, but in the purges that followed over six thousand men and women were executed; twenty thousand more, including children, were jailed. *(National Archives)*

The enemy. "C" and Admiral Wilhelm Canaris, chief of the German military intelligence service—the Abwehr— worked sporadically together in order to kill Hilter while still fighting each other. Canaris *(seated on the left)* was a loyal German who nonetheless hated Hitler and nazism. He was executed in the last days of the war for his part in the July 20 plot. Seated next to Canaris is Reinhardt Heydrich, chief of the Sicherheitsdienst, Hitler's personal secret service, a man considered so dangerous that in 1942 he was assassinated by British agents with "C's" knowledge and approval. *(National Archives)*

Intrepid—William S. Stephenson was appointed over "C's" objections to be chief of the British secret service in the American hemisphere, with headquarters in New York. Such were Stephenson's activities that J. Edgar Hoover and the U.S. attorney general sought to have him recalled to England.

"Q"—Menzies's American counterpart, William J. Donovan. He was a football hero at Columbia, a law school associate of Franklin Roosevelt, a Medal of Honor recipient in World War I, and a brilliant lawyer and politician. FDR made Donovan chief of the Office of Strategic Services, which later became the CIA. "C" and "Q" spent much of the war in conflict over the control and flow of Allied intelligence. *(Donovan Family Archives)*

Colonel Sir Rex Benson, "C's" cousin by marriage and perhaps closest friend and professional associate. He was military attaché in Washington for much of the war while at the same time he reported to "C." *(Benson Family Archives)*

Throughout World War II "C" left England on secret missions only twice. Here he is flying to Algiers in December 1942. While there the commander in chief of the French navy, Admiral Jean Darlan, was assassinated by a Frenchman being trained by Anglo-American agents in secret service operations. *(Menzies Family Archives)*

Major Felix Cowgill, chief of the counterespionage section of Menzies's service. Cowgill's deputy was Kim Philby. *(Cowgill Family Archives)*

Major General George V. Strong, U.S. Army G2, one of "C's" closest allies in Washington. Together they played the major role in ensuring that Ultra, the British penetration of the German and Japanese main codes, remained a state secret in both capitals for almost forty years. *(National Archives)*

Major General Sir Colin Gubbins, chief of the Special Operations Executive, the organization created by Churchill in 1940 with the order to "set Europe ablaze!" "C's" territorial struggle with Gubbins was one of Menzies's sternest tests. *(Gubbins Family Archives)*

Claude Dansey, Menzies's deputy, described by William Stephenson as "a man so evil that he should have gone to the Tower of London." Dansey ran "C's" espionage services.

David Boyle, "an aristocratic odd-job man," was the third of "C's" closest friends. A member of the service throughout Menzies's tenure, he flew to Berlin in the last hours before the outbreak of World War II in an unsuccessful attempt to see Hilter and persuade him not to invade Poland. During the war Boyle was chief of Section "N" of the secret service, the branch responsible for intercepting and opening foreign diplomatic mail.

Sir Alexander Cadogan, the permanent head of the Foreign Office throughout World War II and therefore Menzies's point of contact with the British government. Despite early differences, "C" gradually gained Cadogan's confidence until a point was reached when Cadogan regarded "C" as being one of the best English spymasters to hold that office. They ended the war as firm friends.

Harold Adrian Russell "Kim" Philby—son of a famous Arabian explorer, Cambridge graduate, *Times* war correspondent, and protégé of Menzies. "C" was so impressed with young Philby that he made him chief of the anti-Soviet section at the end of World War II. Unknown to almost everyone, except perhaps "C," Philby was under Soviet control throughout the time he was in SIS, a period that lasted from 1941 until 1951. *(Bettmann Archive)*

Sir Stewart Menzies—"C" to his subordinates, Stewart to his friends, Sir Stewart to the public at large—in the place he loved most, the saddle, shortly before his death in 1968. *(Menzies Family Archives)*

That delay proved fatal both in the outcome of the Battle of Normandy and the survival of the Third Reich. The landings could have failed if Hitler had acted immediately; now they were given just enough time to succeed. The hesitancy of Rundstedt's and Speidel's earliest reactions, the failure of the German intelligence to obtain correct and adequate information or to make realistic deductions, total Allied domination of the air, the brilliance of Allied planning and the boldness and bravery of the commanders and the troops, the bad weather that in fact favored the enemy, the excellence of Allied intelligence of the enemy down to the minutest detail—all combined now to leave the Germans baffled. The assault phase of Neptune was undoubtedly one of the greatest victories in military history.

By the end of D-Day a total of 75,215 Britons and Canadians were ashore on Gold, Juno, and Sword beaches, with 57,500 Americans on Utah and Omaha, a grand total of over 130,000 men. In addition, over 23,000 airborne troops had been landed by the Allied air forces. Except in one place—Omaha—the casualties had been relatively light. British and Canadian casualties were about three thousand men. The total American casualties in both the airborne and seaborne assaults came to about six thousand soldiers. Although the Germans had thirty-six U-boats in the area to attack the great fleets, such was the excellence of the naval plan that Allied naval losses were again negligible.

But at Omaha there was near disaster. The U.S. V Corps ran into a tough, battle-hardened, entrenched, and alerted German formation, the 352nd Infantry Division, which was thought to be inland at Saint-Lô. Instead, its rifle battalions were in the bluffs of the beach. Almost all American casualties occurred at Omaha, and through that misadventure a chain of events almost betrayed to Hitler the invasion's entire plan.

During the evening of D-Day, the Germans came across a small boat rocking in the surf near the mouth of the river Vire. In the boat they found the body of an American officer. When a German intelligence officer examined the briefcase the man had been carrying, he found it contained the operational orders of the U.S. Seventh Corps at Utah Beach, the second of the two U.S. landings. Then, during the afternoon of D + 1, at the seaside village of Vierville, the corpse of another American officer was found, along with the operational orders of the U.S. V Corps, the other main unit of the U.S. First Army. Thus, at the outset of the battle, the Germans had in their hands what General Gunther Blumentritt, Rundstedt's chief of staff, called "the entire scheme of maneuver and order of battle for American units in the first phase of the battle."*

At least one and probably both these captured documents reached the desk of General Max Pemsel, chief of staff to the commander of the German Seventh Army. As Pemsel stated after the war: "During the invasion, the map of the plan of operations lay on my desk for continuous exploitation." Pemsel concluded from his study of the orders that a second landing near Calais was unlikely because the orders showed that "the great expansion of the American bridgehead—according to the plan as far as the inner bay of St. Malo [in Brittany] and eastward—led to the conclusion that this operation required such a large number of American troops that a second landing at another point [such as Calais] was not likely at all." This intelligence was transmitted up through the chain of command through Rundstedt to Hitler. As General Blumentritt claimed after the war, they served to confirm his and von Rundstedt's views that "what was going on in Normandy was the actual invasion."

As a consequence, von Rundstedt ordered seventeen divisions from all parts of Western Europe, but mainly from the Fifteenth Army. These included the SS Leibstandarte Regiment (Hitler's bodyguard regiment, which was stationed near Brussels), two first-class infantry divisions, and one panzer division. Rundstedt's plans were approved by Hitler between June 8 and 10, the orders were intercepted and read by Bletchley, and the great crisis of Neptune, one that was known within the secret circle in London as "the D + 4 affair," then developed with none of Montgomery's armies securely lodged on the far shore. With that development, Eisenhower agreed that a key card could now be played.

With "C" as chairman of the W Board supervising all the key moves of the XX-Committee, the principal player became Garbo, an agent who was under the control of Tomas Harris, in peacetime an

---

*That these orders should have been captured on D-Day and D + 1 is surprising. Neptune security orders prohibited the carrying of more than "the minimum number of papers" during the first four tides of the Neptune assault. Full operational orders—which is what the Germans obtained—were not to be taken ashore at all before June 8 or until D + 2. Until that time only such extracts could be taken ashore as were necessary for commanders and staff officers to conduct operations. The security directive also contained the instruction that "formations will ensure that the risk of valuable information being obtained by the enemy is reduced to a minimum, and that no man carries on his person more written information than is absolutely vital for his task." That Seventh Corps' orders should have been captured so early is the more inexplicable when it is realized that the corps encountered virtually no opposition in its landing at Utah.

art dealer of Anglo-Spanish origins. Since 1942 Harris had been building Garbo up in the enemy's estimation with remarkably detailed intelligence concerning Bolero, the movement of U.S. forces to England for the cross-Channel attack. In what was its most daring stratagem, the W Board obtained Eisenhower's permission to pass information to the German supreme command at about the time the airborne forces were landing, but four hours *before* the first seaborne forces were due to land, intelligence that "the first phase" of the invasion was beginning. The object: to so build up the credentials of Garbo at the outset of the battle that his information would be accepted without question afterward. [35]

At midnight on the night of June 5–6 Garbo went on the air to Madrid and asked his controller to keep the Madrid station open throughout that night, as he was expecting vital intelligence. The Madrid controller agreed, but when at 2:30 A.M. Garbo called Madrid in order to pass the intelligence that the first phase of the invasion was beginning, there was no reply. He called again on several occasions before daybreak, without getting a reply, and assumed that the German operators were asleep.

Garbo was not able, therefore, to transmit the information. That failure required some rapid script rewriting, but Harris was nothing if not resourceful, and a fresh scenario was written and ready for transmission to Madrid at daybreak. In his first and second messages to Madrid on D-Day, Garbo made no reference to the fact that he had been unable to contact the Madrid operator earlier. But having transmitted a bulletin on the movement of Allied forces in England on June 7, Garbo found an occasion to work into his report this paragraph of self-congratulation:

Fortunately this first operation has been robbed of the surprise which the enemy wanted to achieve with it, thanks to information I was able to pass to you [at 0230] on the night of the invasion.

Garbo's controller in Madrid advised Garbo that he had received no such signal, advice that caused Garbo to explode with a fury that was entirely convincing but contrived: "Were it not for my faith in the Führer and the vital importance of his mission to save Europe from the twin tyrannies of Bolshevism and Anglo-American plutocracy, I would this very day give up my work, conscious as I am of my failure." Mortified at the prospect of losing the cooperation of his valued spy, the German controller sent a long signal explaining why Garbo could not get through to Madrid and emphasizing Germany's appreciation for "your splendid and valued work." The German controller added: "I wish to stress that your work over the last few weeks has made it possible for our command to be completely forewarned and prepared." And he concluded: "I beg of you to continue with us in the supreme and decisive hours of the struggle for the future of Europe."

The scene was set, therefore, for what was to prove to be the decisive deception of Neptune. At 7:30 P.M. on June 8, after it had become evident that Rundstedt had ordered the mobile divisions of Fifteenth Army to go to the assistance of Seventh Army in Normandy, Garbo was given a prefatory message to send to his controller at Madrid to ensure that what followed was read personally by General Erich Kuhlenthal, chief of the German service there: "Have had a very busy and anxious day. Hope to give you what I consider to be my most important report to date. Trust you will be standing by at 22 hours GMT."

In the first minutes of June 9, Garbo's wireless operator, who was really a British signals sergeant, began to transmit a message that took 129 minutes to send. In it Garbo reported that his three best agents, Freddy, Dick, and Desmond (none of whom existed and all of whom had been invented by the XX-Committee and paid for Kuhlenthal), had returned to London and reported personally to Garbo on the whereabouts and activities of "Army Gruppe Patton" in eastern and southeastern England. Garbo warned Berlin that the Normandy operation was a trap, and that the main operation was about to take place near Calais. He drew attention to the arrival in London of the U.S. chiefs of staff, the ambiguous statements by General de Gaulle and the Belgian prime minister indicating the imminence of further landings near the Franco-Belgian frontier. He spoke, too, of a visit to the army group by King George VI. And then he concluded with this imprecation:

I trust you will submit my reports for urgent consideration by our High Command. Moments may be decisive at the present time. Before they take a false step through lack of full knowledge of the facts they ought to have at their disposal all the present information. I transmit this report with the conviction that the present assault is a trap set with the purpose of making us move all our reserves in a rushed strategic re-disposition which we would later regret.

Upon reading the report, Kuhlenthal rewrote it and then sent it to the Sicherheitsdienst in Berlin for comment and transmission to

Hitler's headquarters at Berchtesgaden. At H-Hour, Ultra from France sprang to life as the Germans were forced to use their wireless for their most urgent communications. An early Ultra showed that mobile—and very formidable—reinforcements were already on the move from Fifteenth Army in the Pas de Calais Normandy when Kuhlenthal received the trusty Garbo's warning. Air force decrypts showed that the Germans were concentrating large forces of antiaircraft artillery at certain points on the Seine where the divisions would cross into Normandy. Also, alert and action messages were being broadcast by the BBC to the French and Belgian resistance networks in the Calais area, which indicated imminent landings.

When Garbo's warning arrived at Sicherheitsdienst headquarters on the Berkerstrasse in Berlin, therefore, an SD analyst wrote on Kuhlenthal's message:

The dispatch is believable. The reports received in the last week from the [Garbo] enterprise have been confirmed almost without exception and are to be described as especially valuable. The main line of enquiry must now be concentrated on the enemy group of forces in eastern and southeastern England.

Garbo's warning was then sent on to Colonel Friedrich-Adolf Krummacher, chief of intelligence on Hitler's personal military staff, in the Strub infantry barracks near Berchtesgaden. As he read Garbo's report Krummacher underlined the phrases "diversionary manoeuvre," "purpose to entice enemy reserves into bridge-head in order to then launch decisive assault in another place." Krummacher then added this comment: "Underlines the opinion already formed by us . . . that a further attack is to be expected in another place." After "another place" he wrote in parentheses, "Belgium?" During the afternoon of the June 9, Garbo's message was relayed to Colonel General Alfred Jodl, Hitler's chief of operations, who sent it to Hitler with the comment that it might be read in conjunction with the news contained in the intercepted BBC messages activating the Belgian resistance movement.

Later that same afternoon Hitler read the warning from Garbo. Largely because it was from the Pas de Calais that at any moment he intended to launch his missile bombardment of London, Hitler decided that the movement of the Fifteenth Army tank and infantry reinforcements to Normandy should be stopped. He then gave the orders, and early—at about 0730 hours—on Saturday, June 10, Field Marshal Keitel, chief of the German supreme command, telephoned

Rundstedt at his headquarters at Saint-Germain-en-Laye just outside Paris. Rundstedt then directed that "as a consequence of information which has just been received," Fifteenth Army's orders were canceled and the divisions involved were to remain under Fifteenth Army command.

In turn, Hitler ordered reinforcements to the Calais area. On D-Day the Fifteenth Army had three tank and nineteen infantry and parachute divisions. A month later twenty-two infantry and two tank divisions were still there waiting idly and expectantly but fruitlessly for the army group that never existed. And as Sir Ronald Wingate, deputy chief of the London Controlling Section, was to remember of that evening, when it became evident from Ultra in London that Hitler had issued—and then canceled—his fateful order:

It was a frightful movement—there were those big red blobs on the war maps moving towards Normandy all the time. . . . Then Joan Bright [a secretary who kept the "Black Book" of Ultras in the war room] came in and said there was a message which might interest us. . . . We looked at the Ultra—and there it was: Hitler had cancelled [his orders]. . . . [Field Marshal] Brooke's attitude was the oddest. He said that if Hitler was such a bloody fool why had it taken us so long to beat him? Then he stalked off. The P.M. came in with Stewart Menzies and the P.M. said this was the crowning achievement of the long and glorious history of the British Secret Service—or something like that. [36]

9 VALKYRIE

With the Allied armies established in France, Montgomery prepared his forces for the breakout from Normandy. At the same time, both "C" and Donovan were informed that the Black Orchestra's plan for the assassination of Hitler and the seizure of power in Germany were ready. Both spymasters informed their governments. In a long "top secret, eyes only" signal to Eisenhower on June 29, General George Marshall advised that the British chiefs of staff felt "the possibility of German generals taking over from Hitler should not influence strategy at this time," and that the "foundation" of Allied strategy should remain the "continued use of maximum force wherever the enemy can be induced to fight." [37]

With the knowledge that Hitler's assassination might be imminent, Montgomery began to plan his breakout operations Goodwood and Cobra. By late June the main elements of eight panzer divisions had been identified on the Caen sector of the front, sent there by Hitler in the belief that it would be the British who would break out of the lodgment area, that it was from the British army he had the most to fear, and that the British would aim at (a) the missile emplacements in the Pas de Calais because they were making life almost impossible in London and southern England and at (b) Paris because of the old principal of geopolitics that "he who held Paris held France."

Also, Hitler revealed the poverty of his intelligence in Allied territory and the continuing effectiveness of the Fortitude threat against Calais when on July 8 he sent his commanders in the west a fresh directive in which he stated that Army Group Patton "will probably attempt a second landing in the Fifteenth Army's sector, all the more so, as public opinion will press for the elimination of the sites of the long-range weapons firing on London." [38]

But what Montgomery intended to do was continue to pin the Fifteenth Army to the Calais sector by deception and threat and to continue drawing the eight panzer divisions on the British sector in order to "write them down." Then, at the right tactical and psychological moment, Montgomery proposed to unleash the American armies in the Saint-Lô sector against the weakest part of Rommel's front and head across France to the German frontier. That strategy displayed a keen knowledge of the psychological elements of the battle: the German preoccupation with British rather than American intentions; the excellence of the British army in defense; the excellence of the U.S. Army in the offensive; and the knowledge that the German army would collapse or find itself in a civil war with the SS if and when Hitler was assassinated.

As Montgomery prepared his army first for Goodwood, a gigantic attack to *appear* to the Germans as if the Allies were about to break into the Pas de Calais and capture Paris, Hitler himself prepared for the offensive by sacking the entire German supreme command in the west. He kept only Rommel, who remained chief of Army Group B, the main German defensive force in the west; he replaced Rundstedt with Field Marshal Gunther von Kluge, who was until recently commander in chief of the German central group of armies on the Russian front.

As the armies assembled, word reached "C" that an attempt on the life of Hitler was imminent. He passed that information to Clement Attlee. On July 12, eight days before a British-manufactured bomb was due to explode under Hitler's map table at his noonday conference, Churchill was reminded in Parliament of the advice he had given earlier to the German people, that they should overthrow "their Nazi taskmasters." Churchill was asked if he would now make a statement to encourage them further to revolution. Churchill replied: "I am very glad to be reminded of that statement, to which I strongly adhere. I think it has been repeated in other forms by the Foreign Secretary and other Ministers. At any rate, it would certainly be a very well-advised step on the part of the Germans." [39]

As a prelude to Goodwood, RAF ground attack aircraft, alerted perhaps by Ultra, attacked Rommel in his staff car on July 17 on the road near Livarot. Rommel was badly wounded and had to be evacuated from the front. Then, as the German army group was plunged into chaos with the loss of their commanding general, Montgomery's British and Canadian armies delivered their left hook at Caen. Kluge was taken by surprise—he had expected this attack from another direction three or four days later—as fifteen hundred tanks and 250,000 Britons and Canadians attacked the German lines near Caen, jumping off into the fields of high-standing corn by a ghostly artificial moonlight produced by hundreds of searchlights playing upon the undersides of the thick cloud.

Supported by the heavy naval guns of three monitors, *Roberts*, *Mauritius*, and *Enterprise*, at 5:30 A.M. the artillery of an entire British army hit the thick German antiaircraft defenses. Then came the first waves of the 4,500 heavy, medium, and light bombers and fighters that supported Goodwood. The day was fine and clear, with practically no wind, and an infantryman waiting to attack recorded how

high in the sky and away to our left a faint and steady hum caught our attention and, as we watched, it grew into an insistent throbbing roar and the first aeroplanes appeared high up in the pale sky. Then the whole northern sky was filled with them as far as one could see—wave upon wave, stepped up one above another and spreading out east and west till it seemed there was no room for any more. As the first passed overhead guns began to open up on our right and the wonderful hush of the morning was finally shattered. The bombers flew in majestically and with a dreadful, unalterable dignity, unloaded and made for home; the sun, just coming over the horizon, caught their wings as they wheeled. Now hundreds of little black clouds were puffing round the bombers as they droned inexorably to their targets and occasionally one of them would heel over and plunge smoothly into the huge pall of smoke and dust that was steadily growing in the south. Everyone was out of their vehicles now, staring in awed wonder till the last wave dropped its bombs and turned away. Then the guns took up the steadily increasing crescendo the work which the bombers had begun. [40]

It was, as it remains, the mightiest employment of air power in support of an army in history. It was also the supreme moment in the long history of England as a world power. As the offensive ground on throughout July 18, 19, and 20 and finally ended on July 21, astounding news had reached the highest headquarters.

With Omar Bradley preparing to unleash the right hook of Montgomery's offensive, one code-named Cobra, just after noon on July 20, a bomb exploded under the map table in the room where Hitler was holding his main daily staff conference at his headquarters in the East Prussian woods near Rastenberg. It had been placed there by the chief of staff of the home army, Colonel Klaus Schenk Baron von Stauffenberg.

Having excused himself from the conference shortly before the bomb exploded, Stauffenberg watched the explosion from a knoll. When the wooden hut where the conference was taking place disintegrated with the blast, he left the headquarters for the special airfield at Rastenberg convinced that Hitler had been killed. He left assuming, as had been arranged, that the headquarter's communications center was being seized by the head of the German Army Signals Service, General Erich Fellgiebel, who had undertaken to suppress all communications with the outside world after the explosion except those of the conspirators.

But Hitler had not been killed, although four other conferees were either mortally wounded or dead. A heavy upright support of the map table over which the conferees were standing had deflected the blast away from him. His hair was set on fire, his right arm was paralyzed—temporarily—and both his eardrums were affected by the pressure waves of the explosion. One trousers leg was blown off, a weighty object had fallen across his back and buttocks, and he was badly bruised. But because Stauffenberg had left the scene immediately after the explosion, he had not seen Field Marshal Keitel, who had also survived, helping Hitler away from the wreckage of the hut. Had Stauffenberg remained a few extra minutes, the revolution might have taken a different course. Stauffenberg would probably have acted himself to suppress communications and directed that the code word Valkyrie be issued. That, perhaps, would have resulted in the successful seizure of power by the home army and the conspiracy's supporters in all the great capitals.

In the event, however, communications with the outside world had been only partly cut when Fellgiebel learned that Hitler was still alive. Fellgiebel's nerve then failed him, and he did not telephone home army headquarters to warn the conspirators that Hitler was still alive; worse still, when Keitel came to Fellgiebel's office and ordered him to restore all signals services, Fellgiebel obeyed. At that point the plot began to collapse.

As for Hitler, he was convinced that the bomb had been planted by the British secret service and in retaliation ordered that a V1 rocket be fired at maximum tempo against London. Hitler was wrong: Menzies's service had played no part in the attempt to kill him, although the bomb did prove to have been SOE in origin, part of the stores captured in the 1943 *ratissages* against the French resistance movement. While Menzies had received intelligence from one of the plotters' emissaries, Otto John, on or about July 18 or 19 in Lisbon, that an attempt on the life of Hitler was imminent, the Whitehall intelligence community gave the appearance at least of having been taken by surprise at the attack. As Field Marshal Sir Alan Brooke, chief of the Imperial General Staff, recorded in his diary:

*July 21*st. This morning when I turned on the 8 A.M. news I was astounded to hear of the attempt on Hitler's life, although this was exactly what I had been expecting for some time.

Cadogan, the other official immediately involved, exclaimed irritably in his diary on July 21:

Papers full of attempt on Hitler's life. Don't know what it means. Not v. much, I think. Possibly an excuse for a purge. Anyhow, it seems that he has stamped on any opposition. Talk with [Eden] and others about it at 11.30. "Others" rather unduly excited about it. I threw a few little cold douches. . . . 4.30 another meeting with [Eden] and Germany, but we have *no* news.

Churchill visited Montgomery at his headquarters in Normandy on July 20, as Montgomery waited for Bradley to start the Cobra offensive calculated to burst open the German line and start the campaign of movement. Churchill said nothing that has been recorded until July 23, when he remarked to a group of airmen that the Germans had begun to shoot each other, and that "it might be that the fighting might come to an end earlier than we have the right to say." [41] It therefore remains one of the puzzling aspects of the July 20 assassination attempt that so few British officials other than Brooke appeared to take much interest in the implications of the plot. This was even more puzzling in light of the fact that much was known at Broadway about the attempt, although to prevent gossip "C" suppressed circulation of Ultra relating to the plot.

The first signal indicating that an attempt had taken place was decrypted by Bletchley during the evening of July 20. Originated by the German naval command in the west and signed by Grand Admiral Karl Doenitz, the naval commander in chief, the message stated:

(1) Attempt on the Fuehrer's life was made by a clique of Generals who had undertaken a military Putsch. The heads of this clique are General Fromm, General Hoepner, and Generalfeldmarshall von Witzleben.

(2) In place of General Fromm, Reichsfuhrer SS Himmler will take over [as commander in chief of the reserve army in Berlin].

(3) The Navy will institute immediate alarm readiness.

(4) Orders to the Navy in this connection by C. in C. of the Navy only. Orders from Army "H"* authorities are not to be obeyed.

(5) Requests and instructions from the Reichsfuhrer SS are to be complied with.

(6) Arrange for all officers to be informed immediately.

Long live our Fuehrer,

Doenitz, Admiral of the Fleet

Meanwhile, Hitler, Goering, and Doenitz had made a radio broadcast, which was circulated in London at about midnight on 20–21 July, revealing that there had been a plot in the German army to kill Hitler and make peace. That broadcast was followed by a series of odd orders instructing all naval personnel that they were not to obey any army signals and, within the navy, only those signed by Grand Admiral Doenitz. Also, the Fleet Training Unit ordered the cruisers *Scheer* and *Hipper*, which were both in German ports, at thirty minutes past midnight on July 21 that the "sail-training ship *Horst Wessel*" and the cruisers were "to have everything on board ready at short notice without actually raising steam." Further orders would follow. Menzies believed that Hitler or some of his subordinates, particularly Goering, might be arranging their escape.

Following the *Horst Wessel* signals, there was a pause in the special series of decrypts that reached Menzies's desk until this fragment of a proclamation to the German armed forces by Field Marshal

*Army "H" was the official designation of the home army, the center of the revolt.

Witzleben, the titular head of the conspiracy, was intercepted from the naval traffic of the German naval command in Italy:

From C-in-C Armed Forces, von Witzleben.
    To "M" Ops
    FRR* Offizier Cypher
    1. The Fuehrer, Adolf Hitler, is dead. An unscrupulous clique of front-shy party leaders has taken advantage of the situation by attempting to attack the embattled front in the rear and to seize power for self-seeking purposes.
    2. In this hour of great——

The signal was interrupted for some reason at that point, but it was resumed and intercepted by Bletchley a little later:

(2) In this hour of greatest peril, the Government of the Reich has declared a state of emergency in order to maintain law and order, and has appointed me as Commander in Chief of the Armed Forces and also as——

Again the signal was broken off, this time for good, and later Ultra, again suppressed by "C," reflected the fact that there was a little revolt going on within German naval headquarters at San Remo. There were several instances of such minor rebellions, but all they achieved was to feed the firing squads.

As for Donovan's service, the best it could contribute immediately was a summary prepared by an OSS analyst, Walter Langer, who contended that Hitler had staged the attack himself as a repeat performance of the Munich *burbergbraukeller* episode of November 1939 and with the same purpose—to rally the German nation behind him.

Suspecting that "C" was withholding intelligence, Colonel John Haskell, a senior officer of OSS, called on Menzies and *demanded* that "Broadway give us any information on the subject in return for our valuable 'Breakers' material," Breakers being Dulles's code name for the anti-Hitler conspiracy. [42] Dulles was no better informed than "C"; nonetheless, he sent one of his officers, Walter Bell, a son of the bishop of Chichester who had had important contacts with the conspirators, to David Bruce with a short report in which he did not reveal his sources. When Bruce read the bulletin, he wrote in his diary:

---

*The prefix "FRR" was used only for messages to or from Hitler. "Offizier Cypher" was a special variant of the *Shark* U-boat cipher that could be read only by an officer. "M" = German naval command, Italy.

The truth is that, on the positive [espionage, as opposed to negative or counterespionage] intelligence side, Broadway is lamentably weak—especially as regards Germany—and most of the reports they send us are duplicates of those already received by us from foreign secret intelligence services.

What "C" knew and Bruce did not—for Bruce was not cleared to read Ultra—was that there was a very large scale purge going on throughout the German Reich and especially in the higher circles of the German command in Paris. As Bradley prepared Cobra, the SS was arresting the chiefs of the operations, signals, and supply services of the German armies in the west. Nothing could have suited Montgomery better at that date, for Cobra was launched under another terrific bombardment on July 25; it foundered, and then the German front burst open in what Bradley called later "the most decisive battle of our war in Western Europe."

The German front collapsed as Bradley, with the speed and violence of a hollow-charged shell, brought Third Army out of hiding in the woods in the Cherbourg peninsula, and passed it through First Army; it then struck out first for Avranches at the base of the Breton peninsula and then turned right for the great port of Brest and left for Chartres and central France.

With the French nation in a state of general insurrection nourished by arms, munitions, clothes, money, and food delivered by air by SOE and OSS, and with Himmler hanging the first of the eight senior officers involved in the July 20 plot, Hitler made a last attempt to restore his rule in Western Europe.

Despite the breakout, there was still some organization left in the German army in the west. On August 2 Field Marshal von Kluge received a fresh directive from Hitler. With all Patton's supplies passing down the single road to Avranches, if Avranches were retaken, all Patton's spearheads would be cut off root and branch from their supply dumps. They would be virtually surrounded, and when they surrendered, Kluge's panzers could then strike north back into the heart of the Allied concentration area in Normandy. If the plan bordered upon irreality, it lacked nothing in daring.

Kluge replaced all armor in what was left of the German line, concentrated at least four panzer divisions and one infantry corps at Sourdeval, a little metal-working town connected to Avranches by a secondary road that wound through heavily wooded countryside intersected by deep valleys (the area was known as "Little Switzerland"), and then prepared to strike by night through another small town, Mortain, to retake Avranches only twenty or so miles away on the coast.

Little was known at Montgomery's or Bradley's headquarters about the operation until four days later because nothing about it had so far been committed to wireless. But at 2:00 P.M. on August 6, an Ultra was decoded that showed the German air force had been requested to provide nightfighter protection for the Second SS Panzer Division during an attack through Mortain in the general direction of Avranches. [43]

Only a few minutes later the watchmaster at Bletchley received a GAF decrypt that revealed the German Forty-seventh Infantry Corps would attack with the fighting battalions of four panzer divisions. Other decrypts then indicated that the time for the attack was 6:30 P.M. on that day, August 6. These signals were given ZZZZZ clear-the-line priority by Bletchley, and they reached Montgomery and Bradley in time to warn Patton and the commanding general of the U.S. Thirtieth Division at Mortain.

Forewarned, Bradley managed to get the entire strength of Ninth U.S. Tactical Air Force and the RAF's Eighty-third Group, one equipped with the first tank-busting rocket-firing Typhoons, into the air in time to hit the German attack as it jumped off at 6:30 A.M. on August 7. At the start a deep penetration was made, and Avranches was threatened. But in driving west, the German attack created a pocket that became larger the deeper the panzers drove. The farther they drove, the more liable they became to envelopment by three Allied armies, the Canadian First to the north, the U.S. Third to the south, and the U.S. First to the west. Dr. Ralph Bennett, one of the senior watchmasters on duty at Bletchley, recalled the scene at Bletchley as it became clear that the Germans were facing an immense disaster between Mortain and Avranches:

Excitement at the significance of the intelligence we were producing at a moment which might be decisive for the whole campaign was already intense . . . at midnight, but it soon rose still higher. Good fortune sent me on duty then, and I can still vividly recall the exhilaration of the next few hours; in recollection they surpass even D-Day for the volume and importance of the information Ultra produced.

If the Falaise pocket was not completely closed, Bradley halted Third Army's march north to prevent a collision with the Canadians marching south; nevertheless the fighting elements of three armies, the Seventh, Panzergruppe West, and the SS in France, were trapped.

During Montgomery's operations leading up to Falaise, the Germans had lost 2,760 officers and 100,000 men, with only 12 percent of the losses being replaced. Now, at Falaise, they lost 14 generals, 3,219 officers, and 141,046 noncommissioned officers and men.

Even as Kluge sought to rally the front, Himmler's inquisitions established that Kluge, the field marshal commanding the German armies in France, had been party to the plot against the life of Hitler. He was, therefore, already suspect when on August 15 he vanished in the vicinity of Falaise and was not heard from for fourteen hours. At his conference on August 31 Hitler claimed knowledge that

Field Marshal von Kluge planned to lead the whole of the Western Army into capitulation and to go over himself to the enemy. . . . It seems that the plan miscarried owing to an enemy fighter-bomber attack. He had sent away his staff officer, British-American patrols advanced, but apparently no contact was made. . . . Nevertheless the British have reported being in contact with a German general. [44]

The truth of Hitler's assertion, which has never been clarified, is impossible to gauge. Blumentritt, whom Kluge retained as chief of staff to the commander in chief west when Rundstedt was recalled and retired, knew more about this contact than he revealed to his Allied interrogators when he was captured. So did Speidel who, when Rommel was wounded, remained as chief of staff to Kluge as commander in chief of Army Group B. Like General Christiansen in Holland, Speidel may well have had the wireless capability to communicate with "C." That there was radio contact between someone in a high place in the German command and "C" seems evident, for a month later, when Blumentritt visited Hitler's headquarters in East Prussia, Field Marshal Keitel indicated so when he repeated Hitler's statement of August 31 that "according to reliable informations" Kluge "wanted to play the Normandy army into the hands of the Allies."

At the end of the war, *Time* magazine printed a similar report about what Hitler called "the worst day of my life":

The Road to Avranches—One day last August [Kluge] suddenly left his headquarters on the Western Front. . . . With some of his staff, Kluge drove to a spot on a lonely road near Avranches in northwestern France. There he waited, hour after hour, for a party of U.S. Third Army officers with whom he had secretly arranged to discuss surrender. They did not appear. Fearing betrayal, Kluge hurried back to his headquarters.

Whatever the truth, Blumentritt always maintained that on August 14 Kluge set out for the headquarters of Obergruppenführer SS Sepp

Dietrich, commander of the First SS Panzer Corps, at the château of Fontaine l'Abbé near Bernay. Kluge spent the night at Dietrich's command post and left next morning, he said to see Obergruppen-führer SS Paul Hausser, who had succeeded to the command of the Seventh Army when its commander, Dollman, dropped dead of a heart attack.

Kluge set out for the village church of Necy for the meeting with Hausser at between 10:00 and 11:00 A.M. With Kluge was his son, a wireless truck, a small escort, and some aides-de-camp. The weather was clear and perfect for the *jabos*, the low-level Allied fighter bombers that infested the skies over the area through which Kluge drove. As Blumentritt related, Kluge was caught by *jabos* near Ammeville. The wireless truck was destroyed, which prevented Kluge from contacting his headquarters. Kluge collapsed into a ditch and remained there while his aide, Tangermann, found a bicycle and pedaled to the church at Necy where Kluge was to meet Hausser. When Tangermann arrived he discovered that Hausser had come and gone. And (as Blumentritt recorded) when an entire day passed without Kluge returning to his headquarters, or without word being received from anybody in his party, Blumentritt was forced to report to the German supreme command in East Prussia that "in spite of seeking everywhere v. Kluge could not be found and an accident had to be reckoned with."

Hitler then ordered Hausser to take command of the army group for the time being. Kluge arrived at his headquarters at about midnight on the night of August 15–16; Blumentritt reported the fact to OKW, and just after daybreak on August 16 "a most peculiar" signal arrived for Kluge that reflected "the highest degree of suspicion" and as a result "offended the feldmarschall very much."

Later on August 16 Field Marshal Model, who until recently had commanded the northern group of armies on the Russian front, arrived without notice at the Château De La Roche Guyon and took over command of the German armies in the west from Kluge. While retaining the services of Blumentritt, Model relieved Speidel as chief of staff and ordered both Kluge and Speidel back to Germany. Three hours later Kluge took a cyanide pill on the roadside near Verdun.

At about the same time, Stulpnagel, lately military governor of France, was ordered back to Germany to face a court of honor. But instead of doing so, he waded into the Canal des Mort Hommes on the old World War I battlefield of the Somme in 1916 and botched an attempt to shoot himself. Though blinded, he was returned to

Germany, restored to good health, and then hanged for high treason. Throughout the German Reich a total of 4,980 men and women, the remnants of the social elite of Germany, were arrested and executed. The last flicker of military resistance to Hitler's rule and to the Nazi regime was vanquished, eliminating any chance of an early surrender. The process of the nazification of the army was completed, ensuring that the armed forces would fight to the bitter end.

On arrival at his home at Freudenstadt in south Germany, Speidel was arrested by an SS officer and an armed guard. He was then taken to the Gestapo jail on the Prinzalbrechstrasse in Berlin. There, his inquisitors questioned him about his conduct and that of Rommel. The interrogations suggested that both men had had treasonable association with the British. General Speidel defeated all attempts to make him confess to allegations that by his actions he had opened the Atlantic wall to the Allies on D-Day.

But if Speidel saved himself, he failed to save Rommel, who was at his home at Herrlingen near Stuttgart, recovering satisfactorily from his wounds received during the fighter bomber attack in Normandy. On October 14 Rommel received two General Staff officers, Burgdorff and Meisel, at his home. He was given a choice: if he took a poison capsule, which they would provide, his wife and son would be allowed to continue their lives without interference from the state, and Rommel would be given a state funeral at which Field Marshal von Rundstedt would represent Hitler and make an oration on behalf of Germany and the General Staff; if he declined to take the capsule, he would be placed on public trial for having committed high treason against the state and then hanged. Rommel elected to take the former course and was dead by the end of the day.

By September 1, meanwhile, the German army had been defeated in the west, Paris and Brussels and most of France and Belgium had been liberated, and the remnants of the German army was retreating, having lost 500,000 men, half of them prisoners, and a tank army of 2,000 armored fighting vehicles. Montgomery was made a field marshal and then relieved by Eisenhower as land forces commander on the grounds that American public opinion demanded a more prominent place in the command for Bradley.

"C's" hidden presence had ensured that Neptune would become not just a victory, but a triumph. "C" now began to turn his attention to the traditional enemy, Russia. In consequence, his career as Churchill's spymaster entered its most troubled period.

Nine

Overlord

September 1944–May 1945

1 THE NEW DARK AGE

On the night of June 12, eleven V1 flying bombs crossed the English coast. It was a misfire—over five hundred of the missiles were to have been launched, but the bombardment was delayed by the aerial offensive against the launch sites in the Pas de Calais. There was a pause, and three nights later 244 missiles were launched from fifty-five sites, 144 crossed the English coast, and 73 reached London. These killed fifty people and injured some four hundred more. Thereafter, the intensity of the attack mounted, and on Sunday, June 18, the full menace of these deadly little weapons was demonstrated to the Whitehall hierarchy.

That Sunday morning there was a service of thanksgiving for the successful invasion of Europe held at the Royal Military Chapel, a late Regency church of great beauty at Wellington Barracks, a stone's throw from Menzies's headquarters and home. Eisenhower's chief of staff, General Bedell Smith, was to have been present but was forced to cancel. The chapel was crowded with worshipers drawn mainly from the upper reaches of the Allied high command, the military district of London, and the court. Elisabeth Sheppard-Jones would recall what happened just before her legs were blown off:

The congregation rose to its feet. . . . In the distance hummed faintly the engine of a flying bomb. "We praise thee, O God: we acknowledge Thee to be the Lord," we, the congregation sang. The dull burr became a roar, through which our voices could only faintly be heard. "All the earth doth worship Thee: the Father everlasting." The roar stopped abruptly as the engine cut out. . . . The *Te Deum* soared again into the silence. "To Thee all Angels cry aloud: the Heavens, and all the Powers therein." Then there was a noise so loud it was as if all the waters and the winds in the world had come together in mighty conflict, and the Guards' Chapel collapsed upon us in a bellow of bricks and mortar. . . . One moment I was singing the *Te Deum*, and the next I lay in dust and blackness, aware of one thing only—that I had to go on breathing.

A flying bomb had appeared out of the sky low over Broadway. Robert Cecil, "C's" personal assistant, felt it had been hit by ground fire. In falling, a wing touched the roof of Queen Anne's Mansions, another government office block about 100 yards up Broadway from SIS headquarters. This deflected it slightly from its earthward trajectory toward Broadway, the highest building in the street, in the direction of the chapel about 150 yards across the rooftops from Broadway.

The missile hit the chapel at about four hundred miles per hour, and two thousand pounds of aluminized high explosive exploded as Colonel Lord Edward Hay, commander of the Westminster Garrison and "C's" close friend, was taking his place at the lectern to read the lesson. Hay and 130 of the congregation were killed, 68 were seriously wounded, and almost everyone else in the chapel was injured to some degree.

The windows of "C's" headquarters at Broadway were blown in by the blast, the ceiling plaster was brought down in most offices, and the building's foundations were badly shaken by the shock waves. That it did not collapse was due to the fact that it was a steel-framed building. Although there were no casualties at Broadway, where some four hundred of Menzies's staff were at work, fifteen people working in Queen Anne's Mansions, almost next door, were seriously injured by blast and flying glass. In Cecil's view, if the weapon's wing had not tipped the roof of Queen Anne's Mansions, the V1 would have hit the south side of Broadway at about the fourth floor—the SIS executive floor.

Listed by the City of Westminster Civil Defence as Incident 1861, the first report of the explosion reached sector headquarters at 11:27 A.M., for one of the civil defense controllers happened to be driving past Buckingham Palace when the bomb made its dive. His report consisted of three words: "Many shrouds required." Close by, too, was Winston Churchill's wife, Clementine, who was visiting her daughter, Mary. They saw the bomb diving—toward Downing Street, they thought, and noticed many people in the park out for a morning walk throw themselves to the ground to avoid the blast. And as the civil defense controller further reported: "Notwithstanding the enormous amount of debris, it was all removed and the last body recovered within 48 hours. A large quantity of valuable jewellery worn by the casualties was recovered, and many notable people were killed."

Until April 1945 a steady drizzle of flying bombs and rockets struck the British capital and the countryside around it, damaging two million homes and other buildings and killing or injuring some thirty thousand people. To make this latest weapon the greater menace, the Germans were perfecting methods of launching the flying bombs from aircraft and the rockets from submerged submarines. Also, there was evidence of German interest in devising warheads that contained not just high explosive, but also radiological, chemical, and biological contaminants. In an Ultra dated November 1943, a German scientist reviewed evidence that the Russians had used biological warfare agents against the German army, updated by various advices that the Germans were manufacturing at least one nerve gas, Sarin, and might be building a 100,000 kw nuclear pile at Hechingen near Stuttgart with which to produce radioactive poisons. Scant as the evidence was, "C" had now to take seriously yet another new and deadly form of warfare, one that came to be called Cebar.*

A medical doctor and biochemist, Dr. R. Truscoe, was called upon for the inquiry that followed, to study and report on the probability of a Cebar attack against London and the other great cities and the effects of such an attack. Truscoe was described as being "deeply and widely trained in Intelligence," "a man of extraordinary intellect and learning," and "a man who had spent considerable time in Russia" in 1940–41 studying Soviet Cebar capabilities. He began studies of

---

*Chemical, biological, and radiological warfare.

German Cebar capabilities in September 1944, and his report to "C" was both an encouragement and a warning.

Biological warfare had been used on a small scale in World War I by German agents in the United States to infect with anthrax horses and donkeys being shipped to France. Between the wars the Germans gave no serious consideration to Cebar warfare, except in the production of nerve gases known as "G-Agents." But in 1940 the Germans discovered that the French had been researching the production of Cebar agents and thus established a small committee. By 1942 a decrypt of an army high command quoted an order from Hitler that no preparations were to be made for the offensive use of biological warfare, but that intensive studies were to begin into defensive measures against all forms of biological attack. The Blitzarbieter committee was then established under the direction of a certain Dr. Kliewe, a senior medical adviser to the German armed forces who was known to be an expert in biological warfare agents. The committee was divided into four sections: human, veterinary, agricultural, and ordnance.

Work was carried out at the Kliewe Laborator at Giessen, and some field trials of agents were held near Munster. An operation known as the Nesselstedt Project near Posen, Poland, was completed too late to be utilized and was captured by the Russians. Kliewe, reported Truscoe, had concentrated most of his attention on anthrax as an instrument to devastate the cattle population of target countries, thus destroying a major food source. Research was also extended to staphylococcus and the organisms causing typhoid, cholera, and plague. Limited work was done on the preparation of synthetic media suitable for the mass production of bacteria. The combination of mustard gas and biological warfare agents was also considered for use. Work on Rinderpest was abandoned, because of the poor strain of virus produced, but Kliewe's work on the potato beetle and grain rust suggested that these, at least, could be employed as a weapon.

As Truscoe reported, on the basis of his own knowledge and the Broadway files, Himmler was the only influential Nazi who believed in the offensive use of biological warfare. Hitler maintained that only defensive studies were to be conducted until the end of the war. No first-class civilian bacteriologists were diverted from their normal activities to assist in the biological warfare program. Lacking the full support of the German leadership, the program was only moderately successful, although one weapon, the KC50PB bomb, was produced.

German use of biological warfare weapons was not, therefore, to be considered a principal threat. The same, however, could not be said in the field of radiological warfare. There, very small quantities of radioactive waste, or of the metallic chemical element tantalum, could kill, incapacitate, or otherwise neutralize the centers responsible for the supreme direction of the war both in England and the United States. In consequence, Operation Peppermint was undertaken.

Specialist officers were sent to all areas of Britain, equipped with Geiger counters specially produced in the United States, and all commands were instructed to be vigilant for signs that radiological substances had been employed by the enemy, in particular the unexplained fogging of film and the outbreak of "epidemic diseases of unknown etiology."

The missile era had begun. So far, therefore, "C" had watched the world proceed from Victoria's reign, when, as Churchill attested, "the world was fair to see," to the threshold of missiles, atomic bombs, and Cebar. That combination, as Churchill stated on New Year's Day of 1945, constituted "the very darkest time." As the new dark age arrived, the Anglo-American alliance began to disintegrate under the multiple pressures of uncertainty, a war that seemed unending, new forebodings in the direction of science, and the inadequacy of generals and statesmen.

2   "MAJOR STRATEGIC AND POLITICAL ERROR"

As the summer of 1944 ended without a German surrender, Churchill's apprehensions about Russian intentions mounted as the Red Army ejected the Germans from White Russia, entered Poland, Finland, Romania, Bulgaria, and neared the East Prussian frontier. By October they had captured Belgrade and had encircled Budapest. At the end of the year, when the Russian army was about to enter central Europe, the prime minister wrote to Anthony Eden, "Never forget that the Bolsheviks are crocodiles." He felt that Britain was "approaching a showdown with the Russians about their Communist intrigues in Italy, Yugoslavia, and Greece." Soviet activities in Poland caused him to write again to Eden that he feared "very great evil may come upon the world," that the Russians were "drunk with victory" and there was "no length they may not go to." As the old anti-Russian passions erupted, and as Eisenhower's generalship came into question during the Battle for France, Churchill had a fresh vision that might end the war in 1944.

By mid-June, "C" had begun to produce Ultra reflecting Hitler's acute concern for the safety of his Balkans oil, iron ore, chrome, and other raw materials essential to the ability of Germany to continue the war. This concern was not transitory, it was a permanent feature of his strategic thought. If he lost the Balkans, he lost the war, as the kaiser had done when he lost Bulgaria in 1918. It followed, therefore, that he would do all in his power to prevent the loss of the Balkans.

Ever vigilant for opportunities for stratagem, soon after he read the first of "C's" Ultras, Churchill conceived a plan called Armpit. With the object of drawing the maximum number of German forces away from the French and Russian fronts, and to forestall the entry of the Red Army into central Europe, Churchill recommended the elimination of Anvil, the landing of a Franco-American army group on the Mediterranean coast of France, and the use of the forces to be employed in Anvil for a "stab into the armpit of Europe." As Churchill visualized the operation, powerful forces would land in Istria, strike through the Ljubljana Gap in the Julian Alps, gain the Danube plain, and occupy Vienna and Prague ahead of the Russians before marching on southeastern Germany in the area of Munich. It was a brilliant, imaginative concept, but it proved too novel for most of the members of the Anglo-American supreme command. Churchill began to press Armpit on FDR and the U.S. chiefs with all the power and persuasion at his command, while "C" nourished the political and strategical arguments favoring Armpit with a stream of Ultras.

By mid-June Ultra had shown Hitler's concern over the situation that would develop if the Allied armies in Italy managed to get to the Alps that summer. Any Allied landing in Istria—the mountainous peninsula projecting into the northern Adriatic between Trieste and Fiume, and the area in which the Armpit landings were to take place—would be, as Hitler told General Warlimont, deputy chief of operations at German supreme headquarters, "a matter of the utmost danger," one that "could produce catastrophic results." [1]

"C's" decrypts spoke, too, of Hitler's fears concerning the establishment of Allied heavy bomber bases in the Po Valley, from which the Allies would be able to intensify their attacks on those war industries that had been moved to central Europe beyond the easy range of bombers based in Britain. Rather than risk this, Hitler declared, he was prepared to reinforce the Italian front. Other decrypts showed also that Hitler was not concerned about Anvil, that he felt he could withdraw from southern France without sacrificing any territory of strategic or economic value and without giving the Allies any airfields closer to his key war industries than they possessed already. The arguments for Armpit were, therefore, formidable.

Nevertheless, FDR and the U.S. chiefs of staff said no and kept saying no in what became the most furious debate on grand strategy of the war. They rejected the British proposals in language that, Churchill believed, was peremptory to the point of insult, although they were sent an Ultra that, Churchill advised Roosevelt in a special telegram, demonstrated anew Hitler's intense concern for the security of his southern front and his decision to reinforce that front even by taking divisions from the French and Russian fronts. Hitler had anticipated the Allies' next move and shown how greatly he feared it when he spoke of the "incalculable military and political consequences" of any breach of the northern Apennines and had declared therefore that they must be "the final blocking line"—the last line of defense before the Allied armies in Italy entered the inner defenses of the German Reich. [2]

Harold Macmillan was in London and with the prime minister when the reply of the American chiefs of staff came in, and he wrote of Churchill's attitude when he had read it:

It was not only a brusque but even an offensive refusal to accept the British plan. It so enraged the P.M. that he thought of replying to the President in very strong terms; but after consideration it was decided that the British Chiefs should reply formally that they could not change the advice that they were giving to His Majesty's Government to whom they had the duty of giving the best professional opinion which they could form. . . . I left him anxious and a little harassed, and I also strongly got the impression that, in view of the heavy contribution of the American forces to the European campaign and the general situation, we should have to give in if Eisenhower and Marshall insisted upon "Anvil." We can fight up to a point, we can leave on record for history to judge the reasoned statement of our views, and the historian will also see that the Americans have never answered an argument, never attempted to discuss or debate the points, but have merely given a flat negative and a somewhat Shylock-like insistence upon what they conceive to be their bargain. [3]

So Armpit was rejected. Churchill then wrote to FDR a long appreciation weighing the merits of the two operations. "I most earnestly beg you," he wrote in a covering telegram, "to examine this matter in detail for yourself." Churchill also asked the president to "take into consideration the very important information which General Menzies is sending you separately on my instructions." A special meeting of the Combined Chiefs of Staff, the Anglo-American supreme command, was held in Washington on June 29. There Churchill's advocacy was rejected again in terms that reflected the U.S. administration's suspicion of Britons bearing secret intelligence.

Underlying most if not all American attitudes when receiving British intelligence on major strategic issues was the fear that "C" was not above shaping British intelligence to enhance the attractiveness of British strategic proposals, proposals that were in turn intended to use American power to obtain British strategic ends in the Mediterranean theater.

The British representatives on the Combined Chiefs of Staff were "shocked by this dismissal of Britain's most secret source" and "made it clear" that the American military's doubts were not soundly based. Nonetheless, FDR, too, rejected Armpit. "My interests and hopes," he replied on June 29, "center on defeating the Germans in front of Eisenhower and driving on into Germany, rather than on limiting this action for the purpose of staging a full major effort in Italy." In rejecting Churchill's proposal, FDR made no reference to the Hitler directive sent to him by "C," which had seemed to Churchill to be the decisive factor. FDR did make a statement that showed his decision was made not on military but political grounds, for he faced a presidential election. For "purely political considerations" in the United States, he declared, "I should never survive even a slight setback in 'Overlord' " if it were known that he had diverted large forces in the Balkans.

The American decision produced a powerful adverse reaction within the British secret circle. Churchill ordered his York aircraft to be ready to fly to Washington, and he wired FDR that the British chiefs of staff were "deeply grieved," for he considered that here was the "first major strategic and political error for which we two have to be responsible." Churchill warned that by dividing the Allied force in Europe between two theaters, neither force would now be strong enough to defeat Germany that year. He deprecated a suggestion from FDR that the matter should be referred to Stalin for decision, pointing out that Stalin, on a "long term political view," might prefer that the American and British armies "should do their share in France in the very hard fighting that is to come, and that East, Middle, and Southern Europe should fall naturally into his control." He entered a "solemn protest" against the American position, then accepted General Marshall's strategic proposals. These abandoned the southern front as a main sector for an Allied advance into central Europe from which to force Hitler's surrender and to forestall the Russian advance.

When the U.S. Seventh and the French First armies landed near Marseilles on August 15, 1945, they encountered little or no opposition, for most of Army Group "G" had long since been sucked into the Normandy battle.

3 PHILBY'S PROMOTION

After Neptune "C" began immediately to plan for the peace. As antagonisms rent the Grand Alliance and made it seem likely that the peace would be precarious and troubled, his new policy was to place his services in what was a defensive mode, one calculated not only to protect England and the empire, but also to ensure that at the peace, Western Europe and Scandinavia remained secure against Communist and Fascist uprisings.

As part of the new defensive policy, "C" decided to reestablish Section IX, the old anti-Soviet division. The logical choice to be chief of the new section was Felix Cowgill, who had been responsible for anti-Soviet work in the Indian police and had been recruited into SIS as chief of the anti-Soviet section in 1939. Only after the war with Germany had become "serious" in 1940 had Cowgill accepted the post of chief of Section V. If Section IX was established, he would return to anti-Soviet work, in which he was an acknowledged specialist. Cowgill's wartime work against the Axis services had been outstanding; all the enemy services overseas were being defeated, largely through his work and the existence of Ultra. He was still young (forty-two) and fit, and by repute he was as dedicated an anti-Communist as either "C" himself or Vivian.

Yet Cowgill did have drawbacks. Through his zealous defense of the security of Ultra, the disclosure and circulation of which he severely limited, Cowgill had made enemies in high places in the service. Also, he had shown a tendency not to be able to work well with anyone other than the members of his own circle. This was not, it appears, a character defect but rather a reluctance to entrust a secret as priceless as Ultra to anyone he did not know well. His relationship with "C" had been excellent, and Menzies had formed a high opinion of his work.

On the other hand, he had made an enemy of Vivian, and that was dangerous not simply because Vivian had power or influence, but because Vivian was a man who believed in retribution. As an interim measure, "C" appointed Jack Currie, who was approaching the retirement age of sixty. All this was evident to Kim Philby, and by his own account Philby had several conversations with, and wrote several memoranda to, his Soviet controller about the future of Section IX. At length, as Philby recorded, his contact

posed what was to be a fateful question: what would happen if I were offered the post instead of Cowgill? I answered that it would mean a significant promotion and improve my chances of determining the course of events, including my own postings. He seemed satisfied, and said that he hoped to have definite instructions for me by the time of our next meeting.

He had. Headquarters had informed him that I must do everything, but *everything*, to ensure that I became head of Section IX. . . . I was enjoined to conduct my campaign against Cowgill with the greatest care. . . . I should take no overt measures to achieve my goal because, if things went wrong subsequently, I must be able to show that the position had been thrust on me. Every move in the campaign had to come, wherever possible, from someone else. In other words, I must find allies to fight my cause, and the best place to look for them was clearly among Cowgill's enemies. [4]

That Philby did with great skill, playing upon interservice rivalries and presenting himself subtly as the only alternative to Cowgill who would be able to work closely with the Security Service *and* the Americans. By September he had reached the denouement of his controller's scheme to make him head of the anti-Soviet section. The summons soon came, and as Philby went on to record of that critical meeting with "C":

It was by no means the first time I had visited the *arcana*. But on this occasion, Miss Pettigrew and Miss Jones, the Chief's secretaries, seemed especially affable as I waited in their room for the green light to go on. The green light flashed, and I went in. For the first time, the Chief addressed me as "Kim," so I knew that no last-minute hitch had occurred. He showed me Vivian's minute, and out of politeness I pretended to read it. He told me that he had decided to act on Vivian's proposal and offer me the immediate succession to Currie. Had I anything to say? I had. Using the sort of I-hope-I-am-not-speaking-out-of-turn-Sir approach, I said that the appointment had been offered to me presumably because of the well-known incompatibility between Cowgill and his opposite numbers in MI5. I hoped that I would be able to avoid such quarrels in future. But who could make predictions? I would be much happier in the job if I knew for certain that MI5, the people with whom I would be dealing daily, had no objection to my appointment. It would make me just that much more confident. Besides, MI5 approval, officially given, would effectively protect the service against criticism from that quarter.

Within a few days Philby was taking over from Currie. He then returned to see Menzies, for as he explained:

I suggested to the Chief that, to regularize the position of the new Section IX, I should draft myself a charter for his signature. I cannot remember its exact wording. But it gave me responsibility, under the Chief, for the collection and interpretation of information concerning Soviet and Communist espionage and subversion in all parts of the world outside British territory. It also enjoined me to maintain the closest liaison for the reciprocal exchange of intelligence on these subjects with MI5. The Chief added a final clause. I was on no account to have any dealings with any of the United States services. The war was not yet over, and the Soviet Union was our ally. There was no question of risking a leakage. The leakage which the Chief had in mind was a leakage from the United States services to the Russians. It was a piquant situation.

As for Cowgill:

In launching this intrigue I hoped that Cowgill would end by getting himself out. He did. As soon as my appointment became known, he demanded an interview with the Chief. I know nothing of the details of the meeting, but I never saw Cowgill again. He had submitted his resignation once too often. It was a pointless and fatal mistake. Within little more than a year, Sections V and IX were united, under my direction. There was no Cowgill to dispute my path. [5]

Philby was quite correct: the situation was piquant. By the time of his appointment as head of Section IX, it had become arguable that Donovan was on better terms with the Soviet intelligence services than he was with "C."

As a further expression of the "noble credulity" of FDR, and acting in the White House's belief that America and Russia had no problems between them that men of goodwill could not settle, Donovan had flown to Moscow at Christmas 1943 to meet with General P. N. Fitin, head of the Soviet external military intelligence service, and General A. P. Ossipov, who was responsible for Soviet guerrilla, sabotage, and subversion operations in German-occupied territory.

At that meeting, Donovan did something he never did with "C": he proposed a full intelligence alliance between the OSS and the NKVD (the Soviet secret service), in which they would establish missions in each other's capitals. Finding the agenda attractive, the Russians met Donovan immediately and, according Averell Harriman, the U.S. ambassador in Moscow, the "shop talk among spymasters went briskly." Although the Russians volunteered no information about their own methodology, they questioned Donovan "about the particular methods of spying, American style," how "the Americans introduced their agents into enemy territory, how these men were trained, and what special equipment they carried."

To the surprise of the Americans, who were used to dealing with a vast, mysterious, suspicious, and inefficient machine that made decisions almost always in weeks or months or frequently produced nothing but silence, agreement was reached there and then, something that had not occurred before in major matters and would recur only rarely, if at all. It was proposed and accepted that Donovan should send John Haskell to the NKVD; the NKVD would send one of its colonels, A. G. Grauer, to Donovan. Almost as startling was the fact that, in exchange for a telephone number where the NKVD could be contacted, Donovan directed that his agency return to the NKVD the 1,600 pages of NKVD cipher data captured from the Germans by U.S. forces in Italy. The ciphers were copies of those in use at that time between NKVD headquarters and NKVD representatives with the Soviet armies and were therefore of great interest and importance not only to the NKVD, but also to those responsible for Magic and Ultra.

This exchange of missions did not take place, however, largely because the head of the FBI, J. Edgar Hoover, protested to FDR that there were already too many NKVD officials in the United States. At that very moment the NKVD had succeeded in riddling the Manhattan Project, which created and manufactured the atomic bomb. Yet until long after FDR reluctantly directed that the exchange not take place "for the time being," Donovan sent the NKVD large quantities of U.S. intelligence about Germany along with technical devices such as microfilm cameras, readers, and printers. However, Donovan's scheme may not have been as altruistic as it seemed to "C," for as Harriman exclaimed when he heard of FDR's ban on the exchange, the U.S. embassy had

unsuccessfully attempted for the last two and a half years to penetrate sources of Soviet information and to get on a basis of mutual confidence and exchange.

Here, for the first time, we have penetrated one intelligence branch of the Soviet Government and, if pursued, I am satisfied this will be the opening door to far greater intimacy in other branches. If we now close the door on this branch of the Soviet Government after they have shown a cooperative spirit and good faith, I cannot express too strongly my conviction that our relations with the Soviet Government in other directions will be adversely affected.

But Hoover prevailed, and if Donovan displayed an anxiousness to collaborate with the NKVD, he showed no such inclination toward Broadway. As "C" learned, in the late summer of 1943, Donovan introduced a new training program for OSS officers and secret agents going abroad on active service, one that mentioned "colonialism" as an explicit OSS target along with nazism, fascism, and militarism. But the curriculum did *not* mention "communism" as a target, giving rise to the suspicion at Broadway that OSS was prepared to work with the NKVD against the British Empire. [6]

Following that discovery, "C" began to report a widening of "meddling" by OSS in Italy, Arabia, Turkey, Greece, and India. In India, as early as August 1943 OSS Washington was asked by "C" to refrain from political activities in Delhi after the Joint Intelligence Committee had reported that

troubles and difficulties have arisen largely as a result of unnecessary and often [?unwonted] penetration of and interference in India by the personnel of various US bodies. This cannot be compared with our own attempts to secure collaboration with the Americans in the South-West Pacific. This matter now requires clearing up firmly.* [7]

But OSS interference in the affairs of the British Indian government were not cleared up firmly. By 1944 OSS clandestine relations

---

*These complaints were not unjustified. In the Donovan papers there is clear evidence in memoranda form that Donovan's agency was engaging in all forms of espionage against the raj in India without the knowledge even of the U.S. commander in the India-Burma theater, General Daniel I. Sultan. These activities were conducted under the code name Project Bingo, and the large-scale and widespread anti-British operations had as their basis an OSS desire to be in a position to assist U.S. commercial institutions in establishing footholds in the Indian empire. As Dr. William L. Langer, chief of the research and analysis branch of OSS, declared in a paper immediately after the end of the war in Europe in May 1945: "The British may naturally be assumed to take a dim view towards intelligence activities" in British India and Burma. He asked that Donovan should authorize the collection of Indian and Burmese identity papers, passports, motor car licenses, birth certificates, and other papers to enable members of OSS to operate under cover in those countries. He asked also that "intelligence 'stations' " be established at New Delhi, Bombay, Calcutta, Kandy, Colombo, Madras, Karachi, Simla, Rangoon, and Kabul and noted that, with the exception of Simla, Rangoon, and Kabul, "personnel are already operating at the stations mentioned."

with the Indian National Congress were so embarrassing the viceroy, Field Marshal Sir Archibald Wavell, that Wavell made a formal complaint to Churchill. Colonel Eddy, the former OSS chief at Algiers, appeared in Saudi Arabia, then in the British sphere of influence, with an imprest, so Donovan's papers show, of $7 million in silver coin, while Major Subi Sahbi, an American of Levantine origins, was at work in Beirut with a special appropriation of $1 million. In London, Donovan attached an OSS spy, Bernard Yarrow, to the court of King Peter II of Yugoslavia, despite warnings not to engage in intelligence operations in British territory, and at a time when King George VI and Churchill were engaged in complex conversations intended to restore Peter to his throne.

Shortly after the invasion, Menzies was dining at Claridge's with William Stephenson when they were joined by Donovan and Bruce. During the conversation, Bruce mentioned to "C" that, with the campaign developing in Normandy, "a situation might shortly arise when [OSS] would wish to introduce into France agents who had already been trained in the U.K." What, therefore, would be "C's" attitude if such a request was received from OSS? As "C" responded (and Bruce recorded): " 'C' readily agreed to our suggestion that, in the case of agents sent abroad to operate through enemy lines in an American Army zone, it would not be necessary to obtain such clearance from his organization." [8]

"C's" decision to unchain OSS from the constraints under which they had labored in London since they arrived in 1942 was made purely on political grounds: there would only be yet more trouble between Broadway and OSS headquarters if they were not allowed to operate within the Normandy lodgment. Further, with one U.S. Army already in France and four more due to land, plainly the armies might have need of OSS services. Yet "C's" decision produced the very situation that he had been determined to avoid—a situation, reminiscent of World War I, in which secret services of different nationalities had created chaos in the British zone of operations.

There were four British services in the Neptune zone of operations, four or five French services, three Belgian, two German, two or three Russian services, and now there were to be four American —to say nothing of the Brissex and Ossex agents. Everybody seemed to be somebody, and the roads were alive with joyriders, sight-seers, messengers, hangers-on, cooks, signalers and myriad other footloose individuals of all sorts hurtling about the rear areas of the fighting armies looking for lunch, loot, and lodgings. Everybody sought to outdo the rival service or buy up their spies. Everybody seemed to be on missions to obtain intelligence about the enemy that either conflicted with the facts or had been manufactured for cash; Fascist and Communist spies sold each other to the enemy; and by July 7 there was such bedlam in the beachhead that "C" sent Commander Cohen, head of Broadway's French section, to a see Bruce and the Gaulliste section, as Bruce noted in his diary, "to try and evolve some method of introducing order into the disorganized agent situation in Normandy."

But order was less easily produced than chaos could be maintained. Montgomery's security services complained to Montgomery, Montgomery complained to Eisenhower, Eisenhower complained to Strong, his G2, and Strong complained to everyone and was compelled to intervene. General T. J. Betts, Eisenhower's deputy G2, was sent to London to persuade "C" and Bruce each to send four officers to the supreme staff to take charge of the direction of secret intelligence operations. Betts failed. "C" insisted that SIS was not an Allied service, as indeed it was not, although its intelligence was sent to SHAEF (Supreme Headquarters Allied Expeditionary Forces). Bruce declared that he "could not consent to any arrangement which would impair the independence of the American Secret Intelligence Service." [9]

As for relations between "C" and Bruce, these finally collapsed in November 1944 when the OSS team began to meddle in SIS affairs in Belgium. Historically, SIS had maintained the closest links with the Belgian services. Ever since 1916, consequently, "C" had always taken a close personal interest in Belgian affairs and had many friends in the Belgian intelligence services, which had served Britain well in two world wars. But with traditional ties being complicated by modern factors—a powerful and armed Communist party in Belgium and British desire to obtain uranium from the Belgian Congo—"C" was even more anxious to restore the status quo antebellum. The head of the Belgian intelligence service-in-exile, Baron Fernand LePage, a close personal friend of "C," had been returned to Brussels as head of the Sûreté, the new intelligence and security service. With extreme annoyance, he discovered that OSS representatives were attempting to supplant him with Colonel Paul Bihin, who leaned toward OSS more than SIS.

An OSS memo on the subject stated that LePage was "extremely pro-British minded." OSS London complained to General Ganshof, the equivalent of the judge advocate general to the Belgian government-in-exile in London, and as such the political head of the Sûreté, that "we do not seem to be getting the necessary cooperation from" Baron LePage. With that complaint, OSS installed a mission in Belgium called Espinette, commanded by Captain R. L. Brittenham, who in London had cultivated a friendship with Colonel Bihin. According to Brittenham, Bihin was "extremely favourable to the United States, and to the Americans" and had "always shown the greatest desire to cooperate with us and to assist us in our work here. He has repeatedly expressed his desire to see us remain in Belgium in some form."

By early December 1944 "C" was well aware that General Ganshof intended to replace LePage with Bihin as administrator of the Sûreté. Plainly such a change was not in SIS's interests; and on December 7, just before the German attack on the American army in the Ardennes, "C" flew to Brussels in an attempt to persuade Ganshof to retain LePage. But by that time Brittenham had developed a stronger position with the Belgian intelligence services—he had taken Bihin to the United States as guest of OSS Washington, which had prepared a tantalizing itinerary for the Belgian that included a weekend with Cecil B. de Mille and visits to various Hollywood film sets—and SIS's traditional influence in Brussels had been ruptured.

With the arrival of "C" in Brussels—this was only the second time he had been abroad during the entire war—a series of meetings took place in which the German attack in the Ardennes worked greatly to "C's" advantage. It seemed possible that the Belgian service might have to go into exile in London again, where "C" had more access to aircraft the Belgians needed than did OSS. Moreover, instead of attempting to restore SIS relations, he went to work with the Belgians and the Americans to establish Sussex II, an operation that greatly alarmed the Belgians, for it established a system of stay-behind agents should the Germans succeed in reoccupying Belgium. Sussex II also had the effect of reminding Ganshof of the need to maintain the old, close relationship with SIS. The seduction of the Sûreté by the Americans failed, although only temporarily.

There was, however, more to "C's" displeasure than the Belgian imbroglio. On his return to England in late December, "C" discovered that, contrary to all agreements, OSS London had begun illegally to pass German agents under OSS control, men and women "of a very doubtful kind," into England for service in Germany through the OSS air base at Harrington in Northamptonshire without advising either SIS or the Security Service. There was an angry scene in which

Bruce assured "C" that the passage of the Germans across British territory had been an "administrative mistake." "C" then ordered Bruce to remove the agents to France, or he would have them arrested and sent to prison.

It seemed that "C's" authority everywhere was under pressure from the OSS, and especially in Greece. There, OSS agents openly supported the Communists against the Royalists, although Greece was by agreement between the governments a British theater of operations in which Britain supported the restoration of the monarchy. That policy was openly challenged by OSS secret agents, mostly Greek-Americans supported by the U.S. who favored the establishment of a republic.

In foreign affairs, therefore, OSS's conduct was not an expression of native American phobia for imperialism, but an avocation of a new American foreign policy, one intended to supplant England as the principal director of world affairs. That interference was, however, tolerable to both Churchill and "C" until British secret signals concerning the conduct of British forces in Greece were leaked by OSS to Drew Pearson, the Washington columnist, in a fashion that struck at the Grand Alliance itself. Appalled by what seemed to him to be OSS ignorance and irresponsibility, Churchill reacted personally and sent to Donovan what was the most threatening telegram he sent any Allied official throughout the war:

The Prime Minister to General Donovan, private and personal. Off the Record.

I must tell you that there is very formidable trouble brewing in the Middle East against OSS which is doing everything in its power to throw our policy towards Greece for which we have been accorded the main responsibility into confusion. I grieve greatly to see that your name is brought into all this because of our agreeable acquaintance in the past. Drew Pearson's article is a specimen of the kind of stuff that fits in with the campaign of OSS against the British. The OSS activities undoubtedly will have the effect of breeding a local quarrel between them and the British.

I was about to telegraph the president laying out the whole case so that he might have it in mind before we meet in a short time when I realized you were involved. In view of our association I should not like to put this matter on the highest level without asking you whether there is anything you could do to help. If however there is nothing that can be done the whole issue must be raised as between governments. With the great victories we are winning together it would be a great pity to have a lot of public discussion generated about this. [10]

So far as is known, Donovan did not reply to this telegram, although when Menzies's cousin, Rex Benson, was back in Washington on SIS business in December 1944, he met Donovan at a dinner party and found Donovan "much upset over Greece," and Donovan "went for Winston & his intolerance and dictatorship proclivities." [11]

Aware that an outright breach was in the making between Donovan and Menzies, Stephenson sent a most flattering letter to the OSS chief, one calculated to pour oil on troubled waters. For his part, Donovan asked the U.S. adjutant general to confer the Legion of Merit upon Menzies and, when the adjutant general proved dilatory, he sent a telegram to Washington asking that the process by which the medal was awarded be speeded up.

But for all the manifold implications of that citation, relations between SIS and OSS remained broken, and the situation in India in particular remained serious. There, a high official of OSS, Lieutenant Commander Edmond L. Taylor, acknowledged in his statement to the OSS Historical Unit on September 18, 1944: "The British services are always trying to pull a fast one on us. British SOE is very jealous of us, wants to take us over. SIS plays a lone hand. Wavell and Auchinleck, in contrast to Mountbatten, are very jealous of US operations. They have opposed recruiting [of agents] by us in India." And as Taylor's report showed, OSS operations to infiltrate the Indian political and administrative machine were expanding rather than contracting as the war began to reach its end.

4 ULTRA TROUBLE

Shortly after Overlord, Churchill, anxious about Ultra security in Washington, invited General George C. Marshall, on hand in England should a crisis arise, to meet "C." The meeting took place with General Sir James Marshall-Cornwall at "C's" official residence; over drinks, they touched upon their experiences in World War I, and Marshall asked "C" if he was the man who had arrested General Franklin Bell in October 1917 while Bell was on "the Million Dollar Tour" in France. "C" replied that he was not responsible for Bell's arrest, but he had authorized the apprehension of Bell's chauffeur, who was a suspected German spy and one who was driving in a forbidden zone on false credentials. "C" agreed, however, that General Bell had been inconvenienced while the matter of the driver's credentials were being sorted out.

Marshall then said that he was sorry "C" had "got the wrong end of the stick," but he had always understood that Bell had been arrested as well as Damoulakis, the chauffeur, and went on to explain that he had been interested in the case because Bell was a "very remarkable man." He had been Bell's aide when he was commanding general of the Eastern Mobilization District at Governor's Island, New York. Bell had been awarded the Medal of Honor, had been chief of staff of the army, president of the U.S. Army War College, and was in many ways the founder of the modern American army. Somewhat nonplussed, "C" replied that had he known Bell was so distinguished, he would certainly have seen to it that he had a good lunch while he was being inconvenienced, but that the driver would still not have been released until his identity and associations had been checked with Bureau Interallie. But Bell was indignant, voluble, and uncooperative, and that had made matters worse.

Marshall agreed, describing Bell as a "speechifier" and then went on to explain the reason why he had asked about Bell. He had no wish, he said, to suggest that "C's" men had been zealous or discourteous, but he had always wondered how it was that a roadblock "somewhere in France" had had the means to identify Damoulakis as a suspect and how it was that the matter of his credentials had been cleared up within a day. Now that he was chief of staff of the army, Marshall wanted his army to possess the same sense of security and the same organization as the British. It was partly because the British had such an excellent security service, Marshall went on to explain, that he decided if he was appointed to the command of Overlord, as had seemed likely at the Quebec conference in the summer of 1943, he would have taken a British general, Frederick E. Morgan, as his chief of staff. The excellence of British intelligence was another reason, for he was far from being satisfied with his own service.

Menzies replied that he owed much of the high repute enjoyed by his service to Bletchley Park and its cryptographers. But the system was liable to be destroyed at any moment because of carelessness in the use of Ultra, he explained, and asked Marshall if there was someone in Washington with whom he might communicate in an emergency. Marshall said that the new chief of military intelligence, General Clayton Bissell, was an excellent man, and he (Marshall) was reluctant to supervene in Bissell's affairs. But if "C" had an emergency, he could always contact Marshall personally.

Gratified, "C" then turned to the difficult question of special legislation to prevent discussion in the press of communications intelligence matters. Marshall felt the war would be over before such legislation passed through Congress into law, but he had had discussions about this with leading figures in both houses, and he felt there would be some enactment to protect most secret sources. As "C" stated, he felt the special relationship would probably not withstand the loss of Ultra, especially if it led to a prolongation of the war or to serious casualties at sea or on land. As "C" pointed out, new sources were being developed all the time, and some of them might be useful in keeping the peace. At that bold statement—for this was really a matter for the Combined Chiefs of Staff—Marshall was able to assure "C" that, as Menzies had suggested, shared cryptanalytical matters should be kept secret after the war in perpetuity. Marshall agreed to produce the draft of an agreement for the signature of both the president and the prime minister when he returned to Washington.

The conversation then turned to the question of postwar collaboration. In this regard Marshall felt that the United States would establish a permanent intelligence system, and that arrangements should be made by which the two services would work together, especially in the fields of communications intelligence. At that point Marshall asked "C" about the relationship between himself and Donovan, and "C" replied cautiously that Donovan had done a remarkable job of establishing his organization so rapidly and spoke highly of Donovan's counterespionage service, X2. But he also stated that in his view OSS had not as yet matured in its development, and he confessed that there were political and operational difficulties between the two services. Somewhat to his surprise, Marshall staunchly supported Donovan and declared that such difficulties as the Joint Chiefs of Staff had had with OSS were due in some measure to the fact that FDR and Donovan had been classmates at Columbia Law School.*

---

*Marshall said much the same thing of Donovan after the war in a series of interviews with his biographer, Forrest C. Pogue: "At first we had considerable difficulty in dealing with General Donovan and OSS generally. This was composed of a very fine group of men—a rather brilliant group of men—and it was led by Donovan who was a very effective soldier, and had been a very gallant soldier as measured by his Medal of Honour. But he was also a classmate of the president and that presented complications right away, because I could deal with all manner of things in one way, but when I ran into a classmate of the president's, I may have run into a complete stumbling block." See *The Pogue Report*, col. 448.

Although an opportunity arose to discuss OSS activities with Marshall, "C" did not take the matter up because, as Marshall-Cornwall explained, that was something to be settled between governments. Nor did "C" press further on the question of special legislation to protect communications intelligence, which Marshall-Cornwall thought was a mistake. Within ten weeks the two most serious breaches of Ultra security occurred, and to make matters worse, both occurred on the same day, September 25.

By late September 1944 the U.S. presidential election had started, and one of the issues New York Governor Thomas E. Dewey, the Republican candidate, hoped to use to defeat FDR as president was Pearl Harbor. One of the themes of the Republican campaign was that, through Magic, Roosevelt had known in advance of the Japanese intention to attack the United States but had done nothing, "in order to get the country into his war." A parallel theme was that Magic had supplied the president and his administration with so much foreknowledge about the Japanese intention that in ignoring the warnings he was guilty of incompetence and should be impeached. As the campaign intensified, hints of the existence of Magic began to appear in political speeches. For example, Representative F. A. Harness of Indiana told the House on September 11 that "the Government had learned very confidentially that instructions were sent out from the Japanese Government to all Japanese emissaries in this hemisphere to destroy the codes."[12]

"C" and General Clayton Bissell, his American colleague in Ultra, both saw the extreme peril that free public discussion would have for *both* Ultra and Magic, which were by this time closely interrelated. But because of the extreme sensitivity of the controversy—as history had shown, no sensible British government official could afford to involve himself in U.S. presidential campaign matters without the risk of stirring up a hornet's nest—"C" could not intervene directly. He acted indirectly to make Bissell aware of his concern, and it may not have been accidental that Rex Benson reappeared in Washington at this time and hovered between the U.S. capital and New York for the rest of the year, reporting to Stephenson from time to time.

Bissell was quite aware of the importance of the Japanese traffic, especially that of the Japanese embassy in Berlin, which was perhaps "C's" best source on German political and military intentions and in the development of secret weapons such as missiles, jet fighters, and the power units of the new range of German submarines. Bissell required no prodding from "C"; as soon as Harness's remarks became public, he went to see General Marshall to ensure that FDR put a stop to the discussion. As Marshall himself was to state, Magic had become a "a tremendous asset" that was enabling the United States in the Pacific to undertake "one of the most rapid destructions of the shipping of a nation that I think has ever occurred in warfare," and any public discussion of the source was "a very serious matter." [13] It was one that was "loaded with dynamite," and he felt that "something had to be done or the fat will be in the fire to our great loss in the Pacific, and possibly also in Europe."

When Marshall learned that Dewey planned to use this information in his campaign (and alarmed that a renewal of congressional interest in the background of the Pearl Harbor disaster had resulted in separate army and navy investigations), he prepared a letter to Dewey. He asked Dewey to read the first two paragraphs and, if he felt unable to agree with Marshall's proposals, not to read further. The mission of delivering the letter was entrusted to Colonel Carter W. Clarke, of the special branch of the military intelligence service responsible for handling Magic and Ultra. Clarke was directed to take the letter to Dewey at Tulsa, Oklahoma, Dewey's next stopping point on his campaign tour. Clarke was to travel in civilian clothes, he was to tell nobody except Bissell where he was going, he was to make his contact with Dewey unknown to any other person, and he was not to give the letter to Dewey if there was any other person in the room.

On his arrival in Tulsa, he contacted William Skelly, president of the Skelly Oil Company, who arranged, not without difficulty, for Clarke to see Dewey at the Tulsa Hotel. Dewey read the introductory two paragraphs of the letter and then stopped reading and asked Clarke if he was an officer of the regular army and whether "I would give him my word of honor" that he had been sent by General Marshall. Clarke replied that he was, he gave his word of honor, and then, according to Clarke's report of events to Marshall, Dewey

said he did not want his lips sealed on things that he already knew about Pearl Harbor, about facts already in his possession or about facts which might later come into his possession from other sources but which, if they were contained in Gen. Marshall's letter, could not be used because he had given his word on this letter, thereby sealing his lips. He said he would be glad to discuss this matter with me now. I told him I was merely a courier and was not authorized to enter into any discussions about what he knew about Pearl Harbor or about the contents of this letter. He then asked if I were authorized to say to him in the name of General Marshall that if he read the letter through and then stated to me that he already had in his possession the identical information that was contained in the letter, that he would then be released from all obligations to keep silent. I said I had no such authority.

Dewey then added that

he could not conceive of Gen. Marshall and Adm. King being the only ones who knew about this letter. Furthermore he said he could not conceive of Gen. Marshall approaching an "opposition candidate" and making a proposition such as was apparently contained in that letter. He said, "Marshall does not do things like that. I am confident that Franklin Roosevelt is behind the whole thing."

Dewey then proceeded to reread the first two paragraphs but then laid the letter down and went on:

Now if this letter merely tells me that we were reading certain Japanese codes before Pearl Harbor and that at least two of them are still in current use, there is no point in my reading the letter because I already know that . . . I know it and Franklin Roosevelt knows all about it. He knew what was happening before Pearl Harbor and instead of being reelected he ought to be impeached." He then said, "Would you like for me to phone Gen. Marshall and say to him what I have just said to you?" I said, "Governor, this is a subject that should not, under any consideration whatsoever, be discussed or even mentioned over the telephone." [14]

Dewey then returned the letter to Clarke, announced that he would return to Albany on the following Thursday, and that he would then be "glad to receive you or Gen. Marshall or anyone Gen. Marshall cares to send to discuss at length this cryptographic business or the whole Pearl Harbor mess." He promised there would be "absolute secrecy," and the two men then parted. Clarke returned immediately to Washington and reported to Bissell and Marshall, and later on September 27 Clarke received orders to take a second letter from Marshall to Dewey. This letter was very long and set forth the manifold reasons why it was imperative that the matter of the Magic ciphers be concealed now and in the future.*

At Albany Governor Dewey received Clarke at the Executive Mansion. He was not alone but with Elliot V. Bell, a financial journalist turned superintendant of banks for New York State who was Dewey's "economics advisor." As Clarke recorded, Dewey stated that in view of what he already knew about Magic, "and particularly in

---

*For reasons of length and importance, this letter is reprinted in total as appendix G.

view of his trusteeship, he had decided that he could not see me or anyone else alone, that he would not read a letter which he could not keep and which he could not show to or discuss with Mr. Bell, nor would he enter into any further discussion without Mr. Bell being present."

As for Bell, Dewey stated that his associate was "an American citizen and is just as patriotic as any member of the Administration" who knew "all the facts that I know in regard to Pearl Harbor, and I certainly intend that he know the contents of the letter if I read it." If he kept the letter, Dewey went on, no one but Bell and himself would know of its existence or contents, and they would discuss it only between themselves. But what was it that General Marshall was so exercised about? That was the question.

There were, Dewey continued, suggesting that FDR had arranged Marshall's intervention in order to conceal his actions before Pearl Harbor,

at least 12 Senators that I can name for you right now if you desire that know all there is to be known about Pearl Harbor and about how we were reading certain Jap codes before Pearl Harbor and how it is claimed that we are still reading two of these same codes. You know, Colonel, this code business is the worst kept secret in Washington, but I for one want to say to you that I do not believe [that the War Department was still reading the Japanese ciphers] to be a fact.

Dewey sat silent for about three minutes, then proposed that Clarke telephone Marshall "and tell him that I will not discuss the matter with you unless Mr. Bell is present, nor receive the letter unless I can let Mr. Bell read it and then I keep it." Clarke replied that he did not wish to telephone from the Executive Mansion but would go to a pay phone to call; and with that Dewey telephoned Marshall at the Pentagon. While waiting for Marshall, Dewey said: "If, as you say, the Japs are still using two of their codes that they used before Pearl Harbor, why in hell haven't they changed them, especially after what happened at Midway and the Coral Sea?" Clarke offered an explanation, and Dewey then asked why Marshall was "so anxious to stop him from talking when everyone else in Washington knows the story and is talking about it."

At that point Marshall came on the line and authorized Clarke to give the letter to Dewey, to leave it with him, and to discuss the case technically in the presence of Bell. As Clarke opened the envelope Bell remarked:

Colonel, hundreds of people know all about the Midway affair and how most of our other successes in the Pacific have been due to our reading Japan naval codes. Everyone who has ever been out there knows about it and talks freely about it. Why not long ago at a dinner where a large number of people were present I talked to a naval commander who had been out there and had participated in nearly every engagement we have had. He said that they always knew where the Jap ships were and that our people were told by radio where to station their own ships to meet the Japs, and that all this information came from reading Jap codes.

As Dewey and Bell began to read the letter, Dewey remarked that "I'll be damned if I believe the Japs are still using those two codes." Clarke tried to assure him that one of the ciphers "was our life blood intelligence," and that "General Marshall's sole interest in this case is to preserve the only worthwhile source of intelligence that this nation has." Clarke remarked, too, that "the War Department has 10,200 people working in the Signals Security Agency," the Navy Department had "almost 6,000 in their Communications Annex," and that both the army and navy each had "several thousand in tactical field and fleet units engaged in signals intelligence work."

Of the British interest in the continuing security of cryptographic intelligence, Clarke made a startling statement, one that seemed to sober both Dewey and Bell:

Churchill considered this his secret weapon and that it had really saved England. I described how Churchill felt about [the security of the sources], how the Navy prized it so highly and how difficult it had been to break down British resistance [in allowing Ultra to be sent to Washington] because of American lack of security consciousness. I quoted to him Churchill's reported statement about protecting this source, how that in order to protect the source the British had time and again permitted convoys to be attacked rather than divert them from their course and thus blow security.

The candidate then demanded to know: "What in hell do Jap codes have to do with Eisenhower?" Clarke then explained, "The linkage with a general statement on the three types of ciphers used by [the German air force], Abwehr, Clandestine, German Navy, [the Japanese ambassador's] visits [to Hitler], etc. He seemed satisfied." At that Dewey and Bell left the room for about twenty minutes. On their return Dewey made no statement about his attitude toward the problem and, since Marshall had asked for no assurances, he gave none to Clarke. But this extraordinary affair was at an end, and Dewey made no further public reference to the Pearl Harbor dissatisfactions.

For a time, doubtless, he remained of two minds. Given the number of leaks, it was inconceivable that the Japanese were using the same cipher in September 1944 that they had used in November 1941, and that Marshall's intervention was a maneuver by Roosevelt to conceal what really happened in that fateful month. But on the other hand, there were the assurances that they were from no less a man than Marshall, who was well known for his sense of honor and truth.

In due course Marshall sent General Bissell to Albany with samples of the current daily Magic summaries as evidence of the extent to which Magic was helping the United States to destroy Japan's maritime power. But as Clarke's report shows, his statement that Churchill allowed convoys to sail into disaster rather than alert the Germans to the fact that Enigma had been compromised served to show that there was indeed an entire substrata of activity going on in the gigantic war of which Dewey knew nothing. Yet the episode showed that "Top Secret Ultra" was an open secret in Washington.

"C's" concern about the U.S. system's ability to safeguard Ultra and Magic was, unfortunately, greatly inflamed by the second of the two incidents. Even as Clarke was flying to Tulsa to open negotiations with Dewey, a second breach occurred, one that violated all agreements between "C" and Donovan relating to Ultra. Major Maxwell J. Papurt, thirty-seven, X2 chief with U.S. Third Army, was captured by the Germans near Wallendorf on the German frontier, despite the rules stressing that persons with knowledge of the existence of Ultra were not to be placed in a position where they might be captured by the enemy. To make matters worse, captured with Papurt was Gertrude Legendre, a prominent American society woman on leave as supervisor of the OSS message center in Paris, a person who was therefore in possession of knowledge regarding all OSS ciphers in use in London, Paris, and Washington, to say nothing of extensive knowledge of the supreme command and intelligence systems. A third person captured was Lieutenant Commander Robert Jennings, a Texan oilman with OSS in Paris. Both Legendre and Jennings, according to the OSS report on their capture, "are in a position to give away extremely damaging information." [15]

Within a short time the party was at a German headquarters for interrogation. This took time, and the Germans appear to have been slow to deduce that their captives were members of OSS. But when the interrogations began, the Germans learned quickly of the existence of SHAEF's Special Counter-Intelligence (SCI) organization, which operated almost wholly on the basis of Ultra and information collected through the use of double agents.

Although Papurt tried to mislead his interrogators about its purpose, declaring SCI to be concerned with psychological warfare, documents found on Papurt revealed the real names and functions of a total of thirty key SCI agents in the U.S. theater of operations. Norman Holmes Pearson, chief of OSS counterespionage in London, had the difficult task of explaining Papurt's disappearance to "C" and Cowgill.

On the eve of one of the greatest battles of the war, the Battle of the Ardennes, it remained to be seen whether or not the Germans had been alerted to the fact that their most secret ciphers had been penetrated for four years. One ominous sign was the disappearance in December 1944 of the Abwehr Enigma traffic code-named ISK, a mainstay of intelligence about the German secret services since the cipher was first penetrated in December 1941. The disappearance of ISK may have been the consequence of a German administrative measure, for the Abwehr had been absorbed into the Sicherheitsdienst in February 1944. On the other hand, the timing did indicate German awareness that the Abwehr Enigma was compromised. Yet it does not seem that the Germans' concern for the security of Enigma extended beyond that one department, for there was no widespread withdrawal of the machine from service. On the contrary, Enigma remained in German service for at least a year even after their surrender.

As for Papurt, whether by accident or design, on November 29 Allied aircraft bombed the prison camp at Diez near Limburg where he was being held, and, fortuitously for Ultra, he was killed on the eve of a deep interrogation by the Sicherheitsdienst. Papurt was the second person who, having knowledge of Ultra and having been captured by the enemy, had died while in captivity, the other being the chief of Bertrand's P.C. Cadix.

On September 14 Eisenhower's armies stopped on the Siegfried Line. Their supreme command had run out of ideas for defeating the Germans that year. Having rejected Montgomery's proposal for a forty-division tank blitzkrieg to Berlin, Eisenhower's mighty armies limped up to the German border at precisely the moment, through a supreme exercise of the national will, that the German General Staff managed to restore the organization and discipline of their stillpowerful armies. Such was the bankruptcy of Allied strategy that Eisenhower appealed to President Roosevelt for permission to engage in a deception operation intended to lure the German armed forces into either surrendering or deserting. With that appeal, Roosevelt signaled Churchill with a proposal that he, Stalin, and FDR make a joint statement to the German armed forces that—being essentially a compromise of the Casablanca unconditional surrender formula— boiled down to an announcement that the Allies did not "seek to devastate Germany or eliminate the German people," and that upon surrender Germany would be allowed to return to the "civilization of the rest of the world."

There was nothing wrong with such a proposal, except that it was made at a moment of weakness when, through its own iron control and discipline, the German army began assembling in the west for a gigantic offensive intended to shatter the Anglo-American-Russian alliance. Since such a statement would be made when Allied weakness was evident, Churchill counseled against the proposal on the grounds that he and his Cabinet did not think that "the Germans are very much afraid of the treatment they will get from the British and American armies or governments. What they are afraid of is a Russian occupation, and a large proportion of their people being taken off to toil to death in Russia, or as they say, Siberia. Nothing that we can say will eradicate this deep seated fear."

Churchill saw no alternative except to employ the formula of General Ulysses S. Grant: "I fight it out on this line, if it takes all summer." As it had been since September 1939, so it remained five years later.

It was to be a war to the bitter end.

5 THE BATTLE OF THE ARDENNES

With the breakout of the Allied armies complete, at the end of August 1944 "C" felt he had to take some leave. He had had little or none since that snowbound Christmas of 1938–1939, and he had been somewhat stung by a remark of a friend at White's, Sir Archibald Sinclair, secretary of state for air: "Stewart, old chap, you look just like a Staff officer—grey and puffy." After more joshing in this vein, Sinclair suggested that since he was going up to his home, Thurso Castle, to attend to estate matters, "C" might like to fish at their prewar haunts, the Kyle of Tongue and Loch Eriboll. "C" spent ten days on that enchanted coast, and while he was away September 3 passed and the war entered its sixth year, an anniversary marked by the liberation of Brussels.

By September 16 the Allied armies had begun to reach the Siegfried Line, the German frontier fortifications. Eisenhower had 2.1 million men and 460,000 vehicles, grouped into forty-nine divisions. Allied casualties totaled 224,000, 40,000 of whom were dead, less than half the German casualties. To meet the threat to the Third Reich, Hitler had reappointed Field Marshal von Rundstedt as commander in chief in the west, while Field Marshal Model was retained as commander in chief of Army Group B, still the main fighting force in the west. Rundstedt's armies consisted of forty-eight infantry and fifteen panzer divisions, only a quarter of which could be considered at full combat strength: Rundstedt judged their effectiveness to be at most twenty-seven infantry and six or seven panzer divisions against the sixty-odd that Rundstedt incorrectly thought were available to Eisenhower.

One element of the German army in the west, however, was at full strength. The staffs of all higher headquarters were for the most part intact and able to function. The command of the German army, although battered, outflanked, encircled, and apparently destroyed in August, was also intact. As the Allied supply system began to deteriorate through Eisenhower's policy of attacking everywhere all along the line, therefore, Rundstedt began to restore his armies to a degree of fighting strength; and he was just able to do so despite losses totaling 1.2 million killed, wounded, captured, and missing on the eastern and western fronts during June, July, and August.

And if everywhere the Allies saw success and even the imminent prospect of victory, on his return from Thurso "C" saw an Ultra that he interpreted as an ominous sign. It was an order to establish the Sixth SS Panzer Army headquarters under the command of Obergruppenführer SS Josef Sepp Dietrich, an officer with a reputation for *offensive* rather than defensive operations. The primary mission of the new headquarters was described in all early communications as the supervision and rehabilitation of the armored divisions of both the SS and the army on the western front.

This was pure deception, and had it not been for Ultras in the second half of September revealing that Hitler had disengaged two *panzerkorps* consisting of five armored divisions from operations and attached them to the new army, the true purpose of Dietrich's army might not have been divined in London until it was too late. But "C" recalled from his 1918 experience, when the Germans launched no less than five major offensives before surrendering, that it was doctrine for the German army to undertake offensive operations even when confronted with defeat.

While "C" was at Thurso, Hitler had conceived a plan to split the American and British armies in two and either stop or at least slow the Allied invasion of Germany. By the end of October "C" felt so sure that a powerful attack was being planned and mounted that he advised U.S. Army G2's General Kenneth W. D. Strong and General Edwin L. Sibert. As a consequence, guardedly, Sibert issued a warning in his weekly intelligence summary that the disposition of the panzer and panzer grenadier divisions constituted "the key to the enemy's essential capabilities and intentions." In that estimate Sibert was correct, but he misunderstood the function of the group of five armored divisions he was watching; he thought they were there to counterattack a planned U.S. offensive over the river Roer. All subsequent German actions were intended to encourage Sibert and Omar Bradley in that belief.

The plan for the gigantic counteroffensive was presented by Hitler to Rundstedt and Model on November 1. The plan called for Army Group B to attack with twenty-nine to thirty divisions in the area of the Ardennes, through which Germany had struck the Anglo-French armies in 1940 so effectively. The key to success was again surprise, and to ensure surprise both as to the time and place of the operation, it was to take place in December, when the region would be bathed in snow, ice, and fog that would (it would seem to the Allies) make an attack impossible. The political basis for the attack was set forth by Hitler at a meeting with his generals on December 12:

Never in history was there a coalition like that of our enemies, composed of such heterogeneous elements with such divergent aims. . . . Ultra-capitalist states on the one hand; ultra-Marxist states on the other. On the one hand, a dying Empire, Britain; on the other, a colony bent upon inheritance, the United States. . . . Each of the partners went into this coalition with the hope of realising his political ambitions. . . . America tries to become England's heir; Russia tries to gain the Balkans, the narrow seas, Iran and the Persian Gulf; England tries to hold her possessions and to strengthen herself in the Mediterranean. . . . Even now these states are at loggerheads, and he who, like a spider sitting in the middle of his web, can watch developments, observes how these antagonisms grow stronger and stronger from hour to hour. If now we can deliver a few more heavy blows, then at any moment this artificially-bolstered common front may collapse with a gigantic clap of thunder . . . provided always that there is no weakening on the part of Germany. . . . Wars are finally decided by one side or the other recognising that they cannot be won. [Therefore] we must allow no moment to pass without showing the enemy that, whatever he does, he can never reckon on a capitulation. Never! Never! [16]

The point at which he proposed to attack was a one-hundred-mile portion of the Ardennes front held only by four green American divisions. Against that front he would hurl the twenty-eight divisions of 400,000 men, including the ten tank divisions of the Fifth and Sixth Panzer armies. The initial breakthrough was to be assisted by Operation Greif, in which German officers and men dressed in U.S. uniforms and driving U.S. vehicles were to accompany the German spearheads and then fan out behind the Allied line to spread confusion by issuing false orders and seizing bridges and key points. Greif was to be assisted by the dropping of eight hundred paratroopers in the area of Malmédy. Also, to ensure surprise and to further confuse the Allied command, there were to be a series of deception plans intended to mislead the Allies about the capabilities and intentions of Army Group B.

At the same time, all German diplomatic and secret agencies started a concerted propaganda campaign intended in the first instance to create divisions between the American and British government. One aspect of that campaign consisted of an attempt to persuade the British that their American allies were duplicitous and seeking to take commercial and political advantage of a weakened England. The other sought to show the Soviet and American governments that Churchill was seeking to negotiate a separate peace behind their backs. A number of German emissaries contacted their British counterparts before and during the Ardennes offensive to turn the Anglo-Americans against Russia so that they would, in their own interests, join Germany in a crusade against Russian communism. The themes of the campaign were several, insidious, and subtle, and the main danger was that it was difficult, and became more so, to establish which approaches from the Germans represented a genuine attempt to surrender and which were stimulated by Himmler, Kaltenbrunner, and Schellenberg with the intention of making trouble between the Allies.

Meanwhile, "C" had been involved in the more conventional, less political realms of intelligence. These concerned Hitler's capabilities and intentions, which mystified and alarmed the Anglo-American high command to such a degree that in November General Edwin L.

Sibert, G2 of U.S. Twelfth Army Group, sent his deputy, Colonel William H. Jackson, to London to see "C." All "C" could say for sure at that time was that the Germans intended some sort of offensive in the west, but where and when it would come was not clear. "Watch yourselves," "C" counseled, reminding Jackson of German military doctrine, which was to launch a savage attack with all forces available before surrendering.

The first known attention given to the possibility that Hitler would launch a major counterattack was when the Joint Intelligence Committee discussed on November 11 the remarkable resurgence of the German army in the west. After five years of war, Germany remained so innately powerful that Hitler had been able to create, equip, and train a total of fifty fresh divisions. And if the caliber and training of the divisions left something to be desired, as the U.S. official historian observed, "the Germans were much like the giant Antaeus who regained his strength whenever he touched his mother earth."

Despite the Allied aerial bombardment of Germany, and the critical shortages of oil and transportation, through a titanic mobilization of German industry in the late summer of 1944, Hitler was able to stockpile weapons, ammunition, fuel, and food on a vast scale for the western offensive. But of that resurgence the JIC seems to have known little or nothing, for if the committee felt that an attack was brewing, they also felt it would be confined to "a limited spoiling attack" intended to "upset Allied preparations and thus postpone the major Allied offensive, possibly even until the spring of 1945." And as the members of the committee noted: "Such a spoiling attack would be characteristic of German military practise." But the committee also noted, "We do not think that the evidence warrants the conclusion that the Germans are planning a spoiling offensive." [17]

Those last eighteen precautionary words had a fateful consequence. Had they been left out of the bulletin, the Allied intelligence community would have galvanized into watching the accumulating evidence more closely for signs that the German concentration was not for a tactical attack, but for a major strategic counteroffensive intended to change the direction of the war in Germany's favor. Such a warning might have also forced the G2 of the U.S. First Army, Colonel Dickson, to overcome his dislike for OSS and send out parties across the lines into the Ardennes forests. But Dickson had banned OSS from his headquarters for alleged incompetence at the time of the fighting in Normandy. In consequence, when pressure was put on Dickson to remove the ban and allow OSS back into his headquarters in order to undertake line-crossing operations across First Army's front, Dickson refused, declaring, "I don't want a man from OSS, nor a dwarf, nor a pygmy, nor a God-damned soul" from OSS. [18]

Thus the Ardennes forest in front of the First Army's corps of four green divisions was not penetrated by OSS linecrossers. If that had been successfully done, then ample evidence would have been found of concentrations of troops, supplies, and equipment for the impending offensive, for as one of the postmortems on the reasons for the surprise that the German commanders were able to obtain was that on the front of U.S. Eighth Corps, the corps that took the brunt of the attack:

There were some indicators of enemy buildup. . . . Units of the 4th, 28th, and 106th Divisions reported in the last days before the offensive of increased vehicular activity. A woman escapee claimed that the woods were jammed with equipment, and four prisoners of war in U.S. hands reported that fresh troops were arriving for a big attack around 16 or 17 December, certainly before Christmas. Only one of these bits of information (increased vehicular traffic) reached all the way up to 12th Army Group Headquarters—and it was not briefed until the morning of 16 December. [19]

As a consequence of the failure of First Army to reconnoiter its front, the Germans obtained complete surprise on a scale comparable to that which they obtained against the British as early as the Norwegian episode in early 1940. The Germans knew exactly the degree of fighting proficiency not only of the four divisions that were about to be slaughtered, but also much of the whereabouts, strength, and competence of the entire U.S. Army in Western Europe, for as a GC&CS inquiry was to state: " 'Ultra' clearly indicated that insecurity of Allied radio traffic allowed the Germans to form a substantially accurate picture of Allied Order of Battle in the sector South of Aachen."

In short, Dickson and his colleagues up to the supreme commander's G2, General Strong, watched only Ultra; and Ultra was, because of the German's security and deception operations for the offensive, ambiguous. Finding in the mass of Ultra no hard evidence as to the time and place of the attack, they assumed there was to be no attack at all. And there, in the same overdependence upon Ultra, in the tendency not to believe anything unless it was supported by Ultra, was the root cause of the disaster. Yet thinking officers would have seen the menace if everything had been read together in a single file.

During October and November, between forty and fifty Ultras a day were being sent to General Strong at supreme headquarters. These told a great deal about German intentions but not, apparently, enough to convince the G2 system that a major strategic counteroffensive was imminent. In all, there were seventeen messages that, had they been read against the knowledge that could only be acquired by ground reconnaissance, might have placed Eisenhower's higher command in a greater state of alertness. As it was, Ultra contained indications of the strength, date, and probable direction of the offensive.*

Later, in assessing the third major Ultra failure of the war, two of "C's" watchmasters a Bletchley, Peter Calvocoressi and Ralph Bennett, analyzed the meaning of the electronic intelligence the Allies had acquired prior to the assault at Ardennes. Calvocoressi asserted that, although the Germans had tried to enforce wireless silence before the battle, occasional messages popped up that "could give a picture of a large ground force in a definable area and apparently holding its breath before embarking on something special." Also, the Germans had measurably prevented reconnaissance of the area and had given up a lot of railroad data so that Bletchley could predict the order of battle. But, he stated, "we could not give a precise date or the point of attack." [20]

Ralph Bennett found that over eleven thousand decodes were sent out concerning the activities of the German army in northwestern Europe and Italy between October 1, 1944, and January 31, 1945. Bennett held the opinion that, although "Ultra intelligence was plentiful and informative," it did not "point conclusively to an offensive in the Ardennes." In the end, Ultra intelligence pointed to the Germans not attacking; rather, they were assumed to be waiting for the next big Allied offensive.

But neither of these surveys took into account two Japanese diplomatic Ultras, in which "C" usually put so much faith. In one, the Japanese ambassador to Berlin reported on his lunch with Ribbentrop the previous day, during which Ribbentrop asserted that there would be a German offensive in the west. The Japanese ambassador warned Tokyo: "In view of Ribbentrop's record and the general character of similar past conversations, this can be recorded as one of the instances in which truth from the mouth of a liar reaches the highest pinnacle of deceptiveness." [21]

*The evidence for this statement is compiled in appendix F.

Nor did Calvocoressi and Bennett take into account the significant intelligence derived from German prisoners of war who had deserted to the Allies in the month before the offensive actually began. Lieutenant Colonel Willi Kaiser, chief of staff to the German military commander at Strassbourg, stated that at the beginning of November he had attended a lecture given by a *führungsoffizier*, an official of the Nazi party responsible for ideological indoctrination of the troops. The official stated that reserves would be brought up from Germany to "strike a decisive blow on the Western Front," supported by "new weapons." Kaiser had also learned from two other sources of the massing of troups in the west that "the German High Command hopes to achieve a large-scale break-through, because (i) Allied positions in France are not constructed in depth, (ii) the Allies have no reserve divisions behind the actual fighting lines, (iii) the American soldier is war-weary." [22]

However, by December 8 the Joint Intelligence Committee in London had learned enough to feel able to give the opinion that there was "excellent intelligence" that "the enemy was holding just behind his front opposite the Ardennes a concentration of ground and air forces, and steadily building up their strength." The JIC therefore gave a somewhat less reserved forecast of the situation in which it stated that "the enemy was planning some surprise," but "it was not known what it was to be." Both staff and committee drew special attention to the "fact that the enemy had imposed w/t silence." [23]

From that point forward Strong, Sibert, and Dickson appear to have taken a more realistic attitude, one no longer governed by the assumption that if the Germans intended to attack at all, it would be "a spoiling attack," although at no time did Strong calculate that a major offensive was in the wind. But that attitude was itself governed and influenced by the poor relationship between Sibert and Dickson.

On December 10 Dickson distributed his weekly estimate of German intentions. He wrote that it was "plain" the German strategy was "the exhaustion of our offensive to be followed by an all-out counterattack with armor, between the Roer and the Erft, supported by every weapon he can bring to bear." It was also plain that the enemy commander in chief, Rundstedt, "has skilfully defended and husbanded his forces and is preparing for his part in the all-out application of every weapon at the focal point and the correct time to achieve defense of the Reich west of the Rhine by inflicting as great a defeat on the Allies as possible." And as Dickson concluded in the second of the four conclusions he made about enemy capabilities and intentions:

(2) The enemy is capable of a concentrated counterattack with air, armor, infantry, and secret weapons at a selected focal point at a time of his own choosing.

Yet this view so strongly contested at both supreme headquarters and at Twelfth Army Group that Strong telephoned Sibert and directed him to get hold of Dickson and reprimand him for having made such an "alarmist" report. But by the time Sibert found Dickson, who had gone to Paris on leave, the German attack had begun.

Before dawn on December 16, Hitler's three armies struck the American line on a seventy-mile front between Monschau and Trier. The Allied command was taken by surprise, the American front collapsed, and by the next morning panzers were pouring through a fifty-mile gap. That evening the enemy's spearheads were twenty miles inside Belgium. Although for a time Eisenhower seemed paralyzed by the magnitude and ferocity of the attack, he gave Montgomery control of First and Ninth U.S. armies north of the breakthrough in addition to his own command, the British Second and the Canadian First armies.

The battle lasted until January 28, by which time all lost ground had been recovered and the offensive defeated. But Allied casualties totaled almost 77,000 men, all but 1,408 of them American. Of these 8,407 Americans were killed, 46,170 wounded, and 20,905 posted as missing. In the end the Germans achieved nothing, having lost their last reserves of men and equipment on a large scale—120,000 men killed, wounded, missing, or captured, and 600 tanks, 1,600 planes, and 6,000 vehicles lost. So with disintegrating morale they had now to face not only Eisenhower's massed crossing of the Rhine and the envelopment of the Ruhr, but also one of the greatest offensives of the war in Hungary.

On January 14, 1945, "C" received (but suppressed) an Ultra in which Reichsführer SS Heinrich Himmler repudiated the elite division of the Waffen SS, the Twelfth Panzer Division Hitler Jugend. Himmler told the commanding general of the Sixth SS Panzer Army:

I note . . . that detachments of the 12 SS Panzer Division Hitler Jugend, during the fighting in the first battle period of 16th and 17th December, busied themselves behind the front snatching weapons from the dead of another Division—in particular assault rifles 44. That such a course must have an appalling effect on the discipline of the troops is obvious. That the Hitler Jugend Division should have done such a thing is shameful. How can a Division that bears this name behave in so base a manner? This has nothing to do with the scrounging of weapons. Just calmly tell the GoC that for the present I do not recognise this Division, since I do not associate with such people.

Heil Hitler! [24]

The reaction of the Hitler Jugend to that message may be imagined. This repudiation meant the same sort of thing in the SS that a repudiation of the Life Guards by the monarch would have meant in the British army. Meanwhile Allied command had been attempting to establish the root causes of the disaster. No report was published, but there were three conclusions: (a) the encouragement given to Hitler by the severe Allied dissensions, about which he had only to purchase a subscription to *The New York Times* to know all; (b) Eisenhower's insistence upon spreading the attack *everywhere*, the effect of which was to make his command weak *everywhere*; and (c) a failure in intelligence analysis similar to that which had occurred at Kasserine—drawing wrong deductions from correct evidence. In the opinion at least of General Marshall, the man chiefly to blame was General Kenneth W. D. Strong, G2 at supreme headquarters.*

Although Strong had an enormous staff—over one thousand persons—he developed a mind-set in which he believed that the German army could not attack in the west because of (a) the near destruction of the German petrol and lubricants system through bombing, (b) Hitler's apparent preoccupation with the eastern front, and (c) his conviction that if the Germans attacked at all, it would be in order to spoil the forthcoming American attack across the Roer River in the direction of Cologne, not to end the war.

The intelligence procurement system worked with its usual brilliance, but it was defective for two reasons: (a) the intelligence obtained by Dickson was not accepted by Sibert and (b) because of Dickson's antipathy for Donovan and OSS, there was no attempt at large-scale reconnaissance into the Ardennes Forest. The lack of human intelligence was compounded by the inability of the aerial reconnaissance missions to detect the German concentrations in the woods in the fog and low clouds that persisted throughout the preparatory period of the German offensive.

*As General Marshall stated in a series of interviews given to his authorized biographer, F. C. Pogue, "Eisenhower was let down by his English G2." See: *George C. Marshall, Interviews & Reminiscences for Forrest C. Pogue, Transcripts and Notes, 1956–57*, column 317.

In the end, therefore, a single primary conclusion arises from the calamity at the Ardennes. When the Germans attacked out of the Ardennes that icy, misty morning, it was exactly three years and nine days since Pearl Harbor. During that time, the western powers had fought a world war with great skill, courage, and success except in one direction: they had still not learned how to collate and analyze all available intelligence at a single point and draw one set of conclusions. As with the Nazi-Soviet Pact in 1939, so it was at the Battle of Ardennes; most of the intelligence required to make a correct estimate had been procured in ample time, but that conclusion was not reached for a variety of factors.

One, of course, was fatigue: after years of war minds had become dulled from the unending task of scenting the omens. But the main cause of the Ardennes disaster was neither personalities nor incompetence; it was merely a repetition of an old problem: overdependence upon Ultra that had shown itself from Kasserine onward.

But if there was a lesson for Donovan to learn in this, it was apparent that he had not observed it. On January 4, 1945, he met with his principal advisers on the European front, Ambassador Robert E. Murphy (U.S. political adviser at supreme headquarters), Allan Dulles (who had just been appointed to head the large OSS mission in Germany), and Lieutenant Colonel F. O. Canfield (Donovan's representative at supreme headquarters). The purpose of the meeting was to chart the course of OSS policy in the new year. As paragraph seven of the top secret minutes of that meeting stated:

> The subject of the secret penetration of the Russian and British sectors [of occupied Germany] was then discussed. It was agreed that OSS should proceed on the basis that the comparable Russian and British Services would seek to penetrate the U.S. Sector and that OSS should not limit its secret activities to the U.S. Sector. Such penetration should be exclusive of such open arrangements as might be made between OSS and NKVD for exchange of information and missions.

6 GÖTTERDÄMMERUNG

After six years of war, the Teuton furore, begun thirty-four years earlier when "C" rode with the King's Guard of the Life Guards on the return of King George V and Queen Mary to Windsor Castle after their coronation, drew to its dreadful end with a thousand years of European civilization in ashes and ruins. At the same time the incessant and subtle German campaign to split the alliance during the Ardennes counteroffensive had had its effect, especially in the realm of Russo-British relationships. There, through the insidious whispers of German agents, intense suspicions developed in Moscow that Churchill was seeking to make a separate peace with the German General Staff, one intended to free the German armies in the west for concentration against the Russians in the east.

Under the tripartite arrangements established following President Roosevelt's proclamation of unconditional surrender in January 1943, agents of all three governments received orders from their respective foreign offices that all contacts with the enemy were to be reported, that under no circumstances were any agents to engage in political conversations, and that all meetings with enemy agents were to be avoided unless it seemed that vital intelligence might be procured from the enemy emissary. These directives were very rigidly enforced, at least by the British and American secret services. So strictly were they enforced indeed that when in mid-1943 "C" himself received an invitation to attend a secret meeting with Admiral Canaris in one of the Iberian capitals, "C" was directed personally by the foreign secretary, Anthony Eden, not only to reject the invitation but to ignore it altogether. The meeting between "C" and Canaris, therefore, never took place.

The reason for these absolute directives was evident: If the Russians got wind of such conversations they would conclude that the western powers were seeking a separate peace, one that would leave the Germans free to fight the rest of the war against Russia freed from concerns that the Allies would invade western Europe. The Russians were informed about all those contacts that took place in the Iberian capitals and Paris between January and July 1944, when the bomb finally went off under Hitler's map table, and they were readily justified by the vital intelligence procured—intelligence about the morale, strengths, and locations of the German armies in the west and the south.

But with Hitler's preparations for the Ardennes offensive, his agents began to purvey much more insidious fears, ones calculated to play on Churchill's fears of the political situation that would arise if the Soviet armies intruded any further into Central Europe. When the floodgates burst open through the Soviet summer and winter offensives of 1944, Churchill's apprehensions became the greater, a fact that was as well known to Hitler as it was to Stalin and Roosevelt. While "C's" instructions regarding the handling of enemy "doves" were not amended, nevertheless he came under a form of pressure to establish through the "doves" whether the German armies could or could not hold the Russians in the east.

The first major contact between a British and a German agent followed about a month before the Ardennes offensive. On or about November 10, Allen Dulles, the OSS representative in Berne, reported to Washington that he had received information "from a trustworthy source" that Eric Grant Cable, British consul-general at Zurich, was having peace talks with Alexander von Neurath, the German consul at Lugano and son of Hitler's first foreign minister. In a report to the U.S. secretary of state, Cordell Hull, Dulles claimed knowledge that when Neurath asked for evidence of Cable's intentions, Cable produced what Dulles called "a copy of an unsigned document indicating British interest in the organization of an anti-Bolshevist front in Germany and in the preservation of the Nordic race."

While there was room for doubt that Cable's document used any such language, there was no doubt that Cable did see Neurath, and that Neurath was acting in the interests of a group of German generals who were prepared for the second time since D-Day to open the western front to the Allied armies, thus enabling them to occupy Germany before the Russians. Dulles, too, accepted that Cable was having secret conversations with Neurath but added that it was "difficult to judge whether Cable was acting on his own initiative." He considered it unlikely that Cable would be given a "highly confidential task" by the British government because Cable was "a very expansive person who is not considered particularly discreet." In any case, Dulles advised Washington that he would keep apart from these contacts because "of the opportunities which the matter appeared to offer the Germans with respect to the USSR." [25]

Cable's contact was almost certainly known to Whitehall, and there was then, and later, no evidence that the Foreign Office gave an order that the conversations be terminated. But the object was probably not peace but an operation undertaken in accordance with Churchill's desire to establish whether the German generals thought they could hold the line in the east.

The second and still more mysterious contact took place even as Dulles was informing Washington about the Neurath conversations. On November 13, a German officer named Karl Marcus, alias Carlsen, arrived in France, apparently as a deserter from the German army. He told his French interrogators that "he had been sent to get in touch with the British, particularly Lord Vansittart,* and that he would disclose his mission only to a British officer." [26] The French gave him freedom of movement in Paris but told him not to communicate with the British while his case was being considered. Marcus ignored that injuction, made contact with the Chinese embassy in Paris, and the Chinese put him touch with "C's" officer at Eisenhower's headquarters, Guy Westmacott.

According to a memo by "C" to the U.S. and Russian foreign ministers, Marcus described himself as the secretary to and emissary of Kurt Jahnke, the former head of Hitler's personal intelligence office under the control of Rudolf Hess. Jahnke was the man who attempted to arrange a meeting between David Boyle, "C's" representative, and Hitler in Berlin shortly before the outbreak of the war; and he was now, although suspected of being a British informant by the Gestapo, political adviser to Walter Schellenberg.

With the knowledge and permission of Churchill, Marcus was brought to England for interrogation, Churchill expressing no more than surprise that the French should have given Marcus freedom of movement in Paris. The Americans expressed similar surprise that Marcus was in London, but they had little otherwise to complain of for "C" told Donovan that Marcus "seems to possess valuable military and counterespionage information regarding Sicherheitsdienst plans and intentions, German participation in [Communist] activities in Greece, a new German secret weapon, the training of Polish partisans [for service against the Russians], and purported German military intentions in the west." Marcus was "no ordinary deserter" but "represented himself as the political emissary of certain dissident German elements" who believe that "while the USSR, the United States, and France wish the war to continue and Germany to be destroyed, England would work with Germany to counteract Soviet influence and to preserve the Western inspiration of German civilization."

As "C" pointed out, "The similarity with Hess's ideology is obvious." "C's" opinion was that this was "part of the German plan to disrupt Allied relationships" and that in view of "the obvious dangers involved if the British were to give Marcus the slightest encourage-

---

*Formerly Sir Robert Vansittart, Cadogan's predecessor as permanent head of the Foreign Office. He possessed certain private intelligence connections with highly placed Germans, and Marcus, it will be seen, was one of them.

ment" he would be interrogated by SHAEF, not the British government, by British officers in uniform who were instructed to "pay no
attention to any political suggestions which Marcus may make." [27]

The whole question of the desirability of maintaining any contacts
with the enemy came to a head with a note by Donovan to the U.S.
Joint Chiefs that he had received reports from Switzerland early in
December that the Sicherheitsdienst would make "an effort to contact
the 'Western Powers' " and, in what was a reference to Cable's talks
with Neurath, if that contact failed then "Himmler plans to make a
series of disclosures of purported Anglo-American peace feelers to
Germany with the aim of breaking up the Anglo-American alliance
with the USSR."

In the light of that warning, "C" urged his agents to use the
greatest caution in all such contacts in the future, an order that his
agents obeyed to the letter. Similar instructions from Donovan to
Dulles were not so strictly obeyed and, as will be seen, while undoubtedly "C's" agents remained in touch with their "doves," the
American system of maintaining contact proved defective, disastrously so. Furthermore, the dangers inherent in all such connections
were made the greater when, in January 1944, "C" reminded his
principal officers of intelligence of the need for the greatest circumspection on the grounds that it was becoming evident that the Russians
had begun a campaign to discredit "C" personally along with his
service, their object presumably to bring about a loss of confidence
in what was a vital institution.

Consequently, not at any time during the entire history of the
war were contacts with the enemy more dangerous than they were
when, in January 1945, a familiar figure, Neurath, the German consul
in Lugano, reemerged on December 26, his purpose again to arrange
with British *and* Americans agents in Switzerland for a ceasefire in
the west with a continuation of the war against Russia in the east. As
the deputy chief of OSS in Washington, Ned Buxton, reported to the
U.S. Joint Chiefs on December 28, 1944, the head American agent
in Switzerland, Allen Dulles, had commented that "this whole project
appears rather fantastic to him. He believes, however, that the British
know more about the whole matter than they are telling him."

Fantastic or not, Dulles was close to the truth. Marcus, the emissary of Jahnke who appeared in Paris with Chinese assistance in
November and made contact with "C's" representative at Allied supreme headquarters, had facilitated contact with a senior official in
the German hierarchy, Franz von Papen, a figure well known to the

U.S. government and still more so to "C" and his colleagues. A German aristocrat born in 1879, and a former member of the German General Staff, Papen had had a long association with Canaris and the Abwehr. Appointed in 1913 as military attaché to the German embassy in Washington, the Woodrow Wilson government had demanded his recall when it was discovered in 1915 that he was in charge of espionage and sabotage in the United States. After his recall he had served in Turkey and then, when Germany surrendered in 1918, he entered German politics as a member of the Catholic Center Party in the Prussian parliament. In 1932, although politically unknown, President Paul von Hindenburg, who had himself been chief of the German General Staff at one stage, selected Papen to succeed Heinrich Bruning as German chancellor.

In the political maelstrom of Germany in the early thirties, Papen sought to maintain his power by establishing a coalition of the right and center against the left. Although forced to resign in 1932, he did succeed in bringing Hitler to power and his reward was his appointment by Hitler as vice-chancellor of Germany in Hitler's first cabinet. Papen then continued to serve the regime in several capacities, even though several of his closest associates in the General Staff were murdered in the "blood purge" of 1934. As German minister to Vienna he helped prepare the German annexation of Austria in 1938, and from 1939 to 1944 he served as German ambassador to Turkey. Well known in British hunting circles, although so far as is known not in the Beaufort Hunt, Papen developed contacts of an extremely secret nature with the British secret service in Turkey, whose representatives regarded him as an anti-Hitler German nationalist connected to the Canaris group. Papen cannot be described as "a British agent" any more than Canaris, for example, could be so described, but the assistance he rendered to the British service in the events that led up to the attack on Hitler's life on July 20, 1944, were such that "C" authorized a subordinate, probably David Boyle, to warn Papen that he was a marked man when the attack failed.

During the summer of 1944 Papen was recalled to Germany, but he appears to have eluded a Gestapo search and returned safely to his estate on the eastern fringes of the Ruhr, where he remained in residence until he was captured by the U.S. Army in April 1945. During that period, it appears, he acted as political adviser to the German commanders in chief on the western and southern fronts in their attempts to arrange terms with the armies of the western powers in Europe. There is some evidence that he was in contact by clandestine wireless with "C," or, more likely, Boyle's special diplomatic section. Papen's policy appears to have been similar if not identical to that of the German peace emissaries in touch with "C" and Donovan through the Vatican. If that be so, then the essence of the prayers from the German emissaries is relevant and was described by Dulles, the chief U.S. agent in Switzerland, who received this plea for terms through Dom Emmanuele Caronti, Abbot General of the Benedictines:

In the sixth year of war, Germany finds herself alone in the fight against Bolshevist Russia. In the interests of saving mankind, Germany now looks to the highest ecclesiastical authority to intervene with the Anglo-Americans and guarantee absolute secrecy to any negotiations with the Vatican. [28]

For the moment it is necessary to leave Papen at his hiding place outside the Ruhr, seeking to make terms with the British government, and attend to another dangerous matter with which "C" appears to have had connection at this time. This concerned the Yalta Conference between Roosevelt, Churchill, and Stalin early in February 1945, a conference held against a general background of extreme Churchillian anxieties about the reality of the Red Army's intentions. As it seemed at the time, although the conference ended in what resembled a blaze of amity, the Red Army would occupy not only Eastern and Central Europe but begin to appear in Northwestern Europe as well, and especially in Denmark.

On February 6, 1945, at the Second Tripartite Meeting between the American, British, and Russian chiefs of staff, General Alexsei I. Antonov, chief of staff of the Red Army, asked General Marshall whether he had any information regarding the whereabouts of the Sixth SS Panzer Army, the spearhead at the Battle of the Ardennes. This very powerful unit had begun to move east immediately after the failure of the Ardennes offensive; and its whereabouts was of interest to the Red Army General Staff. General Marshall replied that "he had received a message on the previous day which gave definite information of the moves of certain divisions of the Sixth Panzer Army from the Western Front." He promised to get "an exact statement on this matter and give it to General Antonov." [29]

Antonov seemed satisfied at that promise and Marshall asked Brooke, chief of the British staff, to do what he could to satisfy Antonov's request. Neither Brooke nor Marshall, however, controlled Ultra.

"C" did and his permission had to be obtained before Ultra could be given to the Russians. Consequently it was not until February 9, 1945, that Marshall's request was considered and on that date the British chiefs of staff agreed "to inform the Director of Military Intelligence and 'C' of the proposal that *intelligence of a certain character* [emphasis added] should in future be made available to the Russians under certain safeguards and, subject to there being no objection from London, to institute a provision of this intelligence forthwith."

Antonov's request seemed to indicate that the Russians could *not* read either Enigma or Geheimschreiber, for if they had been able to do so they would not, presumably, have asked the Anglo-American chiefs of staff for the intelligence. They would have had it for themselves. Nevertheless both Washington and London sent similar reports to Antonov. They warned that there were two German groupings to watch out for: (1) in Pomerania, a region in north-central Europe, from which the Germans would counterattack toward the Vistula port and city of Torun, and (2) a southern counteroffensive grouping, which included the SS Sixth Panzer Army, located in the region of Vienna and Moravska Ostravá, a major industrial and communications city in north-central Czechoslovakia, for an offensive in the direction of Lodz.

Antonov then manuevered the Red Army to meet the attack on the basis of the Allied intelligence. But when the Sixth SS Panzer Army attacked on March 5–6 it did so not from the directions indicated by the Allied intelligence services but from the direction of Lake Balaton in Hungary. In fact, Antonov asserted, the attack was one of the heaviest of the war, and the Red Army suffered great losses, although through the genius of Marshal Tolbukhin, the commander in chief on that front, and the excellence of Stalin's spies, the Red Army recovered, counterattacked, and took Vienna.

Antonov was, however, courteous enough about the erroneous intelligence when first he wrote to General Marshall about it on March 30, 1945:

A possibility is not excluded that some of the sources of this information aimed to disorientate the Anglo-American Command as well as the Soviet Command and to divert the attention of the Soviet Command from the region where the principal offensive operation of the Germans was being prepared on the Eastern Front. . . . I consider it my duty to inform General Marshall regarding the above with the only purpose that he could make certain conclusions regarding the source of this information.

In closing, Antonov hastened to add that he hoped Marshall would "continue to inform us regarding available data about the enemy"— yet another indication that the Russians could not themselves read either Enigma or Geheimschreiber.

Intelligence continued to flow to the Russians except in one important direction—the secret negotiations that had been going on throughout the Yalta conference period, perhaps without the knowledge of the U.S. government, between Papen and "C's" representatives to arrange a German surrender in the west. Donovan's staff in London were evidently kept informed, for on or about February 27, 1945, Eisenhower felt sufficiently sure of his information to advise the Combined Chiefs of Staff in Washington that:

I have received word via O.S.S. channels of a possible approach by one or more senior German officers with the proposal of facilitating an Allied victory in the West in order to end the war promptly. I understand that O.S.S. has reported the fact in detail to Washington with a copy to London.

I have replied to my informant that, as these reports have gone to my Governments, any action on political levels will obviously be taken at their direction, and that so far as any purely military approach is concerned, the channels should be those which are recognized by the customs and usages of war. However, I have no intention of choking off this channel of possible communication with me. [30]

By that date the U.S. armies had begun to close a gigantic trap around Army Group "B" and its 320,000 officers and men. Mass surrenders had already begun when, in the afternoon of March 23, the eve of Montgomery's massive operation to cross the Rhine, Churchill left London ostensibly to observe Montgomery's operations. While still there on February 24, Churchill received a copy of a telegram sent by Molotov, the Soviet foreign minister, to the British foreign secretary and the U.S. secretary of state alleging that "for two weeks behind the back of the Soviet Union which is bearing the brunt of the war against Germany, negotiations have been going on between representatives of German Military Command on the one hand and representatives of the English and Americans on the other." [31]

That menacing telegram proved to be but the first of a series of allegations that the U.S. and U.K. governments were negotiating a separate peace with the Germans, one intended to prevent further Russian advances into the center of Europe. In that exchange figured anew the question of the "intelligence of a special character" referred to at the Yalta Conference. So serious were Churchill's concerns at the possible consequences of the conversations that, indeed, he doubted the wisdom of allowing his wife, Clementine, to continue her journey to Moscow, where she was to be a state guest of Stalin.

The next Russian telegram indicated the gravity of their attitude. On February 26, Churchill learned that Molotov would not attend the founding conference of the United Nations at San Francisco shortly, and that instead the Soviet government would send instead no more than a low-level delegation. The correspondence relating to the surrender conversations was then elevated to the dangerous level of heads of state. Roosevelt intervened and expressed his regret to Stalin that the surrender conversations had developed "an atmosphere of fear and distrust."

To that telegram Stalin replied on April 3, 1945, in what was his ugliest message of the war:

I have received your message on the question of negotiations in Bern. You are absolutely right that in connection with the affair regarding negotiations of the Anglo-American command with the German command somewhere in Bern or some other place "has developed an atmosphere of fear and distrust deserving regrets."

Using expressions that indicated that he was being kept informed by an agent somewhere in the Allied high command—his informant may well have been Philby making his first appearance as a Soviet spy on the grand scale—Stalin continued:

You insist that there have been no negotiations yet.

It may be assumed that you have not yet been fully informed. As regards my military colleagues, they, on the basis of data which they have on hand, do not have doubts, that the negotiations have taken place and that they have ended in an agreement with the Germans, on the basis of which the German commander on the western front . . . has agreed to open the front and permit the Anglo-American troops to advance to the east, and the Anglo-Americans have promised to ease for the Germans the peace terms.

Stalin went on to declare, revealing the innate suspicion of all official Russians for "C" and his services, that he could not understand "the silence of the British who have allowed you to correspond with me on this unpleasant matter, and they themselves remain silent, although it is known that the initiative [the Cable incident] in this whole affair with the negotiations . . . belongs to the British."

Marshal Stalin then made the gravest allegation against the western powers:

As a result of this at the present moment the Germans on the western front in fact have ceased the war against England and the United States.* At the same time the Germans continue the war with Russia, the Ally of England and the United States. It is understandable that such a situation can in no way serve the cause of preservation [?or] the strengthening of trust between our countries. . . . I personally and my colleagues would have never made such a risky step, being aware that a momentary advantage, no matter what it would be, is fading before the principal advantage of the preservation and strengthening of the trust among the Allies. [32]

President Roosevelt replied that he had received Stalin's message "with astonishment." He reminded Stalin that he had sent a full explanation concerning the talks and expressed the opinion that Stalin's information "must have come from German sources which have made persistent efforts to create dissension between us in order to escape in some measure from responsibility for their war crimes." At the same time, Churchill sent a telegram to Stalin denying the Soviet allegations and also denying that the Germans had stopped fighting in the west. As this signal made its way to the Kremlin, and no doubt gave Stalin a reminder of the fresh power that confronted him in the west, on April 6, 1945, President Roosevelt sent Churchill a portentous telegram—one that foreshadowed, perhaps, as deep a change in FDR's attitude toward Russia as Stalin's attitude was changing toward the west. Roosevelt stated that he was "in general agreement" with Churchill's suggestion that the Allies should meet the Russian armies as far to the east as possible and, again if possible, take Berlin. He added, too, a message that made a powerful impression on the British inner circle. "Our armies will in a very few days be in a position," the president declared, "that will permit us to become 'tougher' than has heretofore appeared advantageous to the war effort." [33]

As to FDR's telegram to Stalin, it produced no retraction from the Soviet leader. Stalin insisted that "It is hard to agree that the absence of German resistance on the western front is due solely to the fact that they have been beaten. The Germans have 147 divisions on the eastern front. They could safely withdraw from fifteen to twenty

*If figures published in 1969 by Seweryn Bialer are correct, it appears that Stalin was not unjustified in his suspicions. In his book *Stalin and his Generals* (New York: Pegasus, 1969, p. 621), Bialer asserts that in the period April 11–20, 1945, 577 German soldiers on the western front were killed and "some" 1,951 wounded. On the eastern front the figures for the same period were 7,587 killed and 35,414 wounded. Again in the same period, 268,229 German soldiers were reported "missing" in the west compared with 25,823 in the east.

divisions from the eastern front to aid their forces on the western front. Yet they have not done so, nor are they doing so."

Stalin then returned to the question of the intelligence sent to General Antonov by Brooke and Marshall in February—information relating to the Sixth SS Panzer Army—and did so in terms that suggested that he believed an attempt had been made by the Anglo-American staffs to deceive him concerning the direction of a massive German counterattack. As Stalin declared:

In February, General Marshall made available to the General Staff of the Soviet troops a number of important reports in which he, citing data in his possession, warned the Russians that in March the Germans were planning two serious counter-blows on the Eastern Front, one from Pomerania towards [Torun], the other from the Moravska Ostrava area towards Lodz. It turned out, however, that the main German blow had been prepared, and delivered, not in the areas mentioned above, but in an entirely different area, namely, in the Lake Balaton area, south-west of Budapest. The Germans, as we now know, had concentrated 35 divisions in the area, 11 of them armoured. This, with its great concentration of armour, was one of the heaviest blows of the war. Marshal Tolbukhin succeeded first in warding off disaster and then in smashing the Germans, and was able to do so also because my informants had disclosed—true, with some delay—the plan for the main German blow and immediately apprised Marshal Tolbukhin. Thus I had yet another opportunity to satisfy myself as to the reliability and soundness of my sources of information. [34]

To that statement, Stalin appended another note on the subject by Antonov:

On February 20 I received a message from General Marshall through General Deane, saying that the Germans were forming two groups for a counter-offensive on the Eastern Front: one in Pomerania to strike in the direction of Thorne and the other in the Vienna-Moravska Ostrava area to advance in the direction of Lodz. The southern group was to include the 6th SS Panzer Army. On February 12 I received similar information from Colonel Brinkman, head of the Army Section of the British Military Mission.

I am very much obliged and grateful to General Marshall for the information, designed to further our common aims, which he so kindly made available to us.

At the same time it is my duty to inform General Marshall that the military operations on the Eastern Front in March did not bear out the information furnished by him. For the battles showed that the main group of German troops, which included the 6th SS Panzer Army, had been concentrated, not in Pomerania or in the Moravska Ostrava area, but in the Lake Balaton area, whence the Germans launched their offensive in an attempt to break through to the Danube and force it south of Budapest.

Thus the information supplied by General Marshall was at variance with the actual course of events on the Eastern Front in March.

It may well be that certain sources of this information wanted to bluff both Anglo-American and Soviet Headquarters and divert the attention of the Soviet High Command from the area where the Germans were mounting their main offensive.

Despite the foregoing, I would ask General Marshall, if possible, to keep me posted with information about the enemy.

I consider it my duty to convey this information to General Marshall, solely for the purpose of enabling him to draw the proper conclusions in relation to the source of the information. [35]

In short, by its tenor and context Stalin's belief was that the intelligence sent to the Red Army was not only wrong but it was also *deceptive* in intent, that "C" had provided the Russians with false information to smother the Russians' attempt to take Vienna, a capital regarded by Churchill as pivotal to the postwar political control of eastern and south-eastern Europe.

Certainly the intelligence given to Antonov was British in origin, for Antonov received it *first* from Colonel Brinkman of the British army staff in Moscow on February 12, eight days *before* similar information was received from Marshall. Moreover, "C" certainly had a safe hand in Moscow by which he could be sure that the intelligence reached Antonov in good time to affect his thinking: Colonel Roderick Napoleon Brinckman was chief of the British army staff in Moscow and a member of White's.

But if the intelligence was *suspect*, there were several reasons why it could not have been *deceptive*, not the least of which was that the Americans in Washington produced an identical estimate of German intentions to that of the British. Unless Marshall and Brooke engaged jointly in a deception (which is not likely given the desire of FDR to make a friend of Russia at Yalta), the American staff must have accepted as true the intelligence upon which the estimate was reached. If it was otherwise then Menzies must have deceived the Americans in order to deceive the Russians, and that seems improbable, too dangerous a stratagem to contemplate unless it *was*, however unlikely, undertaken in conjunction with the American chief of staff.

Indeed, all the evidence suggests that Stalin was outwitted not by his allies, but by his enemies.* Yet the very ferocity of Stalin's accusations demonstrated his conviction that he had been deceived by the western powers in an attempt to use the German army by indirection to keep the Russians as far to the east of Vienna as possible. That belief, read together with his allegations that Eisenhower had secretly negotiated with the enemy to open the western frontier, led to far-reaching consequences. It is not too much to state that if the Cold War had its origins outside the ideological differences between Moscow, London, and Washington, they lay in these charges.

The vehement correspondence between the triumvirs ended on April 11, 1945, when FDR sent another message to Churchill, declaring, "I would minimize the general Soviet problem as much as possible because these problems, in one form or another, seem to arise every day and most of them straighten out as in the case of the Bern meeting. We must be firm, however, and our course thus far is correct." [36] That was FDR's last message, for he died suddenly the next day. He was succeeded by Harry Truman, who was received with a cordiality bordering upon relief at the British embassy, where Lord Halifax, in the course of a long appreciation of the new president, advised Churchill:

Nation at large and Washington in particular seems stunned by the blow of the President's death, and first emotion is one of acute nervousness about the future. The natural instinct of these sheep without a shepherd is to herd together for common security. . . . Assistant Secretary Dean Acheson has been telling his friends not underestimate Truman, whom he had found . . . to be a man of solid sense, wholly Rooseveltian views on international affairs, considerable courage, and guts and, above all, eminently educable [sic]. . . . Truman is warmly pro British, and [he has spoken] about India with trenchant good sense and complained . . . of American ignorance and confusion on the subject which left nothing to be desired. . . . You will I am sure find him to be an admirable representative of the simple, attractive, honest, open-minded American of good-will with whom it is possible to establish from the beginning a basis of close and lasting collaboration. . . . The earlier an attempt is made to mend close Anglo-American links . . . the better for the grand alliance and the world. [37]

Halifax's vision of felicity would not be as easily attained as the British wished. The Americans were tasting global power and authority for the first time, found it congenial, and were not inclined to relinquish

---

*The author investigated Stalin's allegations at length in the National Archives, Washington, D.C. The evidence for this is too lengthy and complicated to use at this point. But Stalin's accusations were sufficiently grave to warrant their inclusion in the text at appendix H.

it easily. But Churchill retained immense authority, partly at least through the excellence of his intelligence services.

One of Truman's earliest acts was to order an end to OSS negotiations with German representatives, although that order was not despatched in time to affect the outcome of the Papen negotiations, which in any case seem to have been conducted entirely by "C's" service. Trapped in the Ruhr pocket by U.S. armies, Model resorted to legal artifice to enable his command to surrender without engaging the Allies in formal discussion—an artifice that suggests strongly the wily hand of von Papen. Reasoning that there could be no formal surrender of a command that did not exist, his issued a simple order telling the 320,000 officers and men of the army group, in effect, to go home. His staff issued discharge papers to the soldiers, the command disintegrated, and the men trudged off looking for a prisoner-of-war camp. Model then went into a deep forest near Düsseldorf and shot himself on the grounds that a German field marshal never surrendered.

As for Papen, at about the same time a patrol from the U.S. 194th Glider Infantry Regiment arrested von Papen at his estate near Hirschberg on the eastern periphery of the Ruhr pocket. He was then interrogated at length personally by Eisenhower's chief intelligence officer, General K. W. D. Strong, and his American deputy, General T. J. Betts. Papen was imprisoned and then arraigned as a major Nazi war criminal. At Nuremberg he claimed to have been a man who had lived "according to the best of my ability in the service of God and my country." One of the few major criminals to be acquitted, Papen may have owed his acquittal to an intercession by "C," for an entry in Cadogan's diary on April 8 showed that "C" was sufficiently pleased with Papen's work in arranging the surrender of the German army group in the Ruhr to send his crony, David Boyle, to the Foreign Office on that day. As Cadogan recorded of their meeting:

Boyle (S.I.S.) called for a longish and not v. useful talk about 6.30. He gave me his ideas of a memorial* to Papen. I had to spray a little cold water.

With Army Group B's surrender, the German Army in the west fell apart and the Third Reich entered its last phase. The German

---

*It is assumed that Cadogan used the term memorial in the legal or diplomatic sense: "A statement of facts drawn up for counsel's opinion. Also, an advocate's brief." A further definition of the term is: "A statement of facts forming the basis of or expressed in the form of a petition to a person in authority, a government, etc."

armed forces began a series of piecemeal surrenders everywhere except on the Russian front, where the Wehrmacht fought to the last cartridge. Yet for "C" there was little diminution in the flow of paper that crossed his desk, for there was a new enemy—Russia. Churchill issued veiled directives in a number of pregnant matters. As Churchill himself told constituents at Woodford, Essex, in 1954:

Even before the war had ended and while the Germans were surrendering by hundreds of thousands, and our streets were crowded with cheering people, I telegraphed to Lord Montgomery directing him to be careful in collecting the German arms, to stack them so that they could easily be issued again to the German soldiers whom we should have to work with if the Soviet advance continued.

When asked whether Churchill's statement was true, that England had prepared for war with Russia using the defeated German army as an ally even before the war had ended, Montgomery replied: "I obeyed my orders!" Pause. "It's true." Asked later in Parliament whether he had intended to fight the Red Army with German soldiers, Churchill replied: "Of course, if they went on." As he explained also, he "distinctly and strongly felt that victory could have become a tragedy in 1945." If the Russians had continued their advance westward, he had felt that they should be warned "that we should certainly in that case rearm German prisoners in our hands, who already, including those in Italy, numbered two and a half million." He had not judged the German army as had others, by their "political label." The majority were "ordinary people compelled into military service and fighting desperately in defense of their native land."

And even as Churchill issued the orders to stockpile German weapons and munitions, "C" had initiated a new cryptanalytical intelligence program against the Soviet government. As the Enigma and Fish programs began to fade with the collapse of the Third Reich, therefore, new intercepts, code-named Bride, began to be circulated within the secret circle. These operations were well developed as the war entered its last weeks with, as it had begun, a plot against Hitler. During a talk with Himmler in early April, Schellenberg, still chief of the Sicherheitsdienst's foreign secret intelligence service, attempted to persuade Himmler to overthrow Hitler and assume the position of Führer and Chancellor of the Greater German Reich.

At Schellenberg's insistence, and with the object of improving his international standing, Himmler promised Count Bernadotte, a Swedish intermediary, that he would release the Danish Jews in concentration camps and then promised to turn over the camps at Bergen-Belsen, Buchenwald, Therensienstadt, and those in south Germany to the Allied armies as each camp was approached. As a first measure Himmler released Jewish and other women from the camp at Ravensbruck. Himmler then discussed his position vis-à-vis Hitler's "continued power and authority in the light of his deteriorating physical condition." [38]

Himmler said that "Hitler's energy was undiminished in spite of the completely unnatural life he led—turning night into day and sleeping at most three or four hours—and that his continuous activity and constant outburst of fury completely exhausted his entourage and created an unbearable atmosphere." It was possible, Himmler thought, that the explosion of the bomb at Rastenburg had affected Hitler's health more seriously than was thought. Himmler "stressed the constant stoop, the pale visage, the severe trembling and also the operation in November on Hitler's ear, the result of the concussion of the brain that he had received at that time."

In Himmler's view Hitler was no longer fit to rule. He suggested obliquely that the way to overthrow Hitler was through his doctors. Schellenberg then arranged a meeting between Himmler, Professor Max de Crinis, a leading Berlin psychologist, and Reichsgesundheitsführer, Conti, where it was decided that Hitler had contracted Parkinson's disease, the main treatment for which was then the surgical destruction of a small area of the brain, a procedure that would entail the risk of Hitler's death on the operating table. At a further conference between Himmler and Schellenberg, Schellenberg stated bluntly that if Himmler was not prepared to have Hitler arrested then the best way to prepare for the peace was that "the doctors must intervene."

At a third conference, held in mid-April, one attended this time by Professor de Crinis, Hitler's personal physician, Morell, an SS doctor, Stumpfegger, and Martin Bormann, head of Hitler's chancellery and Rudolf Hess's successor as deputy führer of the Nazi party. The doctors agreed to recommend "certain medicines for Hitler." These were prepared at de Crinis's laboratory but the "doctor's plot" against the life of Hitler failed as had all the other conspiracies. In all there were eighteen plots in twelve years. Indeed, Himmler proved less efficient in conspiracy than Canaris, who at about this same time was murdered by the SS in Flossenburg concentration camp on the orders of Kaltenbrunner, chief of the Sicherheitsdienst. Canaris was suspended naked on a meat hook, where he remained for almost an hour until he was dead. He was then cremated and his ashes scattered to the winds of Saxony. Canaris's last words were conveyed to "C" later by Colonel Hans M. Lunding, former chief of the Danish intelligence service, who had been in the next cell. Before the execution Canaris had tapped to Lunding in prison Morse:

I die for my country and with a clear conscience. . . . You as officer will realize that I was only doing my duty to my country when I endeavored to oppose Hitler. . . . Do what you can for my wife daughters. . . . They've broken my nose. . . . I die this morning. . . . Farewell.

Thus Canaris died, unmourned by almost all men (except "C," who thought his old enemy was "damned brave and damned unlucky").

"C's" last case of World War II began in late April. Was Hitler alive or dead? If he was alive, then where was he? Here "C's" main informants were not spies but the Ultra decrypts of the Japanese representatives of the Tripartite Commission and the embassy. These told the main story of Germany in extremis. Another Ultra, which was suppressed by "C" in order not to fuel to gossip and speculation about Hitler's whereabouts, dated April 21 showed that on that day Hitler was in Berlin but that his staff and servants were being evacuated by air and road to the Obersalzburg, in the heart of the area known as "the redoubt" in English and the *Reichsverteidigungsstellung* in German. The two words had the same meaning—a fortification, a secret place, a refuge.

The April 21 Ultra was of importance, for on that day Goering (nominally, at least, Hitler's successor) arrived at Obersalzburg and had received "serious information" that "Hitler was no longer able to carry on government outside Berlin." [39] Goering then prepared to assume Hitler's place as Führer and Chancellor of the German Reich. But to be sure Goering sent a signal to the Reichs chancellery in Berlin, where Hitler was last known to be, to establish whether Hitler had or had not "freedom of action." By this stage Ultra had begun to reflect the incoherency and hysteria of the last hours of the German Reich. It was true that Goering's signal elicited a sharp reply from Hitler, which was, apparently, signed by him. Hitler accused Goering of treason and ordered the SS representative in the Obersalzburg, Gottlob Berger, to arrest and execute Goering. But this was not clear evidence that Hitler was alive. Indeed, there was a hint of evidence—but no more—that Hitler might be contemplating flight to Japan.

On April 24, the Japanese minister, Kase, in Berne reported to Tokyo what he called "rather concrete knowledge of the circumstances of the Germans having made preparations for long-distance communications flights to Japan," and the belief of some Germans that "Hitler or the Party leaders will try in the last scene to escape to Japan by this means, whether Japan likes the idea or not." "C" paid special attention to an Ultra of April 12, in which the Japanese military and naval attachés in Berlin jointly asked Tokyo for an immediate decision regarding a German plan to send a special Junkers 290 to Japan from the Luftwaffe base at Bardufoss in northern Norway. The aircraft was to take the great circle route over the Polar region to the Bering Strait, thence over the sea east of Kamchatka to Paramushiro Island in the Kuriles, then Japanese territory. The distance involved was 4,785 miles, which was within the range of a JU 290B.

As the Ultra also showed, whoever was coming intended to remain in Japan. And as the U.S. Navy also noted: "Some months earlier the Germans had proposed sending Air Attaché Kessler [an officer mentioned by Doenitz to Abe as being at sea on his way to Japan in one of the few remaining long-range submarines] to Japan by air across Siberia, but were unable to get [Japan's] consent because of the possibility of complications with Russia in the event of a forced landing." [40] It is evident, therefore, that this was an escape plan for some very high official of the German Reich.

Although neither "C" nor Donovan were able to produce proof positive that Hitler had escaped from Berlin, and that the story of his suicide in the bunker was merely cover for that escape, Stalin at least thought Hitler had escaped. As late as May 23, three weeks or so after the Red Army occupied Berlin and the bunker where Hitler spent his last hours, the Soviet leader told Harry Hopkins, the U.S. presidential agent, according to the official record:

Hitler was not dead but hiding somewhere. He said the Soviet doctors thought they had identified the body of Goebbels and Hitler's chauffeur, but that he, personally, even doubted if Goebbels was dead and said the whole matter was strange and various talks of funerals and burials struck him as being very dubious.

Stalin thought that Hitler, Goebbels, and Borman had escaped from Berlin and had gone into hiding.

Stalin stated, also, that he knew of submarines running back and forth between Germany and Japan, taking gold and negotiable assets from Germany to to Japan with "the connivance of" certain Swiss individuals. He said that

he had ordered his intelligence service to look into the matter of these submarines but so far they had failed to discover any trace and therefore he thought it was possible that Hitler and company had gone in them to Japan.

As late as July and the Potsdam conference between himself, Churchill and Truman, Stalin continued to make statements showing that he disbelieved strongly that Hitler had committed suicide, as members of his bodyguard and entourage in the bunker in those last hours asserted. Nor was "C" able to cast light on the mystery before 1946 when, such was the strength of the rumors that Hitler was still alive, Professor Trevor-Roper was given the task of investigating Hitler's death. Although he subscribed to the report that Hitler was dead, "C" was never able to verify this.

But by April 25, however, it was evident from Ultra that Hitler was not in the redoubt. Nor could he get there, for that day American and Russian troops joined fronts at Torgau, the old town where Martin Luther wrote the documents that led to the Augsburg Confession. America and Russia were now face to face, with every political entity between them in ruins, including England.

The age of the superpowers had arrived.

With Germany cut in half, it could now be only a matter of days before the decision was obtained in the long German march toward *weltmarcht oder niedergang*—world power or downfall. And as it was since the beginning, so it was in the end: "C" had but to sit at his desk at Broadway, or on his bumwarmer, and read the Ultra flimsies coming across his desk to witness what was happening during the last weeks of *das tasenjahrige reich*, the empire that was to have lasted a thousand years—everything that is except Ultra that showed that Hitler was definitely dead.

If Hitler was indeed in Berlin and in the Reichschancellery, then there was no prospect of his escape, for Berlin had been surrounded by the Russians. Hitler had prepared his political and personal last wills and testaments. The former expelled both Goering and Himmler from all posts in the government and also from their membership in the Nazi party, and transferred the power of the state to Grand Admiral Doenitz. In his personal will, he spoke of his affection for Eva Braun, who was at his side and whom he had just formally married.

The Ultra indications were that Hitler carried on the business of chancellor for another twenty-four hours. Then, at 4:00 P.M. on April 30, two hours after two Russian sergeants had hoisted the Red flag over the ruins of the Reichstag, Adolf Hitler shot himself dead. Eva Braun died soon after, having taken poison. But there was never any posthumous evidence of their deaths or that their corpses were then taken into a courtyard to be incinerated with two hundred liters of petrol, as the few remaining diehards made the Roman salute over the pyre. Nor were the ashes of either Hitler or Eva Braun ever found.

All that was truly certain, therefore, was that at last the Reich had expired. Silence came to ruined Europe. The German surrender came on May 7, 1945. It was a total and unconditional surrender coupled with the occupation of the German Reich. Nine million German fighting men laid down their arms amid the ruins. The German General Staff was arrested, and their highest officers were incarcerated in a camp in the Taunus Hills, code-named Ashcan. Bletchley and Colossus II went silent for a period during the celebrations. And then came the last signal of the Third Reich, from Goering to Hitler, and it carried with it a ghostly echo of Teuton dreams of world dominion. Dated April 22, 1945, it had somehow become lost in the torrent of signals of the last few weeks:

My Fuehrer,
I beg you most fervently in the interest of the Reich and the nation to come here into the South German area. I have been able to assure myself sufficiently on my journey that, by making the fullest use of every possibility much can still be achieved for the struggle and that, with the old energy [word or two illegible] resistance can still be offered here successfully. My distress at knowing that you are at this hour in Berlin has no limits.

Hail my Fuehrer!
Your Faithful
Hermann Goering

The Colossi computers had clicked out their priceless intelligence to the end, and the secret of Ultra had been kept.

The golden age of British intelligence had ended.

Ten

Into the Cold War

1945–1952

1 THE RECKONING

World War II ended formally on May 8, 1945, with a BBC broadcast to the world by Winston Churchill. Authorized representatives of the German Reich had presented themselves to the headquarters of General Eisenhower at Rheims and had formally accepted the terms of unconditional surrender.

Churchill exhorted the subjects of the empire only to permit themselves a brief rejoicing as "Japan, with all her treachery and greed, remains unsubdued," and he reminded his audience that "the injury she has inflicted on Great Britain, the United States, and other countries, and her detestable cruelties call for justice and retribution." Therefore "we must now devote all our strength and resources to the completion of our task, both at home and abroad." Churchill's voice broke as he uttered the closing words: "Advance, Brittania! Long live the cause of freedom! God save the King."

His radio broadcast over, Churchill then drove in an open car from the garden entrance of 10 Downing Street and across the Horse Guards Parade to the House of Commons. Everywhere there were great crowds. He entered the chamber at 3:30 P.M., and the Commons rose as a man and cheered and waved their order papers. Having read the speech he had just made over the BBC, he then put his manuscript aside and declared that "all the objectives which we set before us for the procuring of the unlimited and unconditional surrender of the enemy have been achieved."

He recalled that twenty-six years before, at the end of World War I, the Commons, upon hearing the long list of surrender terms that were imposed upon the Germans, were disinclined to discuss them at that time and wished instead "to offer thanks to Almighty God, to the Great Power which seems to shape and design the fortunes of nations and the destiny of man." Therefore, addressing the Speaker of the House, he moved that " 'this House do now attend at the Church of St. Margaret, Westminster to give humble and reverent thanks to Almighty God for our deliverance from the threat of German domination.' This is the identical Motion which was moved in former times."

"C" of course did not attend, as was the custom, for he still did not exist officially. Nor did he attend the dinner given by King George VI for Churchill and other members and advisers of the War Cabinet, for the same reason. But after the dinner Churchill returned to 10 Downing Street to attend to his papers, and in what was one of his first actions of the peace, the prime minister wrote this note to "C" and placed it in a buff despatch box for carriage to Broadway:

My admiration for the work of your Organization cannot be made public. It nevertheless arises from knowledge and constant use of all that has been done. The services rendered, the incredible difficulties surmounted, and the [?victories] gained in the course of the war, cannot be over-estimated. Everyone who has taken part, working at such a ceaseless strain, deserves the most cordial expression of my approval. Will you, within the secret circle, convey to all possible my compliments and gratitude to a large band of devoted and patriotic workers.

There is no doubt of the official opinion of "C" at the end of the war. Churchill told King George VI in Menzies's presence that "it was thanks to Ultra that we won the war." [1] Without Ultra England could not have defeated the German air force in the Battle of Britain, the first major setback suffered by Hitler, and more certainly the Allies could not have won the Battle of the Atlantic. The invasion could not have been launched when it was, if ever, without Ultra. Given the combination of German weapons technology, German morale, and the determination of Hitler's war leadership, Hitler would have turned his might upon Russia. Bloodlet, exhausted, inefficient, Russia would not have survived. In turn, dismayed by the collapse of the Allied strategy and alliance, America would have turned to the Pacific rather than the Atlantic war. When, and if, America returned to the Atlantic, Hitler would have become master of Eurasia at least until 1948, the earliest at which assembly-line production of atomic bombs could have been introduced into the war.

Therefore, the cardinal factor in the Atlantic war was Ultra. That enabled the Allies to assemble the necessary power at the right place and time. Since "C" was director and then director-general of Bletchley, he warranted permanent regard for his direction of that extraordinary establishment, just as he was finally responsible for anything that went wrong there.

At that moment in his long career, Stewart Menzies's reputation, and that of the office of "C," had never stood higher. He was the world master of intelligence and one of Churchill's principal advisers in a triumphant administration that had wrought victory out of defeat without the overwhelming slaughter of World War I. The war casualties of the British Empire totaled 354,652 killed and 470,908 wounded, against the 1,000,000 dead and 2,000,000 wounded of World War I. Against 3,000,000 German dead and 1,000,000 wounded, the United States had 230,173 dead and 613,611 wounded.

Whereas in the First World War the empire had lost 38,834 officers, men who were the national elite, in this war the Royal Air Force, considered to be the "new elite," had lost 70,253 officers. When the officer casualties in the navy, army, and special forces were added to this figure, the total number of officers killed was at least treble the World War I figure. England had lost another generation of leaders.

When that was related to the financial cost of the war—an estimated $150 billion—the empire found itself fatally weakened, physically, spiritually, and politically. The authority of the Crown and the British ruling class had been destroyed, the empire was infected with republicanism, the British electorate was divided, and the worst fears of English statesmen were realized—the European political system had been destroyed. The armies of America and Russia now stood face to face in Central Europe with nothing between them. England was no longer a first-class world power. As the United States withdrew her mighty armies from Europe and prepared to deal with Japan, England was left alone to fight a new, unprecedented, worldwide struggle with the forces of a triumphant Marxism.

It was not long before the first of those symbols of a shattered British ideology—the traitors—began to appear in the British courts. The first to be dealt with was well known to "C." No event affected Stewart Menzies more deeply than the high treason of John Amery, oldest son of Leopold C.M.S. Amery, one of England's leading imperial statesmen. It was a classic case of what Talleyrand had meant when he declared, *"Traihson et une question du date"*—in other words, what is treason today may not have been treason yesterday and may not be considered treason tomorrow.

The tragedy that befell the Amerys epitomized the moral and political dilemma that had beset that British ruling class ever since the Bolshevik revolution. "C" had known Leo Amery since they were at GHQ together in World War I. Their views on the British Empire were very similar, both were praetorians by training and instinct. They had seen a great deal of each other between the wars as, in turn, Amery became first lord of the Admiralty, secretary of state for the colonies, secretary of state for dominion affairs, and then secretary of state for India and Burma in Churchill's government between 1940 and 1945.

The black sheep of the family was John Amery. He had been at Summerfields and Eton, but afterward he had gone wrong. Although he shared his father's politics regarding the dangers of Russian bolshevism, John was continually in trouble. Most of the trouble was of a discreditable sort—dangerous driving, bounced checks, trouble with the ladies. He was made bankrupt for five thousand pounds just before the Spanish Civil War. In an effort to make a man of him, it seems, Leo Amery asked Menzies to employ his son as a spy on the Franco side during that civil war. Young Amery then went to Spain, where he became involved in gunrunning to Franco. He became an ardent Fascist, forming, as did so many of his class at that time, the conviction that communism, not fascism, was the class enemy.

John Amery does seem to have conducted himself with some distinction in Franco's interests, and perhaps also in Menzies's. He claimed to have been given honorary Spanish citizenship as reward for his services to Franco. At the same time he became heavily involved with Jacques Doriot, the former mayor of Saint-Denis, a suburb of Paris, and a Communist-turned-Fascist who, at the outbreak of war, was known as a passionate admirer of Hitler and nazism.

Amery was trapped in France during the French collapse but appears to have done little against the British interest until the establishment of the Anglo-Soviet Treaty upon the German invasion of Russia.

Amery then began to make radio broadcasts in the German interest, but only against Russia, not England. Also, Amery conceived the idea of recruiting British prisoners-of-war at a camp at Saint-Denis to establish what he called the Legion of St. George, to fight not against England, but with the German armies against Russia. While the legion did not go into action against Russia—it seems that Amery was able to recruit only fifteen Britons—nevertheless, by the laws of England, Amery had given "aid and comfort to the King's enemies" and had, therefore, committed high treason, a capital offense.

Amery was captured by Italian partisans near Milan in April 1945 while seeking to escape into Germany in his Lancia Aprilia motor car. He was then turned over by his captors to a Special Operations Executive group controlling the partisans. He was officially classified as "the renegade John Amery" and returned to England to stand trial for treachery. On his arrival in London Amery confessed all.

John Amery was formally charged, "having between June 22, 1941, and April 25, 1945, he being a person owing allegiance to the King, adhered to the King's enemies elsewhere than in the King's realm— to wit: in the German and Italian realms and in those parts of the Continent of Europe controlled by the King's enemies." The ultimate penalty for anyone who pleaded guilty to this offense, or was found guilty of it, was death by hanging.

The prosecution then presented its case, in the course of which Amery's very long statement was read. The thrust of this statement was that at the time he made the broadcasts, and established the Legion of St. George, Amery believed that the world, and particularly the British Empire, stood in greater danger from Russian bolshevism than German nazism. Since that time, Amery asserted, nothing had occurred to make him change his mind. On the contrary, the world stood in greater danger of bolshevism now than it had during the war—a sentiment with which most members of Amery's class, Menzies included, agreed. For that reason, therefore, it was not expected that Amery would be executed if found guilty.

The Soviet *New Times*, an English-language newspaper that had been vigilant throughout the war for any sign that British "reactionaries" were deviating from both the spirit and the letter of the Anglo-Soviet agreement, declared that Leo Amery, who was one of those "reactionaries," and his friends were "using their influence to delay the course of the law." The general impression left by the *New Times* "is one of collusion between Mr. Amery's family, other British persons in high places, and British legal authorities to save John Amery from the penalty for his treason." [2]

Against swelling rather than diminishing concern on the part of the Russian and British extreme left wing that the British ruling class was seeking to protect one of its own, the trial was resumed at the Old Bailey on November 28, 1945. Few thought that John Amery would be hanged if found guilty, but the trial, which was one of the most dramatic ever witnessed at that ancient court of law, ended in enigmatic tragedy. The first sign of drama in the cell below the court where Amery was being held was that the judge did not appear on the bench at 11:00 A.M., when the trial was due to begin. There was no prisoner in the dock, no jury in the box. Amery's counsel, Gerald Slade, K.C., and John Foster, left their seats and hastened to the cells below. According to Amery's brother, Julian, at the last moment his brother decided to plead guilty to the charge in order to spare his family, and particularly his mother, further embarrassment, even though the *automatic* sentence upon such a plea was death by hanging.

After half an hour there was a flurry in the court, the judge, Mr. Justice Humphreys, "entered in shrivelled and eccentric majesty," a man "small in the depths of his red and purple robes." Counsel reappeared, and John Amery was led into the dock looking like "a sick little monkey," one who was "yellow with fear, but behaved well." The indictments against him were read out, that he had made "treasonable broadcasts and speeches," that he had "attempted to seduce British subjects from the allegiance." Amery surprised all by declaring, "I plead guilty to all counts." And at that moment, as the British author Rebecca West, who was present for *The New Yorker*, recorded:

A murmur ran through the court which was horrified, which was expostulatory, which was tinged with self-pity, for this was suicide. If he pleaded guilty he must be sentenced to death, for there is no alternative sentence for treason, and it is not in the power of any judge to substitute a term of imprisonment. There is only the possibility that the Home Secretary may advise the Crown to reprieve the condemned man; and this happens only in certain circumstances, not to be found in any eye in the case of John Amery. In effect, the young man was saying, "I insist on being hanged by the neck in three weeks' time." [3]

Later that same day Amery was taken to Pentonville Prison, London, and lodged in the death cell. He was visited each day by either his father, his mother, or his brother, and sometimes all three. Then, on the eve of the execution, Leo Amery, the great imperial statesman, drove out to Pentonville for the last time. He was accompanied by Captain Julian Amery, lately of His Brittanic Majesty's secret service, and during the ride in the taxicab, Julian noted that his father was scribbling something on an envelope in pencil. At the death cell Julian Amery found out what it was, for during that last meeting, Leo Amery read a few lines of poetry to his condemned son:

> At the end of wayward days,
> He found a Cause.
> It was not his country's
> But who shall tell if that betrayed
> Our ancient laws?
> Was it Treason or Foreknowledge?
> He sleeps well.*

Leo Amery asked his son: "Are you afraid?" John Amery replied: "No, I am your son."

The next morning John Amery was hanged by the neck by the public hangman, Pierrepont, and Moscow Radio made an announcement applauding the action of the Socialist government.

Shortly after Amery's execution King George VI and Queen Elizabeth invited the Amery family to lunch at Buckingham Palace. The Amery family accepted, and the king and the queen each commiserated with Leo Amery, his wife, and their surviving son, Julian, in their great loss.

2 THE WINDSOR LETTERS

In rapid succession, Churchill attended the Potsdam Conference, was voted out of office at the general election in July, and was succeeded by his wartime deputy, Clement R. Attlee, who then formed a Socialist government. Early in August the U.S. Air Force dropped one atomic bomb on Hiroshima, another on Nagasaki, and the Japanese surrendered unconditionally. World War II was over.

*These lines were provided to the author by the Honorable Julian Amery at a meeting in London in April 1984.

"C" intimated to Cadogan that he wished to resign. But Cadogan insisted that it was his duty to remain to see the new government and the country through the transition from global war to peace. Throughout this period of transition from hot to cold war, therefore, "C" pursued a number of urgent tasks in Germany, the most important of which was to find and seize correspondence in the German archives between the duke of Windsor and Hitler and also with the ex-kaiser, Wilhelm II, who had been in exile at Doorn in Holland until his death in 1941. These documents acquired a special significance with the hanging of John Amery.

Toward the end of the war, Lieutenant Colonel Robert Currie Thomson, leader of an Anglo-American team working under the direction of the Combined Intelligence Objectives Committee, entered Germany to locate the records of the Reichschancellery, the chancelleries of Hitler and the Nazi party, and the German Foreign Ministry. In late May Thomson was approached by a former German Foreign Office official, Karl von Loesch, who had an important tale to tell. [4]

In the summer of 1943 Ribbentrop decided to have the archives of his secretariat microfilmed in case the originals were destroyed in an Allied air attack. Some four-fifths of these records were microfilmed: correspondence between Hitler and other heads of states; notes on discussions between Hitler, Ribbentrop, and foreign statesmen; and the main political correspondence with various German diplomatic missions abroad. These were the most important documents of the German Foreign Ministry, and in due course they were placed in Karl von Loesch's custody.

Loesch recognized their importance, and instead of destroying them as he was ordered to do, he put the films into several boxes and then buried them without the knowledge of the Foreign Ministry. At his meeting with Thomson, Loesch disclosed the existence of the film and offered to lead Thomson to where they were buried. Since Thomson's task was intelligence, he began to survey the collection and soon discovered files belonging to the state secretary at the Foreign Ministry, Baron Ernst von Weizsäker. One file was entitled "German-British Relations."

It contained reports from various German diplomats on the political attitude of the duke of Windsor while he was in Madrid and Lisbon at the time of the onset of the Battle of Britain in 1940 (when Brigadeführer SS Schellenberg was sent by Ribbentrop to arrange the abduction of the duke and duchess). Professor George Kent, an

American who also became involved with the archives, stated that the discovery caused "much perturbation" in London.

They did indeed, for as Cadogan, who was still permanent head of the Foreign Office in London and still keeping his diaries, recorded on October 25, 1945: "King fussed about Duke of Windsor file & captured German documents." The king had good reason to be distressed. If those files had concerned any mortal in the kingdom other than the duke of Windsor, they would at the very least have been sent to the director of public prosecutions to establish whether the duke had committed high treason in wartime.

As the documents first revealed, Windsor's earliest recorded conversation with Nazi agents was at Sandringham on the morrow of the death of his father, King George V. As King Edward VIII, Windsor had several long talks with a distant relative, the duke of Coburg, a Nazi agent-of-influence sent to embroil the new king in Hitler's plans for an Anglo-German entente against Russia, which would have led to a German attack.

The second set of documents dealt with Windsor's conduct in 1939–40 while, as a general in the British army, he was attached for intelligence purposes to the Anglo-French Supreme War Council at Versailles. On January 27, 1940, Julius Count von Zech-Burkesroda, German minister at The Hague, advised State Secretary von Weizsäcker that "through personal relationships I might have the opportunity to establish certain lines to the Duke of Windsor."

Those personal relationships almost certainly involved the ex-kaiser, Wilhelm II, who was the duke of Windsor's uncle, and members of the ex-kaiser's household at Doorn. As the documents revealed, Zech was well informed about the happenings within the Supreme War Council and the British government in London. Zech advised Weizsäcker that "there seems to be something like the beginning of a Fronde forming around 'W' which for the moment of course still has nothing to say, but which at some time under favourable circumstances might acquire a certain significance."*

---

*The identities of the members of the Fronde within British society disposed toward a peaceful settlement to the war were not given in this telegram. They were given, however, in other correspondence in the same file. (See: Document 201 from the German minister in Dublin to the German Foreign Ministry, July 22, 1940.) They were Chamberlain (then lord president of the council), Lord Halifax (the British foreign secretary, who was shortly to become British ambassador at Washington), Sir John Simon (chief of the commission that interrogated Hess), and Sir Samuel Hoare (British ambassador at Madrid). Other main figures included the Astors, the marquess of Londonderry, Sir Horace Wilson (head of the British civil service), certain men who were not named but were key figures in the London banking and commercial

On February 19, 1940, Zech wrote again to Weizsäcker to advise that Windsor had said "that the Allied War Council devoted an exhaustive discussion at its last meeting to the situation that would arise if Germany invaded Belgium. The duke indicated that the Anglo-French armies would move forward and occupy as much of Belgium as possible," a revelation that constituted a particularly important aspect of the Allies' war plan in the event, as was expected, that Germany invaded Belgium. That statement alone surely constituted a treasonable statement. The advice that the Allies *would* move into Belgium in the event of a German attack on that country clarified for Hitler what the Allies intended when he attacked in the west and what, therefore, his own strategy and tactics must be. But there were others like it that, even if the Germans were trying to compromise the duke, would at least warrant an examination by the director of public prosecutions. And there was more to warrant such a step, even if Windsor was a royal prince. Zech also reported that the meeting discussed the recovery of the German plan for the invasion of Western Europe from the wreck of a crashed aircraft. That leakage from the duke to Zech through intermediaries was again plainly treasonable, for the discovery that the plan was in Allied hands enabled Hitler to change the direction and weight of his operations in good time and obtain surprise for his operations.

The next document in the Windsor file was a telegram to Ribbentrop from the German ambassador at Madrid, Baron Eberhard von Stohrer, dated June 23, after the fall of France. This telegram related that the Spanish foreign minister "requests advice with regard to the treatment of the duke and duchess of Windsor who were to arrive in Madrid today, apparently in order to return to England by way of Lisbon." The Spanish foreign minister "assumes from certain impressions . . . received in Germany" that "we might perhaps be interested in detaining the Duke of Windsor here and possibly in establishing contact with him."

Ribbentrop informed Stohrer on June 24, asking whether it was possible "in the first place to detain the Duke and Duchess of Windsor for a couple of weeks in Spain before they are granted an exit visa"

---

worlds, and the editor and certain leading members of *The Times*, which was then regarded —by the Germans, at least—as the most powerful newspaper in the world. "C" was not identified with this Fronde at any time, either professionally or socially, although his predecessor, Admiral Sinclair, certainly was. The group was not considered to be treacherous by the Churchill administration, only misguided. Halifax, Hoare, and *The Times* later adjusted their attitudes, but only after England was threatened with invasion.

to proceed on to Lisbon. The next instruction to Stohrer was to advise the duke through a Spanish intermediary that the German authorities in Paris would protect his residence in the French capital, a document that indicated it was the duke himself who had asked the Germans for protection. Then, on June 30, State Secretary Weizsäcker was authorized to issue a statement of political guidance to all German missions abroad. It showed clearly that whatever the Germans said or did, they intended to use Windsor not as an instrument of rapprochement with the British, but as a pawn to achieve England's destruction. As Weizsäcker advised:

Germany is not considering peace. She is concerned exclusively with preparation for the destruction of England.

Then on July 12 the German minister in Lisbon, Baron Oswald von Hoyningen-Huene, sent a most damaging report to Ribbentrop. Huene had heard that Churchill had suggested to Windsor that he go to the Bahamas as governor-general:

As Spaniards from among those around the Duke of Windsor have informed us confidentially on visits to the Legation the designation of the Duke of Windsor as Governor of the Bahama Islands is intended to keep him, far away from England, since his return would bring with it very strong encouragement to English friends of peace, so that his arrest at the instance of his opponents would certainly have to be expected. The Duke intends to postpone his departure for the Bahama Islands as long as possible . . . in the hope of a turn of events favorable to him.

By that remark the duke was referring either to a German approach to restore him to the throne or to the possibility that he might yet to be allowed to return to England. It was not clear from the text, but as the telegram continued, the duke

is convinced that if he had remained on the throne war would have been avoided, and he characterizes himself as a firm supporter of a peaceful arrangement with Germany. The Duke definitely believes that continued severe bombardment would make England ready for peace.

By July 30, 1940, it is clear that, probably through "C," who had an excellent connection with the Spanish foreign secretary, Juan Beigbeder, Churchill was fully advised about the plot to kidnap the Windsors to prevent them from going to the Bahamas. Schellenberg reported from Lisbon that the duke had been summoned to the British legation "for a lengthy consultation," and that a "Sir Walter Turner Monckstone, a lawyer from Kent," had arrived from London. Schellenberg thought this was a cover name for "a member of the personal police of the reigning King by the name of Camerone." In fact Sir Walter "Monckstone" was Sir Walter Monkton, Windsor's lawyer, who had been sent by Churchill to induce Windsor to make a clear declaration that he would accept the post of governor of the Bahamas and leave as arranged on August 30.

By that time Windsor was reconsidering the wisdom of his dalliance with the Germans, and he asked for forty-eight hours before deciding whether or not to have a personal meeting with the Spanish interior minister. On July 31 this report of the duke's attitude was communicated to Schellenberg: "The Duke and Duchess were strongly impressed by the reports of English intrigues being carried out against them and of danger to their personal safety. They no longer feel secure. They say they cannot take a step without surveillance." It was evident that the intervention of the British ambassador and Monkton had been effective, however, for the duke declared that he would have to go to the Bahamas because

no prospect of peace existed at the moment. Further statements of the Duke indicate that he has nevertheless already given consideration to the possibility that the role of an intermediary might fall to him. He declared that the situation in England at the moment was still by no means hopeless. Therefore he should not now, by negotiations carried on contrary to the orders of his Government, let loose against himself the propaganda of his English opponents, which might deprive him of all prestige at the period when he might possibly take action. He could, if the occasion arose, take action even from the Bahamas.

Schellenberg reported after the royal couple had left for the Bahamas that he had "made certain arrangements that ought to make possible resumption of relations with the Duke" in the Bahamas. Schellenberg did not say what these arrangements were, but soon after their arrival in Nassau, Axel Wenner-Gren, the rich Swedish industrialist and German agent-of-influence, arrived in Nassau aboard his private yacht, the *Southern Cross*. Wenner-Gren and the Windsors became intimates in both social and business life in the island, and on several occasions in 1942 and 1943 Churchill expressed anxiety that a U-boat, acting under the control of the *Southern Cross*'s powerful wireless station, would land an armed party in the Bahamas and spirit the duke and duchess away to Germany. Churchill therefore ordered that a platoon of British troops be stationed around the Windsors' home in Nassau.

Having read the Loesch papers, Prime Minister Attlee wrote to Churchill, "Although clearly little or no credence can be placed in the statements made, nevertheless I feel sure that you will agree that the publication of these documents might do the greatest possible harm." Churchill agreed and replied that he "earnestly trusted" it would be possible to "destroy all traces of these German intrigues." The documents were then removed from the German Foreign Office archives at the orders of General Eisenhower and sent by safe hand to the U.S. ambassador in London, John G. Winant, who handed the microfilm to "the British authorities."

The microfilm was then given "the most secret classification and regarded by the few who knew about it, in the words of the new Foreign Secretary Ernest Bevin, as 'a 'ot potato.' " King George VI "contented himself with the reflection that, if the documents were ever to be made public, his brother should be given due warning." The microfilm then vanished, perhaps into the Foreign Office's archives, perhaps into the royal archives at Windsor Castle. [5]

Wherever it was held, it remained beyond the public sight until 1952 and the return of the Churchill government. Then, with the connivance of officials at the Foreign Office, the documents were located, an unauthorized copy was made, and the microfilm was sent to Raymond J. Sontag, editor in chief of the American team involved in the publication of the State Department's *Documents on German Foreign Policy 1918–1945*.

Alarmed, Churchill moved heaven and earth to repossess the microfilm. He wrote to President Eisenhower asking him to exert his power to prevent the publication of documents that represented "a Nazi-German intrigue to entangle and compromise a Royal Prince." If they were published, they might give the impression "that the Duke was in close touch with German agents." This would inflict "distress and injury upon one who has so long enjoyed the hospitality of the United States."

Eisenhower replied that he was "completely astonished" to learn that the microfilm was in the United States and promised to look into the matter. But he did not stop publication. Nor did Churchill's last-gasp proposal to his Cabinet that "publication be postponed for at least ten or twenty years" on the grounds that the documents would "give pain to the Duke of Windsor" and an impression "entirely disproportionate to their historical value." The documents were published in 1957 along with a statement by the British government that they were "necessarily a much-tainted source," and that the duke had "never wavered in his loyalty to the British cause."

Throughout the affair of the Windsor documents, "C" was not concerned with either the reputation or the safety of the duke. What concerned him was the stability of the throne. He appears to have succeeded in delaying publication, for "C's" old friend and colleague, General Sir James Marshall-Cornwall, lately deputy vice-chief of SIS, was editor in chief of the publication project between June 1948 and January 1951.

If there were letters between Windsor and Hitler, or evidence of treasonable communication between Windsor and the ex-kaiser, these were never found, although they almost certainly existed. There were rumors that the actual correspondence between Windsor and Hitler were recovered by Professor Trevor-Roper and Anthony Blunt, the Queen's picture master, and that Kim Philby was the case officer for the operation. Other rumors went further to assert that Philby's and Blunt's knowledge of the letters, the methods used to recover them, and their contents gave both men a degree of power over "C," the palace, and the government when it seemed they were about to be exposed.*

If the entire matter of the Windsor letters appears medieval in its mystery, it must be remembered that *no* British government, Socialist or Conservative, would wish to find itself required to provide evidence for a hanging charge against a royal prince who had once been king of England.

---

*Both rumors perhaps have a basis of fact. There was certainly royal correspondence at Kronberg Castle, the home of Prince Phillip of Hesse, just outside Frankfurt. Hesse was a relative of Windsor. At the end of the war, his family hid the Hesse jewels, heirlooms, and family papers in the cellar of the castle. These were discovered and stolen by U.S. personnel when the castle was taken over as a club for generals and colonels at Eisenhower's headquarters in Frankfurt. At the trial of the thieves, evidence was given that the "royal librarian" did call at the castle and "took into safe-keeping" some five hundred letters that included the correspondence of Queen Victoria with her daughter, the empress of Germany. Whether there was other correspondence was never established, since the "royal librarian" took them away and never returned them, and the thieves did not realize the historical and political importance of the correspondence and, therefore, never bothered to read it.

3 THE BORGIA TECHNIQUE

By early 1946 "C" had re-formed the service to reflect his belief that the only potential enemy was Russia. Nazism was so dead that it seemed it had never existed.

"C" remained chief of the secret service (CSS) and director-general of the Government Communications Headquarters (GCHQ). "C" appointed as his deputy and successor-designate Major General John Alexander Sinclair, last director of military intelligence during the war, despite Cadogan's wish that he appoint a civilian, Cavendish-Bentinck. But Menzies believed that the future "C" must be subject to military law and discipline. Moreover, as he knew well, Cavendish-Bentinck's private life was untidy and could lead him into the divorce courts. Indeed, after a period as British ambassador in Poland, Cavendish-Bentinck asked his wife for a divorce so that he might marry a lady he had known throughout the war. When his wife refused, he brought an action for divorce. His wife countersued for judicial separation, and in the action Cavendish-Bentinck admitted to what the court was told were "extra-marital adventures of an isolated character." With that admission, and although Justice Hodson expressed great sympathy for Cavendish-Bentinck "in the way that he had been treated" by his wife, the court had no choice but to grant the wife's plea. Cavendish-Bentinck then took his plea to the Court of Appeals, which granted him a divorce on the grounds of his wife's infidelity.

But by that time Cavendish-Bentinck, a distinguished officer of the foreign service with a long record, was dismissed on the personal decision of Foreign Secretary Ernest Bevin, for the traditional reason that he was involved in divorce proceedings. [6] According to Cavendish-Bentinck's biographer, Bevin's private secretary, Bob Dixon, stated, "I could have saved [Cavendish-Bentinck's career] if his name had been Smith." But it was not Smith. It was Cavendish-Bentinck, and he was the heir to the duke of Portland. Not only was he dismissed, but he was deprived of all his pension rights. As a consequence, Cavendish-Bentinck found himself at the age of forty-nine without money, without pension, and without work.

He was disqualified for the secret service, and in consequence SIS remained "militarized" for the next seven years, to the irritation of the Foreign Office. "C's" concern, however, was to preserve the character of the service, and, having emerged from the war with an unsurpassed reputation for surefootedness in a tricky world, he found no one in Whitehall to contest him. He believed that John Sinclair possessed the qualities necessary to command Broadway: at over six feet four inches tall he was imposing physically, he was the soul of probity (being a man of God and a good husband), he was discreet, he was cunning in Whitehall, and he was perceptive and cautious in his dealings with subordinates. Above all he was trusty.

With the appointment of Sinclair as vice-chief of the secret service (VCSS), "C" again went outside Broadway for the successor to Claude Dansey, who was now sixty-six, beyond retirement age, and suffering from a serious heart condition that soon killed him. "C's" selection was to prove one of the best appointments he made and showed that he was a better judge of men than he was sometimes given credit for. Air Commodore James Alfred "Jack" Easton was an outstanding staff officer who was only thirty-eight.

Easton accepted the rule that SIS was the senior service and its needs were to be met before others. But he had another rare quality in Broadway: he possessed an excellent mind, which he had developed along the lines of "practical intellectualism." His library of classics was large, his interest in the opera profound, his work capacity vast, his judgment of men excellent, and he was as calm in the office as he had been in the cockpit of a flying boat on a stormy night in the Mediterranean. Easton was liked by the Americans, and in the tradition of British administrators he was self-effacing to a degree— whenever he touched upon his own work, he did so almost shyly and had a queer habit of rolling his eyes heavenward. He was small, slight, and dark, neat in build and appearance, and an avid golfer. He was, therefore, a formidable man and one whom Philby came to fear.

As Philby was to write of Sinclair and Easton from the safety of Moscow: [7]

Sinclair, though not overloaded with mental gifts (he never claimed them) was humane, energetic, and so obviously upright that it was impossible to withhold admiration. Easton was a very different proposition. On first acquaintance, he gave the impression of burbling and bumbling, but it was dangerously deceptive. His strength was a brain of conspicuous clarity, yet capable of deeply subtle twists. Regarding them from time to time in the light of antagonists, I could not help applying to Sinclair and Easton the obvious metaphor of bludgeon and rapier. I was not afraid of the bludgeon; it could be dodged with ease. But the occasional glimpse of Easton's rapier made my stomach flop over. I was fated to have a great deal to do with him.

In the United States, meanwhile, Donovan's OSS had collapsed in the welter of press controversy attending President Truman's interest in creating what became the CIA. The main instrument of Donovan's undoing were reports by Walter Trohan, a reporter close to J. Edgar Hoover, "exposing" the goings-on in the Donovan organization. Trohan published a story that affected "C" personally, although he was not identified. In the *Washington Times-Herald*, under the headline OSS IS BRANDED BRITISH AGENCY TO LEGISLATORS, the story alleged that the British secret service had controlled the Donovan agency throughout the war. The next day in the *Chicago Tribune* a similar story appeared, under the headline BRITISH CONTROL OF OSS BARED IN CONGRESS PROBE. Trohan claimed that OSS had spent "more than $125 million in propaganda and intelligence around the world" but was "scarcely more than an arm of the British Intelligence Service." The two stories "cited a score of items proving the 'tieup; that training of OSS agents in England, British use of OSS for getting information otherwise denied them in the United States, a close connection between OSS and the British passport control office in New York,' the 'headquarters of British intelligence in the U.S.' "

Donovan was relieved of command by presidential order less than a month after the end of the Japanese war. "C's" American policy for a postwar alliance with OSS, albeit a reformed one under fresh leadership, likewise expired. Stephenson's usefulness ended, and he returned to civilian life with a knighthood. While the Truman administration decided upon the form its secret intelligence and special operations services should take, "C" adopted an interim policy that followed a June 16 memo by Air Marshal Sir John Slessor. Slessor advocated "close cooperation" with the United States in both scientific development and intelligence. As Slessor also advocated:

If this proves impractical—and for commercial reasons the Americans make it so, though I believe we have both of us more to gain commercially from cooperation than from competition—then our secret scientific intelligence organization should be extended to cover the U.S. The Americans are insecure people and I do not believe we should have any serious difficulty in finding out all they are doing if we were prepared to spend the money to do so. Conversely their secret intelligence is amateur to a degree and I do not think we should have much to fear from them. [8]

Also, at a meeting of the chiefs of staff committee on November 21, 1945, it was decided that Britain would invite the United States to engage in "100% co-operation" in the production of sigint (intelligence garned from wireless signals), but also agreed that "less than 100% co-operation was not worth having." Substantially, the Americans accepted the sigint pact. An important element in that acceptance was "C's" work in breaking into the Soviet administrative, military, naval, air, and intelligence traffic through a breach in the Soviet cable between Moscow and Vladivostok. When data from that traffic, which was code-named Bride, was related to American work code-named Venona, the Venona-Bride traffic, one of the great secrets of the first years of the Cold War, began to provide "C" and his American counterparts with a major insight into Soviet capabilities and intentions worldwide over a prolonged period leading up at least until the outbreak of the Korean War.

"C" strengthened the relationship further with two other undertakings. This time he sought to illuminate the secrets of Soviet intentions not at first through Russian communications in the ionosphere, but underground.

Soon after the Allied Control Commission entered Vienna, "C" sent Peter Lunn, an official of Section VIII, "C's" communications section, to Vienna. On his arrival in Vienna, Lunn began to look into the extent to which the Russian command in Vienna was using the Austrian trunk telephone and telegraph cable connecting the signals service of the Red Army commanding general with Moscow and the other great capitals of the old Austro-Hungarian empire. As it was with London and Paris, so it had remained with Vienna; Vienna was the hub of the telecommunications network established in 1890–1910 by the old emperor, Franz Josef. To communicate with Belgrade and Budapest from Moscow, all calls had to be routed through the Vienna *centrale*. All calls from the Kremlin to the Hotel Imperial, headquarters of the Red Army in Vienna on the Ringstrasse, passed through along the trunk cable buried, at its most accessible point, beside the main road through the Viennese suburb of Schwechat, which was in the Anglo-French zone of the Austrian capital.

"C" authorized the purchase of a small shop close to the highway, which would sell such goods as Scots tartans and Harris tweed, which the Viennese loved. This shop soon became a large commercial success, providing good cover for "C's" actual intentions, code-named Silver, and a considerable amount of revenue to support them. SIS then purchased a private house and, having run a seventy-foot tunnel to the cable, placed the tap. Thereafter, the tap worked successfully for the British until, at length, its existence was discovered by the

Americans, when it was operated jointly until well into the Korean War.

SIS was able to to establish the nature of the cipher systems in use by a major Red Army headquarters, together with vast quantities of the type required for "Y" or wireless intelligence work—to say nothing of the political and military intelligence it provided on the capabilities and intentions of the Red Army. "C" was now doing to Stalin what he had done to Hitler.

In 1948, with the success of the Vienna tap, "C" moved Lunn from Vienna to Berlin as chief of station, and thereafter Lunn began to examine the telecommunications routes and the geography and geology between the eastern fringe of the British zone in Berlin and the Soviet military, intelligence, and administrative headquarters in the Berlin suburb of Karlshorst. Thus began a joint Anglo-American operation code-named Gold to tap the Soviet underground communications between Red Air Force headquarters at Karlshorst, subordinate commands and airfields, and headquarters in Moscow. Gold required construction of a large tunnel some twenty feet below the surface, one 1,476 feet long and 78 inches in diameter, and the excavation, removal, and hiding of 3,100 tons of earth. It required, too, the installation of special lighting, dehumidifiers, temperature control, telephone tapping, and secure telecommunications between the tap and the point of dissemination to London, where the information was relayed to Broadway and Washington.

The project was not, therefore, completed until February 25, 1955, after "C" had retired. Then six hundred tape recorders began to collect the tapped communications, which totaled 1,200 hours of taping per day and used some eight hundred reels of tape during the lifetime of the tunnel. But Gold lasted no more than eleven months, during which time the Russians became aware of its existence and used it to feed false information into the Allied intelligence system. The Russians closed the operation down on April 21, 1956, when Soviet security authorities raided the tap. It had been betrayed to them by an SIS officer in Berlin, George Behar, alias George Blake.

The chief merit of the Berlin tunnel was that it displayed to the Russians that they had no monopoly on ingenuity. The Central Intelligence and National Security agencies, meanwhile, had been established by President Truman, and a new age had begun in Anglo-American intelligence relations. "C" realized that he did not have the power to fight the Russians worldwide without American assistance; the Americans realized that they could not fight the Russians without Broadway's experience, cooperation, and their intercept and decrypt installations overseas. To London came William Harding Jackson to establish harmony between the Washington and London intelligence communities. He found "C" more than willing to cooperate; for the first time in his career "C" opened the doors of Broadway to a foreign intelligence service, and over a period of six months he passed on the secrets of his trade to Jackson.

While the Americans remained suspicious of British intelligence intentions—as did the British about American proficiency—"C" developed a close working relationship with Jackson, one made the more agreeable by Jackson's wife, the enchanting and clever Adele Astaire, sister of Fred Astaire. Both men shared the belief that the Russians were capable of any mischief, and that extraordinary vigilance and cunning would be necessary if the Soviet services, enjoying as they did the ubiquity of Communists in every country, were to be restrained.

And at all times both men were guided by the new basic policy of the Anglo-American association—the word "alliance" still could not be used accurately. That policy was founded on a powerful nuclear deterrent combined with vigorous offensive intelligence operations to contain the influence of Russian services. And if Jackson never quite overcame his surprise that "C" allowed his senior secretary, Miss Pettigrew, to keep a parakeet in her room adjoining "C's" private office, he never regarded the talkative bird as more than an example of English quaintness.

These were dangerous times, as the Anglo-American association prospered, and Philby came to real power.

4 PHILBY REDUX

Late in 1945, or perhaps early in 1946, the combined code-breaking resources of GCHQ and the FBI—the Venona-Bride traffic—began to provide information about Soviet espionage activities in Washington. One of the signals unbuttoned was of great interest, for it showed there had been a very high level spy either in the State Department or the British embassy who had had access to the secret correspondence between Churchill and Roosevelt. The spy's code name was Homer.

Homer's identity and nationality remained unknown to the State Department and Foreign Office until 1949. Since it was not clear whether Homer was a Briton or an American, the FBI, MI5, and SIS conducted what amounted to a combined operation to identify the individual.

In August 1946, as the Homer case was beginning to evolve, Philby himself received a summons to "C's" office. As Philby related, upon entering the room, "C"

pushed across at me a sheaf of papers and asked me to look them through. The top paper was a brief letter to the Foreign Office from Knox Helm, then Minister at the British Embassy in Turkey. It drew attention to the attachments and asked for instructions. The attachments were a number of minutes that had passed between and within the British Embassy and Consulate-General, from which the following story emerged.

A certain Konstantin Volkov, a Vice-Consul attached to the Soviet Consulate-General in Istanbul, had approached a Mr. Page, his opposite number in the British Consulate-General, and asked for asylum in Britain for himself and his wife. He claimed that, although nominally a Vice-Consul, he was in fact an officer of the NKVD. He said that his wife was in a deplorably nervous state, and Page remarked that Volkov himself was less than rock steady. In support of his request for asylum, Volkov promised to reveal details of the headquarters of the NKVD, in which apparently he had worked for many years. He also offered details of Soviet networks and agents operating abroad. *Inter alia*, he claimed to know the real names of three Soviet agents working in Britain. Two of them were in the Foreign Office; one was the head of a counter-espionage organisation in London. . . . Two Soviet agents in the Foreign Office, one head of a counter-espionage organisation in London! I stared at the papers rather longer than necessary to compose my thoughts. I rejected the idea of suggesting caution in case Volkov's approach should prove to be a provocation. It would be useless in the short run, and might possibly compromise me at a later date. The only course was to put a bold face on it. I told the Chief that I thought we were on to something of the greatest importance. I would like a little time to dig into the background and, in the light of any further information on the subject, to make appropriate recommendations for action. The Chief acquiesced, instructing me to report first thing next morning and, in the meanwhile, to keep the papers strictly to myself. [9]

After several twists and turns, "C" agreed that Philby should go to Istanbul and handle the case personally. Philby set out from London and arrived in Istanbul, but by the time he tried to make contact with Volkov, the Russian had disappeared. Inquiry showed that he was probably the man who, being unconscious and swaddled in bandages, had been hurried aboard a Soviet aircraft in Istanbul at about the time of Philby's arrival. Nearly three weeks had elapsed between the time Volkov offered to defect and Philby's attempt to contact him.

During his return journey, Philby stopped briefly in Rome and called on James Angleton, who had remained in the Italian capital as chief of U.S. counterespionage, even though OSS was being liquidated. Professional to professional, Philby related the story of Volkov's disappearance, probably with the intention of deflecting any American speculation about the real reason for the collapse of the case. After Philby had finished the story, Angleton made a few noncommittal remarks about what a pity it was that so promising a case should have been lost, and then he put Philby on the London plane slightly the worse for drink. Angleton agreed to look Philby up when he was next in London.

When Philby arrived in London, he sent in his report. This caused some unease within the Security Service (MI5), which had been made aware of the Volkov case. Philby's account of what had occurred was not accepted completely, the more so when the Radio Security Service, which had been studying London-Moscow wireless traffic, reported that on the day "C" first told Philby about the Volkov mission, there was a significant increase in wireless traffic from the Soviet embassy in London to the Moscow headquarters of the Soviet intelligence service. Since the length of such traffic could be measured in milliseconds when there was an upsurge of wireless traffic between Moscow and Istanbul of *exactly* the same duration as the London-Moscow messages, it was assumed that the London-Moscow messages were being repeated to Istanbul. Consequently, it could be assumed that the leak in the Volkov case had occurred *in London*.

Among some of the younger members of MI5, that technical advice reawakened interest in the warning of Walter Krivitsky, the Soviet defector who had come to London during the winter of 1939–40, that the Russians had three highly placed spies in London, one of whom was a newspaperman who had worked for the Russian service in Spain during the civil war. It reawakened, too, the suspicions caused by Stalin's statements during the "Bern Affair" of February–March (1945), which Stalin thought were attempts by the western powers to establish a separate peace with Germany. Three occasions showed that he had a spy or spies who were highly placed within either the American or British administrations or both.

Moreover, the technical evidence brought to mind a curious episode that had recently occurred in 1942–43. At Christmas Broadway's decrypts of some of the Abwehr's wireless messages had revealed that a Russian spymaster in Western Europe, Henri Robinsohn, had been arrested in Paris. He had disclosed where he had stored his records, and a digest of these records had uncovered the existence of a Soviet spy in London, David Ernest Weiss, born in Breslau and living in Paddington, London. Weiss was arrested, he agreed to collaborate with Broadway and the Security Service, and he subsequently provided information that led to the arrest and neutralization of a small Soviet espionage network inside the Royal Aeronautical Establishment at Farnborough, Hampshire, where secret research and development work was taking place into jet engines. Also, one member of "C's" counterespionage service, a female secretary, was named and dismissed from the service.

Weiss's information about Soviet spies in place in London was of such importance that some aspects of it were still being exploited in London and Washington at the end of the war and even as late as 1968.

Then, in Ottawa on September 5, 1945, Igor Gouzenko, cipher clerk in the Canadian office of the Soviet espionage service, defected and brought with him a warning that not only were there Soviet-controlled traitors of British origins in the U.S. atomic bomb program, but there was also a Soviet spy code-named Elli in "the headquarters of counter-espionage in London." That statement came to haunt "C," for it was the second such warning to reach him in approximately five weeks.

Upon receiving a telegram from Stephenson in New York that he was proceeding to Ottawa to take charge of the Gouzenko case, "C" again called Philby to his office and suggested that he go immediately to Canada and help interrogate Gouzenko regarding "Elli." Philby hesitated about the mission, perhaps because he felt that if he told his Soviet controller in London, an attempt would be made to liquidate Gouzenko or to take action to ensure his silence. The Soviet service might also arrest a member of Gouzenko's family and hold Gouzenko responsible for that person's life.

But whatever the case, when he returned to "C's" office Philby recommended that an MI5 officer go instead, pointing out to "C" that since Canada was in the empire, it was within MI5's jurisdiction. As Philby pointed out, if he went, it would only cause more trouble between Broadway and MI5 on the recurrent quarrels over jurisdiction in matters of imperial interest. "C" agreed; Roger Hollis, the head of the Soviet service at MI5, was sent to New York, where he was to proceed on to Stephenson's base outside Ottawa. Hollis, however, got no farther than New York, for by Stephenson's own account, "I did not like the look of him and told him to go back to London on the next plane, which he did. He got nowhere near Gouzenko. Nor did I tell Hollis where Gouzenko was hidden." The reason for Stephenson's distrust was that "Elli" might be Hollis. That suspicion was not misplaced, for later there were allegations that Hollis, another Cambridge man, had been subverted by the Soviet service in the 1930s—allegations that were made even more serious by the promotion of Hollis to the post of director-general of MI5.

Stephenson's telegrams to "C" on the "Elli" case confirmed the fears he expressed to Cadogan in 1943—"I have Communists in my organization"—but Gouzenko's statements did not make it clear whether "Elli" was in Broadway, MI5, in the Special Branch of Scotland Yard, in one of the security services of the Foreign Office, the Field Security Services of the armed services, or the scientific establishments. "C" did pass the "Elli" warning to his chief of security, Colonel Vivian, with instructions to establish as quickly as possible if "Elli" was in SIS. In turn, Vivian passed the case to the chief of counterespionage of SIS, Kim Philby. As Easton, who had by then taken up his appointment as assistant chief of the secret service, remembered:

"C" kept at it. He told me about it at our first meeting and raised it with me regularly afterwards. Since Colonel Vivian was the chief of internal security I raised "Elli" with him, and Vivian responded that "he had his best man on it." When I asked who that best man was I was given the name of Philby. I then called Philby to my office and asked what he was doing about "Elli." Philby replied that *he* had *his* best man on the job. This proved to be Philby's closest friend and deputy in counter-espionage, Tim Milne. I saw Milne and Milne was fairly consistent in the view that the suspect was not in SIS at all but in the Security Service. "C" shared that suspicion. When I asked Milne about the reason for his suspicion he replied that there were a number of politically doubtful characters in MI5, including the head of the counter-espionage division, Guy Liddell, who had some very rum friends. In any case, in "C's" mind "Elli" acted like a red-herring throughout the Philby case. [10]

But beyond the belief that "Elli" was in another service, as Easton explained, was "C's" conviction that if "Elli" was in Broadway, then he would prove to be the head of the political section, David John Footman, the man who introduced Guy Burgess to Section D in 1939–40.

In any event, no action was taken to review Philby's record. When

James Angleton arrived in London on leave, he called on Philby as had been arranged in Rome. Philby invited him to attend an interesting ceremony. "C" had put few of his men in for honors at the end of the war, but Philby was one of them. He was made a Companion of the Most Excellent Order of the British Empire, the third in the five grades of the order and one rank below that of a knight. This was conveyed in the New Year's Honors List of 1946, and Philby was "commanded" to Buckingham Palace for the investiture. And as Angleton was to remember, as they were walking away from the palace after the investiture, Philby made a political statement that he had not made before in Angleton's presence: "What this country needs is a good stiff dose of socialism."

This statement surprised Angleton, for until that moment he had regarded Philby as a stalwart of the realm, although perhaps a politically opaque one. But Angleton concealed his surprise and filed it away in his mind for reference. According to Leonard Mosley in his biography of Allen Dulles and his family, the remark "rang bells," and Angleton told Allen Dulles about it later on. "From that moment on, I've been wary of the fellow," Angleton is said to have remarked to Dulles. "You know, he sounded like a Commie. I have a feeling in my bones about him." [11] But again, so it seems, if Angleton had suspicions about Philby, he told nobody in Broadway about them. It is possible that Angleton did not do so because he began to see that Philby might have his uses as a conduit for a deception against the Russians.

By September 25, 1946, the Philby case took yet another turn. Philby married Aileen Furse, with Tomas Harris, Garbo's case officer during Fortitude, as the only witness. That Philby had married Miss Furse bigamously was an astonishing development, for bigamy was then a crime for which the penalty was jail. One wonders why Philby took this dangerous step, for "C" would certainly have sacked Philby had he known that his chief of counterespionage was a bigamist. There are undoubtedly two reasons why Philby took this step:

(1) Since he was rising in the hierarchy of the secret service, and might well rise into the very highest ranks, it would be dangerous if not fatal if it were discovered that he had been married to Lizzy Friedman, the Austrian Bolshevik activist, who by this time was in East Berlin living with Georg Honigmann, a man who was known to SIS *and* MI5 as a Soviet secret agent. Moreover, it is thought that Lizzy Friedman herself had engaged in espionage in the Soviet interest in England in 1943.

(2) Aileen Furse had given birth to three children and was about to give birth to a fourth child when she married Philby. Obviously Philby could not continue to produce bastard children in such large numbers and indefinitely without the fact becoming known within Broadway, and when it *did* become known, the question would be asked, "why doesn't he marry the girl?" and then the reason would emerge—he was already married to Lizzy Friedman, a known Soviet spy. That discovery would in itself cause the inevitable question: "What hold does this suspected Soviet agent, one who is cohabiting with a known Soviet agent in East Berlin, have upon the chief of counterespionage of Broadway?"

Realizing the dangers, Philby took a daring step—he went to see Vivian. At that meeting Philby explained his marriage to Lizzy Friedman, his association with Aileen Furse, and the bastardy of his three children, then asked for leave to request a divorce. This application was approved by Vivian, but Philby underestimated Vivian in supposing that his superior would not check Lizzy Friedman. It was at that point that MI5 advised Vivian that Ms. Friedman was a suspected Soviet agent living with Georg Honigmann, a known Soviet agent in Berlin. In turn, it can be said fairly reliably, Vivian advised "C" about the association. "C's" reaction to Vivian's announcement is nowhere recorded, but as Patrick Seale and Maureen McConville were to write in *The Long Road to Moscow*: "It is a measure of the confidence and affection in which Philby was held by his colleagues that this revelation should seem to add nothing to what he had already confessed to Vivian." [12]

But this statement does appear to underestimate "C" and Vivian as intelligence officers and to underestimate the amount of adverse information there was on Philby in SIS and MI5 files. Late in 1946, after the "Elli" and Volkov cases, Stalin's statements during the "Bern affair" in February 1945, and now the Lizzy Friedman revelations, Philby, despite the great value that appeared to have been placed on his services as chief of Soviet counterespionage, was removed from his post. He was sent as SIS chief to Istanbul, an important but relatively inactive station where the main task was to keep an eye on Turco-Russian tensions.

Philby himself sought to explain this posting with the statement that "the three senior officers of the service, the Chief, Vice-Chief, and Assistant Chief, had no experience of counter-espionage and no practical knowledge of work in the field. But I was not senior enough to benefit from any such dispensation. As all my work for SIS had been concerned with counterespionage at headquarters, I was obviously due for an early change of scene." [13]

Thus, as matters of the highest secrecy were being undertaken by "C" at Broadway, Philby left London to begin learning his trade in the field. And as James Easton, the new assistant director of the secret service, was to acknowledge, "Philby must have had rather a pleasant, interesting, and extended holiday, for we did not use Istanbul much while he was there." In this Philby agreed, for by his own account, he had little to do during the next two years except conduct agreeable expeditions to Mount Ararat and the Turco-Russian frontier and launch some minor espionage agents across the frontier into Soviet Turkestan, where they were not heard from again.

But by September 1949, Philby, who was then thirty-seven and had been in the British secret service for nine years and the Soviet service for sixteen, had completed his two years in the field at Istanbul. He was due for a new assignment. Despite the Venona-Bride decrypts, and all that had preceded them, "C" made a second inexplicable decision regarding Philby. Since Peter Dwyer, the present SIS resident in Washington, wished to return to civilian life, Philby was to be sent to Washington as SIS liaison officer to the CIA—the most important field post in the service.

When Philby accepted—it took him "all of half an hour to decide to accept the offer"—Admiral Hillenkoetter, director of CIA, was given the names of what Easton termed "two or three officers, one of whom was Philby," and Hillenkoetter replied, stating that Philby would be "welcome" in Washington. This suggests that, if "C" was indeed establishing Philby as a high-grade unwitting double agent, then the CIA was party to the stratagem. That is not improbable, for as we have seen, James Angleton had already formed a suspicion that Philby was a Communist. Furthermore, by now Angleton had taken up a high position in the CIA in Washington in which deception was an important element of his duties.

As for Philby, his enthusiasm for his post was boundless. He left Istanbul for London at the end of August 1949, to find that Easton had the "general supervision of relations between SIS and the American services, and it was from him that I received most of my instructions." Easton had considerable knowledge and experience of the personality, politics, and operational intentions of CIA and FBI. At no time, however, was he involved in negotiations concerning deception operations, the most secret of all secret intelligence operations, although he was kept abreast of what was happening in that field, usually during the visits of John Alexander Drew, the British deception expert who used to call regularly at Broadway for evening meetings with "C." Easton later stated emphatically that at the time he gave Philby his briefings, he had not been advised by "C," Sinclair, Vivian, or anyone else that there was any doubt about Philby's loyalty.

According to Philby, Easton gave him a detailed outline of "the elusive patterns of Anglo-American cooperation." But as Easton was to remember, there was one minor incident between Philby and himself that had significance for Easton later:

One morning Philby was in my office when, having learned that his wife had given birth to their fourth or perhaps their fifth child, I decided that it would be in order for me to congratulate him. I did so and Philby replied in that slightly shy, agreeable manner of his: "Thank you, sir. I can think of nothing more rewarding in life than the sight of two rows of heads diminishing in size at the dinner table." I thought to myself, what a decent fellow! What a very fine thing for a man to say! [14]

In due course, it will be seen that Philby's sentiment was to have considerable significance for Easton. Meanwhile, Philby continued to receive his briefings on the most secret matters of English statehood to prepare for him his vital post, one that had been arranged by "C" through Jackson and J. Edgar Hoover.

From Easton, Philby proceeded to other important briefings. One was with "the formidable" Maurice Oldfield, who by now held Philby's old post. Until this moment, it appears, Philby had not been aware of the capability of Washington and London to read certain NKVD traffic, the so-called Venona-Bride signals. But now he certainly knew about it, although it is improbable that Oldfield gave Philby chapter and verse on the source. As Philby wrote of Oldfield's briefing:

Joint Anglo-American investigation of Soviet intelligence activity in the United States had yielded a strong suggestion that there had been a leakage from the British Embassy in Washington during the years 1944–45, and another from the atomic energy establishment at Los Alamos. I had no ideas about Los Alamos. But a swift check of the relevant Foreign Office list left me in little doubt about the source of the British Embassy. My anxiety was tempered by relief, since I had been nagged for some months by a question put to me by my Soviet contact in Istanbul. He had asked me if I had any means of discovering what the British were doing in a case under investigation by the FBI—a case involving the British Embassy in Washington. At the time of asking, there was nothing that I could have done. But it seemed, after my talk with Oldfield, that I had stumbled into the heart of the problem.

Within a few days, this was confirmed by my Russian friend in London. After checking with headquarters, he was left in no doubt that information from the FBI and my own referred to one and the same case. [15]

The Los Alamos spy proved to be Emil Julis Klaus Fuchs, a naturalized Briton of German origins who, as a member of a Communist underground movement while at the university in Germany, came to Britain as a refugee shortly before the outbreak of war. An outstanding physicist, Fuchs was introduced into the British atomic bomb program, Tube Alloys, and in 1943 was sent by the British government with others, having been cleared by MI5, to join the U.S. atomic program in Los Alamos in a key capacity, designer of the implosion system.

The second suspect, Donald Duart Maclean, had been at Cambridge with Burgess and since then had risen to a position of eminence in the foreign service. He became counselor at the British embassy and, as such, chief of the cipher room there. He also became British secretary on the Combined Policy Group, the joint U.S.-U.K. committee responsible largely for acquiring the raw materials necessary to make the atomic bomb. By 1951 Maclean had become head of the American department at the Foreign Office, which handled all diplomatic matters between the United Kingdom and the United States.

Maclean's code name in the Soviet traffic was Homer.

By September, 1949, the time had come for Philby to leave London for Washington, and as he wrote of that moment:

My last call in London was at the Chief's office. He was in the best of form, and amused me with malicious accounts of the stickier passages in Anglo-American intelligence relations during the war. This turned out to be more than just pointless reminiscence. He told me that the news of my appointment to the United States appeared to have upset Hoover. . . . Hoover suspected that my appointment might herald unwanted SIS activity in the United States. To allay his fear, the Chief had sent him a personal telegram, assuring him that there was no intention of a change of policy; my duties would be purely liaison duties. The Chief showed me the telegram, then gave me a hard stare. 'That,' he said, 'is an official communication from myself to Hoover.' There was a pause, then he continued: 'Unofficially . . . let's discuss it over lunch at White's.' [16]

5 WITH PHILBY IN WASHINGTON

Philby sailed for the United States on the SS *Caronia*, a transatlantic liner, at the end of September 1949. It seems impossible that "C" would knowingly have sent a Communist to such a vital post, yet "C's" actions and decisions were not always obedient to ordinary political dictates. World War III seemed inevitable and imminent, and it was a time when the best news that the State Department could give President Truman was that world war was not likely in the next thirty days.

Philby took up his post October 10, 1949. Sir Oliver Franks, the British ambassador, sent Secretary of State Dean Acheson a note introducing Philby as the new first secretary at the embassy. As Philby soon discovered, however, after taking up residence at 5228 Nebraska Avenue, living almost directly across the road was John Boyd, the FBI director of security. Shortly Philby moved to a large brick house on wooded grounds at 4100 Nevada Avenue, explaining to Boyd that with his family arriving, the house on Nebraska Avenue was too small.

Philby's offices were in the annex to the embassy, and his assistant was Miss Jerry Dack, a Canadian lady who kept an alert eye on her boss's correspondence, signals, ciphers, and relationships. His duties were not onerous, except at times of crisis, and his work was strictly confined to acting as liaison officer between SIS, CIA, and MI5. In other words, he carried on no espionage activities against the United States—at least for the British government. He had some responsibility for acting as the medium through which sigint was exchanged between London and Washington. But that sigint had to do almost entirely with matters of intelligence, not military interest. All sigint having to do with the Soviet military, naval, and air forces, and those of her satellites and allies, was handled by specially appointed officers in the British Joint Services Mission with whom, thanks to the strict security compartmentalization then in existence, Philby had little contact.

That compartmentalization was a great barrier to Philby's easy movement about the Washington official community; even his possession of high—but not the *highest*—security clearances did not mean that he could prudently busy himself in affairs that were not his official concern. This applied particularly to all purely American military and intelligence operations. Therefore he was effective as a Soviet agent only in the severely limited realm of Anglo-American affairs.

Indeed, Philby was blocked for other reasons: the suspicion that all SIS officers encountered in Washington and the sensitivity of the Washington intelligence community in general and CIA in particular. Both SIS and CIA had miscalculated badly when in August 1949 the Russians detonated their first atomic explosion, nearly a year before even the most pessimistic prediction. And Philby had to be careful in the questions he asked and the papers he called for; late 1949 was a period of intense war fears inflamed by Senator Joseph McCarthy's hearings. There was widespread belief that all agencies of the U.S. government had been penetrated by the Soviet intelligence service and cryptanalytical knowledge that the British embassy had been penetrated at a high level by Homer. The general atmosphere of the times demanded great vigilance within the administration, and especially at the FBI, which had regarded Philby as suspect from his arrival. But this did not mean that Philby was not strategically positioned as a Soviet spy.

Then, in June 1950, the Korean War exploded. Despite "a year of continuous psychological and political pressure and a number of military false alarms," [17] under Soviet direction the North Koreans succeeded in assembling two corps of armor, artillery, and infantry close to the traditional invasion routes from North into South Korea without being detected by *any* Allied intelligence service. Thus the invasion of South Korea came as a tactical and strategic surprise and constituted the fifth such major surprise inflicted upon Washington in ten years—Pearl Harbor, Kasserine, the Ardennes, and the Soviet detonation of their first atomic device.

The South Korean forces, lacking both tanks and aircraft, were unable to halt the invaders, and Seoul, the South Korean capital, fell quickly. The U.S. government assumed that the Soviet Union had either instigated or acquiesced in the attack, and that produced the gravest crisis since the end of World War II. During earlier crises— Iran, Greece, Czechoslovakia, Berlin, China—the Communists had employed political warfare to achieve their objectives. Now, for the first time, they were resorting to massive military aggression across established frontiers.

Recalling how "appeasement" in the 1930s had brought on World

War II, President Truman felt that "if this was allowed to go unchallenged it would [ultimately] mean a third world war." It was,
moreover, clear to him "that the foundations and the principles of
the United Nations were at stake." [18] Within five days of the attack
Truman committed U.S. ground, sea, and air forces to defend South
Korea. These forces were sent piecemeal, and they were soon overwhelmed. U.S. and Korean forces were quickly penned into a small
redoubt at Pusan on the southern tip of Korea, from which, so it
seemed, it would not be long before they were ejected. Persuaded
that the United States and its allies might be facing the opening
campaign of World War III, the United States began a large rearmament program.

On June 28, 1950, the National Security Council surveyed "all
policies affecting the entire perimeter of the USSR"; debate began
that led to the reestablishment of German and Japanese forces. Emergency fiscal policies were adopted that would permit a major expansion in U.S. military power. Thus only eight months after his arrival,
Philby found himself in what seemed to be a key position in the
Washington polity, one in which he had, at least on paper, more
access to secret U.S. military and political information than any other
foreigner in Washington.

Throughout that period, Philby's closest contact with the CIA was
James Jesus Angleton. Both were deeply involved in Anglo-American
deception operations similar to Fortitude in World War II—the in-
flation of the strength of the United States Armed Forces by deceptive
means to obtain political and military objectives. Angleton's contact
with the British deception agency was John Alexander Drew, who
had played such an important role in the creation of the fictitious
Army Group Patton while involved in both the Bolero project and
the XX-Committee between 1942 and 1944. Drew's point of contact
in London was "C."

But then there occurred a minor but fateful event that once more
displayed the weakness of Philby's tradecraft as a Soviet penetration
agent. In late summer of 1950 Philby received a letter from Guy
Burgess, who by now was employed by the Foreign Office in London,
announcing that he was being sent to Washington as a second secretary at the British embassy and asking whether Philby could accommodate him "for a few days" until he found an apartment of
his own.

In normal circumstances, two Soviet agents would never be connected in such a way; but these were not normal circumstances. And anyway, they had been associated since Cambridge. So it seemed to Philby, therefore, that "there could be no real professional objection to him staying with me." [19] Philby's check with the SIS files showed there was nothing recorded against Burgess politically, so SIS could not object to Philby accommodating Burgess. Moreover, when Philby talked over the problem of Burgess's request with the embassy security officer, Robert MacKenzie, there was no objection from that quarter, either. MacKenzie was well aware of Burgess's alcoholism and homosexuality, and he feared that if Burgess did not stay with Philby, he would find himself footloose in Washington, and it would not be long before he was in trouble, possibly to the embarrassment of the embassy. MacKenzie, consequently, seemed to encourage Philby to accommodate and keep an eye on his old friend.

On his arrival in Washington, therefore, Burgess moved into Philby's house on Nevada Avenue and occupied part of the basement of the house. Soon, however, Burgess began to wander, getting drunk and making passes at other men in the street. It was also not long before he began to attract the attention of the CIA and FBI officers who, from time to time, visited Philby at his home. Moreover, by accident he ran into a friend from Cambridge, Whitney Straight, who knew that Burgess was a Soviet spy. Straight warned Burgess that unless he got out of Washington immediately, he (Straight) would inform the FBI about his loyalties. Consequently, it was not long before Vivian, still the security chief at Broadway, arrived in Washington to check on the situation. Vivian warned Philby that Burgess was getting a bad name, Philby admitted that his guest was "a great nuisance," but that the difficulties would end when Burgess found a suitable apartment. Vivian left Washington apparently satisfied that Burgess's presence at Nevada Avenue presented no great threat to SIS's security.

Burgess's indiscretions, however, increased in frequency and were complicated by his anti-American statements in such places as the Press Club bar in Washington, where regularly he railed against American policy in Asia and the "atomic sabre rattling" that had grown up around the Korean War. It is said that the FBI installed a listening device in Philby's basement, and at the same time James Angleton, whose suspicions were further inflamed by Philby's association with Burgess, managed to affect an association between a CIA informant, Basil, who was a member of the Jewish intelligence service, and

Burgess. Angleton wanted to find out just what *was* happening at Philby's home at a time of intense crisis in world affairs: the entry of the Chinese army into the Korean War on November 30, 1950, General MacArthur's stunning defeat by the Chinese in North Korea, and the growing demand from General MacArthur for permission to use the atomic bomb against the Chinese.

Meanwhile, "C" turned sixty, the mandatory retirement age at the Foreign Office. But no thought seems to have been given to his immediate retirement, by "C" or anyone else, although Sinclair had been deputy for five years and was ready to take over. Both "C" and Sinclair attended a meeting with Patrick Reilly, who by now had become chairman of the Joint Intelligence Committee, at which the question of "C's" successor was brought up, and "in 1950 or possibly very early in 1951 ["C"] joined Sinclair in a recommendation to the [Foreign Office] that Philby should be brought back to Broadway to a high post, with the explicit object of putting him in line for succession to Sinclair's successor, then expected to be Easton." With the eventual retirement of "C," Sinclair would take over that post, Easton would become deputy, and Philby would become assistant chief of the service. [20]

The fact that Philby's promotion was discussed at all seems to indicate that neither "C" nor Sinclair were aware of the truth of Philby's loyalties or even had any suspicions about them. On the other hand, if "C" *was* manipulating Philby, what better way could there be to build Philby up in the estimation of his Soviet employers than to put it about that he had Philby in mind as a successor? Which Soviet controller would cast doubt on intelligence received from a man who, having served them loyally, courageously, and successfully for nearly seventeen years, had now been placed in the line of succession to the post of head of a hostile service?

The suspicion in Washington that Philby might be a traitor was, however, certainly mounting. In February or early March, the FBI wiretap on Philby's home and the embassy had begun to indicate that Burgess was spying for the Russians and that Philby might be involved. This information was then sent to William H. Jackson, "C's" friend and now deputy director of the CIA in Washington. Jackson wanted to warn "C," but it was opposed by a group of CIA officers around Allan Dulles, then the CIA's deputy director of plans, who felt that such a warning might ruin what had become a valuable conduit for the passage of deceptive information to the Russians.

Jackson resigned suddenly on August 3, 1951. There is little doubt that there was severe friction between Jackson and Dulles, who, being an ex-OSS man, was inclined to suspect "C" and his service throughout his career, despite his various statements to the contrary.

The period leading up to the spring of 1951 (when the CIA obtained the information) was also a time of great trial and tragedy for "C" personally. For months his wife had been near death, and on March 13 she died at Bridges Court. She was forty-eight. The death certificate illustrated the fact that her suffering must have been prolonged. Stewart Menzies was deeply distressed by Pamela's passing, for despite the acute medical problem that had afflicted her for almost the entire eighteen years of their marriage, he remained deeply attached to her even to the end, and he was at Bridges Court frequently before, during, and after her death. A gifted woman, "C's" wife had had a tragic life, and much of that tragedy had manifested itself while "C" had been preoccupied by some of the most dangerous periods in the history of the state. If Jackson did send a private warning to "C" about Philby, he may not have received it, and, if it went to Sinclair, Sinclair may well have been unable to act upon the information without proof.

Such, then, was the situation when the FBI and MI5 began the final investigation that led to the identification of Homer. Philby was kept advised by Broadway of all developments in the case, which seems again to indicate that neither "C" nor anyone else had any suspicions of Philby. By April of 1951 Philby was "alarmed by the speed with which [the Homer case] was developing" and perhaps also with the unwanted identification of Burgess. At his meeting with his Soviet controller, Philby proposed that Burgess be induced to commit an indiscretion that would so embarrass the embassy that the ambassador would order his return to London. Then, on his arrival in London, Burgess could warn Maclean that he was in danger of being arrested, so that Maclean, it was hoped, could defect to Moscow.

The Russian appears to have agreed, and Burgess was arrested three times for reckless driving and disorderly conduct while driving his Lincoln Continental in Virginia and the Carolinas in the company of a homosexual prostitute and rapist. On each occasion there were noisy exchanges with state troopers and insulting arguments with at least one judge. The governors of those states protested to the State Department, which then indicated to the British ambassador that Burgess was no longer welcome in Washington.

On his return to England, Burgess warned Maclean that he would shortly be arrested on charges of treason, and *both* men defected from England to Moscow on May 25, 1951. That defection produced rare consternation in the Anglo-American intelligence and diplomatic community in London and Washington. As Philby was to recall of the moment when Burgess and Maclean disappeared:

One morning, at a horribly early hour, Geoffrey Paterson [the MI5 representative at the British embassy in Washington] called me by telephone. He explained that he had just received an enormously long Most Immediate telegram from London. It would take him all day to decypher without help, and he had just sent his secretary on a week's leave. Could he borrow mine? I made the necessary arrangements and sat back to compose myself. This was almost certainly it. Was Maclean in the bag? Had Maclean got away? I was itching to rush round to the Embassy and lend a third hand to the telegram. But it was clearly wiser to stick to my usual routine as if nothing had happened. When I reached the Embassy, I went straight to Paterson's office. He looked grey. "Kim," he said in a half-whisper, "the bird has flown." I registered dawning horror (I hope). "What bird? Not Maclean?" "Yes," he answered. "But there's worse than that. . . . *Guy Burgess* has gone with him." At that, my consternation was no pretense.

Upon receiving that news, Philby sent a telegram to "C" "expressing astonishment at the news of Burgess's departure." Two days later Philby then sent a more thoughtful letter detailing various actions on the part of Burgess which Philby had, 'upon further reflection,' considered suspicious. That letter was read by a young MI5 officer, Arthur Martin, who had earlier attached the correct significance to the sudden upsurge in Soviet wireless traffic between London, Moscow, and Istanbul on the evening after "C" had briefed Philby on the Volkov defection. Upon reading the Philby correspondence to "C" regarding Burgess, Martin felt that the correspondence "did not ring true." This Martin reported to Dick Goldsmith White of MI5. White produced a file on Philby from another MI5 officer, Millicent Bagot, who had recorded her suspicions of Philby. As a result, White met with "C," who decided to bring Philby back to London to "assist MI5 in the investigation into Burgess and Maclean." But if "C" felt that the allegations against Philby were a matter of national security, he did not behave as if there were any cause for urgency or dismay.

During the early evening of June 5, "C" held a meeting in his office at Broadway with John Alexander Drew, the deception agent, who was leaving that night by British airliner for the United States.

After their meeting, "C" asked Jack Easton to write a letter to Philby instructing him that he was to expect a telegram ordering him back to London on friendly terms. Easton then went to his office and wrote a letter on an ordinary airgram letter and gave it to Drew to hand to Philby on his arrival in Washington next day. [21]

Drew arrived in Washington the next day and called at the embassy annex to find great consternation: the news of the disappearance of Burgess and Maclean had at first been suppressed successfully, but it had become clear that the London *Daily Express* had learned of the disappearance and intended to publish on June 6. Drew encountered Philby, who told him how the ambassador had been up all night, and the embassy had been in turmoil over the imminent publication of the disappearance. Philby then asked Drew what news he brought from London, and Drew handed him Easton's letter. As Philby was to record of that letter and what he believed to have been its purpose:

The one I was expecting was a Most Immediate, personal, decypher-yourself telegram from the Chief, summoning me home. At last the summons came, but it took a most curious, thought-provoking form. An intelligence official specialising in the fabrication of deception material flew into Washington on routine business. He paid me a courtesy call during which he handed me a letter from Jack Easton. The letter was in Easton's own handwriting, and informed me that I would shortly be receiving a telegram recalling me to London in connection with the Burgess-Maclean case. It was very important that I should obey the call promptly. While the sense of the communication was clear enough, its form baffled me. Why should Easton warn me of the impending summons and why in his own handwriting if the order was to reach me through the normal telegraphic channels anyway? *There is often a good reason for eccentric behaviour in the secret service, and there may have been one in this case.* My reflection at the time was that, if I had not already rejected the idea of escape, Easton's letter would have given me the signal to get moving with all deliberate speed.

Easton stated in 1986 that he did not encourage Philby to escape but merely advised him of "C's" intention to recall him and to enable him to lose no time in putting his affairs in order so that he would be able to return to London promptly when ordered to do so by "C." That Philby thought the letter an escape warning was, thought Easton, "a sign of his own guilty conscience and also of his state of severe fright." For as Philby had himself concluded in the process of reviewing his situation, "It was an ugly picture," in which he was "faced with the inescapable conclusion that I could not hope to prove my innocence." Nonetheless, he decided against bolting to Moscow on the grounds that "a strong presumption of my guilt might be good enough for an intelligence officer," but "it was not enough for a lawyer."

Philby left Washington about June 12, 1951. On his arrival in London, he went to his mother's flat, lunched, and then telephoned Easton at Broadway. At Easton's request, Philby went straight to headquarters, and once there Easton told him to see Dick Goldsmith White, a senior officer of MI5, immediately. At the meeting, White

> wanted my help . . . in clearing up this appalling Burgess-Maclean affair. I gave him a lot of information about Burgess's past and impressions of his personality, taking the line that it was almost inconceivable that anyone like Burgess, who courted the limelight instead of avoiding it and was generally notorious for indiscretion, could have been a secret agent. . . .

As for Maclean, Philby felt he could "not put a face to him," which was almost true.

Philby's first meeting with White appears to have been little more than a reconnaissance in which White revealed little of anything that he knew about Philby, although he had been suspicious of Philby certainly since the Lizzy Friedman revelations and Volkov's disappearance. But at the second meeting, White began to show more interest in Philby than in Burgess, particularly when Philby made a slip and provided White with some "gratuitous information." That information concerned some rather extensive traveling Philby had done in Europe between 1934 and 1936. White wished to know "who paid for these journeys." Plainly he suspected that the Soviet service had paid for them, and as Philby recognized, with that question "all but the tip of the cat's tail was now out of the bag." As a result of these meetings, White formed the impression that Philby was a Soviet spy, and that it was he who had warned Maclean (through Burgess) that he was about to be arrested and indicted for treason. Philby was therefore in the gravest danger of being indicted for high treason, a hanging offense in Britain even in peacetime.

On June 11 Sir Percy Sillitoe and Arthur Martin, both of MI5, flew to Washington to see General Bedell Smith and J. Edgar Hoover. A week after their meeting, Hoover sent a four-and-a-half-page letter to Admiral S. W. Souers to give to President Truman, setting down what was known about Burgess and Maclean and dealing incidentally with what was known about Philby.

At that point "C" decided to sent Jack Easton to Washington to see Bedell Smith. But he did not tell Easton about Goldsmith White's communiqué, nothing about Philby's involvement in the Volkov affair (Easton had joined SIS afterward), and he enjoined Easton to take the boat to the States rather than fly. He further instructed Easton to tell the Americans nothing more than that Philby was "guilty of nothing worse than gross indiscretion, but that an inquiry was being instituted into all aspects concerning him." Indeed, "C" appears not to have been as alarmed as those around him.

Easton arrived in Washington on July 13 and went to CIA headquarters to see Bedell Smith. Nothing happened. Easton stayed in Washington a few days more and spoke to members of the FBI; Allan Dulles also attended the meetings. But the attitude of the Americans was so unconcerned that Easton sent a signal to "C" asking him not to take any action against Philby until his return. In all, the most remarkable thing about the Washington meetings was that they were unremarkable.

But upon his return to London, Easton was shocked to learn from Vivian that "C" had *not* given him all the information available on Philby; in consequence, Easton had actually unwittingly misled Bedell Smith about Philby's involvement with the Soviet spy ring. As Easton recalled, still astounded after thirty-six years:

I encountered a document that showed that Philby's marriage to Aileen Furse was bigamous, and I recalled immediately Philby's statement to me when I congratulated him on the birth of his latest child—that Philby felt he could think of nothing more rewarding than rows of descending heads at the dining room table. I realised when I read this that this man was an accomplished liar and was therefore capable of anything. The more I read, the more certain I became that Philby was a traitor.

Essentially, there were ten points against Philby:

1. His bigamous marriage to Aileen Furse and the bastardy of Philby's children.
2. His marriage to Lizzy Friedman, a known Communist spy.
3. His close association with Burgess, a defector to the Soviets.
4. The suspect source of his finances while traveling in Europe between 1933 and his appointment to *The Times* in February 1937.
5. Philby's communism at Cambridge and his membership of the right-wing Anglo-German Fellowship, a Nazi-financed organization.
6. The contents of a memo written from Washington about the iden-

tity of Homer that drew a red herring across the entire investigation.

7. The upsurge in Soviet wireless traffic from London to Moscow and Istanbul two days after "C" had briefed him regarding Volkov.

8. His handling of the Volkov affair.

9. His known association with other suspected Communists during World War II at Burgess's flat in 5 Bentinck Street.

10. Shortly after Philby's briefing about Homer there had been another, similar jump in NKVD traffic between London and Moscow.

"C," who had earlier said that he would like to have a long talk with Philby to try and establish what the truth was about his Soviet connections, had decided that Easton was to handle Philby. Accordingly, Easton summoned Philby to his office—Philby was still in London being examined—and at that meeting:

I told Philby of the existence of the paper and went over each point with him. I spoke to him about his bigamous marriage, his various journeys while impoverished, the revelations concerning Lizzy Friedman's associations with a Soviet agent in Germany, that she herself had been a Soviet spy in England in 1943, and drew Philby's attention to the fact that Burgess had visited Philby at Istanbul in 1948. I then pointed out that there was other evidence against him but that I felt he was "making no real effort to defend himself." I asked him why this was. Why did he have no answer to the statements being made against him? Philby attempted to answer each point, but he did so too cleverly. He looked and behaved like a rat in a trap. I let him go. But his attitude was such that everything being said against him was true and that there was therefore a strong presumption of guilt against him.

After Philby had left Broadway, Easton put the entire matter up to Menzies. At that meeting "C" said nothing to indicate how he felt about the matter. But by the end of July or the beginning of August, "C" acted. As Philby was to record, he received a summons from "C," who "told me, with obvious distress, that he would have to ask for my resignation. He would be generous: £4,000 in lieu of pension." Further, as Philby himself related: "My unease was increased shortly afterwards when he told me that he had decided against paying me the whole sum at once. I would get £2,000 down and the rest in half-yearly instalments of £500. The ostensible reason for the deferred payments was the fear that I might dissipate all in wild speculation, but, as I had never speculated in my life, it looked a bit thin. A more likely reason was the desire to hedge against the possibility of my being sent to gaol within three years."

At the age of thirty-nine Philby found himself abandoned by his Soviet friends, unemployable, bereft of the protection of "C," deprived of his passport, and under the deepest suspicion for the gravest of crimes in the British statute book. There was a prolonged period of inaction during which the case against him was being prepared, and it was November 1951 before "C" called Philby back to Broadway. Then Menzies "explained that a judicial enquiry had been opened into the circumstances of the Burgess-Maclean escape," and that Philby was required to give evidence. The inquiry was to be conducted by Helenus J. P. "Buster" Milmo, a barrister, at Leconfield House, headquarters of MI5. Of that ordeal, Philby was to record:

The mention of Milmo indicated that a crisis was at hand. I knew him and of him. He was a skilled interrogator; he was the man whom MI5 usually brought in for the kill. As I drove with the Chief across St. James's Park to Leconfield House, I braced myself for a sticky ordeal. I was still confident that I could survive an examination, however robust, on the basis of the evidence known to me. But I could not be sure that new evidence had not come to hand for Milmo to shoot at me.

At Leconfield House Milmo asked Philby to refrain from smoking, as this was a judicial enquiry. Philby did so, and the enquiry began, Philby seeking to appear as a cooperative ex-SIS officer, his objective to "deny him the confession which he required as a lawyer." Philby wrote in his memoirs:

I was too closely involved in Milmo's interrogation to form an objective opinion on its merits. Much of the ground that he covered was familiar and my answers, excogitated long before, left him little to do but shout. Early in the interview, he betrayed the weakness of his position by accusing me of entrusting to Burgess "intimate personal papers." The charge was so obviously nonsensical that I did not even have to feign bewilderment. It appeared that my Cambridge degree had been found in Burgess's flat during the search which followed his departure. Years before, I had folded that useless document and put it in a book. Burgess, as anyone would have told Milmo, was an inveterate borrower of books with and without the permission of their owners. The aim of the accusation was to show that I had deliberately underplayed the degree of my intimacy with Burgess. It was flimsy stuff and went far to strengthen my confidence in the outcome.

But Milmo produced "at least two rabbits out of the bag which I had not foreseen, and which showed that the chain of circumstantial evidence against me was even longer than I had feared." As Philby related:

Two days after the Volkov information reached London, there had been a spectacular rise in the volume of NKVD wireless traffic between London and Moscow, followed by a similar rise in the traffic between Moscow and Istanbul. Furthermore, shortly after I had been officially briefed about the [Homer] leakage in Washington, there had been a similar jump in NKVD traffic. Taken in conjunction with the other evidence, these two items were pretty damning. But to me, sitting in the interrogation chair, they posed no problem. When asked in Milmo's most thunderous tones to account for these occurrences, I replied quite simply that I could not.

And as Philby continued:

I was beginning to tire when suddenly Milmo gave up. [Arthur] Martin asked me to stay put for a few minutes. When I was invited into the next room, Milmo had disappeared and the MI5 legal officer was in charge. He asked me to surrender my passport, saying that they would get it anyway but that voluntary action on my part would obviate publicity. I readily agreed as my escape plan certainly did not envisage the use of my own identity papers. My offer to send the document that night by registered post was rejected because it was "too risky." William Skardon [the chief MI5 interrogator] was detailed to accompany me back to my home and receive it from me. On the way, Skardon wasted his breath sermonising on the Advisability of Co-operating with the Authorities. I was too relieved to listen, though my relief was tempered by the knowledge that I was not yet out of the wood—not by a long chalk.

Philby was correct. He was not out of the woods by a long chalk. Neither the Foreign Office nor MI5 had any doubt that he was a Soviet agent. "You must accept that as a fact," said Sir Patrick Reilly. But "C" and Sinclair remained loyal to him, as did many others in SIS. Where was the *evidence* that would persuade the director of public prosecutions that there was a case against Philby in law? There were grounds for a strong presumption that Philby was guilty among intelligence officers, but, as Philby had confidently predicted in Washington as he examined his situation, there was precious little *evidence* that could convict him legally. Over the coming months, however, the amount of circumstantial evidence increased inexorably while, at the same time, the case against Philby dissolved into what James Angleton accurately culled as a "wilderness of mirrors." [22] In that

wilderness facts, truth, politics, chronology, history, all became endless, inconsistent, contradictory portraits as those involved sought
without success to explain what had happened and what the consequences would be. The entire affair *suggested* that "C" had indeed
manipulated Philby in some great strategic deception. Yet that solution to the mystery was the *one aspect of the affair that was most
violently denounced.* That, surely, suggested "C" had known the truth
about Philby for a much longer period than he acknowledged, and
his own almost complete silence and his appearance of indifference
to the implications, which he maintained from 1951 until his death
in 1968, was surely convincing evidence that "C" believed he had
done his duty, that he had not been outwitted.

However, most authorities accepted the theory that "C" had been
outwitted. In the end, therefore, we come down to an enigmatic and
challenging statement of Anthony Montague Browne, Churchill's private secretary from 1952 until 1965: "There is one secret left in the
Philby case, and that I may not discuss." And we are also left to
contemplate the inner meaning of Cadogan's equally enigmatic statement in his diary in August 1943: " 'C' about Communists in his
organisation."

Such, then, was the riddle as "C" entered the last phase of his
career. As Easton was to state when confronted with the contradictions: "The best you can do is to present the arguments for the case
that Philby was a manipulation, and those against. Then you must let
the reader make up his own mind." In other words, not even Easton,
the vice-chief of SIS and "C's" nominee as successor, was *quite sure*
that there had not been at least some attempt at manipulation.

6 RETIREMENT

Throughout the Washington phase of the Philby affair, "C" was engaged in what was to prove his last major action in the service of the
state.

After a prolonged period of political confrontation, in May 1951
Dr. Mohammed Mussadeq, prime minister of Persia, nationalized
the Anglo-Iranian Oil Company. It was Britain's largest overseas asset,

and the refinery and oil fields at Abadan were the largest in the world at that time. They provided not only fuel oil for the Royal Navy and British commerce and industry, but also a cash flow to an economy that had been very nearly bankrupted by the costs of fighting World War II. It was recognized by Attlee's Cabinet that if the British acquiesced in what was an illegal nationalization, then other British assets would be seized throughout the world. To complicate the issues and implications of the seizure, there was information in London that the seizure had been encouraged by the U.S. ambassador in Teheran and that American oil companies had advised Mussadeq and supported him financially. In another day, that would have constituted an act of war.

Soon after nationalization, the new Socialist foreign secretary, Herbert Morrison, authorized "C" to organize the overthrow of Mussadeq and his replacement by a more amenable regime. "C" appointed a senior SIS officer, the Honorable C. M. Woodhouse, Lord Terrington's heir and son-in-law of the earl of Lytton, to go to Teheran and arrange Mussadeq's downfall. Later director-general of the Royal Institute for International Affairs, Woodhouse had had a long record of association with Broadway. For the operation, Woodhouse had an equally able deputy, R. C. Zaehner, professor of Eastern religions and ethics at Oxford. Zaehner was also lecturer in Persian at Oxford. He, too, had had a long association with "C," having been press attaché at the British embassy in Teheran between 1943–47 and acting counselor at the embassy in 1951–52.

Zaehner possessed three important agents there, the brothers Seyfollah, Qodratollah, and Assadollah Rashidian, one of whom was a close friend of the shah, Mohamed Reza. A second was a merchant, the third an owner of cinemas. The brothers were regular visitors to London; they kept a suite in the Grosvenor House Hotel overlooking Hyde Park and sent their children to school in England. Their main task was to buy votes in the Iranian Parliament, and for that purpose they not only invested their own money, but they also received suitcases full of English pound notes—in all £1.5 million, so it was said. Woodhouse recorded in his memoirs how he went to the British air base at Habbaniya in Iraq to pick up consignments of arms for the Rashidians' revolutionaries. The Rashidian brothers were provided with wireless to maintain contact with "C" and Broadway.

In October 1952 Mussadeq broke diplomatic relations with Britain. Woodhouse and Zaehner, and their English advisers and associates, were compelled to withdraw. They were replaced by CIA secret agents under the leadership of Kermit Roosevelt, grandson of President Theodore Roosevelt. Woodhouse and Zaehner turned over all their assets in Iran to Roosevelt. These, as Woodhouse wrote, included "senior officers of the army and police, deputies and senators, *mullahs*, merchants, newspaper editors, and elder statesmen, as well as mob leaders." The intention was to arrest Mussadeq and his ministers, capture key towns, and install a prime minister acceptable to both England and the United States. And if there were several misadventures along the way, the operation succeeded, although Britain lost her overlordship in Iran to the United States.

"C" had made his last attempt to maintain England's imperial position in the Orient. The time had come for him to leave. According to Easton, there was nothing curious about "C's" decision, made early in 1952, to retire. While it was assumed by those not close to him that Menzies resigned under the severe pressures created by the Burgess and Maclean affair, and through the suspicions that Philby was a Soviet spy, these beliefs were ill-founded. Through the world emergency caused by the Korean War and the Persian crisis, "C" remained in office for two and one-half years after retirement age, and now, Easton recalled, "C" himself simply was anxious to retire "after thirty-six years in the jungle." With Sinclair sufficiently experienced to take over, he felt the time had come with the fall of the Attlee administration and the arrival of Churchill's second ministry in October.

Although Churchill's Cabinet was composed mainly of men who had served with Churchill during the war, according to Easton, Menzies could have remained as "C" had he wished. But Menzies was comfortably off and felt the need to retire. There was, consequently, no significance in the fact that he chose this moment to leave government service. Menzies sent Churchill a telegram congratulating him on his victory and received a congenial reply by telegram: "Thank you so very much my dear 'C.'"

Then, on February 6, 1952, King George VI died in his sleep at Sandringham at the age of fifty-seven, having recently had surgery for the removal of a cancerous lung. The heir, Princess Elizabeth, was in Kenya with her husband, the duke of Edinburgh, on the first stage of a state visit to British East Africa, Australia, and New Zealand. At the moment of the king's death Princess Elizabeth became, in accordance with a new title enacted in 1949 to keep pace with the reality of politics, Queen Elizabeth the Second, by the Grace of God Queen of the Realm and of all Her other Realms and Territories, Head of the Commonwealth, Defender of the Faith.

With the proclamation of accession, the term "British Empire" formally passed into history, and its remnants became known as "the Commonwealth." Thus Stewart Menzies had remained "C" long enough to witness the liquidation of the empire—a bitter moment for a man who regarded the empire as an estate held in trust. He announced his retirement in a signal to all stations on June 30, 1952. There followed a series of retirement ceremonies and a great volume of letters that did not indicate that "C" was retiring in disgrace or as a defeated man, as his many enemies and critics imagined. On the contrary, the tenor of all the engagements and letters indicated that the state had lost a servant of surpassing ability.

The news soon traveled through the world intelligence community. On July 10, 1952, J. Edgar Hoover wrote in terms that scarcely suggested that, as was also being vouchsafed, "C's" conduct of his affairs had resulted in a trans-Atlantic disaster:

Dear Sir Stewart,

It is with profound regret that I learn of your resignation as Director General, British Secret Intelligence Service.

Your career has been a splendid example of unselfish and unstinted loyalty in the finest tradition and I feel that your retirement is England's loss.

The splendid cooperation you have extended to my representatives in London is very much appreciated and you have my best wishes for every future happiness.

Sincerely,
J.E.H.

Menzies also received many invitations to visit the United States, none of which he ever accepted. Menzies never stepped foot in America.

There were several ceremonies at the Foreign Office. Earlier, when Patrick Reilly told Menzies that the Foreign Office would like to make him a retirement gift and asked "C" what he would like, Menzies replied that he felt he would have need of decanters and glasses. At that the money was collected and a pair of beautiful Georgian decanters and a set of matching glasses was selected by Reilly's wife, Rachel. These were presented to Menzies on July 22, together with a farewell letter from the Foreign Secretary, Anthony Eden. This was framed in terms that again did not indicate that, as was being said, SIS had been defeated by the Soviet service:

My Dear Menzies,

On the occasion of your retirement I am writing to express to you the thanks of Her Majesty's Government for the outstanding services which you have rendered to the State.

Before entering the Service from which you have just retired, you had a gallant and distinguished record in the First World War. For 20 years you have played a leading part in the valuable work which your Service then undertook with very limited resources. You succeeded to its highest post shortly after the outbreak of war had vastly increased its tasks. For nearly six years, with selfless devotion, you carried a personal burden of responsbility such as fell upon few of your colleagues in the whole great machine for the conduct of the war. Since 1945 you have had little respite. You have had to pursue the reconstruction of your Service, on a scale never before contemplated in peace, amid the insistent demands of a new and unprecedented world-wide conflict. *You leave it full of promise for the future.* [emphasis supplied]

By its nature your work can receive no public tributes. For this reason I am all the more anxious that you should know how highly Her Majesty's Government have valued your services. By your retirement they have lost a devoted public servant.

In conclusion, may I say that I hope that you will enjoy for many years the leisure that you have so well earned.

Yours Very Sincerely,
Anthony Eden.

After thirty-eight years in the political underworld "C" had become a private citizen. But even as "C" was settling down to retirement, he was reminded that he could not entirely escape the past. As if to illustrate that nobody really knew "C" in every dimension, and that he never confided everything about his life and work to anyone, a near-tragic incident occurred shortly after Menzies's retirement.

Soon after "C" left Broadway his second secretary, Miss Evelyn Jones, was found near death through an overdose of a controlled substance taken in her flat. She had been "C's" mistress for many years, perhaps going back to 1941, and had sought death rather than face the future alone. Miss Jones was, however, found in time and revived through extensive medical attention in hospital. Having successfully concealed her relationship with "C," except possibly from the chief secretary, Miss Pettigrew, who may have guessed what was going on, nobody else in Broadway knew. Miss Jones's suicide attempt caused surprise and alarm at Broadway: If Stewart had managed to keep a mistress in his private office for all those years virtually without detection, what other secrets had he taken with him into retirement?

7 THE BULLFROGS' CHORUS

"C" returned to Bridges Court at Luckington, that old and silent village between Chippenham and Bath. He was a young sixty-two, fit in limb and wind, he had two and possibly three pensions, and he was reputed to possess "comfortable" private means—not rich by any means, but with sufficient money to do anything he wished to do within reason. Had he chosen, he could have obtained a directorship of a bank or some such institution, but instead he became what he had always been, a country gentleman.

The age did not allow him to revert entirely to harmless pursuits, for he was invited by SIS to write a memoir, for official purposes only. In addition, he was required to attend conferences at Broadway with ever-increasing frequency. He watched Great Britain retreat from the empire through the pages of *The Times*, the *Telegraph*, and *The Tatler* and withdrew into the old world of "the Master," the duke of Beaufort, one of the few remaining pockets of authentic Edwardian England.

"C's" existence—he was always known as "C" to his friends and associates, "Sir Stewart" to the middle and lower classes—began to assume a stately pattern, an agreeable progression of dinners, hunts, shoots, and race meetings, and he became a familiar figure at the big races of the year: the Derby, the Oaks, the Two Thousand Guineas, the One Thousand Guineas, the St. Leger, the Ascot Gold Cup, the Grand National, and the Grand Military Gold Cup. Idle days and hours were spent in gardening—"C" liked dahlias, which grew very well in Wiltshire, phlox, daisies, and large roses and tulips. These all bore English names, and he read only British seed and bulb catalogs.

He hunted regularly with the Beaufort, and he kept two or three horses for that purpose. It was a small world that "C" inhabited; the large dramatics were now in Moscow or Washington. England was becoming the forty-ninth state, and, except in that principality called Beaufortshire, and others like it, the mood was not one of a happy return to old traditions. In Beaufortshire, while the rest of the country struggled to adjust to a new age, one shorn of the empire and dominated by the hydrogen bomb and the strategic bomber, there was rigid adherence to the ancient code. "C" had become as anachronistic in power politics as the Gatling gun, and he knew it.

Stewart Menzies's elder brother, Keith, died on December 7, 1952, at the age of sixty-four. "C" was greatly distressed by Keith's death; another link with the golden days at Eton was gone, and a better epoch had passed, one that Churchill described in his salute to Queen Elizabeth upon her accession as "the august, unchallenged, and tranquil glories of the Victorian era." The world had entered a much less gentlemanly period. But "C's" other brother, Ian, was still alive and well, and they saw a good deal of each other.

With the passing of Lady Menzies, except for the servants, Bridges Court was often empty during the daytime and sounded like it, although things could get very lively during the evenings. After a lifetime of near teetotalism, "C" developed a liking for pink gin and angostura bitters made from Gordon's London Dry Gin, a case of which was sent to him by the directors each Christmas. But he was lonely since the death of Pamela. This made him vulnerable, and late in 1952, having sat down with his daughter, Fiona, and gone over with her the photographs of his "girlfriends," he proposed marriage to the Honorable Mrs. Audrey Chaplin, a rich woman and a daughter of Sir Thomas Latham, chairman of Courtauld's, the pharmaceutical and artificial fiber combine.

Mrs. Chaplin had previously been married to Tim Firkin, the racing motorist. This marriage had ended in divorce with two daughters. In 1928 she had married Lord Edward Hay, who was killed in July 1944 when a flying bomb hit the Guards Chapel at Wellington Barracks as he was reading the Lesson. There was one daughter by this marriage. Lady Hay had then married Niall Chaplin in 1948. The marriage lasted less than a year. She had been well known to Menzies ever since his Eton days, and Menzies had also been professionally associated with Courtauld's, for that company had from time to time provided cover for some of Menzies's agents overseas. But this was not a love match; it was a match between two elderly people who had known each other since youth and desired companionship.

"C's" marriage took place privately on December 12, five days after the death of Keith. The marriage was not a success, however, for both were creatures of habit, and the new Lady Menzies preferred going east to her estate in Essex, whereas "C," of course, had throughout his life gone west to Beaufortshire. Thus, they met for dinner each Wednesday evening at Lady Menzies's town house, the Manor House in Mayfair, then separated—"C" to Wiltshire, Lady Menzies to Essex.

As for the secret service, "C" sought not to involve himself in what were now Sinclair's affairs, but he made himself available when his counsel was sought. He was never, however, completely to escape either Kim Philby or the dark world he had left.

On March 5, 1953, Moscow Radio announced that Stalin had died at the Kremlin of a cerebral hemorrhage; after much rumor there came the news that Lavrenti Beria, head of the Soviet secret service since 1938, had been arrested. As *Tass* announced, paying "C" and his predecessors a backhanded compliment, in 1919 Beria became "a secret agent in the counterrevolutionary services of the Mussavat government in Azerbaijan, which was acting under the control of the British Secret Service. In 1920, Beria was in Georgia, where again he committed a treacherous act, by establishing a clandestine communication with the Menshevik Secret Political Police Department in Georgia, the latter being a branch of the British Intelligence Service." Other bulletins related how Beria had consistently engaged in treasonable activities from 1920 until the present day, along with his executives—six of them—and the death penalty was demanded for, and awarded against, all of them.

By that time "C's" daughter, Fiona, had announced her engagement to the master of the Berkeley hounds, Captain Brian Bell, lately of the King's Royal Dragoon Guards. Bell was an old Etonian, an agreeable man built in the fashion of the heavy cavalry. The Beria affair provided a witty backdrop for their engagement party, which took place at Bridges Court and was attended by the mink and manure set from all over England. "C" was delighted at the union, for he was a great believer in the principle that one should always marry one's own kind.

Following the engagement, Captain Bell moved into Bridges Court for a time, and "C" took him to one side and advised him of the existence of a single cardinal rule of the household: "I do not mind what you do while you are in this house, so long as the servants do not get to hear about it." Obeying this rule to the letter, Bell occupied a guestroom over "C's" bedroom for several months before the marriage, and it was during that time he discovered that "C" might possess limitless calm during daylight but at night it was a very different matter. As Bell remembered:

Since the walls and ceilings were thin, I soon discovered that S.G.M. was suffering from the most appalling nightmares, to do, apparently, with Philby. There was one recurrent theme in these nightmares, which were awful to hear. That was that there was a Russian defector who was taken up in a helicopter over the English Channel and given the choice—talk about Philby or be chucked out without a parachute. They chucked him out.

Having heard this story several times, Bell raised the matter with "C," but all Menzies ever said was that "the man was a damned traitor!" Bell never established whether there was a Russian defector in reality. [23]

Having become engaged when Beria was liquidated, Fiona Menzies and Brian Bell were married at the Church of the Holy Cross at Sherston. The wedding photograph showed that Menzies had lost all the weight he had gained during the war and looked like an aristocratic scarecrow in a morning coat that was everywhere too large for him. Everyone looked happy and delighted; and yet the clouds gathered over Menzies's reputation.

Late in 1955 the government published its White Paper on the Burgess-Maclean affair, and that document reawakened the interest of the press in both London and New York concerning the identity of "the third man." By that time Churchill had retired, Anthony Eden had become prime minister, and Harold Macmillan had become foreign secretary. On October 25, 1955, Colonel Marcus Lipton, a Socialist member, addressed the House of Commons: "Has the Prime Minister made up his mind to cover up at all costs the dubious third man activities of Mr. Harold Philby who was First Secretary at the Washington Embassy a little time ago, and is he determined to stifle all discussion on the very great matters which were evaded in the wretched White Paper, which is an insult to the intelligence of the country?" [24]

Macmillan replied: "Between May 1951 and April 1954, the first thought of those responsible had to be not how much they could tell the public, but what they could do to minimise the harm that had been done. The Security [Service] still had extensive enquiries to make, not merely to reconstruct the story but to improve the Service." But with the defection on April 3, 1954, of Vladimir Petrov, the Soviet secret agent in Australia, Macmillan continued, "a whole new vista on the case was opened up." Petrov had made a statement before a Royal Commission, and the possibility that Burgess and Maclean had been tipped off by someone within the government had now to be seriously considered. Macmillan went on:

In this connection the name of one man has been mentioned in the House of Commons, but not outside. I feel that all Honourable Members would expect me to mention him by name and to explain the position. He is Mr. H.A.R. Philby, who was a temporary First Secretary at the British Embassy in Washington from October 1949 to June 1951 and had been privy to much of the investigation into the leakage. . . . No evidence had been found to show that he was responsible for warning Burgess or Maclean. While in Government service he carried out his duties ably and conscientiously. I have no reason to conclude that Mr. Philby has at any time betrayed the interests of this country, or to identify him with the so-called "Third Man," if indeed there was one.

Anthony Eden then concluded the debate with an appeal for public confidence in the Foreign Office; and as Philby declared at a press conference afterward, triumphant that he had been exonerated publicly by the foreign secretary personally, "As far as I am concerned, the incident is closed." [25] The same thought occurred to many others, including Sinclair, who hoped now to be able to resume operations without having to worry about moles. Menzies, too, resumed his life as a country gentleman and was seen only rarely at Broadway—for the time being, at least.

But it was not long before trouble began afresh in two directions. In the first, Foreign Office officials began to weary of Sinclair's very military manner, his lack of interest in political intelligence, and what they considered to be his overconcentration on preparations for the Third World War—the laying out of agent, communications, escape, and financial networks in Europe against the day the Red Army would roll down to the North Sea, the English Channel, and the Pyrenees.

Second, with Philby's exoneration a movement developed at Broadway to engineer his rehabilitation. Easton would have nothing to do with it, for he was among the small group that had read the report on Philby and was sure of his guilt. The prime movers were Nicholas Elliott and Count Vanden Heuvel, encouraged perhaps by Menzies, who still appeared to be convinced that Philby was guiltless—although, as Easton complained, "he was so sphinx-like and cunning you could never really tell what he thought."

Acting in complete secrecy, and presumably with the support of Sinclair, they argued that Philby could not be left in disgrace for much longer, for he had been cleared of blame as "the third man" even if Dick Goldsmith White of MI5 remained suspicious. It was well known that there had been a movement to get Andre Deutsch, a Czech emigré publisher in London with liberal capital backing, to publish Philby's memoirs if he wrote them. Sinclair thought that would be dangerous. Inside Broadway the belief was that SIS should use its influence to get Philby a job in journalism overseas, but in a place where SIS could still keep an eye on him and bring him in if necessary.

Elliott, who was still in charge of SIS's "outside jobs" department, and Count Vanden Heuvel, now back in London after many years as head of the SIS station in Switzerland, went to see some of the officials of *The Observer* and *The Economist*, and an arrangement was made by which both would retain Philby's services as Middle East correspondent, a position for which he was well fitted—his father, St. John Philby, was still alive and still influential at Ibn Saud's court in Saudi Arabia.

When Philby accepted that appointment, it was intimated to him that while SIS would not reappoint him as an officer, Broadway would welcome his advice on Middle Eastern matters and suggested that he might profitably stay in touch with SIS through the station chief in Beirut. The object here was to enable Sinclair to keep an eye on Philby without having any actual responsibility for him. Upon reflection, it was a neat solution: Philby's silence on difficult matters such as the duke of Windsor was purchased while SIS had distanced themselves from him.

Philby arrived in Beirut in September 1956, shortly before the Anglo-French-Israeli invasion of Egypt. Here St. John Philby was of large importance in establishing his son's credentials as a foreign correspondent. St. John Philby was undoubtedly the greatest living expert on Arabian politics; he introduced Kim to his huge range of friends and confidants, thereby expanding the influence of the Soviet service in Arabia. In general St. John Philby enabled his son to resume to a significant degree his former importance in both SIS and the Soviet service.

Kim Philby's wife, Aileen, died in December 1957; she may have been the last person who knew the truth about Philby's activities. But Aileen, racked with worry and deeply unhappy, died silently. The Cowgills, who had stayed in touch with her despite Kim's intrigues against Felix, thought there was something suspicious about her death, although Philby was in Arabia when she died. There was no investigation. Lucky Kim! they said. With Aileen's passing, it was not long before the small, clannish group of correspondents in Beirut was quivering with other portentous news: Kim Philby was cuckolding Sam Pope Brewer, *The New York Times*'s correspondent. In due course Eleanor Brewer left her husband and became Kim Philby's third wife.

Meanwhile, as Philby was settling in to his new work and play, the Foreign Office's irritation with Sinclair had increased to the point where Sir Norman Brook, secretary of the Cabinet, was asked to undertake an inquiry into SIS and Broadway, which had come to resemble something of a fortress inside Whitehall, an institution that was part of but not connected to the rest of the government. Brook accepted the inquiry and may even have begun work, when there occurred one of those disasters that afflict modern intelligence services in an open society.

In an attempt to moderate the Cold War, Anthony Eden invited to England Nikolai Bulganin, premier of the Soviet Union, and Nikita Khrushchev, who was in the process of denouncing the cult of Stalinism. "B&K," as they came to be called by the British press, accepted, and they arrived at Portsmouth, aboard the Soviet cruiser *Ordzhonikidze*. They were received in circumstances of state and were welcomed almost everywhere in Britain during their ten days in the country. But the Admiralty had been concerned at the turn of speed displayed by the *Ordzhonikidze* during her run down the North Sea and the English Channel, and they had asked Broadway to send an agent to see whether there was anything novel about her hull. Sinclair asked his Foreign Office liaison officer, Michael Wright, to clear the operation with the Foreign Office, but for obscure reasons Wright reported the operation had been cleared when, in fact, it had not been, or at least so the Foreign Office claimed. Believing that he had Foreign Office approval, Sinclair authorized the operation to proceed. However, toward the end of the "B&K" visit, news reached Fleet Street that a British wartime frogman, Lionel Crabbe, had been reported to the Portsmouth police as "missing." That news attracted some attention, although there was no reason at first to link Crabbe's disappearance to the *Ordzhonikidze*. But after "B&K's" departure, the *Daily Mail* discovered that the page of the guests' register of the hotel where Crabbe had stayed had been removed by Portsmouth police "at the request of someone in high authority." That discovery was blasted across the front page of the *Daily Mail*, and the fact that "London" had been involved in the disappearance of "Buster" Crabbe, as he was known to all British frogmen, indicated a sinister trail.

Not unexpectedly, the Eden government was greatly embarrassed by the affair, the more so when a headless, mutilated, unidentifiable corpse in a frogman's suit was discovered near Portsmouth. Shortly there was severe trouble between Sinclair and the Foreign Office; Wright was relieved, and it became evident that, as they used to say in Whitehall, "Sinclair was in for the big chop."

At that point Menzies reappeared at Broadway in the hope that he might save Sinclair's job and prevent the "civilianization" of the secret service; he failed, and Sinclair resigned. At that point, according to Menzies's plan, Easton should have become "C," and, indeed, Eden had approved the appointment. Sir Norman Brook, however, felt it was time to cast off the remnants of the past and do what Cadogan had tried to do in 1945—turn SIS into a modern, civilian department that was part of a modern, civilian government.

When that recommendation came before the government, Easton was in the Far East, "doing a spot of kingmaking" that resulted in one of the most brilliantly successful episodes in the period of transfer of power from colonial to self-government—the establishment of Lee Kuan Yew as prime minister of Singapore, and the consolidation of the Malaysian government of Tengku Abdul Rahman, both in the teeth of major Communist insurgency. He hastened back to London to defend the promise he had received from Attlee and "C" that he would succeed Sinclair. But before Easton could make his case adequately, Brook had recommended that the head of MI5, Dick Goldsmith White, Philby's old antagonist, be made the new "C."

Brook's proposals were accepted, despite a ferocious last-ditch defense of his dynasty by Menzies. His argument, basically, was that the old system of recruitment was best because it had been tried and tested in two world wars and emerged victorious from both, and the only serious cases of treachery had involved not the ex-officers, but the civilians. In particular, he was opposed to the overconcentration of recruitment upon the universities on the grounds that it was well known they were sinks of treasonable thought—was it not at the Oxford Union in 1933 that, by a vote of 275 to 153, the undergraduates approved the motion "that this House refuses in any circumstances to fight for King and Country"? Were the universities not hotbeds of socialism and other riotous, anti-Establishment thought? And look at all the trouble he had had at Bletchley Park during the war, where there was indiscipline amounting to anarchy on occasions! Could university men be trusted to fight Bolsheviks?

In an attempt to get Prime Minister Eden to change his mind and appoint Easton, Menzies called in the many debts owed him by the World War II establishment—men like Churchill, Ismay, Sir Edward Bridges, Marshal of the Royal Air Force Lord Portal, Marshal of the Royal Air Force Lord Tedder, Field Marshal Lord Alexander, and that greatest of *éminences grises*, Sir Walter Monckton, Windsor's lawyer and now the defense minister. But again Menzies did not prevail. His failure marked the end of his power in Whitehall.

Goldsmith White became "C" and, in the spirit of Christ come to cleanse the temple, began to clear out all the great names of Broadway, including most of the ex-officers of "C's" generation. The only senior executive retained by White was Easton, who remained as vice-chief of the service for two years at Goldsmith White's request, "to help me ease myself into the saddle." The intellectuals took over from the professionals at last. Broadway was abandoned (but not the official residence in Queen Anne's Gate) and reappeared in a grimy proletarian quarter called Southwark on the south bank of the Thames, an area where, in those days, no self-respecting man of the old school would be seen dead. Then SIS was integrated with the government.

The only concession to the past was a portrait of Walsingham, Elizabeth I's spymaster. No portrait of Menzies was to be found in the new building. Then the last link with the old order—Easton—departed. He was given the knighthood he would have received if he had become "C" and then, presumably to get him out of the way, was appointed consul-general at Detroit, which enabled him to indulge his greatest passion—golf—for the rest of his days in the agreeable world of the Grosse Pointe clubs.

Meanwhile, knowing nothing of Sinclair's arrangements with Philby, White was appalled to discover that Philby had crept back into the outer fringes of SIS. The time for the denouement in Philby's case had arrived. But White needed proof sufficient to convince a court of law that Philby was a traitor. That did not occur, so it is said, until late in 1961, when the Russians suffered yet another defection—the eighty-second involving a Russian in the rank of captain or above since the end of World War II.

The defector's name was Anatoli M. Golitsin. When he was collected by CIA Helsinki, Golitsin proved to have been "a major in the directorate of the KGB working primarily against targets in the NATO alliance." Golitsin was interrogated first by James Angleton in Washington and then turned over to SIS for questioning concerning Philby. Golitsin provided SIS with a lengthy account that showed Philby had been a spy for the Soviet intelligence service since 1933 and his Cambridge days, and that he was still in the Soviet service; Golitsin even named his controllers in London, Washington, Istanbul, and, presently, Beirut.

Whether the evidence of a Soviet traitor would be adequate to convict a British traitor in a British court was still unresolved when a second, more reliable source emerged. This was Mrs. Solomons, who related a startling story to Lord Rothschild, the inheritor of Rothschild's bank and a man who had served in the Security Service in World War II and was closely connected with Philby and Burgess. Mrs. Solomons stated that during the war she met Philby on several occasions; they became friendly, and eventually Philby told her that he was "engaged on a very secret and dangerous mission in life" and tried to recruit her as a spy in the interests of Russia. Lord Rothschild stated later that he reported this to his former colleagues in MI5, and Mrs. Solomons was formally interviewed by representatives of the Security Service who were still investigating the Philby affair.

MI5 accepted Mrs. Solomons's statement as fact. The statement evidently appeared damning enough to reopen the case against Philby, the more so since reports from Beirut showed that he was drinking extraordinarily heavily even for a man with his "alcoholic" proclivities.

Then, on September 30, 1960, St. John Philby collapsed while with his son in Beirut. He was rushed to hospital, but he recovered consciousness only once, and long enough only to exclaim, "God! I'm bored." He then died and was buried in the Muslim Cemetery in the Basta quarter of Beirut, according to Muslim rites administered by the sheikh of Bashoura. The death of his father left Kim Philby shattered. His moral strength was already sapped by alcohol and almost thirty years of treachery. His new wife, Eleanor, recorded that he was drunk morning, noon, and night, week in and week out, in the winter, spring, summer, and autumn. She did not exaggerate, although those who met him in Beirut during that period all remarked that the inner defenses of the man were probably intact.

White decided it was the time to strike. But he, too, wanted no massive *scandale* such as a major trial. To that extent, therefore, Philby's power remained intact. What White wanted, and what he arranged, was a full confession in return for immunity from prosecution. Nicholas Elliott was sent to Beirut to confront Philby. Undoubtedly, one of Elliott's reasons for dealing with Philby was his desire to settle the scores caused by the ruin of "C," to which Elliott had been practically the only professional witness. The confrontation took place in Beirut on or about January 10, 1963, in a private flat that Elliott had rented for the purpose.

At length, Elliott succeeded in obtaining a general confession of treason and proposed that Philby should put the confession in writing. But Philby hedged at that proposal, stating that he wanted time to think over what he should do. Could they resume their discussion at a later date? Elliott had no choice but to accept and, after dining with Philby and Eleanor, returned to London. Shortly after that dinner, Philby vanished from Beirut. There was a long period of silence, and then, on July 3, the Moscow press announced briefly that by unanimous vote of the presidium, Harold Adrian Russell Philby had been made a citizen of the Soviet Union.

Not long after that, Philby was also made a member of the Order of the Red Banner, conferred as "recognition of conspicuous bravery or self-sacrifice in time of war, special capacity for leadership, or the performance of some action contributing decisively to the success of Soviet arms." The badge consisted of a laurel wreath over the upper part of which was spread the Red flag bearing the words "Workers of all Countries Unite!" Thus Philby became the first Briton to be made a member of both the Order of the British Empire and the Order of the Red Banner. (A year later the Central Chancery of the Orders of Knighthood at Buckingham Gate, London, announced that the name of H.A.R. Philby had been removed from the list of Members of the Order.)

Philby then offered a reason for his treason. "I regard myself," he told the Moscow correspondent of the London *Daily Express*, "as wholly and irreversibly English and England as having been perhaps the most fertile patch of earth in the whole history of human ideas." His conspiracy, he said, had been against "certain temporary phenomena" that prevented England from being herself. What those phenomena were Philby did not say, but by implication he seemed to be pointing at imperialism, capitalism, and "American Democracy."

By 1967, in an interview with a representative of the *Sunday Times*, he recanted that interview and the reason for what he called his "silent war." To betray, a man must belong, he explained. He had not belonged to England or the empire. Therefore he was not a traitor. If he had belonged anywhere, it was to India, where he was born, or Arabia, where his father had spent most of his life. Philby agreed that his conduct had appeared treacherous to those brought up under the canons of Queen Victoria and Edward VII, but, he argued, they were not *his* canons. The canons of his life were "the fight against fascism and the fight against imperialism." Both were, fundamentally, the same fight.

When confronted by the evidence that Philby was a traitor after all, "C" declared to a visitor with his usual limitless calm, that "St. Peter betrayed Christ three times. I was lucky. I was betrayed only once." [26]

But at a time of severe worldwide political tumult and conflict involving Russia, Goldsmith White was compelled to assume that most if not all officers of the service were compromised. A new group would have to be recruited, trained, and deployed. Also, SIS had to assume that all SIS networks in East and West Germany were all also compromised. Almost all networks were liquidated, a process that involved "several hundred" persons. The evidence before him was that the networks in Eastern Europe, the Balkans, and the Middle East were also almost as seriously penetrated or controlled by the Russians. Only the networks in the Far East appeared to him to have escaped Soviet control.

All this was grave enough; but "C's" troubles had only just begun. Until now the Philby affair had constituted a series of intermittent crises that, through the existence of the Official Secrets Act and the "D" Notice advisory bulletins to all newspaper editors except the *Daily Worker*, he and Sinclair were able to control. Now the Philby crisis became what the Foreign Office called "a bullfrogs' chorus," a derogatory reference to the press. As one SIS officer with experience of diplomacy defined that phenomenon: "One croaks, all croak."

In Moscow, Philby was at work on the second of a three-volume memoir. All three, he announced, would be published in the East and the West. The Foreign Office reacted with determination, for it was well aware that during World War II Broadway had been a viper's nest; there were many old scores to settle, and if Philby's memoirs were published, it would unleash a flood of such books that would not only damage the national interest, but also wreck the brilliant reputation established by Menzies and his service during the war. Consequently, a major battle now ensued, one intended to stop publication or at least ensure that if Philby's book *was* published, its worth was destroyed.

At about the same time, the *Sunday Times* began a major examination of the combined Burgess, Maclean, and Philby affairs. Bruce Page, David Leitch, and Phillip Knightley, a team of reporters who specialized in "in depth" reporting, undertook the investigation. Being well-financed with the world resources of the *Sunday Times* at their disposal, and finding many ex-SIS men who were prepared to talk, the three reporters produced well-researched articles that understandably reflected the distinct anti-SIS bias of their informants, most of whom were men "C" had passed over for honors at the end of the war. The articles caused a great sensation and, consequently, in 1968 were published by Andre Deutsch, the London publisher, in book form under the title *Philby: The Spy Who Betrayed a Generation.*

Both the articles and the book were an immense success, and the bullfrogs' chorus lasted for many months. That chorus was fueled from time to time by declarations from one or another of the golden lads. Dr. Goronwy Rees, a fellow of All Souls and a friend of Guy Burgess, was left with an "incurable disposition to doubt and suspect all impeccable authorities [in England]." And as Rees added: "Our security services, in fact, seemed to me a microcosm of that 'great capitalist class' now in the process of internal disintegration, whose structure and organization, modes of behavior and thought, I had found so alien when I first went to Oxford." [27]

All the golden lads that had surrounded Philby, Burgess, and Maclean were interrogated—Cyril Connolly, Tom Driberg, John Lehmann, Phillip Toynbee, W. H. Auden, Harold Acton, Brian Howard, Graham Greene, Malcolm Muggeridge, Claud Cockburn, Evelyn Waugh, Christopher Isherwood. All the rogues, dandies, and orchids were dug out and questioned as London society hummed with the witch hunt for the third man, the fourth man, the fifth man, the sixth man. Every clever pen found the defections symbolic of the decrepitude into which England had sunk through two world wars. A major literary furore developed, one without precedent in modern British literary history, one that went on and on for years, and one that was noticeable for a single element—nobody dared mention Menzies, the unknown dimension in the entire affair.

With the development of a bullfrogs' chorus, it became evident that this was not a national scandal, but a national trauma caused by the realization at last that the world power had been transferred to Washington. The novelist Graham Greene asked, "Who has not committed treason to something or someone more important than a country?" At a later date he compared Philby to the recusant English

Catholics alive under Elizabeth I. W. H. Auden announced that he had become an American for exactly the same reason Burgess had become a Russian—it was the only way to rebel against England. Rebecca West observed that loyalty—Menzies's type of loyalty—had become "dowdy," while "treason has a certain style, a sort of elegance, or, as the vulgar would say, 'sophistication.' "

Recoiling under the welter of words, Felix Cowgill, now in retirement in Dorsetshire, felt that the *Sunday Times*'s articles had libeled him. His resentment was not unjustified, for through his direction, Section V had defeated the German intelligence service as no intelligence service of a modern state had ever been defeated before. That fact was not, however, mentioned in the *Sunday Times*, which failed also (no doubt because of the Official Secrets Act or through ignorance) to mention other matters that might have cast Cowgill in a better light—Ultra, for example.

Cowgill wrote to Menzies at Luckington to advise that he proposed to write a statement for publication in the *Sunday Telegraph*, a Conservative newspaper that often published the opinions of retired officers. Also, Cowgill declared, he proposed consulting lawyers with a view to suit against the *Sunday Times*. Menzies replied with, no doubt, the matter of Edward VIII's correspondence with Hitler in mind, and also perhaps to defend his own knowledge about the reality of Philby's conduct:

Dear Felix,

The article which you found to be so offensive is not one that I should regard as one calling for action as unfortunately we are unable to defend ourselves & once one goes for the Press experience shows that one is unlikely to win. But what possible action could you take except possibly to write a defence to the "S.T." should they be willing to publish it. Again I do not know what the action would be of the "Firm." After all the present incumbents have suffered more than we have & personally I intend doing nothing unless the . . . book forces one's hand. So far I have warded off 4 newspapers [&] 24 TVs. I am however trying to find out if there is any possible action for the likes of us, but I am pretty sure that the action will be to do nothing. What I think about "Kim" is beyond words & that he was seriously considered as the "top" is absurd as we all knew his weakness for drink. But one could not have thought him to have been *an out & out traitor* [emphasis added]. But there are, alas, many such Englishmen as witness the Communists in this country. Of course I should see you, but do nothing until I hear more from a "friend." I wonder what has happened to [Valentine Vivian]—is he unwell as I was told sometime ago? I know very few of those still in work. [28]

Meanwhile, the Foreign Office's campaign to prevent publication of Philby's memoir, *My Silent War*, had been partly successful. First a synopsis and then the manuscript itself appeared in Paris just before Christmas of 1967, but the copyright and authenticity of the work was so successfully muddied that it seemed for a time the bloom was off the book and, as publishers say, "it would bomb." So it might have done, but for the appearance from the wings of Robin Denniston, a director of Hodder & Stoughton, a leading London publishers.

Although his own house had refused to publish the work, as had all other leading London publishers, Robin Denniston, the *Sunday Telegraph* reported, "felt so strongly that the book ought to be published that he took the unusual step of offering to act as London agent for the book in his private capacity and on a no-commission basis."

Denniston gave no reason for his support of a book that was intended, as the text showed plainly, to damage or demolish the reputation of "C" and SIS. However, perhaps a reason lay in his family background. Denniston was the son of Commander Alastair Denniston, chief of GC&CS from 1939 and 1942, when "C" relieved his old friend for incompetence in his management of Bletchley Park. According to Denniston's deputy, H. G. Filby, Commander Denniston was greatly embittered when he was relieved and remained so even after his reappointment as head of the diplomatic code-breaking section in London, although to the world his relations with "C" remained friendly. Indeed, Denniston was so bitter that at a dinner of the diplomatic code breakers at the Cafe Royal after the war (by which time he had realized that he would not get the knighthood he hoped for), his advice in an after-dinner speech to those thinking of making code breaking their career was to find some other occupation, as government service was "not rewarding."

Robin Denniston believed that it was "C" who had been incompetent, not his father. He became a determined enemy of Stewart Menzies by ramming through the publication of Frederick Winterbotham's memoir, *The Ultra Secret*, despite the threats of the British government. And it was Robin Denniston who found Philby's book a home at MacGibbon and Kee, a small but respected London publisher. Although Menzies may have seen the manuscript—a copy was certainly shown to Cowgill—Philby's book, *My Silent War*, was not published until *after* "C's" death. Graham Greene's introduction to the book, and some of the many articles that were favorable to Philby's treason, proclaimed the cult of the antihero, and especially the antihero who made a fool of the Establishment. These served to refuel the bullfrogs' chorus. In its way it was far worse than the Tranby Croft affair, for only the reputation of the future King Edward VII was involved in that incident; the security of the state was involved in this one.

The oddest quality about Philby's book was that there was one man in the British secret world for whom Philby displayed affection—Stewart Menzies, the personification of almost everything about England that Philby was sworn to destroy. Philby revealed an almost filial regard for Menzies, when it might have been expected that he would have reserved his most deadly venom for his old chief. It was almost as if Philby were talking about his father or someone who had played a part in his upbringing—an "uncle," perhaps. But if Philby felt warmly toward his old "C," Menzies did not feel that way about Philby. "That damned blackguard!" he exploded to his son-in-law, Captain Bell, at Luckington Court when the *Daily Express* published an interview with Philby in Moscow.

Following publication of Philby's memoir, Menzies wrote Cowgill that he was "horrified about the Press interviews with 'Kim'—it should never have been allowed & the Press do not seem to appreciate that he was the worst traitor possible & cost lives." Menzies wrote to Cowgill again on December 19, 1967, ending it in kindly fashion with this abjuration:

I received this A.M. news that the F.O. is in touch with you so there is nothing further for me to do. I still feel that you may be wise to do nothing unless your advisers feel v. confident that you will gain a victory—either by an apology or financial gain. Whichever you decide I pray that this will be the end of your troubles altho' I always fear the power of the press! Meanwhile forget for a few days & enjoy yourself at Christmas and receive my best wishes for the New Year.

In the event, Cowgill relapsed into silence as the great effervescence continued. It was at once an attack on the social and political predicament of postwar England and an assault on the ruling class, of which Stewart Menzies had become a symbol. As Malcolm Muggeridge, a Communist turned Christian, rejoiced in an article:

A ruling class which is on the run, as ours is, is capable of every fatuity. It makes the wrong decisions, chooses the wrong people, and is unable to recognize its enemies—if it does not actually prefer them to its friends.

The scandal reverberated until the end and worsened Menzies's marital relations. In her previous marriages, Lady Menzies had paid all the household costs and, it seems, her husbands' bills. And for Stewart Menzies she insisted upon doing likewise. This led to some friction, made even worse by the fact that she drank very heavily and, while not disliking Stewart, was critical of him in public when in her cups. Already limited by geographical and sporting preferences, their life together became clouded by the incessant scandal, which placed a great strain on their marriage and their social life.

At length, while in an alcoholic fit, Lady Menzies denounced her husband in a restaurant for "having let the side down"—the same words "society" had used to denounce Arthur Wilson following the Royal Baccarat hubbub. Lady Menzies meant that Stewart had committed the cardinal sin of the ruling class: through his actions he had brought his class into hatred, ridicule, and contempt with the working and middle classes. After Lady Menzies's denunciation (which was probably only one of many), Stewart Menzies spent more and more time alone at Bridges Court.

The end for Stewart Menzies was not far off. In 1967, just after his seventy-seventh birthday, he was hunting with the Beaufort near Silk Wood. As usual he rode his horse *at* rather than *over* a fence. Never an elegant rider, and being fierce and exuberant in the chase, he caused his hunter to stumble and fall. This time he was thrown badly, and his horse rolled over him. Winded and bruised, he was taken by the hunt Land Rover to the Lansdowne Nursing Home, a big Georgian house just under the lip of the Lansdowne plateau— Claude Dansey had died in the same place of his heart attack in 1947. Here, Menzies spent ten days recovering and was told that he now had "a heart condition," that he must take nitroglycerin pills to demolish the plaque in his cardiovascular system, and that he must hunt no more.

Not to be able to hunt depressed him greatly. According to Bell, he spent much of his time at the garden gate at the back of his property, watching (through a keyhole) a vixen who was in cub. When she had her cubs he fed them by tossing mutton bones over the garden gate. And when they were old enough to move about, he told nobody about them, least of all the Beaufort.

As for the Philby affair, barely a week passed without some fresh development. "The incessant, untrue, unfair publicity that went on and on without any attempt by the government to give a correct version of the facts certainly sapped my ability to control myself," Cowgill was to remember. "I wrote to Stewart Menzies and suggested that something must be done to get the truth out. It was wrecking my life and I am sure it was wrecking every one else's involved."

With the spring of 1968 came the cruelest blow. In April Hugh Trevor-Roper published his view of the Philby literature in *Encounter*. This article was a long, merciless indictment of the Secret Intelligence Service during the period 1941–45, the epic years in which Menzies had been "C." While Trevor-Roper treated Menzies personally with respect and even affection, he was caustic and contemptuous of SIS's achievements, organization, and executives. This disturbed Menzies very deeply, for he had thought highly of Trevor-Roper's future and had prevented his court-martial and ruin at the hands of Vivian. But the strange thing, as Bell stated, was that "not once—except when Stewart made the expostulation about Philby being 'a blackguard'—did SGM ever show that he was affected by the controversy. His calm was such that I began to wonder whether or not, after all, it was SGM, not Philby, who had had the last laugh. But I never found out because SGM would never discuss the case with me."

Even so, "C" could hunt no longer, his reputation seemed to have been destroyed along with that of the service he had created, his third marriage brought him no solace, and he was suddenly old and tired. Soon after Trevor-Roper's article, early in May of 1968, Mrs. Greville-Collins, his neighbor at Luckington Manor, happened to see Menzies while she was attending to her flower beds by the hedge that separated their properties. She bade him good morning and thought how distinguished he looked—his features had become very *fin de race* toward the end, just like those of his grandfather, Graham Menzies, in the portrait at Hallyburton.

To her surprise, Menzies announced that he thought he was going to die shortly and was going up to London to do so. A little later she heard that Menzies's groom had shot his two hunters. She felt that her neighbor could not be long for this world, for if he had intended to remain in it, he would never have shot his horses—he was too fond of them. As far as was known, "C" caught the train at Badminton Halt and was not seen again, at least in Luckington.

At the end of the month *The Times* announced that Major General Sir Stewart Graham Menzies, K.C.B., K.C.M.G., D.S.O., M.C., had died on May 28, 1968, at Sister Agnes's, the King Edward VII Hospital for Officers in Beauchamp Place, London, S.W.1. He was in his seventy-eighth year and had died at a place of distinction in the midst of the Philby scandal-of-state, not far from where he was born into the Royal Baccarat scandal-of-state in 1890.

The tributes followed. None were more important than that of Dick White:

My Dear Lady Menzies,

May I say how grieved I was by the news of Stewart's death. . . . He was invariably most kind and helpful to me and I admired his achievements, especially those of wartime, very much indeed. He is undoubtedly the greatest name in modern intelligence. On returning to the Office today I found enclosed letter from the London liaison officer of the C.I.A. I think that you would like to know that Stewart's reputation with the Americans was a great one. Nicholas [Elliott] has kept me in close touch with events. I send you my most sincere sympathies in your great loss. By those in a difficult world who knew Stewart he will not be forgotten. He was a great and gay man with great powers of endurance as the war years showed.

Yours Sincerely
Dick White

Wilderness of Mirrors

On May 31, 1968, *The Times* took what was then the unprecedented step of publishing a full obituary of "C."

Major General Sir Stewart Menzies, K.C.B., K.C.M.G., D.S.O., M.C., head of Britain's Secret Intelligence Service—which became known as MI6—from 1939 to 1951, died on Wednesday in London at the age of 78.

To become head of the Secret Intelligence Service in the third month of a great war, with fresh tasks and new men pouring in; with Admiralty, War Office, Air Ministry and Foreign Office pressing for attention to their needs; with sparse moneybags suddenly swelling; and enemy activity creating new problems and new opportunities almost daily—that was an ordeal to test a superman. Menzies would have been the last to claim for himself such quality. Indeed, standing up to the superman who was then Prime Minister probably caused him the most wearing concern. His direct access to Winston Churchill and the Chiefs of Staff must have been a source of pride to 'C'; many a brilliant offering of intelligence was he able to bring to them. But they were also exacting, critical and often quite unaware of the problems that accompany the search for secret information.

In 1939, the Secret Service, like the fighting services, had suffered for years from under-manning and under-spending. Menzies's predecessor, Admiral 'Quex' Sinclair, had his work cut out to decide how to use his limited resources under governments which were seldom confident of what the right targets for intelligence should be. Certainly between the wars Germany was not the main target, and the fluctuations of British policy towards Moscow created problems of loyalty of which much has lately been heard. The swift and ruthless overrunning of the Continent by the Germans in 1940 made it necessary to start again from scratch over most of occupied Europe. True, outstanding success was won by men and women of allied Secret Services, notably the Norwegian one and later by the Resistance in France and the Low Countries; but the war was to show that the agent was no longer the first arm of intelligence work and that information won by technical means—above all by the study of wireless traffic—was becoming more important and increasing the authority and scope of the Service Directors of Intelligence.

It was in this rapidly changing Whitehall that Menzies's charm and intuitive gift were so valuable; even Philby paid tribute to it. He was overloaded, like all the men then in power, with paper-work and his assistants did not, perhaps, rise to the challenge of world war. Nothing in their peacetime experience had prepared them for the tasks laid on them as first Germany, then Italy, then Japan became an enemy—and as Soviet Russia after 18 months became an ally. The brilliant men brought in from outside—scholars, writers, bankers, journalists—raised the quality of the Service's work but they did little to lighten its administrative burdens.

The pressure was at its worst in the period after summer 1940 when Churchill was searching in every direction for offensive openings. Target succeeded target in rapid sequence: Norway, the Canaries, raids on France, Madagascar, Syria. It was not understood that the channels used by Menzies and his men needed long and patient preparation. (Who in his senses had thought of Norway as an intelligence target during the period between the wars?) To meet the criticisms of the Service Directors of Intelligence Menzies accepted the appointment to his own office of their nominees who were given the rank of deputy directors. The "commissars" made little difference. The vital work was being done elsewhere, under Menzies's direction it is true, by the code-breakers and analysts working on whatever the operations of war might bring to their desks.

Menzies's retirement in 1951 [sic] passed unnoticed by the general public because newspapers were observing the Whitehall request that the head of MI6 should not be embarrassed by identification and publicity. In the past two or three years, books and articles, published here and abroad, had made the convention no longer enforceable. The former chief was obliged, therefore, to hear and read critical accounts of his department's war work—some of it unfair or at least unanswerable—without being able to reply. One source, but not the only one, of this criticism was his former officer, the traitor Kim Philby; and it was the searching investigation of the Philby affair, and of its connexions with the Burgess and MacLean defections, that brought MI6 into glaring and unfavourable light.

To a man who could rightly claim—as Professor Trevor-Roper wrote recently—that the enemy intelligence services had been mastered and outwitted in war by his own service this was a galling experience. The one person who could have spoken up decisively in his defence—Winston Churchill—died before the sensation began. Whether historians will ever be allowed to assess his work is highly doubtful. If they are, they will doubtless note that Britain in peace time tried to get intelligence on the cheap. It was necessary to rely extensively on personal contacts in the world of finance, shipping, the Services, the press and so on. If that network—inadequate for war—was on an old-boy basis, so are most networks, whether in the party state or the democratic one.

As the spider in the centre of such a network Menzies was suitably equipped by birth, by education, by connexion and by first war experience. A man of different background might not have been so much liked by his staff, so approachable, so successful in working with and initiating the Americans and able to survive five years at Churchill's right hand. If his death should provoke more curiousity than respect, that is one of the penalties of holding an office in which it is impossible to answer back to critics who can never be perfectly informed.

The *main* reason for the publication of the obituary was political. Through the Soviet secret service's artful political warfare—begun in January 1945 with the object of demolishing the British service's reputation for omniscience and omnipresence—and the British government's own blundering in its handling of the Philby case, the Russians had secured a major propaganda victory. But there was more to the obituary than politics.

There was rumor that Stewart Menzies had committed suicide in despair, so it was said, at the defeat of the service that he had created and that he had admired so greatly. Those rumors, when investigated carefully, proved quite untrue and, in origins, no more than fevered village gossip that developed from another rumor—that Menzies had had his colts, Silver Beaker and Golden Beaker, shot.

In fact, Menzies had not ordered his horses destroyed (at least in the period alleged). They passed to Menzies's daughter, Fiona, under the terms of her father's will and they were raced for a period *after* Sir Stewart's death. One, Silver Beaker, ran two races after Sir Stewart's death but fell in the second and was destroyed in August 1968. The other, Golden Beaker, ran twenty more races until it became too old and then was put out to grass. Three years after Menzies's death, in August 1971, Golden Beaker passed on. The rest of the innuendo about "C's" death proved no more substantial.

"C's" death certificate showed that Stewart Graham Menzies had died at the age of seventy-eight of "1a. Broncho-pneumonia; 1b. Cerebral vascular accident; 1c. Ischaemic heart disease." A doctor from whom I sought advice about these complaints did state that they were all "complaints of antiquity" and that there was nothing exceptional or mysterious about any of them.

I continued my inquiries because a biographer should know as much about the end of the life of his subject as he does about its beginnings. I sought and obtained a meeting with "C's" son-in-law and daughter, Captain and Mrs. Brian Bell. They told me that Stewart Menzies had been in Sister Agnes's Hospital for about ten days prior to his passing. They visited him there, and he revived once or twice, on one occasion asking if he might see his black and white mongrel dog, Spot, to whom he was devoted. Although the ward sister disapproved, Spot was brought to Menzies's room.

As the Bells related, the funeral service was held in the Church of the Holy Cross at Sherston Magna, a small market town on a hilltop in Wiltshire, at 3:00 P.M. on July 1, 1968. The Church of the Holy Cross was in the same parish as Luckington church, but the church at Sherston was used more frequently because Luckington church had an infirmity of the belfrey that made it unwise to ring the bells too often.

Immediately after the funeral service, Captain Bell escorted the Daimler carrying the coffin to the City of Bath Crematorium in Haycombe Cemetery on Shrophouse Road, a modern installation on the lip of the beautiful Valley of Englishcombe. There he attended the brief service before the committal. The coffin was definitely present at this service and the municipal authorities later confirmed that Sir Stewart Menzies was cremated there on that day.

Another important point was, perhaps, that a large number of letters of condolence from persons prominent in the Anglo-American intelligence community had survived. All spoke of the great service Menzies had rendered to the state and the Grand Alliance, and two spoke for the rest. The London representative of the Central Intelligence Agency, Bronson Tweedy, wrote to Sir Dick White, on June 4, 1968, on behalf of the director of central intelligence in Washington, Richard Helms:

My service, and Dick Helms quite specifically, were saddened by the news of Stewart Menzies's death. As Dick said in a brief telegram to me, "those of us who knew this legendary figure mourn his passing." From the affectionate tones in which I have heard him mentioned over the years by his former subordinates, I can only conclude he will occupy a prominent and honourable niche in whatever Valhalla exists for intelligence officers. . . .

Later, in Menzies's letter file, I found that Rex Benson had gone to see "C" at Sister Agnes's shortly before his death. They talked for a time and it had seemed to Benson that his old friend was on the mend. But Stewart died two days after Benson's visit. Benson's letter of condolence to Lady Menzies observed sadly that "C" was "the last of my old Eton friends." In reply Lady Menzies wrote to Sir Rex: "I so loved what you wrote about Stewart—My thoughts linger on the Eton days, lovely, lovely, lovely days." That was the last correspondence between the Menzies family and Benson. Within a fortnight Benson himself had died and with his death the last of Impey's golden lads had passed on. Such were Benson's services to the state that a service was held in his memory at St. Paul's Cathedral.

In all, therefore, it seemed clear that Stewart Menzies's passing was entirely natural. Yet there remained a miasma of mystery about his death even now, largely because he had no known grave. The peculiar circumstances attending this fact then emerged in equally queer measure.

Some time before his death, Menzies discussed his will with Lady Menzies and, while not revealing whether he had money or not, suggested that perhaps he should make Lady Menzies a beneficiary, leaving his property to his daughter, Fiona. Lady Menzies could be very imperious, and believing as she did that a man who had been in government service all his life could not possibly have any money worth speaking of, replied that she would prefer that his estate went to Fiona.

Stewart Menzies accepted this and gave the requisite directions to his lawyer. At the same time, he stated that he would prefer to be cremated, although it it is uncertain about whether he gave any instructions about where his ashes were to be scattered. The result of these imperfect instructions was that after the cremation the ashes were delivered to Lady Menzies's home in the Manor House, Mayfair. Almost coincidentally with their delivery, and while in one of her imperious moods, Lady Menzies learned that Sir Stewart had died a rich man by British standards. At the rate of exchange pertaining at the time of his death his estate represented not far short of $1 million, which was very much more than everyone thought he was worth, including Lady Menzies. This wealth, according to Fiona Bell, came not through inheritance but was the result of "sensible investments."

Probate provoked an outburst in the course of which Lady Menzies banished the box containing Stewart's ashes to the cellar of the Manor House. There they remained for the next sixteen years. When asked where Sir Stewart was buried she would reply that he would be scattered with her ashes at her estate at Theydon Mount in Essex, and assurances that this would be done were given to Menzies's daughter, Fiona. However, the fact that "C" had no known grave served to nourish the rumor about his death.

By 1984, with Stewart Menzies's ashes still in the basement of the Manor House, Lady Menzies was only rarely *compus mentus*, and it seemed to all who met her that she could not live much longer.

This caused considerable anxiety with Mrs. Ford, Lady Menzies's secretary, who knew that the ashes of Sir Stewart were in the basement but had received no instructions about their disposal should Lady Menzies die. Fearing that they might well be thrown out in the housecleaning that would follow her passing, and uncertain as to what she should do, Mrs. Ford communicated her anxieties to me. I related Mrs. Ford's statement to Captain Bell, and he acted immediately to recover them.

Although Lady Menzies was still alive (but in another world for most of the time), Fiona Bell drove to London and Lady Menzies's secretary handed over the box containing Sir Stewart's ashes in the hall. Mrs. Bell then took them to Luckington and on November 11, 1984—Armistice Day—the remains of "C" were at last committed to hallowed soil, a matter that would have been of importance to him, for he had been a God-fearing man. Later a gravestone was placed at the spot where "C's" ashes were buried. The inscription stated:

Sir Stewart Menzies,
1890–1968
Chief,
Secret Intelligence Service,
World War II
RIP

Thus did Stewart Menzies take his last great leap in the dark. The fever called living was conquered at last.

But of course, as in life, so in death. With Stewart Menzies there was never one enigma without a second. It seemed at the time that this completed my inquiries into the life and fate of Stewart Menzies. He ranked with the greatest of the English spymasters, if only because Winston Churchill would have replaced him so rapidly had he been anything less than a proficient spymaster and a trustworthy man. In fact, I was prepared to say that he had been the greatest spymaster in English history. But it seemed impossible to make that estimate of "C" while the Philby affair remained unexplained.

The history of that affair, and the government's handling of it, seemed to hint at some strategic deception operation involving "C" and Philby. I had encountered a pattern with which I was familiar, a pattern of confusion, contradiction, evasion, and half-truth that besets a government when it seeks to deny a secret service action. Yet if measured against logic one could conclude only that "C" died a defeated man—surely he would not have allowed a traitor to roam across his most secret service for eleven years? Knowing the man as I did, however, it seemed illogical, however, that mere logic could dictate "C's" epitaph.

As I peered more closely into the Philby affair, Colonel William R. Corson, a U.S. intelligence officer of the period, made an astonishing statement that supported "C." In a history of the Washington intelligence community, *The Armies of Ignorance*, Corson examined the relationship between James Angleton, the CIA's head of counterespionage, and the Israeli intelligence service:

Over time, not only during the Truman years, the relationship produced some remarkable results and intelligence coups. One in particular is worth mentioning briefly. It involved the identification and subsequent manipulation of three British intelligence officials who were soviet spies. The three were [Donald] Maclean, who was in charge of the chancery at the British embassy in Washington between 1944–48; Guy Burgess, who was posted to Washington in 1950 as the second secretary in the British embassy; and Harold Adrian Russell Philby, known commonly as Kim Philby, who served as England's anti-Soviet intelligence chief and who in 1949 was the British SIS representative in Washington, working in liaison with the CIA and the FBI. As a result of the American-Israeli secret intelligence connection, each of these three spies was identified, Maclean's identification leading to Burgess' and thence to Philby's. By itself the mere act of identifying these Soviet spies is noteworthy; but the subsequent manipulation, which included providing them with intelligence disinformation to mislead the Soviet, makes the overall operation a classic one. In the course of manipulating them— playing on their personal, physical, and moral weaknesses and vanities— the CIA's small band of secret intelligence professionals were able to discover the identities of other Soviet agents in place in the United States and elsewhere, and to use that information to thwart Soviet subversive initiatives in a wide variety of government, business, and scientific endeavors.

Corson seemed to support the notion that there was more to the Philby affair than met the eye, and his statement seemed to explain why, despite the bullfrogs' chorus, "C" displayed the equanimity he did for so long: he knew the truth.

Nor was Corson alone. Others still more centrally placed hinted from time to time that there had been a maneuver, a stratagem. During discussion about Philby's memoirs, *My Silent War*, Sir Maurice Oldfield, Philby's successor in Washington and one who became "C" himself, remarked to Phillip Knightley of the London *Sunday Times* that the memoir was an accurate account of Philby's conduct "*as far as they go.*" What did they conceal? Knightley asked. There was, of course, no reply. Then, in 1984, William E. Colby, a former director of CIA who had held a succession of high posts within that organization for a quarter of a century, met me at the Waldorf-Astoria Hotel in New York on my return from a prolonged research trip to England concerning "C." He asked me: "Did you learn anything new about Philby?" His manner suggested that there *might* be more in the Philby case than the official British version.

But that question was a matter of nuance. There were more substantial grounds for doubt in 1982 when Nicholas Bethell, a British author, peer, and parliamentarian, brought a Freedom of Information Act suit against the Central Intelligence Agency, after CIA's rejection of his application to read the CIA's files on some operations in Albania that had involved Philby. The CIA's counsel, Louis J. Dube, advised the court that if these documents were released to Bethell then the Soviet government would be able to make an estimate of the accuracy or otherwise of the intelligence provided by Philby while he was in Washington. If access was denied then the Russians could not know definitely whether the information given them by Philby was true or false. The court rejected Bethell's plea on the grounds that U.S. national security would be endangered if it succeeded.

Dube's statement clearly suggested again that Philby had been manipulated as a conduit for the passage of deceptive intelligence to the Russians. But if this was correct, who manipulated Philby, when, and what was the nature of the false intelligence passed to him? Again, there was no answer, no evidence. It was possible that Dube's statement was calculated to embarrass Philby in his relations with his Soviet hosts. But if Dube's statement was sincere, then it meant that all established beliefs about the Philby case were erroneous and that there was, as Anthony Montague Browne said, a secret left. Not surprisingly, Dube's statement provoked speculation in Washington that Philby had, after all, been a controlled hostile agent. A leading CIA watcher, Tad Szulc, wrote an article to that effect for *The Washington Post*.

At about this same time, I had occasion to interview James Angleton, who passed away in May 1987, in connection with certain chapters in my biography of William J. Donovan. Although Angleton had hitherto evaded interviews about matters that occurred while he was in the U.S. counterespionage service, as he explained because "in counterespionage a case may last a lifetime and it is better that the other side does not know what you know," he did admit that his service had doubts about Philby's loyalties since 1947, largely through

Philby's handling of the Volkov case and his remark to Angleton after they left Buckingham Palace: "What this country needs is a good healthy dose of socialism." He admitted also that he had had contact with Philby through intermediaries since Philby defected to Moscow. When I asked Angleton whether Philby had stopped his self-destructive drinking, Angleton replied: "Yes, he stopped it from the moment he arrived in Moscow." He claimed also to be able to get a message to Philby "whenever the need arose." That the chief of U.S. counterespionage should have had such a facility seemed very odd to me, for was Philby not a traitor and a defector?

Then, on a visit to New York in January 1986, I raised these various statements and hints with Commander Dunderdale, "C's" colleague since 1926. Dunderdale was still with "C" in 1952 when Menzies retired and was, it was evident, knowledgeable about the inner politics of the Philby case. He was not, however, forthcoming about any of the matters I have related, until I mentioned something I had been told by General Edwin L. Sibert who, after being G2 to Bradley and Eisenhower in Europe, was brought into the CIA as an assistant director. Sibert, who became a good friend of mine, remarked over drinks one evening at his home in Maclean, Virginia, that Philby had been "used" to pass fictitious information about the effectiveness of Strategic Air Command and the size of the U.S. atomic arsenal at the time of the Korean War. When I related that statement to Dunderdale, a man in his early eighties, Dunderdale visibly shed twenty years and became what I imagined must have been his official self. Gone for the moment was the amiable bon vivant and raconteur. "It would be improper for me to discuss such a matter," he ejaculated, adding that any discussion about "*that matter* should be shown to H.M.G."

That is, more or less, what I did do. I went to see Sir Patrick Reilly, the man who had been "C's" personal assistant for a time during the war and who, during the Burgess and Maclean affair in 1951, was "C's" master as chairman of the Joint Intelligence Committee. I presented Reilly with all the facts and rumors, and the theorem, and he wrote an opinion of them. In that opinion Sir Patrick pointed out that:

["C"] was then near retirement. He had a strong [deputy] to whom he was relinquishing the reins. ["C"] was deeply and emotionally committed to belief in P's innocence. If "C" had been manipulating Philby, then he did so unknown to his deputy, Sinclair, or to my knowledge anyone else in London. The story implied that "C" put Philby in positions where he could do grave damage to SIS. Why should he get involved in such an operation for the Americans? Was it conceivable that "C" sent Philby to Washington, running a fearful risk of grave trouble with the Americans—unless he did so with the knowledge and approval of the Americans? Was there any evidence that he had such permission?

As Reilly continued:

The theory implies that in the first half of 1951 "C" allowed all the exchanges between MI5 and the FBI to go through Philby, thus enabling a traitor [Maclean] to escape. This would have been at least collusion in treachery.

As an afterthought, Sir Patrick then stated that the theory that Philby was controlled by "C" would make sense "only if 'C' had got himself into something over a long period from which he could not extricate himself."

I then asked James Easton for his opinion of the Philby affair. He wrote to me the following:

In the minds of those close to "C" and the C.I.A. the more that this hypothesis is examined, pro and con, the more firmly is the use of Philby rejected as inconceivable for the reason that in the positions which Philby held in S.I.S. and in his last post (Washington) would have made the damage he could do far outweigh any potential benefit which which could have been derived from his attempted deception. . . . his guile and cunning serve to emphasize how extremely devious and clever he could be and getting himself into the best positions he could to serve his Russian master.

With these characteristics and with his overall knowledge of what went on in Intelligence circles, I have little doubt that Philby would not have been slow to detect it if he had false information planted on him for onward passage.

I began to come to the conclusion that, for all his experience, skill and cunning Stewart Menzies had in fact been duped by Philby. But even as I began that process, some new half-facts came light. On May 10, 1987, even as Easton was writing to me, the *Sunday Telegraph*, a London newspaper with a reputation for reliability, published an interview with the British novelist Graham Greene, who had remained a close friend of Philby since their service together in the counterespionage branch of SIS.

This interview showed that, as Angleton had intimated, there *had* been some form of official communication between Philby in Moscow and London, in this case, a high official of Menzies's service, Maurice Oldfield. Oldfield was the same officer who had taken part in Philby's briefing for his mission to Washington. He had been recruited into the service during Menzies's time and had been in turn Philby's successor as chief of the anti-Soviet section, he replaced Philby as SIS representative at Washington, and he had then become in turn assistant chief, vice-chief and then chief of the service in 1976. Thus Oldfield and Philby were well and favorably known to each other, at least until Philby's relief. Moreover, they may even have been close friends, for Oldfield was not an establishment man like Menzies but a meritocrat of humble origins.

Graham Greene was not only a close friend of Philby, he was a Socialist although for prolonged periods he was ideologically opposed to the Russian brand of Marxism. A Catholic, he wrote the foreword to Philby's memoir, *My Silent War*, his chief point being: ". . . who among us has committed treason to something or someone more important than a country? In Philby's eyes he was working for a shape of things to come from which his country would benefit." By that statement Greene meant the world movement toward Marxism. In Greene's view, Philby was motivated by reasons similar to that of the English Catholics who, in the reign of Elizabeth I, worked against English causes in what they believed were the more praiseworthy interests of the pope. There was a certain legitimacy about that statement, for as with the English papists, Philby was indeed the embodiment of Rudyard Kipling's poem about the man with two separate sides of his head, one loyal to English ways, the other to Marx. His treachery was ideological, not venal or sexual.

During the interview, the journalist, Anne-Elisabeth Moutet, attempted to lead Greene into a discussion of his association with Philby, especially that part of it that continued after Philby's defection to Moscow. During this aspect of their discussion, Ms. Moutet recorded, Greene was markedly evasive. But he did admit to a correspondence with Philby, one that was "largely on private matters." But Greene added enigmatically that " 'if there was anything political in it, I knew that Kim would know that I would pass it on to Maurice Oldfield, so it was either information or disinformation.' "

Greene would not state whether he in fact passed Philby's letters to Oldfield, nor did he state whether Oldfield had written to Philby. All that Greene would admit was that in a span of some fifteen years Greene received "seven or eight" letters from Philby. With similar reluctance he admitted to two meetings with Philby in Moscow in 1986–87. But then Greene made a further statement of some significance in the context of Philby. As Ms. Moutet recorded: "[Greene] doesn't hide his dislike of America, which contrasts strongly with his

regard for Gorbachev, and even for Andropov [Gorbachev's predecessor, a career officer and then chief of the KGB]." And as Greene
said in the context of Andropov:

Any change in the Soviet Union will have to come from the KGB . . . because
they take the youngest and the brightest and they train them and they send
them abroad where they learn about the world. Whereas the army are really
a bunch of Napoleonic old men.

To my mind it seemed possible that Greene, a man of nimble
wits, was hinting that Philby was, or had been, a sort of "human
hotline" between officials of the secret service in London and the
KGB in Moscow. In the world of secret service this was sufficiently
implausible to be plausible—"C" did have a long history of contact
with hostile agents ever since, it would seem, Baron von Treeck
arrived in Luckington in 1936. For years, to take another example,
"C" had kept contact with Admiral Canaris even across the lines of
battle, his purpose to establish the inner politics of Berlin. Such
connections were, indeed, one of the principal reasons for having a
"C" at all. It was not at all improbable that Philby performed that
function for "C's" successors. It would have been entirely characteristic of "C," a man who operated beyond the law for much of his
career, to say to Philby: "Now look here Kim, we know about you.
But I don't want to have to send papers to the Director of Public
Prosecutions. They'll hang you, and that would cause a stink in Coronation Year that the P.M. [Churchill] does not want. Bugger off to
Moscow, lie low, keep quiet, make connections and get in touch with
me when the need arises."

Certainly such a stratagem would not just be in keeping with "C's"
character. Such a maneuver would, if it took place, provide an acceptable reason for the rumors and contradictions in the Philby case,
the most tantalizing of them being Anthony Montague Browne's enigmatic statement: "There is one secret left in the Philby case, and that
I may not discuss." It would explain too how it was "C" managed to
conduct himself with complete equanimity throughout the long ordeal
of the bullfrogs' chorus before his death. "C" alone—except for Churchill, a prime minister to whom deception and maneuver came
naturally—knew the truth.

But it must be admitted all of these shards of information are
worthy of nothing more than speculation and conjecture. "C's" closest
colleagues in intelligence undoubtedly believed that "C" had been
outwitted by Philby. In the end, therefore, we are confronted with

a riddle unique, probably, to the world of Stewart Menzies. There are those who believe that there was much more to the Philby story than has been admitted, including myself, and there are those who do not share that belief.

As this book was, in the language of the trade, being put to bed there seemed some reason to accept that "C" had at least attempted a stratagem against the Russians and involving Philby, but that, as "C's" closest colleagues in intelligence undoubtedly believed, Philby had outwitted "C." I concluded that we were, therefore, confronted with a riddle unique to the world of Stewart Menzies and secret intelligence and sources. There were those, I decided, that there was much more to the Philby story than had been admitted, and there were those—the majority—who did not share that belief.

In that spirit, therefore, I laid down my pen. But even as I did this some startling fresh evidence suddenly surfaced. It was from a British journalist, Chapman Pincher, an individual who had done much important work in the sphere of counterespionage in Britain in the forties, fifties, and sixties. What Pincher declared in a 1987 book entitled *Traitors: The Labyrinths of Treason* was that "*before* the defection of Burgess and Maclean" there "no less than *nine* Britons were under special surveillance as suspect Soviet agents." These included Burgess and Maclean, David Footman, and, as Pincher added, "almost certainly Philby." All nine suspects were "subjected to physical and telephone surveillance during which time Philby was given the codename "Peach" while Footman was code-named "Flaxman," after a London telephone exchange. The watch was maintained by the Security Service and, in the case of Burgess, he was under suspicion and surveillance as a suspected Soviet spy "before he left London on Foreign Office posting to Washington." Indeed, so suspect was Burgess in London that the special surveillance on him was extended to Washington without the knowledge of the Foreign Office. The FBI was not informed of these suspicions, and as Pincher stated of Philby personally:

> While my informant cannot be completely certain from memory that Philby was on the List of Nine before the Burgess and Maclean defection, the odds are that he was. [Guy] Liddell and the [wartime] MI5 chief Sir David Petrie had both been suspicions of him. . . .

Following that disclosure, it seemed to me that it was not now as improbable as it had seemed that "C" used Philby for some stratagem against the Russians during the Korean War period, perhaps with

Philby's cooperation, perhaps not. If Pincher was correct, then Burgess was certainly used by "C" in Washington and, since Burgess was living with Philby, *both* were were being manipulated.

What, therefore, was the nature of the stratagem? It is not impossible to see the hand of "C" and James Alexander Drew, the British deception agent, in an operation similar in theory and practice to that of "Document 'X'" in 1918 and Fortitude in 1944: to mislead the enemy about American strength. If that was so in this case, then the inquirer might usefully look into the true status of both Strategic Air Command and the U.S. atomic arsenal, both of which were in a woeful state when the world appeared to be on the brink of World War III.

In the end, however, we can make a sure judgment only of Menzies as a spymaster. Cumming lasted fourteen years and Sinclair sixteen. "C's" term was thirteen years. No American or Russian spymaster—"C's" principal rivals—lasted as long as Stewart Menzies. None achieved as much as he did in World War II. There was little to choose between "C" and his predecessors, except that the dangers during "C's" term were greater and more complex than in earlier times.

The only real difference was that Cumming and Sinclair passed into history with the affections of their colleagues, although by 1987 there was a tendency to regard "C" with more admiration than he received while alive. During his lifetime "C" he was seen as a remote, guileful, devious, overly ambitious, privileged man, one who defied judgment—an enigma. Only now can we see that he was not an ordinary bureaucrat, one whose reputation rested upon the abilities of other men, but an extraordinary individual. He was a man who began life on a horse at the side of the sovereign and ended it as the ultimate weapon of Armageddon, the nuclear-tipped strategic missile, was being introduced. At each step of his transition he survived and even prospered.

During his career he presided over *the* great technological revolution of his time—the penetration of Enigma. And if he could not understand Turing's paper "On Computable Numbers," he did possess the ability to form and keep a team that did. Above all, in the end he won. I believe that he was the greatest British spymaster, greater even than Walsingham, the man who stole the secrets of the Spanish armada. "C" suffered his ignominy silently, whereas Walsingham did not. It may be said therefore that in Stewart Menzies the Right Reverend Edmund Warre, "C's" headmaster at Eton, succeeded in his high purpose. He made a man who, as with Plato's guardians, was prepared to defend the state in war when he was young and, when he was older, to become "magistrate, ruler and law-giver." To the end he maintained that bearing of effortless superiority and unassailable primacy that, they said with pride, was the hallmark of the Eton man. He trod a dangerous path faultlessly, picking his way with great skill. And in the end his epitaph should read:

At a desperate time in world history he was the right man in the right place at the right time.

The work for this volume officially began in February 1983 and was completed in January 1986—thirty-nine months. During that period, I do not recall a waking hour in which I did not spend at least part in a private or communal debate on some aspect of the life of Sir Stewart Menzies. At the end of the thirty-nine months I found myself just as interested in him as when I began work. Such a large commitment of time and thought was justified, I felt, because I was studying a man who, for ordinary mortals, was a ghost—and a very strange one at that.

During his long career as an intelligence officer, he was seen everywhere, and yet he was nowhere. His influence was everywhere in the highest realms of activity, especially in the years 1939–52, yet officially he did not exist. Yet he did, and Winston Churchill had, according to his authorized biographer, Martin Gilbert, "in excess of fifteen hundred meetings" with "C."

Even so, there was little or no trace of these meetings—no minutes, few agendas, few letters between the two men, although thousands of such documents existed. They all were locked in the secret archives of England; consequently, scholarly men thought that here was one biography that could not be written. But the scholarly men were incorrect. Provided the author was prepared to undertake a task not unlike that of a wild pig hunting for truffles, there was ample spoor and evidence of his activities.

Several diaries were kept by men who were close to "C." A relative had taken the trouble to obtain and paste in heavy albums every newspaper report of the activities of "C's" family and of "C" himself from before the turn of the century until the 1950s. British records contained numerous direct references to him and his work; Churchill's papers, likewise. The American archives, which rarely refered to "C" personally, often made reference to what his men did at his direction. The papers of "C's" principal American colleague (and rival), William J. Donovan, were particularly revealing about "C," his men, and their activities, provided the author was prepared to examine and weigh each folio of myriad documents. There were newspaper and magazine archives on both sides of the Atlantic and many men and women who knew him and were prepared, now that he was dead, to talk about him. And there was a box of "C's" personal papers; these proved vital to my task. In all, therefore, it was possible to offer a comprehensive portrait of the man, his work, and his times.

A large number of men and women devoted much time to giving or finding recollections and information. First there was "C's" family: Captain and Mrs. Brian Bell (son-in-law and daughter), who spent many hours helping me reconstruct "C's" private world, although the experience of being questioned on intimate matters was alien to them and not always welcome—they had had to live with "C" through the dreadful years of the Philby affair. David Benson, son of the late Sir R. L. Benson, "C's" cousin, friend, and colleague in secret service, set aside two luncheons and two afternoons to discuss the Holfords and "C" with me. He also entrusted to me an ammunition box, one embossed with the coat of arms of George IV, crammed with that treasure, his father's diaries from about 1908 to 1960. "C's" nephew, Alastair Graham Menzies, opened several important doors.

Mrs. Avilde Lees-Milne (a cousin of "C") and her husband, James, extended their hospitality and recollections of the man, his family, his associates, and his times and in turn led me to Mrs. Joan Lindsay (present laird of Hallyburton, the family estate in Perthshire). Mrs. Lindsay and Alastair Graham Menzies arranged for me to meet Victor M. G. Wombwell, lord of the manor of Newburgh Priory, Yorkshire; and Wombwell was able to transport me back to the days of Graham Menzies, founder of the dynasty from which "C" sprang, and forward through the days of Edward VII (who stayed at Newburgh Priory frequently), through the First Battle of Ypres (where Wombwell was wounded while serving as adjutant to a battalion of the Seaforth Highlanders), through the Second World War, and up to the time of "C's" death.

Outside "C's" family, but within his private circle, there was Major Gerald Ashton Gundry, secretary of the Beaufort Hunt 1938–51 and joint master of the hunt from 1951. Major Gundry extended me much hospitality and time at his home, explaining the social and political life of that most exclusive of all hunts in the prewar period. General Sir James Marshall-Cornwall, a close friend and colleague of "C" in both world wars, told me much about life in the strange artificial vivaria they both inhabited for so long. Miss Mary Lutyens, the biographer of Krishnamurthi, gave me important insights into "C's" life in the twenties, as did Sybil Dowager Countess De La Warr, Lady Avice Spicer's aunt.

Sheila D. Herringshaw of Highcliffe, near Bournemouth, spent many hours poking into the past concerning Jack Graham Menzies's death; Colonel A. D. Meakins, keeper of the Household Cavalry Museum at Combermere Barracks, Windsor, provided much valuable information about the personalities, manners, and mores of the Household Cavalry in the reigns of Edward VII and George V. In this, Colonel Meakins's staff, William Johnson, Edward Woodbridge, and Bernard Greene, all provided invaluable advice and assistance.

Field Marshal Sir Roland Gibbs, lately chief of the Defence Staff, was able to obtain the records of "C's" military career. Lawrence Impey, the only surviving son of Edward Impey, "C's" housemaster at Eton, spent a day with me in recollection about SGM's youth and life at Eton before World War I. Michael S. Moss, author of *The Making of Scotch Whisky* and archivist at Glasgow University, gave me much invaluable guidance on that ruthless trade, the whiskey industry, in the late nineteenth and early twentieth centuries. Brian Spiller of the Distillers Company Limited, London, and Dr. Ishabel Barnes of the Scottish Records Office were most helpful regarding the Menzies family's estate, financial, historical, and trade interests. Major Roger Courage, of headquarters, London district, made an important intercession in regard to Stewart Menzies's career in the Life Guards. Kingsley James of Windsor did major photographic work for this volume, as did Hill & Saunders of Eton.

Duncan Chalmers, now the number three at the Public Records Office at Kew, placed at my disposal his vast knowledge of Prime Minister Churchill's records and those of the Cabinet, Foreign, Air, Admiralty, and War offices. Cyril Mills had much of interest to relate about the management of the double agent Garbo and "C's" role in the timing of the Fortitude deception. Rodney Dennys, a member of Section V of SIS at The Hague, provided important information and guidance relating to the Venlo incident and its aftermath. Colonel Felix Cowgill and his wife, Mary, devoted two entire days to a discussion on the operations of Section V, Philby's role therein, their relations with Philby and Colonel Vivian, their view of the Philby intrigue, and its effect upon themselves—and also provided me with two excellent lunches; Robert Cecil and Sir Patrick Reilly spent more time than they could afford to discuss "C" and the inner politics of the secret service.

Sir James Easton's recollections were of high importance; he gave me several excellent lunches at the Grosse Pointe country clubs. Kim Philby was quite right in one matter—the excellence of Easton's mind. Sir William Stephenson gave me three or four hours each day for ten days in Bermuda to discuss life and work in Churchill's secret circle. Others in the secret circle—Sir Stuart Milner-Barry and I. J. Good of Bletchley, Commander W. F. Dunderdale, Colonel Claude Arnould and Commander Kenneth Cohen of Broadway, Colonel John Bevan, General William H. Baumer, Roger Fleetwood-Hesketh, Colonel S. Lohan, Colonel E. Putzell, the former executive officer of OSS—all gave me more of their time than they could really afford. Martin Gilbert, Churchill's official biographer, Anthony Montague Browne, Churchill's private secretary, Sir John Colville, the diarist and another of Churchill's private secretaries—all gave me much food for thought or pointed me in the direction of truffles.

The Honorable Julian Amery bore with me during two extensive sessions relating to the events that led to the execution of his brother, John Amery, an awful business if there ever was one. Ranald Boyle very graciously told me what he could about the activities of his father, David Boyle, and his relationship with "C." At Eton College, first Patrick Strong and then Paul Quarrie, Strong's successor as librarian, gave me the run of their archives room, where I found much information that enabled me to reconstruct "C's" career at Eton and those of "C's" colleagues, and also to fill out my collection of photographic portraits. Mr. Quarrie's hospitality was memorable because of his custom of offering me a glass of sherry served on a silver salver before lunch in the medieval splendors of the library. Corelli Barnett, keeper of the archives at the Churchill Archives Center, and his excellent assistant, Marion Stewart, made several major collections of documents available to me, including that vital document, the Cadogan manuscript diaries. At the National Archives in Washington there were those devoted and tireless archivists, John Taylor, Dr. Robert Wolff, George Wagner, Edward Reese, Tim Mulligan, Tim Nenninger, Leroy Jackson, George Chalou, Dr. Gustafson, Dr. Haynes, Sally Marks, Mrs. Nicastro—all proved to be congenial servants of this work. So were Warren Orvill at the Truman Library, David Hait at the Eisenhower Library, and Robert Parks at the FDR Library, who made a number of very important contributions, including the diaries of Adolf A. Berle. Mrs. David K. E. Bruce gave me special access to her husband's diaries at the Virginia Historical Institute in Richmond, for which I am profoundly grateful. At Ypres, Belgium, and Hull, England, the librarians and their staffs provided much information on the great battle there and, at the latter institution, about the Royal Baccarat Scandal and the Wilson shipping line.

Otto C. Doering, Jr., Donovan's law partner and executive officer in OSS, spent many hours away from his law practice to advise me on the inner politics of OSS, Washington at war, and the early relationship between the British and American secret services. I was privileged to spend an evening at the home in Washington of General T. J. Betts, who held a number of central posts in the wartime and postwar Anglo-American intelligence communities. On many occasions I tried the patience of Henry B. Hyde, chief of OSS SI at Algiers and later in Switzerland, and of James Jesus Angleton, and David Donovan, my friend and neighbor and Donovan's son, who guided me on the political attitudes of his father and on the intricacies of some aspects of the Anglo-American relationship.

Mr. Giddy, managing director of the best book shop in the world—Hatchards on Piccadilly—took my telephone calls, found and air-freighted the volumes I needed, and was ever vigilant for publications that might be of service. The young and gifted Richard Aldrich, of Corpus Christi College, an historian and writer with a great future, saved more than one important passage in this work from extinction through his astonishing knowledge of the files at the Public Records Office and of the available manuscript diaries. The ninth duke of Portland took time away from his own memoirs to give me lunch at the House of Lords and then spend much of the afternoon offering me insight into the world of the wartime Joint Intelligence Committee. Charles Grey, lately of the CIA in Paris and, before that, Commander Dunderdale's friend, agent, and pilot, spent another afternoon in Paris relating for me the story of Dunderdale's escape from Paris. Dr. Summer, chief historian at the U.S. Army War College at Fort Carlisle, Pennsylvania, found and offered me the diaries and recollections of General Van Deman, founder of the U.S. military intelligence service, and General Nolan, General John J. Pershing's G2. These gave me much of importance concerning the Anglo-American intelligence relationship during and after World War I.

Major General Edwin L. Sibert, G2 first to Bradley and Eisenhower and then assistant director at the Central Intelligence Agency, was an important eyewitness to events within the secret circle between 1942 and 1952. My good friend James MacGuarquar of Washington led me into the paths of truth regarding the early stages of U.S. involvement in the postwar Albanian operations; Robert B. Joyce gave me more treasure—his unpublished memoirs regarding the post–World War II intelligence world.

Professor F. H. Hinsley, vice-chancellor of Cambridge University and director of the official history, *British Intelligence in World War II: Its Influence on Strategy and Operations*, gave me another insider's view of the relationship between "C" and the cryptanalytical world. Guy Vansittart, "C's" neighbor at Luckington, recalled the prewar world of Beaufortshire, enabling me to build upon what Gundry had told me. Tom Childs, a leading New York lawyer, spent many hours in agreeable conversation concerning the half-world between the Roosevelt administration, Congress, and the British missions to Washington and New York at that fateful time in world history, the Battle of Britain. William E. Colby, a former director of the CIA, corrected me where he could on certain aspects of the Philby affair. Dr. Allard, the U.S. Navy historian, provided me with vital studies relating to the Sealion and Harpoon deception operations. Dr. Telford Taylor gave me lunch at the Harvard Club in New York City and told me the American side of the problems that besieged the Anglo-American Ultra relationship.

One regrettable point needs to be made. Since I had no address for the present Secret Intelligence Service, and no name to write to for information, I asked a man who had had contact with that illustrious body to ask the present "C" whether the service would like to assist me insofar as it was able in the preparation of this work on their greatest chieftain. I received no reply to my invitation. Perhaps after all SIS does not now exist.

Lastly, a special note of thanks is owed to Edward Chase, who suggested this study and started me off. An equally special note is due to Hillel Black and Alan Brooke, who carried the main burden of the work, and to Edward Novak, who put the book to bed. Without their interest, diligence, and understanding of the problems of authorship in a subject such as this, my work would not have seen the light of day.

I am indebted to all. But in the end, of course, as it was with "C," so it is with his biographer. I, alone, am responsible for the facts and interpretations contained in this volume.

ANTHONY CAVE BROWN

Eton & Broad Run, Virginia
April 1987

Appendixes

Appendixes

APPENDIX A

While little has survived concerning Menzies's tradecraft during his early career, there is a document entitled "Notes on the Working of Agents" published as an appendix to the 1929 final report on British secret intelligence in the Rhineland between 1919 and 1929, and part (at least) of the modus operandi discussed there must have derived from the Menzies period. Certainly it shows the attitude of the British service in penetrating the Nazi party and, at about the same time, the Abwehr, the new German espionage and counterespionage service:

1. First step is to try and exchange conversation with prospective agent, with the object of finding out what type of a man he is, i.e., talkative, indifferent, or an enthusiast on any particular subject.

   Secondly, going very gently, see if he accepts small offers of cigarettes or beer, and ask him casually for a little information, some harmless questions, but of such a nature that will cause him to show by his answer if he is likely to become an agent or not. An important point: when he is considered reliable, and his information is accurate, tell him the truth in return as far as is consistent with safety.

2. *Types and Characteristics of Agents.*

   Possible reasons why a man gives away information: (a) Desire for money. (b) Dislike of the person or persons about whom he gives information, e.g., political party informers. (c) Desire to try and win a position where he hopes to obtain protection from his own people or police.

Types.

   The following are examples of the various types of agents: (a) Pacifist informers on militarists or republicans on monarchists, Communists on the police or vice-versa. (b) Agents in the pay of the political police who are "put on to" [a British agent] to find out what [his service] is trying to find out, or in what he is interested. This type may be told to sacrifice some true information in order to gain confidence of [a British agent]. (c) Indiscriminate agents, who are continually asking if there is anything they can do, if there is any information they can provide. This type can be either dangerous or merely annoying. (d) Men as the same type as (b) whose aim is to make friends with [a British agent], offering to give information in order to find

761

out his system of work and facts about the routine of his office. (e) Lastly, there is the casual informer, or, in the journalistic parlance, the "penny-a-liner," who will give odds and ends of disconnected information in return for cigarettes or drinks.

3. *General Method of Handling Agents, and Precautions.*

(a) Keep the agent's identity secret and do not expose him to unnecessary risks. (b) Do not give an agent too much money at a time. In the spending of it he may attract attention to himself and, indirectly, to [the British service]. (c) Do not tell him more than he needs to know; there is always the risk that an undesirable person may obtain the information. (d) If possible, [a British agent] should try to hide his real identity and address. There may come a time when it is necessary to cut off all communications with an agent. (e) If possible, try and gain some influence over him. Find out something about him, that would cause him unpleasantness with the police or his party. It may prove useful later if he tries, or threatens, to go over to the other side.

Precautions.

(a) An agent sometimes urges [a GHQ agent] to meet him in some hotel, cafe, or restaurant, and becomes embarrassing in his demands. Probable reason: There is someone there from the other side, who wants to identify the [GHQ agent] as a [GHQ agent], and your agent is trying to give you away. (b) Whenever possible, do not interview someone, particularly in a discreet enquiry, with a set plan in your head. Certainly try to turn the question round to the subjects in which you are interested, but do not force it. He may be cleverer than you. (c) Try to find out something beforehand about the person to be approached, his interests, etc. (d) Avoid arousing suspicions by doing silly things: e.g. smoking obviously English cigarettes, etc. (e) If you think you are suspected, make sure, or you may fall into a trap. (f) Once you have made a statement keep to it. Contradictions make you nervous and the agent suspicious. The general principle for a [British agent] is to obtain as much information as possible, without giving any way.

4. *Points of Importance in the Work of a [British agent].*

(a) *Watching a house.* Keep on the same side of the street as the house you are watching. Stand in a doorway where, to all appearances, you are on your own doorstep. (b) *Meeting agents or informants.* Do not meet them where you are known, or in places patronised by police or German agents. If the conversation is interrupted by a waiter or a stranger, do not suddenly stop talking; change the subject. Do not produce documents. (c) *Passing information in the street, and signalling to another [British agent].* Do not walk straight up and say what you have to say; ask for a match or give some similar excuse. In signalling, avoid using as a signal the blowing of one's nose or looking at a watch. Such actions are apt to be done from force of habit and one may do them without thinking, with possibly far-reaching results. Drop a glove or a stick. (d) *Making notes.* Make as few as possible. Write on a newspaper or with a short piece of pencil on a piece of paper in the pocket. Never carry documents likely to connect you with the Army. (e) *Enquiries in hotels.* Never trust porters, waiters, or hotel proprietors. Try to make friends with the victim by sitting at the same table with him. Intercept his letters from the rack and return them, with apologies for the mistake. (f) *"Telling the tale."* Do not masquerade as someone about whom you know nothing, i.e. do not say you are a Dutchman unless you speak perfect Dutch; the other man may be one too. (g) *Use of telephone.* Never use a telephone when speaking to agents. Danger of being overheard or intercepted. (h) *Women agents.* It is easier to get information out of a woman, but more dangerous. Make use of jealousy if possible. Information about one woman through another. . . . (m) *Following a suspect and being followed.* Keep a fair distance, varying it according to the traffic. Keep on the same side of the street as suspect, or you may get blocked by a tram. If suspect takes a car and you cannot get another, take the number and get in touch with the driver of it. If suspect goes into a large building with several doors, go in on his heels or you may miss him. On following him into a cafe, keep your hat and coat and pay the waiter at once. Delay in getting out may cause you to lose him. When being followed, make use of the tram.*

*British intelligence Corps Library, Ashford, Kent: "Memorandum on the Work of the Section of Civil Affairs & Security," General Staff, British Army of the Rhine, December 12, 1929.

APPENDIX B

CHRONOLOGY DURING THE INVASION PERIOD

It does seem that Sealion was more of a deception operation, one similar in size and intention to those launched later during the war by the Allies in England themselves, than a plan for an actual military operation. The question arises, therefore, how much Menzies knew or deduced that Sealion was a deception, if anything at all. And if he knew, was Churchill so informed? And if Churchill was informed, did he advise President Roosevelt? Part of the answer to these questions lies in the sequence of events relating to Barbarossa, the German invasion of Russia, and how much Menzies knew of that operation, if he knew anything at all. For Barbarossa ran in exact parallel to Sealion. The chronology of these events was important in two directions: (a) in establishing what Menzies knew of them; (b) in establishing that Sealion was a deception for Barbarossa.

June   SIS reports German infiltration of Romania.

June 2   In a conversation with Rundstedt, Hitler stated that "now he imagined England was ready for peace, he would begin to settle the account with Bolshevism."

June 14   Foreign Office advised Sir Stafford Cripps, new British ambassador to Moscow, that Russians "were alarmed by German victories in France." Cripps in Moscow and Churchill in London send warnings to Soviet government of "danger it stood in from Germany." Cripps warns Molotov that "according to our information," Germany intended to "turn east."

June 26   Churchill sends Stalin a warning in much the same terms.

June 27   Churchill tells Prime Minister Smuts of South Africa that "if Hitler fails to beat us here he will probably recoil eastwards. Indeed, he may do this without attempting invasion." These views *not* sent to the chiefs of staff.

July SIS reports that the Soviet military attaché in Berlin had warned his government that Germany was preparing to attack Russia. Another SIS agent, however, one in contact with Ribbentrop, reported that a German war with Russia was "out of the question at present."

July MI London begins to accumulate evidence of increases in the size of the German army, the number of its motorized and airborne divisions, and its concentration in southeastern and Eastern Europe.

July 2 Hitler's first Sealion directive.

July 2 JIC expects that while Germany would make peace overtures to Britain, she might be planning (a) invasion, (b) attack against Russia, (c) a Balkans expedition, (d) an attack against Egypt or Gibraltar. JIC believed that "it seems improbable that [Germany] would wish to take on [Russia] before she had finished with us."

July 2 Foreign Office "cast some doubt on" Germany's determination to invade the United Kingdom, and that Germany would invade the Ukraine.

July 2 MI London insists that Germany will give "absolute priority to" Sealion.

July 16 Hitler's second Sealion directive.

July 19 Hitler offers to make peace with England in a speech to the Reichstag.

July 29 Hitler orders preparations to begin for five-month blitzkrieg against Russia beginning May 1941, major operations against the United Kingdom being deferred to the autumn of 1941 or to 1942.

July 29 Jodl briefs the senior officers of Section L of the German supreme command that "Hitler had decided to rid the world 'once and for all' of Bolshevism by a surprise attack on Soviet Russia to be carried out at the earliest possible moment, i.e. in May 1941." Section L instructed to "produce a draft of a preparatory order for the immediate transport, movement, and accommodation of the bulk of the Army and Air Force to occupied areas of Western Poland. . . ."

July 31 At a conference at Berchtesgaden, Hitler states: *"Russia is the factor by which England sets the greatest store. . . . If Russia is beaten, England's last hope is gone.* Germany is then master of Europe and the Balkans. . . ." *"Decision: As a result of this argument, Russia must be dealt with. Spring 1941."*

August 1 Hitler issues Directive 17 headed "Conduct of Air & Sea Warfare against England." It is noted by Section L that no reference is made to *land* warfare.

August 1 Soviet government denounces warnings from Britain as an attempt to drive a wedge between Russia and Germany.

August 5 German army planning staff completes a plan for the invasion of Russia.

August 5 JIC concludes unanimously that Germany & Russia "had the best of reasons for avoiding an open clash."

August 22 Czech SIS advises that the German army intelligence branch responsible for the Soviet Union had been expanding since June, and that the Abwehr's counterintelligence activities against Russia were being increased as a matter of urgency. The Abwehr in Romania being reinforced by specialists in the Ukraine, Crimea, and Caucasus.

September SIS circulates reports throughout this month of increasing Soviet, German, and Finnish military movements.

September 11 Hitler decides to send army and air missions to Romania after Romania asks Hitler for protection against Russia and other Balkans countries. The real task of the missions is to protect Romanian oil and prepare Romania's facilities "in future operations."

September 26 SIS reports countrywide German infiltration of Romania.

September 29 Czech intelligence reports German occupation imminent of Romania.

October The London "intelligence authorities" collect "incontrovertible evidence" that Germany is preparing a large-scale Balkans campaign.

October 7 Chairman JIC in letter to MI London disputes MI's view that "the time will never come . . . when it will be safe to say that invasion of the UK is off."

October 12   Hitler cancels Sealion except as a deception operation to deflect attention from his Russian preparations.

October   Churchill in London and Cripps in Moscow return to speculative warnings of Germany's intentions regarding Russia, and earlier dissension between the Foreign Office, which felt that Germany would attack Russia, and MI London, which felt not, reappears.

October 27   MI finds no evidence to support "an early falling out of thieves."

October 31   MI London reports evidence of a "vast program" of motorization in the German army and "steady" movement of divisions from Western Europe to Poland. New mechanized divisions would be ready for operations "in Russia" or Egypt by spring 1941.

October 31   Churchill advises his senior military commanders that Germany "would inevitably" turn on Russia during 1941 for the sake of her oil. This view shared by the Foreign Office.

November   First press reports—in the *Neue Zurcher Zeitung* and the *Chicago Daily News*—appear of the coming Russo-German war.

November   SIS Helsinki reports that Abwehr officers were reporting that Germany would attack Russia in the spring.

December   SIS reports in November and December that Balt aristocrats are openly saying they would soon regain their estates "in the wake of the German Army."

December   SIS reports that Keitel had announced German intention to remount Sealion in spring. This and other such reports rejected as deception by JIC.

December   Czech intelligence advises SIS that German attack on Greece through Bulgaria and Yugoslavia was planned for March 1941.

December 18   Barbarossa directive released. This laid down that Russia was to be defeated in one rapid campaign "even before the conclusion of the war with England." It was of "decisive importance that the intention to attack should not become known." No whisper reaches Whitehall.

January   The Foreign Office learns that Russia and Germany had renewed their economic agreement and had signed a pact of friendship.

January 1   SIS reports from Polish intelligence that "considerable amount of west to east road and rail construction was taking place in Slovakia."

January 6   Churchill refers anew to Hitler's intention to open "a great campaign in the east of Europe."

January 9   Hitler reaffirms his intention to invade Russia at the middle or by the end of May 1941.

January 20   Perhaps at Churchill's initiative, the Defense Committee debated, inconclusively, whether Germany's object was a drive against the British or an attack on the Russians into the Ukraine and the Caucasus.

January 23   MI London calculates that the German army was now about 250 divisions, "stronger than is necessary for actual operations, excluding a war against Russia," which was "unlikely for the present."

January 31   SIS reports that preparations for the invasion of Russia were "almost open." Troops were arriving in Poland from France. Russian speakers were being recruited into the army and Russian emigrés into German intelligence units. Preparations for operations included the building of a continuous chain of airfields along the railway line from Poznan to Lodz.

February 5   Polish intelligence reports circulated in London that large numbers of German troops were reaching East Prussia, most of them armored, and that there was rail congestion between Berlin and Warsaw.

February 21   Sam E. Wood, U.S. consul-general at Geneva, was in touch with an anti-Nazi German named Respondik, who had excellent contacts with the anti-Nazi group within the German General Staff; Wood sends to Cordell Hull, U.S. secretary of state, full details of Barbarossa directive. Cripps was, it is thought, informed of this development by his U.S. colleague in Moscow.

February 24   Churchill states that Russia was now in an unenviable position, and her attitude was one of making concessions to Germany in order to gain time.

February 24   Cripps states that Germany would attack Russia "not later than the end of June." Cripps announces this at a press conference at Moscow on February 28. Cripps revealed no source of his information except, in a conversation with

Deputy Foreign Minister Vyshinski, that the information was in his own opinion "based on reliable sources."

March 5　MI London notes SIS reports of the eastward movement of first-class German divisions and their replacement of positions formerly held in Eastern Europe by second-class divisions.

March 24　Churchill decides to send substantial reinforcements from the British to the Middle Eastern garrison.

April 27　JIC decides that Sealion unlikely.

May 31　Chiefs of staff advised that Germans were concentrating large army against Russia.

In sum, this chronology shows that Churchill was being kept accurately informed about Hitler's true intentions—that Russia, *not* England, would be Hitler's main target for 1941. There is room for conjecture, therefore, whether the U.S. Congress would have been so ready to grant lend lease to Britain in February 1941 had these facts been known at the time.

During the course of the entire pre–Pearl Harbor affair, "C" sent forty-one Ultra decrypts to Washington. Of these only the most significant are cited here. On November 25 he sent a decrypt of a telegram from the foreign minister, Tokyo, to the Japanese diplomatic representative at Turkey, which stated, "Should negotiations break down, that part of the situation in which the Japanese Empire is involved will be critical." On December 1 "C" showed how the Japanese ambassador at Hanoi was discussing with the foreign minister, Tokyo, that he imagined the Japanese Cabinet would decide in a day or two whether "it is to be peace or war," and that if it was to be war, then the military preparations in Indochina were such that "an advance would be possible within ten days or so." "C" provided several *Blue Jackets*—diplomatic decrypts—showing Japanese concerns for the strength of the wireless signals over which the "winds" messages were to be transferred, the security of their cipher systems, and the need to destroy all cipher machines and systems at all diplomatic outposts upon receiving the "winds execute" messages.

Particularly revealing was the decrypt of a signal from the foreign minister, Tokyo, to Japanese representatives at Rome and Berlin, Japan's allies, that it was "possible that circumstances may necessitate your having a special interview with [Hitler and Mussolini]." On December 2, five days before Pearl Harbor. "C" provided a most secret message from the Japanese foreign minister to the Japanese ambassador at Berlin, in which he stated that "a breakdown is inevitable" in U.S.-Japanese relations, "despite the sincere efforts of the Imperial Government." The empire, therefore, now had to "take the most serious decisions." The Japanese ambassador should inform Hitler that

the attitude of Britain and America has recently been provocative and they have continued to move troops into all parts of Eastern Asia. To meet this we too have been compelled to move troops, and it is greatly to be feared that an armed collision will occur and we shall find ourselves in a state of war with Britain and America. You should add that this may happen sooner than is expected.

The foreign minister added that while "we will not relax our restraint on the Soviet," it was in the South China Sea that "we lay most emphasis, and that we propose to refrain from deliberately taking positive action" against Russia.

On December 3, the day on which Menzies sent the critical decrypt discussed at such length by the Pearl Harbor inquiry, he also sent a further decrypt in which the Japanese ambassadors at London and elsewhere were instructed in regard to their cipher machines and systems: "Please exercise the greatest care and, in particular, with regard to the methods of dismantling and breaking up the essential parts, carry them out in accordance with instructions." In 1941, such instructions were considered to be the harbinger of war.

That ominous bulletin was followed on December 4 by a further decrypt from "C" that revealed Japanese instructions for the withdrawal of embassy staffs, reporters, and Japanese businessmen from London, together with directions regarding the closing of the embassy in the event of war. Another decrypt of December 4 sent by "C" revealed orders to begin destroying cipher machines and systems at the Washington embassy. On December 5, two days before Pearl Harbor, "C" further despatched a decrypt that showed Tokyo had ordered London, Hong Kong, Singapore, and Manila to "discard" their cipher machines, Batavia's had been returned to Tokyo, and instructions had been issued to burn copies of all but two telegraphic codes held in Washington, Canada, Panama, the South Seas, Portuguese Timor, Singora, Chiang Mai, and all British and Dutch possessions. That signal was an endorsement of the intelligence that, in preparation for war, the Japanese government was dismantling her entire cipher system throughout what she intended would be the zone of her operations.

Also on December 5, all consular posts were ordered to burn all ciphers and all files of in and out telegrams and all secret and confidential documents. In addition, this order contained the statement, "These are precautions envisaging any Emergency." On Saturday, December 6, Stewart Menzies sent to Washington a very long decrypt containing a new and special code to be used in "telegraphing secret code words to notify the critical condition of the situation." Reflecting the extreme human tensions of the moment, that and subsequent telegrams ordered all Japanese official personnel to "redouble your attention to your duties and maintain your calmness and self-respect."

Very early on the morning of Sunday, December 7, 1941 (by

London time, about five hours ahead of Washington and twelve hours ahead of Pearl Harbor), "C" transmitted the first decrypt relating to the pact between Germany, Italy, and Japan and further news that it was probable Germany and Italy would declare war on the United States if war broke out between American and Japan. It began:

In view of the increasingly obvious desire of the United States and England to bring to naught a just New Order with all the armed forces at their disposal and to cut off the means of existence of the German, Italian, and Japanese peoples, the German Government, the Italian Government and the Japanese Government have, in order to ward off these grave threats to the existence of their peoples, jointly resolved on the following. . . .

Each power then undertook to "fight together with all the resources at their command until victory is achieved over the United States and England," and each also undertook "not to make a separate armistice or separate peace with the United States or England without full mutual understanding." This agreement was to come into force on the "day of the 12th month of the 16th year of the Showa Bra Era, i.e. . . . December 1941 or the . . . day of December of the 20th year of the Fascist Era."

Later on December 7, at 11:50 hours "OMT," a transmission error for Greenwich Mean Time (GMT), there came not the "winds execute" message expected, but a message in the code words sent by "C" to Washington on December 6. That message included three code words: *hattori, koyanaqi,* and *minami.* These meant, as "C" advised Washington, "Relations between Japan and Great Britain and the United States are extremely critical." Shortly, too, the "winds execute" message was heard in various parts of the world. In the United States, all that was heard was "West wind, clear," which meant that war with England, not with the United States, had broken out.

APPENDIX D

This document is the only known SIS battle report to come into the public domain. It was located in the Donovan papers and was given to Donovan by Lieutenant Colonel R. E. Henderson, "C's" director of training. As Henderson stated in a note to Donovan, some of the names of those involved in the espionage rings had been doctored to prevent the Germans, Italians, and Vichy French from discovering their identity.

The SIS Group "Tom Brown's" Battle Report:
1. During the period of actual hostilities, the following four groups were operating in Tunisia:
   A "Tom Brown" Group
   B Y.Y.Y. Group
   C "Hirondelle" Group
   D Lulu-Dupont Group

2. All four groups were closely interrelated, while the Lulu-Dupont Group was eventually dissolved, the former coming under control of "Hirondelle" and the latter gravitating to the Y.Y.Y. Group. For the sake of clarity, however, each will be dealt with as a separate entity.

3. *"Tom Brown" Group.* At the commencement of the Tunisian Campaign this Group consisted of the following principal members:
   Jacob Mifsud ("Tom Brown")—Leader.
   Stephen Negley—W/T Operator.
   Ian Hurley
   Madeleine Marchand
   Frederic Arnoux
   Francois Berthelmot
   Nicolas Muntz
   Pierre de Chardon
   Marcel Odin
   Danielle Prevost
   Jacques Fossard

4. *Release from Prison.* At the date of the Allied landings, the first four of the above list were all confined in the Civil Prison in Tunis. Upon the arrival of the Germans on the night of 13th–14th November, they were released

773

by the French authorities, and these four . . . found temporary sanctuary in the house of Jacques Frossard, the "Commis-Greffier" [assistant clerk of the courts or keeper of civil documents].

5. *Re-organization.* "Tom Brown," whose energy and enthusiasm were unquenchable, took prompt steps to reorganize the group, to repair and instal one of the W/T sets hidden at the time of his arrest, and to establish contact with Alpha on 17th November 1942. During his confinement, "Tom Brown" had become associated with a party of Gaullist supporters, and, upon their release, these were anxious that "Tom Brown" and his group should join them in sabotage operations. This suggestion was vetoed by London, and "Tom Brown" was instructed to confine his activities to the procuring of information. Funds to finance to group were provided by Dupont [of the Lulu-Dupont] team.

6. *Co-ordination.* On 28th November Major Proctor [controlling "Tom Brown" group] left Alpha for Algiers for the purpose of coordinating the work of the Tunisian groups, supplying their W/T requirements and avoiding duplication of information, the volume of W/T traffic having reached a proportion which was causing anxiety in London from a security angle.

7. *Branches Established.* On 30th November a branch of the "Tom Brown" group was established at Bizerta, and shortly afterward a second branch was started at Ferryville. Negley was W/T operator working between the two places, while "Tom Brown" himself secured a job as chauffeur in [the Tunis Public Works Department], which enabled him to travel daily between Tunis, Ferryville, and Bizerta. The team in Bizerta consisted of de Chardon and Berthelmot, while those working in Ferryville were Muntz and a Gaullist sailor whom "Tom Brown" had recruited in prison (name unknown). Merville acted as a link between the two substations, carrying communications by pedal-cycle.

8. *Number of Messages Sent.* From the end of November, 1942, up to the date of his arrest on on 24th February 1943, "Tom Brown" was prolific in his supply of information. 585 messages in all were sent by his group in the short period of four months.

9. *Hunted by Gestapo.* On 30th November, 1942, Alpha received the information that the Gestapo were hard on the heels of "Tom Brown" and his associates [presumably through Bletchley's reading of the Abwehr and Sicherheitsdienst's traffic]. Their meeting-place and respective lodgings were promptly changed, and thenceforward the principal members of this group appear to have led a veritable "Robin Hood" existence, never remaining in one place for more than a week or two and frequently escaping across the roofs of the native town, while the Gestapo were hammering on the door of their hastily vacated quarters.

10. *Loyalty to Group Leader.* It is perhaps appropriate the mention here the tremendous loyalty and personal affection accorded to "Tom Brown" by all who came into contact with him. His name became a myth in the Tunis underworld and his unlucky arrest and deportation to Germany constituted not only a grave loss to our Service, but a genuine grief to many of his friends.

11. *Finances.* Money was an ever-present need with "Tom Brown" and his rapidly expanding organization, whose numbers had by now increased to approximately 21, including sub-agents, runners, and helpers. Dupont was supposed to provide the necessary funds, but "Tom Brown" (like nearly all our other agents) found this unsatisfactory and unreliable. Indeed, of all our 45–50 "workers" in Tunisia, Dupont was the only real disappointment, and even he was never deliberately disloyal or treacherous—a good record. "Tom Brown" also had misunderstandings with Lesage, whom he frequently characterises as disobliging and un-cooperative. This friction, however, may to some extent have been due to inter-group jealousy and complete incompatability of temperament, "Tom Brown" being the reckless, debonair adventurer, and Lesage the careful, calculating organiser. The financial situation was eventually eased by a generous loan from Philippe Simon, manager of the Star Shoe Factory, Tunis.

12. *Martin & Raffles.* On 10th November, 1942, Pilot-Officers Martin and Raffles crashed at Bou Ficha. They succeeded in making their way to Tunis and soon afterwards they contacted "Tom Brown" who quickly put them to work. The language difficulty rendered them unsuitable for outside work, but they willingly offered their services as codists and general inside assistants.

13. *Distribution of Members.* By the middle of January, the location of the principal members of the group was as follows: Tunis: "Tom Brown," Leader; Arnoux, (i/c agents); Hurley, (i/c Information); Negley, (i/c W/T). Bizerta: De Chardon, Berthelmot. Ferryville, X. Sacarello, Achmet. The remainder of the "team" were distributed at strategic points, while many of them (including of course "Tom Brown" himself) circulated constantly from one point to another.

14. *Family Anxieties.* A point which is perhaps worth mentioning and which is repeatedly brought out in W/T messages is the anxiety of "Tom Brown" and others of his group, owing to lack of news of their families. A study of the circumstances suggests that this anxiety could have readily been alleviated by brief but regular, reassuring messages from our side. While it was true that no preoccupation was likely to undermine a character such as "Tom Brown," the same does not apply to less resilient temperaments.

15. *French Police Network.* In early January 1943, "Tom Brown" decided that much valuable information would be available, were it possible to es-

tablish a network of informers and sympathisers among various departments of the French Police. Contact was accordingly made with Peter Sanguinetti of the "Service de Sûreté Tunisienne" [the Tunisian Security Service], who in turn enlisted a number of others including the following:

Superintendant Desyeux (Chief of Sûreté)
Superintendant Lefevre (Service de Surveillance Territoire)
Ginot (Of the Immigration Office)
Enor Mizraim (Arab Inspector)

16. *French Police (contd.).* The police sub-group supplied much valuable military, air, and shipping information, and, in addition, it was invaluable in warning our agents when danger threatened. Sanguinetti's team was also helpful in supplying our friends with stolen or forged identity cards. (N.B. A study of the various activities of the various Police Departments in Tunis during this period discloses an almost impenetrable maze of intrigue and double-crossing.)

17. *Liaison with "Hirondelle" Group.* The group headed by Andre Boyer ("Hirondelle") had landed by submarine at Cap Bon on 28th December 1942, and shortly afterwards contact was made with "Tom Brown," who was able to render them an initial service by taking charge of the two soldiers (Dowd and Fegan) who had accompanied them ashore. In return "Delle" (as he was called by all his friends) and Harry Marks, both W/T experts, were of great assistance to Negley ("Tom Brown's" chief operator), who had been having recurring trouble with both the Bizerta and Ferryville sets. After "Tom Brown's" arrest, "Delle" came to the financial aid of Arnoux ("Tom Brown's" successor), and co-operation between the two groups remained cordial until the end.

18. *Andree Tours.* In this connection, the somewhat obscure relationship between "Tom Brown" and Mme. Andree Tours is of interest. M. Tours (Andree's husband) had been in charge of the sabotage section of the original North African group (led by Legrand). He is personally acquainted with [General Maxime] Weygand [the former French commander in chief in French North Africa] and [General Charles] de Gaulle and he had a brother, naturalized British, serving with the R.A.F. Mr. Tours had been arrested in Tunis in June 1941, and was not released until November 1942, when he succeeded in contacting our Algiers station and was eventually sent to the United Kingdom.

19. *Andree Tours (contd.).* Andree Tours followed her husband from France to Algeria, thence to Tunisia where she was herself imprisoned as a Gaullist. While in prison she became acquainted with "Tom Brown" and was released with him in November 1942. When "Tom Brown" reformed his group, Mme.

Tours volunteered for working in sorting and assessing information, and she proved herself an intelligent and valuable assistant.

20. *Andree Tours (contd.)*. After the arrival of "Hirondelle," Mme. Tours was used as "agent de liaison" between the two groups, and she soon became intimate with Harry Marks, the number two of the "Hirondelle" group. It has been hinted that she "deserted" "Tom Brown" for Marks; it has been even insinuated that [she] was in some way connected with the former's betrayal. There is no shadow of evidence to support either of these suggestions. Mme. Tours is naturally reticent about the entire affair, but a point of interest is the fact that, at the conclusion of the Tunisian campaign, she was able to recover and hand to our representative a number of letters, photographs, and documents (including a diary)—all the private property of "Tom Brown," which (she says) had been hidden by friends at the time of "T.B.'s" final arrest. The condition of the papers show that they had been buried, but where or in what circumstances had not been ascertained.

21. *Funds Provided by Mr. Ffoulkes*. A fresh financial crisis arose in early January 1943, when Mr. Ffoulkes came to the rescue of the group by advancing a substantial sum from his private funds. Mr. Ffoulkes is the English Protestant clergyman, resident in Tunis, who remained in the city throughout the Axis occupation. Although harrassed both by the Germans and the Italian police, he was never actually confined and was thus able to render many small services to the Allied Cause.

22. *Assessing Value of Information*. The first and second weeks in January 1943 constituted the peak period of the "Tom Brown" group. Their information embraced practically every branch of enemy activity, including enemy intentions and French political tendencies. *Military, air, and shipping intelligence was voluminous—indeed, for reasons of security, it was necessary to curb the almost continuous flow of messages. In this connection and for future reference, stress is laid upon the extreme importance of mentioning sources when transmitting military information. Unless clear distinction is made between first-hand and second-hand information, it is impossible for the competent military authority to assess its value, while errors occur resulting in a loss of confidence. Despite repeated warnings, "Tom Brown" and his group were consistent offenders in this respect, which suggests that their training had not sufficiently emphasized the point.**

23. *First Arrests*. The first mishap occurred on 11th January, 1943, when Mme. Grasse and one other Gaullists were arrested in the restaurant "Chez Maurice" [in Tunis]. Mme. Grasse knew most of the members of the "Tom

---

*The italicized portion of paragragh 22 of the Tom Brown Battle Report was emphasis provided by Donovan in order, presumably, to ensure that his agents did not repeat these mistakes.

Brown" group, as "Chez Maurice" was a favorite meeting-place. Just how much she divulged to Soult [of the Commissaire Special] and his gang is a matter for speculation. It is certain, however, that she was later appointed prison wardress and used as a "stool pigeon" by Massat, the Governor of the Civil Prison.

24. *Arrest of Berthelmot and de Chardon & Berthelmot's Escape.* The prelude to a series of far graver misfortunes was the arrest on 15th January, 1943, of the French Police Inspector Guillot, accused of associating with Gaulliste and British agents. Guillot, a weak, vacillating creature, was cross-questioned and undoubtedly roughly-handled by Soult at his headquarters at 41, rue Hoche. Under pressure, he betrayed the whereabouts of Berthelmot and de Chardon. It is possible that he also gave information concerning "Tom Brown," Arnoux, and others. At all events, seven days later (20th Jan) Berthelmot and de Chardon were arrested in Bizerta and taken to Tunis for interrogation. While awaiting the arrival of the notorious Soult, a momentary lack of supervision enabled Berthelmot, although still handcuffed, to effect a clean getaway. A friendly garage employee, named Turville, removed his handcuffs, and after various adventures, he succeeded in rejoining "T.B." and resuming his work with the group.

25. *"Tom Brown's" First Plan to Cross Lines.* Early in January 1943, a number of problems (financial, technical) arose which made it desirable that "T.B." should, if possible, personally contact either Major Proctor or our Algiers representative. Arrangements were made accordingly for him to cross the lines in the Poohoomul district on or about January 21st. He was to don Arab disguise and assume the identity of Sheik Ilidar. Upon the receipt of the disturbing news of the arrest of Berthelmot and de Chardon, these plans were temporarily abandoned.

26. *Arrest of Muntz.* Next to be arrested, on January 23rd, was Muntz, one of the early members of the group, who had rendered valuable service finding flats and "hide-outs" for hard-pressed fellow workers.

27. *French Police Documents Handed over to the Gestapo.* In attempting to ascertain the causes (other than treachery) for the gradual denouement of the whole of the "T.B." group, the following interesting facts have come to light. When the Germans arrived in Tunis in November 1942, the Prefect of Police, M. Fahy, removed the documents and identification papers of British agents then in prison and had them sent to El Rak, where they were concealed in the cellar of a villa. Some weeks later the Americans occupied this area for a short time, but it was eventually recaptured by the Germans, and the hiding-place of the police records was revealed to them by a Tunis lawyer, M. Fioravanti. From that moment, the Gestapo were in possession of the names and particulars of many of our agents at work. Fioravanti was

arrested when the Allies finally entered Tunis, but was released by the turn-coat, Calatroni, controller of the Judiciary Police.

28. *Arrest of "Tom Brown" and Berthelmot.* It will be remembered that "T.B.'s" trip through the lines had been postponed on account of Berthelmot's and de Chardon's arrest. Fresh plans were drawn up in February and it was decided that "Tom" and Berthelmot (who had rejoined his old chief after his escape) were to cross over to Allied-occupied territory in the Rouleville area, on or about 22nd February. Both men assumed Arab disguise and set out on the journey from which they were destined to return as prisoners. While attempting to cross the lines, they were detected, and in the revolver duel which ensued, Berthelmot was badly wounded in the shoulder.

29. *Berthelmot's Martyrdom.* The prisoners were brought back to Tunis and Berthelmot was hurried to Soult's office, first aid for his wound being refused. The proceedings which followed were reported to French Police Inspector Grigolati (one of Sanguinetti's pro-Ally team) by an eye-witness, Lieutenant Capaletti, an Italian officer attached to the S.S. Although exhausted and suffering from loss of blood, Berthelmot maintained a complete sangfroid, and during a long night of interrogation and torture, resolutely refused to reveal anything. Indeed, he so taunted Soult and his fellow-inspectors that the blackguardly Soult finally lost all control and finished him off by shooting him in the neck with a revolver. The third-degree methods employed by Soult on this occasion appear to have been so revolting that [a] German SS officer who was present was unable to stomach the scene and finally left, declaring that these were "Russian methods!"

30. *Arnoux Assumes Leadership of the Group.* As can be imagined, the arrest of "Tom Brown" and Berthelmot and the murder of the latter, was a very heavy blow to the remaining members of the group. However, the importance of continuing their work was appreciated by all and the group reorganized its activities under the leadership of Arnoux.

31. *Arrest of Negley & Madeleine Marchand and W/T Set Discovered.* For two weeks all went well and a considerable amount of valuable information was transmitted to Alpha and thence to [British] 1st Army H.Q. Then on 8th March, while walking down the rue de Belgique, Negley and his friend Madeleine Marchand were recognized by one of Soult's men and were promptly arrested. Almost more serious than these arrests was the fact that, upon searching Negley's apartment, one of the W/T sets was discovered together with a coded message.

32. *Arnoux & Laters Arrested.* Three days later (11th March) Arnoux, the deputy leader of the group, was arrested in the native quarter of Tunis, and this disaster was quickly followed by Laters' arrest on 17th March. Laters,

while not in fact one of "T.B.'s" team, was closely associated with them, having acted as an 'agent de liaison' between the Y.Y.Y., Lulu-Dupont and T.B. Groups.

33. *Concerning Guillot.* While there is no actual proof that Guillot (the self-confessed betrayer of Berthelmot) gave information leading to the apprehension of Negley and Arnoux, it is significant that this whole series of misfortunes closely succeeded his (Guillot's) arrest and interrogation.

34. *Hurley Becomes New Leader.* Things were looking black indeed, and for some days the remaining members of the group were obliged to take cover and temporarily to suspend activities. The leadership of the new decimated group devolved upon Ian Hurley. After the arrest of all his friends, this stout-hearted North countryman found sanctuary with a friendly carpenter, Verdurier, who had already afforded refuge to others of the group. He reorganized the available personnel and for over a month continued to keep Alpha supplied with vital military information.

35. *Co-operation of Hirondelle Group.* The various accounts of group activities during this final stage (12th March–15th April) were confused and contradictory. It is clear, however, that, owing to the reduced ranks of the "T.B." team, much of their work had perforce to be handed over to the Hirondelle group. H. Marks made two successive trips to Ferryville in order to effect repairs to the W/T set, and Tarbant was installed there as operator.

36. *"Coup Final"—Hurley and Mme. Prevost Arrested. Hurley's Interrogation.* The "coup final" occurred on 15th April, when Hurley, his friend Danielle Prevost, and Verdurier were all arrested in Tunis. Negley was denounced by an Italian, Simone, who occupied the flat below him. When the police came to arrest him, Hurley made a last desperate effort to escape by leaping from a second storey window. Unfortunately he only succeeded in breaking a leg and was quickly recaptured. At the time of his arrest his real identity was unknown, and he might have got away with his story of being a Spanish petty thief, had it not been for a slight carelessness in his disguise. Hurley's hair was naturally red but it had been dyed black some time previously. Unfortunately the dye had not been renewed, with the result that the roots disclosed the natural red shade, while the ends remained jet black. Hurley was taken to police headquarters by Commissioner Soresi (a friend of Calatroni) and the customary third-degree interrogation followed. Realising that the "game was up," Hurley admitted his identity but resolutely refused to disclose any information regarding the past or present activities of himself or his associates.

37. *J. Fossard Leaves Tunis.* The only remaining member of the group now was Jacques Fossard who, it will be remembered, had given refuge to "Tom Brown," Negley and others in the early days. On the advice of friends, he left Tunis and eventually succeeded in crossing the lines near Hafiz-ad-Djin.

38. *Whole Team Wiped Out.* The whole of Tom Brown's gallant band had been liquidated, and their only future intercommunication was through the thick walls of the Civil Prison or during chance encounters in the exercise yard.

39. *High Grade Morale and Low Grade Security.* The whole "esprit" of Tom Brown's team was based on great daring and disregard of danger, and these admirable and lovable traits brought them many recruits. On the other hand, this same daring (often amounting to rashness), together with a taste for good fellowship and good living, were largely responsible for their final undoing. This particularly applies to Negley and Madeleine Marchand who habitually went together to restaurants, cafes and other public places, regardless of the immense risk. In the type of work in which they were engaged, overconfidence is as great a pitfall as faint-heartedness.

40. *Summing Up.* In assessing the work of the "Tom Brown" group, several points stand out: (i) The amazing speed with which the group was organized for work; (ii) The immense volume of information transmitted over a comparatively brief period; (iii) The good morale of all members and their strong personal devotion to "T.B."; (iv) The relatively bad security of the leaders.

41. *Lessons to Be Learned.* Of all the stories of the Tunisian groups, that of "Tom Brown" is by far the most glamorous. The whole episode is packed with adventure, hair-breadth escapes, rapid recovery from reverse and individual heroism under duress. Perhaps the two outstanding lessons to be learnt are (a) what can be achieved under brilliant leadership, and (b) the inevitable result of over-confidence and lack of security precautions.

APPENDIX E

This document was considered by Dr. R. V. Jones, "C's" chief scientific officer, to be one of the most important relating to the missile crisis of 1943 and a model of an agent's report. It was written by Amniarix, the young female spy in the Alliance network in France headed by the famous Marie-Madeleine Fourcade:

Information communicated by a captain on the active list attached to the Experimental Centre in question

On the island of Usedom (north of Stettin) are concentrated laboratories and scientific research services to improve existing weapons and perfect new ones. The island is very closely guarded. To gain access, besides a military identity card, requires three special passes:

> *Sondergenehmigung* on watermarked paper
> *Zusatz* an orange card
> *Vorlaufigergenehmigung* on white paper

The administrative services are at Peenemunde and at Zempin. Research is concentrated on:

(a) bombs and shells guided independently of the laws of ballistics.

(b) a stratospheric shell.

(c) the use of bacteria as a weapon.

Kampfgruppe KG 100 [a Pathfinder unit of the Luftwaffe] is now experimenting with bombs guided from the aircraft by the bomb aimer. These bombs could be guided from such a distance that the plane could remain out of range of AA fire. Accuracy is perfect if the plane does not have to defend itself against fighters.

It appears that the final stage has been reached in developing a stratospheric bomb of an entirely new type. This bomb is reported to be 10 cubic metres in volume and filled with explosive. It would be launched almost vertically to reach the stratosphere as quickly as possible. The source speaks of 50 mph vertically, initial velocity being maintained by successive explosions. The bomb is provided with *Raketten* and guided to specific targets. The bomb is said to be fuelled with 800 litres of petrol, necessary even in the experimental stage, in which the shell is not filled with explosive, to enable it to carry. The horizontal range is slightly over 300 miles. Trials are said to have been made, without explosive charge, from Usedom towards the Baltic and to have reached as far as Konigsberg. The noise is said to be as deafening as a Flying Fortress. The trials are understood to have given immediate excellent results as regards accuracy and it was to the success of these trials that Hitler was referring when he spoke of "new weapons that will change the face of the war when the Germans use them."

Difficulties have developed quite recently, only half the bombs hitting selected targets accurately. This recent fault is expected to be remedied towards the end of the month. The trials have been made by Lehr-und-Erprobungskommando Wachtel.

Colonel Wachtel and the officers that he has collected are to form the cadres of an anti-aircraft regiment (16 batteries of 220 men), the 155 W, that is going to be stationed in France, at the end of October or the beginning of November, with HQ near Amiens, and batteries between Amiens, Abbeville, Dunkirk.

The regiment will dispose 108 (one hundred and eight) catapults able to fire a bomb every twenty minutes. The army artillery will have more than 400 catapults sited from Brittany to Holland.

The artillery regiments will be supplied with these devices as and when there is a sufficient production of ammunition.

Major Sommerfeld, Colonel Wachtel's technical advisor, estimates that 50–100 of these bombs would suffice to destroy London. The batteries will be so sited that they can methodically destroy most of Britain's large cities during the winter.

Reinforced concrete platforms are reported to be already under construction. They are expected to be fully operational in November.

The German experts are aware that British experts are working on the same problem. They think they are sure of three to four months' lead.

APPENDIX F

Summarized below is the Ultra intelligence available at Allied supreme headquarters, U.S. Twelfth Army Group; and U.S. First Army, relating to German capabilities and intentions before the Battle of the Ardennes in December 1944.

October 14, 1944
Ultra indicates that Sixth Panzer Army was under the personal direction of Hitler and was undergoing a rest and refitting programme.

October–November 1944
Throughout November and December the German state railways key was broken. This revealed large-scale train movements into the concentration area between Cleves and Roermond behind the Ardennes forests and mountains.

November 2, 1944
Army Group "B" calls for fighter protection for the unloading of important troop trains during the next two days at various points in an arc of some twenty miles' radius from northwest to southwest of Cologne, an area just to the east of the Ardennes. One of the earliest decrypts was of particular importance, for it indicated that German troops of unspecified formations in unspecified numbers were detraining in the general area of Kall-Gerolstein-Bitburg. These places were within 10–15 miles of the Ardennes front in a sector held only weakly by U.S. First Army.

November 3, 1944
The German state railways key revealed on this date two movements, one of 41 and the other of 28 trains. The first carried the 352nd Volksgrenadier Division. The contents of the second train were not revealed but its arrival was notified to 7 Army and 5 Panzer Army, thus suggesting that the 352nd was reinforcing those two armies, both of which were to be used in the Battle of the Bulge.

November 3, 1944
The request for fighter aircraft protection was repeated with high priority at dawn on November 3, 1944. During the next 45 days before the attack "thirty or more" similar signals were decoded and transmitted to SHAEF,

12th Army Group and U.S. 1st Army. This was an average of two signals every three days. All requests for fighter protection came from Army Group "B," then the main German formation on the Ardennes front. In general, all signals referred to the need for air cover of trains in the area (a) Cologne-Aachen-Munchen-Gladbach. With increasing frequency, "and sometimes almost shrill urgency," these signals referred to the special need for air protection of the Rhine crossings between Bonn and Koblenz, with a growing emphasis on the southern half of the area—that is to say, the area directly behind the Ardennes from which the attack was delivered.

ca. November 10, 1944
The German state railways key reveals that the command echelon of 6 Panzer Army moving westwards from its training area. Another decrypt revealed that 12 SS Panzer Division moving westwards. The contents of 17 more trains were delivered to 7 Army and 5 Panzer Army. These signals revealed that troop transports were being given priority, that they might be crossing the railway bridges over the Rhine, and that four armies in the center or the front were concerned but not the 15th Army at the northern or the 19th Army at the southern extremities of the western front. On two of the three separate days on which these railway movements took place, requests for fighter protection for railway transports were intercepted.

November 10, 1944
The Director-General of Transport *demanded* that 6 Panzer Army tell all its formations to ensure strict punctuality, as otherwise the "prescribed timetable" could not be observed nor delays made good. Only the previous day, the official complained, 22nd SS Panzer Division had fallen 36 hours behind schedule. The Panzer Lehr Division was 24 hours before schedule, 12 SS about 12 hours so far as could be ascertained. This signal was sent with the highest priority—ZZZZZ—to SHAEF, 12th Army Group, and U.S. 1st Army that same day.

November 21, 1944
Ultra reveals that 9 and 10 SS Panzer Divisions were around Eusenkirchen, southwest of Cologne.

ca. November 23, 1944
A series of orders for aerial reconnaissance began. These continued throughout the last week of November, and conveyed an increasingly urgent note. All signals focused interest in two areas (a) the approaches to Liege, an important Allied supply center (b) along the Prum-Houffalize axis toward the Meuse crossings at Dinant and Givet. All requests for such reconnaissance emanated from Army Group "B."

November 24, 1944
Ultra reveals 2 SS Panzer Division at Munchen-Gladbach.

November 26, 1944
Ultra reveals 1 SS Panzer Korps southwest of Cologne, preparing to take command of Panzer Lehr Division, and 1, 2, 9, 10 & 12 SS Panzer Divisions. 116th Panzer Division took delivery of a few Panther tanks on December 1st. This concentration of armor should have suggested the imminence of a German offensive on the scale of May–June 1940.

November 29, 1944
Army Group "B" requests aerial reconnaissance of the Meuse crossings from Liege to Givet. This request was repeated daily. As the period developed, night reconnaissance was requested as well. Ultra reveals what the reconnaissance observers were instructed to look for: Were Allied reinforcements moving up? Where were the Allied tank concentrations and supply dumps? Ultra then revealed that the day flights were "entrusted for safety" and "as a matter of the greatest urgency" to the Arado 234 jets of Detachment Sperling.

First days of December 1944
Ultra reveals that OKW, the German supreme command, had ordered Field Marshal Albert Kesselring, C in C of the German armies in Italy, to surrender 1,000 trucks to 6 Panzer Army.

December 2, 1944
Army Group "B" asked with "special urgency" for fighter protection to be given to troop movements in the Moselle valley area. These decrypts revealed that a total of nearly 200 trains carrying 12 different formations were to be unloaded in the Eifel and Saar districts, while a further 40 were destined for Alsace. [In all, some eight hundred trains were used in November and early December to move Sixth Panzer Army westward. Ultra accounted for almost 400 of these movements.

December 5, 1944
Ultra reveals that a big conference of commanding officers was convened for this date at an airfield outside Koblenz. The purpose was not stated, but summonses were sent to all main fighter formations—Jagdkorps 1, Jagdivisionen 1,3,5, and Jafue Mittelrhein, the fighter control unit for the Middle Rhenish area.

ca. December 7, 1944
Ultra reveals that a Luftwaffe fighter control post had reported 35 Me 109 fighters serviceable out of 60, and about 70 Fw 190s out of 108. On the 10th, a further Ultra showed these figures had suddenly risen. On the day before the German offensive began they stood at 164 fighters serviceable, almost equally divided between Me 109s and Fw 190s, out of 340. There were crews available for half as many more. This was a much larger number available for operations than at any time in a long time past.

December 8, 1944
Detachment Sperling instructed to secure good photographs of the Meuse
crossings and of the road junction at Ciney.

December 10, 1944
Ultra reveals that all SS units were observing wireless silence—intelligence
of especial significance to those looking for evidence of an imminent SS
attack.

APPENDIX G

This is the letter written by General George C. Marshall, chief of staff of the U.S. Army, to Governor Dewey, the Republican presidential candidate in September 1944, when Dewey threatened to make public the existence of Magic and Ultra in an effort to embarrass President Franklin D. Roosevelt.

TOP SECRET

For Mr. Dewey's Eyes Only.   27 September 1944.

My Dear Governor:

Colonel Clarke, my messenger to you of yesterday, September 26th, has reported the result of his delivery of my letter dated September 25th. As I understand him you (a) were unwilling to commit yourself to any agreement regarding "not communicating its contents to any other person" in view of the fact that you felt you already knew certain of the things probably referred to in the letter, as suggested to you by seeing the word "cryptograph," and (b) you could not feel that such a letter as this to a presidential candidate could not have been addressed to you by an officer in my position without the knowledge of the President.

As to (a) above I am quite willing to have you read what comes hereafter with the understanding that you are bound not to communicate to any other person any portions on which you do not now have or later receive factual knowledge from some other source than myself. As to (b) above you have my word that neither the Secretary of War nor the President has any intimation whatsoever that such a letter has been addressed to you or that the preparation or sending of such a communication was being considered. I assure you that the only persons who saw or know of the existence of either this letter or my letter to you dated September 25th are Admiral King, seven key officers responsible for security of military communications, and my secretary who typed these letters. I am trying my best to make plain to you that this letter is being addressed to you solely on my initiative, Admiral King having been consulted only after the letter was drafted, and I am persisting in the matter because the military hazards involved are so serious that I feel some action is necessary to protect the interests of our armed forces.

I should have much preferred to talk to you in person but I could not devise a method that would not be subject to press and radio reactions as to why the Chief of Staff of the Army would be seeking an interview with you at this particular moment. Therefore I have turned to the method of this letter, with which Admiral King concurs, to be delivered by hand to you by Colonel Clarke, who, incidentally, has charge of the most secret documents of the War and Navy Departments.

In brief, the military dilemma is this:

The most vital evidence in the Pearl Harbor matter consists of our intercepts of the Japanese diplomatic communications. Over a period of years our cryptograph people analyzed the character of the machine the Japanese were using for encoding the diplomatic messages. Based on this a corresponding machine was built by us which deciphers their messages. Therefore, we possessed a wealth of information regarding their moves in the Pacific, which in turn was furnished the State Department—rather than is popularly supposed, the State Department providing us with the information—but which unfortunately made no reference whatever to intentions towards Hawaii until the last message before December 7th, which did not reach our hands until the following day, December 8th.

Now the point to the present dilemma is that we have gone ahead with this business of deciphering their codes until we possess other codes, German as well as Japanese, but our main basis of information regarding Hitler's intentions in Europe is obtained from Baron Oshima's messages from Berlin reporting his interviews with Hitler and other officials to the Japanese Government. These are still in the codes involved in the Pearl Harbor events.

To explain further the critical nature of this set-up which would be wiped out almost in an instant if the least suspicion were aroused regarding it, the battle of the Coral Sea was based on deciphered messages and therefore our few ships were in the right place at the right time. Further, we were able to concentrate our limited forces to meet their naval advance on Midway when otherwise we almost certainly would have been some 3,000 miles out of place. We had full information of the strength of their forces in that advance and also of the smaller force directed against the Aleutians which finally landed troops on Attu and Kiska.

Operations in the Pacific are largely guided by the information we obtain of Japanese deployments. We know their strength in various garrisons, the rations and other stores continuing available to them, and what is of vast importance, we check their fleet movements and the movements of their convoys. The heavy losses reported from time to time which they sustain by reason of our submarine action, largely result from the fact that we know the sailing dates and routes of their convoys and can notify our submarines to lie in wait at the proper points.

The current raids by Admiral Halsey's carrier forces on Japanese shipping in Manila Bay and elsewhere were largely based in timing on the known movements of Japanese convoys, two of which were caught, as anticipated, in his destructive attacks.

You will understand from the foregoing the utterly tragic consequences if the present political debates regarding Pearl Harbor disclose to the enemy, German or Jap, any suspicion of the vital sources of information we possess. The Roberts' report on Pearl Harbor had to have withdrawn from it all reference to this highly secret matter, therefore in portions it necessarily appeared incomplete. The same reason which dictated that course is even more important today because our sources have been greatly elaborated.

As another example of the delicacy of the situation, some of Donovan's people (the OSS) without telling us, instituted a secret search of the Japanese Embassy offices in Portugal. As a result the entire military attaché Japanese code all over the world was changed, and though this occurred over a year ago, we have not yet been able to break the new code and have thus lost this invaluable source of information, particularly regarding the European situation.

A further most serious embarrassment is the fact that the British government is involved concerning its most secret sources of information, regarding which only the Prime Minister, the Chiefs of Staff and a very limited number of other officials have knowledge.

A recent speech in Congress by Representative Harness would clearly suggest to the Japanese that we have been reading their codes, though Mr. Harness and the American public would probably not draw any such conclusion.

The conduct of General Eisenhower's campaign and of all operations in the Pacific are closely related in conception and timing to the information we secretly obtain through these intercepted codes. They contribute greatly to the victory and tremendously to the saving in American lives, both in the conduct of current operations and in looking towards the early termination of the war.

I am presenting this matter to you in the hope that you will see your way clear to avoid the tragic results with which we are now threatened in the present political campaign.

Please return this letter by bearer. I will hold it in my most secret file subject to your reference should you so desire.

Faithfully yours,
(sgd) G. C. Marshall

In the matter of Soviet allegations after the Yalta Conference that the Allies deliberately gave the Red Army chief of staff, General A. A. Antonov, deceptive intelligence relating to the whereabouts of the SS Sixth Panzer Army (commanded by Obergruppenführer SS Sepp Dietrich) and thereby almost caused a disaster on the Russian front, the known facts about Dietrich's movements and those of his army were themselves beclouded by a desire to mystify and mislead the Allies as to his whereabouts and intentions.

Schellenberg's statement to Masson, chief of Swiss intelligence, early in February showed a clear indication to deceive when he mentioned gratuitously that Dietrich and his army had gone to the defense of Berlin.

As to the record of the movement of the Sixth SS Panzer Army, it is known that on January 3 Hitler formally abandoned the objectives of the Ardennes offensive. On January 8 he ordered the withdrawal of the Sixth SS Panzer Army into reserve to meet an Allied counteroffensive. But on January 12, 1945, the Red Army launched its mightiest offensive on the eastern front between Hungary and the Baltic.

Warned that the eastern front might not survive the Russian offensive, on January 16 Hitler ordered Dietrich's six panzer divisions to move to Hungary, for (as Hitler declared) the outcome of the war hinged on holding the Hungarian oil fields. The Sixth SS's heavy losses in men and equipment having been made good while in reserve in the west, the movement began by rail on or about January 22. It was made in great secrecy, partly to deny to the enemy any information that might result in aerial attacks on the trains and partly to prevent the Russians from discerning Hitler's plans in the relocation of the divisions.

For cover purposes, therefore, Sixth SS Panzer Army was called "Higher Engineer Commander Hungary," and the rail movement consisted of two parts. Dietrich's two panzer corps totaled six divisions, but in order to mislead the Russians, he and his headquarters did not travel to Hungary with the divisions but instead moved in behind the German Ninth Army, which was stationed between Berlin and Stettin. Dietrich's mission there was, to all appearances, to help the Ninth Army prevent the Red Army from trapping two German armies on the Baltic coast of Pomerania. He arrived behind the Ninth Army in the first week of February and, probably to enhance the belief that the rest of the Sixth SS Panzer Army was arriving in that sector, was actually seen to be making a plan for operations in the Stargard area against the Soviet Second Guards Tank Army.

In reality Dietrich's six panzer divisions were heavily concealed in and around the Bakony Forest of Hungary, awaiting orders to move into a position between lakes Balaton and Velenzca. The fact that Dietrich was behind Ninth Army was, no doubt, reflected in Ultra, which gave rise to the assumption by military analysts in London, Moscow, and Washington that he would attack there. How it became apparent that Dietrich and his army then moved from Pomerania to Moravská Ostrava is not clear, but it was military deception usage to suggest that a prominent general was anywhere and everywhere except at his true location. It is probable, therefore, that when Dietrich vanished from his location behind Ninth Army, the suggestion was put about by the German deception organization, which had shown itself to be effective before the Ardennes battle, that he was relocating at Moravská Ostrava. That made sense, for there was need for such an army in Army Group Center, which was badly under strength.

On February 22 Dietrich attended a conference with Hitler and the group commanders for the south and southeast. The code name of this operation, which involved three armies, was *Fruelingserwachen*—"awakening of spring"—and its purpose was to put greater distance between the Russians and the Nagykanizsa oil fields of Hungary. A subsidiary purpose was the destruction of three Soviet armies and one Bulgarian army. Neither the presence of Dietrich nor his army was detected when the army moved into its jump-off position between lakes Balaton and Velencza on March 5, and when they did jump off, the Russians, expecting as they were to meet Dietrich much farther north, received a severe fright. Their casualties were heavy, and if the German counteroffensive failed, it did so not because of Marshal Tolbukhin's generalship, but because of poor terrain conditions: so secret was *Fruelingserwachen* that Dietrich was forbidden to make a terrain reconnaissance before the attack and thus advanced in the belief that the ground over which he was to fight would be frozen hard.

In fact it proved to be wet and marshy, and as a consequence 147 of his tanks sank up to their turrets in the deep mud. Fifteen of them were Royal Tigers, seventy-ton tanks equipped with the eighty-eight-

mm gun. The attack then collapsed, and the Red Army, having recovered from its surprise, made a counteroffensive that resulted in
the capture of Vienna on April 13.

If there was an Allied deception, and its motive was to keep the
Russians out of Vienna and enable the Allied armies in Italy to capture
it first, as Stalin suggested, then it failed in its purpose, for on that
date the nearest army in the west, Patton's Third, was at Jena in
eastern Germany while the nearest army in Italy, the British Eighth,
was still in the Po Valley preparing to cross the Julian Alps.

APPENDIX I

On June 6, 1968, the day after the funeral, *The Times* published a bittersweet letter by "C's" leading "Honourable Correspondent," Sir Rex Benson, Stewart Menzies's cousin by marriage, colleague, and closest friend. It read:

SIR STEWART MENZIES

Lieutenant-Colonel Sir Rex Benson writes:

Much has been written and no doubt more will come from those who were closely associated with Stewart Menzies during his 35 years of invaluable professional work in the Secret Intelligence Service, which, commencing in 1915, lasted up to his retirement in 1951.

Stewart went out to France with the British Expeditionary Force in 1914 as a subaltern in the 2nd Life Guards—an "Old Contemptible" as they were later named. He earned rapid distinction winning the M.C., but his unusual qualifications were soon recognized in 1915 when he was seconded from his regiment and started his long career in the Secret Intelligence Service at G.H.Q., as a result of which he eventually became "C" between the two wars.

As a boy at Eton from 1904 to 1908 he and his elder brother Keith joined up with my elder brother Guy and myself and spent four blissful years, seeing each other and messing together daily under the tutelage of Edward Impey, an almost ideal housemaster, who, apart from his uncanny knowledge of youth, was always prepared to defend his boys from any unjust attack from whatever quarter. Impey had a profound love and admiration for the works of Kipling and Co. and Kim. He was wont frequently to read out and quote to us as youngsters. He never—and quite justifiably—had a high opinion of our scholastic abilities, but it was from him that we learnt discipline, the value of initiative and leadership.

On the playing fields Stewart was a beautiful athlete, winning the steeplechase, probably the most coveted race to win at Eton. As a football player he captained the XI. He was also Master of the Beagles and President of "Pop"—the Eton Society. He had a friendly, happy disposition, not easily ruffled, and a good judgment, which developed as he got older.

He had a habit of plying you with questions and like "Kim" of "acquiring knowledge" which he put to good use in his later professional life; but he rarely imparted his observations to any but his intimate friends, keeping them to himself for future reference.

After he left Eton his mother married my uncle, Sir George Holford, and we both spent several of our leaves from the Army, which we joined about the same time, hunting with the Duke of Beaufort's Hounds from Weston-birt. Stewart looked on the Duke's country as his home and it was only last year after a bad fall out hunting that he began to lose his health and his zest for life.

He will be sadly missed by the few of us whose nostalgic memories of him go back to our boyhood and by his devoted wife Audrey, who looked after him during the few years of his life as his energy began to fail.

> And we all praise famous men—
> Ancients of the College;
> For they tried to teach us common sense—
> Tried to teach us common sense—
> Truth and God's Own Common Sense
> Which is more than knowledge!

SOURCES, NOTES, AND BIBLIOGRAPHY

CHAPTER ONE

[1] The information concerning Graham Menzies's personal and business affairs was derived from the following sources: interviews with Mrs. Joan Lindsay, William D. G. Menzies's daughter-in-law; Mrs. James Lees-Milne, a first cousin of Stewart Menzies; Michael S. Moss, author of *The Making of Scotch Whisky* (Edinburgh: James & James, 1981), and also the archivist of Glasgow University; an interview with Mr. Moss; a letter from Brian Spiller, historian to the Distillers Company Limited, to ACB, May 28, 1971; David Bremner, *The Industries of Scotland* (Edinburgh: 1869); Alred Barnard, *The Whisky Distilleries of the United Kingdom*; DCL Histories Series: *Caledonian Distillery*, Haymarket, Edinburgh; the contents of Graham Menzies's will filed at the Scottish Record Office, Edinburgh; and the Blairgowrie, Perth, and Dundee *Advertiser* newspapers.

[2] D. P. Menzies, *The "Red and White" Book of Menzies* (Plean, Stirlingshire: privately printed, 1908).

[3] Information concerning the Wilson brothers' business and personal affairs obtained from Hull Public Library, copies of documents entitled: *Taylor, Ellermans: A Wealth of Shipping*, pp. 247–51; Thomas, *Pioneer Shipowners*, pp. 61–67; C. A. Manning Press, *Yorkshire Leaders, Social & Political* (Leeds: McCorquodale, 1892), pp. 226–27; P. M. Pattinson, article in *The Banyan Tree*, journal of the East Yorkshire Family History Society, no. 8, 1980–1981; monograph, "Thomas Wilson: A Mystery Resolved," *anon.*

[4] Randolph S. Churchill, *Winston S. Churchill*, vol. 2, *Young Statesman* (Boston: Houghton Mifflin, 1967), p. 192.

[5] *The Hull Times*, February 12, 1887. All quotations from that source unless otherwise stated.

[6] *The Dictionary of National Biography* (London: Oxford University Press, 1917), supplement, January 1890–1911.

[7] Phillip Mason, *The English Gentleman* (London: Deutsch, 1982), p. 21; Christopher Hollis, *Eton: A History* (London: Hollis & Carter, 1960); and C.R.L. Fletcher, *Edmond Warre, D.D., C.B., C.V.O*, sometime headmaster and provost of Eton College (London: Murray, 1922), p. 214.

[8] Bernard Darwin, *The World That Fred Made* (London: Chatto & Windus, 1955), p. 117. Interview with Lawrence Impey, England, 1984. Interviews with the Eton College Librarian, Paul Quarrie, 1984.

[9] Martin Green, *Children of the Sun* (New York: Basic Books, 1976), p. 116.

[10] Eton College *Glossary*, 1924 edition.

[11] Shane Leslie, *The End of a Chapter* (London: Constable, 1916), p. 41.

[12] *Regimental Standing Orders: The Household Cavalry* (London: Regimental Headquarters, Household Cavalry, 1956).

[13] Interview with Mrs. Joan Lindsay, Laird of Hallyburton, April 1, 1983.

[14] Scottish Records Office: declaration in respect of J. G. Menzies by the Forfarshire Commission, May 14, 1912.

[15] *The Ladies Pictorial*, July 27, 1912.

[16] *The Yorkshire Herald*, July 18, 1912.

[17] PRO, London: FO 371/25986.

[18] Barbara Tuchman, *The Proud Tower* (New York: Macmillan, 1962), p. 14.

[19] *Griffith's Club Guide*, 1907.

[20] For a full account of the involvement of the De La Warr and Lutyens families in Theosophism, see Mary Lutyens, *Krishnamurti: The Years of Awakening* (London: Rider, 1984), p. 21 *et seq.*

[21] All details regarding Rex Benson's journey to and sojourn in India from his unpublished journals, c. 1904–1914, and interviews with his son, David Benson, Singleton, Sussex, 1984 and 1987.

[22] Household Cavalry archives, Combermere Barracks, Windsor, Great Britain: recollections by F. W. Buckley.

[23] William Manchester, *The Arms of Krupp, 1857–1968* (London: Michael Joseph, 1969), p. 325.

[24] PRO, London: Second Life Guards war diary, file no. WO/95 1155.

[25] The reference to the Maggi soup advertisements is in Imperial War Museum, British Expeditionary Force, GHQ 1b section: bulletin for October 4, 1914.

[26] R. A. Lloyd, *A Trooper With the Tins* (London: Hamish Hamilton, 1926), pp. 110–14.

[27] Household Cavalry archives, Combermere Barracks, Windsor, Great Britain: diaries of Lord Tweedmouth, entry for October 23, 1914.

[28] *Ibid.*

[29] *Ibid.*

[30] Imperial War Museum, archives branch, London: document of unknown provenance, "Adolf Hitler: Baptism of Fire," IWM ref. no. DS/Misc Reel 1.

[31] Eugene Davidson, *The Making of Adolf Hitler* (New York: Macmillan, 1977), p. 74.

[32] Sir George Arthur, *The Story of the Household Cavalry* (London: Newnes, 1934), pp. 101–103.

[33] PRO, London: Second Life Guards war diary, file no. WO/95 1155. Letter beginning "Dear General," dated October 16, 1923, on Dorchester House notepaper.

[34] Arthur, pp. 101–103.

[35] Manchester, p. 377.

[36] Lloyd, p. 102.

[37] Interview with General Sir James Marshall-Cornwall, London, February 1984.

[38] This paper is in the Household Cavalry Library at Combermere Barracks, Windsor, England, and is part of a collection of descriptions by officers and troopers of the regiment's part in the First Battle of Ypres.

[39] Tweedmouth diaries, *op. cit.*, and statement by SGM in conversation with his son-in-law, Captain Brian Bell.

[40] SGM papers.

[41] *Ibid.*

[42] Rex Benson diaries and journals, 1904–1914.

[43] This incident is referred to in the official history of the Essex Yeomanry in World War I, a privately printed volume found by the author at Ypres Public Library. Almost certainly the volume may be obtained through a major British library.

[44] Imperial War Museum, London: Kirke diaries, entry for March 2, 1916.

[45] SGM related the fact of his gassing to his son-in-law, Captain Brian Bell. Information concerning the use of gas on May 25, 1915, derives from PRO, London: Second Life Guards war diary, file no. WO/106/389 051901. This report appears to bear the initials "SGM."

CHAPTER TWO

[1] James Marshall-Cornwall, *Wars & Rumours of Wars: A Memoir* (London: Leo Cooper/ Secker & Warburg, 1984), p. 32. For a more detailed discussion of the Charteris episode see also J. M.-C., *Haig as Military Commander* (London: Batsford, 1973), p. 135 *et seq.* All quotations relating to the Charteris affair from these sources unless otherwise stated.

[2] Sir Paul Dukes, *The Story of 'ST 25'* (London: 1938), p. 35.

[3] Archives of the Intelligence Corps, Templer Barracks, Ashford, Kent, Great Britain: anonymous poem by an officer of GHQ 1b entitled "Just a Minute," c. Spring 1917.

[4] National Archives, old military records branch, Washington, D.C.: Central Special Intelligence Bureau, MI-5(F), "Preventive Intelligence Duties in War," published as IP book 19, April 1918, in file 11013–21, August 5, 1918. All quotations regarding NPI from that source unless otherwise stated.

[5] Archives of the Intelligence Corps, Ashford, Kent, Great Britain: an untitled paper on World War I intelligence written by Major R.M.C. Woolrych c. 1940.

[6] R. J. Drake, "History of Intelligence, British Expeditionary Force, France, from January 1917 to April 1919," filed as WO/106/45 at the archives department, Intelligence Corps, Templer Barracks, Ashford, Kent, Great Britain. Hereafter referred to as Drake report.

[7] Brigadier General John Charteris, *At GHQ* (London: Cassell, 1931), p. 261. All quotations relating to Charteris and U.S. intelligence from that source unless otherwise stated.

[8] National Archives, old military records, Washington, D.C.: record group 120, "Moreno Papers," letter Drake to Quekemeyer concerning Angelo Damoulakis, dated November 1, 1917. All quotations about the Damoulakis incident from that source unless otherwise stated.

[9] National Archives, diplomatic branch, Washington, D.C.: papers of Edward Bell, Office of the Counsellor, U.S. Embassy, London, item no. 800/M 341 in the "Secret File."

[10] "G.S.O.," *G.H.Q.* (London: Allan, 1920), p. 239.

[11] SGM papers, "Extracts from 'Particulars of Service Intelligence Duties during the war,' rendered upon Brevet-Major S. G. Menzies, D.S.O., M.C., General Staff (I), General Head-quarters."

[12] Imperial War Museum, archives branch, London: letter from R. J. Drake to S. Payne Best, dated September 18, 1947, in the S. Payne Best collection.

[13] Winston S. Churchill, *The Great War*, vol. 3, p. 1376.

[14] Letter with enclosure from Captain A. C. Turner, intelligence officer, H.Q. Base Section 3, Service of Supply, American Expeditionary Force, Goring Hotel, London, to assistant chief of staff G-2 SOS., AEF., dated June 10, 1918: "Information re Billing Case." In record group 120, Records of American Expeditionary Force to France, secret service section, item no. 138.1. All quotations from that source unless otherwise stated.

[15] Robert Cecil, " 'C's' War," in *Intelligence and National Security Review*, May 1986.

[16] National Archive, diplomatic branch, Washington, D.C.: papers of Edward Bell, letter from Bell to Leland Harrison, chief of the Office of Counsellor, January 14, 1919.

[17] *Ibid.*, letter from Bell to L. Lanier Winslow, dated July 23, 1919.

[18] National Archives, old military records branch, Washington, D.C.: record group 165, telegram by General Marlborough Churchill, dated November 22, 1920, in record group 165, MID 9771-945-52.

[19] Sir J. W. Wheeler-Bennett, *King George VI* (New York: St. Martin's Press, 1958), pp. 501–502.

[20] For the origin of these epithets, see the jacket copy of: Anthony Read and David Fisher, *Colonel Z: The Secret Life of a Master of Spies* (London: Hodder & Stoughton, 1984).

[21] For a comprehensive expression of Churchill's anti-Bolshevik opinions, which he never really modified, see Chapter 24, "The Poison Peril from the East," in Martin Gilbert, *Winston S. Churchill*, vol. 4, *The Stricken World, 1916–1922* (Boston: Houghton-Mifflin, 1975), beginning at p. 412.

[22] This report was obtained from U.S., not British, files, although it was originated by a British agency. It is in National Archives, Washington, D.C.: USMID 9771-188-2, Directorate of Intelligence, special report no. 3, "Indian & Egyptian Conspirators in England and the Remedy," July 1919. All quotations relating to the fedais and the Countess De La Warr from that source unless otherwise stated.

[23] Information from Robin Cecil.

[24] Martin Gilbert, *Winston S. Churchill*, vol. 4, pp. 422–25.

[25] Claire Sheridan, *The Naked Truth* (New York: Harper & Brothers, 1928), p. 153. All quotations from that source unless otherwise stated. See also the U.S. military intelligence file on Claire Sheridan, record group 165, National Archives, old military records branch, Washington, D.C. This file deals with Ms. Sheridan's association with Kamenev and Trotsky, and also contains the evidence that Ms. Sheridan became a Soviet fellow-traveller.

[26] Christopher Andrews, *Secret Service: The Making of the British Intelligence Community* (London: Heinemann, 1985), p. 295 *et seq.*

[27] Interview with Commander W. F. Dunderdale, Popham, Hampshire, Great Britain, 1968.

[28] Interview with Guy Vansittart, Mayfair, London, 1984.

[29] SGM papers.

[30] Central Intelligence Agency, Washington, D.C.: historical study entitled "The Trust."

[31] There is a major file on the 1933 Vickers case in PRO, London.

[32] Churchill College Archives Centre, Cambridge, Great Britain: untitled document, 21 pages, dated December 2, 1944, filed as "Denn 1/4." Hereafter referred to as the Denniston report.

[33] Brigadier General C. G. Higgins, "Whites's," an article in *The Field*, July 8, 1939.

[34] SGM papers: one of a collection of anecdotes by SGM in the possession of his daughter, Mrs. Fiona Bell. Captain Bell stated that SGM told him that this incident occurred at Dorchester House in 1923.

[35] Interviews with Dowager Countess Sylvia De La Warr, London, April 1984.

[36] Somerset House, London: last will and testament of Sir George Lindsay Holford, April 27, 1927. All statements and quotations relating to Holford's estate from that source unless otherwise stated.

[37] See *Wiltshire Chronicle* and *Bath Chronicle & Herald*, November–December 1928, for the reports of this major event in the social history of Wiltshire and Gloucestershire.

[38] Interviews with Countess De La Warr.

[39] *Kelly's Handbook of Distinguished People*, 1938.

[40] *Evening Standard*, London, November 16, 1932.

CHAPTER THREE

[1] Elizabeth Monroe, *Philby of Arabia* (New York: Pitman, 1973), p. 17. All quotations in section 1 relating to the Philby family from that source unless otherwise stated.

[2] Andrew Sinclair, *The Red and the Blue* (Boston: Little Brown, 1986), p. 39.

[3] Robert Rhodes James (ed.), *Chips: The Diaries of Sir Henry Channon* (London: Weidenfeld & Nicolson, 1967), p. 36.

[4] Frances Donaldson, *Edward VIII*, pp. 203–204.

[5] Kenneth Young (ed.), *The Diaries of Sir Robert Bruce Lockhart*, vol. 1, 1915–1938 (London: Macmillan, 1973), p. 263.

[6] *Documents on German Foreign Policy* (London: HMSO), series vii, vol. 4, document no. 8015/E576522-4. All quotations regarding the duke of Coburg's talks with King Edward VIII from that source unless otherwise stated.

[7] Fritz Hesse, *Hitler & the English* (London: Wingate, 1954), pp. 21–23.

[8] Albert Speer, *Inside the Third Reich* (New York: Avon, 1970), p. 133.

[9] Donaldson, p. 218.

[10] Joachim von Ribbentrop, *Memoirs* (London: 1954), p. 70.

[11] Donaldson, p. 264.

[12] M.R.D. Foot, *SOE in France* (London: HMSO, 1966), p. 3.

[13] The biographies of Stevens and Payne Best are found in National Archives, microfilm

reading room, Washington, D.C.: RSHA records, T175, Sicherheitsdienst interrogation of S. Payne Best and Captain R. H. Stevens, microfilm reel R649, frame 216, p. 87. All quotations from that source unless otherwise stated.

[14] William J. Donovan papers, U.S. Army War College, Fort Carlisle, Penn.: telegram for "Q" from British Security Coordination, New York, dated March 26, 1942; memo from J. C. Wiley to WJD, dated July 16, 1942; letter from Charles H. Ellis to WJD, dated September 11, 1942. All documents relate to proposals for a similar subsidy to be paid to the Archduke Otto's movement by the U.S. government.

[15] PRO, London: Cab 104/43, "C" to General Sir Hastings Ismay, dated November 15, 1938.

[16] *Ibid.*

[17] Interview with Commander K.H.S. Cohen, London, April 1983.

[18] Imperial War Museum, archives branch, London: S. Payne Best collection, letter from SPB to Dansey, dated October 11, 1946.

[19] David Dilks (ed.), *The Cadogan Diaries, 1938–1945* (New York: Putnam, 1972), p. 238. This statement is made in an editor's note to Cadogan's diary entries on the subject of Goerdeler for the mid-December 1938 period.

[20] Andrew Boyle, *The Climate of Treason* (London: Hutchinson, 1979), p. 93.

[21] PRO, London: Cab 27/627, "Summary of Information from Secret Sources," by G. Jebb, dated January 19, 1939.

[22] PRO, London: FO 800/270, letter from Cadogan to Henderson, dated February 29, 1939.

[23] Hinsley *et al.*, vol. 1, p. 46; and PRO, London: FO 371/21732.

[24] For a full account of the Schmidt incident, see David Kahn, *Kahn on Codes* (New York: Macmillan, 1983).

[25] Gustav Bertrand, *Enigme* (Paris: Plon, 1965), p. 64.

[26] C. Andrews and D. Dilks (eds.), *The Missing Dimension*, article by Jean Stengers entitled "Enigma: The French, the Poles and the British, 1931–1940," p. 126 *et seq.*

[27] *Ibid.*

[28] See Peter Calvocoressi, *Top Secret Ultra* (New York: Ballantine, 1980), p. 117 *et seq.*

[29] Interview with Commander W. F. Dunderdale, New York, January 1986. All quotations relating to the transportation of the Polish equipment and data to London from that source unless otherwise stated.

[30] Bertrand, p. 64.

[31] Harold Nicolson (ed.), *Diaries & Letters, 1930–1939* (New York: Atheneum, 1966), p. 415.

[32] PRO, London: FO 371/23686, minute from R. A. Butler to Cadogan, dated August 25, 1939.

[33] National Archives, German military records section, record group 165: final report of the interrogation of Walter Friedrich Schellenberg, c. July 1945; and David Boyle, *With Ardours Manifold* (London: Hutchinson, 1959), pp. 286–89. Boyle states that he went to Berlin through a tip from Otto Kiep, the former German representative in London of the council for nonintervention in the Spanish civil war, to Boyle through Theo Kordt, the German charges d'affaires in London. This may well have been so and Boyle's version is not incompatible with the statement by Schellenberg concerning Jahnke's attempts to arrange a meeting between Hitler and "an English intelligence agent."

[34] Hinsley *et al.*, vol. 1, p. 57, footnote. It is noted that, as Hinsley states, the Foreign Office files relating to Venlo have been closed until the year 2015 because "they contain references to technical matters and to individuals." Whether they contain anything relating to policy matters is not clear from Hinsley's statements.

[35] John Colville, *The Fringes of Power: 10 Downing Street Diaries 1939–1955* (New York: Norton, 1985), p. 40, entry for Friday, October 13, 1939.

[36] Walter Schellenberg, *The Schellenberg Memoirs*, (London: Deutsch, 1956), p. 89.

[37] National Archives, diplomatic branch, Washington, D.C.: 862.002 Adolf Hitler/211, telegram from the U.S. embassy in Berlin to the State Department, dated November 9, 1939. All quotations regarding the Munich incident from that source unless otherwise stated.

[38] All statements about assassination in this paragraph are found in National Archives, modern military records branch, Washington, D.C.: *Reichsführer SS und Chef der Deutschen Polizei*, microfilm reel R649, frame 216, p. 87. Hereafter referred to as Himmler report.

[39] Interview with SGM.

[40] *The New York Times*, November 28, 1939.

CHAPTER FOUR

[1] H. R. Trevor-Roper, *The Philby Affair: Espionage, Treason, and Secret Service* (London: Kimber, 1968), p. 72. All quotations attributed to Trevor-Roper are from that source unless otherwise stated.

[2] P. J. Stead, *Second Bureau* (London: Evans, 1959), p. 28.

[3] The papers of Sir Eugen Millington-Drake (John Henry Vandersteganl), in the custody of the Macnaghten Memorial Library at Eton College. Having presided locally over British diplomatic and intelligence operations concerning the *Graf Spee*, EM-D collected documentation from all the nations and individuals involved, including the Germans and the Uruguayans, presenting it in a privately printed book entitled *The Drama of Graf Spee & The Battle of the River Plate*. All quotations from that source unless otherwise stated.

[4] Churchill College, Cambridge: Cadogan ms. diary, entry for December 23, 1939.

[5] Unless otherwise stated, all quotations involving "C" and the German invasion of Norway derive from PRO, London: Prem 1/435.

[6] *The Memoirs of General Lord Ismay* (New York: Viking, 1960), p. 116.

[7] Winston S. Churchill, *The Second World War*, vol. 1, *The Gathering Storm* (London: Cassell, 1948), p. 594.

[8] Colville, *The Fringes of Power*, p. 121.

[9] Gilbert, *Winston S. Churchill*, vol. 6, p. 314.

[10] Cadogan ms. diary, entry for May 16, 1940.

[11] Colville, p. 141.

[12] P.M.H. Bell, *A Certain Eventuality* (London: Saxon, 1974), p. 31.

[13] Gilbert, p. 358.

[14] Colville, p. 144.

[15] *Hansard*, June 18, 1940, cols. 51–61.

[16] Warren F. Kimball (ed.), *Churchill & Roosevelt: The Complete Correspondence*, vol. 6, *Alliance Emerging* (Princeton: Princeton University Press, 1984), p. 40, item no. C-11x.

[17] *Ibid.*, p. 41, item no. R-5x.

[18] *Ibid.*, p. 23.

[19] *Ibid.*, p. 24.

[20] T. F. Troy, *Donovan and the CIA* (Washington, D.C.: CIA, 1981), p. 31 *et seq.* See also the CIA's "OSS & British Intelligence." These two documents are closely related and hereafter referred to as the Troy report.

[21] Interviews with Sir William S. Stephenson, Bermuda, January 1986.

[22] Troy report, *op. cit.*

[23] U.S. Army War College, Fort Carlisle: Donovan papers, vol. 34.

[24] Churchill College, Cambridge: journals of Admiral John Godfrey. Hereafter referred to as the Godfrey journals.

[25] Troy report, *op. cit.* All quotations concerning Donovan's tour are taken from that source unless otherwise stated.

[26] Godfrey journals.

[27] U.S. Army War College, Fort Carlisle: Donovan papers, vol. 34, letter from WJD to SGM, dated August 27, 1940.

[28] *Ibid.*

[29] Colville, p. 139.

[30] C. Andrews, *Secret Service: The Making of the British Intelligence Community* (London: Heinemann, 1985), p. 448.

[31] Colville, p. 210.

[32] In the duke of Windsor affair, all quotations from: PRO, London: FO 371/24249; Michael Bloch, *Operation Willi: The Plot to Kidnap the Duke of Windsor, July 1940* (London: Weidenfeld & Nicolson, 1984); National Archives, modern military records branch, Washington, D.C.: final report of interrogation of W. F. Schellenberg, *op. cit.* All quotations from these sources unless otherwise stated.

[33] Gilbert, *Winston S. Churchill*, vol. 6, p. 705.

[34] FDR Library, Hyde Park, N.Y.: see diaries of Adolf Berle for September and October 1940 for frequent discussions of the duke and duchess and their pro-Nazi activities.

[35] Colville, p. 205.

[36] James Leutz (ed.), *The London Journal of General Raymond E. Lee, 1940–1941* (Boston: Little, Brown, 1971), pp. 144–45.

[37] All information regarding "C's" sources in Berlin from National Archives, modern military records branch, Washington, D.C.: final report of the interrogation of Schellenberg.

[38] F. H. Hinsley, *British Intelligence in the Second World War*, vol. 1. p. 434. All predictions by Churchill and others regarding German intentions toward Russia are taken from this source unless otherwise stated.

[39] All quotations relating to the Polish service in Poland at this time from National Archives, modern military records branch, Washington, D.C.: final report of the interrogation of Schellenberg.

[40] PRO, London: Cab 120/746, Churchill to Ismay, dated August 5, 1940.

[41] Colville, p. 298.

[42] Robert Bruce Lockhart diaries, 1939–1962, p. 62.

[43] See Foot, *SOE in France*, pp. 7–8, for the fuller official account of the formation of SOE from which the author's account was derived in part.

[44] Kim Philby, *My Silent War*, p. 2.

[45] *The Memoirs of Lord Gladwyn*, p. 101.

[46] Cadogan ms. diary entry for September 3, 1940.

[47] All data relating to the London blitz, and especially those incidents involving SIS headquarters, were gathered from the Civil Defence files, which are held by the Westminister City Library, Buckingham Palace Road.

[48] U.S. Navy Archives Center, Washington Navy Yard, Washington, D.C.: paper by Office of Naval Intelligence, "Espionage, Sabotage, Conspiracy: German and Russian Operations 1940 to 1945." Excerpts from the files of the German naval staff and from other captured German documents, 190 pages, declassified February 15, 1972. This document discusses how operation *Shark* replaced *Sealion*, the intention being to provide cover for the transfer of the German armies in the west to the east to undertake Barbarossa, the invasion of Russia.

[49] Kimball, *Churchill & Roosevelt*, vol. 1, p. 78, item C-34x.

[50] Epigram by Sir William Stephenson, in introduction to *Hitler's Secret War in South America, 1939–1949* (Louisiana State University Press, 1981).

[51] All quotations concerning Menzies-Popov are taken from Dusko Popov, *Spy/Counterspy* (London: Weidenfeld & Nicolson, 1974), p. 58.

[52] Interviews with Colonel F. H. Cowgill, Dorset, Great Britain, April 1983.

CHAPTER FIVE

[1] PRO, London: Cab 120/767, dated August 21, 1941.

[2] SGM papers.

[3] *Ibid.*

[4] Letter, from D/CSS to CSS, dated January 6, 1941. In private possession. All quotations between Vivian and Menzies from that source unless otherwise stated.

[5] H. R. Trevor-Roper, "The Philby Affair," in *Encounter*, April 1968, pp. 27–29.

[6] Philby, *My Silent War*, p. 46.

[7] Benson diary, entry for February 6, 1941.

[8] *Ibid.*, entry for February 21, 1941.

[9] *Ibid.*, entry for February 26, 1941.

[10] Warren F. Kimball, *The Most Unsordid Act: Lend-Lease, 1939–1941* (Baltimore: Johns Hopkins, 1969), p. 186.

[11] Benson papers: all quotations relating to Benson's appointment and instructions taken from that source unless otherwise stated.

[12] Donovan papers: the intelligence agreement excerpted from the military conclusions of the ABC-1 staff conversations in Washington, D.C., March 1941.

[13] Benson diary, entry for May 1, 1941. All Magic texts relating to Pearl Harbor are found in U.S. Department of Defense, *The "Magic" Background of Pearl Harbor* (Washington, D.C.: Government Printing Office, 1977), vol. 1 (February 14–May 12, 1941), section 61, "Germany Plans to Attack Russia," pp. 21–22. The texts are in *ibid.*, Magic no. 75.

[14] Benson diary, entry for May 13, 1941.

[15] *Ibid.*, entry for May 20, 1941.

[16] F. H. Hinsley *et al.*, *British Intelligence in World War II: Its Influence on Strategy & Operations*, vol. 1, p. 263.

[17] PRO, London: Cab 120/789, letter from Jebb to Ismay, dated March 10, 1941.

[18] *Ibid.*

[19] Cadogan ms. diaries, March 31, 1941.

[20] Information regarding *Shark* and *Harpoon* found in U.S. Navy, Washington Naval Yard, historical section, Washington, D.C.: ONI, "Espionage, Sabotage, Conspiracy, Germany-Russia, 1939–1945." All references to *Shark* and *Harpoon* taken from that document unless otherwise stated.

[21] Hinsley *et al.*, p. 443.

[22] *Ibid.*

[23] In the Crete operations, see D. D. Eisenhower Library, Abilene, Kansas: paper entitled "The Use of 'U' in the Mediterranean and Northwest African Theatres of War," by Group Captain R. H. Humphreys, October 1945; Churchill, *The Second World War*, vol. 3, p. 240.

[24] PRO, London: Prem 3/22/44, July 10, 1941.

[25] Churchill, vol. 3, p. 319.

[26] PRO, London: Prem 3/395/2, "Prime Minister's Warning to M. Stalin About the German Danger, April 1944," ff. 36–40, undated.

[27] Hinsley *et al.*, vol. 1, p. 456.

[28] Colville, *The Fringes of Power*, pp. 385–86.

[29] Major Graham Donald, "The Story of Rudolf Hess," in *The Journal of the Royal Observer Corps*, October 1942.

[30] James Douglas-Hamilton, *Motive for a Mission* (Edinburgh: Mainstream, 1979), pp. 158–65.

[31] PRO, London: Prem 3/219/7, letter and report from the duke of Hamilton to the prime minister, May 18, 1941.

[32] Douglas-Hamilton, *Motive for a Mission*, p. 177.

[33] Colville, p. 386.

[34] Robert E. Sherwood, *Roosevelt & Hopkins: An Intimate History* (New York: Harper, 1948), p. 294.

[35] Colville, p. 387.

[36] Douglas-Hamilton, p. 180.

[37] PRO, London: Prem 3/219/7, report on the custody and movements of Rudolph Hess, by General Sir A. Hunter, director of prisoners of war, f. 141, May 22, 1941.

[38] Douglas-Hamilton, p. 197.

[39] Robert E. Sherwood, *Roosevelt & Hopkins*, p. 294.

[40] Cadogan ms. diaries, entries for May 12 and June 11.

[41] Churchill, *The Second World War*, vol. 3, p. 49; see also PRO, London: Prem 3/219/7, f. 174, minute for the Secretary of State for Air, April 6, 1945.

[42] Gilbert, *Winston S. Churchill*, vol. 6, pp. 983, 1040.

[43] Hinsley *et al.*, vol. 2, pp. 59–60.

[44] Office of the Chief of Military History, United States Army, Washington, D.C.: translation of *History of the Great Patriotic War of the Soviet Union*, vol. 1, *Preparation and Unleashing of the War by Imperialistic Powers*, p. 17.

[45] British government paper: "Treaty for an Alliance in the War Against Hitlerite Germany and Her Associates in Europe and Providing also for Collaboration and Mutual Assistance Thereafter," London, May 26, 1942. Published by HMSO, 1942.

[46] Hinsley *et al.*, vol. 2, pp. 58–62.

[47] *Ibid.*

[48] Colville, p. 439.

[49] T. F. Troy, *Donovan & the CIA*, p. 42.

[50] The report is in the Donovan bound files at Fort Carlisle, Penn., vol. 34.

[51] Churchill, vol. 3, p. 97.

[52] Benson diaries, entry for May 27, 1941.

[53] Anthony Cave Brown, *Donovan: The Last Hero* (New York: Times Books, 1982), p. 171.

[54] Troy, p. 57.

[55] Donovan papers: Dansey to WJD, July 15, 1941, in "Congratulations" file, microfilm reel 32, U.S. Army War College, Fort Carlisle.

[56] Donovan papers: W. D. Whitney to WJD, "Detailed memorandum of our talk with Stallforth at 1647 30th Street, N.W., at 5:00 P.M."

[57] Donovan papers: see "Exhibits," microfilm reel 101, U.S. Army War College, Fort Carlisle.

[58] PRO, London: Cab 120/815, dated November 1941. All quotes pertaining to Ismay memorandum are from this source unless otherwise noted.

[59] Donovan papers: OSS history section file "W" for interviews with Lieutenant Colonel Paul West.

[60] FDR Library, Hyde Park: Berle ms. diaries, entry for September 5, 1941.

[61] *Ibid.*, entry for September 27, 1941.

[62] *Ibid.*, entry date obscured.

[63] Donovan papers: note to FDR from WJD, dated December 12, 1941. See CIA file on the Donovan-Roosevelt correspondence, January 14, 1942, U.S. Army War College, Fort Carlisle.

[64] Kimball, *Churchill & Roosevelt*, p. 249.

[65] J. C. Masterman, *The Double-Cross System in the War of 1939 to 1945* (New Haven: Yale University Press, 1972), p. 79.

[66] *Ibid.*, pp. 196–97.

[67] *Ibid.*, pp. 80–81.

[68] U.S. Congress, PHI, part 37, Clausen investigation.

[69] U.S. Congress, PHI, part 35, Clausen investigation: letter from Kirk to Commandant, 14th Naval District, Pearl Harbor, dated October 14, 1941.

[70] *Ibid.*, p. 148: memorandum of the JAGD for secretary of war, dated September 14, 1945.

[71] *Op. cit.*

[72] Rear Admiral Edwin T. Layton *et al.*, *"And I was There:" Pearl Harbor and Midway —Breaking the Secrets* (New York: Morrow, 1985), p. 215.

[73] U.S. Congress, PHI, part 35, Clausen investigation, exhibit 8, p. 686 *et seq.*: "The following documents comprise intercepts obtained from British sources. They consist of 41 documents extending over the period 21 November 1941 to 22 December 1941."

[74] U.S. Congress, PHI, part 36, pp. 4335–36. Emphasis supplied to indicate that part of the signal derived from Ultra.

[75] *Ibid.*, p. 4337.

[76] *Ibid.*, telegram, from CSS to Jones.

[77] *Ibid.*, p. 4359.

[78] PRO, London: FO 371/27893, transcript of telephone call between FDR and WSC.

[79] Churchill, *The Second World War*, vol. 3, pp. 539–40.

CHAPTER SIX

[1] Robert Rhodes James (ed.), *Chips: The Diaries of Sir Henry Channon* (London: Weidenfeld & Nicolson, 1967), p. 316, entry for January 5, 1942.

[2] Kimball, *Roosevelt & Churchill*, vol. 1, editorial note about India on pp. 447–48.

[3] Berle diaries, entry for March 5, 1942.

[4] Interview with Sir James Marshall-Cornwall.

[5] Robert Bruce Lockhart, *Diaries, 1939–1962*, p. 242.

[6] Donovan papers: letter from Whitney to WJD about signation, dated April 16, 1942, microfilm reel 101.

[7] Interview with Otto C. Doering, Jr.

[8] Interview with I. J. Good.

[9] Ronald Lewin, *Ultra Goes to War* (London: Hutchison, 1971), p. 184.

[10] Hinsley *et al.*, vol. 2, p. 655.

[11] *Ibid.*, p. 657.

[12] Interview with Sir Stewart Milner-Barry.

[13] Hinsley *et al.*, vol. 2, p. 657.

[14] *Ibid.*, p. 26.

[15] Kimball, vol. 1, item C-32/1: letter from WSC to FDR, dated February 25, 1942.

[16] Hinsley *et al.*, vol. 2, p. 27.

[17] Bertrand, *Enigme*, p. 112. All statements relating to Bertrand's operations in 1942 from that source unless otherwise stated.

[18] Churchill College, Cambridge: memoir on GC&CS by Denniston, filed as document no. Denn 1/4, December 2, 1944.

[19] Brown, *Bodyguard of Lies*, p. 221. The fact of "C's" involvement was conveyed to the author in an interview with Sir Colin Gubbins, Tarbuth, Isle of Harris, Outer Hebrides, Scotland, August 1970.

[20] Final report, Schellenberg, *op. cit.*

[21] *Ibid.*

[22] Brown, p. 221.

[23] *Ibid.*

[24] Final report, Schellenberg, *op. cit.*

[25] Interview with Sir Patrick Reilly.

[26] Letter supplied by Reilly.

[27] PRO, London: Cab 120/57, Dill to Ismay, dated April 9, 1942.

[28] Berle diaries, entry for May 2, 1942.

[29] Eisenhower Library, Abilene: since only MacArthur's version of the security arrangements governing the use of Ultra by U.S. commanding generals has survived, that version is used here. It is known that Eisenhower received similar, if not identical, instructions. In any case, a letter from Marshall to Eisenhower relating to the use of Ultra, but dated May 1944, has been found, and the terms are not very different to the MacArthur version.

[30] F. W. Winterbotham, *The Ultra Secret* (New York: Harper & Row, 1975), pp. 90–91. All quotations attributed to WWW from that source unless otherwise stated.

[31] Hinsley *et al.*, vol. 2, p. 548.

[32] Philby, *My Silent War*, pp. 105–106.

[33] For the meeting between Groussard, Churchill, and "C," see P. H. Stead, *Second Bureau, op. cit.*

[34] PRO, London: Chiefs of Staff Committee, COS (42) 141st meeting, May 6, 1942; and 152nd meeting, May 16, 1942: memorandum by the chief of the General Staff, dated May 12, 1942.

[35] Foot, *SOE in France*, p. 231.

[36] PRO, London: Chiefs of Staff Committee, *op. cit.*

[37] Macmillan, *War Diaries*, p. 23.

[38] See Donovan microfilm, Lisbon–Washington cables, 1942, for a full account of the Solborg incident. All quotations from that source unless otherwise stated.

[39] Donovan papers, Torch file: memo from Buxton to Donovan, "North Africa Mission," dated July 9, 1942.

[40] Terence Robertson, *The Ship with Two Captains* (New York: Dutton, 1957), p. 108.

[41] *Ibid.*, p. 110.

[42] Eisenhower Library, Abilene: see Eisenhower diary for November–December 1942. All quotations relating to the Eisenhower–Giraud exchange from that source unless otherwise stated.

[43] Final report, Schellenberg, *op. cit.*

[44] Macmillan, p. 23.

[45] *Ibid.*

[46] All quotations relating to Gustav Bertrand drawn from his memoir, *Enigme.*

[47] Kimball, vol. 2, p. 7, message C-193.

[48] PRO, London: Cab 120/530, December 29 and 30, 1942.

[49] *Ibid.*

[50] Interview with Carleton Coon.

[51] From an after-action report by Coon. The passage was entitled "VIII: Postscript: The World After the War: OSS-SOE: The Invisible Empire." This was not in WJD's papers, nor in Coon's memoirs, *North Africa Story*, having been excised by the editor. Coon voluntarily sent this segment of what was his final operational report to the author.

[52] Brown, *Donovan: The Last Hero*, p. 271.

[53] Interview with Sir Patrick Reilly, Ramsden, Oxfordshire, April 1942.

[54] Winterbotham, *The Ultra Secret*, p. 99.

CHAPTER SEVEN

[1] Hinsley *et al.*, vol. 2, p. 4 and footnote.

[2] Churchill, *The Second World War*, vol. 2, *Their Finest Hour*, p. 337.

[3] Hinsley *et al.*: see app. 1, part 2, "Intelligence Bearing on Security of Ultra."

[4] Gilbert, *Winston S. Churchill*, vol. 6, p. 1243.

[5] PRO, London: Cab 122/242, corr. between British embassy and, with others, General W. S. Smith, secretary of the U.S. Joint Chiefs of Staff. All quotations about the Ultra/Magic leak taken from that source unless otherwise stated.

[6] Layton, *And I Was There*, p. 413.

[7] *Ibid.*

[8] Hinsley *et al.*, vol. 2, pp. 413–14; and see app. 1, part 2, "Intelligence Bearing on Security of Ultra."

[9] Benson diaries, entry for August 16, 1943.

[10] Hinsley *et al.*, vol. 2, pp. 645–46.

[11] Eisenhower Library, Abilene: diaries, entries for February 17 and April 17, 1943.

[12] Hinsley *et al.*, vol. 2, p. 647.

[13] *Ibid.*, p. 596.

[14] *Ibid.*, p. 648.

[15] Patrick Beesly, *Very Special Intelligence* (New York: Ballantine, 1977), p. 168.

[16] *News Chronicle*, London, July 29, 1943.

[17] The letter from Churchill to Eden is cited in the *Sunday Times* of December 9, 1979; and see Gilbert, *Winston S. Churchill*, vol. 7, pp. 729–30.

[18] Philby, *My Silent War*, pp. 62–63.

[19] *Ibid.*, pp. 64–65.

[20] Letter, Roald Dahl, dated October 4, 1985; and telephone interview.

[21] *Communism in India* (Government of India confidential publication, Delhi: 1932), pp. 17–18. Located at the India Office Archives, Lambeth, South London, 1983.

[22] Dahl interview.

[23] John Morton Blum, *The Price of Vision* (Boston: Houghton Mifflin, 1973), p. 358.

[24] Dahl letter, dated October 4, 1985, and telephone interviews.

[25] Churchill College, Cambridge: Wilkinson diaries.

[26] Benson ms. diaries, entry for December 25, 1943.

[27] *Ibid.*, entry for January 24, 1944.

[28] *Ibid.*, entry for February 3, 1944.

[29] Interviews with Ernest Cuneo.

[30] Untitled, unpublished ms. by Henry B. Hyde, New York, relating to his experiences as chief of OSS SI Algiers.

[31] Donovan papers: OSS historical section monograph entitled "The Algiers Office: Spanish Zone Operations," undated but c. 1944–1945.

[32] Note in OSS SI war diary, Operation Sussex, in modern military records branch at the National Archives, Washington, D.C.

[33] PRO, London: Cab 120/93, dated August 1, 1943.

[34] Gilbert, *Churchill*, vol. 7, p. 459.

[35] Donovan papers: OSS historical section interview with Colonel John Toulmin, chief, OSS Cairo, December 5, 1944. See vol. 3, T–Z.

[36] Donovan papers: decrypt captioned "Translation of XX-619 (London X1N-396)," undated but internal evidence shows that the conference opened on July 1, 1943.

[37] Larry Collins papers and interviews with Collins, June 1986. Note: For the purpose of his own writings, Collins undertook a long and thorough investigation of the Dericourt case. These findings, he subsequently passed to this author.

[38] Donovan papers: "Translation of XX-619."

[39] *Ibid.*

[40] Foot, *SOE in France*, p. 257.

[41] *Ibid.*, p. 303.

[42] Interview by Larry Collins with M. Buckmaster, a transcript being provided to this author.

[43] Foot, pp. 308–309.

[44] *Ibid.*, p. 278.

[45] *Ibid.*, p. 307.

[46] *Ibid.*, p. 308.

[47] Interview with Sir William Stephenson.

[48] Robert Marshall, "Wartime Spies and the Web of Deception," *The Listener*, May 1, 1986. Note: *The Listener* is a production of the BBC London.

[49] *Ibid.*

[50] Donovan papers (French files): copy of paper by General G. de Benouville *et al.* on clandestine conditions likely to be encountered in Germany after the Allied occupation. Hereafter referred to as Benouville report.

[51] Foot, p. 311.

[52] *Ibid.*

[53] Brown, *Bodyguard of Lies*, p. 322.

[54] R. V. Jones, *Most Secret War* (London: Hamish Hamilton, 1978), pp. 351–53. All quotations relating to the Frank and Thoma incidents from that source unless otherwise stated.

[55] The file on the V1's and V2's is one of the largest in the records of the War Cabinet Office during World War II. All data and quotations relating to the missiles was extracted from Cab 120/748 unless otherwise stated.

[56] For an account of Noah's Ark and Amniarix's exploit, see Jones, pp. 373–75.

[57] *Ibid.*

CHAPTER EIGHT

[1] Hinsley *et al.*, vol. 3, pp. 51–52.

[2] *Ibid.*, p. 480.

[3] Eisenhower Library, Abilene: SRH-026, letter from Marshall to Eisenhower, dated March 15, 1944.

[4] Unless otherwise stated, all quotations relating to the "Suicidex plan" taken from National Archives, modern military records branch, Washington, D.C.: OSS war diary, Sussex Operation.

[5] National Archives, modern military records branch, Washington, D.C.: OSS ETO SI war diary, vol. 3, p. 27.

[6] *Ibid.*, p. 49.

[7] Virginia Historical Institute, Richmond: operational diary of Ambassador D.K.E. Bruce, entry for August 13, 1944.

[8] PRO, London: JIC (43) 325 (U), August 1, 1943. All quotations concerning CX108 taken from that source unless otherwise stated.

[9] PRO, London: Cab 69/6, note by minister of economic warfare, dated January 11, 1944.

[10] PRO, London: Air 8/1749, letter from Glyn to Ismay, dated July 30, 1943; extract from minutes of Defence Committee, D.O. (43) 7th Mtg., dated August 2, 1943; minute from ACAS (I) to CAS, dated August 1, 1943.

[11] H.M.G. Lauwers, author of the epilogue to H. J. Giskes, *London Calling North Pole* (London: Kimber, 1953), p. 176.

[12] Patrick Howarth, *Intelligence Chief Extraordinary: The Life of the Ninth Duke of Portland*, p. 175.

[13] PRO, London: Cab 120/827, VCOS to deputy prime minister, dated December 1, 1943.

[14] PRO, London: Cab 69/6, note from minister of economic warfare, dated January 11, 1944. All statements attributed to Selborne from that source unless otherwise stated.

[15] PRO, London: Cab 120/827, P.M./44/1, memo from Eden to Churchill, dated January 5, 1944.

[16] PRO, London, Cab 120/827, minute from WSC to Ismay, dated February 10, 1944.

[17] Unless otherwise stated, all data and quotations relating to the Vermehrens are taken from Donovan papers, biography 440A, in "U.S. Government Biographical Records,

New York," February 11, 1944. Note: These biographical records consisted of the copy of the British security indexes sent to New York when OSS X2 became an authorized recipient of ISOS in 1942. They had been brought up to date by OSS X2 in New York. These are used for the purposes of this work because the British copy remained classified in 1986.

[18] Gilbert, vol. 5, *The Prophet of Truth*, p. 226.

[19] National Archives, modern military records branch, captured enemy documents section, Washington, D.C.: interrogation of Walter Friedrich Schellenberg, in record group 165 (records of the War Department general and special staffs), undated but c. July 1945, p. 65. All information and quotation relating to Schellenberg from that source unless otherwise stated.

[20] Chester Wilmot, *The Struggle for Europe* (London: Collins, 1965), p. 217.

[21] Gilbert, vol. 7, p. 760. All quotations by McCloy from that source unless otherwise stated.

[22] Eisenhower Library, Abilene: letter from Eisenhower to General Brehon B. Somervell, dated April 4, 1944.

[23] Arthur Bryant, *Triumph in the West: A History of the War Years Based on the Diaries of Field-Marshal Lord Alanbrooke, Chief of the Imperial General Staff* (New York: Doubleday, 1959), p. 152, entry for June 5, 1944.

[24] Washington National Records Center, Suitland, Maryland: record group 331, Med. Allied Air Force section, signal entitled "Enemy Appreciations of Planned Intentions," dated May 25, 1944.

[25] G. A. Harrison, *Cross-Channel Attack* (Washington, D.C.: Office of the Chief of Military History, 1950), p. 237.

[26] Bertrand, *Enigme*, p. 161 *et seq.* All quotations from that source unless otherwise stated.

[27] All statements and quotations regarding Canaris's visit to the Paris convent derived from interviews with Colonel Ollivier, the mother superior Sister Frede, and Commander Dunderdale.

[28] Harrison, p. 275.

[29] Interview with Anton Staubwasser; and his paper for General Speidel, "The Alert Problem during the Night of the Invasion, June 5–6, 1944."

[30] *Ibid.*

[31] *Ibid.*

[32] Harrison, appendix G, "Divisions Available to Germany on 6 June 1944," p. 471.

[33] Howarth, *Intelligence Officer Extraordinary*, p. 186.

[34] General W. Warlimont, *Inside Hitler's Headquarters*, p. 427.

[35] Interview with Sir Ronald Wingate, deputy chief of the London Controlling Section, the main deception bureau for the invasion. See also Sefton Delmer, *The Counterfeit Spy* (New York: Harper & Row, 1971). All statements attributed to Garbo are from Delmer unless otherwise stated. Also, interview with S. Delmer.

[36] Interview with Wingate.

[37] George C. Marshall Research Foundation, Lexington, Virginia: # War 58039, "Eyes Only" message from Marshall to Eisenhower, June 29, 1944.

[38] L. F. Ellis, *Victory in the West*, vol. 1, p. 322.

[39] Brown, *Bodyguard of Lies*, pp. 740–41.

[40] *Anon.*, cited by Ellis, first in *Welsh Guards at War* (1946), then in *Victory in the West*, vol. 1, p. 339.

[41] Gilbert, vol. 7, p. 861.

[42] Virginia Historical Institute, Richmond: Bruce diaries, entry for July 28, 1944.

[43] All quotations relating to Ultra and the Mortain battle were from Dr. Ralph Bennett, *Ultra in the West*; and interviews with F. W. Winterbotham.

[44] Brown, p. 784 *et seq.* All quotations relating to the attempt of Kluge to surrender from that source unless otherwise stated.

CHAPTER NINE

[1] Warlimont, *Inside Hitler's Headquarters*, p. 469.
[2] John Ehrman, *Grand Strategy*, vol. 5, *August 1943–September 1944* (London HMSO, 1956), p. 353.
[3] Macmillan, *War Diaries*, p. 476 et seq.
[4] Philby, *My Silent War*, pp. 68–70.
[5] *Ibid.*, p. 74.
[6] Donovan papers: *Secret* "Advanced Training Program" for "ATU 11." Copy in possession of author.
[7] Howarth, *Intelligence Chief Extraordinary*, p. 181.
[8] Virginia Historical Institute: Bruce diaries, entry for June 11, 1944.
[9] *Ibid.*
[10] National Archives, modern military records branch: SHAEF SGS 332.01, WSC for Smith for Donovan, August 24, 1944.
[11] Rex Benson, diaries, entry for December 6, 1944.
[12] Quoted in David Kahn, *The Codebreakers* (New York: Macmillan, 1967), p. 604.
[13] George C. Marshall Research Foundation, Lexington, Virginia: "George C. Marshall Interviews and Reminiscences for Forrest C. Pogue: Transcript & Notes, 1956–57," released in 1986. Hereafter referred to as Pogue report.
[14] National Archives, modern military records branch, Washington, D.C.: National Security Agency paper SRH-043, "Statement for the Record of Participation of Brig. Gen. Carter W. Clarke, GSC in the Transmittal of Letters from Gen. George C. Marshall to Governor Thomas E. Dewey the Latter Part of September 1944," in record group 457. Hereafter referred to as Clarke report.
[15] Captain Akeley P. Quirk, U.S.N.R. (Retd.), *Recollections of World War II*, pp. 58–59.
[16] Citing Führer conference, fragment 28, December 12, 1944, see Wilmot, *The Struggle for Europe*, p. 578.
[17] Howarth, p. 189.
[18] General Edwin L. Sibert, papers: transcript of interview by Forrest C. Pogue, U.S. official military historian, of General Sibert and Colonel William H. Jackson, deputy director CIA, May 11, 1951.
[19] National Archives, Washington, D.C.: records of National Security Agency, "Post Mortem Writings on Indications of Ardennes Offensive December 1944," in SRH 112, record group 457.
[20] Peter Calvocoressi, *Top Secret Ultra* (New York: Ballantine, 1981), pp. 51–52.
[21] National Archives, modern military records branch, Washington, D.C.: records of the U.S. National Security Agency, SRH 112: "Communications Intelligence (Comint) in the Prelude to the Battle of the Bulge," undated.
[22] Sibert papers: paper entitled "German Assault Army, *Stossarmee*," promulgated by HQ U.S. Seventh Army, December 10, 1944.
[23] PRO, London: Adm 223/107, paper entitled "The Value and Use of Special Intelligence in J.I.S. Work," c. May–June 1945.
[24] PRO, London: CX/MSS/C400, January 14, 1945.
[25] Donovan papers: memo from Donovan to secretary of state, dated December 13, 1944.
[26] Donovan papers: memo from Buxton to the Joint Chiefs of Staff entitled "Nazi Attempt to Contact British," dated December 26, 1944.
[27] *Ibid.*
[28] Donovan papers: unsigned, undated memo probably by Charles Cheston, deputy director OSS Washington, to Joint Chiefs of Staff, entitled "RHSA Attempt to Obtain Papal Intervention for Peace," dated January 18, 1945. Marked "Top Secret."
[29] Virginia Military Institute: the papers of George Catlett Marshall, minutes of the Argonaut Conference, Second Tripartite Military Meeting, February 6, 1945.

[30] PRO, London: Prem 3 198/2, February 27, 1945.

[31] PRO, London: Prem 3 198/2, telegram British ambassador Moscow to London and Washington, f. 107.

[32] PRO, London: Prem 3 198/2, telegram FDR to WSC, April 5, 1945.

[33] *Ibid.*, f. 53.

[34] *Stalin's Correspondence with Churchill, Attlee, Roosevelt & Truman 1941–45* (London: Lawrence and Wishart, 1958), pp. 209–10.

[35] *Ibid.*, pp. 210–11.

[36] F. L. Loewenheim, *Roosevelt and Churchill*, p. 709.

[37] PRO, London: Prem 4/27/9.

[38] Schellenberg interrogation, *op. cit.* All quotations from that source unless otherwise stated.

[39] PRO, London: CX/MSS/C486, April 21, 1945, received by "C" on April 25 due to a backlog in decryption and translation at Bletchley.

[40] National Archives, Washington, D.C.: Top Secret Ultra, "Japanese Reaction to German Defeat," publication of Pacific Strategic Intelligence Section, commander in chief United States fleet and chief of naval operations (OP-20-3-G50), dated May 21, 1945. In record group 457, records of the National Security Agency, paper no. SRH 075.

CHAPTER TEN

[1] Bertrand, *Enigme*, p. 256.

[2] PRO, London: FO 369/3174, file on "British renegade: John Amery." Also, interviews with the Hon. Julian Amery.

[3] Rebecca West, *The Meaning of Treason* (London: Virago, 1982), p. 150 *et seq.*

[4] Interviews with K.M.H. Duke and Professor George Kent; and *Documents on German Foreign Policy, 1918–1945* (London: HMSO, 1962), series "C." See also *Documents on German Foreign Policy, 1918–1945*, series "C," vol. 6 (Washington, D.C.: State Department, 1983). All quotations and documentation from these printed sources unless otherwise stated.

[5] Michael Bloch, *Operation Willi*, see app. 1, p. 230ff.

[6] Howarth, *Intelligence Chief Extraordinary*, p. 222. All quotations regarding Cavendish-Bentinck's marital predicament from that source unless otherwise stated.

[7] Philby, *My Silent War*, p. 85.

[8] PRO, London: Air 2/12027, June 16, 1945.

[9] Philby, p. 89.

[10] Interviews with Sir James Easton, Grosse Pointe, Michigan, July 2–3, 1986.

[11] Leonard Mosley, *Dulles* (New York: Dial, 1978), p. 284.

[12] P. Seal and M. McConville, *Philby: The Long Road to Moscow* (London: Hamish Hamilton, 1973), p. 97.

[13] Philby, p. 97.

[14] Interview with Easton.

[15] Philby, pp. 111–12.

[16] *Ibid.*, p. 112.

[17] R. K. Sawyer, *Military Advisors in Korea* (Washington, D.C.: Office of the Chief of Military History, 1969), p. 114.

[18] Harry S. Truman, *Years of Trial and Hope*, p. 333.

[19] Philby, p. 126. All quotes attributed to Philby from this source unless otherwise stated.

[20] Interview with Sir Patrick Reilly.

[21] Interview with Easton. All quotes from Easton taken from interview with the author unless otherwise stated.

[22] Interview with James J. Angleton.

[23] Interview with Captain Brian Bell.

[24] Boyle, *The Climate of Treason*, p. 440.

[25] *Ibid.*

[26] Interview with Sir Ronald Wingate.

[27] John le Carré, in the introduction to *Philby: The Spy Who Betrayed a Generation*, p. 23.

[28] F. H. Cowgill papers.

INDEX